Industrial Marketing

INDUSTRIAL

MARKETING

RALPH S. ALEXANDER
Professor Emeritus
School of Business
Columbia University

JAMES S. CROSS
Manager, Statistical Research Department
Sun Oil Company

RICHARD M. HILL
Associate Director and Professor of Marketing
Graduate School of Business Administration
University of Illinois

Third Edition · 1967
RICHARD D. IRWIN, IN.C
Homewood, Illinois

Third Edition

First Printing, June, 1967
Second Printing, May, 1968
Third Printing, April, 1969
Fourth Printing, March, 1970

Library of Congress Catalog Card No. 67–17053

Printed in the United States of America

PREFACE

IN THIS THIRD EDITION of *Industrial Marketing* we have tried to bring the textual material as nearly up to date as possible in such a highly dynamic marketing area. In addition, we have sought to make a number of changes that will, we hope, further improve the text as a learning tool. The following revisions and additions are probably the most important.

1. Since the book is organized around the managerial approach, we have included in the first chapter a short section on management, outlining its functions and problems. This is for the benefit of the student who approaches the study of Industrial Marketing without benefit of a previous course in management.

2. We have expanded our treatment of industrial buyers, giving much greater detail about the buying organization and process and such buying tools as value and vendor analysis.

3. The chapter on planning has been completely rewritten to present, we hope, a much more sophisticated and realistic picture of the planning process.

4. Chapter 8, "Managing the Product Offering," has been partially rewritten, and significant additions have been made, although we have tried to retain the scholarly flavor the late Ross Cunningham imparted to the original.

5. We have tried to sharpen the treatment of marketing channels in Part IV and have made important additions to it.

6. A significant portion of the material devoted to the management of pricing has been rewritten to reflect recent changes in thinking and improvements in technique.

7. A separate chapter on "Organization for Industrial Marketing" has been included.

8. We hope that the chapters on "Managing Personal Selling," "Managing Industrial Advertising," and "Special Media and Sales Promotion" have been strengthened by extensive revision and the addition of considerable new material.

9. The chapter on physical distribution has been almost entirely rewritten to reflect the profound changes that have occurred in that area.

Our treatment of the mathematical technique in managing marketing reflects our concept of it as a tool of management rather than its goal. We have tried to indicate problems where mathematical analyses and model building will prove useful in their solutions; and to segregate the general factors that should go into each such model; but we have refrained from including the models themselves. We feel very strongly that each model must be specific in order to include the special conditions under which the firm using it must operate and the objectives management wishes to achieve.

We have added a few new cases and omitted several that were in the previous revision. This reflects our feeling that it is more important that a case be good than that it be new. If a case involves a problem that is timeless, the case itself is timeless. When we find better cases than the ones we have, we will include them; but we feel that change for the sake of change is of doubtful value.

To help in nullifying the usefulness of fraternity case solution files, we have made several changes.

1. We have presented the cases in alphabetical order at the end of the text.

2. At the end of the Table of Contents we have inserted a table indicating the parts of the text to which each case is applicable.

3. At the end of each part of the book we have listed the applicable cases.

4. In the Instructors' Manual we will include a list of questions on each case. These questions are of two types: major, which we feel may be useful as the basis of formal, fairly sophisticated reports (several of these should be equivalent to the usual term paper) and minor (which may be used as the basis of class discussion, as class quizzes, or as "quickie" exercises to be prepared outside of class). The manual will include a further discussion of these questions.

June, 1967   RALPH S. ALEXANDER
                                                      JAMES S. CROSS
                                                      RICHARD M. HILL

TABLE OF CONTENTS

CASES APPLICABLE TO EACH PART

CASES	PARTS							
	I	II	III	IV	V	VI	VII	VIII
Acme Chemical Co. [p. 551]								x
Agex Oil Co. (A) [p. 556]						x		
Agex Oil Co. (B) [p. 559]						x		
Agex Oil Co. (C) [p. 562]						x		x
Barry Corp. [p. 570]			x	x		x		
Childers Co. [p. 575]				x				
Coccidiostats for the Birds [p. 579]	x		x					
Collis Co. [p. 582]						x		x
Cundy-Betts Corp. [p. 590]	x	x	x					
Hancock Co. (A) [p. 600]					x			
Hancock Co. (B) [p. 604]			x			x		
Heflin Chemical Supply Co. (A) [p. 611]	x			x				
Heflin Chemical Supply Co. (B) [p. 615]				x		x		
Jackson Chemical Co. [p. 622]			x			x		
Kendall Mills [p. 629]		x	x		x		x	
Leland Lock Co. [p. 635]	x	x	x					
Margeann Co. [p. 638]			x		x			
Meadows Co. [p. 642]		x		x			x	
Ordway Co. [p. 648]				x				
Reynolds Products Co. [p. 653]							x	
Silas Oates Co. [p. 663]		x	x	x		x		
Taylor Marine Supply [p. 670]			x	x				
Thomson Electric Welder Co. [p. 675]		x				x		
Velting Machine Co. [p. 677]		x					x	

Basic Considerations

A STUDENT beginning the study of a subject is wise at the outset to seek a general understanding of its nature, its dimensions, and its place in the scheme of things. So in Part I, we present a general concept of the kinds of things that are handled in the process of industrial marketing, its functions and importance in the economy, the kinds of agencies through which it is carried on, and the characteristic features of industrial and institutional demand that set the climate within which the industrial marketer must operate.

We have chosen to adopt the management approach in our study of the subject. In fact, the book might be more accurately titled, The Management of Industrial Marketing. We are aware that some who use the book may not have had introductory courses in management or the opportunity to read general books on that subject. Therefore, in a section of Chapter 1 we have presented an outline of the more important activities involved and problems encountered in management.

Those who have had courses in management or have done a reasonable amount of reading in the subject probably will gain little additional enlightenment from this outline, but they may meet a somewhat different point of view. If the instructor chooses to waive the study of the outline for those in this category, he has the blessing of the authors in doing so.

Chapter 1

<><><><><><><><><><> THE INDUSTRIAL MARKETING

SYSTEM AND MANAGEMENT

IN ITS SIMPLEST TERMS, a market is composed of buyers and sellers, exchanging goods and money. It is usually helpful, however, to also think of markets in terms of the channels that bring buyers and sellers together, as well as of the relationships between these buyers and sellers in the marketplace. A market system, therefore, includes at least three elements—participants, distribution channels, and relationships.

PARTICIPANTS

One way to identify participants in the system of industrial marketing is to think of the national economy as composed of three broad divisions—extractive industries, manufacturing industries, and using or consuming units. The flow of products is predominantly from the extractive industries, through the manufacturing industries, to using and consuming units. While there is a backflow of products (capital goods and operating supplies) from manufacturing industries to the extractive industries, the volume is small compared to the movement of products from manufacturers to ultimate consumers, (individuals and households buying for personal satisfaction), government, business users, and exporters. The general nature of this flow is depicted in Figure 1–1.

It is apparent in this illustration that manufacturing industries form a complex with both external and internal product flows. Externally, the complex faces in two directions: (1) procuring raw and semifinished materials from the extractive industries while supplying them with capital goods and supplies; (2) selling capital goods, supplies, and consumer goods to households, government, business and institutional users, and exporters. Internally, it is engaged in the process of exchanging semifinished products, component parts, operating supplies, and finished capital goods among the constituent manufacturing establishments.

Industrial marketing—as opposed, for example, to agricultural marketing, which we will not discuss—encompasses the movement of material

3

FIGURE 1–1.   Product Flow Diagram

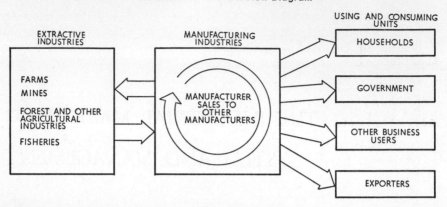

from mines as well as the return flow of goods to mines, farms, fisheries, and other extractive enterprises. It also includes the movement of goods to government, nonmanufacturing business users, and exporters, as well as between units within the manufacturing complex itself. The approximate dimensions of this flow as well as the relative importance of the broad classes of participants in it are shown below.

Producers	*1965 Income**	*Purchasers*	*1965 Outlay**
Manufacturers	170.4	Households	431.5
Services[1]	74.6	Government	136.2
Financial institutions	61.0	Business[2]	106.6
Construction companies	28.3	Exporters	7.0
Transportation companies	22.9	Gross Outlay	681.3
Communication enterprises	11.2		
Farms, forestries, fisheries & agricultural services	21.0	Less indirect business taxes, capital consumption allowances, and statisti-	
Mines	6.4	cal discrepancy, plus remainder of	
Importers	4.3	subsidies minus surplus of govern-	
		mental enterprises	122.3
Middleman (wholesalers & retailers)	83.6	Total	559.0
Government and governmental enterprises	75.3		
Totals	559.0		

SOURCE: *Survey of Current Business,* July 1966, pp. 8, 9, 15.
* In billions of dollars.
[1] Includes electric, gas, and sanitary services, 1966.
[2] Investment expenditure, i.e. plant, equipment, and net addition to inventories.

The most important group of business and industrial users is manufacturers, whose purchases probably amounted to approximately $266 billion in 1965.[1] Included in this category are construction companies,

---

[1] 1965 *Annual Survey of Manufactures, General Statistics for Industry Groups and Industries,* p. 4. This exceeds outlay for business given in the preceding table, because the latter value represents investment alone rather than gross expenditure for materials and supplies.

transportation companies, commercial and financial enterprises, and institutions. Government includes state and local as well as the federal government. In terms of dollar value, the major portion of exported merchandise is made up of goods for use in further production or provision of services.

Therefore, on the supply side of the distribution channel the major participants in the industrial marketing system are manufacturing and mining establishments. On the demand side of the system is a family of business and industrial users, government agencies and departments, and exporters. Because of their importance as industrial customers, it is often meaningful to distinguish original equipment manufacturers (OEM's) from other manufacturers. The original equipment manufacturer is one who buys a material or component to incorporate into a product he makes and sells. For example, a diesel engine maker who buys filters and gear boxes for use on his engines is classified as an OEM customer by suppliers of filters and gear boxes. For use in their businesses, other manufacturers buy products such as lathes, typewriters, and paper towels. The same manufacturer might, of course, be classified as an OEM account by some suppliers and as a user account by others.

Producers and users of industrial products are linked by a third group of participants, industrial middlemen. These may be identified as manufacturer's branches, merchant wholesalers or distributors, and agents. Manufacturer's branches, which are wholly owned subsidiaries of manufacturing companies, usually perform a substantial array of marketing functions. The branch may stock commodities received in carload or truckload lots. This permits the manufacturer to combine the more expensive small lot shipments from the branch to customers in its territory with lower carlot or trucklot rates over the longer distance from factory to branch. Such facilities are customarily referred to as branch *houses.* A branch *office*, on the other hand, does not carry stocks and serves primarily as headquarters for the field sales force. The branch office is usually intended to afford a convenient organizational unit through which to manage selling activity. Orders are forwarded to the home office or to a franchised distributor or other cooperating middleman located in the territory covered by the office.

Merchant wholesalers or distributors are independently owned firms that buy products from manufacturers and resell them in the same, or almost the same, form to users and OEM's on their own account. They can usually be identified as *general* or *specialty* houses. The general merchants—or general-line houses, as they are often called—handle a wide variety of industrial supplies and minor equipment, which they sell to a diversified group of customers. The specialty houses may confine their stock to a particular category of products, such as office equipment, abrasives, or electrical supplies, or they may limit their market to a given trade or industry, such as hospitals and medical clinics, or hotels and restaurants.

Several types of agents participate in the marketing of industrial products. The most important of these in terms of both number of establishments and volume of sales are the *manufacturer's agents*. These firms represent only sellers, whom they serve on a commission basis. They typically represent a limited number of principals, and the relationship between principal and agent is usually a continuous one. Although manufacturer's agents do not take title to merchandise, many carry stocks on consignment. They ordinarily sell only a portion of the client-producer's output, and they limit their activities to specific geographical areas.

Sales agents operate in much the same manner as manufacturer's agents. They represent a limited number of sellers on a more or less continuous basis and charge a commission for their services. Unlike manufacturer's agents, however, sales agents usually sell to a given trade or industry group wherever its members can be found and do not limit their activity to any specific area. They are also likely to dispose of the entire output of the principal. By making an arrangement with a single sales agent, a producer can solve his entire problem of choosing marketing channels; if he markets through manufacturer's agents, he must make arrangements with a number of them if he expects to reach his entire market through this channel.

Brokers play no very significant part in industrial goods marketing, but they can provide some very useful services. While brokers negotiate and facilitate sales, they do not take title to the merchandise involved and ordinarily bear no responsibility for it or its condition. Often, they never even see the products they sell. In most circumstances, brokers possess no merchandise other than samples to which they may have temporarily taken custody as a convenience to clients. They receive a commission for their services, paid by the client on completion of an agreement and delivery of the merchandise. Brokers are most useful in marketing goods that are standardized or can be conveniently described by grade or trade designation. A variety of materials, some supplies, and a few small tools and items of equipment fall into this category.

While *commission merchants* play a highly significant role in the marketing of agricultural products, there is no reason why the average industrial products maker should want to consistently consign merchandise to an agent with whom he has no continuing contractual relationship and who may or may not be able to sell it. As a rule, commission merchants do not enter into long-term relationships with a producer, and may negotiate sales without the specific approval of their principals since they have physical custody and control of goods they sell.

CHANNELS

The participants in the industrial marketing system are linked by both direct and indirect channels. The direct channel is traditionally defined as one in which the producer controls the distribution of his products from factory to user or OEM customer. Normally, this control is administered through the manufacturer's branch house or office, although some manufacturers administer their distribution system direct from the home office without subsidiaries.

The indirect channel is identified by the presence of independent middlemen who limit the control a manufacturer can exercise over the distribution of his products. The extent to which control is diluted is determined by the type of independent middlemen employed, as well as by the relationships that prevail between manufacturers and middlemen and between the middlemen themselves.

At the risk of oversimplification, it may be useful to identify some of the more common channel arrangements through which industrial goods reach user and OEM customers.

1. *Manufacturer to branch house or branch office to customer*. This is the direct channel and is usually implemented through the manufacturer's own sales force. Typically, a system of branch houses is relied on for physical distribution of products sold.

2. *Manufacturer to distributor to customer*. Usually, manufacturers sell to wholesalers through a small sales force and ship goods to them in quantity lots, which are then sold in broken lots or individual items by the distributor's salesmen. There are, however, numerous variations of this general pattern. For example, some wholesalers drop ship, that is, order merchandise sent direct from the manufacturer to the customer. While the drop shipper is responsible for delivery and payment, and takes legal possession of merchandise, he does not physically handle it.

Other distributors depend heavily on manufacturer's detail men or missionary salesmen to sell products they stock, while they concentrate their own efforts primarily on physical distribution. In still other cases, the manufacturer's salesmen travel with the distributor's salesmen for the purpose of training and stimulating them to sell the manufacturer's products. As a rule, manufacturers who employ detail men or whose salesmen instruct and assist distributor salesmen are attempting to win some of the benefits of direct distribution without incurring all its costs.

3. *Manufacturer to agent to customer*. The agent customarily makes initial contact with customers and performs a complete sales function, often supplying technical service where needed. Orders are referred to manufacturers who ship direct to the customer.

4. *Manufacturer to agent to distributor to customer*. This arrangement is sometimes used in markets composed of small and scattered customers whose combined volume is large enough to support marketing efforts. In a few industries, the agent is replaced by a superjobber or warehouse distributor who sells only to other wholesalers.

5. *Mixed arrangement*. Each of the preceding channel arrangements, of course, represents a general type or class, and manufacturers create many variations within each of them as well as hybrid arrangements including two or more channel types. A manufacturer may use one channel for one product or group of products and another for a different product group,

or reach one group of customers through one channel and use a completely different channel for another customer group. He may sell direct to customers who are large, or potentially so, while using middlemen to serve smaller buyers. Manufacturers may even act as middlemen themselves, buying products from other manufacturers to fill out or supplement their own product lines, which they sell direct. In every instance, of course, it is the requirements of the market that dictate the makeup of the channel arrangement.

In later chapters, we will explore in much greater detail the operations of the units in these marketing channels and the problems the industrial goods manufacturer meets in selecting channels and units in them, as well as in managing his relationships with them and their relationships with one another.

THE RELATIONSHIPS

The relations that exist among the participants who comprise the various distribution channels for industrial products may be most easily identified as formal and informal. Among the formal relationships are the various contracts of sale and franchise agreements, which define the respective responsibilities and rights of buyers and sellers. The most significant of the informal relationships are loyalty, confidence, and reciprocity.

Contracts of Sale

Unlike the casual arrangements accompanying the sale of most consumer products, the formal contract that stipulates the responsibilities and liabilities of each party to a sale is present in many exchanges between industrial buyers and sellers. The complexity and detail of the sales contract naturally vary with the characteristics of the product or products involved, amount of the sale, nature of the services to be rendered, and number and character of the parties included.

Aside from the clarity and concreteness a formal statement lends to any agreement, a sales contract has certain benefits from a marketing standpoint. It enables salesmen to know precisely what the company is and is not prepared to do in behalf of its customers and products. The contract also serves to minimize deliberate misrepresentation. Knowledge that the terms of an offer will appear in writing as part of a contract is an effective brake on ill-considered claims and empty promises.

Moreover, it is no exaggeration that minimizing misunderstanding and argument about the exact terms of an agreement can save hours for salesmen and sales executives alike. As any businessman can testify, dealing with customer complaints can be a distasteful and time-consuming task, which often has its roots in misunderstanding or inadequate information.

When sales transactions involve products of a technical nature, as well as substantial sums of money and the ability to meet production schedules, having the exact terms of an agreement written down for all parties to read can avoid much embarrassment and friction later.

Franchise Agreements

Some form of continuing contractual arrangement is usually sought by manufacturers who market through independent middlemen. Such agreements are often in effect for an indefinite period, subject to cancellation by either party on proper notice. They generally summarize the services and prerogatives the manufacturer intends to give his outlets and what he expects of them in return. When some form of protection is offered or implied, the agreement is usually referred to as a *franchise*.

Franchises vary in the protection they afford the parties and in the obligations they impose on each. An *exclusive franchise* usually designates the distributor as the sole outlet for the manufacturer's products in the middleman's marketing area, and commits the producer to supply substantial aids—technical, financial, administrative, and promotional—to the distributor. Legally, the manufacturer cannot bind the distributor to reciprocate by handling no competitor's products; practically, he can bring powerful pressures to bear toward this end. He can also ask the distributor to commit himself to perform certain specific functions in promoting and marketing the products, such as carrying a standard stock, rendering certain designated services, and distributing sales promotion materials. This is a fairly typical arrangement in the heavy equipment industry, in which the distributor's inventory commitment must be substantial, and technical service to the buyer-user is vitally important. It is not uncommon in other phases of the industrial goods business.

A far more common relationship is the *selective franchise*, in which the manufacturer limits the number of distributors who carry his products in a market area. While such selective distribution has definite advantages over so-called blanket distribution, under which a producer sells to every middleman who can be induced to buy, the manufacturer's control over the middleman is substantially less than in the case of an exclusive franchise.

Loyalty

Industrial buyers may go to considerable lengths to help suppliers whose products and services they value. It is not unusual for buyers to permit valued suppliers to test new or redesigned products in their plants, to achieve greater flexibility and efficiency in planning production runs by placing orders well in advance of need, and to participate in joint research efforts. Buyers have also been known to assist trusted suppliers in financing machinery or inventory. Such actions can scarcely be attributed to charitable motives, but are based on the mutual advantage that both parties anticipate.

Suppliers who can be depended on to deliver what is ordered when it is needed, to render good service, and to cooperate with the buyer in meeting special requirements are not easy to find. The buyer tends to be loyal to such suppliers in order to hold their loyalty to him. Such loyalty is especially important to the buyer when the product to be bought is not a standard item but must be made to rigid specifications, when it is of small value but vital to the buyer's operations, and when the supplier's capacity cannot be easily or readily increased.

By the same token, a buyer who can be depended on to cooperate with a seller in product testing, market studies, advance placement of orders, inventory or equipment financing, and supplying timely information regarding design changes and price structure on his own products is a valued customer. Such customers can reduce a manufacturer's promotional and research costs, and can provide a reliable means of evaluating the effectiveness of his marketing effort versus that of competitors.

Confidence

A powerful force in cementing relationships between suppliers and buyers of industrial goods is confidence. When asked what single factor has the most influence on their bestowal of patronage, a high percentage of purchasing officers will reply confidence.

This confidence is a feeling of certainty that the supplier will do what he promises or will spare no effort or cost in trying to do it, that his claims with respect to his products and services can be accepted without serious question, and that he can be counted on to help execute special projects and to go all out to aid in emergencies. These are the chief elements in the buyer's confidence, but not the only ones; others are peculiar to individual cases.

Of course, the buyer enjoys an emotional satisfaction—mainly a sense of security—in dealing with suppliers in whom he has confidence. But, primarily, buying on the basis of the elements just outlined puts money in the bank for his company. The lack of any or all of these assurances may be costly enough to more than offset significant price concessions offered by less trustworthy suppliers.

Buyer confidence is not something a manufacturer gets as a natural right. He must earn it by performance over a period of time. No amount of advertising or salesmanship can equal a record of delivering the goods and services.

To be really solid, the buyer–seller relationship must be cemented by confidence on both sides. The seller must feel that the buyer will not abuse the seller's services or the terms on which he sells, that he will use the product for the purpose it is intended and in the manner prescribed, and that he will not make exhorbitant claims for adjustments.

Perhaps the importance of confidence in industrial marketing relationships arises from a mutual recognition of the weakness of the legal contract as an instrument of exchange in a business that is highly complex, often extremely technical, and fraught with intangible factors that are hard to measure but are very important in terms of use and cost. In a contract, it is usually possible to describe with some exactness the goods that are involved, but it is virtually impossible to put in writing the services that often constitute an almost equally important part of the transaction.

Neither party wants a suit to compel the other's compliance. The seller fears loss of the buyer's patronage and alienation of other buyers, and the buyer hesitates before the risk of incurring a bad reputation in the supplying trade. In the final analysis, the most potent sanction of an industrial purchase and sale contract is not legal action to enforce the letter of the agreement but the will of the two parties to carry out its intent.

Reciprocity

A manufacturer of industrial goods often is both a seller to and a buyer from the same firm. He thus has opportunity for using his purchases to generate sales by a threat, overt or implied, to withdraw patronage unless it is reciprocated. This practice has ethical as well as broad, companywide policy implications. For this reason, we will delay our discussion of reciprocity until a later chapter, when we have become a bit more familiar with the background of the issues it involves.

THE DIMENSIONS OF MANAGEMENT

It is the task of the industrial goods marketing executive to use management tools to sell and distribute his firm's products through the marketing agencies, just described, to the buyers, whose broad patronage motives we have outlined. This job has unique aspects due to the nature of the business, but, in the main, management is management wherever you find it. So perhaps we can understand a little better the nature of the task as we study its several parts if we first briefly review the elements or subfunctions of the general activity we call management. Later, we will return to each of these elements to discuss in detail its specific applications to the marketing of industrial goods.

For our purposes, the job of management may be conveniently divided into the subfunctions of planning, organization, staffing, supervision, and control. There is always a temptation to feel that such a listing has chronological implications. This is not necessarily so. Usually, plans are being made; organization structures are being changed; personnel is being lost, recruited, or shifted about; and supervision and control are being exercized at the same time and by the same man.

Planning

Planning in industrial marketing as anywhere else involves collecting and analyzing information, and using it to make decisions. Some information, such as sales and costs, comes to the manager almost as a matter of course in his daily routine. Other facts, particularly those concerning shifts in general business or industry conditions, changes in the market, and the effectiveness of competitive activities, must be sought and procured often at considerable cost.

A basic part of planning is trying to forecast not only what general business and market conditions will be during the planning period, but also what competitors will do and how effective their activities will be as well as how effective the company's marketing efforts will be. This may involve expensive marketing research.

In the light of the facts disclosed and their analysis, the manager must decide what marketing objectives are feasible. In selecting the goals for emphasis, he must try to choose those that will help most in attaining overall company objectives. He must then determine the best method for achieving these objectives with the resources the firm has available. In addition, he must set up policies (general courses of action to deal with problems that recur in substantially similar forms), programs (lists of things that must be done in order to carry out a project or achieve an objective), procedures (lists of subactivities that must be performed constantly or recurrently, and their assignment to specific persons), and schedules (any of the lists above, with dates of initiation or completion or both). Along with these plans for physical activities, the manager must prepare an estimate of their costs and their results in terms of dollars of sales—a budget.

In the course of their unfolding, plans must be constantly reexamined and sometimes changed in response to changed conditions or evidences of mistakes in their original preparation. Planning is a continuous process.

Organization

The principles and concepts of organization that apply to business generally also apply to industrial marketing operations. Whenever one man cannot perform an activity alone, the need for organization arises. The process of organization requires (1) an enumeration of functions that must be performed, (2) a grouping of related activities, (3) a definition of the relationships among these activities as well as those among the different individuals performing them, and (4) establishment of a structure that will combine the different activities in an integrated operation.

Operational Groups. Operational grouping begins with the identification of subfunctions or specific activities that must be carried on. This requires a reasonably exact definition of the purposes the marketing department, for example, is expected to fulfill, from which the subfunctions necessary to each purpose can be deduced. Each of the subfunctions may, in turn, be broken down into minor activities. These subfunctions ordinarily must be combined into related groups. This is necessary whenever activities are too numerous and varied to be directly supervised by a single person.

Except in the very small company, where a functional basis is the logical choice, marketing activities may be grouped on several different bases. The functions, such as selling, advertising, and research, are the primary bases for grouping even in large companies. However, the more numerous the personnel involved, the more diverse the products and services offered, the greater the variety of customers served, and the larger the area over which sales are solicited, then the more likely it is that other bases may be used for primary grouping.

In companies that offer a diverse assortment of products, marketing activities are often grouped on a product basis. If customers belong to different industries that buy different combinations of a company's products and use them differently, industries or customer groups often represent the logical basis for grouping. A geographical basis is often used by companies that market nationally or internationally.

Other factors that influence operational grouping are the need for specialization, the importance of coordination, company policy, adequate control, the ability of available personnel, and executive interest.

Delegation. Management must create operating units to perform and supervise each of these groups of activities. The manager must decide (1) what specific tasks shall be performed in each unit and (2) how much authority the supervisor of the unit shall have to commit the resources of the company. There is likely to be a series of delegations down to the level at which subordinates need no further assistance in performing assigned tasks. Where there is a series of authorizations and assignments running down the chain of command, there will be a corresponding series of responsibilities in the opposite direction.

Delegation involves three elements—assigning tasks, granting authority to use resources to carry them on, and fixing responsibility for the results. Ideally, these three elements should increase and decrease together, a change in one being accompanied by a corresponding change in the others.

The process of delegation is hedged about by limitations; some are implicit in the act itself, and some stem from the circumstances in which the delegation takes place. The benefits of delegation depend in large part on the extent to which these limitations are recognized and heeded. Sometimes, subordinate managers are merely given vague but heroic orders to get the job done. Again, they may be given fairly detailed instructions, but fail to make these instructions clear when they redelegate to their own subordinates. In either instance, results are seldom satisfactory.

A crucial issue is how much authority subordinates will be given to decide what is to be done. That is, to what extent should the authority to *make* decisions, rather than simply to implement them, be delegated? Should a salesman, for example, be given authority to decide where he will solicit business, what approach he will employ in his solicitation, and how he will distribute his time among the customers he solicits. Should an advertising manager be free to decide the sales message to be carried by advertising media, the audience this message will be aimed at, and the basis on which its success will be judged?

How much decentralization of decision a company may seek depends on several considerations. There are inherent limitations in authority itself. It is not the same as obedience. The only authority an executive really has is what his subordinates are willing to accept. Because of personal feelings, employees will either refuse to do some activities or will do them only halfheartedly. Simply assigning authority does not always get things done.

Delegation may also be restricted by the ability of the personnel, the effectiveness of control, the importance of decisions to be made, organizational distance (the number of layers separating the marketing manager from the lowest echelon of his department), the importance of consistency in policy matters, and the growth characteristics of the enterprise. But some delegation is forced by limited human capacity in upper level positions. The alternative to it is the use of staff assistants. This, however, introduces questions of structural arrangement.

Organizational Structure. The structure of an organization refers to the overall arrangement of its operating divisions and supporting departments. Structure results from the way the work of the enterprise is divided, the number of operating units created, the number of levels each is separated into, the distribution of authority, and the need for supporting or service units. These decisions are, in turn, shaped by the objectives, policies, and size of the enterprise.

A diversified product line policy requires a form of marketing organization different than one specializing on a single product or a limited number of them. The diversified firm tends to group selling activities on a product basis and to develop a larger marketing operation, with more layering, than the specialized house. The specialty manufacturer is apt to place heavy emphasis on technical service and to build his marketing organization around field salesmen and sales engineers. Size creates complexity of structure and increases the number of levels.

Industrial marketers are too varied to permit much generalization about the pattern of organization structure. But we can identify some key issues that will be useful in our later study of industrial marketing organization.

How should authority be scaled and distributed? Should it flow only from superior to subordinate, or directly to each employee or group concerned? Should it flow horizontally as well as vertically? Should authority to plan as well as to act be delegated, and if so, should delegation be to individuals or to committees or to both? At what level should planning authority be centered? Should it be high or low in the organizational structure? In seeking answers to these questions, the chief alternatives are line and staff relationships, functional relationships, and committees.

When formal line relationship is used, the manager divides the work among his immediate subordinates who, in turn, allocate and delegate it down the line to those who produce products, sell them, and perform supporting services. Authority runs downward; responsibility, upward; and communication should take place in both directions.

But when too much emphasis is placed on the line relationship, delays, mistakes, and confusion occur. Only the top level can coordinate or provide specialized assistance, professional counsel, or advice.

The line relationship works well for small enterprises and is a good place to begin an examination of structure in large ones. A line system usually provides the basic organizational framework of a company and of each of its separate divisions. When it becomes overburdened, staff may be used to assist the line managers in their work. The staff units extend in a horizontal fashion, while the line units develop downward, ending in contacts with workers, customers, vendors, government agencies, and others.

The true function of staff is advisory and service in nature. Theoretically, a staff officer has no authority except over another member of the same staff. He supplies information and recommends plans to a line executive, who may or may not transform them into action. Staff men do the things a line executive would do if he had enough time and energy. The staff officer must assist rather than command; he must convince rather than order.

But the inability of line managers to be expert in all the functions their subordinates perform often gives rise to the need for *functional authority*, usually exercised by a staff officer. This means that employees have direct contact with a number of different superiors. Instead of having only one boss, an employee may receive instructions from several, each specializing in a particular function.

Functional authority clearly involves multiple supervision and divided responsibility. Unless its use is carefully defined and consistently controlled, it is apt to create confusion and frustration. If, for example, the controller has authority over expenses, he can become virtually a second general manager, because expense enters into almost every decision. Staff men with functional authority may burden lower echelon managers with procedural detail or conflicting instructions. But in a business so highly technical as the average industrial goods firm, the use of functional staff authority can hardly be avoided.

In essence, a committee is a special form of staff. Both its strengths and its weaknesses arise from the assignment of tasks to a group rather than to an individual. Each committee member has a part in the decision-making process, but he cannot act independently. Committees should be incorporated into the organizational structure at places where group judgment is needed or where cooperation is vital. Group judgment and cooperation are especially needed in situations—so numerous in industrial marketing—that cut across department lines or fall between the areas of existing line or staff units.

The Span of Supervision. This is the question of how many persons should report to one supervisor. Involved are at least two subsidiary questions: (1) What determines the number of subordinates a manager can supervise? (2) What are the practical limits to the number of levels of supervision?

How many subordinates a manager can supervise is partly a matter of individual capacity. In general, the abler the subordinates or the simpler and more similar their jobs are, the more subordinates one superior can direct. The more technical, complex, and distinctive each subordinate's job is, the fewer of them one superior can manage. The right number of levels of supervision is largely a matter of the effect of increased layering on communication, overhead costs, and morale.

Parity of Authority and Responsibility. A grant of authority creates a duty in the receiver. Logically, this responsibility cannot be greater than the power granted, nor should it be less. Nor can an executive delegate part of his own responsibility by delegating a part of his authority. He simply becomes responsible for the acts of his subordinate.

The Unity of Command. The responsibility of a subordinate to a superior is essentially personal. It represents an obligation not only to try to accomplish desired results, but to account to the superior for the degree of success he achieves in doing so. It follows, then, that the superior–subordinate relationship will work better if each subordinate is responsible to but one superior.

The greatest danger to this unity of command is the unrestricted or careless use of functional authority. This begins innocently enough with the quest for economies of specialization and the need for technically expert opinion. The controller is given authority to prescribe accounting procedures throughout the company; the purchasing officer, to prescribe how and where all purchases are made; the personnel manager, to specify how employees shall be classified, to maintain their records, and to schedule vacations.

The line manager finds himself with a number of superiors, in addition to his immediate boss who controls promotion. This breeds frustration, buck-passing, and politicking, with lowered efficiency.

Staffing

The manager must staff his organization. This involves recruiting candidates for the various positions, examining and appraising their qualifications, choosing those to be employed, inducting them into their positions, and providing basic training for their jobs. It is usually sound policy to fill upper echelon positions by promotion rather than from outside.

In firms of any size, most staffing usually is done by a specialized department, personnel. For technical jobs, those requiring special skills such as salesmen, and for managerial positions, the personnel staff usually merely collects and analyzes information and otherwise helps the responsible executives in the work of selection and training.

The industrial marketer must staff not only the positions in his department but also those in his marketing channel. This task is usually so highly specialized that the personnel staff can offer little help. It involves crucial decisions in the marketing effort.

Supervision

When the objectives of an enterprise have been decided, a framework of policies and programs incorporating these goals has been established, and an organization that fits them developed and staffed, management is ready to put its plans into operation.

Supervision is the task of fitting together all the pieces of a plan or program and of making sure that all the functional groups involved in it work together as a smoothly operating whole. The activities involved in supervision may be classified as coordinating and securing cooperation, instructing, directing, motivating, and stimulating personal involvement of those supervised.

Coordination. Coordination can be achieved only when the various people involved in a project can be induced to cooperate willingly in a common effort and are willing to adapt themselves to the constraints of a master plan. The purchasing agent, the sales manager, the controller, the design engineer, the production manager, and the personnel director must be willing to subordinate their respective needs and operating problems to a common course of action. If they are not able to agree, a superior may impose an uneasy and not always entirely effective cooperation upon them.

Despite the importance of proper organization and communication, the real burden of securing cooperation falls on the supervising executive. The better the organization, the less onerous his job will be. But he can not escape responsibility for it. He must not only see to it that the activity in his own department is planned and carried on, but also that his operations promote balance and unity in the total company effort when combined with those of other departments. In this process, he must guide and instruct his subordinates, explain and interpret what they are asked to do, restrain some, encourage others, and reconcile or arbitrate honest differences of opinion. His most effective tools in the work of coordination are policies and programs.

The logical time to coordinate all marketing activities with each other and with financial, production, and personnel operations is when they are being planned. During the planning stage, the manager has the best opportunity to compare different plans, assess their consistency, and determine whether or not the proposed timing and sequence of action in different units will produce an integrated pattern of operation. Inconsistencies are much easier to correct in the overall planning stage than when they have been worked into the plans of operating departments. To change them later may require changes in the plans of several departments. Every operation that involves more than one or two steps must be scheduled. This requires estimating the time needed to perform each step, determining the order in which the steps should be taken, and fixing the completion target date for each step.

The chief means of assuring consistency, timing, and meshing of operations at the company level are policies and long-run programs. The policy framework provides standing answers to the basic questions of direction, purpose, and tactics, and serves to knit together the activities of various units in a common effort. Long-run programs define the goals to be aimed at over a future period longer than a year, and the progress each year's operations are supposed to make toward them. The long-run program indicates what management hopes to achieve, what efforts will be demanded to achieve it, and when they should take place. It sets guideposts for subordinate units.

At the operating unit level, the chief means of coordination is the short-run program, typically the budget. This is concerned with the specification, timing, and sequence of action on a month-to-month and day-to-day basis. A short-run program usually covers the length of the budget period—a year or less. If properly drawn, a budget merely represents a costing and pricing out of activities and expected results embraced in a detailed plan. If the various parts of such a plan are properly dovetailed, they supply a guide to the way in which the activities of various units must fit together to achieve the end result.

Instruction. When plans have been approved, they must be communicated to line managers in the form of official instructions. These must be reworked and passed on down to the lowest echelon in the organization, i.e., to the doers. Everyone who has a part to play in the action defined by a plan must have a clear idea not only of what he is supposed to do and when he is supposed to do it, but also why it has to be done and how it fits in.

To be effective, instructions must be accurate, understandable, and complete. As they filter down from one executive level to another, they must become more specific and detailed. In the process, their original intent and emphasis are apt to be changed, and they may even be interpreted in the interest of the transmitting executive.

The clarity and completeness of routine instructions can often be improved by the use of standard operating procedures. For example, if it is decided to give each salesman a bonus for every new account he lands, procedures for handling the computation and payment of bonuses must be worked out in the payroll, accounting, and personnel areas.

Effective direction demands that an executive either should see to it that his instructions are carried out or should rescind them. This has a salutory effect on both him and the receiver. It means that before he issues instructions he must try to predict the kind of impression they will make; this should serve as an effective break on dogmatic or inflexible rules and stipulations. The practice puts subordinates on notice that the boss means business.

Supervision, the Personal Touch. In most cases, the supervisor–subordinate relationship should be a very personal one. It is the supervisor's task to train those under him, to stimulate them, to protect their group interests, to try to understand and help solve their personal problems (sometimes off-the-job as well as on-the-job ones), to build their morale, to interpret and represent the company to them and them to the company, and to give praise when it is earned and administer discipline when it is deserved. He has to be a cross between a benevolent big brother, an impartial Simon Legree, and an understanding friend.

Supervision at any level is a combination of communication, teaching, leadership, discipline, inspiration, and guidance. No man can do it perfectly. But every manager owes it to his firm and to his people to try to supervise as well as he can.

Motivation. Instructing subordinates and counseling them with regard to their performance will be of little avail unless they want to follow instructions. Motivation may be positive—rewards or negative penalties. Generally, both must be used. The basic motivation for work is money, so a fair level of pay and a sound system of wage scales is a primary requirement in inducing people to put forth their best efforts. But management cannot stop there; it must seek to tap the reservoir of intangible motives.

Any deprivation of a man's higher-level needs, such as association, independence, achievements, or status, will affect his behavior almost as strongly as hunger or thirst. People may put forth only minimal effort, even in response to high wages, good working conditions, ample fringe benefits, and steady employment. By satisfying physiological and safety needs, management may shift the motivational emphasis to the social and psychological areas. It must satisfy these needs, also.

Management cannot by any act or decision directly satisfy these higher-level human needs. It cannot endow its people with self-respect, or the respect of their associates, or the sense of self-fulfillment. But management can set up conditions that enable and encourage the employee to create these satisfactions for himself.

Usually, this means allowing as much opportunity as possible for self-direction. This does not imply that management abdicate control or abandon leadership. It does suggest loosening some of the constraints of formal organization and permitting employees greater freedom to direct their own activities through greater delegation of authority, encouraging acceptance of responsibility at the bottom of the organization, and allowing participation of employees in making decisions that affect them.

Control

Control is basically an attempt to learn what is happening—how well a plan is working out in execution.

It is an aid to planning because a knowledge of what will work and what will not work is vital to that activity. It serves as a guide to supervision, since it indicates the parts of the plan that are going wrong and need revision or supervisory emphasis to make them go right. It may warn a manager of the failure of a project in time to enable him to salvage parts or to cut his loss by abandoning it.

Control represents the final phase in a continuing cycle of planning, organizing, coordinating, and directing that defines the responsibilities of a manager.

Keeping operations in line with plans requires not only a definition of satisfactory performance, but also a current feedback of information about performance and a comparison of this with desired results. The exercise of control thus involves at least four essential steps: (1) defining standards of performance, (2) developing an information feedback system, (3) establishing procedures for reporting and comparing operations with standards, and (4) taking appropriate action. All these processes should be carried on in a constructive spirit, in search of answers to "What went wrong and how can we make things work better?" instead of "Who is to blame?"

SUMMARY

In this chapter, we have sought to do two things. First, we have examined the nature of the industrial market. This involves a glance at (1) the participants (the extractive industries, the manufacturing industries, and the various types of establishments that use industrial goods; (2) the industrial marketing channels (branch houses and offices, distributors, and agents) and the most usual patterns in which the channel units are arrayed; and (3) the basic relationships that govern the behavior of industrial buyers and marketers (formal, such as contracts and franchises, and informal, such as loyalty, confidence and reciprocity).

For the benefit of the reader who lacks familiarity with the dimensions of management, we have outlined briefly the various activities that comprise it, such as planning, organizing, staffing, supervision, and control, together with an indication of some of the problems the manager meets in dealing with each of them.

Chapter 2

◇◇◇◇◇◇◇◇◇◇◇◇◇◇◇◇◇◇◇◇◇◇◇◇◇◇ THE DEMAND FOR

INDUSTRIAL GOODS

THE CHARACTERISTICS of the demand for industrial goods may perhaps be treated most effectively by separating these characteristics into three general groups: (1) those related to product types, (2) those related to the derived nature of demand, and (3) those related to the nature of the customer. In discussing the first and second groups, we will examine factors that influence the total value of sales realized by all industrial sellers. Discussion of the third group will emphasize the conditions and qualities that induce customers to patronize one marketer rather than another.

MARKET LEVELS AND PRODUCT TYPES

One of the unique characteristics of demand for industrial goods is that it may encompass any or all levels of the market from raw materials to finished products. It is useful to identify these different product-market levels not only because of the added insight about demand for industrial goods that can be gained, but also because of the advantage to the marketer of considering his products in the light of the conditions and manner in which they are most often bought. The proper choice of distribution channels and the most effective means of promotion often depend on the way in which buyers classify products.

It must be remembered, of course, that one cannot be very specific or precise in identifying these levels because of the tremendous variety of products involved. This problem can be partially eliminated, however, by using the following general classifications: major equipment, accessory equipment, fabricating or component parts, process materials, operating supplies, and raw materials.

Major Equipment

This category includes large machines or other tools whose unit purchase prices are so great that expenditures for them are apt to be charged to a capital account. The cost of such items therefore becomes part of the buying firm's capital structure rather than a current expense. Some items of equipment, such as automatic measuring and control devices, would also be included in this category even though they are not expensive and their cost is often charged to current expense. Since such items are vitally important to proper operation of the expensive machines they are attached to, they are often bought in much the same manner as the machines.

Major equipment is of two general types—multipurpose or standard machines and special-duty or single-purpose machines. Multipurpose equipment can be used by a number of different industries or by many firms in the same industry. By minor adjustments or changes of parts, standard machines can be adapted to several kinds of work within the general type of operation they are designed to perform. The substitution of dies or parts in a standard stamping machine, for example, enables it to stamp a variety of shapes and sizes.

Single-purpose machines, on the other hand, are designed to perform one particular operation and no other. A grinding machine, for example, may be designed to smooth a number of surfaces of varying hardness and have its abrasive elements set in an intricate and very exact planal relationship. Such a machine could become useless if the end product is changed so that the intricate grinding operation is no longer needed.

Typically, multipurpose machines tend to have a much longer life than single-purpose equipment, and the demand for them is likely to extend throughout several kindred industries. Since the original purchase price of such equipment can usually be amortized over a longer period than can the cost of single-purpose machines, annual fixed costs of its use are apt to be lower than those of more specialized equipment. The built-in versatility of standard equipment also makes unnecessary the detailed study of customers' production problems so characteristic of sales efforts in behalf of specialized machinery. As a result, the purchase of standard equipment is likely to involve much less preliminary planning and negotiation than the purchase of more specialized equipment.

Demand for special equipment is often confined to a single industry, even to one firm in the industry, because much of it is made to the buyer's specifications. Consequently, the negotiation of a purchase agreement often requires the closest kind of cooperation between the technical and sales staffs of buyer and seller. Since the value of the equipment may be destroyed not only by use but by relatively minor changes in design of the end product it is used to produce, the timing of purchases is usually determined by the incidence of model changes in the end product. The end product may not even be produced by the buying firm if it is a components or process materials house. The more limited application and life span of such machinery allows a relatively short period of time over which its purchase price may be amortized, and requires that the dollar benefits of using it be considerably greater than for other more standardized equipment.

Since the unit price of major equipment is sometimes very high, its purchase may involve financial problems for the buyer. Therefore, firms that market such equipment must usually be prepared to arrange loans for their customers, to help them float issues of securities, to negotiate with investment concerns, such as insurance companies, to buy the equipment and lease it to the using firms, to make sales on an installment basis, or to lease their own products instead of selling them.

Minor or Accessory Equipment

Minor or accessory equipment is machinery used in an auxiliary capacity. Its unit price is usually much less than that of major equipment, and its cost is generally charged to current expenses, although small or poorly financed buyers sometimes place it in a capital account. For this reason and because of the relatively small amounts involved, such purchases are likely to be made in a more routine manner, to involve less negotiation, and to require the approval of fewer executives in the buying firm than is the case with major installation items.

Most minor equipment items are standardized and suited to the performance of a function involved in more than one of the operations of a business. For example, small lathes, fractional horsepower motors, and small tractors may be used in carrying on activities in several different departments or at several different stages in the production process. They are also likely to be useful to many different types of business. For these reasons, their demand is usually horizontal in nature in that it is not confined to one industry. As a result, the organization for marketing them must be much more widespread than is that for items of major equipment. Minor equipment must be sold through many more outlets, and the relations between the buyer and the maker can be less direct and immediate.

Fabricating or Component Parts

It is characteristic of American industry that, except in rare instances, a single establishment does not carry through the entire production process from raw material to finished product. Typically, the work of production is carried on by a series of plants, often under diverse ownership, each performing a single operation or homogeneous group of operations on the material. As the process approaches the final, finished product stage, the work of production becomes more and more a matter of assembling finished parts, bought from different suppliers, into an article ready for use and final sale. Almost the entire production process of some industries is one of assembly. Even large integrated manufacturers like the major automobile producers, which have long sought to control their supplies of component parts through ownership of subsidiaries, still find it necessary to buy items from thousands of small suppliers.

Components are often bought on the basis of specifications prepared by the purchaser, although many of them, such as batteries and tires in the automotive industry, are standardized according to the specifications of the parts manufacturer. In either case, the buying firm probably will want to include commitments for an entire year's supply or a stated percentage of a year's supply in one contract. In order to assure uniformity of quality, a buyer is under pressure to concentrate his purchases of components parts with as few suppliers as possible, although to provide continuity of supply, he may need more than one source.

In awarding purchase contracts for parts, the buyer is apt to place heavy emphasis on uniformity and reliability of quality as well as on the certainty and regularity of the seller's delivery service. This emphasis arises because it is especially important to keep the stocks of component parts as small as possible. Since their value is usually high in relation to the cost of the materials in them, they are very expensive items to carry in inventory. If a buyer can rely on the quality and delivery service of his supplier, he can reduce to a minimum his stocks of these highly expensive materials. For these reasons, component parts are usually bought directly from the maker.

Some component parts retain their identity in the finished product. This offers buyers the opportunity of enhancing the sales appeal of their end products by incorporating in them a component of known market acceptance. On the other hand, if the replacement market offers a component maker a possible sales volume greater than the requirements for original installation, the manufacturer of the finished product may enjoy a decisive advantage in bargaining with the parts maker. In the tire business, for example, it has been shown that the car owner who needs a new tire exhibits a strong preference for the make that was on his car when he bought it. Tire manufacturers, therefore, have shown a willingness to make substantial price concessions to the automobile-producing firms in order to get their tires installed as original equipment.

Process Materials

Process materials closely resemble component parts in that they usually enter into and form an indistinguishable part of the finished product. A pharmaceutical house may buy the acetate or acetyl of salicylic acid and an inert carrier or binding agent, mix them together, form them into tablets, put them into a container carrying its brand, and sell them as aspirin tablets. A food manufacturer may buy a variety of ingredients, mix them in proper proportions, and sell the resulting material on the market as a cake mix.

A few process materials either are broken up and dissipated in the production process without entering into the final product, or they act to bring about changes in the materials that enter into the product without themselves undergoing material change or forming a part of the finished article. A catalyst, for example, sets off certain chemical reactions without undergoing any change itself; it therefore can be used over and over again.

Process materials differ from component parts chiefly in that most of them cannot be identified so that they can be recognized in the finished product. For very few of them is there a replacement market. As a result, little is usually to be gained by advertising a process material over the head of its industrial user to the buyers of the product it is employed to make. There are a few examples of such advertising, but they are not common.

Process materials tend to be bought on specifications prepared by the buyer or according to standards developed by the trade, often with the help of government agencies. For example, fine chemicals are usually bought and sold on the basis of U.S.P. standards, although one supplier may gain some advantage over another by building a reputation for exercising extreme care in making sure that the quality of every lot he sells conforms exactly to the standard or exceeds the standard by a constant ratio in purity or other desirable properties. However, this standardization is sufficient to throw considerable emphasis on price and service as competitive factors in the sale of process materials.

It is not unusual for a firm to buy certain types of process materials on requirements contracts or to purchase them speculatively, sometimes for future delivery. The negotiation of such contracts may be a matter of considerable importance to both the buyer and the seller and may be handled at high executive levels.

Operating Supplies

Operating supplies do not become a part of the finished product, but for the most part are continuously worn out or used up in the process of operating or facilitating the operation of an enterprise. Such items as paints, soaps and detergents, oils and greases, cleaning materials, pencils and ink, typewriter ribbons, and stationery belong in this category.

The typical operating supply is needed by many different firms in many different industries. The functions which such goods perform are likely to be common to many types of enterprise. This means that they must be marketed on a widespread basis. The methods by which they are marketed more nearly resemble those under which consumers' goods are sold than do those of any other type of industrial goods.

Supplies are generally bought in small quantities, although some purchasers are willing to enter into blanket or open-end contracts whereby they commit themselves to buy their entire requirements of certain items from one, two, or three suppliers for a designated future period. When supplies are bought currently without benefit of such blanket contracts, their purchase usually takes place in a routine manner and according to a set pattern, which remains unchanged over considerable periods of time. When they are bought on blanket contracts, the contract may be the subject of much negotiation, but the work of placing delivery orders becomes a matter even more routine than in the absence of such contracts.

Operating supplies are usually standardized at least within the brand designations of the makers, although occasional buyers purchase on specifications they prepare for their own use. For this reason, there is little need for direct contact between the buyer and the seller. Because of the wide areas over which they must be sold and the smallness of the unit purchase, it is both difficult and uneconomical to establish and maintain such contact. They are likely to be marketed on an indirect basis through middlemen.

Purchasing agents and marketers of industrial goods often speak of MRO (maintenance, repair, and operating) items. In this category, they usually lump operating supplies and at least the less expensive articles of accessory equipment. This is often a useful grouping, because these kinds of items tend to be bought in much the same manner and hence must be sold through the same kinds of channels and by the same methods.

Raw Materials

Raw materials are the basic materials of industry. They usually have undergone only such processing as is necessary for convenience in handling and transportation or for standardization to facilitate their use or purchase and sale.

Raw materials are supplied chiefly by agriculture and the lumbering, mining, and fishing industries. Those produced by agriculture are generally marketed in fairly small lots through elaborate marketing systems. Since their distribution is highly specialized and is in itself a separate subject of study, it will be given only incidental treatment here.

The industries, other than agriculture, that extract raw materials exhibit a strong tendency to integrate their extraction with the performance of at least the early processes of refinement and fabrication. In some industries, this integration is carried well along into the production process. For example, very few firms that use steel shapes or forms in their operations buy the raw iron ore or even the refined steel billets. The steel companies carry the production process from the ore in the ground through to the point where they are able to offer rods, beams, sheets, and other shapes to suit the purposes of their customers. The oil companies carry the process of integration through from the well to the industrial consumer, although there is a brisk trade among them to secure special kinds of crude, to dispose of excess supplies of it, and to offset shortages in their own crude production. Such transactions are generally negotiated at very high levels and involve large quantities. The mechanism for negotiating them is usually relatively simple and direct, although the details of the bargaining process are often infinitely complex.

When raw materials are traded in on the open market, they are usually bought and sold on the basis of recognized standards, expressed in terms of either grade designations or sets of specifications. Agricultural raw materials are usually vended on the basis of systems of grades sponsored and administered by the federal government. Chemicals may be marketed by grade or by specification; minerals may be sold by grade, by specification, or by the vein from which they were dug.

Various kinds of agents, especially brokers, are an important element in the system for marketing the part of the supply of raw materials that does not move in integrated channels. Much of the supply is usually controlled by integrated firms, and much of that part of the supply sold on the market consists of (*a*) an integrated firm's excess production over its own needs, (*b*) an integrated company's purchases to supply shortages in its own production of materials, and (*c*) an integrated company's purchases of materials with special characteristics that its own controlled sources of raw materials cannot supply. Thus, many of the buying and selling firms do not possess well-organized departmental units to make such purchases and sales. They do not do enough of this kind of business to justify maintaining such a unit. Therefore, this work is often done at irregular intervals by some executive as an addition to his usual duties. He does not have time to keep up with the market or to maintain adequate contacts with customers or sources. The agent offers both information and contacts when they are needed. Brokers, often operating almost entirely by telephone, are usually a feature of the unintegrated portion of demand for a raw material.

DERIVED DEMAND

Derived demand refers to the indirect way in which the need for industrial goods is generated, i.e., from the demand for the consumer goods or services they are used to make or provide. For example, the demand for sheet metal is derived from the demand for products made of sheet metal as is the demand for machines that cut and shape sheet metal. In general, the demand for industrial goods tends to depend on and fluctuate with the demand for the goods and services they are used to produce.

Demand for an item used in maintenance and repair depends on general business activity and is usually determined by sales (expected as well as actual) of all the various articles produced by the manufacturing complex. By contrast, demand for a material or component at any particular time depends on the probable demand for articles to be made from it during the relatively near future (one or two production cycles) as estimated by the managers of firms that use the material in fabricating or processing operations. Demand for a piece of specialized machinery, on the other hand, is determined to a great extent by long-run forecasts of demand and profit possibilities for products the equipment is used to make. Such forecasts would normally cover a 3- to 10-year period, but are sometimes projected as many as 20 or 40 years into the future.

This characteristic of derived demand often causes the manufacturer of a material or piece of equipment to promote the sale of the product his machine or material is used to make. For example, the Pure-Pak Division of Ex-Cell-O Corporation, which produces machines that make paper milk containers, found it profitable to advertise in national consumer media, stressing the advantages of buying milk in paper cartons. The Timken Roller Bearing Company used to remind the public that the Broadway Limited "rolls on Timken bearings." The United States Steel Company promoted in consumer media the use of household furniture made of steel. In 1965, Du Pont of Canada set up a program to train shoe clerks of about 100 retail stores concerning the properties of Corfam, its synthetic leather product. Many other similar examples could be cited.

Manufacturers who sell to OEM buyers, and who identify their products so they can be recognized as part of the finished article, are often forced by the presence of derived demand to select their customers with discretion. Otherwise, the prestige and reputation for quality that prompts this identification will be lost if the product is used in conjunction with supplementary materials of a shoddy nature or the product it is incorporated into is of substandard quality or poor workmanship. It is known that several textile firms that emphasize the identity of their products in their promotion are rather selective in their choice of customers.

When the use of a manufacturer's product adds salability to the buyer's end product, derived demand can provide the manufacturer with a potent sales appeal. Some years ago, for example, the Reynolds Metals Company introduced an aluminum foil wrap to be used in packaging. One of the buyers of this material was a firm selling dried fruits. The firm advertised that its product was wrapped in aluminum foil, although the foil itself was concealed by an outer pasteboard container. A moderate increase in sales resulted. The metals company subsequently persuaded its customer to redesign its package so the foil would appear on the outside. When the new package was test marketed, it produced a dramatic increase in sales. The redesigned package, using foil on the outside, resulted in a more salable product for the fruit processor and a better customer for the metals company.

As a result of its derived nature, the demand for industrial goods may fluctuate violently because of changes in the tempo of business operations and subsequent shifts in inventory objectives. Typically, an industrial buyer's inventory objectives are expressed in terms of the quantity of an item necessary to satisfy operating needs for a stated number of days. Once the desired number of days of supply is determined, it is the purchasing officer's responsibility to adjust purchases and commitments to buy so that the stock of an item is always as close as possible to the amount necessary to sustain operations at the current and projected rate for the desired number of days. While this is an extremely difficult feat to achieve with accuracy, particularly with an inventory consisting of thousands of items, it nevertheless represents the objective toward which purchasing management works. For example, a purchasing agent is said to be buying on a 60- or 90-day basis.

When business conditions are bad, the number of days of stock established as the inventory goal is likely to be reduced due both to the easier availability of goods, accompanied by at least the prospect of lower prices, and to the uncertainty of future demand for the end product. When business is good and expectations are bright, the number of days of supply is apt to be increased for the opposite reasons. These changes in inventory level have a multiplier effect when they are translated into purchase commitments. For example, if a firm operating on a three-month inventory experiences an increase in sales that steps up the use of material A by 100 units per month, its purchases of material A during the first month after the change are likely to be increased by 400 units. The firm would, of course, need an additional 100 units to support increased production during the current month and 300 additional units to build up a three-month inventory to support the new rate of production.

This bulge in purchases may be diminished somewhat if the buyer decides to spread his inventory buildup over two or three months instead of concentrating it in one. This he may very well do so that before making such a drastic inventory commitment he can assure himself that the sales increase is a continuing one and not a one-month flash in the pan. In either event, the increase in demand experienced by supplier firms is considerably greater than the increase in sales realized by the buying firm.

A drop in sales tends to make an even greater difference in purchases. Let's assume, for example, that a given firm sells 1 million units of its product per month and carries a 3-month supply of needed materials and parts in inventory. This means that the firm maintains an inventory of 3 million units of needed materials and parts and buys 1 million units each month to meet production requirements and maintain its 90-day stock. Suppose now that sales fall to 800,000 units per month and production declines proportionately. The company now needs only 2.4 million units of materials and parts in stock in order to achieve its 90-day inventory objective. It must reduce inventory by 600,000 units of materials and parts.

If management seeks to make the entire adjustment during the first month after the change in sales, the firm will place orders for only 200,000 units instead of the previous 1 million units. If management decides to spread the adjustment over the following 2 months, purchases will be reduced to 500,000 units per month. When many companies widely follow such procedures, it tends to cause a change in the demand for certain types of industrial goods entirely out of proportion to the decrease in demand for consumer goods, which initiated the adjustment.

Because of the derived character of demand for industrial goods, financial considerations also have considerable leverage in determining how much of an item will be purchased. Such considerations are especially influential in the market for industrial equipment. This influence can be readily appreciated when it is understood that industrial purchasers are keenly interested in the effect of their acquisitions on the net profits of their companies and, in some cases, even on the financial structure of their firms.

The purchase of materials influences profits chiefly through its effect on the cost of end products and on their physical attractiveness. Of course, the availability and speed with which materials can be procured influences the capital structure of a firm because of the working capital required for inventory. The more difficult it is to procure supplies of a given material, the greater the stock of the material that must be carried in inventory.

An equipment purchase affects profit as a result of both its initial cost and its effect on the cost and attractiveness of the end product. The obsolescence rate of equipment also affects capital structure through the size of reserve funds that must be established to replace it. The impact of such influences on the profit position and capital structure of buying firms is greatly multiplied by the forces of inflation and technological improvement.

The case of the Thompson Products Company[1] is a classic example of the part financial considerations play in the demand for industrial equipment. In 1942, Thompson Products bought a Warner Swasey 3A saddle lathe for $12,000. This was depreciated on the company's books on a 14-year basis, so that by 1956 the Thompson Products Company had retained in its capital structure from cash inflow the sum of $12,000 as a depreciation reserve. In addition, it found that the lathe could be sold for $1,000 in the used machine market. But the price of a lathe of the same make and model was now $35,000, so it would be necessary to borrow or apply from retained earnings $22,000 in order to restore Thompson Products' production equipment to the 1942 level of efficiency. The firm netted about 9 percent on sales before taxes. Income taxes took about 52 percent of this; so that to find the $22,000 Thompson Products had to commit the earnings from almost $500,000 worth of sales.

But this was not all the bad news. In 1942, the Warner Swasey 3A

---

[1] Reported in *Sales Management*, February 20, 1959.

saddle lathe was the machine best suited for its purpose. By 1956, a new and improved model selling for $67,000 had been developed. So if Thompson Products wished to retain in the 1956 technological environment the same position it had occupied in 1942, it had to raise $54,000 of new capital or apply that sum from retained earnings, thereby reducing by that amount the funds available for new ventures. To earn this amount, Thompson Products had to sell $1.250 million worth of goods and services.

This saga illustrates the effect of financial considerations on the demand for industrial equipment; it also explains why many managements use the so-called cash flow method of analyzing the effect of equipment purchases on their financial situation. Without going into the intricacies of the method, it should be pointed out that net cash flow represents money that flows into a business but does not flow out again in the current course of business—mainly charges for depreciation and reserves and net profit.

In addition to its general implications about the demand for certain types of industrial goods, this discussion suggests that industrial marketers should be prepared to analyze the effect the purchase of their products is likely to have on the profit position and financial structure of buying firms. They should also prepare their salesmen to talk in terms of the cash flow method in communicating the results of such an analysis to the prospective customer.

Elasticity of Demand

Over short-run periods, the demand for many industrial products is likely to show a reverse elasticity. Ordinarily, when the price of an article declines, its demand tends to increase; when its price advances, the demand for it tends to fall. Precisely the reverse is true of many industrial materials and some supplies in the short run. This is probably due largely to the training and experience of most buyers. When the price of a material declines, a purchasing agent is likely to withdraw from the market to the extent his inventory position will permit, until he has an opportunity to study the situation and decide whether in his opinion the decline is merely a temporary fluctuation or represents the beginning of a continued downward trend. This means that even a small price decline sometimes has the effect of drying up demand for a time until the general market situation clarifies. If the market condition remains uncertain, buyers are likely to purchase from hand to mouth until it becomes more settled.

On the other hand, if the price of a material advances, the careful buyer is likely to wonder whether the increase portends the beginning of a general advance. If he concludes that this is the case, he is apt to make more than usually heavy commitments for his firm. The executive charged with the buying work of an industrial concern always looks good to his management when during a period of advancing prices the firm is able to use materials bought at lower price levels, or when during a period of falling prices the concern is able to use goods bought at current, or nearly current, prices. The resulting beneficial effect on the company cost structure lends flexibility to the firm's pricing practices for its end products.

These observations as to the reverse elasticity of industrial demand apply more accurately to the sum total of a given material sold than to the amount disposed of by an individual supplier, and to general price fluctuations more than to those of a single seller. For example, when the price of a standardized material declines slightly or one supplier lowers his price, purchasing agents who must buy to maintain stocks are likely to divert their purchases to those sources offering the lowest prices, and at the same time shrink the amount of their total commitments while studying the market. Therefore, decline in the price of a single supplier may increase his sales while diminishing those of competing sellers by an amount in excess of that diverted to the price-cutting supplier.

It should also be understood that this observation applies almost entirely to the short-run behavior of demand. Over the long run, a decline in the price of a material whose purchase cost constitutes a primary factor in the expense structure of concerns using it is likely to increase the total sales of that article, since such a cost reduction is apt to make possible a decrease in the price of the goods made of the material and, in turn, increase the demand for them. This effect is limited in its scope, because comparatively few materials play such a large role in the cost structure of their end products that a reduction in their prices, in the proportions likely to occur, will make possible any significant decrease in the end product prices. In order to cause any appreciable effect on the price of an end product, moreover, the reduction in the price of its primary material must usually extend over a long period.

To repeat, the price change responsiveness of the overall demand for an industrial material depends to some degree on how important its price is as an element in the general cost structure of the using firm or of its end product. If the cost of a material represents a significant element in the cost structure of the average using firm or of its end product, a lowering of its price is apt to cause enough saving in the cost of the end product to make possible a reduction in its price, with a resulting increase in the demand for both the end product and its primary material. If, on the other hand, the cost of a material constitutes only a small fraction, say a few percent of the end product cost, a shift in its price may make a change in the end product cost so small that no significant movement in the end product price is justified, and there will be little or no shift in overall demand for the material.

If a product is of minor importance to the buyer, a shift in the price of a single supplier is likely to cause little change in the volume he sells. The small differential involved may easily by nullified by slight savings in inventory carrying charges made possible by the superior services of the regular supplier or by the added costs of buying such a product separately instead of as part of a large order from the regular supplier, whose price remains unchanged.

When quality or consistency of quality in materials and components is a matter of prime importance but not easily checked, demand responds very little to changes in the price of any individual supplier. For example, a customer who experiences good results in the use of a complex chemical or electronic part made by one supplier is not apt to shift readily to a new source simply because the old one drops his price. The buyer is likely to fear that imperceptibly slight or hidden differences in the chemical or physical properties of the two items will cause undesirable changes in the performance of his end product. A drastic price reduction may even rouse suspicions that the price-cutter has debased quality in some way that is not readily apparent. By contrast, demand for materials bought and sold on the basis of recognized standards tends to respond actively to price changes by individual suppliers.

On the whole, demand for equipment is likely to be less responsive to shifts in price than demand for materials, supplies, and components. Equipment price usually appears in the cost structure of the end product either as an element in factory overhead, which includes other items that cannot readily be identified with the product, or as a general depreciation figure. Both these figures usually include the capital charges on a number of machines, and are allocated on some basis that appears reasonable to the cost accounting executives. Therefore, it is a remote likelihood that a price reduction for a given piece of equipment will cause an end product cost reduction big enough to make possible a general price cut, with a resulting increase in demand for the end product and, eventually, for the equipment. Such a chain of causation may occur, but it is not common. It is more likely to happen with single-purpose, special machines than with multi-purpose machines whose capital charges are apt to be spread over the costs of many end products.

Even changes in an individual equipment marketer's price are not likely to bring about proportionate changes in the demand for his goods. Costs of operation, repair, and maintenance, precise suitability for the job, ease of adjustment, speed and productivity of operation, and other similar considerations are fully as important as, if not more important than, price in influencing patronage. Moreover, the buyer often prefers to use machines all of one make to perform one sequence of operations or to equip one unit of his shop. This preference may be due to the way their functions dovetail, because such an arrangement facilitates repairs and lessens downtime or because the stock of repair parts needed is reduced. Some equipment makers have capitalized on this tendency of buyers by selling packages of machines, each containing the units necessary to equip a certain type of shop or to perform a closely related group of operations. Undoubtedly, the machines in such a package are often made to function better when they are all used together than when tools of other makers are interspersed among them.

For these and other reasons, demand for industrial products, both on an industrywide basis and on the basis of the individual maker, is usually sticky in its response to price change.

CUSTOMER MOTIVES

In addition to its derived or indirect nature and the number of product-market levels at which it is present, demand for industrial goods is also characterized by a measure of economic objectivity stemming from the nature of the industrial customer. Unlike the ultimate consumer, the industrial buyer is motivated by profit considerations and must be prepared to justify his purchases on the basis of measurable performance. Consequently, the professional buying staffs of businesses, government agencies, and institutions are interested in benefits that will be reflected in the cost and/or profit experience of their enterprises. For the most part, the factors that influence the patronage motives of such buyers are product quality, price, and service, as well as the saving that can be anticipated from a given combination of product, price, and service. A study made by E. J. Nouri, reported in *Sales Management*, April 2, 1965, showed that industrial buyers ranked patronage in the following order of importance:

1. Quality.
2. Technical assistance.
3. Service.
4. Price

Product Quality

The industrial buyer tends to define quality as the characteristics of a product that suit it for the purpose for which he intends to use it. He probably wants these characteristics to be present in the article in precisely the degree needed to make it suitable for his purpose and no more. He is almost as reluctant to pay for extra quality (over and above a reasonable safety factor) that he does not need as he is to buy goods of inferior quality. And he is likely to feel that if unneeded quality is there, he pays for it regardless of the price.

For example, a firm bought stainless steel discs chamfered on one side at a price of 18 cents each. The chamfering was not needed, and when discs without this feature were bought from another supplier, the cost was 5 cents each. A firm using a specially made hex head cap screw found that by a slight change in its end product, that in no way affected the end product's performance, it could use a standard screw with a resulting reduction in price from $4.90 a hundred to 30 cents a hundred. In buying radiators, the Ford Company specified 120 tubes per unit. One bidder offered radiators with 140 tubes, which increased the weight 15 percent. The Ford purchasing department helped him to redesign his product to meet the specifications exactly at a much lower price.

A quality characteristic that increases the life expectancy of a piece of industrial equipment supplies a powerful patronage incentive. A manufacturer of rock bits found that by using electrode-type electric salt bath furnaces for hardening the bits he could increase their life by four or five times, with resulting increase in sales. A maker of brakes for giant trailer trucks developed a drum manufacturing method that increased their period of effective operation by about 600 percent. Such an increase in the life of a piece of equipment has additional appeal in that it reduces the annual depreciation a buyer-user must charge against the product.

The industrial buyer's patronage is also likely to be strongly influenced by a quality characteristic of a material or machine that makes his end product more attractive to customers. For example, the firm that makes a compressor that runs without sound perceptible to the average human ear will have a powerful appeal to manufacturers of refrigerators, deepfreeze units, and room air conditioning equipment. It is difficult and often impossible for either the industrial marketer or his customer-user to measure the value of such a benefit in dollars. In spite of this, an industrial good that adds to the attractiveness of the end product draws patronage.

Consistency in the quality of materials, supplies, and component parts is a patronage motive almost as important as the level of quality itself. The specifications for an industrial good will almost always include a range within which the quality of different units may vary. This is known as tolerance. When the product of an industrial marketer has consistency of quality, every unit can be counted on to fall within a quality range suitable to the buyer's purpose.

Assured consistency of quality greatly reduces the need for meticulous inspection and testing of incoming shipments, and does much to assure that the end product is of uniform quality. For some materials, consistency diminishes shutdown time and repair costs for delicate machines unable to handle materials of varying quality without adjustment, or machines that may be damaged by imperfections in the materials on which they are used. Consistency may enable the user-buyer to reduce the inventory he must carry, because if different shipments from the same source vary widely in quality, the buyer must carry enough stock to enable him to inspect, reject, and replace a shipment without shutting down his operation. Since different uses of a material and the conditions under which it is used may affect the range of tolerance permitted, the marketer may find it necessary to study customer plant operations to ascertain the degree of quality consistency each buyer needs.

Price

While price has a very potent influence on patronage demand, it is usually not the most important factor. Quality and service are generally of equal or greater importance. It is true that a lower price is perhaps the most obvious piece of evidence a purchasing officer can submit to his management to show that he is doing a good job. But its apparent usefulness for this purpose may be illusory.

If a buyer who has a choice between product A, which exactly fits the need of his firm, and product B, which falls short of need but can be had for a lower price, insists on purchasing product B, he may be generating trouble for his firm and undermining his own effectiveness. The people who use the product will soon learn its shortcomings and complain that the purchasing department is not doing the job it was set up to do. If they lose confidence in the purchasing officer, his relations with them may degenerate into bickering and open conflict. One of the industrial buyer's most valuable assets is the confidence and cooperation of the operating executives whose units he serves. In spite of these facts, one of the most common managerial complaints about purchasing officers is that they overemphasize price as a factor in patronage.

In comparing prices, most purchasing officers go beyond quoted figures and compute the relative costs of different materials, pieces or machines in use, or as components of the cost of the finished product. This takes into consideration a variety of factors, such as the amount of scrap or waste resulting from the use of a material, the costs of processing the material, the units of service actually delivered, the amount of work a machine will do, the power it needs, and a host of other characteristics that generate or minimize costs.

For example, the price of a paint may be low, but it may be costly to apply. The coal with a low price per ton may be high in volatile material, ash, or fusable elements and low in B.t.u.'s. In buying soap, a New York hospital analyzed the products of seven suppliers. The liquid soaps ranged from 20 to 35 percent and the paste soaps from 35 to 61 percent in dry soap content (the ingredients that do the cleansing). This analysis showed that one brand with a relatively high quoted price cost 38 cents per pound of dry soap, while another with a lower quoted price cost $1.41 per pound of dry soap content. *Sales Management*, December 3, 1965, reports that Kaiser Aluminum Company was able to take power transmission tower tonnage away from steel. While the aluminum towers cost more, costs of installation (by helicopter in rough areas) were less (by $600,000 for 450 towers in one contract) and maintenance expenses were much less.

The techniques used in making these comparisons are a part of what the purchasing profession calls "value analysis." This part of the process involves trying to determine for each industrial good the effect its use will have on the final cost of the end product. The wise industrial marketer will inform himself about the techniques used in value analysis and will compare his own products with those of his rivals so that he may use the results in his product improvement work if they are unflattering or in his selling work if they are favorable.

Value analysis also includes an attempt on the part of the buyer to compute the costs of making the most important products he buys. This knowledge gives him a powerful leverage in the negotiation process. Such an attempt involves breaking down the item into its component parts or materials, determining the processes that must be used in fabricating the article and its components, the operations involved in assembling it, and the probable cost of materials and processes. Value analysis groups can often come surprisingly close to determining the actual cost of making many of the industrial goods bought by the firms that employ them. This is especially so with machinery and component parts. It is less likely to be true of chemicals and similar materials, since there may be wide variations in yield that cannot be accurately estimated.

Needless to say, the application of these two techniques sometimes yields contrary results. Industrial good A, with a wide margin between its price and its cost, may provide a smaller addition to end product cost than B, which shows exactly the opposite cost-price relationship. In such a case, there is a little question which the wise buyer will choose, and little he can profitably do to force the marketer of A to reduce its price. The producer of A has what amounts to a monopoly, within a price range equal to its differential advantage in contribution to the cost structure of the customer's end product. In such a case, the buyer benefits from value analysis only in that he knows what he gets for what he pays; he knows at what points the supplier may become vulnerable to pressures for reduced prices; and he has a factual and analytical basis on which to decide whether to make the article or to buy it.

Not all industrial buyers make use of the techniques of value analysis. Its intensive use is probably limited to large firms whose volume of purchases justifies the expense of an organizational unit of specialists. The buyer for a smaller firm probably employs some value analysis techniques on an informal basis, but cannot afford an intensive or specialized program. The purchasing officers of the large firm with a well-staffed value analysis unit sometimes find that as a result of its work they are able to suggest to their suppliers changes in design, materials, or production processes that will reduce their costs and thus enable them to lower prices. This is not a usual procedure, and probably happens most often when a large firm, well staffed with technical specialists, buys from a small concern that cannot afford such talent.

From the standpoint of the student and, to some extent, from that of the practical marketer, the point of this discussion lies in the fact that the comparison of industrial suppliers' prices is usually not the relatively simple process of matching quoted figures assumed in economic theory, but is a much more complicated operation, often involving factors that are peculiar to the production or marketing processes of the buyer and are in large measure hidden from the supplier.

Service

Service has many facets; each provides its own series of benefits that influence buyer patronage. The most important types of service are technical, repair and maintenance, delivery, information, and sales contacts.

Technical. Problems of a technical nature frequently arise in connection with the use of industrial products. In some cases, vendors are able to rely on their salesmen to supply the expert help users need to solve these problems. In other cases, salesmen must be buttressed with a force of trained specialists to whom they or users can refer difficult problems, or from whom they can get advice and consultation in handling them. In either case, the amount of training needed by a sales force is considerable. If a salesman is to provide the service himself, he must be given thorough technical training in the product's uses so that he can diagnose and prescribe for the difficulties likely to arise in the buyer's plant. Even if the technical service is provided by a force of specialists who do nothing else, the salesman must be trained to recognize and describe the various types of technical problems that develop so that he can give the specialist some idea of the kind of service needed.

Some industrial marketers seek to supply their customers with written material they hope will enable the customer himself to handle all but the most complex and difficult technical use problems. For example, the Diamond Alkali Company, which sells basic chemicals to about 60 industries, in one year distributed some 8,000 copies of its *Chlorine Handbook*, 4,000 copies of its *Chromium Chemical Handbook*, and 8,000 copies of its *Silicates Handbook*, containing highly detailed technical information about the properties and uses of those types of chemicals. Merck and Company, maker of fine chemicals, publishes and distributes the *Merck Manual* and the *Merck Handbook*, exhaustive compendiums on the characteristics and behavior of diseases and on the properties and uses of chemicals employed in the treatment of disease.

The customer who has learned to rely on the technical advice and help of an industrial marketer in solving his materials use problems may be hard to win away from that marketer by other appeals. One such unsolved or improperly solved problem may cost much more than the savings resulting from a substantially lower price for the material of a competing supplier.

Repair and Maintenance. For some kinds of equipment, repair and maintenance service, especially the parts supply service, is a very important patronage influence. Many equipment users prefer to make their own repairs, because by doing so they can save shutdown time of machines that affect the operation of an entire production complex, such as an assembly line or a processing group. Some of them maintain special shops within the plant for this purpose. Such plants generally carry stocks of parts from which they can draw to make repairs. Sometimes, such stocks include only the parts that must be replaced most frequently. Other firms carry standby machines to be used in case of breakdowns, and order parts as needed. The result is that no small fraction of the parts business is conducted in an emergency atmosphere. For these reasons, speed is a vital element in the service of supplying parts and replacements.

An added factor emphasizing the importance of speed is that even though the need for any part may occur very rarely, its timing is highly unpredictable and it is very urgent when it happens. The result is that a user who wants to be able to repair any breakdown that may occur must carry many parts he may not need for years and some he will never need. Thus, inventory is very high in relation to use. One firm found that in order to avoid shutdowns and stoppages of production it was forced to carry at all times about one and one half times the value of the parts it used annually.

A concern can reduce these uncertainties by preventive maintenance, but it cannot eliminate them. The size of the stock the user must carry to supply his erratic needs will be materially reduced if his supplier offers a satisfactory parts service with the following essential features:

1. Adequate and representative warehouse stocks at points convenient to using centers backed by adequate factory stocks.
2. Prompt handling and delivery of all orders.
3. Reliable delivery information and promises.
4. Willingness to give service out of the ordinary routine in emergencies.

The marketer of equipment to whom parts service is a vital patronage factor may find that he cannot market through distributors unless they carry adequate and representative stocks of parts and maintain satisfactory facilities for delivering them.

Reliability. Reliability is one of the strongest service patronage factors. In its essence it consists of assurance that the supplier will do what he promises to do. It has three important facets—quality, delivery, and production.

The importance of consistency in quality, which is an element of reliability, has already been mentioned. This characteristic also involves care on the part of the marketer in learning precisely what is wanted and in seeing to it that this is what is delivered. If items are made to stock, this is mainly a matter of inspection and order handling. When industrial goods are made to order, it really involves one phase of reliability in production.

Reliability in production is important mainly, if not entirely, when goods are made to order or on contract. It consists in a thorough understanding of specifications or other forms of quality description and a rigid compliance with them so that the buyer can be sure that what he orders is what he will get. This same understanding also gives assurance that the supplier will be able to make the items contracted for, without delay and postcontract negotiation of changes in specifications, price, or delivery dates. A third phase of production reliability involves exact compliance with delivery promises for goods made on contract. Most buyers understand and are willing to make allowances for failures to finish and deliver goods on time because of strikes and natural calamities, but failures stemming from lesser causes are not easily forgiven, and a reputation for failure is a powerful deterrent to patronage.

Reliability in production is most important as a patronage factor in the demand for equipment. But it can also be highly important when materials or components are bought on blanket contracts for delivery as required during the contract period. Coupled with speed and certainty of delivery, reliability becomes a vital patronage factor when the buyer operates on the basis of moving materials or components direct from the receiving platform onto the production line, and protects his production continuity only by nominal reserve stocks.

Reliability in delivery consists of two elements—speed and certainty. Speed requires the supplier to maintain adequate and representative stocks in or near using centers, to handle orders efficiently, and to use the proper means of transportation. These are costly activities, and the vendor must constantly balance the expense of speed in delivery against the patronage attracted by the value of its benefits to the user-buyer. In the sense that the buyer can count on a supplier to deliver what is ordered within a specified number of days, certainty of delivery is clearly a strong patronage factor.

The benefits accruing to the buyer from both these elements of reliability in delivery are primarily related to the amount of stock he must carry in order to avoid shutdowns. If a supplier offers a high degree of both speed and certainty of delivery, the buyer may reduce his inventory to the minimum. If a supplier's delivery service is usually speedy but erratic, the buyer must base his inventory on the longest experienced lead time between ordering and receiving. Often, a supplier whose delivery service is slower but more certain than that of a rival enjoys a definite patronage advantage. The benefit the buyer gains from reliability in delivery is one he can readily value in dollars and cents. The marketer can also calculate it roughly and balance its probable pulling power against his cost of supplying the service.

The Selling Service. It may seem odd to classify an industrial marketer's selling activities as a service to the buyer, since their primary purpose is the purely selfish one of getting business for the marketer. The industrial buyer's function is to buy, not to be sold. In the process of buying, however, the purchasing agent may make use of at least some, if not most, of the supplier's selling efforts if they are properly made. He is apt to be partly influenced by the marketer's selling efforts in placing his patronage, to the extent that those efforts help him in getting the maximum benefits for his firm.

Many industrial marketers are aware of this, and they train and stimulate their salesmen to organize their work around the central idea of being of service to the customer. Industrial advertising and sales promotion material often has this as its central theme, also.

Probably the most important kind of service the average industrial buyer expects to get from the marketer's salesmen and sales material is information. The information may apply to several subjects, the most usual of which is the marketer's own product and service.

Industrial buyers want this kind of information to be exact and accurate. For example, they may be cold to such claims as: "This paint contains more white lead than any other"; "The finish is very high grade"; "We will install some time next week." They prefer such statements as: "This paint contains 42.6 percent white lead"; "The acidproof enamel is baked at 320 degrees"; "We'll be here at 2:15 Tuesday to install." If a salesman does not know the exact answer to a question, buyers prefer that he admit the fact, make inquiry from his superior, and report his findings promptly. Neither the salesman nor the writer of advertising or promotional material can properly present such information unless he has adequate technical or experience background as well as proper training concerning the materials, methods of manufacture, properties, uses, and operational behavior of the products he sells.

The purchasing agent also looks to vendor's salesmen for information about new products, not only those offered by a salesman's own firm but by his industry or by any other trade from which the buyer's firm may purchase. This is a very important facet of the salesman's information service. It may also be supplied by the marketer's advertising and promotional material.

Furthermore, buyers depend on salesmen for information about the trade or industry. In the course of visiting many firms in an industry, salesmen acquire facts about general trends, new developments, changes in personnel, and other trade information of interest to buyers. One type of industry information a buyer usually receives with mixed emotions from a supplier's salesman is that of a confidential or semiconfidential nature about the buyer's competitor. He is glad to have the information, but in supplying it the salesman loses his confidence for the buyer knows that thereafter he cannot tell the salesman anything about his own business that he is not willing to have broadcasted to his competitors. In addition, out of the normal routine salesmen may provide odd bits of information of value to the buyer's firm.

Personal factors are no insignificant element in the demand for industrial goods because of their influence on the buyer's evaluation of vendors' selling services. While business is business and the industrial purchaser should regard his contacts with sellers' representatives as part of it, when those contacts are pleasant he will function much more smoothly and effectively than when they are frustrating or disturbing. Consideration for the buyer's time, expressed by refraining from calling without specific purpose, by promptness in keeping appointments, and by telling his story quickly and clearly and leaving when it is told, adds greatly to the value of the salesman's service. Respect for the purchasing department's position and prestige in the organization of the customer firm, expressed in refraining from back-door selling (going around the purchasing officer to call directly on operating or designing executives), is also an element in its value.

Savings

Demand for the goods or services of a particular industrial marketer may be materially increased because of the savings buyers are able to enjoy from the use of his products or from the way he markets them. A report commonly submitted by the purchasing officer to his management deals with "Savings Effected." Mere reductions in price, unless they are peculiar to the purchasing officer's firm or are obtained through his negotiations, do not usually appear in these reports. The savings most commonly reported are those resulting from changes in the articles bought or changes in the way they are bought or delivered that manifest themselves in improvements in the cost structure of the firm or its products.

Saving of Materials. A buyer may prefer one material or machine to another because the preferred article makes possible a lower cost of materials in the finished product. For example, a stamping firm that made deep automotive oil pans installed a 750-ton deep drawing press that not only increased the rate of production but also decreased loss in the form of scrap from 3.5 percent to less than 1 percent. Another concern that made rock bits suffered from a high percentage of rejects in its finished product. Installation of two electrode-type electric salt bath furnaces for neutral hardening and drawing of paving breakers, road chisels, and other items almost completely eliminated the rejects, with a consequent increase in the output of end products per unit of material, as well as a saving in the labor cost per usable unit of output. Another firm that used a hydraulic press for extracting cottonseed oil installed a chemical solvent extraction unit, with the result that 33 additional pounds of oil were obtained from every ton of seed. The substitution of synthetic for natural sandstone millstones for grinding cornstarch enabled another firm to obtain 5 percent more starch per bushel of material.

Saving of Labor. A material or machine may be preferred because it makes possible a saving of labor. For example, the chemical solvent extraction unit just mentioned made it possible for 4 men to do the work formerly done by 12, with consequent cost reductions. The National Acme Company placed on the market a new machine to replace an old one that required the constant attention of one man to operate it; one man could run two or three of the new machines.

Such savings in labor may be enjoyed if there is less need for maintenance work to keep a machine going or to process a material. For example, in a chemical plant it was necessary 6 times in every 24 hours to loosen and retighten the electrode clamps on a phosphate furnace. Each such operation involved the work of 3 or 4 men with wrenches for about 12 minutes. An air-powered tool was installed, enabling one man to do the job in three minutes. Through savings in power, labor, and downtime of the furnace, the tool paid for itself in five days' operation.

A carpet company used cotton needle and knife ropes that wore out and had to be replaced every four months. A change to nylon ropes made possible substantial savings in labor, repair, and maintenance costs, and in shutdown time while the ropes were being changed.

Saving in Processing. A material or a piece of equipment may be bought because it is easier to process or because it protects more expensive equipment from damage. For example, a firm working with vinyl plastic material found that the plastic sometimes had in it tramp pieces of metal that ruined the rolls in calendering. A magnetic separator was tried but would not work. The company then installed an electronic metal detector that stopped the conveyor belt when metal approached the rolls. During the first half hour of its operation, this gadget saved $2,000 in rolls that otherwise would have been ruined.

Saving in Transportation. Savings that motivate purchases may appear in the form of lower transportation costs on the finished product. An example of this may be found in cement-lined hot-water tanks made from carbon steel. The maker changed to high-strength steel with a yield point of 50,000 pounds. While the steel was more expensive per ton, the shipping weight of the tank was reduced 18 percent, with a resulting cut of 16 percent in freight charges that covered the additional cost of the steel and permitted a net saving of 10.8 percent.

Saving in Time. A particularly strong motive for industrial buyers is the possibility of increased output within a given period of time. This often results in substantial savings in cost of production. The substitution of manufactured for natural sandstone millstones for grinding cornstarch, mentioned previously, increased production from 1,500 to 4,500 bushels a day, with considerable savings. The machine brought out by the National Acme Company, noted earlier, produced 75 pieces of product an hour, as against 7.5 pieces per hour turned out by the one it replaced. A maker of quality coffeepots annealed his copper five times with very accurately controlled heat and skilled labor. His metallurgists worked with a supplier's technicians and found that by using properly processed copper strip four annealings could be eliminated at an annual saving of $10,000.

Increased productivity has its own appeal and constitutes a buying motive in its own right. It is especially important during a period of high business activity, when buyers' plants are working to capacity to meet demand. On the other hand, when business is not so good and manufacturers are seeking methods to cut costs, the savings usually enjoyed as a result of increasing productivity constitute a powerful buying motive.

Saving in Inventory. One industrial supplier or product may be favored as against another because he or it makes possible a reduction in the buyer's inventory. A hardware manufacturer who bought and stored a large number of items of special material differing only in slight particulars was induced and aided by a supplier's representative to prepare simplified specifications, many of them standard, for about 225 out of 360 of these items. This change made it possible for him to buy in larger quantities, reduced his clerical work in buying and recording his inventory, and enabled him to significantly reduce the amount of materials he held in stock. The entire operation effected a saving of $25,000 a year. Needless to say, he developed a pronounced partiality for the cooperating supplier.

Savings from Safety. In some circumstances, safety provides a strong motive for buying industrial goods. Safety is important to the buyer from the purely commercial standpoint, in addition to humanitarian considerations, because it tends to reduce his costs of liability insurance, to improve the morale of his working force, and to prevent or diminish the damage and interruption of production that inevitably accompany any sort of accident.

Assurance of Supply and Patronage

Assurance of supply is vital to the purchasing officer. If the supply flow of an item is interrupted, probable resulting shortages will cause shutdowns of production operations. When a shortage threatens, the buyer may be able to avoid a shutdown by purchasing emergency orders from suppliers with whom he does not ordinarily deal, but such orders may be expensive.

In spite of all that any supplier can do, his flow of goods to customers may be interrupted by strikes, accidents, fire, or natural catastrophies, such floods, storms, or snow. Thus, no buyer can be even reasonably sure of continuity of supply so long as he purchases entirely from one supplier. Of course, if a material or component or machine is made to the buyer's individual specifications, and especially if its manufacture requires special machinery and has a long production cycle, he usually has little choice. He must rely on one supplier.

In the absence of such limiting factors, the purchasing officer is likely to buy an article from at least two suppliers, splitting his business between them. One probably will be preferred and will get the lion's share, but neither can get all of it. This is a matter of very great importance to the industrial goods marketer, since it limits not only the amount of business he can get from any one customer, but also the share of the total market he can hope to capture.

Usually, the purchasing officer administers this policy on the basis of individual items. Some buyers apply it across the board by establishing a maximum dollar amount they will purchase from any one supplier. This is not a particularly intelligent practice, since it limits the buyer's use of a good supplier who is highly diversified and it discourages the vendor from improving his existing products and creating new ones.

It behooves the industrial marketing manager to try to learn the policies his most important customers follow in seeking continuity of supply and to plan his operations in conformity with them. Otherwise, he may waste time, money, and effort in reaching for volume that he simply cannot get.

SUMMARY

In this chapter, we have discussed two phases of the demand for industrial goods. We first treated the more important factors that influence the overall demand of all industrial goods buyers. One of these is the varying nature and uses of the products themselves, whether they are items of major equipment, either special purpose or multipurpose, minor or accessory equipment, component parts, process materials, operating supplies, or raw materials. We called attention to the effect the derived nature of demand for industrial goods exercises on its behavior, and to various factors that influence its elasticity.

In the second part of the chapter, we discussed the most important factors that influence the individual industrial buyer in placing his patronage—in choosing among competing suppliers. The factors we treated were product quality, price (not the quoted figure but price in use), service (technical, repair and maintenance, reliability, and selling), savings in use, and the desire to assure the continuity of supply against hazards over which the individual supplier has no control.

CASES APPLICABLE TO PART I

PART II

The Industrial Customer

OF THOSE who have anything to do with a business, the customer is the most important. All others are expendable. He is not. If the business offers him the goods he needs and wants, at prices he regards as reasonable, accompanied by services that facilitate his use of them, and purveyed by marketing methods that conform to the way he wants to buy, the business has a good chance of success. The supplying firm that lacks any or all of these factors suffers under a very real competitive handicap.

So the wise industrial marketer makes it his business to try to understand the characteristics of possible buyers of his products, to know the various steps in the procurement processes they follow, and to study the methods by which and the bases on which they choose among products and suppliers. The next three chapters present a general discussion of these background considerations.

Chapter 3

◇◇◇◇◇◇◇◇◇◇◇◇◇◇◇◇◇◇◇ BUYER CHARACTERISTICS

SUCCESSFUL MANAGEMENT of the marketing function begins with a knowledge of the buyers to whom marketing effort is directed. An adequate knowledge of industrial buyers includes, at least, an awareness of their characteristics, an appreciation of how they usually reach buying decisions, and an understanding of the manner in which these decisions are generally implemented. The present discussion identifies the various types of industrial buyers, and discusses their characteristics in terms of number, size, geographical distribution, and organization of the procurement function. The buying decision and its implementation are treated in the remaining chapters of this part.

TYPES OF BUYERS

Industrial customers have already been broadly identified as businesses, institutions, and governmental units. Businesses include such diverse types of enterprises as manufacturers, construction firms, commercial establishments (retailers and wholesalers who buy equipment and supplies for use), transportation companies, service companies (hotels, laundries, and recreational enterprises), and certain professional groups (doctors and dentists). The most important of these various business customers are manufacturers. Probably next in importance in terms of volume of purchases are construtcion firms, followed by service companies, transportation companies, and commercial establishments, approximately in that order.

While manufacturing, construction, service, and transportation companies buy all kinds of industrial goods, commercial establishment purchases are confined largely to furniture and fixtures, cleaning and packaging materials, office supplies, and business machines and their accessories. Aside from office and other categories of supplies, purchases of the professional group are limited to specialized types of equipment. The same is true to a lesser extent of institutional buyers, although educational institutions are likely to have broader and more varied needs than other institutions.

Units of government may be divided into (1) departments of federal,

51

state, and local governments and (2) administrative units, such as school districts and sanitary districts. Administrative units enjoy a substantial degree of independence in allocating purchases. Also included in the government category are the government-created, autonomous agencies, such as the Tennessee Valley Authority and the Port of New York Authority. As a result of rising expenditures for defense and the expansion of government into areas formerly reserved to private enterprise, the importance of governmental units in the market for industrial goods has increased at an accelerated pace over the past two decades.

BUYER POPULATION

The basic unit for classifying nonmanufacturing businesses and institutions is the reporting unit. A reporting unit is generally a single establishment or a group of similar establishments under one control. It is an operating entity, which the Census Bureau counts once in each county in which it operates. Thus, all nonmanufacturing establishments that belong to a given firm are grouped into a single reporting unit if they are in the same county and engaged in the same kind of business.

Manufacturing businesses are classified on the basis of establishments, each representing an economic unit that produces goods or renders services, such as a mine, a factory, or a shop. An establishment is characterized by physical location, distinctive activity, and reportability. It is not identical with a business firm or legal entity, since either might consist of more than one establishment. As a consequence, the number of reporting units is smaller than the number of establishments and the average size of a reporting unit is larger. However, since the purpose here is not to compare one category with another but to present a general picture of the industrial market, lack of comparability between manufacturers and non-manufacturers does not impair the usefulness of data on reporting units.

The number of reporting units in the industrial market and the general categories to which they belong are given below.[1]

Industry Category	Number of Reporting Units
Agriculture, forestry, and fisheries	29,285
Contract construction	319,205
Finance, insurance, and real estate	325,243
Manufacturing	298,930
Mining	29,114
Retailing and wholesaling	1,083,206
Services	935,797
Transportation, communication and other public utilities	128,659
Unclassified establishments*	50,217

* Includes reporting units that could not be classified in any major industry group because of insufficient information, as well as all institutions not included in other categories but covered by the Federal Insurance Contribution Act.

[1] *County Business Patterns,* United States Summary, 1965.

Government buyers of industrial goods include not only procurement departments of the federal government, of which there are 8, but also about 4,500 agencies of states, counties, and cities of more than 10,000 population.[2] This omits many subsidiary governmental organizations, such as school districts, sanitary districts, and the like, which also buy industrial goods.

SIZE DISTRIBUTION

Industrial buyers vary widely in size from the alley machine shops with no employees or a small municipality governed by a town board to such giant organizations as the general Motors Corporation or the Department of Defense. Although the industrial market is not one market but many, an important aspect of any market or market segment is the size distribution of buying units that comprise it. An awareness of the variations in size of at least the major categories of industrial buyers is basic to an understanding of the problems in serving them efficiently.

There are several ways of measuring size, but unfortunately the best way is not always a practical one because of the paucity of data. The most readily available measure and the one used here is number of employees. Where other more appropriate measures are available, such as value added in the case of manufacturers, these will also be used.

The class of buyers with the most even distribution of size, relatively speaking, is manufacturers. As indicated in Table 3–1, about 66 percent of all manufacturers have fewer than 20 employees, while 16 percent have between 20 and 49, 8 percent have between 50 and 100, and only about 10 percent have more than 100 employees. In contrast, 80 percent or more of the reporting units in all other industries have fewer than 20 employees, and only in mining and in transportation, communication, and other public utilities is the proportion of reporting units in the 0 to 19 class less than 90 percent of the total number in the class. Moreover, only in the last two industries is the proportion of reporting units with 100 or more employees more than 1 percent of the total. And in both mining and transportation, the number of reporting units with more than 100 employees is, at most, 4 percent of the total.

No such comprehensive data is available for measuring the size distribution of all industrial buyers on any other basis, such as sales volume or value of purchases. However, considerable information is available on what is undoubtedly the most important category of industrial buyers—manufacturers. For example, data are available for manufacturers on value added by manufacturing, a more meaningful index of size than either employment or value of sales. It is interesting to note that in 1965 only 28 percent (81,434 reporting units) of the total number of manufac-

[2] *Census of Governments*, U.S. Department of Commerce, 1962.

TABLE 3–1

Size Distribution of Industrial Buyers by Industry

| | Percent of Total Reporting Units by Employment-size Class | | | | |
	Less than 20	*20 to 49*	*50 to 99*	*100 to 499*	*500 or more*
Agricultural services, forestry, and fisheries....................96	3	1	0	0	
Contract construction................92	5	2	1	0	
Finance, insurance, and real estate......93	4	2	1	0	
Manufacturing.....................66	16	8	8	2	
Mining...........................80	12	4	3	1	
Retail and wholesale trade...........93	5	1	1	0	
Services..........................94	4	1	1	0	
Transportation and other public utilities......................83	10	4	3	0	
Unclassified establishments..........97	2	1	0	0	

SOURCE: *County Business Patterns*, United States Summary, 1965.

turers had an annual value added of less than $500,000 per unit, on the average, while less than 3 percent of the total (6,353 reporting units) had an average value added in excess of $1.116 million.[3] This means that most manufacturing establishments fall into a relatively narrow range of size from $500,000 to about $1 million in value added per establishment.

GEOGRAPHICAL CONCENTRATION

The manufacturers' part of the industrial market is also rather concentrated geographically, as indicated by the fact that 14 states in the northeastern portion of the nation account for about 60 percent of the total value added by manufacturing. Indeed, 13 additional states—8 in the South Atlantic region and 5 in the Pacific region—account for another 22 percent of total value added. Thus, 37 states contribute about 82 percent of the total value added by manufacturing in the United States.[4]

From the marketing viewpoint, the most meaningful measure of size is the value of purchases. Total value of purchases by manufacturers in 1965 was slightly more than $200 billion.[5] Over one half of this figure, $109.3 billion, was accounted for by manufacturing establishments in 7 states.[6] Only 5 other states had a value of purchases by manufacturers in excess of $5 billion.[7]

Even these figures do not indicate the full measure of the concentration

---

[3] *Annual Survey of Manufacturers*, 1962. Percentages personally computed.

[4] *Ibid.*

[5] Calculated by subtracting total value added from total value of shipments.

[6] Leading states and value of purchases by manufacturers in billions of dollars for 1965 are as follows: New York, 20.4; California, 19.0; Pennsylvania, 15.5; Illinois, 15.0; Michigan, 14.8; Ohio, 13.4; and New Jersey, 11.2.

[7] Massachusetts, Indiana, Wisconsin, Missouri, and Texas.

of the manufacturing industrial market. The 1963 Census of Manufactures shows that 10 of the 3,000-odd counties in the United States contain 25.5 percent of the total manufacturing establishments, with 21.1 percent of the people employed in manufacturing, producing 20.8 percent of the total value added, and making 14.6 percent of the total capital expenditures of such establishments.

If the market of an industrial goods producer depends primarily on the number of manufacturing establishments, he will find about 38 percent of it in 30 counties. If number of employees is the best index of his market, he can reach about 34 percent of it in 30 counties. If the best index is value added by manufacture, 35 percent of his market lies in 30 counties, and if the purchase of his product involves a capital expenditure, 28 percent of its market is in 30 counties. The same 30 counties do not appear in all these categories, but most of them are in all lists. In specific industries, the concentration is even more marked than these figures indicate.

Other classes of industrial buyers, such as state and local governments, institutions, construction enterprises, transportation and other public utility companies, retailers and wholesalers, banks and insurance companies, and service establishments, tend to follow the size distribution of the populace they serve. Although data concerning the size distribution of these classes of buyers are neither plentiful nor very specific, it is to be expected that the largest and most important of their number will be found in the population centers and the smallest in the more sparsely populated areas. Therefore, one would expect to find the largest of the nonmanufacturing buyers in New York, California, Pennsylvania, Illinois, Ohio, Texas, Michigan, New Jersey, Massachusetts, Florida, and Indiana—the 11 states in which 55 percent of the population resides.[8]

Governmental units and institutions are, of course, located in all parts of the nation, and with the exception of procurement agencies of the federal government their geographical distribution, at least on a volume basis, is probably closely related to that of the population. Since governments and institutions serve the populace, it is probable that the most important industrial buyers of this type tend to be concentrated in the major population centers

Available data concerning other types of buyers indicate that with the exception of agricultural enterprises, mining, manufacturing, transportation and other public utilities, and the wholesale trade, over one half of all business and institutional buyers are located in eight states—California, Florida, Illinois, Michigan, New Jersey, New York, Ohio, and Texas. Agricultural enterprises and companies in transportation and other public utilities are the most widely dispersed geographically, but even in these industries over one half of the reporting units are concentrated in less than a dozen states. Mining establishments are the most geographically concen-

---

[8] *Current Population Reports*, Series P-25.

TABLE 3–2

Geographic Concentration of Nongovernmental Industrial Buyers

Percent of Total Reporting Units by State

Industries	Calif.	Fla.	Ill.	Iowa	Ky.	Mass.	Mich.	Mo.	N.J.	N.Y.	Ohio	Okla.	Pa.	Tex.	W.Va.	Wis.	Total by Industry (Per cent)
Agriculture, forestry, and fisheries	11.5	6.4	4.1	3.3		3.1			3.3	6.4	3.7		3.7	6.0			51.5
Mining	4.2	3.9			5.5							8.2	8.4	19.2	7.0		52.5
Contract construction	10.1		5.4				3.6		4.3	8.2	5.2		5.9	6.0			52.6
Manufacturing	9.7		6.1			3.8	4.5		4.9	15.5	5.1		6.4		7.0		56.0
Transportation, communication, and other public utilities	7.4		5.6			3.0	3.3	2.8	3.6	9.3	4.5		6.4	5.5		2.8	54.2
Wholesale trade	8.4	2.8	5.9				3.7	2.8	3.2	13.5	4.7		5.7	5.6			56.3
Retail trade	8.6	2.9	5.4				4.2		3.6	9.6	5.1		6.1	5.5			51.0
Finance, insurance, and real estate	8.0		8.6						3.6	17.1	4.3		4.7	4.9			51.2
Services	10.8	3.4	5.4				3.9		3.5	10.9	5.0		5.8	5.6			54.3
Unclassified establishments	12.2	4.5	5.5				3.0			11.3	3.5		3.3	7.4			50.7

SOURCE: *County Business Patterns, United States Summary*, 1965.

trated of all business and institutional buyers; 6 states account for 52 percent of all reporting units. For further detail concerning the geographical concentration of nongovernmental industrial buyers, see Table 3–2.

ORGANIZATIONAL CHARACTERISTICS

Organization of the procurement function has striking similarities in all types of operations, regardless of the nature of the buyer's principal activity. However, government purchasing has certain unique features that warrant giving it separate treatment in this discussion. The type of purchasing organization required by business and institutional buyers is influenced by such factors as size of operation, place of purchasing function in the overall organizational structure, and policy concerning relations with suppliers. The type of purchasing organization used by governmental bodies is essentially determined by the level of government—i.e., federal, state, or local—and the size and complexity of the unit's administrative structure.

Business and Institutional Buyers

The Influence of Size. The volume of purchases made by many small institutional and business buyers, i.e., those employing no more than 20 persons, is probably not great enough to warrant personnel who specialize in buying. Purchases by manufacturers in this size group amounted to only about $6,000 per establishment in 1963.[9] Such small buyers may well have a one-man purchasing operation conducted by the chief administrative officer or delegated in whole or in part, along with other duties, to another official such as a shop foreman or office manager. In either case, buying is likely to be a part-time activity relegated to moments when the officer's attention is not required by the function for which he is primarily responsible. As indicated in Table 3–1, most nongovernmental industrial buyers belong to this category.

It is quite probable, therefore, that in most small organizations purchasing is still assigned to shop foremen or office managers when not retained by the chief executive—a pattern that existed almost universally before the development of scientific management and modern principles of organizational structure.

It is likely that many medium-sized businesses and institutions (those with less than 100 but more than 20 employees) have purchasing departments but employ no more than two or three persons in each of them. An American Management Association study of 147 representative industrial firms indicates that, on the average, fewer than 2 percent of all employees

---

[9] *Census of Manufactures*, General Statistics for Industry Groups and Industries, MC 63 (P), 3, 1963. Purchases computed by subtracting value added from value of shipments.

on the payroll of the typical company are involved in purchasing.[10] Since buying is seldom confined to the purchasing department, even in large firms, it is likely that a small unit could satisfy the needs of most medium-sized establishments. In companies of all sizes, purchases of capital equipment and important raw materials (particularly of a speculative nature) are often made by persons outside the purchasing department, usually by members of top management.

Among larger establishments, i.e., those with 250 or more employees each, probably all have some form of specialized purchasing staff. Although details of organization vary substantially from one enterprise to another, some generalization about departmental organization is possible. The most common pattern is that of specialized buyers under the general supervision of a chief purchasing officer who is concerned with policy

FIGURE 3–1

Internal Organization of a Purchasing Department

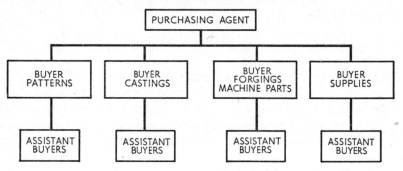

making and other administrative matters as well as with buying. Generally speaking, a buyer is assigned to a specific commodity or group of commodities for which he is responsible. This responsibility usually includes selecting suppliers, placing orders, and expediting shipment, and may embrace other activities related to the purchasing function, such as value analysis, inspection of incoming shipments, and control of inventory. (See Figure 3–1).

The allocation of commodities to different buyers is commonly made on the basis of similar physical characteristics (castings, machine parts, nonferrous metals) or of use characteristics (operating supplies and raw materials) or major source of supply. In the last instance, all items normally purchased through merchant wholesalers, for example, might be assigned to one buyer, while those bought through agents and brokers would be assigned to another, and anything purchased directly from manufacturers to a third.

Of course, numerous modifications of this general pattern are dictated

[10] George H. Haas, *et al., Purchasing Department Organization and Authority* (American Management Association Research Study No. 45 [New York, 1960].

by local conditions. A firm may use a single commodity in such volume that success or failure depends in large part on its proper purchase. In such a case, a major executive may assume responsibility for its purchase, while other items continue to be bought through the purchasing department. Examples of such commodities might be textiles for clothing, leather for shoes, or grain for breakfast cereals. Administrative policy may permit using departments to specify brands or trademarks on requisitions. This severely limits the freedom of the buyer in filling requisitions.

A buyer who has acquired valuable experience and know-how in the purchase of a particular commodity may continue to be responsible for its purchase after being assigned to another position or department. Such a situation is usually undesirable and of short duration, but it is not uncommon in firms going through a period of expansion or adjustment following a merger or acquisition. While these exceptions to the authority of purchasing officers to select suppliers and place orders are significant, they do not substantially alter the recognition of buying as a specialized management function.

When the volume of purchases has grown beyond the capacity of the simple organizational pattern depicted in Figure 3–1, it is no longer feasible for each buyer to be personally responsible for all the detailed procedures involved in purchase transactions. As a rule, buyers are relieved of the clerical and routine tasks to permit them to become specialists in evaluation of quality, selection of vendors, and negotiations. Similarly, departmental activities such as value analysis, economic research, traffic and routing, and other special services are usually segregated and assigned to staff positions, which function in support of buying operations.

The chief executive of large purchasing departments, often titled Director of Purchasing, is more concerned with policy and other administrative duties than with the actual work of buying. He may be responsible for trade relations, coordinating purchasing policies and procedures with those of other divisions, and representing his department at executive and interdepartmental meetings, and may be responsible to top management for the overall conduct of the purchasing function. His participation in buying is ordinarily limited to major contracts and commodities that involve substantial outlays and/or have important policy implications. The chief purchasing officer may also participate in the initial consideration of new sources of supply or new materials likely to affect product design or production methods.

An assistant director of purchases is also fairly typical of large purchasing departments. He is customarily in direct charge of the buying staff, and in many companies he reviews all purchase orders before they are released to vendors. Typically, the assistant director also supervises office services and any staff specialists who may have been appointed for traffic, value analysis, disposal and salvage of surplus and waste materials, fol-

FIGURE 3-2

Internal Organization of a Large Purchasing Department

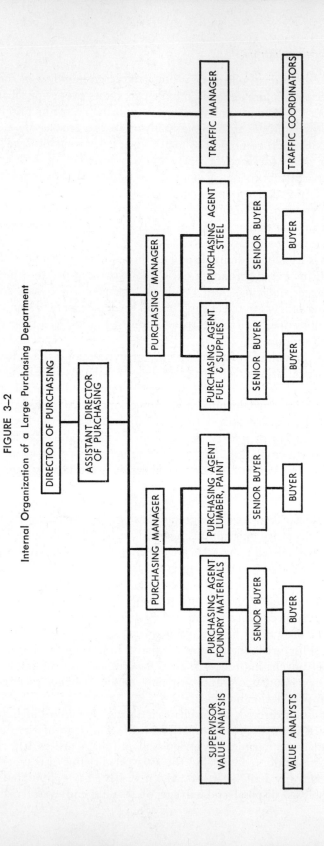

low-up, and expediting. If inventory control is within the jurisdiction of the purchasing department, a stores manager also reports to the director of purchases, along with the assistant director. Generally speaking, such officers are line managers and are on the same organizational level. (See Figure 3–2)

For the most part, institutional purchasing departments are organized in a manner similar to those of industrial companies where the size of the operation makes it feasible to concentrate this activity within a single department. (See, for example, Figure 3–3.)

FIGURE 3–3

Internal Organization of the Purchasing Department in a Large
Educational Institution

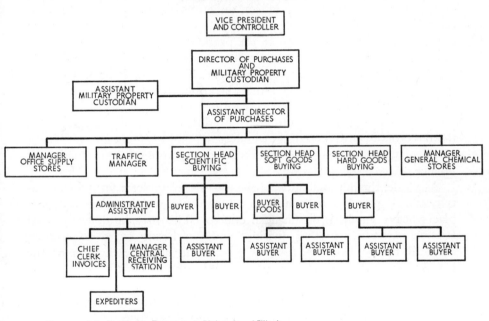

Courtesy of the Purchasing Department, University of Illinois.

Position in Company Organization.   Although substantial variations exist in individual cases, it is possible to identify several patterns of relationship between purchasing and other functional departments in businesses and institutions. In one pattern, the officer in charge of purchasing reports to the president or general manager, along with the heads of production, marketing, finance, personnel, and other functional departments. This pattern is commonly found in medium-sized firms and institutions. It is also found at the branch plants of companies in which purchasing is decentralized, with rather autonomous departments at the plant level. (See Figure 3–4.) Where this pattern prevails, the head of purchasing usually has sufficient status and authority to preclude the subordination of his activity to that of any other line function.

FIGURE 3–4

Company Organization with Purchasing Department in First Echelon

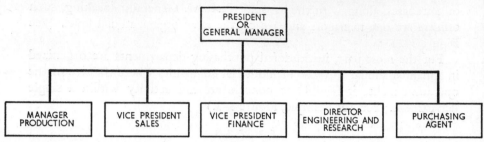

In large single-unit enterprises (or large plants of multiunit enterprises), the chief purchasing officer sometimes is in the second tier of executives, and reports to an operations, production, or financial vice president who, in turn, reports to the president or general manager. (See Figure 3–5.) The position of the purchasing department in such organizations tends to be a subordinate one in which emphasis is on service and support of a particular division rather than on materials procurement as an independent contributor to cost control or profits. This is less true when the purchasing agent reports to a vice president of operations, along with the directors of manufacturing, engineering, and maintenance, for example, than when he reports to an executive responsible for production or finance.

As a rule, the purchasing department is placed under a financial executive, as in Figure 3–6, only in those companies in which top management places heavy emphasis on financial control. This may be done to avoid friction between operating divisions and purchasing or to concentrate financial responsibility as fully as possible in a single division of the company. Concentration of financial responsibility is sometimes sought by industrial firms that are primarily assemblers rather than manufacturers of the products they sell. In this instance, the cost of purchased materials is a very large share of the end cost of the finished product.

During recent years, there has been increasing executive emphasis on

FIGURE 3–5

Company Organization with Purchasing Department in Second Echelon

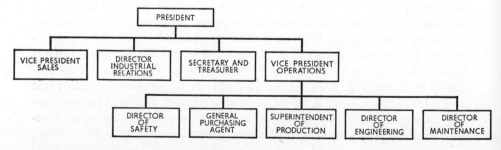

managing inventory. In some companies, this has resulted in the appointment of a director of inventory control, whose business it is to set and
administer standards and policies for all kinds of stocks, materials, goods in
process, and finished goods. This executive usually reports to the president. Sometimes, the purchasing department has been placed under his
control on the theory that since procurement is the chief means by which
stocks of materials may be increased or decreased he should have authority over it. This tendency is not widespread, but it is something that the
wise industrial marketer will watch carefully.

A third pattern characteristic of multiunit enterprises, particularly
those whose various plants or divisions are in different industries, is one
that separates the operational and administrative phases of the purchasing
function. Separate purchasing departments are established at the plant or

FIGURE 3-6

Company Organization with Purchasing in Second Echelon

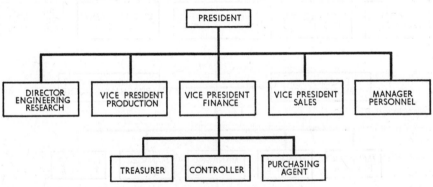

division level, while a general purchasing department at company headquarters serves the entire organization in a staff capacity. (See Figure 3-7.)
The headquarters purchasing staff ordinarily counsels top management on
procurement and materials policy, does research relevant to the overall
conduct of purchasing in the company, coordinates procurement policy
with other functional area policies at the company level, and may establish
training programs for buyers and provide assistance to divisional departments on specific purchasing problems. In some instances, the home office
purchasing staff may also have buying responsibility for major raw materials and capital equipment, and for items on which maximum quantity
discounts can be earned only when the needs of all plants are consolidated.

At the plant level, the head of the purchasing unit often reports
directly to the plant manager. Within the general framework of policies
and procedures established by the home office, he usually has authority to
procure all requirements of the plant in which he is located without
approval from headquarters.

There are good reasons for branch plant autonomy with regard to the purchasing function in large multiplant companies. A substantial saving in inventory can often be achieved through a reduction in the time required to place and receive orders. Channeling orders through the home office in a large, diverse company usually consumes more time than placing them directly from the plant at which the requisition originates. A local purchasing agent is usually more aware of local conditions that affect the speed and economy of procurement, such as transportation and storage facilities, climatic conditions, and local laws or customs, than are personnel at the home office. Then, too, if the branch plant manager is responsi-

FIGURE 3–7

Multiplant Company Organization with Divided Purchasing Responsibility

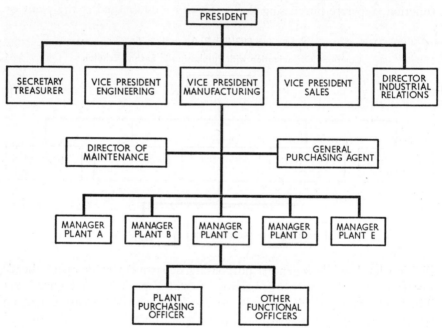

ble for achieving a specific profit objective, he should logically have control over purchasing because of the effect of expenditures for material and equipment on plant operating costs.

There are numerous variations to this general pattern. In some large companies, purchasing is combined with traffic management in the staff organization at the home office. In other companies with production-oriented top managements, the purchasing agent serves in a staff capacity to the vice president of manufacturing, who exercises line authority for production operations in branch plants. In still other instances, purchasing is included in a service division, along with public relations, traffic management, economic research, legal counsel, and other specialties, whose director reports to the president. In these firms, each separate operating division or plant customarily has a purchasing agent who reports to the general manager of the plant or division. In all instances, though, the operating phase of purchasing is separated from its policy phase, and the two are conducted by different groups within the company.

The Influence of Policy.   Since organization is a means, not an end, its characteristics reflect the nature of plans and policies to which management is committed. Plans for cooperative research with selected suppliers for improvement in cost and performance of purchased items requires personnel who know both the company's product needs and the technology of the products in question, and are free from the day-to-day routine of purchasing activity. This usually necessitates creation of a staff position to the head of the purchasing department, or a line position if product research (i.e., value analysis) is to be a continuing function of the purchasing department.

A policy of giving preference to local suppliers in a multiunit company often necessitates a certain amount of decentralization in the purchasing organization. The more widely dispersed are the plants and the more diverse the products they produce, the greater is the need for decentralization if local suppliers are to be favored without impairing the efficiency of procurement.

The policy with perhaps the most significant effect on organization of the purchasing function is that of reciprocity. This is particularly true of multiunit companies. The urge to select vendors on the basis of their value as present or potential customers is almost always present. It is greatly intensified during periods of depressed business activity, when every means of leverage may be exerted to make sales. The multiunit firm that adopts reciprocity as a standard operating plan is usually obliged to center responsibility for selecting suppliers and placing orders at the home office. The home office purchasing staff is in the best position to determine how orders should be placed so as to derive the greatest sales benefit for the company as a whole. In a single unit firm, a policy of searching out reciprocal arrangements may reduce the purchasing department to a bookkeeping operation, since the sales department dictates placement of orders.

In multiunit companies, a policy of filling needs internally to the fullest extent possible also tends to centralize purchasing responsibility at the home office. Such a policy reduces the number of necessary plant-level purchasing decisions. Instead, a process of matching needs and resources internally is used. In this situation, purchasing becomes largely a clearing house operation. As a consequence, it can usually be carried out most expeditiously in the home office. A centralized purchasing staff is also often in the best position to place orders outside the company for needs that cannot be filled internally, since the final determination of which needs cannot be met internally must be made by top management.

A policy of meeting product needs internally also tends to deemphasize the independence of the purchasing function in large single-unit companies. Depending on the extent to which make-or-buy decisions tend to favor making the needed product, the purchasing department will be placed under production or engineering rather than being made independent of these functions.

Governmental Buyers

Buyers for governmental departments and agencies belong either to federal or to state and local units. For the most part, governmental purchasing units are organized in a manner similar to those of businesses and institutions handling the same volume of orders. (See Figure 3–8.) There is, however, a greater emphasis on the clerical function in governmental purchases because of the more detailed procedures demanded by statutory requirements and a multiple authority relationship characteristic of government. The head of the purchasing department in a governmental unit frequently reports to a board of elected officials, who review and approve his decisions. Occasionally, however, the purchasing agent may be responsible to a city manager, a governor, or other official of comparable rank.

Federal Purchasing Organization. Purchases by the federal government are administered through four major types of offices: the General Services Administration, the purchasing offices of civilian departments and agencies, special purchasing agencies, and the Department of Defense. The General Services Administration was created in 1949 by the Federal Property and Administrative Services Act to direct and coordinate federal purchasing, as well as to centralize procurement of goods and services needed by the various branches of the federal government. The major procurement agency within the General Services Administration is the Bureau of Federal Supply.

While the various governmental departments may obtain their requirements by placing requisitions with Bureau of Federal Supply warehouses, they may also buy directly from suppliers by means of open-end contracts issued by the Bureau of Federal Supply. Departments with special requirements are also authorized to buy directly from suppliers on a bid basis. The departments of Agriculture and Commerce, the Veterans' Administration, the Federal Security Agency, the Federal Trade Commission, and the Tennessee Valley Authority are some of the units that buy directly from suppliers on a bid basis through their own purchasing offices. The major share of military needs is also purchased on a direct bid basis.

From time to time, Congress authorizes special programs designed to fill some extraordinary need of the government. Such programs are temporary in nature and are typically administered by special agencies established for the purpose. While procurement for these programs is often handled through existing government purchasing offices, it may be made through private trade channels. Among the better known of these pro-

FIGURE 3–8

Organization Chart, Department of Purchasing, Contracts, and Supplies, City of Chicago*

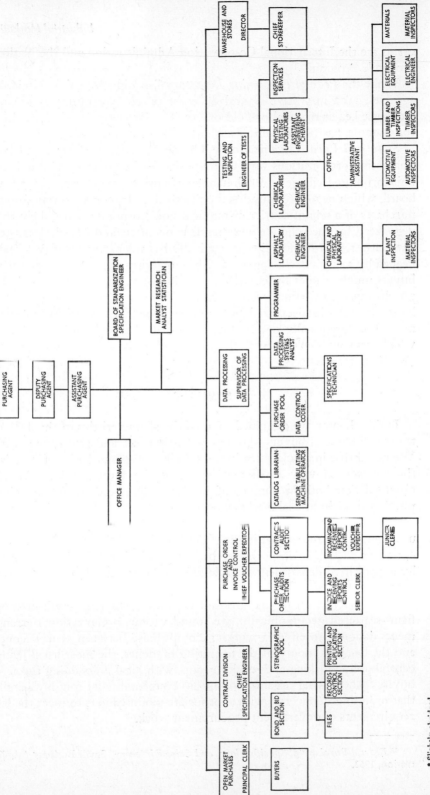

* Slightly abridged.
Courtesy of John Ward, Purchasing Agent City of Chicago.

grams are the International Co-operation Administration and the National Stockpile Program.

While the *Federal Purchasing Directory* lists only 24 major purchasing agencies, each may have several different purchasing offices at separate locations, i.e., at regional or field offices. The Department of Agriculture, for example, has 18 such offices authorized to buy independently.[11]

State and Local Organization. The characteristics of state and local purchasing organizations vary with the size of the governmental unit. An unincorporated village of 500 inhabitants is probably governed by a town board, which negotiates purchases collectively. Depending on its size, the purchases of a school district or public school corporation are likely to be negotiated by the school superintendent or an elected board of trustees. By contrast, a large municipality typically has a department of purchasing headed by a city purchasing agent who supervises the work of specialized buyers much as does his counterpart in industry. (See Figure 3–8.) The purchasing organizations of state governments tend to resemble those of large cities, with specialized personnel grouped in a specialized department. Both are usually responsible to a board of accounts or city council, which reviews departmental decisions and possesses veto power over individual transactions.

SUMMARY

In this chapter, we examined some of the characteristics of the different types of industrial buyers—businesses, institutions, and government units. We noted that in all classifications the bulk of the purchasing power is in the hands of a very small percentage of the buying units. We also observed that both in number of buying establishments and in volume purchased the industrial market is highly concentrated geographically.

We examined the organization of the purchasing function within the using units. We found that in the typical small establishment the buying is done on a part-time, unspecialized basis. In the larger units, it is performed by a specialized department, with individual buyers handling special products or groups of products and staff men carrying on certain supporting activities, such as value analysis and expediting. In large multidivisional firms scattered geographically, we found various organizational arrangements designed to effect a working compromise between central control and the local autonomy of the operating branches, the most usual being a central policy making and service group, with local units doing the actual buying. The buying organization of governmental units roughly parallels that of business concerns, with appropriate modifications to meet the legal requirements of government procurement work.

------

[11] *Federal Purchasing, Specifications, and Sales Directory*, Small Business Administration, 1962.

Chapter 4

XXXXXXXXXXXXXXXXXXXXXXX THE BUYING PROCESS

DESPITE DIFFERENCES in the size and organizational structure of businesses, institutions, and government departments, the types of commodities purchased, or the sources from which they are obtained, a buying procedure common to most purchasing departments can be identified. This procedure consists of three general steps: the recognition of need, the decision regarding specific means and sources for filling this need, and completion of the purchase transaction. While these steps are so obvious as to make any discussion of them appear pedantic, they are important enough in shaping marketing plans to warrant more than perfunctory recognition. Each represents significant opportunities for the industrial marketer. To a substantial degree, success in industrial marketing depends on the ability of the seller to fit into the customer's buying process and to supply the assistance necessary to win his patronage and loyalty.

RECOGNITION OF NEED

The buying process begins with the recognition of need and an accurate description of its extent and character. To initiate a purchase, the need itself must not only be identifiable, it must also be translated into a meaningful request to the purchasing department to take action. Since purchasing is a service function, recognition of need must usually include some form of authorization to buy.

While needs invariably emerge from using departments, their origin may not always be in the demands of manufacturing operations or the programmed replacement of worn and obsolete equipment. Need may also arise from the expansion of plant and facilities to capitalize on a favorable market position, from efforts to improve efficiency, and from the introduction of new products. All of these origins of need represent opportunities for creative marketing and are the kind of phenomena on which industrial marketing research should focus.

While needs originating within a company may come from a number of different levels, sooner or later they must be translated into requests for specific products. These are then forwarded either directly or through a stores or stock department to the purchasing department for buying action. If responsibility for stores and inventory control is assigned to the purchasing department, it is incumbent on purchasing to anticipate the needs of using departments far enough in advance to prevent an excessive number of rush orders.

The translation of need into a request for the purchase of specific products is usually accomplished by means of a *requisition.* (See Figures

FIGURE 4–1

General Purchase Requisition

ELECTRO-MOTIVE DIVISION

GENERAL MOTORS CORPORATION

PURCHASE REQUISITION NO. 270285

ORDER PLACED WITH ______ DATE ______

DELIVER TO ______

ATTN: ______

P.O. # ______ DATE ______ BUYER ______

CHARGE ACCOUNT ______

If shipment is to be made at a location other than Plant No. 1, La Grange show complete address.

ROUTING ______

F.O.B. ______ TERMS ______

The above portion to be completed by Purchasing Department

LAST PURCHASED FROM ______

QUANTITY	EMD PART NO.	VENDOR NO.	DESCRIPTION	PRICE

REQUESTED BY ______ APPROVED BY ______ APPROVED BY ______

This requisition will not be accepted until approved by authorized personnel as listed in Standard Procedure No. 67.

EMD 219 C

4–1 and 4–2.) The requisition indicates the desired quantity and quality of materials designated by the using unit, and authorizes the purchasing department to procure them. However, the requisition is not the only instrument used to translate need into authorization for procurement. If production is planned on the basis of orders—i.e., if products are sold before they are produced and there is no production for inventory—need may be formalized by a bill of materials. This usually consists of a list of materials needed to complete a certain project or to make the products specified in the customer's order. It typically originates in the production planning or engineering department, and it includes the amounts needed and the delivery schedules desired, as well as the specification of materials.

A continuing need, particularly for standard materials, supplies, or materials purchased by specification, may also be translated into authorization for procurement by establishment of minimum inventory levels, order points, and standard order quantities. In such instances, when the

FIGURE 4–2

Production Purchase Requisition

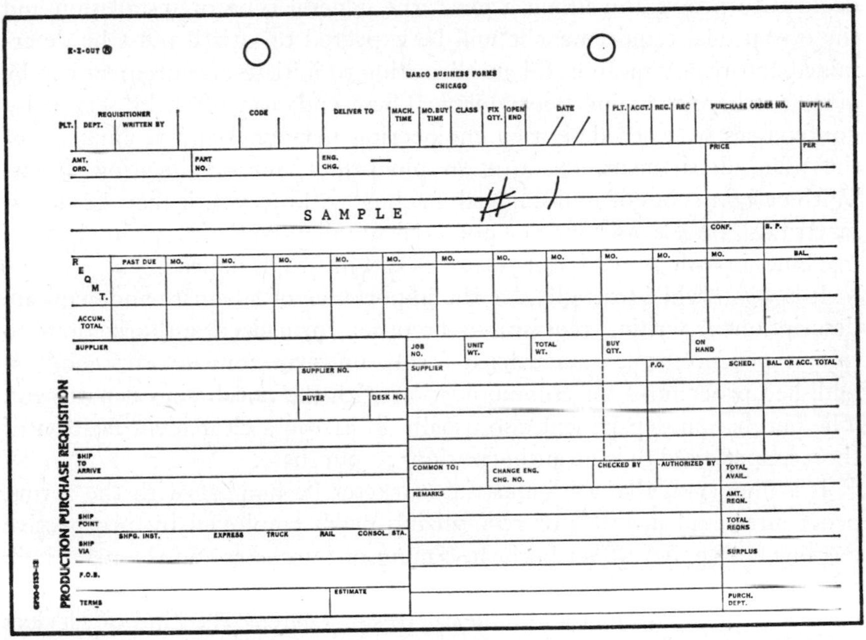

stock of an item reaches a level designated as the order point, the buyer is automatically authorized and obligated to place an order for the designated quantity. The order point and standard order quantity are usually calculated to maintain an average inventory of sufficient amount to achieve a planned stock turnover objective.

In addition, the budget may be used as authorization for purchasing when it is advantageous to buy in volume on a semiannual or annual basis. In such cases, the budgeting process usually includes making projections of the number of units of each end product the firm plans to produce during the budget period. Executive approval of the budget results in the translation of output figures into requirements for materials and authorizes the purchasing department to make commitments with suppliers for these requirements. Such commitments generally call for delivery of all or some stipulated share of the total requirements during the budget period.

The translation of need into some formal document authorizing purchase is somewhat more involved for major equipment than for materials, component parts, and supplies. Questions must be answered with respect to the best use of available capital funds, the desired rate of return on invested capital, alternative uses of available capital funds, operating costs, the effect on the company's tax liability, and technical service. Many of these questions can be answered only by top management, design or engineering specialists, or operating managers. Consequently, recognition of need for capital equipment often includes an extended investigation of its urgency and of available ways by which it may be satisfied. If it is decided to proceed in filling a need, the general type of installation and the operational requirement it will be expected to satisfy must be determined before any meaningful authorization to initiate procurement can be given to the purchasing department. These ends can often be served by conferences between design or engineering personnel and technicians of the using department, resulting in blueprints and specification sheets. With certain types of nonstandard machinery, however, it may be necessary to call on the assistance of potential suppliers to design prototypes of machines in order to arrive at the exact specifications desired.

It is worthwhile to emphasize the importance of adequate and accurate description in writing requisitions or other formalized authorizations to initiate procurement, standardized forms, uniform nomenclature, and established procedures for communication with the purchasing department. The purchasing department also usually insists on a clear identification of those empowered to issue authorizations to purchase.

It is important that the industrial marketer be familiar with the forms, procedures, and methods of recognizing needs employed by prospective customers, for they affect both the timing of purchases and the manner in which they are made. The nature of purchasing procedures and methods employed by a customer also indicate, to some extent, the kind of services the buyer expects and the appeals likely to influence the buyer and to direct his patronage, and the persons in the buying firm to whom the appeals must be made.

DECISION REGARDING MEANS AND SOURCES

For purposes of discussion, decisions regarding the best means and sources to fill a recognized need may be separated into two phases: (1) the analysis of alternatives and (2) the choice of an alternative or some combination of alternatives.

Analysis of Alternatives

The major alternatives available to the industrial buyer in filling needs are: (1) to produce the item or items himself, (2) to call for bids from a select group of suppliers, or (3) to negotiate with interested vendors for the best combination of quality, service, and price.

Make or Buy. The decision to extend a company's manufacturing operation to cover particular supplies and parts involves far-reaching economic and social implications. Consequently, all that can be attempted here is a brief summary of the conditions that might lead a firm to produce rather than purchase needed products and the conditions that usually serve to restrict such action.

Occasionally, manufacturers are forced to make some of the products they might otherwise purchase because no suitable suppliers exist. This was true of some companies producing dry cereal for breakfast foods, for example, when they were unable to buy suitable roasting equipment. In other instances, companies may use such small quantities of some special item that vendors are not interested in producing it.

Firms that depend on materials or equipment of unusual properties or design sometimes manufacture them to preclude any interruption in supply or variation in quality, or to protect the design of their equipment— particularly, equipment of advanced technology. A company may also find it cheaper to manufacture a particular item than to buy it, although circumstances that generate such opportunities are rather unusual. It may happen that while the cost of manufacturing is no lower for the buyer than for vendors, an exhorbitant market price prevails as the result of a monopolistic supply situation, legislative practices, or collusion among vendors. Moreover, the company capable of manufacturing even a small part of its own requirements is in a stronger bargaining position in negotiating with vendors than is one that cannot produce any of its requirements.

In periods of depressed sales, a manufacturer may choose to make rather than buy certain items in order to utilize idle productive capacity. Even in periods of normal demand, management may decide to manufacture rather than buy certain items as a means of spreading overhead and reducing the share of overhead expense that must be charged against the company's end products.

While some circumstances argue in favor of manufacturing rather than purchasing a part of a company's requirements, several weighty considerations deter many firms from taking such action. One such deterrent is lack of administrative or technical experience in making the required articles. To manufacture an item as a sideline may involve new equipment, new skills, and new supervisors. Moreover, every time another unrelated production unit is added to the original organization there is certain to be some loss of cohesion and unity in management, which is sure to produce a new set of technical and supervisory problems.

An equally serious possibility is that of losing market position in the company's own major products. This could happen as a result of the obsolescence or outdated design of components or fabricated parts used in the end products and manufactured by the company as a sideline. The price of a strong market position is usually constant research effort directed toward improved product performance and lower production costs. Companies that produce their own materials as a sideline can rarely afford sufficient research to keep abreast, much less ahead of, firms for which such products are of major concern. As a consequence, it is likely to be only a matter of time until the company producing a needed article as a sideline falls behind its major producers in quality and cost improvement. If the quality of its sideline component or material is a factor in the performance of the company's major products, the results of manufacturing instead of buying may well be disastrous.

The decision to make rather than buy can also result in a substantial loss of goodwill if the volume of discontinued purchases is sizable. Losing the goodwill of suppliers can have an adverse affect on the sales volume of a company in a number of ways. If reciprocity plays a part in marketing effort, the effect of curtailing purchases is readily apparent. If the displaced supplier is one through whom the manufacturer's end product is sold, the probable adverse effect on sales is equally apparent. The value of promotion received through the auspices of friendly suppliers is less obvious but nonetheless significant. The customer of any given vendor is very likely to be a supplier to other customers of this vendor. Good relations with vendors, whose success will be enhanced by the success of their customers, can promote word-of-mouth advertising of a very effective kind. The opposite result can be produced by rebuffed and resentful vendors.

A long-term consequence, which almost invariably plagues a firm that manufactures any substantial part of its own material requirements, is inflexibility in the use of materials, parts, and supplies. As a purchaser, a firm can buy from any source that offers the best combination of price, quality, and service. It is free to substitute items, shift from one source to another, or split orders among competing sources as terms and conditions warrant. This freedom is lost to a firm whose management is committed to procurement by manufacture.

Competitive Bids. A very substantial volume of both standard and special items is purchased on the basis of competitive bids. Government units and most public institutions are required to purchase on the bid system. Under the governmental system, a contemplated purchase is advertised well in advance so that any interested supplier may have time to submit a bid. After a set date, no bids will be accepted, and all bids received by this time are opened, usually in the presence of the bidders themselves. The bids are made public, and the lowest responsible bidder is awarded the order. If no bids are acceptable, the purchasing agent ordinarily has no alternative but to reject them all and initiate the procedure again, calling for new bids.

The chief disadvantage of such a procedure is that decision hinges solely on price. This can be alleviated, of course, by making the requirement of quality and service so definitive and unmistakable that price is the only real variable. To assure that quality and service will not be scanted in delivery, each bidder may be required to submit a performance bond along with his bid.

As a general rule, business buyers use the bid system primarily as a means of exploring or identifying the price factor. No market price exists for many nonstandard materials, complex fabricated products on which design and manufacturing methods vary, and items made to the buyer's specification. In these circumstances, asking for competitive bids is the simplest way of exploring price and evaluating the reasonableness of quoted prices. (See Figure 4–3.)

Having received competitive bids from a group of reliable suppliers, the buyer can select the lowest price offered or weigh it alongside other considerations. If there is a wide range of quotations, both excessively high and excessively low bids may be open to the question: Do the bidders understand the requirements? On the other hand, insignificant variation or identity in quotations is often ground for suspicion of collusion. Whether or not the low bid represents the best price must, in the end, be judged by comparison with other offers, with past experience, with the prices of similar products, and in light of the buyer's own knowledge of market conditions.

Selecting suppliers who will be invited to submit quotations often involves paring down a sizable list of sources to a relatively small one. If items are bought frequently, the purchasing department may have developed an approved list of firms invited to submit bids. While firms are periodically added to and dropped from this list, it usually remains intact for considerable periods of time.

In the case of nonroutine purchases, selecting suppliers to whom requests for quotations will be sent may involve not only a review of past experience with the suppliers under consideration, but also often on-site inspection of their facilities, extensive interviews with salesmen, and inquiries to purchasing agents in other firms who may have patronized them. The more important the purchase, the more exhaustive the investigation.

Negotiation. In the firm that cannot manufacture needed items, or whose management chooses not to manufacture them, the purchasing agent who must procure materials or equipment not suited to purchase on a competitive bid basis must negotiate with prospective suppliers. The process of negotiation may begin with a bid that is later modified to reflect additional factors pertinent to the company's needs, which come to light during interviews between salesman and buyer. Negotiations may also be carried on simultaneously with a number of competitive vendors until enough information has been passed back and forth to enable the buyer to choose the vendor or vendors he will patronize. The advantage

FIGURE 4–3
Request for Quotation

THE **Magnavox** COMPANY

REF.

DATE

REQUEST FOR QUOTATION

YOUR REPLY MUST BE
RECEIVED BY ▼

- ALL QUOTATIONS MUST BE SUBMITTED IN ACCORDANCE WITH TERMS ON THIS REQUEST.

  THIS REQUEST FOR QUOTATION CONSTITUTES NO OBLIGATION ON THE PART OF THE MAGNAVOX COMPANY.

- WE RESERVE THE RIGHT TO ACCEPT ANY PART OR ALL OF YOUR QUOTATION ON THE PRICES QUOTED UNLESS OTHERWISE NOTED.

- THE CONDITIONS CONTAINED IN OUR REGULAR PURCHASE ORDER FORM WILL BE THE CONDITIONS UPON WHICH AN ORDER WILL BE PLACED IF YOUR QUOTATION IS FOUND ACCEPTABLE.

- ANY SUGGESTIONS FOR REDUCING COST WITHOUT AFFECTING QUALITY WILL BE WELCOMED AND CONSIDERED.

IS YOUR COMPANY A "SMALL BUSINESS CONCERN" AS DEFINED IN ASPR 1-701? ☐ YES ☐ NO

IS YOUR COMPANY LOCATED IN A "LABOR SURPLUS AREA" AS DEFINED IN ASPR 1-802.2? ☐ YES ☐ NO

ITEM	QUANTITY	PART NUMBER AND DESCRIPTION	VENDOR # 1	VENDOR # 2	VENDOR # 3

SUMMARY

IMPORTANT INSTRUCTIONS

I   TOOLING

A   QUOTATION ON TOOLS SHALL BE BASED ON ESTIMATED PRODUCTION OF [   ] PIECES AT RUN RATE OF APPROXIMATELY [   ] PCS. PER MO./WK.

B   FURNISH WITH QUOTATION A BREAKDOWN OF TOOLS REQUIRED BY TYPE AND ESTIMATED TOOLING TIME. ON CONSUMER PRODUCT DIVISION TOOLING, DRAWINGS, PHOTOGRAPHS OR SKETCHES OF THE TOOLING MUST BE SUPPLIED AT THE SAME TIME THE SAMPLE PARTS ARE SUBMITTED FOR APPROVAL.

C   TOOLING SHALL BE MAINTAINED IN OPERATING CONDITION AT NO ADDITIONAL COST TO MAGNAVOX.

D   TOOLING CHARGED AGAINST MAGNAVOX OR AMORITIZED IN PIECE PRICE SHALL BE SUBJECT TO REMOVAL FROM SELLERS PLANT AT THE DISCRETION OF MAGNAVOX.

E   TOOLING SHALL NOT BE USED FOR PRODUCTION OF ANY PARTS OTHER THAN FOR MAGNAVOX WITHOUT ITS WRITTEN PERMISSION.

F   SAMPLE PARTS FOR THE APPROVAL OF TOOLS SHALL BE FURNISHED ON A NO CHARGE BASIS.

G   TOOLING INVOICES MAY BE SUBMITTED FOR PAYMENT ONLY AFTER SELLER RECEIVES WRITTEN APPROVAL OF SAMPLE PARTS.

II   PIECE PARTS

A   IF PRICE DOES NOT INCLUDE FINISHING SO SPECIFY.

B   PRICES QUOTED SHALL BE GUARANTEED FOR A PERIOD OF ONE YEAR FROM TOOL PURCHASE ORDER DATE AND SHALL BE APPLICABLE TO ANY QUANTITY RELEASED AT A GIVEN TIME AGAINST THE TOTAL QUANTITY SPECIFIED IN THIS REQUEST FOR QUOTATION.

III   DEVIATION

A   ALL EXCEPTIONS AND DEVIATIONS FROM DRAWINGS MUST BE DETAILED IN YOUR QUOTATION.

RETURN QUOTATIONS TO THE ABOVE ADDRESS TO ATTENTION OF:

NAME

TITLE

TERMS

F.O.B.

QUOTATION SUBMITTED BY:

SELLER COMPANY NAME

AUTHORIZED SIGNATURE   DATE

M-1251-1 REV. 5-65   PERMANENT FILE COPY

of negotiation is that all pertinent factors can be brought under discussion and analysis. Accordingly, details of requirements can often be adjusted to take advantage of the special strengths of particular suppliers, with the result that price, quality, or service advantages that would otherwise be missed can be achieved.

It is probably true that most major purchases by businesses, private institutions, and numerous governmental agencies and departments are negotiated. This method is almost always used in the purchase of new products, because with no experience in manufacturing such products bidders would have to inflate their quotations to allow for more than the normal contingencies. If a substantial margin should be paid, which in the light of subsequent manufacturing experience proves unwarranted, the business or institutional buyer, unlike the federal government, has no legal recourse by which to force renegotiation of the contract.

The successful negotiation of a purchase contract requires skill and experience. The buyer must be cognizant of the cost situation of his own firm as well as that of vendors. He must be able to assemble facts meaningfully, to establish realistic price limits, and to appraise the effect of general economic conditions on the supply situation in industries from which the company fills its needs. Since a purchasing program is no stronger than its sources of supply, it is short-sighted to drive a bargain that will make the firm's patronage unattractive or weaken the vendor as a reliable, continuing source of supply. On the other hand, the buyer must seek every advantage of price, service, and quality to which his company is legitimately entitled.

Negotiation between buyer and seller almost always involves some form of strategy, which is conditioned by the needs of the buyer relative to the eagerness of the vendor for his patronage. The supplier who urgently needs additional volume, who is uncertain that he will get the buyer's order, and who knows there is a limited amount of time to reach an agreement will negotiate in an entirely different manner than he would in the opposite situation. By the same token, the buyer who knows that the seller has little competition, who has little solid information on which to base a price analysis, who does not have much business to offer the supplier, or who is under some pressure to fill a need for a using department will also conduct negotiations in an entirely different manner than he would if the opposite situation existed.

It is also true that the vendor eager to get his foot in the door of a company, or to become established in an industry, is often willing to make special concessions. Similarly, the vendor without accurate records of cost is likely to have a rather wide range of acceptable prices to permit special arrangements. Moreover, that a given vendor has the lowest price does not always mean it is low enough; he may still be using his plant inefficiently. If this is true, and if other qualities of the vendor make him attractive as a source of supply, it is the responsibility of the purchasing agent to convince him of this and help his management to reduce its cost to a minimum without diluting quality. The purchasing agent who has suc-ceeded in developing alternative sources of supply is in a much stronger position to induce vendors to inaugurate cost-reduction programs than is the one without such alternatives.

Negotiations may take on a highly technical character, either because of the products involved, the amount of the purchase, or the implications for design, production, or other operations of the company. In these situations, a team of buyers may be employed, including representatives from engineering, finance, marketing, production, and the legal staff, as well as the purchasing department itself. A similar team is often used by the vendor to make a comprehensive and detailed presentation to the customer. When such teams are involved, negotiation may be protracted and include a great deal of technical data.

Characteristically, alert purchasing departments have specific goals in view when negotiating with prospective suppliers. These objectives often incorporate a range of possibilities to permit flexibility. However, they are usually established on the basis of a careful examination of the company's needs and alternatives as well as the recognition that suppliers must make a profit, too.

Selecting the Alternatives

A decision to manufacture rather than purchase an item as well as a decision to call for firm competitive bids determines the means of procurement as well as the source. The process of selection is completed in the first and will be automatically determined in the second. If, on the other hand, it is decided to purchase rather than manufacture or to negotiate rather than to call for bids, the buyer must select a vendor to receive the order or group of vendors among whom it will be divided. Although the complexity of the selection process varies with the nature of the purchase, it is determined in no small degree by the buyer's conception of what constitutes a good supplier and the usefulness of available information about suppliers.

Characteristics of a Good Supplier. To a considerable extent, all purchasing officers look for much the same qualities in the suppliers they patronize. Honesty, of course, is a prime consideration. Any evidence of a prospective vendor's dishonesty—to his customers or his employees, or in past dealings with the buyer—will generally result in his being given a low priority as a possible supplier. Equally basic is the capacity of a prospective supplier to meet the buyer's requirements with respect to quality, quantity, and delivery time. Any doubts about a supplier's ability to deliver commodities that consistently meet the buyer's specifications in the amounts and within the time period required will give the supplier a low priority, regardless of any other consideration.

Sound financial condition is another quality generally sought in a supplier as assurance that if given an order he will be able to maintain sufficient inventory, production facilities, and personnel to deliver it on the time schedule required. In addition, such qualities as a reputation for research, advances in technology, and alertness to new developments in the industry are usually desired in suppliers. Vendors able to make suggestions and recommendations that effect cost reductions, product improvements, or better service to customers are especially valued.

Experience in manufacturing the products desired and location may be important considerations to buyers. The manufacturing experience weighs heavily in the case of a highly technical or very expensive product. Vendor location is an important consideration if the buyer wishes to avoid high freight costs, to lessen the risk of damage in transit, or if a policy of developing local sources of supply is being pursued.

Information Sources. Numerous sources of information are typically used by purchasing agents to determine the extent to which prospective vendors possess desired qualities. The most reliable and accessible source is usually the buying company's own records. If these have been properly kept, they should reveal such information as suppliers' promptness in response to requests for quotations or other data, promptness in handling rejections, acknowledging orders, and settling complaints, certainty of delivery, and the extent of suppliers' cooperation with engineering, research and development, production, or other departments trying to solve some problem.

Vendor salesmen are, of course, an important source of information, particularly for vendors with whom the buyer has had no previous experience. Salesmen serve as a source of information not only about their own companies, but also about developments in the industry they belong to. It is perhaps unnecessary to mention that salesmen should be sufficiently conversant with the technical properties of their products and with their company's policies concerning prices and services to provide the information requested by buyers. Although purchasing agents generally make it a practice to interview every vendor representative who calls, they have specific informational needs which the representative must be able to supply, either during the interview or at some reasonable time thereafter. Any failure or undue delay in this regard lessens the possibility of a favorable attitude on the part of the buyer.

Catalogs are another common source of vendor information used by purchasing departments. Distributors' catalogs, which usually contain a considerable assortment of products of various specifications and prices from a variety of sources, are particularly useful, as are catalogs distributed by equipment and machinery manufacturers, containing specifications, prices, and sources of replacement parts as well as original equipment. Many vendors attempt to invite more frequent use of their catalogs by including in them trade and product information of a general nature frequently needed by customers.

The value of catalogs to buyers and the frequency of their use depends on the form in which they are published and the ease with which the material they contain can be found, as well as on the way in which they are indexed and filed in the purchasing office. A properly designed and compiled catalog, conveniently indexed and filed, is a ready reference that is likely to become a permanent record in the buyer's office. Such a permanent record is an ever-present reminder of the vendor who issues it, and a continuing instrument of promotion for him between salesmen's calls.

Other frequently used sources of information about prospective vendors are trade journals, advertising, and trade directories. Trade publications are numerous and represent a wide range of quality. Nevertheless, virtually every trade is served by informative journals, read extensively by persons with particular interest in the industry or industries they cover. A good trade journal is not only a source of general information about an industry, such as new products, new techniques, new personnel, and other news events, but it also contains the advertisements of many present and prospective suppliers.

Although the value of advertising to industrial buyers is a matter of dispute, it is generally conceded that they read advertisements and consciously or unconsciously are influenced by them. Purchasing agents undoubtedly find promotional literature useful to the extent that it contains sufficiently detailed information about the advertised product to enable them to match its properties with known or contemplated needs of their companies. Such promotional literature either produces immediate inquiries or is filed for future reference when the contemplated need for an advertised product arises. Much industrial advertising, nevertheless, is thought to be sheer waste as far as producing sales is concerned. This is probably due to a lack of appreciation of the purchasing function by some advertising managers and agencies. But no such indictment can be applied indiscriminately. In spite of its waste, there is ample evidence that industrial advertising does provide buyers with useful information concerning vendors and their products.

Trade directories also vary considerably as to their accuracy and usefulness, but most purchasing offices probably maintain a fairly complete file of standard and specialized directories. Such standard references as, for example, Thomas' *Register of American Manufacturers* and MacRae's *Bluebook* are widely consulted, as are many of the more specialized directories. For the most part, trade directories list leading manufacturers alphabetically by name as well as by products made. In addition, such information as number of branches, addresses, affiliations, and, in some instances, financial standing are often included.

CLOSING THE TRANSACTION

Selecting a vendor or vendors leads, of course, to placing an order, which, in turn, sets in motion procedures for following up the order, checking the invoice, receiving and inspecting the incoming shipment, and completing records of the transaction.

Placing the Order

Placing an order almost invariably involves the use of a purchase order form (see Figure 4-4), even in an emergency situation when usual proce-

FIGURE 4–4

Purchase Order Form

INTERNATIONAL HARVESTER COMPANY

CENTRAL PURCHASING DEPARTMENT

401 NORTH MICHIGAN AVENUE, CHICAGO, ILLINOIS 60611

TELEPHONE AREA CODE 312 527-0200

PURCHASE ORDER

PURCHASE ORDER NUMBER

THIS PURCHASE ORDER NUMBER AND OUR PART NUMBER OR CODE MUST APPEAR ON EACH INVOICE, PACKING LIST, SHIPPING CONTAINER AND CORRESPONDENCE.

SHIP AND INVOICE TO OR SHIP TO

INVOICE TO

G.O. BUYER	REQUISITION NO.

THIS ORDER IS GIVEN AND ACCEPTED SUBJECT TO ALL CONDITIONS HEREIN AND PRINTED ON THE REVERSE SIDE HEREOF.
SEND ACCEPTANCE OF THIS PURCHASE ORDER DIRECT TO LOCATION TO WHICH INVOICE IS TO BE SENT.

TERMS	F.O.B.	VIA	DATE
ACCOUNT NUMBER	DELIVER TO	P.O. COPIES REQUIRED FOR	

FEDERAL EXCISE TAX ▶ ☐ FOR FURTHER MANUFACTURE · SEE EXEMPTION CERTIFICATE ON REVERSE SIDE ☐ FOR RESALE · SERVICE (EXEMPTION CERTIFICATE NOT APPLICABLE.)

DELIVERY SCHEDULE: MATERIAL MUST BE SHIPPED TO ARRIVE AT OUR LOCATION ON DAY INDICATED.

JAN.	FEB.	MAR.	APRIL	MAY	JUNE	JULY	AUG.	SEPT.	OCT.	NOV.	DEC.

STATE SALES AND USE TAX ▶ ☐ FOR USE ☐ FOR USE NONTAXABLE ☐ FOR RESALE-REGISTRATION NO.

QUANTITY	OUR PART NUMBER OR CODE	SUPPLIER NUMBER AND/OR DESCRIPTION	PRICE

INSTRUCTIONS: Invoice in DUPLICATE

Mail all invoices and bills of lading same day goods are shipped. Render a separate invoice for each shipment against this purchase order if partial shipments are made. Provide packing list in each shipment.

GFX-50 EA-G.O. M.T

INTERNATIONAL HARVESTER COMPANY

BY____________________

dures are set aside. It is also true that all conditions of the purchase agreement may not be stipulated in the purchase order. Some vendors may insist that the purchaser sign a sales agreement that affords them a degree of protection not specifically assured by the buyer's purchase order. How unyielding the vendors are in such matters usually depends on the extent to which a strong seller's market exists in the commodity being purchased, the complexity of the transaction, and the relative bargaining strength of the two parties.

The layout and routing of purchase order forms defy generalization, largely because the purchase order is a legal document and opinions vary widely on the manner of presentation that will provide the best protection. There is general agreement that the conditions governing relations between buyers and sellers are of paramount importance, but there is no general agreement as to how these conditions can be properly stated in a legal document. It is generally agreed, though, that any satisfactory purchase order form should contain such essential items of information as

FIGURE 4–5

Form Used for Releasing Quantities of an Item under an Open-End Order

PURCHASE ORDER RELEASE AND SHIPPING SCHEDULE
EMD 720-L

SUPPLIER COPY
ELECTRO-MOTIVE DIVISION
GENERAL MOTORS CORPORATION • LA GRANGE, ILLINOIS

SERIAL NO. 294749

TO:

THIS PURCHASE ORDER RELEASE AND SHIPPING SCHEDULE SUPERSEDES ALL FORMER SCHEDULES FOR THIS PART.

PART NO.
SCHEDULE
DATE

ORDER STATUS

ORDER NUMBER	ORDER DATE	ORDER SERIES	MEAS.	TOTAL RECEIPTS	LAST REC. CONSIDERED DATE	LAST REC. CONSIDERED QUANTITY	SUPPLIER CODE

RATING CERTIFICATION

PART DESCRIPTION	DELIVER TO: PLANT	DELIVER TO: WHSE	M F B

SHIPPING SCHEDULE
DO NOT FABRICATE MATERIAL FOR PERIODS MARKED WITH ASTERISK (*) RELEASED FOR MATERIAL ONLY

SCHEDULE TOTALS	BALANCE DUE	TOTAL RELEASED	PREV. RELEASED	CHANGE IN RELEASE	CUMULATIVE AVAIL.	EXCESS AVAIL.	

EACH MONTH'S SHIPMENTS MUST BE SHIPPED ON THE SCHEDULED DATES OR IN EQUAL WEEKLY SHIPMENTS THROUGHOUT THE MONTH.

CHECK "RECEIPTS" WITH YOUR FIGURES AND ADVISE IMMEDIATELY IF ANY DISCREPANCY.

ELECTRO-MOTIVE DIVISION
GENERAL MOTORS CORPORATION

J S Voller
DIRECTOR OF PURCHASING

BY ______
BUYER

the date of issue, name and address of the firm receiving the order, the quantity and description of goods ordered, date of delivery requested, shipping instructions, prices, terms of payment, and a serial number to permit easy tracing of the order.

Placing a purchase order does not always create a contract until it has been accepted by the vendor, not merely acknowledged by him. In consequence, some buyers insist on an acceptance from the supplier, except for insignificant, emergency, or routine purchases. The form of acceptance may vary from a verbal confirmation that an order has been received—quite common in telephone orders—to a detachable stub on the purchase order or an acceptance copy of the order itself. Either the stub or the acceptance copy can be signed by the vendor and returned to the buyer.

Without prompt acceptance of his order by the vendor, the buyer can only assume that delivery will be made by the date requested or that prices will remain as initially quoted. Such information is especially important to buyers if delivery dates are uncertain and prices are subject to fluctuation. Vendors who fail to accept orders promptly in such circumstances are not likely to be honored with much repeat business.

Firms that sell products used in volume and purchased repetitively over a period of time, such as maintenance and repair items and production line requirements, usually suggest *blanket* or *open-end* orders to buyers. Such orders include all terms and stipulations needed for the purchase of a given product or products over a considerable period of time. For example, an engine manufacturer may purchase his predicted requirement of hose connectors for the coming year in a single order. Subsequently, releases of specific quantities may be made against the order as required by his production schedule. (See Figure 4–5.) In some instances, it may be possible to tie the preparation of purchase order releases into the production scheduling procedure and forward them to the purchasing department for transmission to the vendor. It is not unusual for such open-end orders to remain in effect until changes in design, material specifications, or conditions affecting price or delivery make new negotiations desirable or necessary.

Order Follow-up

Ideally, it should not be necessary to follow up an order. But purchase orders are not always prepared so that vendors can interpret them accurately, and vendors themselves are not always fully cooperative. They do not always honor the delivery dates to which their salesmen have committed them, and when running short of material they may shift production to other orders without notifying either their sales departments or their customers. Suppliers have also been known to give priority to the more profitable orders on their books, and to view such contingencies as labor difficulties and mechanical breakdowns with more optimism than conditions warrant. Consequently, there is almost invariably a need for some kind of follow-up procedure.

Although follow-up procedures in current use are too varied to permit much generalization, responsibility for initiating them usually rests with the buyer who places the order. His more intimate knowledge of who should be contacted in the vendor firm and the greater likelihood that he can get prompt action without jeopardizing friendly relations with the vendor usually account for his key role in follow-up action. Follow-up procedure itself may involve no more than a telephone call, a series of letters, or a questionnaire. On the other hand, it may include a group of

FIGURE 4–6

Expediting Form

UNIVERSAL BLEACHER CO.
1303 N. McKINLEY AVE. -- P.O. BOX 640
CHAMPAIGN, ILLINOIS 61823

Purchase Expediter

USE WINDOW
ENVELOPE
FOR RETURN.
FOLD HERE

PLEASE REPLY IMMEDIATELY

☐ BY PHONE

☐ BY WIRE

☐ ON THIS FORM

PLEASE SAVE YOUR TIME AND OURS, BY COMPLETING THIS
FORM RATHER THAN WRITING A LETTER. FORM MAY BE
RETURNED IN A #10 WINDOW ENVELOPE. FOLD AS
INDICATED AT UPPER LEFT.

DATE

OUR PURCHASE ORDER NO.	YOUR INVOICE NO.	YOUR ORDER NO.	INVOICE DATE	INVOICE AMOUNT	REFERENCE

ORDER INFORMATION
1. ( ) Please rush PRICES.
2. ( ) Acknowledge our order and give SHIPPING DATE.
3. ( ) Please mail us ACCEPTANCE COPY of our Purchase Order.
4. ( ) Is this order considered COMPLETE?
5. ( ) Please inform us about items BACK ORDERED.
6. ( ) CHANGE made on above order. Please acknowledge.

SHIPPING INFORMATION
7. ( ) RUSH shipment. ADVISE earliest shipping date.
8. ( ) Will you SHIP on date requested?
9. ( ) WHY did you not ship as promised? WHEN will you ship?
10. ( ) IF SHIPPED advise method.
11. ( ) What PARTIAL shipment can you make and WHEN?
12. ( ) When can BALANCE of order be shipped?
13. ( ) Please make certain order is SHIPPED VIA_____
14. ( ) Please make SHIPMENT RELEASES as shown under Remarks.

ACCOUNTING INFORMATION
15. ( ) We require_____INVOICE COPIES.
16. ( ) INVOICE enclosed RECEIVED IN ERROR.
17. ( ) We are RETURNING attached invoice.
18. ( ) PURCHASE ORDER NO. incorrect or missing.
19. ( ) PRICE ☐ TERMS ☐ DISCOUNT ☐ do not agree with quotation.
20. ( ) Please forward CORRECTED INVOICE or CREDIT MEMO for following
       reason:
       ( ) Quantity incorrect.   ( ) Extension incorrect.
       ( ) Should be F. O. B. destination. ( ) Unit price incorrect.
       ( ) Material wrong or defective.
21. ( ) SALES TAX not applicable. Exemption No. is_____.
22. ( ) We have no record of RECEIVING INVOICE NO._____
       shown on your statement. Please send duplicate invoice.

REMARKS

SERVICE AND OTHER INFORMATION
23. ( ) If order has been shipped, MAIL INVOICE today.
24. ( ) Please forward CERTIFIED WEIGHT slip.
25. ( ) Please forward SHIPPING NOTICE.
26. ( ) Please show PURCHASE ORDER NUMBER on papers referred to or
       attached.
27. ( ) Material not received. TRACE AND ADVISE.
28. ( ) Please forward receipted FREIGHT BILL.
29. ( ) We have NO RECORD of transaction covered by your invoice. Advise
       date of shipment, name of person placing order and furnish signed
       delivery receipt.
30. ( ) Please complete and return our REQUEST FOR QUOTATION
       dated_____.

SIGNED

*Reply*_____

DATE   SIGNED

PLEASE RETURN THIS COPY TO SENDER WITH REPLY
PINK COPY IS FOR YOUR RECORDS

specialists, expediters, who spend virtually full time keeping suppliers on schedule. Expediters are often vested with considerable responsibility and spend much of their time on visiting suppliers' plants to investigate deliveries and to keep shipments moving.

Handling the Invoice

The receipt of an invoice is not only notification of shipment, it is also notification of what has been shipped and the exact nature of the vendor's claim against the buyer. Since no transaction is complete until the invoice has been verified and the claim against the buyer paid, the way invoices are handled is a matter of some consequence. A common practice is to attach to the invoice a list of items to be verified as soon as it is received. If any information called for by this checklist does not appear on the invoice or if any information appearing there does not agree with the purchase order, the invoice is ordinarily returned to the vendor for correction. In many cases, a special form is used for this purpose.

Even though the return of an incorrect invoice is a routine operation for both buyer and seller, it represents much lost motion and adds nothing to the efficiency of the buyer or to his estimate of the seller. Many marketers do not include invoicing in the marketing function. Nevertheless, careless invoicing by a vendor, which requires the customer to spend a disproportionate amount of time in checking and returning his invoices for correction, can have a deleterious effect on repeat business. While buyers are not apt to be very reticent about such annoyances in their interviews with salesmen, it is not unusual for salesmen to be indifferent about following up such complaints.

There appears to be considerable difference of opinion as to whether invoice verification and approval is a function of purchasing or accounting. In practice, every conceivable arrangement involving both departments can be found. As a general rule, however, it is the purchasing department that authorizes payment and must be satisfied that the terms of the purchase agreement have been met.

Receipt and Inspection of Merchandise

With the exception of large, multiunit companies, the receipt and inspection of incoming merchandise is usually centralized in a single unit, either directly or indirectly responsible to the purchasing department. The receiving unit commonly reports incoming shipments on some form

FIGURE 4–7

Form Used for Reporting Receipt of Purchased Merchandise

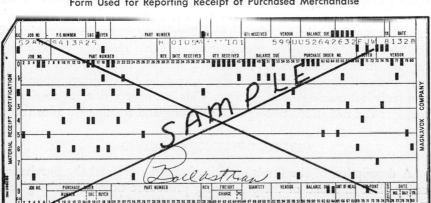

of "materials received" memorandum. (See Figure 4–7.) Typically, copies of the memorandum are forwarded to the purchasing department to be checked against the invoice, to the stores department for entry in inventory records, and to the using department as notification of fulfillment of its requisition. In some companies, a copy is also sent to the traffic division.

In addition to the verification of quantities received, it may be necessary to verify quality as well. In many firms, inspection of quality is limited to a representative sample of each shipment. Some receiving departments have a specialized inspection division whose personnel determine how and when inspection of incoming shipments will be made.

Completing the Records

Completing the purchasing record requires that copies of the various documents relating to an order be assembled and filed, so that if they contain any information the department wishes to keep it may be transferred to the appropriate permanent records. While filing and assembling documents is largely a routine matter, decisions as to what items of information and which documents should be retained involve judgment and planning. While legal minds tend to argue for keeping all formal documents indefinitely, it is fairly common practice to classify purchasing documents on the basis of their importance and retain only those regarded as most important. For example, a purchase order is much more important than a requisition because it is evidence of a contract with an outside party. Less important documents that contain certain items of information management wants to keep (delivery dates, number of rejects, handling of complaints) would be transferred to permanent records, such as a vendor file, and the documents themselves discarded.

THE PURCHASING OFFICER

What manner of man is it who directs this purchasing process? As a group, purchasing officers are very able business executives. Their attitudes toward their jobs are more nearly professional than those of most other groups of businessmen, accountants excepted. Various studies indicate that more than half of them are college graduates with some kind of technical or administrative specialization, and that this ratio is increasing rapidly. In his contacts with purchasing officers, the industrial salesman may increasingly expect to deal with men who have college educations and technical training or experience. This is a matter that the marketing manager can not afford to forget in selecting and training his sales force.

MULTIPLE INFLUENCE IN BUYING

A description of the firm's organization structure and the purchasing unit's place in it and of the purchasing procedure does not quite give a clear picture of the areas of influence that bear on the buying decision. To a very considerable extent, this decision is likely to be a multiple one rather than the work of a single person. In the average firm, several persons bring to bear on the buying act varying degrees of influence applied at various stages of the process.

A 1959 study of 106 industrial firms, made by the McGraw-Hill Publishing Company, indicated that in over 38 percent of the companies at least four persons influenced buying, and that in almost 78 percent of them three or more persons exercised such an influence. A similar study, made by the Marketing Services Division of Dun and Bradstreet in 1958, indicated that the number of persons who influenced buying in the average firm was 8.7.

This characteristic varies in nature and intensity among the several types of industrial products. When major equipment is to be bought, the design and development unit, the engineering department, and the production executives are likely to play a decisive part in determining the kind of machine to be bought and in preparing the specifications for it. In this process, it is not unusual that operating supervisors, such as the foreman, works manager, or master mechanic, will be consulted. If sizable sums of money are involved, top management in the person of the chief executive officer or the chief financial officer or both are apt to exercise power of approval or veto. The purchasing officer performs mainly the functions of negotiation and follow-up.

When a component or major material is to be bought, the design units of engineering, research, and production are apt to play stellar roles in preparing specifications and comparing the merits of suppliers. Marketing is likely to be consulted if the item exercises a significant effect on the salability of the end product. Since large commitments of current funds are involved, top management often retains the power of approval or veto. The purchasing officer is likely to limit his participation to negotiation and follow-up, although negotiation may be wholly or partially taken out of his hands when requirements contracts are transacted, as they often are, by high level executives of both the buying and the supplying firm.

The choice of auxiliary equipment and MRO items may be influenced by the operating executives, often at the supervisory level and sometimes even by the workers who use them. Occasionally, specifications are set by a unit of the engineering department.

When the cost of a basic material looms large in the cost structure of a firm, some member of top management is likely to exercise a decisive influence on the timing of its purchase, the amount in which it is bought, and the supplier. The engineering department usually prepares specifications or determines the grades of materials to be bought. The marketing department probably will influence the choice of suppliers of all products in whose procurement reciprocity plays a significant part.

This fact of multiple buying influence is very important to the industrial marketer. It means that he cannot be content to make contact with and tell his story to the unit of a customer company that is officially charged with the work of purchasing. In each customer organization, he must try to locate the individuals who have the final power of decision with respect to his product or who exercise a significant influence on that decision, and then devise ways to contact them and get to them information about his product and service. And he must do this without antagonizing the purchasing officer within whose province these matters ostensibly fall.

SUMMARY

This chapter is based on the proposition that the industrial marketer must know his customer and the way he buys. Therefore, it has been organized around the several recognized steps in the buying process. We have noted the various ways in which a need for a product or service is recognized, and how this recognition is translated into a request or authorization to buy. The three major alternative methods by which the need may be satisfied were outlined: (1) to make the product or service, (2) to request competitive bids, (3) to negotiate a purchase. The more important factors involved in selecting a supplier and the sources of information about suppliers were discussed briefly.

We also indicated the important features of the purchase order and the steps in handling and consummating it: follow-up, handling invoices, receiving and inspecting merchandise, and completing the purchase record. Finally, we presented brief discussions of the purchasing officer and of the multiple influences that affect the buying decision. Much of our ensuing discussion of the problems of organizing and managing the process of marketing industrial goods is based on the assumption that the reader has at least a rudimentary knowledge of industrial purchasing procedure. The successful marketer must have much more than a rudimentary knowledge of it.

Chapter 5

◇◇◇◇◇◇◇◇◇◇◇◇◇◇◇◇◇◇◇◇◇◇◇◇◇◇◇◇◇◇◇◇◇◇◇◇ VALUE AND

ALYSIS

THE TECHNICAL NATURE of t   many industrial products as well as the   have placed a
high priority on the prope   rnative means
of filling them. To these   leveloped two
kinds of programs with in   ccause of their
bearing on the choice of   These are value
analysis, sometimes calle   provement, and
vendor analysis.

Most value analysi   conceptual roots in
the ideas of work si   Mogenson in the
early 1930's. The p   ng transaction with
the definition of de   sing department and
he endeavors to procure   st. By comparing the
quality and price of a supplier's prod   andard, value analysis
seeks to measure the extent to which the produc enables him to do this.
The essence of quality is suitability. To the extent that an item incorporates features or properties that do not contribute in some significant way
to either the efficiency of the production process or the salability of the
buyer's end product, its value is impaired. Value improvement, therefore,
begins with an analysis of the purpose or function an item is purchased to
fulfill. The objective, of course, is to effect a revision of the specification
or quality definition of the item that will permit a reduction in its cost
without impairing its suitability.

It is apparent that value analysis cuts across lines that customarily
divide functional responsibility. Although the determination and definition of quality requirements are the responsibility of using departments
rather than purchasing, purchasing clearly has responsibility for value.
Consequently, the systematic search for the most economical means of

satisfying requirements of using departments has been widely accepted as
a legitimate extension of purchasing activity. This involves the effort to
recast the technical description of purchased parts, materials, components,
and equipment so that their specifications will more accurately reflect
their purpose or function.

The Process of Value Analysis

The search for improved value generally proceeds in two stages: (1) a
review of existing product specifications in the light of use requirements
and (2) the identification and elimination of unnecessary cost factors.

Review of Product Specifications. The need for value analysis arises
from several situations that may result in product specifications that do
not completely match use requirements. Products are often developed and
marketed on tight schedules that allow little time for investigation of all
possible avenues of low-cost manufacturing methods and processes. Later
reviews of these products may be chiefly concerned with making minor
improvements rather than with scrutinizing specifications with regard to
both manufacturing and customer requirements. Moreover, it is not unusual for manufacturing technology to advance so rapidly that a product in
production only a few years may contain significant excess cost elements
unless it is periodically reviewed in the light of new methods and technology. Antiquated make-or-buy policies may limit the consideration of
offers by outside specialty suppliers. Such situations can result in thousands of dollars of excess cost, not as a result of something that is done
wrong, but as a result of something that is not done at all, viz., periodic
scrutiny of the parts, components, subassemblies, and materials that enter
into the end product of the buyer.

While such reviews of specifications do not imply distrust or dispar-
agement of the engineering skill and judgment represented in the original
statement of need, they do recognize the ever-present possibility of improvement in specification and design. These reviews also recognize that
in mass production no unit saving is too small to be worthwhile. A
difference of one cent per unit, where thousands of units are being
produced annually, can result in substantial savings or losses. For example,
a leading automobile manufacturer realized savings of $64,000 per year
simply by changing one small component from a forging to an equally
serviceable screw-machine product. While the new product was only
$\frac{1}{10}$ of 1 cent cheaper per unit than the forging, 16 were used in every
car.

In essence, those reviewing specifications seek to determine what the
material or part under consideration contributes to the end product, what
is the minimal function it must perform to give the end product the
desired performance capabilities, and how much this minimal function or
contribution is worth. Depending on the nature of the product, these
questions will raise such detailed inquiries as: Does the part or material

used need all its features? What else would perform the same function? Can it be made at lower cost? Can it be obtained from another dependable supplier for less? The purpose of such questions is to determine how equivalent performance can be achieved at lower cost and how the combined knowledge of engineering, manufacturing, and purchasing personnel can best utilize alternative materials, newer processes, and abilities of specialized suppliers to speed this achievement.

Identifying and Eliminating Unnecessary Costs. Establishing that the cost of a particular part or material is unnecessary or unreasonable involves the analysis of its price as well as of its function or contribution. Although many cost factors may be subsumed in a supplier's price quotation, price analysis ordinarily begins with the cost of production. The supplier's basic production cost may be relatively fixed by the design, materials, and methods specified by the buyer. If it can be assumed that buyers select suppliers whose production methods are efficient and whose costs are competitive, price analysis invariably focuses on design, materials, and production methods. This is almost always the case, even though there is some variation among suppliers on other factors that influence price, such as overhead charges, distribution and promotion costs, quantity differentials, profit margins, and pricing policies.

Careful appraisal and analysis of design, materials, and production methods often points the way to elimination or modification of unnecessary features of design and the cost of the manufacturing operations they entail. The result is usually a part or material with properties that more economically satisfy the use requirement intended for it. An example of this identification and elimination of unnecessary cost is provided by a manufacturer of timing devices who purchased the motor that activated the timing mechanism from a leading supplier of electrical appliances. Since the motor represented the most expensive part of the end product, it was selected first for investigation when a value analysis section was established in the company's purchasing department. Disassembly of the motor revealed that most of the structural components were made of brass. Since the primary function of the structural members was to provide support and rigidity to the motor housing, substitution of a cheaper metal or alloy of adequate strength seemed possible. A conference was arranged with members of the supplier's design and engineering staff and representatives of several primary metal suppliers to study the design and materials of the housing. As a result, aluminum alloy was substituted for brass in all supporting members of the motor housing, with a reduction in price that saved the buyer $15,000 annually.

The Value Analysis Program

A program of value analysis is an organized sequence of investigation aimed at challenging existing product specifications, design, and production methods. Such programs normally begin with the organization of a value analysis group consisting of representatives from purchasing, engineering, manufacturing, accounting, and other departments with a functional interest in the product under study. The purchasing representative is generally called on for information regarding supplier capabilities and to provide liaison with suppliers to solicit their suggestions and draw on their store of knowledge and technical capacity. Engineers typically supply technical evaluation of suggestions, while the manufacturing representative appraises them in the light of his knowledge of production methods and processes. The role of the accountant is usually that of cost analysis and verification of cost-price data. Other specialists, such as marketing officers, may be called on for their ideas and evaluations of suggestions as to end product customers' preferences, attitudes, and problems.

Along with the establishment of an analysis group must be a procedure for selecting what the group will study and how the study will proceed. The first usually presents no problem, since few products are so well designed and manufactured as to discourage any thought of significant improvement. The issue is usually which parts, materials, and components have a value analysis priority, and this is usually decided by the importance of their contributions to the total cost of the buyer's end product or service. This is not always the case, however. The sales department of a company may occasionally quote prices below cost in order to get the company's foot in the door of an important account. If such quotations have the approval of top management, the value analysis group may be called on to try to salvage some profit out of the order. But it is generally agreed that such activities do not represent the best use of value analysis and should be confined to rare occasions.

When criteria for identifying products to be analyzed have been chosen, value analysis programs usually proceed with the determination of the product's (part, material, or component) function, the identification of alternative means of performing its function, the testing of each alternative, and the formulation of a recommendation. Determining the function of a part, material, or component is perhaps the most important of these steps, because it requires a clear, succinct statement of what the product does and it leads to the identification of other means of doing it. For example, a shovel moves dirt, but what else could be used to move dirt—a broom, a blast of air, a stream of water? Gasoline provides energy through combustion, but what else provides energy—light, chemical action, fermentation? What else could be used to write with instead of a pencil or to preserve food instead of a can or a refrigerator?

Ideas generated by the identification of function are then tested and appraised, often with the cooperation of prospective suppliers. After a cost analysis of the most promising ideas has been completed, proposals are typically submitted to the appropriate engineering, design, or production official for approval.

The implications of this kind of program for the industrial marketer are significant. Normally, a new product is developed and produced for a limited, exploratory market in order to determine its need and acceptance. If accepted, it increases rapidly in sales during its growth period and ultimately levels off. To get this device into production and up to projected sales volume often requires the expenditure of considerable engineering effort. Once this volume is reached, however, engineering, design, and other creative talent tends to be directed toward the development and manufacture of other new products. Unfortunately, this is the juncture at which imitative competitors tend to enter the market and endeavor to take business away from the originator. Such invasion of the originator's market is usually successful if he ceases to make continued improvements in the performance or cost of his product. It is at this point that value analysis can be a most effective tool in weeding out unnecessary cost and maintaining the competitive vitality of the original product. This is also the point where suppliers (sellers) with an appreciation of value analysis and a positive program for contributing to it can strengthen their position with customers who may have considered them as marginal.

The need for this kind of work persists throughout the life of an industrial product. Value analysis may even be worthwhile in making deletion decisions. When a product is sick or suffering the infirmaties of age, value analysis may suggest production changes or product modifications that reduce cost or increase marketability to prolong its profitable life. On the other hand, such a study may confirm the conclusion that the product has outlived its usefulness and should be deleted.

The industrial marketer can use value analysis of his own and competing products to supply his salesmen with information about the competitive strengths and weaknesses of his product in use, which the salesman can translate into selling appeals. The salesman gains strength from a knowledge of his products and those against which he must compete.

VENDOR ANALYSIS

In reality, a supplier represents an extension of the buyer's manufacturing or operating capacity without the attendant implications of ownership and control. The quality of a supplier's product must not only match the specifications of the buyer, but his delivery performance also must conform to the buyer's manufacturing schedule or other operational timetable. The vendor's price is an indivisible part of the total cost of bringing materials from the vendor's plant to the point of usage in the buyer's plant, office, or other facility. Any delay in delivery or deviation in quality adds to the buyer's procurement costs.

In consequence, buyers must be certain that their suppliers meet the standards of performance and quality for which their own operations have been planned. Rapid advances in product technology and the spiraling investment in goods and services characteristic of many industries have given an air of urgency to ways of accurately assessing vendor capabilities. Most of these ways are concerned with the identification, definition, and measurement of vendor capacity to satisfy the buyer's particular requirements.

To the extent that buyer requirements can be satisfied by materials available commercially and marketed on official or generally accepted specifications or standards, a buyer requires commodities rather than capabilities. However, when requirements are unique, calling for special design, performance, or reliability features, or when they entail expensive tooling, extended periods of preparation, high setup costs, and involve large quantities of material over extended periods of time, the purchasing department's job is primarily to buy capabilities rather than products.

Evaluating Vendor Capacity

To the extent that the buyer recognizes vendors as extensions of his own resources and operational capacity, he must appraise them in terms of their technological, productive, financial, and management capability.

Technical and Production Capability. A vendor's capability in technology refers to the excellence and extensiveness of his design and development engineering, production engineering, test engineering, and tool engineering. Adequate know-how and sophistication in these various phases of engineering is necessary to assure consistency in the quality of products before, during, and after production. Vendor production capability refers to the efficiency and completeness of his manufacturing facilities and practical know-how, as well as the means to extend or supplement them through both subcontracting and procurement.

Analysis of a vendor's technical and production capability usually involves on-site inspection of his facilities and visits with his key officials in production, purchasing, engineering, and sales. The trained mind and the experienced eye can quickly appraise conditions in the vendor's plant, observe the variety of standard and special equipment used, the adequacy of inventories to support production schedules, and the orderly conduct of manufacturing operations. Such visits can also afford the opportunity to observe testing and quality control procedures, as well as the assortment of products and components manufactured.

Financial Capability. A vendor's financial capability is usually measured by his credit standing, cash flow, equity, and working capital. Of equal importance is the ease with which the vendor could augment capital funds through borrowing or additional investment. Financial ratios, particularly those that indicate liquidity, are important tests of financial capacity. A good profit record over a period of years is a reliable indication that the vendor will be able to raise more funds, if necessary, from

creditors or investors.[1] By the same token, vendors with a large net worth
are usually able to raise funds readily because the owner's investment
provides a cushion of safety for creditors. Similarly, a large net worth to
debt ratio provides a basis for more credit.

The volume of sales the vendor has predicted and plans to make is also
an indication of financial soundness. A company with annual sales typically within a range of $500,000 to $1 million, for example, would probably find itself in difficulty if it attempted to increase sales to $5 million a
year, even if it had previously been in a strong financial position. On the
other hand, a firm with a sound financial position should be able to
support a modest increase in sales without difficulty.

Financial analysis often brings to light weaknesses that make a vendor
undesirable as a supplier. The types of firms likely to fail financial tests are
new firms of limited net worth and experience, rapidly expanding firms,
firms that refuse to divulge information about their financial condition—
secrecy often hides weaknesses—and small firms, because there is generally greater uncertainty about their ability to command additional funds if
they are needed.

Management Capabilities. The ability of a vendor firm's management
to plan, organize, integrate, and control its facilities, manpower and materials, time, and cost is a critical but elusive quality. In evaluating it, buyers
usually seek to identify the vendor's key management people—their titles,
responsibilities, experience, and extent of formal education. The nature of
a vendor's planning, scheduling, and inventory control systems also indicates management's caliber. Equally revealing is information about machine and manpower loading, how requirements are released—by job, by
lot, or by forecast—and whether the company requires certifications and
tests of quality from its own suppliers.

Once the buyer's system of evaluation has eliminated those vendors
who do not qualify for patronage, it is common practice to rate those who
remain in the light of experience with them.

Rating Vendor Performance

The objective rating of vendor performance is a matter that eluded any
form of measurement criteria for years. But significant progress has been
made recently in this direction, particularly among large buyers, through
the development of and experimentation with vendor rating systems.

A vendor rating system entails the establishment of performance rating
standards so that the buyer can validly distinguish between good and
marginal suppliers. The purpose of the rating sytem is to supply tangible
guidelines that will improve judgment in all areas of resource selection.

---

[1] The net profit record itself may not show the full success of the company,
particularly a small company, because the drawing account of the owner may include
more than reasonable salaries and expenses.

Past experience with a vendor's quality and delivery is important for this purpose as is past experience with his services—technical, financial, and managerial. Past prices, however, are usually not significant, and quoted prices are significant only to the extent that they can be expressed in terms of the value of the product quality, delivery, and service package offered by the supplier.

As a rule, rating systems reflect the cost buyers must incur, supplier by supplier, in satisfying their requirements. For example, suppliers may be rated on product quality in terms of three categories of cost—defect prevention, defect detection, and defect correction. The sum of these quality costs for each supplier is then expressed as a percent of the total value of materials purchased from him.

Delivery performance is similarly rated by expression in terms of acquisition and availability costs. These costs represent such expenditures as follow-up and expediting time, telegraph and telephone expense, field expediting and surveillance costs, and premium transportation charges, as well as manufacturing losses due to supplier's delivery failures and resulting shortages. These, too, are usually expressed as a percentage of the value of materials purchased from each source.

Suppliers are also rated in terms of the value they contribute to the buyer in addition to product quality and delivery performance. Such added values are loosely classified as service and given a variety of cost equivalents. When price, quality, and delivery considerations produce comparable ratings, it is evident that service ratings could have a decisive influence in the choice of a preferred supplier.

A Vendor Rating System.[2] The Development Project Committee on Standards for Vendor Evaluation of the National Association of Purchasing Agents recently published several different plans for vendor performance evaluation. Although these plans represent a considerable variation in method and approach, all rely on the four major procurement variables as bases for measurement, viz., price, product quality, delivery, and service. In the interest of brevity, we will limit our discussion to the plan that has probably elicited the widest interest. The *cost ratio plan* incorporates a vendor performance evaluation formula that enables a buyer to factor a vendor's price on the basis of tangible performance criteria. The formula incorporates a quality rating, a delivery rating, and a service rating in such a way that a minus (−) weight favors the vendor and a plus (+) weight detracts from him. The individual factor ratings are compiled separately and then combined into the final composite rating. Let us examine the nature of these ratings.

The Quality Rating. The quality rating is a composite of the percent of the total number of defective items purchased by the buyer from a

        [2] Much of the material presented in this section was provided by William D. Kellner, Manager, Purchasing Support, the General Electric Company.

given supplier, multiplied by a disposition factor. The number of defective items purchased is determined by sampling, whereas the disposition factor is a weight based on the standard cost of disposing of defective material and expressed as a decimal fraction. The various ways in which defective items are disposed of and the relative costs of each are given under *disposition factor* in Table 5–1. In a fairly representative company

TABLE 5–1

Quality Rating

Formula
   1.00 + % defective (disposition factor)

Percent Defective
   Number of defective units in a sample lot divided by the number of units in the sample

Disposition Factor
   Use as is....................................05
   Scrap and reorder..........................14
   Return and reorder.........................15
   Rework:
      a) Billed to vendor......................03
      b) Absorbed..............................43

Example

Units Inspected	Units Rejected	Dispositio
100	50	Use as is

$$\text{Quality Rating} = 1.00 + \frac{50}{100} \times .05 = 1.025$$

experimenting with the cost ratio plan, the cost of using a defective item involves writing of a quality data report and having a conference that includes the quality control engineer, the project engineer, the incoming material inspector, and, occasionally, the customer. To scrap and reorder a defective item in this company requires a written quality data report, a letter to the vendor requesting corrective action, dispostion of the inventory of defective items, issuance of a second purchase order, and a second incoming inspection. If a defective item is returned to the vendor and reordered, the cost elements are a written quality data report, a letter requesting corrective action, a shipping notice, packaging of material, issuance of a replacement purchase order, and a second incoming inspection. As a last resort, the company may rework defective items and use them. If this alternative is chosen, the costs incurred include a quality data report, the scheduling of manufacturing operations necessary to rework the material, direct labor, and attendant overhead cost. If the vendor accepts the cost of reworking, then the only cost incurred by the buyer is that of billing the vendor.

The example shown in Table 5–1 assumes a sample lot of 100 pieces drawn at random from the vendor's shipment, of which 50 were found to be defective. If the decision was to use the defective pieces, the vendor's quality rating would be 1.00 plus 50/100 × .05, giving a value of 1.025.

The Delivery Rating. In developing the rating system for delivery performance, company management established standard costs resulting from improper delivery. A weighted cost factor was then assigned to the different delivery possibilities from two weeks or more ahead of schedule to more than six weeks late. Costs that entered into the standard cost base from which the weights were derived were the expense of idle factory time and replanning created by delinquent shipments, as well as travel, telephone calls, and living expenses created by the necessity of expediting delivery. Application of the delivery rating is shown in Table 5–2.

It will be noted that delivery two weeks or more ahead of schedule is given a penalty rating(+), as is delivery more than one week late.

TABLE 5–2

Delivery Rating

Formula
    Delivery rating factor and expediting factor to be added to or subtracted from quality rating

Delivery Rating Factor
    a) 2 weeks or more ahead of schedule...........................+.01
    b) 1 to 2 weeks ahead of schedule...............................−.01
    c) 0 to 1 week ahead of schedule................................ .00
    d) 1 week late...+.01
    e) 2 to 3 weeks late..+.05
    f) 4 to 6 weeks late..+.10
    g) More than 6 weeks late.....................................+.20

Expediting Factor to Be Added to Delivery Rating
    a) 1 vendor contact.. .00
    b) 2 to 3 contacts..+.01
    c) 4 to 5 contacts..+.02
    d) More than 5 contacts.......................................+.03
    e) Delivery information supplied voluntarily.......................−.01

An early shipment (in excess of two weeks ahead of schedule) in this company causes a premature expenditure of planned inventory funds, while a shipment one to two weeks ahead of schedule eliminates expediting and affords some flexibility in processing material through the inspection routine. Delivery on or no more than one week ahead of schedule is typical. Penalties understandably go higher with progressively delinquent shipments.

The delivery factor is supplemented by an expediting factor shown in the lower half of Table 5–2. The weighting used here is also a standard cost, computed from the history of telephone and telegraph expense incurred to expedite shipments. A contact is defined as a prepaid telephone or telegraph toll. Although vendors are expected to voluntarily provide shipping information, one expediting contact per purchase order is usually considered routine.

The Service Rating. Vendor performance of the various business functions normally associated with his product is given a service rating, and the weights used are based for the most part on judgment (see Table 5–3). Vendors are expected to promptly handle requests for quotations and rejected material, as well as to acknowledge purchase orders by return mail. Cooperation and assistance given by the vendor in resolving purchas-

TABLE 5–3

Service Rating

Formula
  Service factor to be added to or subtracted from quality rating

Promptness in Replying to RFQ
On time	0.00
Late	+0.005

Promptness in Handling Rejection
Within 1 week	0.00
More than 1 week	+0.005

Promptness in Acknowledging Order
Within 1 week	0.00
More than 1 week	+0.005

Cooperation
Solve engineering, QC, manufacturing problems	−0.005

Vendor Trip Required	+0.01

Supplied All Special Documents with Order
Yes	0.00
No	+0.005

Financial Status*
Satisfactory	0.00
Needs special attention	+0.01

Facility Survey
Adequate	0.00
Outstanding	−0.005

Salesman Calls
Regularly	0.00
Infrequently	+0.005
Helpful	−0.005

Vendor Has Participated in Seminar, Value Engineering Workshop, or Engineering Conference in Past 6 Months
Yes	−0.01
No	0.00

*Need not be reported if last report is less than 2 months old.
  RQF—request for quotation
  Q.C.— quality control

ing problems are greatly appreciated by most buyers and, under this system, earn an extra credit. On the other hand, if the buyer must travel to the vendor for any reason other than a goodwill or routine visitation, a demerit (+) weight is given. Frequently, special documents, certifications, or catalogs are required with shipment, and these are identified in the purchase order. If a vendor fails to supply them with the shipment, and as a result the work of processing it through the inspection and receiving routine is delayed, the vendor is also given a demerit (+) weight. The importance of a vendor's sound financial condition is also recognized in this system, and if a buyer is obliged to give special attention to the vendor's financial status he receives a demerit (+) weight.

The company used in this illustration conducts a survey of vendor facilities before awarding contracts to new and untried vendors. This is done to verify the firm's ability to maintain a consistent level of product quality and production volume. A vendor with above-average facilities justifies greater confidence in his ability to perform as agreed than one whose plant and equipment are considered to be just average for the industry. Consequently, vendors in the above-average category are given a higher service rating than those in the average.

TABLE 5-4

Vendor Rating

Commodity Code	Vendor Code	Quality Control Rating	Delivery Rating	Service Rating	Composite Rating
HA	0971	1.025	+.05	+0.005	1.08
HA	1121	1.15	−.01	.00	1.14
HA	1340	1.075	+.12	.00	1.195
HA	1590	1.43	.00	− .02	1.41
HA	2697	1.03	.00	+ .01	1.04

Example					
	Vendor Code	Price Quoted	Vendor Rating	Cost to Stock	
	0971	$30.00	1.08	$32.40	
	1590	24.00	1.41	33.84	
	2697	28.00	1.04	29.12	
	1121	26.00	1.14	29.64	

This company also expects vendors to maintain good communications with the company's purchasing agents. Salesmen who familiarize themselves with the company's problems and provide assistance in solving them are of real value, and this is reflected in the weighting factor. Vendor participation in educational activities is also a factor in the rating system, because both vendor and customer usually share their benefits.

The Composite Rating. In Table 5-4, the quality, delivery, and service ratings are combined for five vendors of the same commodity. The top half of the table gives the results of quality, delivery, service, and composite ratings. Use of the composite rating in factoring the prices of four vendors who bid competitively is illustrated in the bottom half of the table.

The decision on which vendor to select becomes less difficult when it can be demonstrated that vendor 1590, whose price is lowest, is not the vendor with the most economical offer. A purchasing agent could readily justify a decision to buy from vendor 2697. However, if delivery is an important factor in the contemplated purchase, he would be justified in paying a few cents more to buy from vendor 1121, who has the best delivery rating.

Most of the data used in such systems are programmed into a computer. The only manual collection of information is ordinarily represented by a checklist that buyers execute for each purchase to supply ratings for service and expediting. This data is also added to the captive data of the computer, and cost elements and weighting factors are periodically reevaluated.

Vendor Analysis and Marketing

The importance to the industrial marketer of knowing how he is or may be rated by the purchasing departments of his customers can scarcely be overstated. In many companies, the purchasing department controls more funds than all other departments combined, and represents the seller's chief contact with using departments. While the precise nature of vendor rating systems used by purchasing departments vary substantially from one company to another, all are aimed at enabling the purchasing agent to reap the greatest possible benefits for his company per dollar expended. The successful marketer must therefore formulate his plans with full recognition of the type of analysis his performance will be subjected to and the standards it must satisfy. If an awareness of customer needs is the point where market planning begins, the criteria by which customers appraise marketing performance suggest the goals toward which marketing plans should be directed.

SUMMARY

In this chapter, we have examined two types of analysis used by buyers to appraise a supplier's effectiveness: value analysis, which applies to products, and vendor analysis, which deals with the character and capacity of the supplier and the operating relationships between him and the buyer.

Value analysis involves the review of product specifications in relation to requirements, the identification of unnecessary cost elements, and suggestions for their elimination. This is a cooperative activity requiring participation by several groups of specialists, such as engineering, manufacturing, and accounting, usually under the leadership and coordination of purchasing.

Vendor analysis is usually a purchasing department activity, with incidental contributions from other areas. It seeks to appraise the capability and actual or probable performance of the vendor in the areas of technology, production, financial strength, and management. Several mathematical systems have been developed for rating vendors; all rely on four main variables—price, product quality, delivery, and services surrounding the buying transaction. We have described one of these systems in some detail.

This chapter brings to a close our study of the industrial buyer. We are now ready to tackle some of the problems in trying to market goods and services to him.

CASES APPLICABLE TO PART II

Planning for Industrial Marketing

THE PROCESS of planning is probably more important in industrial than in consumer goods marketing. The large units in which industrial goods are usually sold, their technical character, and the multiple buying influence that so often affects their sale require the very close cooperation of a number of persons from different functional areas of the marketing firm to accomplish the average sale. This teamwork can be achieved most effectively by planning. The general framework and procedure for planning the marketing of industrial goods are outlined in Chapter 6.

The raw material the planner deals with is information. Chapter 7 presents a discussion of the most useful types of such information and the sources they come from, with special emphasis on marketing research.

Product management is not strictly a planning activity nor does it fall entirely within the marketing province. But it is so fundamental to the marketing process and marketing considerations usually play such a dominant role in it that it seems desirable to treat it here. The provision of salable products may be considered one of the steps toward planning successful marketing operations. We try to convey some understanding of this in Chapter 8.

Chapter **6**

◇◇◇◇◇◇◇◇◇◇◇◇◇◇◇◇◇◇ THE ROLE OF PLANNING

IN INDUSTRIAL MARKETING

THE MARKETING activities carried on by a manufacturer of industrial goods are an integral part of the company's total operating system. In a well-managed firm, they must be carefully meshed with production, finance, research, and other functions of the business to make the maximum possible contribution to the companywide objectives.

Marketing management, stripped to its essentials, is much the same as the management of other business functions. It consists of (1) making plans, (2) carrying them out, and (3) controlling them by measuring what is done against suitable standards and then rectifying failures. The essence of planning is an organized thought process before taking action. This chapter will discuss its role in the management of industrial marketing.

Although the essential elements of marketing management are the same as those for other business functions, the process of planning for it is more complex than in other functional areas because in much of his work the marketing manager must deal with customers, prospects, distributors, and competitors, operating within a constantly changing technological, social, and political environment. He is concerned primarily with people and ideas, and only to a minor degree with physical things. His relationship with people outside the company is basically of a persuasive character, with little, if any, possibility of direct control through authoritative sanctions. Furthermore, there is inevitably some degree of conflict of interest in business relationships with distributors and customers, as well as with other groups in the market complex.

This indicates that in planning the marketing manager must cope with a dynamic and volatile environment of great uncertainty and difficulty that makes it hard or impossible to forecast the results of particular marketing efforts. All of this represents a real challge to competent management. Success depends not only on skillful and aggressive adjustment to shifting market forces, but also on bold innovation that can itself change the market environment. Because of the lead time that must elapse

107

between concept and fruition in most product and marketing programs, the industrial marketing manager in his analytical and decision-making processes must learn to live in the future, despite all its frightening uncertainties.

The three most important areas of general marketing decision are: (1) What should be the product mix and the effort put behind each product line? (2) What markets should be cultivated and with what intensity? (3) What mixture of the tools of marketing should be used and in what proportions in order to bring products and markets together to yield desired objectives? Actually, decisions in the first two areas are necessarily merged, since products cannot be considered without relation to particular groups of customers or markets, and markets are meaningless except in the framework of their expected consumption of specific products. Thus, what is really involved is an extensive series of product-market combinations, which are either presently in existence or represent feasible objectives for the company. Overlaid on these product-market combinations are the selling methods that are in use or might be used.

From this complex of facts and relationships, decisions concerning the most desirable allocation of company resources must be reached. The first two of these areas are ultimately matters of top management decision, although the marketing manager and his staff must do much of the primary work of exploration, fact-finding, analysis, and recommendation. The third is apt to be largely or entirely within the marketing department's area of decision, with top management's role largely confined to criticism and approval.

The problems of managing industrial marketing vary with the different types of operations involved. In later chapters, we will analyze the product mix and the various components of the marketing mix. This chapter will be devoted to a general consideration of the role of planning in the total marketing management process.

Only within the past few years has the need for emphasis on marketing planning begun to be widely recognized. In part, this is a result of the increase in the number of firms that have adopted the market concept wholeheartedly and have become customer-oriented in all of their operations to a degree only rarely true 15 to 20 years ago.[1] Effective adjustment to present and future needs of customers requires careful consideration both of the direction and scheduling of many types of activities. Competition has become keener, the technological revolution has produced more and more products with a faster pace of change, vastly improved data processing systems are being widely adopted, new industries are developing, the technical content of products has increased and become more

---

[1] For a discussion of implementing the marketing concept see Arthur P. Felton, "Making the Marketing Concept Work," *Harvard Business Review*, July–August, 1959, pp. 55–65; and J. W. Keener, "Marketing's Job for the 1960's," *Journal of Marketing*, January, 1960, pp. 1–6.

complex, and new types of management decision aids have become available.

All these factors add up to more complex marketing operations, higher costs, and increased uncertainty. Greater emphasis on the planning function in terms of more detailed plans, better information on future trends, more complete integration with company objectives and total operations, and forms of organizing that will assure planning a continuously high urgency rating offer industrial marketing management important tools to cope with its increased responsibilities.

BASIC CONSIDERATIONS

Perhaps our study of planning for industrial marketing may be more realistic if we first emphasize a few platitudes so commonly accepted that people tend to forget them. Plans deal entirely with the future. The future may be good or bad, pleasant or painful, but it is always and forever uncertain and, therefore, fraught with risk. Planning is an attempt to reduce its uncertainties and protect against its risks. Therefore, the essence of planning lies in an attempt to foresee the areas of uncertainty, to appraise the chances or probability of the occurrence of various possible events within those areas, and to plot a course of action that will take advantage of the beneficial aspects of those most likely to occur and avoid or minimize their damaging features. It is also designed to cause certain things to happen that will be beneficial to the company.

Marketing planning for industrial goods is much more difficult and, at best, is much less exact than that for most consumer goods. The demand for consumer goods depends on people in the mass, their income, and their willingness to spend it. Population changes tend to occur slowly, and since they arise in part as a result of shifts in the birth rate many of them can be foreseen before their influence becomes effective in the marketplace. Income shifts also tend to occur gradually and to conform to trends that are often discernable. Willingness to buy is a more volatile element, but even here consumer purchasing behavior for most products tends to change slowly over relatively long periods.

Since the demand for industrial goods is derived from that for consumer goods, it is subject to all the uncertainties that beset consumer purchasing performance. In addition, it suffers from factors of risk that do not affect the market for consumers' goods, or influence it only mildly. The total demand for a material, component, supply, or piece of equipment may be changed profoundly and abruptly by changes in technology.

For example, an improvement in the technique of making castings may increase the demand for castings and reduce that for machined parts and the equipment that machines them; technical developments in making and using plastics may take business away from metals; electronic transistors largely destroyed the market for tubes; the development of synthetic fibers invades the market for textiles; if Du Pont's synthetic leather proves itself in use, the tanner's market will suffer.

This uncertainty of total demand is augmented for the individual firm by the fact that most of the volume of an industrial product is usually bought by a small number of large users. A shift of patronage by any one of them is apt to subtract heavily from the sales volume of one supplier and add greatly to the total sales of another. Thousands or millions of ultimate consumers shift their collective patronage slowly. By a single act, any one of a dozen or half-dozen industrial goods buyers can significantly change the patronage balance in the typical trade.

THE END RESULTS OF MARKETING PLANNING

Logically, it might seem that we should discuss the end products of marketing planning at the close of this chapter after we have examined the process itself. We have chosen to treat the subject briefly here on the theory that we can better understand the process if we first gain a reasonably clear notion of what it is intended to accomplish. We can aim better if we know what we are shooting at.

In discussing the operating end results of marketing planning, we will move from the very general to the highly specific in much the same way the process itself must progress—objectives, policies, procedures, programs, schedules.

Marketing Objectives

An objective is an end or goal that is sought. The marketing objectives of a firm must grow out of its general overall objectives. In theory, a business concern has but one objective—to make as much profit as possible, to maximize profit, as the theorists state it. Really, it is probably rare that this is the sole objective of a firm, or even its primary goal. This is not to deny that profit is almost always a prime objective, but it does raise the question of how much profit the average management sets as its goal.

Theoretically and legally, top management should set goals that are for the best interest of the firm. Practically, it is inevitable that personal or group interest gets mixed into management thinking about company objectives. This is especially true with respect to profits. Management almost always has a profit goal, but how near this target approaches the maximum that can be made depends on the need management has for profits.

This varies with different companies, but certain elements are almost always present. Top management almost invariably keeps control of the company through the votes of the stockholders, and it needs profit sufficient to be able to pay dividends big enough to keep them reasonably happy and quiescent. It needs enough profits to build up a surplus as a reserve against bad periods, so that the firm can pay dividends consistently in lean years as well as fat. It needs enough profits to finance new ventures and planned growth, either out of retained earnings or by borrowing on terms made favorable by an earnings record attractive to lenders. Whatever the profit goal may be, it vitally affects the planning of marketing activities.

Almost every management has as one of its most important goals the survival of the firm. This objective may be diametrically opposed to that of maximizing profit. Over considerable periods such objectives as expanding the firm's share of the market, entering a new market and establishing a position in it, developing or maintaining a full product line, or creating a company image may command the central place in management thinking. Keeping on the legal side of the various governmental regulations is always a highly influential objective and one that often demands a limited profit goal.

In planning the activities of his area, the marketing manager must understand the overall goals of his company and the emphasis top management attaches to each one. Then, for his own department he must translate this understanding into a set of objectives that conform to the broader goals and are designed to aid in achieving them.

How ambitious should objectives be? Within the limitations of the company goals, the industrial marketing manager may have considerable leeway in picking his targets. The maxim, "Hitch your wagon to a star," is not always a sound guide in making this choice. A target that is manifestly impossible challenges only the rare person; it discourages others and tends to become meaningless.

On the other hand, a goal that is too low supplies no incentive, offers no challenge, and is likely to lead to complacency and a false sense of security. Probably the desirable compromise is to shoot for a target that can be achieved but that will strain the muscles and test the will of the organization in its attainment. This is a nice problem in managerial judgment.

Policies

A marketing policy is a course of action established to obtain consistency of marketing decisions and operations in recurring or essentially similar circumstances. It is a guide to specific decisions within an area. Examples are: to emphasize quality as our primary appeal, to rely on manufacturer's agents as our sole outlets, to market through only one outlet in each marketing area, to be competitive in price but not a price leader.

Marketing policies, like marketing objectives, should be consistent with and implement companywide policies. The marketing manager plays a dual role with respect to them. He must see to it that marketing plans conform to long-standing policies. It is also part of his job to examine these continuing policies from time to time to make sure that the situations that gave rise to them have not changed so as to render them obsolete; if they are, he must move to revise them. An outworn policy deadens executive ingenuity and fetters management in attempting to meet new obstacles and exploit new opportunities. In addition, he is expected to develop policies to cover new recurring situations in which they can be useful. Policies thus play a dual role in the process of marketing planning; they both guide it and are an end result of it.

A companywide policy is usually stated in very general terms; otherwise, it may tie the hands of operating executives in handling unusual situations. This means that as it moves down the managerial hierarchy, it must be interpreted in terms of the operating conditions and problems of each level. In the process, it tends to become more specific and, all too often, twisted from its original meaning and purpose. This throws on the marketing manager a dual responsibility (1) to see to it that company policies are accurately reflected in the policies of the marketing area and (2) to make sure that as departmental policies are transmitted down the line they are properly interpreted and understood. This duty is especially important in the industrial goods field because success is so dependent on close cooperation among the several units in the marketing area, and between the marketing department and other functional areas of the business.

Procedures

A procedure is an item-by-item description of who is to do what, and often of when and how he is to do it, in carrying out a recurring process. A routine for handling orders is an example. Another at a somewhat higher level is a listing of the things that are to be done, the decisions that are to be made, and who is to do what in the course of deleting products from the line. A procedure, like a policy, is a continuing pattern that may last through many marketing plans—for example, the routine by which budgetary marketing plans are drawn. Unlike a policy, a procedure is strictly a nuts-and-bolts affair.

Adequate procedures are necessary if recurring operations are to be carried on effectively. They are vital in attaining a long-term objective, implementing a continuing policy, or carrying on a recurrent operation that involves the concerted action of a number of persons or divisions of the business, especially when the action required of each is not a primary part of his job. A procedure is often not thought of as a plan; but if it is not made a part of the planning machinery, even the work of planning is not likely to get done, for it fits the above description pretty snugly.

Programs and Schedules

These are the planning process results the operating people live with most intimately. Only rarely is long-range planning carried to the point where its results are expressed in the detailed lists of things to be done that constitutes a program or, if the element of timing is added, a schedule. Most short-range and project plans are cast in the form of such programs or schedules. The most familiar of these is the budget or, rather, the background documents from which the budget is drawn. The budget is simply an expression of the dollar costs of the things we propose to do in carrying out our plan and of the dollar results we expect to obtain by carrying it out.

If a marketing plan is to be really effective, the programs and schedules expressing it must be very detailed. For example, the work of each salesman may be planned to the point of indicating the number of calls he is expected to make on each customer or prospective customer, and perhaps a rough approximation of the time he expects to spend on each product or group of products. The advertising plan may detail the space or time to be used in each publication or station or network, together with a listing of the implementing activities involved in getting the space or time and filling it. This may be broken down by products or groups of products or by groups of customers. The marketing plan for a large company may constitute a sizable volume or series of volumes. It may represent weeks or months of work on the part of the marketing staff.

This is a process that can be easily overdone. It can and sometimes is carried to such detail that the time and money spent on it exceed any possible value that can be gained from it. One industrial marketing manager was heard to remark in the midst of his budget planning season, "I have to spend so much time planning around this place that I can't get any work done." He is not alone in that feeling, and perhaps the opinion is justified.

The general theory that should govern this matter is simple and easy to state. The work of planning should be extended to, but not beyond, the point where an additional dollar spent in planning will add something more than a dollar to the income from performance or subtract something more than a dollar from its cost. This principle is easier to state than to apply in specific cases. But the mere process of thinking in these marginal terms is apt to cause the manager to discard habitual planning activities that are of doubtful effectiveness and may even lead him to introduce new planning features whose value has not been previously appreciated.

SPECIFIC PURPOSES OF MARKETING PLANNING

Our broad statement at the beginning of this chapter, outlining the purposes of marketing planning, covers the waterfront but leaves much to be desired in the way of specifics. Our understanding of the process may be enhanced by an examination of the detailed uses that various parts of the business may make of a well-constructed marketing plan.

Coordination of Effort

One way to run a business might be everybody's pitching in and doing the best he can in his particular job without too much regard for what anybody else is doing. In fact, when our whole economy and the various business units in it were smaller and simpler, that was approximately the accepted theory of management. If the marketing department sold all it could, and production turned out the largest volume it could at the lowest cost it could achieve, and finance conserved every penny as carefully as possible, success was assumed to be the outcome.

The vast increase in the scale and scope of business operations, the extensive development of complex and specialized technology, and the constant growth in the dynamic character of business enterprise made this theory no longer workable. It is vital to the success of the modern firm that the activities of the various functional divisions be coordinated. This can be accomplished best by planning. Through the relation of the marketing plan to the overall plan for the firm, top management can to some extent coordinate marketing activities with those of other functional divisions.

But the principle goes farther than this. The marketing manager himself finds that he must direct the activities of a variety of specialists, some of whose functions are highly technical and whose special interests are often in conflict. He, too, needs a plan to give some assurance that all units of his department work together for the benefit of the whole. This is especially necessary in the industrial goods business, because in this field technology is most important and change is more than ordinarily rapid.

Help to Production Planning

It once was the job of the marketing department to sell what the production department could make. With the shift from a sellers' to a buyers' market, it has become more nearly the job of production to make what marketing can sell. But in businesses that manufacture to stock, production can do this properly only if it knows what marketing will sell long before the sales are made. Even when goods are made to order, production must be able to plan its needs for materials, facilities, and manpower ahead of the time when orders are received.

So it is that before production can plan what to make and when to make it, marketing must plan what it will sell and when the goods will be needed for delivery to customers. One of the chief purposes of marketing planning is to provide a guide to production planning.

In general, the consumer goods marketer can do this better than his industrial goods alter ego because he can forecast his sales more accurately. The average consumer good is ultimately bought by hundreds of thousands or millions of people, whose buying habits change slowly and no one of whose purchases looms large in the total. On the other hand, most industrial goods are bought by only a few customers, and usually the bulk of the volume of any one article is taken by a couple of dozen firms at most. They can change their patronage very quickly, and a shift by any one of them drastically upsets any forecast made by the supplier in reliance on its business.

Planning Equipment and Facilities

When a manufacturer considers buying a piece of equipment, he must be assured of a need for the productive capacity it will provide during the period of its amortization. Otherwise, its purchase price can not be recaptured out of its earnings. Therefore, he must ask: Can marketing sell what this machine can make during its operating life? If equipment and facilities are to be bought intelligently, marketing must plan far enough ahead to indicate whether they will be needed to make the products required to service sales profitably.

Aid in Planning Finances

The financial executive is charged with the job of providing the working capital invested in inventories and accounts receivable, and the fixed capital sunk in equipment and facilities. If the marketing manager can plan his activities far enough ahead to indicate with accuracy that X years from now sales volume will require certain specific additions to equipment, the financial manager can start making arrangements to have the money ready to buy the added machines. When capital, especially of the long-run type, must be raised on a crash basis, it is usually pretty expensive, and the extra expense lasts over a long period.

If the marketing manager can plan his annual sales by months, the financial executive can foresee how much capital will be needed in inventory to service each month's sales and how much will be tied up each month in outstandings. He can also forecast monthly needs for materials and wages. He is able to construct a chart showing when and in what quantity funds will flow out of cash, and when and how much money from sales will flow in to replace it. This enables him to foresee the need for bank loans and to provide for them ahead of time.

Promoting Sounder Decisions

When action occurs without plan or according to plans that are very general or sketchy, emergencies are frequent and often crucial. The process of management then becomes one of handling a series of crises by decisions made under pressure. Part of the process of planning is an attempt to foresee difficulties or situations that may require decision and, in an atmosphere of calmness and relative freedom from stress, to determine what to do about them when or if they arise. Such decisions are apt to be sounder than those made against time and under the whip of immediate necessity.

Facilitating Delegation

If a plan is carefully drawn and implemented on paper, the process of carrying it out can be delegated. Even the authority to deal with emergencies may be largely passed on to subordinates, because under a well-conceived plan most of the emergencies that occur are likely to be minor ones. Most of the major emergency situations should have been foreseen and provided against in the plan.

In fact, when operating plans are drawn well ahead of the time for action, much of the planning work itself and the decisions that go with it can be delegated to subordinates near the point where the action may be expected to take place, subject, at most, to higher executive review and approval. This is especially important in marketing, because such delegation tends to build, throughout all levels of the organization, the enthusiasm and personal commitment so vital to effectiveness in an activity whose success depends largely on intangible factors and human relationships.

Facilitating Control

A well-drawn plan may provide a standard against which to measure performance. "Are we doing what we planned to do?" If the program is well implemented and accepted by personnel in the lower operating levels of the organization, it is apt to stimulate those on the firing line to check their own performance against what they set out to do and to seek to remedy failures before they become serious enough to draw the attention of the higher executives. This is the essence of good control, and, it is especially important in marketing because failures at lower levels are apt to spread to other areas faster and with more devastating impact than those in almost any other functional area.

Marketing planning may serve other purposes that vary with different firms and situations. We have limited our discussion to those that seem to be fairly common to all companies and circumstances.

KINDS OF MARKETING PLANS

It is useful to distinguish three kinds of marketing plans:

Long-range plans, which cover more than 1 year, sometimes as many as 5 or 10 or even 20 years.

Short-range plans, which cover a year or some fraction of a year and which generally assume final summary form as the marketing part of a budget.

Project plans, which may cover less than a year or extend over a number of years. Examples are a plan for introducing a new product, breaking into a new market, or acquiring a larger share of an old market.

It must be understood that the marketing plan should be and usually is the marketing part of an overall company operating plan.

Long-Range Marketing Plans

During recent years, there has been an increasing tendency to emphasize long-range planning. In the industrial goods field, this kind of planning involves an attempt to project into the future existing trends in the market for the consumer end products the industrial product is used to make, to forecast technological developments in both the end product industry and the industry that supplies it, to foresee shifts in competitive relationships and customer alignments in both industries, to determine the position the planning firm wants to occupy in the total market thus envisioned, and to construct a rough program of the steps to be taken to capture that position.

The resulting document is of great use to management in determining the direction and emphasis of research. For example, as an outcome of such a study, which indicated that due to the growing percentage of old people in the population geriatrics would become increasingly important during the late 1960's and the 1970's, a medicinal materials company shifted some of the emphasis of its research from the objective of keeping people alive to that of making the added years worthwhile. Longe-range planning also helps management in decisions concerning the purchase of equipment and the provision of facilities. Since these things influence the capital requirements of the firm, it also helps in planning financial needs.

The marketing manager probably gets less guidance from long-range plans than do his opposite numbers in research, production, and finance. They may help him somewhat in channel selection and management and, theoretically, in making short range plans, since if long-range planning is done on a five-year basis, for example, the five interim annual budgetary marketing plans put end-to-end should be designed to achieve the objective of the long-term plan at its terminal date.

Regardless of the long-range plan's usefulness to the marketing manager, he is very definitely and actively involved in its preparation. His organization is on the firing line in the market, where the trends that shape the future are becoming apparent. He should have access to one of the two trade grapevines (the other is research) most sensitive to the direction in which technical developments in customer industries are moving. He and members of his staff are the persons in the company best qualified to estimate the value of new markets and the appeal of possible new products.

Short-Range Marketing Plans

The short-term marketing plan consists of a volume of sales and sometimes of other objectives the firm will try to achieve during the coming operating period as well as a schedule of the activities it will carry on in order to reach the objectives. Often this is set out in great detail. When sales are priced out and the activities are costed, the result becomes the marketing part of the company budget, a statement of planned cash inflow and outflow for marketing costs.

To be most useful, the marketing plan should be expressed at least initially in physical units—pounds or tons or machines to be sold on the one hand and man-hours of work, pages of space, and minutes or hours of air time to be used in selling and delivering them on the other. These can then be translated into dollars on the basis of forecasted prices and rates. If the process is short-cut by making the estimates initially in dollars, the planning process may be perfunctory and unrealistic and may lose much of its usefulness as a tool of management.

The short-term marketing plan may serve a number of managerial purposes if it is carefully done. If forecasts are properly made and alternative possibilities thoroughly considered, many matters can be decided in a relatively relaxed atmosphere that would otherwise assume the proportions of crises. The net effect may be to change the daily business life of the operating marketing executive from a succession of major and minor crises into a series of minor crises, but with resulting improvement in the soundness of major decisions.

It also facilitates delegation of authority and responsibility. Once the marketing plan is set up in some detail, the manager can delegate to his subordinates the job of carrying it out, and he must intervene only when significant departures from it become necessary or when it is not going properly.

This suggests a third major use of the short-run marketing plan as a tool of control. It constitutes a statement of things we propose to do and events we will try to make happen. This is a way of describing a standard of performance. By checking what is actually done and achieved against this standard, management may be alerted to the need for reconsideration, decision, and action.

Project Plans

Project plans are sometimes also called special purpose plans. They deal with special problems or objectives that may be very important for a time but are not likely to recur. Their period of importance may be a few months or a number of years. The activities and costs they generate and the results they promise are likely to be closed into and made a part of the overall plans and budgets of the firm or department. But management may find it desirable to keep the plans for them separate in preparation, execution, and control.

Consider the case of the firm that added a new product to its line of industrial materials. Potential sales of it were estimated to be about $10 million annually. But management foresaw a five- to seven-year period of market development, during the early part of which yearly sales would probably be only a few hundreds of thousands of dollars and costs half a million or more. The new product was assigned to a marketing manager, whose departmental sales of other products were about $20 million a year.

After two years, management became dissatisfied with progress. A study of the situation showed that the marketing manager was not spending enough money on the new product's development, because the cost of doing this work was closed into the general budget for his department and made its profit result look bad. His attitude changed when he was asked to prepare three marketing plans and budgets, one covering his operations without the new product, one for the new product, and one combining the two. In its review and control work, management dealt with each of these separately.

The moral of the incident is that special projects are not apt to receive the attention they deserve unless they are set apart in planning and control. Of course, only those projects of considerable significance in relation to the welfare or objectives of the company should be treated in this manner.

MARKETING FORECASTING

Since all plans are made for an uncertain future, a vital part of planning is the attempt to forecast with reasonable accuracy those future events that will make up the environment within which the plans must be carried out. The most important elements that must be forecasted in preparing the marketing plan are dollar sales and marketing costs. In order to estimate dollar sales, the planner must forecast physical units sold and price per unit during the planning period. To arrive at a cost figure, he must determine the things that must be done to carry out the plan and the cost of doing each one. He can usually estimate costs much more accurately than sales, since wage and service rates tend to be much less volatile than prices and customers' buying behavior. So the key figure in most forecasts is sales volume.

Long-range forecasting tends to be much less accurate than short-range. The farther the forecaster tries to peer into the future, the hazier its outline becomes. The long-range planner in the industrial goods field must try to foresee the behavior of consumer demand for the end products made from or by his goods during the next 5 or 10 years. He must also attempt to foresee the changes that will occur in the technology and competitive relationships in his industry and in customer industries as well as what the trend of general business conditions will be during the period. He must then try to appraise the effects of these changes on the need for his products and on his competitive position in his industry.

For example, during the late 1950's a fine chemical company, which make medicinal materials sold to proprietary and ethical drug houses for compounding and resale under their own brands, tried to forecast its business during the 1960's and 1970's. Its managers studied population trends and forecasts—noting that during these years the over-60 and under-7 age groups promised to constitute a larger than usual percentage of the total population—income trends, and trends in people's attitudes towards expenditures for health. They also examined the trend away from druggist compounded prescriptions toward the count-and-pour type, and the development of socialized medicine, medical service plans, such as Blue Cross and Blue Shield, and group medical plans. They took account of the tendency of proprietary houses to make their own ingredients and of fine chemical firms to get into the compounding business. They tried to foresee the areas in which technological breakthroughs were most likely to occur during the 20-year period. They looked into the political glass darkly to discern probable changes in governmental attitudes and actions with respect to public health. They examined trends in the operations and influence of retail and wholesale druggists in the business. On the basis of all the forecasts resulting from these studies, they constructed a picture of the environment within which they thought their company would have to operate during the period.

A firm that makes and markets a basic material such as steel and steel products must try to project trends in gross national product, particularly in heavy metal-using industries such as the automobile, construction, machinery, railroad, airplane, steamship, and communications businesses. The firm would also try to foresee in these customer industries technological developments that might affect their use of steel products. It cannot afford to neglect a careful study of the possibilities for development of additional uses for steel substitutes, such as aluminum, plastics, glass, and perhaps new materials now in the test-tube stage or merely an idea in a chemist's mind. It must also try to foresee in the steel industry itself technological breakthroughs that may adapt steel to new uses. Nor can a steel firm forget the inroads that usage during the 20-year period are likely to make on the reserves of iron ore. It must estimate the effects this depletion may have on the costs of steel and thus on the prices of steel products, on the competitive position of steel in relation to other materials, and on company volume and profits.

As you can readily see, the work of planning these explorations into the future, summarizing their findings, and drawing conclusions from them is essentially a function of top management and top management staff. It is equally apparent that much of the information sought lies in the marketing area, and that marketing personnel is likely to have the background needed to make intelligent estimates of many factors vital to long-range forecasting. Consequently, the work of assembling much of the material, analyzing it, and drawing initial conclusions from it is likely to fall on the marketing manager and his staff.

Making long-range forecasts is a relatively new activity for most firms. Comparatively few have been doing it in any systematic way for very long. On the other hand, many concerns have for many years made forecasts of sales and costs for periods of a year or less. As a result, the techniques of short-run forecasting are somewhat more highly developed than those used in long-range planning. All forecasting methods are based primarily on the technique of projection. It can hardly be otherwise. Inevitably, what will be grows largely out of what was and what is.

Whether we use the newest and keenest tools in the statistician's kit or rely on less systematic methods—even on judgment or hunch—we start our forecast by projecting the trends of the past and present into the future. This is done in two chief ways, by means of statistics and by the use of imagination and judgment. By one approach, we build from the general (an overall industry estimate) to the particular (an estimate for the firm and its divisions); by the other, we move from the particular (an estimate for each potential customer) to the more general (an estimate for the firm).

The Statistical Approach

In using the first approach, we seek one or more statistical series that seem to be indicative of sales for all industry or for our particular industry. The types of series most commonly used for industrial goods are:

Gross national product.
The Federal Reserve Index of Physical Production.
Personal income.
Inventories, wholesale, retail, manufacturers'.
Construction contracts awarded.
Car loadings.
Price indices.
Corporate profits.
Durable goods orders received.
Unfilled orders.

By statistical methods, chiefly the correlation method, we analyze the past behavior of one or more of these series, seeking to observe patterns of behavior that conform to and, if possible, lead in time the pattern of sales in our industry. By a further use of statistical tools, we project these predictive series into the future to establish an estimate of future sales for the industry. We then determine the probable share of the market for our firm on the basis of past performance and our proposed plans for the period. Finally, this can be broken down into estimates by products, geographical areas or other divisions of our company.

There is no need for us to detail the statistical techniques used in this work of analysis and projection. In books on statistics, they can be and are treated much more completely and competently than we can possibly do here. It is enough that we understand the conceptual basis underlying the task.

This essentially statistical approach has certain elements of strength and weakness. Its greatest strength probably lies in its almost complete freedom from the bias that inevitably colors all forecasting attempts that lean heavily on human judgment. By the same token, it is less subject to the reasonable doubt and criticism that is almost certain to attach to any forecast that is the result of opinion. The probable sales figure is like the traditional horse race in that there is always room for legitimate differences of opinion about both.

A statistical forecast is based on an observed and proven tendency of sales to vary along with, and perhaps somewhat after, some other statistical series or combination of series in the past. It may, in addition, be grounded on a distinctive pattern observed to be characteristic of the behavior of sales or of the related series in the past. Even the part of the forecast that depends on the effect of our planned marketing efforts can often be developed from a pattern derived by observing and measuring changes in the behavior of sales when efforts of similar kind and intensity have been applied in the past. In this process, the only matter of opinion that opens the door to the frailty of human bias is the assumption that because certain patterns of behavior and relationship have prevailed in the past they will continue in the future. The statistical method has about it an aura of science and certainty, which lends a feeling of confidence to those who use its results.

One of the great weaknesses of the method lies precisely in this basic assumption that the pattern of the past will project itself into the future. The assumption gains soundness if a causal relationship can be proved to lie at the basis of the pattern—that is, if it can be shown that changes in the predictive statistical series or combination of series cause changes in sales, or that the past pattern of sales was caused by factors that are reasonably sure to operate in the future. Too often, this can be done only or largely by eliminating all other factors that might have caused the pattern. This can readily become a tenuous and highly uncertain process.

In the industrial goods field, the process of proving the assumption is especially difficult and its results less reliable, because the chain of causation must run through so many levels from ultimate consumer end product demand, through the highly dynamic environment of technology and operating methodology, to the demand for materials, components, or equipment. When we seek to pin it down further in forecasting the sales

of a single firm, its validity is even more thinly diluted by the big-three or
-four or -five characteristic of the average customer industry. A change of
patronage by one big using firm, which may result from numerous
unpredictable factors, including many entirely within the buying firm
(shifts in intracompany political influence, changes in top management
personnel or policy, death, promotion, or retirement of a chief purchasing
officer or even of a buyer), may upset the most carefully calculated
statistical forecast for an individual supplying firm.

When an overall statistical forecast for a firm is broken down among its
customer groups or geographical divisions, it tends to lose its soundness,
since a market is not a monolithic solid but a fluid body with innumerable
eddies and currents characteristic of its several customer or geographical
parts. These often are not significant enough too have much effect on the
total figure, especially since they may offset one another, but they may
cause the breakdown to be entirely unrealistic in specific areas.

For this reason, salesmen often display little or no personal acceptance
of or commitment to territorial sales estimates arrived at by the statistical
method; they tend to dub them "home office whiz-kid stuff." This tendency is emphasized in the industrial field by the fact that the average
salesman's volume, like that of his firm, is heavily concentrated in the
hands of a few customers. This lack of personal commitment on the part
of the men in the field tends to subtract heavily from the usefulness of the
statistical forecast as a tool for planning and controlling field operations.

The Judgment Approach

The other approach to forecasting sales depends largely on human
judgment and imagination. It may be applied on at least two levels within
the organization—the executive personnel and the field force.

Jury of Executive Opinion. When this method is used, several executives, whose background or job assignments may be assumed to equip
them with some market familiarity, are asked to estimate what sales will
be during a coming period. This may be done in one of two ways. The
group may meet in conference and discuss the matter until an overall
figure or a figure for each product or customer group or geographical
area is agreed on. Or each member of the jury may be asked to submit his
own estimates, which are then averaged or otherwise combined to arrive
at a common figure or figures.

This is a relatively inexpensive and speedy method of forecasting.
Aside from executive time, it usually requires only assembling past sales
figures—sometimes past marketing cost figures—with a general summary
description of business conditions and apparent trends, and making this
background information available to the participating executives to guide
their deliberations.

On the other hand, it is no improvement on the statistical method in
achieving acceptance and personal commitment on the part of the field

force. The men in the field are apt to feel that they are at least as well qualified as their bosses to guess what the future will be in their respective territories. Who can deny that their feeling may be justified?

Furthermore, the method may possess either a considerable element of built-in bias or carelessness, according to the process used in carrying it out. If the executives meet in conference to make their estimates, the opinion of each man is almost certain to be subjected to considerable pressure of intracompany politics, with the effect that the estimates finally agreed on can hardly be said to be unbiased or systematic. On the other hand, if each member of the group sets down his own estimates and submits them to be averaged, he knows that he will not have to defend them before his fellows, but that they will be hidden behind the anonymity of an average. The probable result is that only the most conscientious among them will devote to the estimating process the careful analysis and study that its significance deserves.

This method also suffers a loss of accuracy when its results are broken down by products, customer groups, or geographical areas—perhaps to a lesser degree than does the statistical technique, but still to an extent that is significant. While the men in the office, as part of their jobs, try to keep informed about conditions in the field, they are inevitably insulated to some extent against the impact of purely local factors that affect the volume opportunities of individual salesmen. This is even true of the executives in the marketing area. They may be told about such factors by the men in the field but are often at a loss to know whether they are hearing reasons or merely excuses for failure.

The jury of executive opinion method of forecasting is apt to be a none too satisfactory compromise between the costs of getting a reasonably high degree of accuracy and the dangers of planning without it.

Grass Roots Method. What might be called the grass roots method of forecasting relies on the use of the salesman's intimate knowledge of the needs, attitudes, and intentions of his customers. It is the most expensive technique, but also often the most useful in the industrial goods field.

One firm implemented the method about as follows.

1. About the middle of August each salesman received from the home office a sheet that looked like this.

Customer	Sales			Budgeted Sales This Year	Planned Sales Next Year	Number of Calls Planned Next Year	Comment
	Year Before Last	Last Year	This Year to Date				
Customer Jones							
Product A							
B							
C							
Total							
Customer Smith							
Product A, etc.							

All the columns reporting past performances were filled in at the home office. Those involving plans were blank.

2. The salesman also received a summary statement of top management's expectations of general business and industry conditions, expected price changes, planned product line changes, and general advertising and promotion policies during the coming year. Copies of all these documents went to the field sales supervisor.

3. Between the middle of August and the middle of September each field supervisor spent about a day with each of his men, preparing a sales estimate and selling plan for the man's territory. In the course of this session, they discussed each customer and prospective customer and set down an estimate of sales of each product or product group to him. They also decided what field action, in the form of sales calls, etc., would be required to achieve this objective.

4. As these estimates were received at the central office, the marketing executives reviewed them. Those that did not seem to make sense were questioned, and the field men were called on to explain them. For example, a salesman who during the first 7 months of the current year had sold 600 pounds of a material to a customer whose annual take had never been more than 1,000 pounds estimated that during the coming year he would sell this same customer 600,000 pounds. When questioned, he reported that according to his information the customer was about to introduce a new end product which, if successful, would increase his total annual take of the material to about 1 million pounds. Of this amount, the salesman expected to get 600,000 pounds, since he had worked with the customer during certain stages of the development program.

5. After all adjustments were made, the individual estimates were priced out and summarized by products or product groups, customer groups, and in total. The summary was the forecast.

One big advantage of this method lies in the high degree of personal commitment it achieves among the men in the field. Since a man sets his own objective, he will leave no stone unturned to achieve it. The plan will work out if he can possibly make it do so. This is a matter of high significance. No amount or quality level of control, supervision or leadership can get out of the field force a performance that even approaches one resulting from the enthusiastic devotion of the men themselves to objectives they have had a hand in setting.

The grass roots procedure, if properly carried out, has an advantage in that, in the course of it, a detailed plan of work can be prepared for each field salesman, and this plan is directly related to the needs and problems of each customer. In fact, it and the sales objectives are the result of an analysis of the probable requirements of the customer, made primarily by the two people in the marketing firm who are closest to him and should know most about him—the salesman and his immediate supervisor. This is a plan that grows out of the conditions in the territory and should be realistic in relation to those conditions if it is nothing else.

On the other hand, the method is expensive. It uses up at least one selling day for each man on the force. In addition, it claims at least as many days of the supervisor's time as he has salesmen under him, not to mention the time he must spend in planning the individual sessions and reviewing their results. If the scheme is to work, one or more home office people fairly well up in the marketing executive hierarchy must review the objectives very carefully. All this adds up to a lot of company employee time and money.

This matter of cost is much less a drawback to the industrial goods marketer than to consumer goods manufacturers. A firm that markets direct to tens of thousands of retail stores through a sales force of a thousand men is apt to find its cost prohibitive. We have pointed out that the prospective buyers of many industrial products number only a few hundred or, at most, a thousand. The number of salesmen needed to serve them is likewise small, and the cost of the grass roots forecasting procedure is modest. This is less true or not true at all of some maintenance, repair, and operation supply items that are bought by many firms in many industries.

The firm that sells through distributors is not likely to find the method particularly useful. Its salesmen contact the distributors, and their knowledge of the users' operations and intentions is, at best, secondhand. The whole success of the procedure depends on that knowledge being intimate and detailed. This drawback is especially characteristic of the business in supplies.

If a firm markets through manufacturers' or sales agents who do not carry stocks, some modification of the method can be used. Since it ships direct to user-buyers on orders received through the agents, the marketing manager is in a position to know who these buyers are and how much each has taken. The agent's knowledge of his customers probably is reasonably complete. Considerable difficulty may be experienced in getting the cooperation of agents because of (a) the time element involved, for each agent may represent 10 or a dozen manufacturers, (b) the necessary disclosure of information they consider confidential, and (c) the fear that the results may be used against them when the time comes to negotiate renewal of the agency. It is not impossible for a firm that has built a record of cooperation and fair-dealing with its agents to overcome this reluctance.

By no stretch of the imagination can a grass roots forecast be said to be unbiased or free from the influence of personal interest or opinion. The smart salesman might even be expected to manipulate the process for his own benefit and at the expense of the accuracy of the forecast. For example, he might consistently underestimate expected sales, with the result that the forecast for his territory would be too low and he would look good to his management when his actual sales exceeded the forecast.

Experience with the method indicates that this defect is more apparent than real. The average salesman is an optimistic, self-confident soul who tends to plan more than he can do. Sales executives have found that individual estimates must be pruned just about as often as they must be padded to approach realism. Then, too, an observant field supervisor should know enough about each salesman's territory and the customers in it to be able to spot serious over- or underestimates and ask embarrassing questions about them. The home office reviewers also are able to question individual customer estimates that are too far out of line with past performance trends. Most of those who have used the grass roots method have not found underestimating a serious drawback.

The grass roots method of forecasting is used very widely in the industrial goods field. The relatively small number of customers who comprise the market for many industrial goods products and the direct contact between producer and user that this characteristic makes possible and that the technical nature of many such articles demands tend to make this technique applicable in planning their marketing.

Some firms combine the statistical approach with either the executive jury or the grass roots method, checking the results of one against those of the other. If they agree, the executives can feel that they are planning on fairly sound grounds. If discrepancies appear, the planners then explore the specific areas in which differences occur and try to uncover reasons for them so that they can be reconciled into a reasonably realistic figure. Probably a little of this goes on in all forecasting work for industrial goods. Even though a firm is devoted to the statistical approach, its planners probably can not afford to neglect attempts to make special checks on the expected operations and buying intentions of very large customers. If the grass roots process is to produce realistic results, it must go on in the expected atmosphere of general business, industry, and customer trade conditions as forecasted by methods that are largely statistical.

Almost every sales forecast involves an effort to foresee two things: (a) what sales will be if we drift with the tide or continue to do what we have been doing, (b) how this figure will be modified by changes we propose to make in our production and marketing activities. During recent years it has become the fashion to call these activities the "marketing mix." Let's explore some of the problems involved in planning the marketing mix.

PLANNING THE MARKETING MIX

The components of the marketing mix are certain to vary from company to company according to each firm's objectives, competitive position, strengths and weaknesses, and personnel skills. The elements almost always present in the marketing mix of an industrial goods company are:

Advertising	Delivery service
Sales promotion	Special jobs or putups
Personal selling	Quality
Technical service	Price

The use of any one of these to gain sales volume costs money. The central problem in planning the marketing mix is to find the combination that will result in the maximum net cash inflow, that is, cash inflow minus cash outflow.

In principle, the answer to this problem is very simple. It involves the application of marginal analysis; that is, the use of each component should be pushed to the point where the return from an additional dollar spent on it exactly equals the return from an additional dollar spent on any one of the others. A top limit is placed by the maximum amount of money the firm can afford to spend or by the point at which an additional dollar spent on any one or all of the components will not bring in a cash flow of more than a dollar; usually, it is the former. While this principle is simple, any attempt to apply it is bound to be infinitely complex. This complexity arises not so much from the mathematical problems involved as from the difficulty of forecasting results of the use of the different components. If the results of applying each element in the mix could be accurately foreseen, a mathematical formula could be developed that would make the principle readily workable.

But it is very difficult to forecast the results of the future use of a tool unless its results can be measured once it has been used. This is now possible with only a few of the tools we have mentioned, such as direct mail advertising or promotional material designed to bring in orders or inquiries. With most of them, though, the measurement of results is at the present time largely a process of more or less intelligent guessing and the exercise of seat-of-the-pants judgment. In spite of the lack of adequate means to forecast the results of marketing action, or even to measure them, the marketing manager cannot avoid trying to do so. Unless he does, he cannot plan. During recent years, much study has been devoted to attempts to improve both measurement and forecasting in this area. We may expect that during the coming years, these efforts will be continued and probably intensified. Students and practitioners of marketing will be wise to keep themselves aware of the direction and progress of such efforts.

At this point, we might suggest what seems to be the most promising approach to the problem. Much of the work that has been done has been devoted to measuring what might be called the preliminary or intermediate rather than the end results of marketing effort.

For example, most attempts to measure the effectiveness of magazine and trade journal advertising have sought to discover whether a given advertisement was noticed, read, or remembered; the radio and TV rating services report the number of people who listened to or viewed a program. This is only the beginning of the story. In order to be an effective marketing tool, a piece of advertising copy must call attention to itself so that prospective customers or persons who influence buying will read it or listen to it; it must get its message across to the buying or influencing group; it must convince them; and it must motivate them to adopt a pattern of thought or action desired by the advertiser. A certain conviction or action is the end objective of the advertisement. But none of the usual tests of effectiveness even approach this point.

Part of the reason for this lies in the fact that the end objectives of many advertising pieces and campaigns are not clearly stated or even envisaged by those who prepare them, or if they are, the goal of each advertisement differs somewhat from every other, which makes it impossible to measure all of them with a single tool. The measurement of effectiveness of a marketing tool is a job that each marketing manager must do or have done for himself.

This suggests that the job of measuring the effectiveness of an advertisement—or, for that matter, the use of any other marketing tool—must begin when the use of that tool is planned. For example, if when we plan an advertising campaign we set down its objectives in the most specific terms we can command, in the form of numbers, if possible, we can then seek to develop some method of checking its results after publication.

Suppose a campaign has as one of its objectives attracting inquiries. We might ask ourselves: How many inquiries are we shooting for and how many dollars of business do we expect to get from them? We must have some such figures in mind when we decide whether the campaign will be worth its cost. It should not be too difficult to set up a system of records and analysis that will tell us how near we come to our goal.

Consider a less tangible objective, creating or changing a customer attitude or company image, for instance. When we decide to do this by an advertising campaign, we must believe that the attitude, once achieved, will be worth more dollars to our firm than we propose to spend for the advertising. Why not decide what we think the change really will be worth to us? Then, by attitude surveys we can check the degree to which we actually achieve the desired change and what return we really get on the money spent. It is true that all these dollar value appraisals would be made on very nebulous bases; but the fact is that we must make such an appraisal, usually subconsciously and on much more nebulous grounds, every time we make a decision about such advertising. The appraisal is apt to be more careful and accurate if we bring it out in the open and set it down on paper as part of our marketing plan. *Industrial Marketing*, May, 1966, reports such an operation. A firm that makes electrical fixtures checked the effect of an advertising program on customers' attitudes toward the company. The study showed the following percentages of favorable attitudes toward several patronage factors:

	Percent Favorable		
	1961	*1964*	*1965*
Product quality....................40		44	54
Product development................40		49	56
Product style.......................39		50	59

Once we build a background of experience in this area, we should find that it has predictive possibilities and that we can plan with more precision and confidence. Some such concept as this seems to offer possibilities for applying the marginal analysis to the problem of determining the marketing mix with results that will not be completely accurate but should be practically useful. But until we can measure, we cannot predict; until we can predict with some rough approach to accuracy, we cannot plan with confidence or soundness.

STEPS IN MARKETING PLANNING

For purposes of discussion, we may find it convenient to divide the planning process into several steps or stages. The divisions we use here are not necessarily standard or universal. Other writers and practitioners may prefer other breakdowns perhaps as good or better than the one we find most convenient. It should also be recognized that the chronological implication of the list of steps we shall use is largely false. In a typical planning operation, a number of them may be going on simultaneously and at least one of them—the collection of marketing information—must go on all the time if it is to be done properly.

Nor is the planning process itself so distinct from operation in either timing or nature as our treatment would imply. While carrying out the current plan, the marketing manager must be preparing others for the future and, at the same time, making such amendments to the current one as may be demanded by changing conditions and newly discovered information.

Collecting Information

Before you can do much intelligent planning about a thing you must know about it. This is true of even the simplest situation. The more complex the problem, the more complete your information about it must be if your plan to solve it is to be realistic and sound. The technical nature of most industrial goods and the derived character of their demand cause the problems of marketing them to be naturally complex. The increasingly dynamic character of our technology and the growing interdependence of the different parts of our economy are constantly increasing that complexity and thereby multiplying the information needs of the marketing manager of industrial goods.

When we think of information, we normally think only of facts. But the marketing manager must broaden his concept of the term to include opinions, attitudes, and even rumors; what people think or feel is true or even suspect or fear may be true often influences their buying behavior more than what actually is true. This is less the case in the field of industrial goods than in the consumer goods market, but the industrial marketer who ignores the emanations of the trade grapevine is courting trouble.

All planning must deal with the future, and the future grows out of the past and the present. Thus, it is helpful to the planner to know what was and is, but it is much more vital to him to have some idea, however incomplete, about what *will* be. Therefore, the most useful kind of information for the marketing planner is the on-going kind that indicates trends rather than the static kind that simply represents what the situation is at a particular time without indication of the direction in which it is moving or the speed of its motion. Trends are usually the most important form of marketing information.

Information About What? Of course, the marketing planner needs to know all he can learn about the market, its extent, its geography, its depth, the people and firms in it, trends within it, its purchasing power, and any other items of information about it that he can use in his conscious analysis of it or that will add breadth or depth to his understanding of it.

It is especially important for the industrial marketer to know every scrap of information he can get about his product, what it is used for, the techniques of its use, the difficulties its users encounter in their operations and the methods they have found to overcome those difficulties, its weaknesses and its points of strength. It is particularly important that he keep up to date with respect to changes in the technology of the using industry that may affect the applicability or performance of his product.

He needs to know as much as he can find out about the channels or outlets through which he can move his goods to market. Changes constantly occur in the marketing services rendered by individual outlets or types of outlets, and in the struggle for power and influence that incessantly goes on among them. In this area, he cannot be content with knowing general trends, but must extend his information service to cover the behavior and fortunes of individual outlets.

The industrial marketing planner, much more than his consumer goods counterpart, must know his customers. It is not enough for him to be informed about the firms that use or can use his products. Within each customer firm, he must ferret out the individuals who exercise buying power or influence, and must learn the selling appeals that are apt to motivate them. He is likely to find it worthwhile to study even the internal politics of important customer concerns to discover shifts in power and influence that are taking place or are likely to occur. An especially important area of customer information is that of new end products in the planning or development stage which may, in due course, cause a demand for new materials or equipment.

He needs somewhat the same kind of information about his competitors, particularly about the men who make or influence marketing and pricing decisions. In addition, he must find out all he can learn about their present products vis-à-vis those of his own firm to discover where his competitive product advantages and weaknesses lie. An especially difficult area within which to obtain competitor information is that of product planning and development, but it is necessary if we are to avoid being outgunned in product quality, uses, or appeal. A knowledge of a competitor's delivery and service performance and of his reputation for being helpful to customers and keeping his promises is very much worthwhile.

Of course, an elementary kind of information, which is usually much easier for the industrial marketer to get than for his consumer goods counterpart, is his own sales. For the many industrial goods houses that sell direct to users, getting this information is merely a matter of arithmetic analysis. It is simply a process of putting the raw data of the accounting records into usable form by classification according to customers, products, areas, etc., and discovering relationships between them. When agents are used, the same is true since shipments are generally made direct. When a firm markets through distributors, the process is much more complicated and difficult, and the resulting data are much less complete and reliable.

The marketing planner must at all times keep abreast of changes in general business conditions and of shifts in the business climate or weather within his own and customer industries. This is usually not too difficult, since many publications and commercial services make it their first order of business. The trick is to decide which items from among the welter of reported fact and opinion are significant and worthy of reliance.

Sources of Marketing Information. Some marketing information is to be found inside the firm or can be picked up in the course of the normal contacts of the people in the firm. Some must be obtained from outside the company.

Outside information comes from two sources. Much material about the average industry is published. Some must be gathered and analayzed by marketing research. Both these sources will be discussed in the chapter on marketing research, so we will not treat them further here.

Most marketing managers recognize that outside marketing research must be planned and organized. Not so many of them realize that the same is true of information gathering within the firm. Most managements maintain a unit to analyze sales; many organize the analysis of marketing costs; but very few set up and administer any organizational unit or system for mobilizing and analyzing the flow of marketing information that more or less automatically enters the average business concern at various points from president to office boy. Fewer still seek to stimulate and train the company personnel with public or trade contacts to observe and report the fragments of marketing information that naturally come before their eyes or into their ears.

Salesmen, repairmen, technical service men, research men, purchasing department people, public relations men, and executives at all levels are naturally exposed to fragments of information that, collected and fitted together, might present a fairly complete library of marketing information. An executive in one industrial goods company remarked, "Somewhere in this company there is somebody that knows anything we need to know about customers, competitors, products, and the market, but how can we find him when we want him?" His statement, like the fabled hoop snake, had a sting in its tail. The organization problem involved in mobilizing this widely scattered and fragmented internal information is monumental, and very few firms have found even a moderately satisfactory solution. In fact, only a few firms have tried to organize it. More might find it worthwhile to do so.

Setting Objectives

A second step in planning marketing is the setting of objectives or goals for the marketing activity. We have already pointed out that, in the main, the goals of a firm's marketing division should grow out of and be designed to contribute to the achievement of its overall objectives. It is usually not a good idea for the marketing planner to be content with setting general objectives for the entire marketing area. He should go further and see to it that these are broken down into goals for different parts or functions of the total marketing activity, such as geographical divisions, products or product groups, customers or customer groups, advertising, personal selling, and even individual salesmen.

Finding and Selecting Methods

Once the marketing manager knows what he wants to accomplish, he usually finds that there are several ways of trying to do it. Usually, not all of these are obvious. Sometimes, the best ones must be sought in the imagination of the planner or in his creative analysis of the situation. Usually, each method consists of a certain combination of the tools of marketing, such as advertising, sales appeals, personal selling, the various sales promotion devices, pricing, delivery, credit, technical service, and the various other customer services all used in a certain pattern—a *marketing mix*. The number of marketing mixes available to achieve a given objective is limited only by the inventiveness and ingenuity of the planner in conceiving different proportions in which the marketing tools may be used or variations in the method of their use. The crux of his problem is to find and choose the best one or, at least, one that is better than any his competitors may hit on.

This is certain to be more or less a hit-and-miss operation that depends heavily on executive judgment and feel until methods can be developed to measure and so to forecast the effects of the use of the several marketing tools. So far, this has not been done satisfactorily. In the section dealing with forecasting, we have suggested a possible method of approach to the problem.

Implementing the Plan

Before a marketing plan can be considered complete, it must be implemented in the form of a program or list of very specific actions to be taken or things to be done and, usually, of when they are to be done. This process of implementation does not necessarily wait until selection of the marketing mix is completed. In fact, often it is hard to judge the extent to which a proposed method is feasible or practical until it has been implemented on paper in some detail.

A systematic method of doing this, known as "program evaluation review technique," or PERT, has been developed. It consists of four steps.

1. Visualize all individual tasks in a project as clearly and in as great detail as possible.
2. Draw up a visual network of the tasks to show sequences and paths that individual parts of the work must travel to completion.
3. Make three time estimates for each task:
  Optimistic.
  Most likely.
  Pessimistic.
4. Seek to locate critical paths and points that may prove to be bottlenecks because of tight or slack time elements.

All these activities add up to a lot of time and expense. But unless the planning process is overdone, it makes possible an increase in marketing effectiveness that is well worth its cost.

SUMMARY

In the course of our discussion, we have emphasized the need for marketing planning in the industrial goods field. We noted the end results of the marketing planning process in the form of marketing objectives, policies, procedures, and programs or schedules. We examined the chief purposes of industrial marketing planning: coordination of marketing effort, guidance to production planning and to providing equipment and facilities, aid in administering finances, adding to the soundness of decisions, facilitating delegation and control. The processes and uses of long-range, short-range and project plans were contrasted.

We examined the problem of forecasting, contrasting the use of the statistical and the judgmatical approaches. The problem of planning the marketing mix was outlined, and its dependence on adequate tools to measure the effectiveness of marketing activities was emphasized. Finally, we outlined the several steps in marketing planning: collecting information, setting objectives, finding and choosing methods to achieve them, and trying to precheck the feasibility and effectiveness of these methods.

Chapter 7

<diamond ornament> INDUSTRIAL

MARKETING RESEARCH

THE BASIC TASK of marketing management is that of preparing plans, executing them, and controlling operations to achieve the most profitable allocation of company resources to current and future market opportunities. Management may be aided in these efforts by marketing research, which the American Marketing Association has defined as "the systematic gathering, recording, and analyzing of data about problems relating to the marketing of goods and services."[1] Marketing research uses powerful investigative and analytical techniques, drawn largely from the behavioral and physical sciences, to narrow the areas of guesswork and enable executive judgment to produce better decisions.

The need for such assistance in decision making stems mainly from the constant changes characteristic of industrial markets. If they were static or changed very slowly, the matching of product lines and marketing methods to market opportunities would not pose difficult problems. Executives could learn from past experience and avoid repeating past errors.

But industrial markets, far from being static, are constantly seething with change. Increasing technological expenditures produce a continuous flow of new products, new processes, and new materials, which make obsolete existing products and methods. The semiconductor produced a new industry and permitted significant improvements in a vast range of products. New plastic materials are replacing traditional fibers, metals, and films. Mechanization and automation are revolutionizing industrial processes. From the large expenditures on national defense and space efforts are coming new and exotic products. Changes in living habits and tastes of the general public call for different types of consumer products and thus have an impact on the industrial market. For example, the shift to the suburbs with more single residences and outdoor living, the boating boom, and growing amounts of leisure time have called for different products and have had an impact on the suppliers of equipment and materials used in making them.

---

[1] "Marketing Definitions, A Glossary of Marketing Terms," compiled by the Committee on Definitions (Chicago: American Marketing Association, 1960).

As a result, the executives of an industrial goods company are frequently faced with marketing problems, unknown in their previous experience, that pose major uncertainties. Managers are well aware of these risks, and many of them have organized marketing research departments to gather and analyze information that enables them to reduce the reliance they must place on intuition or hunch.

THE USE OF INDUSTRIAL MARKETING RESEARCH AS A MANAGEMENT TOOL

Several studies have traced the development of industrial marketing research from the mid-1920's, when the first few formal marketing research departments were formed, to the present time. Perhaps the most authoritative source of information about organization, budgets, subject matter of research studies, and compensation of marketing research personnel is to be found in a series of surveys published by the American Marketing Association. The latest one, in November, 1963, provides this information for industrial product manufacturers, consumer manufacturers, retail and wholesale establishments, and other company members of the association.[2]

This survey shows that more than half of all respondent companies have formal marketing research departments, while another quarter of them report that one man is assigned to marketing research functions. Among the smaller companies (annual sales less than $5 million), 20 percent have formal departments. This proportion rises steadily as company size increases; 9 out of 10 of the largest firms have formal departments.

Data gathered on the year in which marketing research departments were organized indicates that there has been a steady, rapid growth in the use of marketing research. Table 7–1 shows this information for consumer

TABLE 7–1
Dates of Organizing Marketing Research Departments

	Consumer Products Manufacturers	Industrial Products Manufacturers
1958–62	37%	51%
1953–57	30	24
1948–52	15	14
1943–47	9	5
1938–42	4	4
Before 1938	5	2
No. answering this question	250	412

[2] Dik Warren Twedt (ed.), *A Survey of Marketing Research* (Chicago: American Marketing Association, 1963).

and industrial products manufacturers broken down by five-year intervals.

Among industrial products manufacturers, it is noteworthy that over half the respondents organized marketing research departments during the last 5-year period, and 75 percent indicated that their departments had been established for 10 years or less. Since the date of this survey, the function of marketing research has continued to expand; the major difficulty is the lack of qualified managerial personnel.

Research Activities Performed

Since marketing research is a type of intelligence service to aid management in problem solving and decision making in every aspect of marketing operations, it is proper to ask, first, how far such a broad mandate of assistance is actually found in the industrial market and, second, to what extent there may be differences in research activities between manufacturers of industrial goods and those of consumer goods.

Evidence bearing on the first question can be found in Table 7–2. In it, the first column shows the percentage of the reporting companies that carry on each of a number of different types of marketing research activities in four basic categories: advertising research, business economics and corporate research, product research, and sales and market research. The second column shows how many companies carry on these activities through a marketing research department, while the last two columns indicate how frequently other departments within the business or outside firms are used to undertake or assist in this work. Of the reporting firms, 9 out of 10 carry on studies of short- and long-range forecasting, studies of business trends, new product acceptance and potential, competitive product studies, development of market potentials, market share analysis, determination of market characteristics, sales analysis, and the establishment of quotas and territories.

The bulk of this work is handled by the marketing research department. In certain areas, other departments, such as advertising, commercial development, corporate planning, economics, or research and development, are assigned primary responsibility for research activities. Typically, a number of staff as well as operating units within larger companies combine their efforts in handling large-scale marketing research projects. It is, therefore, extremely important that good liaison be maintained among the participating units so that the particular skills and knowledge of each may be used effectively. Often, marketing research serves as the contracting agent in hiring outside research firms. As indicated in Table 7–2, advertising research and distribution channels and cost studies are among those most often contracted out to specialized research firms.

TABLE 7–2

Analysis of Marketing Research Activities Performed by Industrial Companies with Formal Marketing Research Departments

Research Activity	Percent Doing	Marketing Research Done by Department	Entirely or Partly Done by Another Department	Done or Aided by Outside Firm
Advertising Research:				
a) Motivation research..................	17	8	4	8
b) Copy research.......................	37	6	12	21
c) Media research......................	53	11	19	26
d) Studies of ad effectiveness............	57	16	18	26
e) Other.............................	13	8	2	4
Business Economics and Corporate Research:				
a) Short-range forecasting (up to 1 year).........................	92	72	24	1
b) Long-range forecasting (over 1 year)....	91	77	19	1
c) Studies of business trends.............	90	78	13	2
d) Profit and/or value analysis...........	83	32	55	1
e) Plant and warehouse, location studies....	76	40	41	2
f) Diversification studies................	84	62	32	2
g) Purchase of companies, sales of divisions............................	81	41	52	2
h) Export and international studies.......	72	41	35	2
i) Linear programming.................	41	10	32	—
j) Operations research..................	45	14	33	1
k) PERT studies.......................	35	6	29	—
l) Employee morale studies..............	48	5	39	5
m) Other.............................	7	7	1	1
Product Research:				
a) New product acceptance and potential...	92	83	17	3
b) Competitive product studies...........	92	78	19	3
c) Product testing.....................	81	31	54	2
d) Packaging research design or physical characteristics	59	16	43	6
e) Other.............................	5	4	1	—
Sales and Market Research:				
a) Development of market potentials......	94	92	6	1
b) Market share analysis.................	94	89	8	1
c) Determination of market characteristics.	92	89	6	2
d) Sales analyses	94	74	27	—
e) Establishment of sales quotas, territories.	90	57	42	—
f) Distribution channels and cost studies...	80	55	33	8
g) Test markets, store audits.............	36	21	14	6
h) Consumer panel operations............	21	10	6	7
i) Sales compensation studies............	73	32	41	3
j) Studies of premiums, coupons, sampling, deals...........................	20	9	10	2
k) Other.............................	6	6	—	—
Number of Companies Answering.....309				

SOURCE: Dik Warren Twedt (ed.), *A Survey of Marketing Research* (Chicago: American Marketing Association, 1963)

ORGANIZATION AND OPERATION OF
INDUSTRIAL MARKETING RESEARCH DEPARTMENTS

Since the marketing research department is primarily concerned with marketing operations, logic suggests that it should report to a top marketing executive. Industry practice tends to support this view, as shown in the survey referred to above. Among industrial products manufacturers, 67 percent of the marketing research directors report to a marketing executive with a title such as vice president of sales, marketing manager, director of sales, general sales manager, or sales manager. In the earlier survey, published in 1957, only 59 percent of the marketing research directors reported to an executive in sales or marketing management. In the 1957 survey, it was found to be much more common for the marketing research director to report to the president or executive vice president or to another official in corporate management, such as the assistant to the president or division vice president.

It may be argued that a research department should not be placed under a marketing executive, because he might be loath to authorize studies that threaten to reveal inefficiencies. However, the risk of such limitation of action appears to be less today than it was 15 or 20 years ago because of the trend toward placing an executive of broad experience and capacity at the top of all marketing operations. Such a man welcomes help in improving efficiency of operations. Some feel that a marketing research department should contribute to other functions of the business as well as marketing, and that it can do this effectively only if it reports to a president or executive vice president. There is some logic to this point of view, and departments with a broad scope of operations will sometimes have the words "business research," "commercial research," or "economic planning" in their titles.

Regardless of the exact title of the executive to whom the research director reports, what is important is that his chief should be genuinely interested in the benefits marketing research can bring, should know how to use research effectively, and should have sufficient stature within the organization to take the action indicated by the studies.

The compensation of the directors of marketing research in industrial companies increases gradually with the size of the firm. The American Marketing Survey showed that the median salary paid by companies with annual sales under $25 million was $12,000. The largest companies, with sales over $500 million paid a median salary of $20,000. The spread of salaries around the median figure for the smallest companies showed that about 25 percent of the companies paid over $14,800 and 25 percent paid under $8,800. Among the largest companies, the range was from $15,500 to $22,000.

The industrial marketing research department is usually small in terms of number of full-time employees. The smallest companies in the survey, if they had a research unit at all, had only one man assigned to it. Among the companies with sales over $5 million, the median number of employees was 10. One quarter of the larger firms had more than 22 employees, and one quarter had less than 6 employees.

An essential characteristic of the successful marketing research department is that it strictly preserves its staff function in helping various operating department executives to solve problems. The director of marketing research must be willing to let others take the credit and be skillful in planting seeds of thought that may later lead to requests for studies. An empire-builder temperament is unlikely to produce the most effective type of research operation. In fact, the marketing research department is such a good training ground that the director often has difficulty in holding personnel when openings appear in the management of a growing company.

A new department must earn the respect of company executives; it cannot expect to gain acceptance simply by issuance of memoranda from top management stating that a department has come into existence and should be used by the operating executives. It is wise to start a department on a small scale, with a director, a senior analyst, a secretary, and possibly a statistical clerk.

With such a modest start, some important objectives are accomplished. First, the investigations conducted by the department must be selected with the greatest care in terms of their real value to the company. This means that the first efforts of the department, because of their importance to management, will create a favorable impression and speed up the process of acceptance throughout the organization. Second, a small department will always have a backlog of important assignments, and there will be little danger that it will have to search for things to do and run the risk of creating antagonism among the operating departments. Third, the budget will be modest and less likely to draw pruning attention in periods of poor business. In some cases, overexpansion during the beginning period has led to abandonment of the department when sales and profits dropped. A veteran marketing research director commented:

With respect to the "dos" and "don'ts," I feel that the infant market research department should subdue the temptation to look important by acquiring an imposing staff and facilities. As essentially a staff department, it does well to remind itself that economy waves can fall heavily on it. Therefore, it seems prudent to keep the staff to a hard-working minimum.

An essential ingredient for successful operation of an industrial marketing research department is the proper attitude on the part of top management. Unless top management is truly sympathetic with the factual approach in solving business problems and is willing to create a favorable environment, the effort is likely to fail. The top manager who adds a marketing research department because it seems to be the fashionable thing to do, without any real understanding of his obligations and responsibilities in using such a staff group effectively, is likely to be disappointed and unable to hold competent staff in the department. One marketing research director comments:

A department's usefulness is also further limited by the cooperation which it receives from the other departments and divisions of the company. This, I think, necessitates a thorough selling job on marketing research to all officials and departments affected by the establishment of the new function. Duties of the department and the type of work that will be performed should be thoroughly explained.

The department manager should be a sales-minded person in order to induce the most effective utilization of his department's services. Some firms place at the head of a new department a company man who is thoroughly familiar with the firm and its method of operation and has earned the respect of his fellow executives. Such a man may not have the technical knowledge necessary for some types of marketing research work, but this can be supplied by the men he hires. Although there are clearly two sides to this question, some evidence suggests that the initial heading of the department by a company man can facilitate its growth and acceptance within the business more than a director from the outside. This approach has the important limitation, however, that an outsider may bring to the company's problems a breadth of view that cannot be duplicated by the inside man.

The director of marketing research should be represented on management committees that bear directly or indirectly on the work of his department. A chief function of marketing research is to supply information to aid management in reaching decisions, and if the director is in a position to know executive thinking he can more effectively guide the work of his department.

The department work should be carefully programmed, and management should aid in establishing priorities of studies to be undertaken. So far as possible, the first projects chosen should be those that promise significant cash savings or improvements in efficiency. The more dramatic these can be, the better for the acceptance of the department. In one company, a department became permanently established on the basis of a study of delivery costs, which pointed the way to large economies; in another, a careful study of inventories and orders made possible a reduction in inventory investment of over $1 million.

It is important that the marketing research department not be burdened by routine assignments that are repetitive in character. It may prove necessary for a department to undertake certain types of recurrent analyses not being prepared within the company. Once the value of such analyses has been proved as regular operating tools for management, the department should seek to shed the responsibility for preparing them. If it does not do so, flexibility is lost and the general level of personnel is downgraded.

In recent years, the trend toward decentralization of management in many companies has posed problems for effective organization of marketing research. In such circumstances, marketing research may be organized three major ways.

1. A centralized marketing research department with:
   a) Individuals or groups of individuals specializing on the problems of the various operating divisions.
   b) Branch departments physically located in the divisions but reporting to the central marketing research director.
2. Autonomous marketing research departments in each product or geographic division.
3. Separate divisional research departments reporting to divisional management but operating with the consulting assistance and general guidance of a headquarters marketing research staff.

The arguments in favor of a centralized department revolve around fuller use of personnel and research results, greater specialization of personnel, more emphasis on improving research techniques, greater stature within the company, and greater contribution to top management policy setting. Important disadvantages are that the work may be inefficient if marketing problems vary widely between divisions, and divisional executives do not view such staff as real family members of their operating teams. Also, divisional executives often feel that they cannot get the help they need at the time they need it and resent the necessity for competing with other divisions for research service.

At the other end of the spectrum, complete autonomy of divisional marketing research departments may be undesirable unless the marketing problems encountered are completely dissimilar in nature. The best arrangement seems to be divisional departments reporting to divisional management, but operating with informal guidance and consultation from a headquarters staff marketing research department. Such a central staff can assist on unusually difficult assignments, aid in recruiting and screening personnel, and can exercise a degree of persuasive quality control over research methods. This is a delicate kind of relationship, but it can be achieved, given the right people at the headquarters level and in charge of divisional departments.

Expenditures for Marketing Research

Industrial marketing research budgets expressed as a percentage of sales are shown in Table 7–3. Companies in the lower sales volume brackets spend relatively more for marketing research than the larger firms. In each volume bracket, however, there is a considerable spread in the size of

TABLE 7–3

Industrial Marketing Research Budgets as a Percentage of Sales

Annual Sales Volume (Millions)	*(1) Median Budget*	*(2) 25% of Companies Spent More than*	*(3) 25% of Companies Spent Less than*
Under $5........................	0.30%	1.00%	0.08%
$5–$25..........................	0.20	0.40	0.10
$25–50..........................	0.10	0.20	0.03
$50–$100........................	0.10	0.20	0.03
$100–$200.......................	0.08	0.13	0.03
$200–$500.......................	0.05	0.10	0.02
Over $500.......................	0.03	0.10	0.001

SOURCE: Dik Warren Twedt (ed.), *A Survey of Marketing Research* (Chicago: American Marketing Association, 1963).

expenditures, as indicated in columns 2 and 3 of the table. This is particularly noticeable in the category of companies with annual sales of over $500, where 25 percent of the respondents spent more than 0.1 percent of sales on marketing research, while another 25 percent spent less than 0.001 percent. Undoubtedly, among the second type staff groups other than marketing research undertook marketing studies. Nevertheless, the data suggest that the question, how much should be budgeted for marketing research, is not a simple one.

While reference to past company and industry ratios, such as those in Table 7–3, may provide a useful starting point in determining the size of the budget, many other factors, such as type of industry, type of product, width of product line, and geographical coverage are influential. Even more important are management's basic objectives in terms of diversification, growth, and profitability. It is true, of course, that short-term profits can be increased by reducing the cost of staff groups such as marketing research. It is also a fact that a research department, like any other organization, may become unwieldy and unproductive if it does not have well defined goals and if the benefits of its use are not regularly compared with its cost. It is evident, however, that in most companies a substantial and growing research program is needed to meet the basic objectives of the firm.

Marketing managers could probably do much to expand the use of marketing research and increase its effectiveness if they would try to weigh the estimated cost of each proposed research project against the estimated value of the benefits to be expected from it. The cost of a contemplated marketing research can usually be estimated with some accuracy. But estimating the value of the benefit we may expect to gain from it is bound to be a nebulous process, for the benefit is almost certain to be intangible—usually, an increase in the soundness of executive decisions.

However, this benefit is no more intangible than many other objectives for which business managers spend money, such as creating or strengthening a company image, building a reputation for quality or service, or developing an attitude among customers. In the final analysis, the issue to research or not to research boils down to the difference between the cost of researching and the cost of failing to research.

The cost of failing to research depends on at least two factors. One of these is the effect that the information the research is designed to disclose is expected to have on the soundness of decision. This can be measured by comparing the likelihood or chances of a wrong decision with and without the research information. For example, we may estimate that with the information we already have our chances of making a wrong decision are 40 out of 100, and that with the research information they will be 25 in 100. The amount of this difference depends primarily on the significance of the missing facts, the extent to which they bear on the heart of the problem or are merely peripheral, and on the density of our ignorance about them. If they are merely incidental or if existing facts afford a fairly sound basis on which we can guess what the missing ones must be, research will probably do little to improve the soundness of our decision.

A second factor consists of the dollars that ride on the decision. If a company's sales run into the hundreds of millions and the decision affects less than $100,000 of this volume, with a possible net profit of only $6,000, the cost of a wrong decision cannot be very great relatively, and we cannot afford to spend very much on research to avoid it, certainly not as much as $6,000.

These factors are intangible, but with a little ingenuity their value can be estimated. Such estimates may be wrong, just as any estimate may be wrong. But if management makes its marketing research decisions on the basis of honest estimates of the pertinent factors, less useless research will be done. By the same token, total marketing research activity is likely to be expanded because all parties will have greater confidence in it and a better understanding of its usefulness.

Use of Marketing Research Consultants

In small marketing research departments, it is probable that at times more urgent studies need to be done than the size of the staff will permit. Rather than expand the staff for such peak loads, frequent use of consulting organizations is made to carry out specific studies. There has been a substantial growth in specialized marketing research organizations over the past 20 years, and many companies make extensive use of them, especially in the consumer goods field and to a somewhat lesser degree in the industrial goods field. Such a consulting group brings wide experience in handling assignments for many types of clients, and this breadth of experience is often an important ingredient in the service they render.

There are fewer consulting organizations with wide experience in industrial marketing research than in the consumer research field. Thus, it is very important to choose wisely the consulting firm to carry out an industrial marketing research assignment. In many such studies either an engineering training or a very practical mechanic-type contact with the field is required for best results. It is, therefore, important to inquire into the background and experience of the staff of an organization, particularly of those members to be assigned to the study. Most important, however, is a careful check with firms that have made use of the consulting group under consideration. No reputable concern will hesitate to tell a prospective client the names of companies for which it has done work. An effort also should be made to learn the names of some clients who may have been dissatisfied with its work. Judgment must be applied, of course, in interpreting information from such sources, as sometimes there have been personality frictions that in no sense reflect on the basic competency of the research group.

In using an outside research organization, it is important to recognize that a substantial period of education is essential before a study can be intelligently formulated. Both the marketing research department and management must be patient during this educational process, and must be willing to cooperate fully with the consulting organization in disclosing pertinent information.

METHODS OF INVESTIGATION AND ANALYSIS

Let us now consider the investigation procedure used in solving marketing research problems, and examine the basic types of studies most commonly made.

Before undertaking a formal marketing research project we should first ask: Is this investigation really necessary? The information sought may be readily available in company files, in trade journals, or from government or industry sources. Often, it can be obtained for the cost of a telephone call. Even though the information thus gathered may be incomplete or not oriented precisely toward the question posed, it may be good enough so that expensive field surveys or other types of primary research can be avoided.

Investigation Procedure

When a formal research project is established, several well-recognized procedural steps must be taken to insure its success.

1. Definition of the problem and preliminary statement of objectives sought in investigation to solve the problem.

2. Exploratory investigation among informed sources to check the validity and completeness of the preliminary objectives and the fundamental significance of the problem itself.
3. Determination of the types of data needed, the methods to be used in gathering the data, and the types of analyses to be made. This planning step should also include means for securing adoption and implementation of the results of the study. At this point, a dummy report often can be prepared, showing the types of data that will result and the ways in which they will be presented. This dummy report serves to achieve a meeting of the minds between the marketing research group and the executives who will later use the results. It also serves as an important preselling step.
4. Collection of data:
   a) Design of sample (if sampling is involved).
   b) Gathering data from secondary sources, such as published material and internal records, and from primary field sources through personal interviews, telephone interviews, and mail questionnaires.
5. Analysis of data that have been collected.
6. Presentation of solution to problem in manner that will achieve the most effective implementation of the results.
7. Later follow-up to learn of the effectiveness of the study and of difficulties encountered in implementing the findings.

Preliminary Statement of Objectives

On-the-hoof marketing management problems do not come in the sharply defined, carefully stated, and exactly classified form in which one usually encounters them in the textbooks. Something seems wrong, and the manager must find out what it is, what causes it, and what to do about it. Or plans must be made, and the manager must decide what they shall be designed to achieve, what areas they shall cover, and all other details about them. Symptoms are obscure, often conflicting, and hard to appraise.

So the first job of the marketing research director is to get an accurate definition and statement of the problem. Such a statement is best if it can be compressed into a single one-sentence question or, failing that, into several one-sentence questions.

Such a statement of a marketing management problem usually points the way to a list of the items of information needed to solve it. Some of these are already known. Gathering those unknowns, together with their analysis in relation to the known data, determines the objectives of the research.

In the initial stages of a research project, it is wise to set down all these matters as simply and concisely as possible in writing so that everyone who has anything to do with it knows precisely what the research is designed to accomplish. This heads off much muddled thinking and wasted effort at later stages.

Exploratory Investigation

The purpose of this step is to gather key information from a range of informed sources so that the true dimensions of the problem become apparent. This very often results in a major revision of the preliminary statement of objectives and practically always in a more precise formulation of them. It may also be found that the problem has taken on a different shape and must be redefined. It may be helpful to follow successful research procedure in both the physical and social sciences by phrasing key hypotheses or statements of assumed relationships between two or more variables. These hypotheses are then either verified or disproved by the ensuing investigation.

In this exploratory phase, the emphasis is on obtaining data about each major aspect of the probem from a few carefully selected sources. First, the company files should be searched for pertinent past studies or reports. Spot checks and quickie analyses of sales records should be made. Company executives, division sales managers, salesmen, and friendly customers may be interviewed. A brief literature search will often reveal information of value. Trade paper editors, well-informed distributors, market research men in related but noncompetitive lines, government personnel, and others may be interviewed. Such interviews, though possessing some general structure of approach, should be distinctly open-end so that every aspect of the problem field can be touched on.

Detailed Planning of Investigation

The exploratory phase of the study results in a final statement of objectives, and frequently indicates the most fruitful methods by which the problem can be studied. With a precise statement of objectives, it is possible to plan in detail the types of information needed, the sources it is to be gathered from, and, in general, a comprehensive program of study. This plan will include not only a timetable but also an estimate of costs likely to be incurred. It will contain a description of the method of gathering each type of information. When information has to be sought in the field, as opposed to published literature or internal company records, a sample usually must be designed because it is rarely feasible or desirable to attempt a complete census of any industry market.

Design of Samples in Industrial Marketing Research

The design of samples for industrial market studies presents some important differences from the typical sample design for consumer marketing research. These differences tend to be of degree rather than kind.

Samples are necessary in marketing research because time and expense do not permit complete censuses of the groups being studied. With proper care, it has been found possible to estimate the characteristics of total groups by gathering information from a sample of them that is representative of the whole. In order to be able to measure the precision of results obtained from a sample, the sample must have been designed according to probability concepts, and the units in it must be interviewed without a significant amount of substitution. A probability sample is one in which each unit in the market being studied has an equal chance of being selected in the sample, or at least a known probability of being included.

In consumer research, it is possible to design such samples and to adhere to them reasonably well, although it must be admitted that complete coverage of a probability sample is rarely achieved, both because there are some refusals and because the number of callbacks necessary to reach the more elusive members of the population may raise costs to an excessive level. This difficulty has led to the development of various means for estimating the characteristics of the not-at-homes. The use of probability samples has increased significantly in consumer research over the past several years, although quota or judgment samples are still used. This increase in the use of scientific sample designs has significantly improved the precision of consumer research.

In the industrial marketing field, several important factors affect the sample design problem. Typical industrial products, especially those that find vertical markets, have a much smaller number of buying and using units than do typical consumer products. On the other hand, products that find a horizontal market have tens or hundreds of thousands of possible buyers. A second difference is the wide variability that may exist between manufacturing establishments in the extent and nature of product use. This may be because using establishments are in different industries, or because even within a single industry technical experience and manufacturing practices may differ substantially between companies. Third, in industrial markets it is very common for a few companies to account for the major share of the purchases of a commodity. It is not at all unusual to find half a dozen firms buying 70–90 percent or more of the materials or specialized equipment used by an industry. A fourth difference, which relates more to interviewing than to the design of the sample, lies in the multiple-purchasing characteristic of industrial companies and the consequent complexity of the purchasing process. Unless this is adequately recognized in interviewing procedure, the results will bias the sample.

In view of the heavy concentration typical in many industry markets, and the possibility of high variability in the purchasing practices and attitudes among companies in each industry group, it has been customary to stratify an industrial sample according to size of firms, and to insist on complete coverage of the largest concerns. This use of what amounts to a census approach on the upper stratum is considered by some to be a denial of the possibility of really using samples in industrial marketing research. This point of view is fallacious, because complete coverage of the large concerns is simply an essential part of the sample design. For firms of medium and small size, a census would be clearly inappropriate, and a sample should be drawn.

In industrial marketing research, it is more difficult to plan a sample in detail and follow the plan exactly than it is in the consumer field. This stems, again, from the high variability among industry markets, and even among companies in the same industry. It also is due to the difficulty of predicting the variations in purchasing practices and attitudes among different firms. Although the exploratory phase of the study is of tremendous help in this respect and enables more precise sample planning than would otherwise be possible, careful study of the results obtained in the beginning part of an industrial market survey often indicates that the sample should be modified. For example, it may be found that certain industry markets believed to be important for a product under study turn out to have little, if any, use for it and may be eliminated. It may also be found that other groups, although seemingly homogeneous, actually differ widely between companies in their use of the product. This means that more interviews must be made in such a group to be sure that the picture is reasonably complete. The reverse of this situation occurs when several interviews among the companies in one industry market show a very uniform pattern of behavior, and it may be feasible to reduce the number of interviews planned for it.

These characteristics of the industrial market have led some writers to emphasize qualitative as opposed to quantitative marketing research. This confuses rather than clarifies an already difficult field of investigation. It is quite clear that before management can have faith in marketing research as an aid in solving its problems, it must feel certain that research results accurately represent the major tendencies in the field—in other words, that they *do* have quantitative significance. The term "qualitative" often seems to be used to emphasize the importance of getting a complete picture of the complicated purchasing practices of industry. Any sound investigation will seek enough and only enough information to help solve the problem at hand. Some of it is almost sure to be quantitative. Sound marketing research, both industrial and consumer, has both quantitative and qualitative aspects.

Methods of Gathering Field Information

In gathering field information, three major methods may be used: (*a*) personal interview, (*b*) telephone interview, and (*c*) mail questionnaire.

Personal interviewing may be carried on by members of the marketing research department, by part-time interviewers hired and supervised by department personnel, by research firms that specialize in marketing surveys, and, in some cases, by salesmen or other types of company employees. In general, industrial interviewing requires a higher level of knowledge, intelligence, and adroitness than does the typical consumer survey. In part, this is because it is often not possible to develop a definite questionnaire form that, after adequate testing, can be used uniformly throughout the survey. Industrial respondents are skilled in the particular matters they are being asked about; such matters are their livelihood. Thus, the interviewer needs a better understanding of the nature of the problem being studied than does the average interviewer in the consumer field.

Another factor that calls for a higher grade interviewer arises from the difference in practices between companies, which again makes a standardized questionnaire of limited value. Instead, it is customary to employ an interview guide, which covers the basic subjects to be discussed.

It is generally agreed that an interviewer should not take detailed notes during the interview, although jotting down complicated data is essential if it is to be recorded accurately. Usually, the interview write-up should be made as soon as possible after the session; some organizations insist that this be done before the next call is made. It is helpful to plan the interview guide with spaces so that it can be used for recording the results of the interview. The interviewer should be trained to record the results sufficiently clearly to avoid the necessity of rewriting before analysis can be undertaken. A portable dictating machine may be helpful, provided the interviewer organizes his notes effectively before using it.

The field personnel of the marketing research department or of a marketing research organization should be equipped by training and background with enough understanding of the needs and problems of the respondents to permit effective discussion. With such capable interviewers, the length of an industrial interview can be much longer than a consumer interview; 40 to 45 minutes may be considered typical. It is possible to make interviews of this length because businessmen are very much interested in their own operations and are surprisingly willing to talk about them.

The use of salesmen as interviewers for industrial marketing studies is generally considered to be of limited application, although a few marketing research men feel that they can be used effectively. The major limitations arise from the temperament and personal characteristics of the average salesman, who by nature is an extrovert and not inclined to analyze things objectively and in detail. He resents paper work and fights additional demands for it. Second, the salesman regards his relationships with his customers as most precious and crucial to him, and is unwilling to jeopardize them by requesting information he feels the customer may not wish to give or may regard as impertinent. A third limitation is the expense of this use of salesmen's time as opposed to their major function of selling. Good salesmen are costly, both in terms of salaries and expenses, and have developed special skills that should be used to increase company sales and build customer goodwill. Diversion of their time to market survey work can be justified from a cost standpoint only if they have idle time that otherwise would be wasted. When the demand for the product line is highly seasonal, there may be such idle capacity.

On the favorable side, salesmen regularly gather and enter on their call reports information of great value to the market analyst, particularly with regard to competitors' activities. The salesman recognizes that such information is of value to him personally, as well as to the company. Firms with considerable experience in using salesmen for field work have found that cooperation is reasonably good when they limit the information requested to what the salesman views as important to himself and the company, and what he can secure readily in the course of his regular work. Even in these instances, however, it is vital to explain the objectives of the investigation and to instruct the salesmen very carefully in ways to obtain the information and in how it should be recorded. The problems of communication in adequately instructing salesmen in these matters are tremendous, and in some instances may be almost insurmountable.

Telephone Interviewing

Telephone interviewing has a very real place in industrial studies that do not involve gathering lengthy or complicated information. Along with personal interviewing, telephone interviewing has the merit of making possible a controlled contact with the sample selected. It also saves travel time and expense. There seems to be little significant resistance on the part of businessmen to telephone interviewing. The telephone is so much a way of life to many executives that this approach seems perfectly normal to them. Moreover, a telephone interview requires less of the respondent's time than would a personal call.

Telephone interviewing has limitations, particularly in studies that require interviews with several people within an organization, some of which must be made jointly in conference. Second, it is not practicable over the telephone to hold long or detailed discussions. Third, some studies require the respondent to consult company records in order to provide useful responses. Even in personal interviews, this may require a high degree of persuasive skill on the part of the interviewer; it is much more difficult in a telephone interview and almost always requires a second call. Some researchers have had good success in writing to interviewees in advance of telephone calls, asking for cooperation in assembling the needed information.

Mail Questionnaires

Mail questionnaires suffer from the danger that respondents will consist mainly of individuals or companies especially interested in the particular inquiry. Thus, even mail surveys that yield such high returns as 50 to 75 percent cannot be assumed to be representative of the entire market group to which the mailing was made. The nonrespondents may consist almost entirely of companies that do not use the particular product or whose interest in it is limited or unusual.

Before the results of a mail questionnaire survey can be used as a basis for marketing decisions, some means must be found to estimate the characteristics of the nonrespondents. The methods for doing this all rely basically on sampling them to gain responses, which can then be analyzed to estimate the group's characteristics. One method is to circulate the questionnaire again to the nonresidents, with a different letter and a stronger appeal for cooperation. Sometimes, several remailings are made. A second method is to conduct personal interviews among the nonrespondents; a third is to make telephone interviews. In sampling the nonrespondent group, personal interview and telephone interview methods yield more reliable results than additional mailings, because returns from mailings are subject to the same type of bias as were the original returns. Since many surveys relate to the conditions or amount of use of product lines, it is vital to know the proportion of users to nonusers among the nonrespondent group.

In planning the sample of nonrespondents, care should be taken to include a suitable range in size and business characteristics. It is good practice to design two such samples to be equivalent in composition, and to separately analyze the results from each. A small number of differences suggests low variability and the uselessness of further samples. On the other hand, if the variation is large additional samples are required to get a trustworthy indication of the character of nonrespondent companies.

Measurement of the bias introduced by the inevitable partial return of a mail questionnaire may seem sufficiently complicated and troublesome to make the mail technique far less desirable than personal or telephone interviewing. This is not necessarily true, since the total cost of a mail questionnaire survey is likely to be substantially less than that of an equivalent study conducted by personal interview. Some industrial marketing research men have made extensive and ingenious use of the mail questionnaire method and feel that it permits them to contribute much important information that would not have been worth the cost of the more expensive type of investigation.

Also, a mail questionnaire has certain specialized uses in studies designed to uncover industrial market opportunities for a particular product or line. As an example, when the Dewey and Almy Chemical Company expanded the production capacity of its plants for making synthetic rubber sealing compounds, additional markets were needed to use the excess capacity. To uncover these markets, a preliminary exploratory questionnaire was prepared. This was sent to 1,500 companies with 100 or more employees, selected from the *New England Directory of Manufac-*

turers. It was believed that the New England area included a range of industry wide enough so that this exploratory questionnaire would reveal most, if not all, of the trades using adhesives in significant volume. It included the following questions: (1) Do you use adhesives? (2) What types? (3) What average monthly consumption? (4) For what end use? Questionnaires were returned by 43 percent of the manufacturers, of whom nearly three quarters used some type of adhesive. About one quarter of the companies that used adhesives had need for the types manufactured by the Dewey and Almy Chemical Company.

The marketing research director selected 14 of the industry markets that appeared to be important enough for more detailed study. These markets were then analyzed carefully by personal interviews and further mail questionnaires.

Another example of the exploratory use of a mail questionnaire was a double postcard sent to several thousand companies throughout the United States, asking whether they used rope and, if so, in what quantities and for what purposes. From the returns, detailed plans could be made for a market study covering the uses of rope.

Analysis of Data

The analysis and interpretation of data require full understanding of the objectives of the study and how they relate to the management problem under attack. Further, since the number of interviews in a typical industrial marketing study is far less than that in the usual consumer market survey, it is essential that the information in each interview be completely utilized. Coupled with this is the importance of the small number of large companies that represent large shares of the industry market and whose influence must be carefully evaluated in analyzing and interpreting the data.

The very great importance of an intimate knowledge of the survey suggests that the analysis should be carried out by the individual in charge of it, and that he should do at least a portion, and perhaps the major portion, of the field work. This point of view has much validity. Certainly, the analytical work must be carefully set up and supervised by the analyst most closely concerned with the project. It should certainly be carried on by someone who has had experience in industrial marketing research, preferably a staff member who has worked on the particular assignment.

Although it is essential that the analysis reflect the quantitative weight of market evidence, especially as it is influenced by the importance of various users whose replies are being evaluated and analyzed, the process requires the exercise of intelligent judgment and cannot be merely a simple tallying of answers. Particular attention must be paid to the variability of practices between companies and markets. An industrial market that appears initially to be essentially homogeneous may turn out to consist of several segments each of different importance, and with somewhat different requirements.

Presentation of Results

The presentation of results must be as effective as possible in persuading the executive for whom the study was conducted to implement its findings. To this end, it may contain persuasive discussion to explain and justify the reasons for the recommended solution. This material can also be very valuable to the executive in working with his subordinates to put the plan into effect.

This is not to suggest that a marketing research report should be a special pleading document, like a lawyer's brief which emphasizes facts and analyses favorable to the course of action he seeks and ignores or depreciates those unfavorable. It should impartially present all the facts the study has disclosed and indicate the significance of the ones that deny as well as those that support the conclusions. Once all the facts are in, it is perfectly proper and desirable for the writer of a report to present in detail his appraisal and balancing of the data to justify his conclusions. To the man who must make the decision, the researcher owes not only a complete statement of the facts he has found and his analysis of them, but also his opinion as to what they mean in terms of action and his reasons for that opinion.

Often an oral as well as a written presentation can be effective. This is especially desirable when a study deals with matters that affect the work of a number of units in the organization. The people in those units are apt to be much more effective in implementing a decision if they understand the factual and analytical background that gave rise to it. This is especially apt to be true in the industrial goods field. It is good for the morale of the marketing research department to have this presentation made by the man who did most of the work on the study or was in direct charge of it, with such sideline support from his manager as seems necessary.

In our discussion on planning a study, we stressed that the planners should think ahead to the implementation of results and point their work to this end. The process of achieving later use really begins during the first three stages of the study, and particularly in the preparation and discussion of a dummy report. This dummy report indicates in understandable form the kind of information that will be derived from the study, and facilitates two-way communication between the executive and the marketing research department. It is also desirable to maintain good communication throughout the course of the study, as early field work may require some modification of the original plans.

Follow-up of Study

Even if acceptance of the report has apparently been complete and the recommended course of action adopted, there is still need for a regular system of follow-up by the marketing research department. In part, this is to determine how well the recommended procedure is actually working and so test the validity of the original analysis. Such review may bring to light unsuspected factors either not recognized or given inadequate attention in the original study. Also, since changes in the industrial market can at times be very rapid, a situation existing at the time the field data were collected may have substantially changed while the proposal was being implemented. The follow-up step may also reveal deficiencies in planning for implementation and may suggest better methods of achieving this all-important objective in future studies.

In the event that the recommendations of the report are not accepted, it is the responsibility of the director of marketing research to determine the reasons. He may find that communications are at fault or that management is motivated by factors outside the marketing area. The morale of marketing research personnel will be improved if they are given a full explanation of why the results of their efforts have not been favorably acted on.

FIVE BASIC TYPES OF MARKETING RESEARCH STUDIES

Although an industrial marketing research department may conduct many different types of studies, five provide vital information in solving many marketing problems: (1) measuring the size of markets; (2) analyzing sales results; (3) sales forecasting; (4) analyzing customers' buying practices, motives, and attitudes; and (5) analyzing competitors' marketing activities.

Measuring Size of Markets

Market-size measurements enable management to know for each product what share of the market the company has obtained and what trends are operating. Thus, they aid in planning selling programs, in designing sales territories, in setting standards for distributors and salesmen, in evaluating new products, is achieving effective advertising, and the like. Without such knowledge, it is easy for a company to be satisfied with its own rising sales curve when, in fact, the industry in total is growing at a faster rate. Conversely, a declining sales curve can cause deep concern among executives when the firm may be actually winning an increase in its share of a market that is declining in total.

The industrial marketing executive wants to know the total United

States sales for each of the important product types he sells. Thus, the sales manager of a metal specialties producer would like to know total sales of metallic pigments as well as total sales of powdered metals of various kinds. The manufacturer of milling machines and lathes requires total industry sales figures that can be related to his own performance in each of these lines. An aluminum producer would like total sales by various forms of the product, such as sheet, bar, structural shapes, forgings, and the like. Thus, in the simplest and broadest concept, market-size measurements consist of total industry sales of a particular product type to industrial users throughout the United States. Imports should be included in these figures, and exports, of course, excluded.

Market-size figures are sought by marketing executives on a monthly basis, if possible. Provided the time lag between occurrence and distribution of such figures is not excessively long, monthly figures are helpful in closely following industry movements, especially during shifts from a sellers' to a buyers' market. Quarterly figures are next best; lacking these, fact-minded executives insist on annual figures, even though they must be based on estimates if there is no regular industry or government-sponsored program for collecting sales data.

Despite the great value of total market-size figures in indicating overall marketing performance of the company, they do not provide a division of total sales among industry segments, such as the railroad industry, construction, appliance manufacturing, the automobile industry, and petroleum refining. Shipments are, in general, synonymous with sales, but figures for production, which sometimes are the only information available, are not necessarily the same as sales and must be used with this limitation in mind.

For the manufacturer of a product with a vertical market, market-size information is likely to be relatively simple, consisting of figures for the single industry he serves. He should be aware, though, of the possibility that the type of material or equipment he makes may, as a result of technical change, become suitable for use in a different industry either as is or in a modified form.

It is usually very much worthwhile for the marketer of a product with a horizontal market to have market size figures for each of the industry segments that make up his total market. Otherwise, without knowing it he is apt to direct his promotional and selling emphasis toward segments whose sales possibilities are small, or toward industries in which he dominates to such an extent that additional sales increments come hard and are costly, and he may ignore segments whose possibilities are lush and relatively unexploited.

In addition to sales figures for various markets, it is highly desirable to have a breakdown by end use. In some instances, of course, the market and end use classifications coincide, as would be true for papermaking equipment in the paper industry and for plastic materials used by the plastic-molding industry. Usually, however, the using companies in a market make a variety of products, and the seller of a material, machine, component, or supply does not know to which of them his product is applied unless he gathers end use information. This is important, because the product mix of manufacturers in a seemingly homogeneous market can cover a wide range. For example, there are over 1,000 paint manufacturers, but only a portion of them produce metallic paints. A producer of metallic pigments cannot safely assume that the geographical distribution of his market is coextensive with the dispersion of paint manufacturers in general. Actually, the two differ markedly.

Measuring Territorial Subdivisions of Markets. So far, the discussion of market-size measurement has been focused on measuring total market size for a product line. Many of the sources of information useful for measuring total size can also be applied to territorial measurements. Such measurements are vital to management because they provide the basis for planning and control of field selling and advertising programs.

Industrywide figures on production or sales cannot be used for territorial measurements, nor are consumption data gathered on enough products to make this source useful. One way of attacking the problem is to develop some index or series of indexes by which the total market can be broken down into geographical units small enough to use in laying out sales territories. Another general procedure is to break down the total market into the different industry markets that use the product. It may then be possible from governmental, trade association, and trade directory data to determine the number and size of the companies within each geographical unit, such as a county or state. Knowing the share of the total market represented by an industry market, the analyst can allocate this amount to each geographical unit by use of some measure of size, such as number of employees.

The obvious danger in this procedure is the assumption that each company in the particular industry market has the same kind of need for the product, and that the extent of the need is accurately measured by number of employees or whatever other size measure is used. Although the validity of this assumption usually varies widely among different product-market situations and is probably never complete in the strictest sense, the general approach is useful, and with careful judgment it can be employed to arrive at an estimate of market size by geographic areas that serves all practical needs. Here, the company's past sales history and the detailed knowledge of the sales force and district managers can be very helpful.

A method of validating such a geographical index of market size is to make a customer-by-customer analysis of several salesmen's territories that have been intensively covered and for which the firm has unusually complete and accurate information on the total consumption of customers and prospects. If this information tallies reasonably closely with estimates derived from the market index, the index can be used with reasonable safety across the board. If there is little relation between the two, further analysis may indicate methods of refining the index to usable form. At worst, the index approach may have to be abandoned or supplemented by liberal applications of executive judgment.

If an industrial goods firm has served an industry for a long time and its management has been information minded, its records probably contain the names and locations of all the firms in the using industry—customers and prospects—together with enough information about each one to enable the analyst, with the help of the salesmen and operating executives, to make a close estimate of the total needs of each for the several products his company sells. These estimates can be totaled by counties, states, or other spatial units to get usable geographical market-size figures.

Market Measurement for New Industrial Products. Industrial products are usually first introduced by one or a very few producers. The industry markets and end uses for some new products may be well defined, but usually they are not, and a period of experimentation and product adjustment must elapse before the market pattern begins to emerge clearly. Because new products are new, industrial buyers are reluctant to purchase them in quantity; performance characteristics are unknown, and frequently the price level is high. When a new product replaces one of long-standing usage, there is a problem of acceptance by the buyer's production employees. If the characteristics of the industrial buyer's end product are changed by the use of the new product, he must consider possible adverse reactions from his own customers. The amount and quality of promotional effort expended by the sellers of the new product may vary widely among industry markets, end uses, and sections of the country.

Thus, a knowledge of the industry production and sales of the new product during the period of market development will obviously be of great interest to management. It does not, however, accurately reflect market opportunities. For effective planning of new product marketing programs, it is necessary to introduce the concept of market potential. Market potential represents an estimate of the total possible purchases, within a given time period, of all industrial buyers who have a use for the product and might purchase it if it were effectively brought to their attention. Market potential estimates should be sought in total, by industry market, by end use, and by geographic areas. Because these estimates involve a forecast of buyers' behavior, care should be taken to make them as realistic as possible. This is particularly necessary when they are used to aid in decisions regarding new plant and equipment or significant expansion of the sales force.

The need for estimating market potentials is greatest during the early stages of the product's life cycle. It may begin when the product is in the idea stage. Unless the market potential is large enough to promise a profit, management is not justified in spending money to research the idea or do engineering development work on it. At this stage, estimates of potential must usually be in terms of order of magnitude rather than exact figures. When research has developed a product in the test tube or on the drawing board, marketing research can often produce much more exact estimates of potential to guide management decisions on whether to make it and introduce it in the market and on how the introduction process shall be done. If final decision on these matters is postponed until pilot operations have made small quantities or prototypes of the product, even more reliable estimates can be made.

Despite wide differences among industrial products, there is a rough similarity in the shape of their growth curves. Growth in a new product almost always is rather slow for some time, often for several years, and then there is a period of quite rapid increase, followed by gradual leveling off, and usually eventual decline. Once a product is well into the growth phase of its history, industry sales become more and more accurate as a reflection of market opportunity and can largely supplant estimates of market potential, which, at best, suffer from substantial areas of incomplete knowledge and uncertainty.

Even for a well-established product there is real need for the concept of market potential. The alert marketing research department is always searching for untapped markets, which spring up as a result of technological developments and changing social and economic trends. Such markets may be quite outside the normal sales operation of the company, and can be uncovered only by imaginative and purposeful search.

In measuring the size of the market in total, by industry markets, by end uses, by territory, and for established as well as new products, much of the needed information can be derived from published data. As indicated above, every possible use should be made of readily available sources before resorting to expensive field investigations.

Government Sources of Market Data. Probably the most important source of published data is that provided by government agencies. Although most of the agencies issue lists of their own publications, these lists are not always up-to-date and, in any event, do not indicate the nature of studies that may be in progress or have been completed but not published for one reason or another. Therefore, it becomes very desirable for the market analyst to visit Washington from time to time to become acquainted with the personnel in the various government agencies that publish information in his fields of interest. This enables him to become familiar with present and projected data-gathering activities and to enlist expert assistance in interpreting reports that have been issued. Quite often, valuable, nonconfidential information not published may be made available to him.

Since most of the data collected by government agencies is originally entered on a schedule or questionnaire form, it is helpful to examine the schedules used in collection. Government agencies cannot publish every possible arrangement of data, and often special tabulations can be prepared at modest cost, provided they do not reveal the operations of individual companies. These may be extremely helpful in providing more detailed cross-classifications of data, and particularly in more closely identifying the geographic locations of producers of specific types than are revealed by the overall location pattern of the industry.

A limiting characteristic of government information is found in the strict legal requirement that confidential data be handled so that the operations of individual companies or plants will not be disclosed. This means that in industries with few companies and manufacturing plants it is not possible to publish data by geographic areas unless several companies are in an area. Thus, there are many industries for which a detailed territorial breakdown of production cannot be obtained.

Trade Associations as a Source of Market Data. A major source of information on markets is the trade association with a statistical program covering production, sales, and other activities of member companies. Although the number of associations with such programs is smaller than in previous years, in part because of antitrust suits, this source deserves careful review by the market analyst.

A basic limitation is that one or more important firms in the industry may not be members of the association. Certain managements may believe that the benefits of membership are not enough to justify the costs, or may fear the risk of government antitrust suits. Competitive jealousies may be so intense that one or more important producers refuse to support the association. Sometimes, the feeling is directed toward the association itself because its actions have caused resentment. If a substantial block of total industry product sales is made by nonmembers, the statistics as a measure of market size must be used with caution. Furthermore, members may not be regular in their reporting, and the industry coverage achieved is thus constantly shifting.

Associations are sometimes reluctant to disclose such shortcomings of their statistical series, and the market analyst must become thoroughly familiar with collection procedures and industry coverage before using these data for market-size measurements. If the omissions and other limitations are known, however, association data may be extremely valuable. Gaps in the information may be filled in by estimates of product sales of nonmembers or noncooperators.

Trade associations vary in their policy regarding the issuance of statistical information for use by nonmembers. When market-size measurements are sought for products currently being produced, the company is usually a member of the association, and the material is available to the analyst. This is not true when a firm that makes a material or component wants to use the end product statistics of its customer trade association to estimate the market for its own product. And if the purpose of the study is to evaluate a new product in a new industry, the restriction of association data to members only is a real limitation. A *Directory of Trade Associations*, containing descriptions of their activities, is published by the Department of Commerce.

Market-size measurement information may be secured from other published sources. Many trade journals publish annual statistical numbers, containing production and/or sales figures of the important product groupings in the industries they serve. When government or association data exist, they are usually reproduced in these issues, but often the figures are estimates compiled by the editorial and research staffs of the periodicals. Such estimates may involve a substantial amount of field checking with individual producers and with well-informed personnel throughout the industry, and are sometimes widely accepted as being the best available measures. Data from the *Census of Manufactures*, of the mineral industries, of agriculture, and other sources provide bench mark information on which estimates for succeeding years are based. Some examples of trade papers with well-established annual statistical reviews are *Chemical Engineering*, *Modern Plastics*, *Automotive Industries*, *Steel*, and *Oil and Gas Journal*.

In addition to annual numbers covering all aspects of the markets they serve, many trade papers publish special reports on particular products. For instance chemical magazines frequently publish detailed analyses of demand and production trends, end uses, competitive situations, and other market data about such basic chemicals as sulphur and ammonia.

Trade magazine publishers and trade associations issue directories that list producers and distributors in the industry, classified by various product groupings and often arranged geographically. Many of these contain substantial information about each company, covering such items as names of key personnel, product lines, branch plant and branch office location, type and amount of machinery, productive capacity, and the like. These directories may also contain various types of overall market information useful in arriving at market-size measurements. State industrial directories can be helpful in many studies.

There are also specialized services that contain valuable product and market information. For example, the *Chemical Economics Handbook*, published by the Stanford Research Institute on an annual subscription basis, contains a comprehensive collection of statistical data and charts on all phases of the chemical industry. Several handbooks published in different industries have useful information on raw materials consumed, types of manufacturing process, industry statistics, and the like.

Input-Output Analysis. An important tool was placed in the hands of the industrial marketing analyst with the publication of the 1958 *Industry Relations Study*.[3] This technique, originally conceived by Professor Was-

---

[3] See Morris R. Goldman, Martin L. Marimont, and Beatrice N. Vaccara, "The Industry Structure of the United States, A Report on the 1958 Input–Output Study," *Survey of Current Business*, U.S. Department of Commerce, November, 1964.

sily W. Leontief of Harvard University, was further developed by the U.S. Bureau of Labor Statistics in the form of input–output tables based on the year 1947. The 1958 survey was undertaken by the Office of Business Economics of the U.S. Department of Commerce in cooperation with the Departments of Agriculture, Labor, and Interior.

The basic output distribution table lists 86 industries in a column at the left side and the same industries across the top of the table. Each row of the table shows the percentage distribution of the output of a particular industry to all other industries. In addition, the proportion of goods and services moving from each industry to final consumption is indicated. Thus, information is provided on the market pattern for the output of each industry. For example, in the primary iron and steel industry 90 percent of the output is sold to other industries, being distributed widely among 55 different categories. In the farm machinery and equipment industry, on the other hand, only about 17 percent of the output is sold to intermediate consumers in 7 industries.

A second table shows the direct requirements of each industry for the output of other industries. Thus, to produce $1 of output the motor vehicle and equipment industry needs to purchase rubber costing $0.028; glass, $0.010; and steel, $0.085. The remainder of the dollar is distributed among 66 other suppliers of goods and services, including imports; a residual of $0.290 represents value added by the motor vehicle industry. This information is useful to an analyst in the steel industry, for example, who wants to know the direct effects an expansion in the automobile industry may have on steel. Using this table, he can also trace secondary effects, and by a chain of repeated calculations he can determine the total effect on the steel industry of a given expansion in the automobile industry. Supplementary tables have been calculated to show the total impact on each industry resulting from a given amount produced and sold by every other industry. Periodic updating of these tables and a planned expansion to a 400-industry matrix should materially increase the value of this analysis to the industrial marketing researcher.[4]

Internal Company Records and Surveys. Most manufacturing companies have important internal sources of information about products and their markets. The sales department continually assembles data on customers and prospects and on the activities of competitors. The salesmen's call reports often contain much information about customers' total purchases, sources of supply, amounts bought from each source, the end use of the product, production equipment employed, and the like. In addition, the sales department may make special studies that provide figures on size of markets. Although such reports rather quickly get out-of-date, they often afford a foundation on which it is relatively easy to build a current structure. The accounting department, in preparing financial statements

---

[4] See Wassily W. Leontief, "Proposal for Better Business Forecasting," *Harvard Business Review,* November–December, 1964; and "Industry's Slide Rule is Updated by Eleven Years," *Business Week,* November 21, 1964.

for the business, maintains records that are an invaluable source of information about markets.

Other departments of the business may have useful information. The purchasing director must know a great deal about the supply situation for the wide range of products he buys, including the size of the industries that make them and much detail about individual suppliers. The research and development department is well informed about certain product groupings, especially the technological trends that may affect their future market size. Other departments of possible value include traffic, finance, and legal. Few companies have good indexing systems to readily locate useful reports, and it is up to the analyst to do his own searching.

Field Investigation. If neither published sources nor internal company records and studies provide adequate measures of market size, a field survey by personal call, telephone, or letter and mail questionnaire may be required. In such a study, salesmen may be very useful as field interviewers because of their detailed knowledge of and access to customers and prospects. More often, field interviewing is done by personnel in the marketing research department or subcontracted to independent marketing research firms. Usually, such field work covers people who are well informed in the industry, such as trade paper editors, trade association executives, large volume distributors, and large volume users of the product. In addition, it almost always includes the major suppliers. Such an approach to competitors or possible future competitors clearly requires that the interviewee be duly warned of the competitive aspects of the inquiry.

Despite the resulting on-guard nature of such interviews, much of value can be discussed without revealing confidential data, and a certain amount of information trading can be done. Estimates of industry total figures in the absence of any solid statistical data are, at best, informed opinion, but by cross-checking estimates gathered from competitors and other sources it is often possible to develop an order-of-magnitude idea of the market size adequate for planning purposes. Similarly, estimates can be obtained of the market shares of different suppliers. Such a survey may disclose not only the range of end uses for the product, but also some idea of their relative importance. It should be designed to uncover technological trends that may affect the use of the product and its various end use industries.

Sales Analysis

Sales analysis provides management with sales results classified in a variety of ways to reveal important aspects of present and past sales accomplishments. Sales volume is one of the most important marketing factors affecting profits. Other important determinants are the dollars of gross margin yielded by sales of the various product lines to different customer groups and expenditures incurred in marketing. Sales analysis provides basic data for appraising the profitability of current and past operations, and for planning future activities.

Measurement Units Used in Sales Analysis. Sales of industrial goods may be analyzed in dollars or in physical units, such as yards of cloth, tons of coal, barrels of crude oil, and others. Although dollar value is used most commonly, physical units are frequently employed and are more meaningful than dollar figures for products whose price fluctuates widely over relatively short periods of time. For example, the price of cotton gray goods very closely follows that of raw cotton. If dollar volume alone were used for purposes of recording and analyzing sales, it would be difficult to compare sales accomplishments over time without using an index to adjust for changing price levels.

Sales data usually are derived from the invoice prepared when a shipment is made to a customer. The total value of all invoices sent to customers within an accounting period, such as a month or a year, represents total gross sales. Returns and allowances are deducted from this figure to yield net sales.

When industrial products are manufactured after the receipt of orders, either because purchasing specifications require special designs or features or because a plant is oversold and must schedule production ahead, there may be a time lag of weeks or months between placement of the order and preparation of the invoice. When the lag is substantial, the data generated from the invoice lose much of their value in reflecting current sales operations, and records of unfilled orders become a necessary part of the sales information system. Unfilled orders do not necessarily match later shipments, because orders may be canceled or changed. Cancellations are likely to be quite large when there is a shift from a seller's to a buyer's market. Buyers expect price levels to soften and, unless protected by price guarantees, try to cancel earlier commitments. Also, if business activity declines, buyers' requirements for equipment and materials may likewise decline. Despite these uncertainties, many firms with a time lag problem make extensive use of unfilled order data.

The basic unit of sales information consists of the sale of a specific product to a specific customer. A typical invoice may contain several lines, each giving the number of units, a description of the product item, the price per unit, and the extended amount obtained by multiplying unit price by quantity. These, with other items of information on the invoice, may be analyzed to give any desired arrangement of sales data in any degree of detail. Detailed information on sales of individual items, such as sizes, colors, and similar variations, may be necessary for planning production or other purposes. In many instances, however, such detail is not necessary, and accumulation of sales of individual items into product totals is enough.

Similarly, it may be useful to analyze sales made to each customer, breaking this figure down further into such product classifications and other detail as may be required. Sales may be grouped by customers of similar type as, for example, steel companies, railroads, chemical producers, automobile companies, bakeries, and others. At times it may be useful to classify sales by amount of customer purchases or by size of order. Sales by salesmen are obtained by adding sales made to all of the customers in each man's territory. This is useful in evaluating salesmen's performance, in planning and administering compensation plans, and for other purposes. As in other analyses of sales data, product sales can be broken down in as much detail as may be desirable, provided the basic unit of information—sales of a single item to a single customer—has been preserved in the recording system.

By grouping sales results for salesmen or manufacturer's agents according to sales district or sales division lines, the sales performance of the districts or divisions is obtained. Finally, the aggregate of sales results from the several districts or divisions yields the total sales figures for the company, except for customers that may be handled from the central office, or house accounts, as they are commonly called. Sales in different geographic areas may be analyzed to uncover the effects of weather or other factors, which may vary in their impact on industrial purchases in different sections of the country. Studies may also be made of the sales by various types of distributors used.

Trend Analysis. By grouping sales information according to regular time periods, the analyst may reveal upward or downward trends and disclose seasonal patterns. Trend analysis is extremely important, both in evaluating past performance and in planning future activities.

Share-of-Market Analysis. To measure the position of the firm and its products in its various important markets and the trend of its position is one of the most valuable services marketing research can perform through sales analysis coupled with estimates of industry sales. Such studies are tremendously useful in uncovering both weaknesses and strengths in products and in marketing performance, and in disclosing opportunities for expanding sales and profits.

The rapid improvement and wide use of electronic data processing equipment permits much more complete and much more rapid flow of information about sales activity than was formerly available. Machines can communicate to machines over telephone lines, and the aggregate results of far-flung operations can be available in a very short space of time. It is also feasible to analyze information in great detail; management must actually resist the temptation to ask for more reports than it can use effectively.

Sales Forecasting

The process of making a sales forecast includes two chief elements: (1) an estimate of what sales are expected to be for particular products, territories, and industry markets under the assumption of an unchanged pattern of company activities; and (2) an adjustment of this estimate in the light of changes the company plans to introduce in its products or marketing program during the forecasting period.

Sales forecasting builds on knowledge of market size and trends as well as on past history as interpreted by sales analysis. There are two general approaches to forecasting. The first is to estimate the general level of business activity expected during the coming period and from this to project a total sales figure for the company. This figure is then broken down among product groups, customer groups, and geographic areas on the basis of past relationships. Some adjustment must be made for known factors likely to affect sales of each group or area. For example, trends in capital spending by industry is a particularly important factor. Forecasts of capital spending are made in the quarterly capital appropriation survey of the National Industrial Conference Board, under the sponsorship of *Newsweek*, and in the new plant and equipment expenditure series issued by the Securities and Exchange Commission and the Department of Commerce.

The second approach is to build up a sales forecast by making a sales estimate for each of the industry markets the company sells to. This may be extended to making estimates of sales to each account during the coming period. These can be totaled to get a total estimate for each customer industry; this estimate may then be checked against the general outlook for the industry.

Most forecasting procedures make use of indexes of overall economic activity, such as gross national product, industrial production, construction, disposable income, etc., combined with estimates of future activity in the important industry markets the company sells to, and estimates secured from the sales and distributor organization. These forecasts are adjusted by the expected results of specific actions the company plans to take during the coming period, such as increases or decreases of marketing effort, additions and deletions of products, and increases or decreases in productive capacity.

One of the most important uses of a sales forecast is in production planning. In one company that manufactures power transmission equipment, such as V-belt drives, mounted bearings, pulleys, flexible couplings, and speed reducers, the inventory of stock items numbers over 3,000. These 3,000 items group into about 90 commodity lines, of which about a dozen represent the bulk of total sales. In each line, the market research department sets up a sales pattern, which gives the distribution of sales by sizes within the line. This pattern is based upon sales during the preceding three years and is revised once a year. The forecast then consists of the best estimate of the level of sales in the period ahead, expressed as a percentage of the basic sales pattern. For example, dual-duty sheaves might be expected to sell at a level representing 130 percent of the basic sales pattern. With this information, a clerk can use the pattern to calculate a specific forecast for each size. The forecast committee may also decide that a suitable order point in terms of inventory for this commodity line should be 35 percent of the forecasted annual sales.

From this information, the marketing research department in this company provides for the 90 commodity lines production planning data that take into account forecasts of sales and inventories on hand. The forecasting committee consists of the production manager, general shop superintendent, assistant sales manager, assistant secretary and treasurer, and the market research manager. Monthly sales forecasts are developed by using seasonal indexes calculated from past sales experience. Each district sales manager estimates his sales for the coming year, both for his district as a whole and for his major customer accounts. The company's experience has been that the managers usually assume the coming year will be the same as the previous one, except for specific accounts they know will change. The market research manager has found it necessary to revise such estimates both upward and downward, depending on the general outlook.

The complexity of forces at work that affect the levels both of general business activity and of specific industries is such that forecasting can never become an exact science. But the marketing executive will find that an orderly approach to forecasting will make possible more efficient operations. Sales forecasting is not something a marketing executive can choose to do or not do as he wills. Lack of careful analysis in arriving at a forecast results in a forecast just as truly as the most elaborate procedure, and decisions must be made on the basis of forecasting whether or not it is done systematically.

Customer Buying Practices and Attitudes

Studies of customer buying practices and attitudes form an important guide in planning effective industrial marketing programs. These practices may vary both among industry markets and among companies within an industry market. Usually, however, some general patterns can be uncovered. Not only is this type of information valuable in planning general programs, but also it is especially useful to the sales manager and the advertising manager. It is perhaps of more crucial value to the advertising manager, because while a salesman may learn from experience that certain approaches do not work or may sense that he is not reaching the right people in the customer firm, this kind of evidence is not readily available to the advertising manager. Thus, improperly conceived advertising programs can be carried on for some time before it becomes apparent that they are pointed at the wrong people and appeal to the wrong buying motives.

The manufacturer of a material or component part often finds it worthwhile to study the buying behavior of customers for the end products his material or parts are used to make. For example, *Sales Management*, July 15, 1966, reports a study of people's bed-buying habits, made by Jones and Laughlin Steel Company to guide a possible campaign to increase wire sales by getting consumers to buy bigger double beds or single beds instead of doubles. Two singles require more wire in the springs than does one regular-sized double.

Among the more important questions to be answered about the buying practices and habits in each industry market are:

1. What functional activities are sufficiently affected by the purchase so that the men responsible for them have something to say about it?
2. What part in the purchasing procedure does each of these men play?
3. What language do they understand best?
4. What buying appeals are most likely to favorably influence them?
5. What are the most effective and economical ways of transmitting the selling messages to these men?
   a) If through salesmen, what should their qualifications be?
   b) If through advertising, what media should be employed?
6. How can buying appeals used in advertising best be presented to fit peculiarities of the men and the media?
7. How rapidly is delivery required?
8. What are the service needs?
   a) In connection with sale?
   b) After sale?
9. What are the customary discount structures and credit terms?
10. How important is reciprocal buying?

Several studies of industrial buying procedure have been made. These studies show the similarities and differences in practice, but are not sufficiently detailed to guide the planning of a particular company's marketing program. Marketing research or an aggressive and alert sales force should learn and report the buying practices of specific markets and important customers.

The addition of new products, even when used by the same markets, raises questions about buying habits and practices that past experience with other product lines does not fully answer. Some new products must be marketed to new markets. At times, the sales volume of existing product lines can be increased by invading new markets. In both these instances, it is up to the marketing research department to help develop customer information to guide sales and advertising.

Such data must usually be developed through field investigation. This may involve calls on a sample of the companies in an industry market, with special emphasis on those buying in large quantities. When a small fraction of the total number of firms in an industry has a large fraction of the total business, sometimes as high as 80–90 percent, it may be necessary to include all the very large companies in the sample because their buying practices may differ considerably. Another source of information is sellers of noncompetitive products used by the industry market. It may be worthwhile to call on competitors.

Studies of Competitors

Knowledge of competition in all its aspects is an important resource to the management of an industrial goods house. It has become even more significant in recent years because of the stepped-up pace of research and development activities, which has resulted in more, and a greater variety of, new products and new processes. The general tempo of technological development has increased, often bringing competition from unexpected sources. Quite clearly, the most obvious competitor is the company that makes product lines of a similar type. But competition may also come from substitute products, or from completely different means of accomplishing the same results. For example, the market for laboratory chemicals has been limited by the use of electronic and other mechanical devices for making chemical analyses.

A second reason for more detailed knowledge of competitors' activities arises because marketing research as a management tool is increasing, especially among industrial goods producers. As competitors organize the marketing research function and make effective use of it, their skill in marketing operations is bound to increase. This increase in competitive marketing skill must at least be matched and, if possible, improved on.

In the earlier discussion of measurement of market size, emphasis was placed on industry total sales of particular product classes and the shares of that total captured by different suppliers. Such information is in one sense the most important single type of competitor data that a company needs to know. But it does not tell how this share has been achieved—whether through unusually well-designed product lines, through good distributing service, by effective advertising or aggressive selling, by excellent technical service, or other means. Information on the basic goals and objectives of competitors, their organizational structure, pricing policies, acquisition and diversification plans and other similar information aids in defining the task of marketing management.

Of high importance are the financial results of competitors' operations. Although it may be difficult or impossible to trace the contributions of various product lines to a rival's total financial result, nonetheless, by piecing together bits of information estimates can sometimes be made as to the probable production costs and margins of different lines.

Unfortunately, not all companies are willing to provide detailed financial information to reporting organizations such as Moody's or Dun & Bradstreet, particularly concerns in which the ownership interest is closely held. In such situations, considerable ingenuity is needed to develop useful information. Careful search of government proceedings and hearings before various regulatory agencies, as well as court cases, may provide worthwhile data. In making competitive studies, the marketing research department will find salesmen's reports very useful because they often contain detailed information on competitive activities. Trade journals frequently provide useful information of this sort. Other sources include personal calls, telephone calls, and mail questionnaires among customers, prospects, and distributors.

Detailed information on competitors is of great value to the sales manager. A knowledge of the territorial deployment of competitors' salesmen and distributors helps in laying out salesmen's territories and gives a guide to the intensity of coverage needed. In addition, knowledge of competitors' relations with particular important accounts is invaluable in interpreting trends and in indicating the need for countermeasures.

Knowledge of competitors' products and selling practices can be included in training the sales force. It enables the salesman to cope more effectively with competitive action and to capture the confidence of customers and prospects. Competitive information is also a real help in developing sales forecasts, because one of the elements in forecasting most difficult to appraise is the impact of competition. Anything that can be learned, not only in terms of the nature and magnitude of competition as it currently faces the company but also in terms of competitors' plans for the future, is of importance. The methods used in collecting such information should not only be legal in order to avoid any charge of commercial espionage, but also should conform to accepted ethical standards.

SUMMARY

We began our discussion of marketing research by showing the extent to which it is used in the industrial compared with the consumer goods field. We also gave some indication of the extent of its use in specific areas, such as advertising, economic, product, and sales and market evaluation. We discussed its place in the company organization structure and in the company budget. The use of outside marketing research agencies was described.

The steps in conducting marketing research were outlined; statement of objectives, exploratory investigation, planning the research and designing samples; gathering information, analysis of data, presenting of results, and follow-up. The chapter concluded with a discussion of the five most important types of marketing research: measuring the size of markets, analyzing sales results, forecasting sales, gathering information about customers, and studying competitors and their marketing activities.

Chapter 8

◇◇◇◇◇◇◇◇◇◇◇◇◇◇◇◇◇◇◇◇◇◇◇◇◇◇◇◇◇◇◇ MANAGING THE

PRODUCT OFFERING

PRODUCT MANAGEMENT is not strictly a marketing activity. It involves consideration of factors of production, finance, purchasing, labor relations, and general management as well as marketing. So most product decisions are made at the top management level.

But the growing realization in management thinking of the paramount importance of the customer to the success of the firm has caused the marketing manager to have much more voice in decisions about products than he once did. The core of product management lies in offering the products the customer wants and needs, in the quantities he wants, and when he wants them. Since the marketing manager has closer contacts with the customer than any other executive of the firm, he plays an increasingly important role in product management.

In our economy, very few concerns make and sell only one product. Some industrial goods houses confine their activities to a single *line of products*, by which we mean a group of articles that serve the same general purpose or are otherwise so closely associated that customers want to buy them together. Examples are abrasives, grinding machines, power transmission equipment, and materials handling equipment. Many firms spread their activities over a number of product lines. The entire product complex of a firm is called its *product mix*.

Some of the most difficult problems of product management cluster around the question: What should belong to our product mix? Closely allied to this is the range of items or varieties to be offered within each product line. There are important questions of price levels to be charged, quality standards, and guarantees to be offered. Quality as a consideration includes the whole range of product specification and design. It also involves the question of whether the company wishes to be a leader in design or a follower of others who carry on the pioneering work.

The degree of custom manufacturing to meet the needs of individual buyers versus quantity production of a limited range of product types is a significant problem of product-planning policy. An important consideration is the type and amount of engineering and other services to be offered prior to, during, and after sale. For some industrial goods, engineering service is vital to a successful selling program and to continued customer goodwill, even though it requires large expenditures and is subject to abuse.

Determining how much of each product line to manufacture and when it should be made is an important part of the product-planning task. Related closely to this is the practice to be pursued in warehousing stock. These questions are affected by the ability of management to forecast sales. Mistakes in judgment resulting in overproduction are painfully apparent and may cause substantial loss. Those that result in underproduction and inability of a company to take advantage of market demands are much less apparent, but can be just as serious to the welfare of the firm.

Another type of product decision relates to the dropping of items or even of entire product lines. This activity tends to be less well organized than many others connected with product planning. It is more satisfying to add items than it is to drop them, and many manufacturers have been shocked by the large number of slow-moving or unprofitable products that come to light in a critical review of their offerings.

Finally, there are questions about the procedure by which new articles are to be added to the product mix. The development of new products within the company itself through research and development activities is a very common method. Other methods are copying unpatented products of other firms, negotiating royalty arrangements, and purchase from outside sources, either of the product itself with manufacturing and sales rights or of an entire company with its product mix and its manufacturing and marketing organization.

PRODUCT PLANNING AS A COMPETITIVE WEAPON

Industrial marketing is characterized by keen competition. Competitive behavior takes several main forms: the product-planning and development activity that shapes the product mix being offered, the price levels at which these products are sold, the services rendered the customer, and selling and advertising programs. Of these forms of competition, product planning is probably the most important. Furthermore, its stature as a competitive weapon seems to be increasing.

The economy of the United States is growing steadily and becoming increasingly dynamic and complex. More customers request special product variations to meet real or fancied needs. Buyers are increasingly critical as the purchasing function becomes more professional. Technical research is growing rapidly in importance and has resulted in vastly improved products, materials, and manufacturing processes. Many companies find that from one third to one half of their total sales are of products that were not being produced 10 years before.[1] Another factor contributing to the increasing importance of product policy is the higher break-even point characteristic of modern industry, which results mainly from the widespread adoption of mechanization and automation. Unless the product mix is properly adjusted to market needs, sales may be too low to support the high fixed cost.

One difficulty in effective management of product planning and development is that the product mix of a company is shaped by a multitude of forces, many of which are not within the control of its executives. This means that a considerable amount of product management effort must consist of skillful adjustment to shifting market opportunities and to competitive action. Since the area of direct control is smaller than in many other types of management activity, it is vital to follow a purposeful policy rather than to drift with the tide.

Every manufacturing company is to some degree unique in that it has its own history behind it, particular personalities who have shaped its growth, its own inventory of skills and know-how, a certain assembly of production equipment and labor, a distinctive sales organization, set of market contacts, and fund of goodwill. These aspects of the enterprise represent both strengths and weaknesses in relation to which decisions regarding the product mix must be made. It is management's responsibility to take them into account in looking ahead to determine the product policy most profitable during the foreseeable future.

These strengths and weaknesses of the firm are not immutable over time. Effective correction of company weaknesses and continued growth in corporate strengths require forward planning. The formulation of a product-planning program for 5 years, perhaps 10 years, ahead can provide a significant guide to changes in the enterprise deemed desirable and feasible.

The fundamental forces affecting the product mix of a manufacturing company will be discussed in the first section of this chapter. Second, the appraisal of company strengths and weaknesses will be considered as a means of formulating a sound product-planning policy. The third section will briefly discuss the organization structures used in implementing product-planning and development policy. The fourth section deals with the process of developing new industrial products, and a final short section treats product deletion.

DETERMINANTS OF PRODUCT MIX

Product policy implies a course of action or set of principles thought through in advance so as to result in a consistent pattern of decision and

---

[1] Booz, Allen and Hamilton, *Management of New Products* (Chicago, 1960), p. 1. These conclusions were supported by a survey made by the A. C. Nielsen Company in 1963, and reported in *Sales Management*, September 6, 1963.

action regarding the product mix. Careful attention by top management to the formulation of product-planning policy is by no means standard practice. In the absence of such a policy, decisions regarding the product mix of a company are likely to be based on the pressures of the moment. Although such decisions usually take account of the dominant characteristics of the company, they often do so on an intuitive basis and incompletely.

Let us seek to identify the fundamental determinants of the product mix of a company in order to understand a little better the problems of making product policy. Management's role consists of adjusting the resources of the enterprise to these forces as skillfully as possible, and of guiding the firm along product paths that will lead to future growth and profit. We will limit this discussion to the determinants that are fundamental, and will make no effort to treat in detail the various specific reasons or motivations underlying company product action.

Changes in the product mix of a company involve changes in the design of individual products already in the mix, changes in the variety of present product lines, the addition of products new to the company, and the elimination of products formerly in the product mix. A new product is one new to the particular company, and usually involves significant tensions, difficulties, and adjustments during its assimilation by the manufacturing, sales, and other departments within the company. By this definition, a new product need not be new to the market, only to the company. It should be born in mind, though, that the problems of introducing a hitherto unknown product differ widely from those of adding one already known to the market but new to the company.

Technical Research and Development

The most potent factor tending to broaden and diversify the product mix both of industry as a whole and of the typical firm is scientific research. Much of this is now done by business concerns or under their sponsorship. In certain areas, such as electronics and aviation, most research is sponsored and paid for by the government, although the actual work may be done by scientists in educational institutions, research foundations, and the laboratories of business concerns. In other areas, most research is done in the laboratories of individual firms, although some of it is carried on by academic scientists either on their own or on grants from industrial concerns.

Comparatively little industrial research is basic in the sense that it is directed to the discovery of new principles or knowledge. By far the greatest industrial use of research and development is in the application of existing knowledge to the development of new products and processes or the improvement of existing ones. The rate of technological change is accelerating, and technical research is unquestionably the most basic force affecting the product mix of the individual company. It underlies a number of the other determinants of product policy, which we will discuss.

Changes in Competitors' Product Mixes

A second important determinant of a firm's product mix is found in the changes in competitors' product offerings. Closely related is the introduction of competitive products by companies not now considered to be competitors. This has happened increasingly in recent years, with the growing tendency of industrial firms to enlarge their product mixes and to include product lines in fields and markets not previously served. Changes in competitive products represent a direct challenge to a company, and if the change is a truly significant improvement, it may prove disastrous unless it can be matched or surpassed within a reasonable length of time. This matter of the time element explains why firms seemingly in a solid product position spend large sums on research to discover new products that render their present ones obsolete. When asked why his firm was doing this, one chief executive replied, "If we don't, some one else will."

In addition to changes in their product designs, competitors may make changes in their overall product mix and put a firm at a competitive disadvantage. As will be pointed out later, there are important forces favoring a product mix of considerable breadth. Broadening product lines may be a real advantage in distributor relations and in lowering selling costs.

The number of competitors may change. An increase in numbers is likely to result in keener competition and lowered profit margins. Significant increases in numbers of competitors is especially likely in industries where the capital investment necessary for entry is modest. In such situations, a product that enjoys a rapid increase in sales is likely to attract many new entrants into the field, some of whom will not survive the period of consolidation, or shakeout, as it is sometimes called. In industries that require large investment, increases in the number of competitors are less dramatic. When they occur, the new competitors tend to reach for volume by cutting price, which reduces both the total sales and the gross profit rate of the original innovator. The result is that as soon as a firm introduces a new product on the market, it starts research to improve it and to find new products to replace it when competition develops.

Changes in Market Demand for Product Lines

Although declines in demand are most disturbing to management and may result in an expansion of the product mix in an effort to replace lost business, upward changes are also of significance. Management's responsibility is to capitalize as fully as possible on expanding product fields just as much as it is to meet the challenge of declining markets. These changes in product demand are of various types.

Shift in Customer's Product Mix. The industrial marketer, by definition, sells his product to other businesses either for incorporation in their products or for use in running their businesses. Materials that enter customer products are therefore vulnerable to changes in the product lines manufactured by customers. If the customer is himself an industrial goods producer selling to other industries, his shift may be triggered by changes *his* customers have found necessary. Such a chain reaction may have several links, all within the field of industrial marketing. In contrast, the immediate customer may be a manufacturer of consumer goods, and a change in his product mix will have repercussions because of his efforts to satisfy ultimate consumers more precisely with his offerings. The widespread use of annual models in the consumer field introduces a regular periodicity to changes and intensifies the need for planning ahead. Many annual models are designed years before they appear, and the seller of components or equipment who fails to establish and maintain sales and other contacts through which to learn about such changes, and to provide materials or equipment to facilitate them may suddenly find his product obsolete.

In addition to the product demand shifts brought about by customers' changes in product line design to meet their own customer needs, some regular customers may engage in diversification programs that expand their product mix and offer opportunities for sale of additional quantities or for modification of the seller's product mix to capitalize on additional business available from them. Since diversification programs often grow out of a decline in business or the fear of a future decline, there may well be concurrent drops in demand.

Some customers may pursue a policy of simplification of product mix. If this is confined to dropping low-volume items, the decline in their purchases will not be large. However, a drastic simplification of the total product mix, involving the elimination of some lines that are selling in substantial volume, will cause a significant shrinkage in purchasing requirements.

Changes in Availability or Cost of Materials or Components. A material or part used in making an end product may become scarce or its price may go up so as to distort the competitive relationships in either the components or the end product market. This necessitates product modification or change by the firm that makes the components.

For example, during recent years the price of tin has been increasing, until in 1965, as reported in *Sales Management*, January 1, 1965, the cost of the tin needed to coat a tin can was about four times that of the aluminum required for the same purpose, and the price of the combined steel and tin sheet in a tin can was greater than that of a sheet composed entirely of aluminum. The United States Steel Company developed a vapor coating process for coating light-gauge, flat-rolled steel sheets with aluminum. It thus sought to retain the steel tonnage that had formerly gone into tin cans, even at the expense of expanding the market for its competitor material, aluminum.

Changes in Manufacturing Processes. Changes in manufacturing methods by customer firms may affect the demand for the supplying company's product. This is most likely for manufacturers of major special-purpose machines, since a change in the manufacturing process may render them obsolete. A producer of raw or processed materials can also be affected because of the considerable freedom of choice that exists among the materials of which a product may be made. A change in a customer's manufacturing process may result in a larger yield from each unit of material, so that he needs to buy less of the material to produce the same output.

Shifts in Location of Customers. Transportation costs are important for many types of industrial goods. These costs limit the geographical extent of the market that can be profitably served by an industrial marketer, and any shift of customers out of this market area can result in major declines in sales and the necessity for replacing this lost business with other products. Sometimes, migration of customers or potential customers into the area economically served by a producer helps offset losses from outward migration. Some manufacturers, however, have been so closely tied to particular industries—for example, textiles—that large-scale migration becomes a death sentence unless the supplier also moves.

Changes in Levels of Business Activity. The examples just given of changes in product demand are based upon market changes of various types. There may also be changes in demand because of seasonal fluctuations in the industries served. Nearly every producer faces some type of seasonal pattern of sales, and also is vulnerable in greater or less extent to major shifts in the level of general business. Some companies have extended their product mix by adding lines whose seasonal patterns offset those of their present lines, and thus have obtained a reasonably even rate of total production and sales activity throughout the year. This consideration also applies to distributors who may feel the need for a product mix that evens out seasonal fluctuations.

In somewhat similar fashion, some companies have sought to add product lines less sensitive to business-cycle fluctuations than are their existing ones. Many manufacturers of machinery, particularly in the major equipment groups, are concerned about their sensitivity to cyclical drops in demand and would like to meet this drop through diversification. Cyclical fluctuations are often of the rolling type in that demand does not decline in all industries at the same time. When this happens, a supplier who diversifies to sell to a number of industries may diminish the sharpness and extent of the decline in his sales volume.

In addition to changes in general business activity, there may be variations in local or regional markets or in individual industries.

Government Controls. The last several decades have been a period of war and general tension in international relations. It seems certain that for many years in the future there will be a high level of government spending for national defense, coupled with the possibility of limited-scale military action. Under such conditions, certain materials are of great strategic importance, and the government may take steps to limit their usage for civilian purposes in order to manufacture military material or to build stockpiles. Such government controls have widespread ramifications through industry, and tend to cause major changes in sales volume for particular product lines. When there is no possibility of substituting materials, little product action can be taken. Frequently, however, such a tight material situation may encourage experimentation and research on substitute materials to perform the function. This leads to changes in product offerings.

Difficulties in Predicting Product Demand Changes. Although marketing research is of great assistance in measuring trends in demand for products and thus aids in predicting future demands, considerable uncertainty will always remain. This has led some managements to diversify product lines in order to spread the risk of unforeseen declines in demand for particular items.

Forces Tending to Broaden Product Mix

Several forces have the effect of tending to broaden the product mix of the industrial goods marketer. Let us briefly discuss the most important of them.

Industrial Buyers Prefer to Buy Several Product Lines from One Source. The industrial buyer prefers to buy several products from one source of supply instead of a single item or line from each of several sources. This preference stems from the time saved in purchasing, from the benefits of reliance on a single source for technical service and for settling of complaints, from pooling shipments of several products at lower transportation costs, and from the possibility of price savings on quantity purchases. Furthermore, because the combined purchases of several lines represent a sum large enough to be quite important to the supplier and his salesman, the buyer may feel that he will get more service and attention than he would if he dealt with several suppliers.

Interestingly enough, while the industrial buyer's tendency to protect his continuity of supply of each important article from such risks as fire, strikes, and other disturbances by splitting his purchases among two or more suppliers might be expected to limit the effect of this factor on expansion of suppliers' product lines, it actually has precisely the opposite effect. If the split is made by simply dividing total purchases of each article among several suppliers, the effect is to reduce the total volume of sales each manufacturer of the article can hope to get. If his finances or facilities enable him to handle more than that, he must get it by making and marketing some other product. If the buyer seeks to achieve his purpose by the less intelligent method of placing a limit on his dollar purchases from any one supplier, he not only limits the supplying firm's potential volume but also makes it impossible for the supplier to increase his sales except by adding items that can be sold to some other industry. This usually involves adding a new line to the product mix.

Industrial Salesmen Can Effectively Sell Several Lines. Provided the product lines sold by an industrial salesman do not require a high degree of technical knowledge or a radically different type of knowledge for each line, it is feasible for him to sell several products. There is, of course, an inevitable dilution of his knowledge and selling skills and time as the number of product lines is increased, and he reaches a point where the addition of further lines will drop the level of his sales skill below the needs of the customer. It is important to be sure that the salesman is at least above this threshold of competence for most of the accounts he will be selling to. It is to be expected that some customers will require more technical help than he can supply, and usually an industrial producer provides for this by having a technical service department to back up the salesman.

Marketing Costs Reduced by Several Product Lines. When a salesman is handling a number of product lines, the fixed cost involved in customer contacts is spread over the sales of the several products. With several product lines, there is more chance that his call will coincide with a buying cycle in one of the lines, and thus there is a higher probability of making sales than would be true if he handled a single product line. This increase in sales volume per call results in a lower percentage of direct sales expense. Marketing costs are also reduced by spreading the expense of company institutional advertising and marketing administration over several product lines.

Special Put-ups Incubate New Products. Every manufacturing company has a particular structure, a particular product mix, particular behavior patterns, and other factors that distinguish it from other manufacturers. These differences affect it's needs for purchased products. Thus, the buyer finds it necessary to make many compromises in product specifications between his ideal needs and what the market offers. If such compromises become too expensive or inconvenient, he may ask his supplier to produce special variations, which are often called special put-ups. A few of these may be found to serve a fairly general need among customer firms, and may be added to the supplier's line, thereby broadening it.

Several Products More Appealing to Distributors. Many manufacturers market through industrial distributors. The manufacturer of a single product line may find that its sales represent such a small proportion of the total sales of his distributors that it receives little attention, so he has little bargaining power with the distributor in efforts to improve sales effectiveness. As the number of a manufacturer's product lines increases, assuming that they fit into the distributor's markets and capacities, the relationship improves, and he is able to get more help from distributors and finds them generally more receptive to suggestions regarding sales and inventory coverage as well as selling methods.

Unutilized Capacity. Perhaps the most important single force driving manufacturers to broaden their product mix stems from unutilized capacity in some part of the business. This may be in production equipment, in the marketing organization, in the research department, in financial capacity or in management skills—in fact, in any aspect of the enterprise. The existence of unutilized capacity usually stems from changes of the types just discussed. In some instances, these changes can be foreseen with adequate analysis, while in others they are very difficult or impossible to predict.

Another source of unutilized capacity arises because increases in production or marketing capacity can rarely be made in small increments. This is particularly true of production facilities, which are usually made up of complexes of machines interrelated in function. When demand outruns existing facilities and a new equipment complex is bought, there may be a period in which it is not totally utilized in satisfying existing demand, and there is pressure on management to find new products to keep it busy. Similarly, when a marketing organization is set up to serve a particular market for a single product line, it often becomes apparent that the salesmen could handle other lines as well, and pressure is generated to find products they can sell profitably.

The management of a profitable firm may not find it necessary or desirable to pay out all profits in dividends to stockholders. Retained earnings become part of the capital of the company and must be put to work instead of being allowed to languish in the cash account. The management of the average profitable company must constantly search for new product opportunities to put its earnings to work.

Utilization of By-products. Many industrial processes involve by-products as an inevitable concomitant of production of the main line. It is rare that some use cannot be found for what would otherwise be waste, and considerable effort and attention may be applied to the problem of getting the maximum possible return out of such by-products. If successful, this leads to expansion of the number of lines in the product mix.

The various forces just described are largely external to the business and tend to mold the product mix of a manufacturing company. The company, of course, does not assume a passive role in this, but may attempt to innovate in both products and marketing methods and thus have an impact on the environment. The task of management is that of skillful adjustment plus forward planning. The influence a company can bring to bear in shaping its product mix is greatly affected by its character and by the circumstances in which it operates. Let us examine some of them.

APPRAISAL OF COMPANY STRENGTHS AND WEAKNESSES

In many respects, a business enterprise may be compared to a human being. Definite flows and rhythms of activity characterize it. A company has a physical structure of a certain size and shape, and a power to perform that reflects its strength and endurance. Intelligence of a certain level is brought to bear in the combined efforts of the people who constitute its management and work force. It has certain behavior patterns that are the product of past environment and policy and do not change rapidly. A company may display imagination in its activities, or may not; the degree of alertness and response to both internal and external challenge varies widely among firms. There is room for argument about whether the people in a firm create and maintain the corporate character or the corporation attracts people who fit into its character and personality. Perhaps the firm's chief difference from the human organism is that a corporate form of organization makes possible an indefinite life span, whereas the life span of a human being is finite.

The variety of the forces that influence the particular product mix an industrial marketer offers to buyers makes it especially important that management develop product-planning policy with the greatest care. Not only will such a policy guide the addition of new products that mesh well into the company's accustomed operations, but it will indicate the general directions in which management should move to correct practices, which, if unchecked, will cripple its earning power in future years.

A well-conceived product policy also charts the general course the company is to follow, and thus enables research personnel and others throughout the organization to move in directions that give promise of profitable returns. In the absence of such a chart, considerable manpower and funds are liable to be committed to projects later abandoned when management really faces up to its decision to move the product into semiworks or full-scale manufacturing and sales. Such mistakes are not only costly to the enterprise, but also can have unfortunate effects on the morale of the organization. Finally, a product policy tends to assure that worthwhile opportunities will not be overlooked because middle managers do not know what top management wants.

A sound product policy must be thought through for several years in advance, because a substantial number of years may elapse between the decision to move ahead on a promising idea and the time when a resulting new product is actually earning profits for the company. In fact, there is no area of business management decision where so long a time lag exists between an initial green light to explore a new idea on a limited scale and the final goal of profitable operations. The situation is aggravated because financially during this time everything is going out and nothing is coming in.

The general policy guides for product planning, which result from the appraisal processes being discussed, find their application in defining the general areas of product search. In considering specific new product ideas, however, management does not always keep these general product policies in sufficiently sharp focus to aid in the screening process. For such applications, these guides should be translated into a series of questions, checklists, or formulas to make certain that all aspects of product suitability are taken into account in arriving at a decision.

Appraising Company Capabilities

The general method of appraising a company's capabilities is to take an inventory of its present position and to trace the route by which it has arrived there. An important part of this procedure is to make continuous comparisons with competitors. Such comparison is not limited to industrial marketers who make comparable product lines, but should be extended to those who make goods that can serve as satisfactory substitutes for the firm's products. Although the yardstick of competitive practice is reasonably adequate for most situations, in some cases competition may be so weak that other yardsticks must be found in order to make sound appraisals of company capabilities. Such yardsticks may have to be adapted from analogous situations and, while necessarily crude, are nonetheless useful.

A detailed appraisal of capabilities is beyond the scope of this discussion, because it would involve an extent and depth of coverage not necessary to illustrate the general idea and because many of the details are peculiar to the individual company and have no general application. It will suffice to consider the appraisal in terms of product mix, production facilities, processes, materials and labor, research and development, technical service, marketing organization and activities, financial resources, executive groups, and ownership groups.

Product Mix Audit. The first step here is to analyze sales, gross profits and net profits, if at all possible, or if net profits are not available by products, contribution of each product or product group to general overhead and net profit for the most recent annual accounting period available and for a period of several years prior to that time. A 10-year period is normally adequate, while anything less than a 5-year period will not present a very complete picture. The exact period chosen depends not only on the availability of records, but also on the timing of any major fluctuations in business levels of the industry in which the company operates, as well as major fluctuations in general business.

The amount of detail in which such an analysis should be made depends on the character of the product mix itself. Certainly, product lines should be studied separately, and probably the most important items within each line. In addition to analyses by product lines and some items within each line, important additional information will be gained if the distribution of such product sales and profits can be shown by industry markets. Another dimension of experience that can be very useful in appraising the present product mix relates to the end uses of different product lines. Thus, the sales volume of electric motors is spread among a wide range of industries. Yet, the nature of the end uses of these motors represents a considerably smaller listing.

The type of analysis just sketched is incomplete as a reflection of the adequacy of the product mix unless it can be compared with similar information about competitive companies. Although at times it may be possible to obtain detailed information about individual competitors, the more usually accessible information is limited to sales and often consists of estimates of total industry sales. This makes it possible to calculate share of market figures by various product lines and, in some cases, to analyze them by industry markets and, at times, by end uses. Such share-of-market figures are a measure of total company sales performance for particular product lines. This performance includes not only the product but also the price at which it is sold, the amount and quality of the marketing effort expended, and similar factors. Because the influence of the product is so important in the total result, it becomes necessary to separate this from the total picture of sales results and to analyze product attributes in comparison to those of competitive product lines. Thus, it is possible to judge the skill of the company in keeping abreast of or ahead of competitive product offerings. In such comparisons, the effect of services offered should not be ignored.

Coupled with these analyses, a field survey measuring the attitudes of customers and prospects regarding the company and its product offerings can be very helpful.

Production Facilities, Processes, Materials, and Labor.   There should be an analysis of the production activities of the company in terms of equipment and other facilities used, processes of manufacture, materials used, and labor force. This analysis would likewise be historical, for past behavior is often the most accurate basis on which to forecast future behavior. In addition to a detailed description of the plant and equipment devoted to various product lines, the study should include measurement of the degree of utilization and some indication of production efficiency.

The type of production know-how possessed by the company personnel is also important. For example, in the chemical business one company is highly skilled in applying many of the techniques of large-scale production to what is essentially a small-quantity operation, while another is equally skillful in wringing the last fraction of a penny out of cost through large-scale operations in making and marketing chemicals by the carload or trainload. A firm that makes specialty castings has developed unique skills in metallurgical manipulation and precision in making exactly the products its market needs.

Comparisons with competitors' practices in production should also be made. Much can be learned about the alertness of a company by studying the degree to which it has been an innovator of new methods of production or has been quick to adopt such improved methods.

Comparisons of production costs by product lines with competitive costs, when available, reveal both strengths and weaknesses. It is rare that a company is equally efficient in the production of its various products, and this pattern often suggests promising areas for new product expansion. This information about competitors is hard to come by, since cost information is usually carefully guarded and different methods of allocating costs make comparison difficult. Shrewd guesses can often be made on the basis of fragmentary facts.

Research and Development. The size and types of activities carried on by the research and development staffs and the history of changes over a period of several years indicate the growth or lack of growth and the activities in which these groups have concentrated and presumably have special skills. Of even more importance, however, is the record of actual accomplishments of the research and development staffs over a period of time in terms of product improvements, development of new products, and assistance in uncovering new applications of old products. It is difficult to find yardsticks to measure the efficiency of research. One of the most useful comparisons is to study the research activities and accomplishments of competitive companies. Such comparisons will reveal the role management expects its research and development group to play in each of the companies covered.

It is also important to understand the areas of research within which people have special skills and know-how. For instance, a firm whose research group is especially skillful in inorganic chemical research will be handicapped in moving into a product area that requires organic research.

Technical Service. Many industrial products require some degree of technical service in the selling program. This need arises primarily because customers do not know exactly how to use the product, or because particular customers want to use it to get special unusual effects in their end products or want to use it under unusual conditions.

If the service needed is relatively simple, a properly trained salesman can handle it. If it is complex, a teamwork operation probably will be necessary. The salesman uncovers the need for service, gets a general picture of the problem, and calls on a technical service unit in the home office to do the work. A reputation for rendering good technical service is hard to get and not easy to keep. Not all firms have it that think they do. This is a point in our appraisal where we may find a customer attitude survey worthwhile.

Marketing Organization and Activities. One prime function of the marketing division of an industrial goods company is to maintain adequate contact and communication with user customers and prospects, or with the various types of distributors who handle the company's product lines. It is important to know how the sales force is organized in terms of product lines handled and markets served, and whether the organization structure is flexible enough to absorb new products or new product lines without complete rebuilding. The quality of the distributor organization may be a source of major strength or weakness. There are never enough competent and aggressive distributors to satisfy all competing sellers, and some companies have been more successful than others in attracting and holding a strong distributor organization.

The skill of industrial advertising managers and industrial advertising agencies varies widely, and this potential resource justifies careful assessment. The present activities and the past contribution of the marketing research department to decision making will provide some indication of its value as a source of company strength. Finally, a very important marketing resource may be the goodwill the company has earned among customers in its markets. This is intangible and difficult to measure, but may be very important in facilitating the successful introduction of new products.

Throughout the evaluation of these various aspects of the company's marketing talents, comparisons with competitive facilities will make possible more meaningful judgments on strengths and weaknesses. Another factor of special importance is the degree to which the marketing organization and the distributor organization are currently working at capacity. As was pointed out earlier in this chapter, one of the important forces tending to broaden the product mix is that buyers prefer to purchase several product lines from one salesman and that a salesman can sell several product lines with reasonable effectiveness. One of the real strengths of a company may be found in excess capacity in some phase of its marketing activities and the opportunity this offers for the efficient marketing of new product lines.

Financial Capabilities. The financial capabilities of a company and its financial history are relatively easy to measure, and they represent one of the most important controlling factors in planning for new products. The successful introduction of a new product may require a substantial investment in research and development work, in various types of technical and marketing studies, in a careful program of product evaluation, in the construction of a semiworks manufacturing plant, in the addition of new plant and equipment, and in outlays for market development work. Besides knowledge of the funds available for allocation to new products, it is vital to assess management's willingness to spend them for this purpose. This is particularly true in companies whose stock is closely held. The ownership interest may not wish to assume the risks of new ventures, even though substantially higher rates of return might be secured.

The investment necessary to add a new product or line to the established product mix varies widely. Production of some types of chemicals and of certain metals demands a large-scale investment and makes it impossible for a company with limited resources to consider entry into such fields. In contrast, entry is relatively easy in industries where capital requirements are low. Such industries tend to be characterized by keen competition and low rates of overhead expense. Companies accustomed to operating in high-investment industries are justifiably cautious about entering low-investment fields because experience has shown that they may have great difficulty in effectively competing on price.

As with the other aspects of an enterprise's resources, evaluation requires comparison with competitive financial resources. For example, if a manufacturing company is planning to embark on a particular new product program, the financial ability of competitors to follow suit is an important consideration.

Capabilities and Attitude of the Executive Group. One of the most important factors in appraising a business is the judgment, skill, imagination, alertness, and physical vigor of the top executives and the middle management group. In part, this has already been revealed through the study of each aspect of the company's activities over the recent period. However, a certain amount of good fortune may have aided a mediocre team of executives, and it is desirable to be coldly objective in assessing the capacities of this group. One important characteristic is to be found in the age distribution of the executive personnel. If they are bunched at certain age levels, the company may face serious problems of retirement in a short span of time. Another factor to be investigated is the extent to which the company has a definite and well-thought-out program for uncovering and developing executive talent.

Two vital factors are the willingness of management to continue spending money on a promising new product until its potentialities are developed, and the courage and judgment to cut its losses and pull out when a product's early promise proves illusory. For example, consider a firm that has been operating in a field where the product development period is three or four years before pay-off begins. If it adds a product line that requires five or six or seven years to develop past the break-even point, top management may get discouraged and pull out when the turning point is just over the next hill, unless the chief executives thoroughly understand the nature of the new venture and are emotionally committed to it.

Finally, there is the question of how nearly the executive group is working at capacity level. If the key executives are spread thinly over a vast range of problems and responsibilities, this may preclude additions of new products whose success depends on careful executive attention and follow-through. In order to secure the most realistic interpretation of executive strengths and weaknesses, some consideration should also be given to competitors' executives.

ORGANIZING FOR PRODUCT PLANNING AND DEVELOPMENT

From our discussion so far it is evident that effective management of the product mix requires an unusually broad understanding of the company as it is and as it hopes to be, and of its competitive relationships, not only among its immediate group of rivals but also among producers of alternative or substitute materials, which often provide keen competition. However, the real core of the organization problem lies in the fact that product planning and product development cut across the entire operation of a company to a degree that exceeds any other function of comparable significance. The marketing department, the production department, the research department, the financial group, the legal counsel, and others are inevitably involved in the process of developing new products.

The scope of the product-planning and development task varies widely among companies in the same industry, depending on the method of operation that has evolved over a period of time. Some firms stress innovation of new products and have strong research groups. Others do not attempt to pioneer to the same degree, though they conduct a limited amount of research in the belief that this activity will pay for itself. Still others pursue a follower policy and copy new products that have proved successful. Such major differences in management philosophy obviously are reflected in the size and importance of the research function, and in the organization of the product-development process.

The essential product management jobs to be performed in an average company include:

1. A review of the product mix at regular intervals, and decision making on redesigning, adding, or dropping product lines or items.
2. A continuous radar-type monitoring of external forces, such as declines and growths in demand for particular products and in particular markets, product changes in competitive offerings, changes in technology, and so forth.
3. Carrying on technical research of the type appropriate to the particular company situation and dealing with both products and processes.
4. Providing for adequate technical service to customers in the application of present products, and assistance in evaluating any special requirements.
5. Securing adequate market-development effort, both during the process of evaluating or developing a new product and in introducing the product and expanding demand when it is ready for sale.
6. Carrying on a purposeful search for new-product ideas.

7. Achieving coordination and minimum-time requirements in the whole product development process from the initial idea through preliminary appraisal into technical research, semiworks, full-scale production, and market introduction.

Various organization arrangements of the development function are found in different companies. Although some of this variety reflects particular company situations, much of it stems from the fact that there is no clear-cut, obvious, or generally accepted way to organize for effective performance of a business function that is so inherently heterogeneous in its nature. Furthermore, management's appreciation of the need for a well-thought-out organization and procedure for the purpose varies among companies. This seems to be especially true of firms whose product lines are fairly stable and who do not create large numbers of new products. In such companies, the essentially sporadic nature of additions to the product mix tends to lead management to ignore the values of a well-worked-out procedure. Conversely, in companies where change in product mix is constant it is more likely that some definite assignment of responsibility for procedure will be made.

Types of Organization

In one form of organization, the president or some other top executive takes an interest in new product development and devotes time and attention to seeing that proper activities are undertaken. This has the advantage that the new product coordinator can speak with authority, and there is less danger of jealousy and friction between the departments that must participate. The danger, however, is that such major executives are usually so busy solving critical problems that they do not have adequate time for new product development, even though they recognize its vital importance. In an alternative arrangement, the top executive has a staff assistant who speaks for him and acts as coordinator and expediter.

A second plan of organization gives the research director and his staff substantial authority in making decisions regarding the product mix and in managing the development process. Many research directors feel that this is the most logical procedure, and point out that their job is to insure company profits in future years through development of salable products and through continuous reductions in production cost. With this arrangement, however, it is usually considered desirable to have one or more committees made up of key people from marketing, production, general management, finance, and sometimes the legal department. The function of such committees is to review the recommendations of the research director regarding projects he believes should be worked on, and also to evaluate projects at various stages in their development. As the semiworks stage is approached, in which a substantial commitment of funds may be involved, there is usually an approval procedure that often involves a committee. The approval of key personnel is also essential when the decision is made to move ahead with commercial-scale manufacture and market introduction. Despite the use of such committees, the essence of this arrangement is that the research department acts as the coordinator of the effort.

The third organization arrangement is to assign the responsibility of product planning and development to a special department. The functions of such a department and its relations to the other departments within a business are usually carefully delineated. This approach recognizes that management of the product mix is a definite job, which will be done more effectively by fixing responsibility. There is substantial evidence that this approach to product planning and product development is on the increase.

A variation of the product-planning department is the new-product or commercial development department found in certain companies. Such a department is most likely to be used when the company has several main operating divisions, each with its own research and product-planning groups. It is assumed that these operating departments are capable of managing their particular product lines, but that they will not be interested in exploring or competent to explore lines substantially outside their present fields of activities and interests. Thus, new-product departments have evolved on the basis of providing for exploration of interesting new products and new applications that otherwise would not be developed. Such departments frequently are empowered to produce and sell small quantities of new products as one means of determining whether there is a real market need and what is the extent of that need. This type of organization unit is on the increase. A 1965 study made by Booz, Allen and Hamilton, which embraced 54 well-managed firms, showed that, in 1956, 12 of them had new-product departments; in 1960 the figure was 28; in 1965 it was 46. In 1965, these firms introduced 366 new products, 67 percent of which were successful—a figure well above the usual batting average.

Even in companies without new-product departments, analogous situations may arise, usually as a by-product of a research program. A research director may have faith that the new product has a field, but he may be unable to persuade his management that it is worthwhile to spend money on it. Some companies definitely recognize that this situation may arise, and the research department is empowered to undertake small-scale production and sale. Sometimes, this is done with the active blessing and support of top level executives, sometimes with their tacit acquiescence, and now and then without their knowledge.

Another type of organization places responsibility for the product line on a product manager. In a number of industrial companies, several product lines may be sold by the same sales force, but for each line there may be product managers who have a staff relationship to the sales force and who work through the manager of the sales force in their relations with the salesmen. If the other duties of the product manager leave him adequate time to carry on the product-planning responsibilities, this arrangement may work reasonably well.

It is necessary that an overall procedure be developed and well understood throughout the organization for development of new products. If this is not done, a product manager may meet much resistance from other departments. In particular, production department executives, who believe, with some justice, that they are being judged on their cost performance, tend to resist anything that might slow up production and thus raise costs. This type of resistance is encountered during the stage of transition of a new product from research and development into regular manufacturing operations. It must be recognized as a natural and inevitable situation, and steps must be taken to get around it. In one company, the research department had in its own budget a fund, which could be used to assist production groups in various plants in the experimental process of adapting new products to production procedures.

Some companies conduct their product management work largely through committees. This may work reasonably well, provided there is either one individual who takes the product-planning and development function as a major responsibility or, less desirable, the procedure is so well spelled out that action cannot be avoided or unduly delayed. For such committee activity to be fruitful, however, a considerable amount of staff work must be carried on by someone in preparing material for committee consideration so that meeting time can be spent efficiently. Although committees are essential working tools in a product-planning and development program, they appear to be used most effectively as an adjunct to a staff group with responsibility for seeking the most profitable product mix.

An American Management Association study, reported in *Sales Management*, July 5, 1963, showed that 35 percent of the companies reporting had a vice president as head of their new-product planning and development work. In 50 percent of the firms, the man in charge of new product work, whatever his title, reported to the chief executive officer. In this year, 58 percent of the firms had product-planning committees, as against 33 percent in a similar study in 1959. Of the total product planning committees, 69 percent were headed by members of top management, while in 1959 the figure was only 31 percent.

Despite the variety of organization forms in use, one central fact emerges: effective product planning and development require clear-cut recognition of the function and definite assignment of responsibility for it at a very high level. In the following section, we will discuss typical sequences of activities in the development of new industrial products.

MANAGING NEW-PRODUCT DEVELOPMENT

The details of the process of new-product development vary from firm to firm. Certain types of activity must be carried on by every company, regardless of how the details may be arranged. We will direct our attention to these activity types.

Let us assume that the company has an adequate technical research department and various staff groups concerned with development engineering, technical service, marketing research, and market development. To further simplify our study, let us assume that top management has organized for the administration of product planning and product development by setting up a product-planning department responsible for making decisions regarding the product mix, coordinating the activities of various company departments involved in product development, making up schedules of activities, and following through to see that the entire operation runs smoothly. Once a particular new-product development project is on the books, one man from this product-planning department is likely to be appointed project supervisor. His responsibility will terminate only when the product is in full-scale production and is being marketed through the regular company organization or when it is dropped as unsalable or unprofitable.

Complicating Factors

Several fundamental characteristics pervade the entire new-product development process and complicate its management. The first is that all functional units of the enterprise are involved at various points, and many of them throughout the entire process. They must be carefully mobilized and their natural resistance to cooperative action overcome. Second, many different types of activity must be carried on concurrently. Practically all of these are necessary prerequisites to later activities. Thus, there is an acute problem of skillful timing with the establishment of target dates and follow-up to determine progress. Failure to do a careful scheduling job, coupled with persuasive expediting, will not only result in confusion and frustration but will also stretch out the entire process longer than is necessary. For products that require a substantial amount of technical research and development work, the period from the original concept of the idea until sales return a net income stream to the company is typically in the 5- to 10-year time span. Acceleration of this process without incurring excessive risk is obviously desirable.

A third fundamental element in new product development is the need for several stopping points at which the project is considered in all of its aspects and decisions are reached—whether it should be abandoned, put on the shelf, or continued at a given rate of work. There is no set number of such stopping points, although the most obvious occur at the point of preliminary screening of new product ideas, at the time substantial amounts of expenditures are authorized for research and development and market development programs, at the time of moving into semiworks manufacture and market or use testing, and at the time of decision regarding full-scale manufacture and marketing. The process of reviewing the project in its manifold technical and economic aspects at each of these stopping points becomes increasingly more detailed and thorough as larger and larger amounts of company resources must be committed by decisions to continue it.

Another basic characteristic is that new products that are quite similar to the present line in production and selling characteristics will not require a process of development so elaborate or so long as those that are more alien to the established knowledge and know-how of the company organization.

Stages in Development Process

These factors complicate selection of the most pertinent outline of activities or stages of activities for consideration. There is a temptation to make a detailed listing, which has the disadvantage of being confusing and also of implying time sequences among activities that may be concurrent. The other extreme is to present a very few stages in the process. This has the merit of overall simplicity but means that each stage requires substantial examination. The outline adopted here is in the midzone between these two extremes and consists of the following steps:

1. Finding new-product ideas.
2. Preliminary appraisal of new product ideas and selection of projects.
3. Research on products and markets.
4. Research on manufacturing process.
5. Semiworks operations in production and marketing.
6. Transition to full-scale production and marketing.

With the exception of the second step, we have left out the appraisals that are likely to be made near the end of one stage and the beginning of the next.

Finding New-Product Ideas. An adequate flow of new-product ideas is essential to the most efficient management of new-product development. These ideas should be reasonably relevant to the capabilities of the enterprise, and they should be gathered in sufficient number to present a real choice of opportunities. Securing relevant ideas depends in large part on the formulation of a product-planning policy based upon careful appraisal of the enterprise and the communication of this policy throughout the organization so that each individual or group is aware of the kinds of new-product fields the company is most interested in. This procedure not only stimulates thinking in desired areas but also diminishes the number of ideas that must be discarded because of their inherent lack of suitability. Otherwise, people who submit ideas are often not aware of the yardsticks by which they are judged and become discouraged when they are consistently turned down.

Of course, the danger in utilizing a product-planning policy statement of this sort is that company personnel will develop blinders, which lead them to ignore new-product ideas with such large profit potentials that management might wisely disregard the limitations of the enterprise and set up an entirely new manufacturing and selling organization to exploit them. This danger is probably more fancied than real in most situations, although it must be accepted as a risk. It can be avoided in part in the process of communicating the product-planning policy by stressing the willingness of the company to enter completely new fields, provided the growth and profit potentials appear sufficiently compelling. In fact, this can be made one of the planks in the policy platform.

Finding new-product ideas involves both the identification of the many sources from which they may be derived and purposeful efforts to stimulate maximum flow from each source. Means of stimulating idea flow consist primarily of gaining and holding the interest of individuals and groups within the organization. It is very important that adequate machinery be set up for acknowledgement, prompt review, and communication of the decision to the submitter as quickly as may be feasible. Delay is usually interpreted as lack of interest on the part of management and discourages originality more quickly than any other single factor. Financial rewards have their place in the picture, and here again prompt administration is highly important. Some companies have experimented with suggestion systems as a means of encouraging new-product ideas, and when properly managed they have been of some value. They appear to be less effective, however, in encouraging new-product ideas than in developing suggestions for other phases of company operations.

The major sources of product ideas include field surveys of users, prospects, and distributors, as well as surveys of related or different markets, the research and development staff, the technical service staff, salesmen, executive personnel of the company, analyses of competitive product mixes, analyses of company sales, the patent department, inventors, literature search, and various outside sources such as trade associations, professional societies, trade shows and exhibits, and so forth.

Field surveys represent a definite effort to uncover industrial needs for product modifications and for new products. Although a technically trained salesman should always be alert to such needs, he is often too busy selling to devote adequate attention to searching out new product opportunities. Furthermore, a field survey may be directed as much to the research personnel of customers and prospects as it is to their buying and production personnel. The research groups are working on products the customer will have in production sometime in the future. Since the new-product development process often takes years, an intelligent search for ideas must look to the period ahead, rather than strictly to the present product lines of customers. The same kind of forward thinking applies to new materials or equipment that may serve future manufacturing processes.

In addition to the study of present customers and prospects, a new-product field survey may well be directed at related markets or, in some cases, entirely new markets, provided there is a logical reason for considering entry into them. In one progressive manufacturing company, a new product was developed for the printing field because the company had unusual manufacturing know-how that could be applied to the product. Prior to that time, no sales had been made to the printing industry, and therefore it was necessary to recruit, train, and operate a new sales force. When this had been done, the company management realized that the sales force was capable of handling more than one product line for the printing trade, and so it undertook a study of printing to uncover new items that could be made efficiently with the company's know-how and manufacturing facilities. This study revealed that there was a real opportunity for an article that would appreciably increase labor productivity in one aspect of the printing operation.

The research and development departments represent unusually fruitful sources of new-product ideas. Many of the men in research and development are highly imaginative and are accustomed to working with new concepts. Although they are not always fully aware of the commercial requirements of new products, this limitation can be met in part by communication of the product-planning policy and more largely through the efforts of the research director to create in his staff an understanding of cost and profit problems. One important characteristic of research workers as a source is that they are typically thinking ahead to future technology and are not too heavily influenced by current industrial practices.

In addition to ideas that may spring from research workers themselves, an active program of research in a company inevitably produces many by-products in terms of possible materials or equipment not among the primary objectives of the research effort. When a research project directed to a certain end turns up new-product ideas not contemplated in its original purpose, they are usually shelved in a "possible project" file for examination at a future time. Too often, they are forgotten. These by products frequently represent promising opportunities, either for development by the company or for sale or license to other firms. One chemical company found it very worthwhile to review the new-product projects it had placed on the shelf (because they did not fit company needs closely enough), and, through license arrangements or sale, to exploit these properties and derive some income from them.

The technical service staff is in close contact with the problems of applying company products to customer needs. Such staffs frequently are specialized by customer industries and thus have an intimate knowledge of their changing needs. The technical service group usually handles customers' complaints about the technical characteristics or performance of the product. These complaints sometimes suggest new-product ideas. In general, though, the technical service group probably will suggest improvements of present products rather than new products.

The sales force as a source of product ideas suffers from a tendency to closely relate ideas to present product lines, and particularly to variations of those lines, in order to meet specific customer desires. However, the salesman is in an unusually good position to uncover opportunities for new products because of his day-to-day contact with customers and the necessity of thorough familiarity with competitive products and activities. If he is alert and has the right kind of contacts with his customers, he may be able to pick up some indications of the direction of their product planning and research, which may provide tipoffs about materials and equipment they are likely to need in the future.

The value of the industrial sales force as a source depends somewhat on the distribution policy followed by the company. If sales flow mainly through distributor channels, these provide a sort of insulation between user and company with regard to detailed knowledge of the user's needs and desires. However, even here an alert sales force will maintain close contact with some of the larger customers of distributors, and will attempt to learn all they can from the distributors and their salesmen about problems and conditions of product use. More new-product ideas will come from salesmen when a considerable portion of sales are made direct to user accounts.

Executives in sales, production, research, and general management have perspective on the needs and probable future course of the company. They represent a source of new-product ideas that should be well adjusted to company capabilities. Some of them are likely to possess an intuitive sense of profit opportunities and of the proper timing for maximum exploitation of such ideas. In addition, they are apt to have access to the high-level trade grapevines that often carry surprisingly accurate news about the product planning and research of customers and competitors, which is a raw material for new-product ideas.

An obvious, and often rewarding, source of product ideas can be found in an analysis of the product mixes of competitors. This is particularly important in determining questions about the breadth of the product line to be handled by the company sales force or by the distributing organization. The concept of a full line is somewhat difficult to define. We have indicated that it is often desirable to sell more than one product line through a sales force, but the point of diminishing returns is difficult to identify. The breadth of the product line competitors appear to be selling successfully may serve as a crude yardstick in thinking through one's own product-mix policy.

Analyses of company sales results by product lines and by items are useful in indicating the need for the redesign of existing products when sales decline and growth opportunities when sales increase. Such analyses should not be limited to product lines, and major items within each line but should include a breakdown by type of industry to which sales are made and, if possible, by end uses.

The company patent department is often a fruitful source of ideas because its members are trained to think in terms of new products. In the course of patent searches and in writing patent descriptions for company inventions, ideas may occur to them.

Free-lance inventors represent a source of ideas, although it appears they are not so important as they once were. This is partly a reflection of the complex technology of our day, which makes it more difficult for the individual working alone to create viable products. Nonetheless, companies still add worthwhile products brought to them by free-lance inventors. And they also turn them down, as was illustrated by Xerox, which was refused by at least two blue-chip firms before it was finally introduced.

An obvious source of ideas may be found in literature searches, both in United States publications and in foreign journals. In one instance, a piece of medical equipment was developed in a foreign country and secured extensive adoption in hospitals there. It later appeared in the United States through import channels. The practice of following foreign technical literature enabled one company to have similar equipment on sale before the imports appeared.

A variety of other sources of new-product ideas may be found outside the company. These include professional society meetings, trade shows and exhibits, government research programs and publications, university research activities, consulting organizations, and others. The problem is to be sure that these sources are tapped without excessive expenditure of time and energy.

By an orderly and imaginative effort to stimulate the flow of product ideas, a satisfactory pool of them can be developed for consideration in the preliminary screening process. The mortality of new-product ideas is very high. Some years ago, the Commercial Chemical Development Association[2] questioned 20 chemical firms about the mortality rate of new-product ideas in their experience. It was found that in order to obtain one successful new product an average of:

540 possibilities in the idea stage were considered at the research level.
448 were eliminated during screening conferences.
 92 were selected for preliminary laboratory investigation.
  8 were sufficiently promising to warrant further development.
  7 were dropped as unsalable or unprofitable before or during the semiworks stage.
  1 survived and was placed in regular production.

[2] H. M. Corley (ed.), *Successful Commercial Chemical Development* (New York: John Wiley & Sons, Inc., 1954).

An average of six years and two months was required from the time an idea was originally investigated in the research department until full-scale production was attained.

This study indicates the scale of shrinkage that takes place in the original fund of new-product ideas in the chemical industry as they are developed into products that eventually are marketed. Another study covering companies in a number of industries shows an overall ratio of 40 to 1 from the screening stage to successful introduction.[3] A study by the National Industrial Conference Board, reported in the *New York Times*, October 25, 1964, showed that 1 out of every 3 products put on the market by the 87 reporting companies failed. Adding new products is a risky business, and they need to be picked carefully.

Preliminary Appraisal of New-Product Ideas. This step has two major purposes. The first is to eliminate ideas that are clearly unworthy of further consideration and investigation. The second is to select from among the remainder those with enough promise to be set up as new-product projects for exploratory work by the technical research and development staffs. Two steps seem desirable in this process. First, the product-planning staff may measure each new-product idea against the general product-planning policy of the company. This permits a substantial reduction in the number, and the remainder will be those that merit more careful consideration. The product-planning staff may, as a second step, gather certain readily accessible data on each idea to provide the new-product committee with additional information on which to base judgment.

A new-product committee normally consists of executives from marketing, production, research, and general management, with others brought in as the occasion requires.

In this preliminary appraisal process, much reliance is properly placed on the experience and judgment of the executives present. Because of the multiplicity of factors that affect the desirability of pursuing any specific new-product idea, it is often useful to develop a checklist of questions to be answered. The checklist approach has the merit of preventing the omission of vital factors in the heat of a discussion session. If the company product mix is fairly homogeneous, one such checklist may serve the purpose; if not, it may be necessary to have more than one. Generalized types of checklists have been published by the United States Department of Commerce. One of these relates specifically to industrial products.[4] Although it is essential that the entire range of factors be considered, it is not necessary that detailed information be available at this stage. The emphasis is, rather, on uncovering possible weak points that might lead to a decision to drop the idea.

Major factors for consideration usually include such things as expected

[3] Booz, Allen and Hamilton, *op. cit.*, Chart 7, p. 11.

[4] Gustav E. Larson, *Developing and Selling New Products* (Washington, D.C.: United States Department of Commerce, 1950), pp. 51–58.

profit potential of the new product, the competitive situation, the general adaptability of the company to the new product, and the scale of investment that would be necessary in relation to the funds the company has available. Marketing considerations include the approximate size of the market, the trends operating within it, marketing methods that would be necessary for successful sale, price structures, and so forth.

Many new-product ideas involve problems of technical design. Thus, it becomes necessary to judge the technical feasibility of the idea and estimate the likelihood of success in solving technical problems. Production considerations also enter in the form of the nature of production facilities required, approximate costs of production, availability of materials, and continuity of their supply. At times, legal considerations also enter, both as to the patent situation and as to hazards that may accompany customer use of the product.

Meetings of the new-product committee to conduct preliminary appraisals should be held at regular intervals. The committee will probably also consider projects that were approved at earlier meetings and have now reached a point requiring more detailed consideration.

Several firms have attempted to develop formulas to use as tools in making new-product decisions. Such a formula worked out for use by a fine chemical house is shown in Figure 8–1, with some changes to protect confidential information. A critical total score was worked out by applying the formula in retrospect to a number of products the company had introduced and comparing scores with actual performance.

Such a formula assures that all the factors generally significant in a new-product decision are considered in a systematic, uniform manner. But its use has dangers. When men have a formula, they tend to quit thinking. Any new-product idea may have one feature that outweighs all others and that is not general in the sense that few other ideas or none have it. A formula is apt to be disastrous if used by a committee or staff group composed entirely of conformists. It may work very well for a group that contains one or more highly vocal people who always look for the unusual in every situation.

Although the use of formulas in making new-product decisions is growing slightly, it is still confined to a relatively small number of companies.

Research on Products and Markets. This stage covers the technical, economic, and market research carried on after an idea has been selected as a new-product project in the preliminary appraisal. The amount of technical research necessary will vary greatly, depending on the difficulties involved in achieving a satisfactory product. The more nearly similar the new product is to those currently being manufactured, the less likely is the need for significant amounts of technical work. During this stage, the physical properties of the new product are discovered, small quantities are prepared in the laboratory, research on possible uses is initiated, preliminary work on patents starts, and preliminary estimates of production costs

FIGURE 8–1. Formula for Selecting New Products

		Total Possible Score
Estimated volume of sales (annual) :[1]		10
under $250,000 .... Not considered		
$250,000–1 million	2	
1–5 million	5	
5–15 million	10	
15 million and up	7	
Market protection:[2]		20
Product patentable	20	
Chemistry highly complex (nonpatentable) ...	15	
Much production know-how needed (non-patentable)	15	
High investment needed (nonpatentable)	10	
Marketing factors:[3]		10
Technical service needed	4	
Sold to present customers	6	
Sold to a new trade	4	
Sold to both	6	
Bulk:[4]		10
Made and sold in carloads or trainloads	2	
Made and sold in truckloads	5	
Made and sold in drums	10	
Made and sold in smaller quantities (unless value very high)	7	
Estimated net profit on investment:[5]		20
Less than 6% after taxes .... Not considered		
6–7%	6	
7–9	10	
9–10	15	
10 plus	20	
Nature:[6]		15
Involves human health	15	
Involves animal health	10	
Involves nutrition (human or animal)	10	
Other	7	
Kind of research needed:[7]		10
Biological and organic	10	
Other	5	
Special factors:[8]		5
Government clearance needed	5	
Other	?	
		100

[1] A product with less than $250,000 annual sales is apt to get lost in the shuffle and not receive proper managerial attention. The larger its sales volume above about 10 to 12 million, the more likely the product is to be worth the attention of giant competitors, such as Du Pont or Monsanto.

[2] This company is very good at highly complex chemistry and has a lot of production know-how in dealing with it. Relatively high investment keeps out the quonset hut and reconverted garage competitors.

[3] This company is strong in its technical service. Products sold to present customers can be handled by the present sales force and marketing channels. Those sold to a new trade are harder to introduce but not subject to volume limitations imposed by customer purchasing officers.

[4] This company is not good at handling carload business but in applying large-scale techniques to relatively small batches or production runs.

[5] This company's average earnings on investment are about 7.5 percent after taxes. To carry on the necessary research and build retained earnings to finance new projects, it must net that or more.

[6] The company has a traditional position in the field of public health and nutrition, and its people are oriented in that direction.

[7] Management has found it difficult to organize and conduct research outside the field of special competence and interest of its scientific personnel. A laboratory is more than a lot of apparatus and the scientists to man it.

[8] Management has developed great skill in presenting products to government regulatory bodies so as to secure their prompt action and, generally, their approval. Nothing crooked is involved here, but merely a thorough understanding of the regulatory standards used and the tests and facts and the manner of their preparation and presentation that these bodies demand. Confidence engendered by careful testing and honest reporting is also heavily involved.

are made. Some industrial products, especially materials and supplies, lend themselves to limited field distribution of sample quantities, and thus permit preliminary evaluation of their suitability to the needs of selected consumers. The market development staff should also prepare a study of the economic possibilities of the new product.

Research on Manufacturing Processes. In point of time, this stage may overlap research on the product and market. The technical groups study the most feasible methods for producing the new product and development information needed for patent application. Quality control problems are investigated, and plans made for handling this problem in the semi-works and later stages. The market development staff continues the search for prospective users of the new product and carries on the limited field testing possible with laboratory quantities. This testing work is usually done by selected customers who agree to cooperate, often in return for assurances of early supply if the product proves satisfactory.

Market development groups and marketing research groups at this stage begin work on a suitable product name and package. Also, there should be careful review of the product design to make sure that all feasible suggestions gathered by the limited field evaluation have been incorporated. As a result of process-development research in this stage and product research in this and the earlier stages, together with marketing and economic data, it is possible to prepare a report containing recommendations for follow-up action in the new-product project. The project should then be reviewed by the new-product committee in the light of the study and action taken on moving into the semiworks stage, undertaking further work if information seems inadequate, conducting further research if testing has shown serious product defects, or perhaps abandoning the project.

Semiworks Stage. This portion of the development process has as one of its major objectives testing of the proposed method of manufacture by actually building a limited-scale plant and producing the article in small quantities. Since larger amounts of the product are available, the market development group can conduct reasonably full-scale testing with a limited number of customers. Total production at this stage, of course, is quite small, and the quantity available must be allocated carefully in order to get the maximum amount of market information. The technical groups continue work on process development until the operating problems at the semiworks level are solved. They also carry on use research and develop information needed for patent applications. At this point, it is also possible for a technical service group to become familiar with the use problems of the new product.

The market development group continues its program of field evaluation and sales, and with the larger quantities available it should be able to more nearly approach actual conditions of later marketing. The sales organization can start to become familiar with the new product and perhaps engage in actual sales training. During this period, also, promotional strategy for the new product should be worked out and decisions reached concerning selling methods to be used.

About this time, the brand name of the new product is chosen, and if it must be sold in a container, package design is determined. Perhaps at this point, we might be wise to briefly discuss these matters. Neither the brand nor the package plays in industrial marketing a part so important as in consumer goods. But they are significant enough to justify careful attention.

Industrial goods that are highly standardized and sold in bulk, chiefly materials, are usually not branded. The same usually is true of component parts made to specification for the buying firm or not interchangeable among the end products of competing customers. For example, tires, batteries, and spark plugs that are interchangeable among different makes of cars and command an active replacement market are branded. Most castings and machined parts are not.

Major machinery tends to be sold under the name of the maker, although subsidiary brands are sometimes used to distinguish different types or sizes of a machine. This may be true of tractors and construction equipment, for example. Auxiliary machines are usually sold under brand. Process materials are quite generally branded, as are operating supplies.

In marketing industrial goods, the brand function of identifying and distinguishing the maker's product is much more important than its job of exerting a positive persuasive force at the point of sale, as in consumer goods. As a result, there is much less need for brands to be catchy, to have euphony, to sing when pronounced. But there is some point in their having a technical or scientific flavor. Such brand names as Kazon, Zembide, Nicarb, and Glycamide illustrate this tendency. The trick seems to be to pick a name near the scientific or chemical designation of the material or article, but not so near that it is legally indefensible. In originating names, some firms seek to reenforce imagination with science by using computers to develop a large stock of pronounceable combinations of the letters in the alphabet. The results are sometimes weird.

When a firm makes and markets a family of industrial products, special problems of branding arise. In the consumer goods field each one of a family of products must stand on its own feet at the point of sale, and there is no compelling reason for a family brand, since ultimate consumers tend to rely more on what they know about the product than on what they know about its maker in choosing articles. The industrial buyer, on the other hand, is heavily influenced by what he knows about the manufacturer of a product. So a family brand or a family resemblance among brands is highly important. But as the number of products in the family grows and becomes diversified, such a family brand system may become highly complicated and bewildering.

One solution to this dilemma is to use one overriding brand, preferably the company name or the dominating element in the company name, that applies to all products, and a system of subsidiary brand names that apply to individual products. For example, the Irwin Equipment Company might make and sell the Irwin Earth Master for heavy excavation jobs, the Irwin Little Giant for finer earth-moving work, the Irwin Ditchdigger's Delight, and similar but perhaps less euphonious and more dignified brands for other construction implements. This is not the only solution, but simplicity and consistency are attributes to be earnestly sought.

The primary purposes of the industrial goods package are to protect the contents and to facilitate handling. Its use as a promotional device is definitely secondary, since the buyer usually does not have the package before him when he orders the product. But the package can contribute sales appeal if its size and shape facilitate handling by the user's material handling equipment and it fits snugly into the standard shelving or other storage facilities generally used in his warehouses, and if its color scheme is such that it can be readily located and recognized on his shelves or storage floor.

Certain materials that are corrosive, or must be delivered under pressure, or that deteriorate if exposed to air, or absorb moisture, or evaporate rapidly, to mention only a few of the many hazards, must be sold in packages that are fairly costly and often heavy. This adds to the cost of transportation and may create a package return problem that always contributes a high nuisance value and leads to disputes and misunderstandings. The manufacturer of such products can wisely afford considerable research to develop nonreturnable packages in which to deliver them.

The same is true with packages that are very heavy. For example, a firm that sells gases used in refrigeration and air-conditioning units packaged its product in two sizes of steel containers, the larger weighing 72 pounds with contents, and the smaller 40 pounds. The distributors' service men had to lug them over roofs and down into basements and other awkward places. Aluminum containers with overall weights of 64 and 35 pounds, respectively, cost more but won the hearts of service men, and so the business of the distributors who employed them.

The makers of certain kinds of industrial materials and equipment face legal hurdles in introducing new products. For example, before the producer of a chemical used in medicines can market it, he must gain approval of the Food and Drug Administration by supplying evidence that it will do what he says it will do, and will have no more than allowable toxic side effects. In order to gain clearance, he must submit the results of approved independent clinical tests to satisfy the Administration.

This requirement has both good and bad effects on the manufacturer's marketing activities.

1. It delays the introduction of the product. Not only does it take a long time to complete clinical tests, but after they are submitted the manufacturer must await completion of any supplementary tests the Administration decides

to make and the slow unwinding of its bureaucratic red tape, which is further delayed by chronic undermanning due to the niggardly policy of Congress in dealing with its budget.

2. The conduct of such clinical tests and presentation of their results in a form that suits the needs of the Administration is an art in itself.

3. The timing of the Administration's release may bear no relation to the ebb and flow of demand. Many diseases are seasonal, and the release of a product at the end of the season may lose the maker a whole year in its introduction to the market. Nor can the time of release be forecast with any accuracy. So marketing plans must be prepared in detail and then held in abeyance, often to become outdated before they can be put into effect.

4. On the other hand, once the Administration issues a release, this in itself goes far to assure users that the product will do what is claimed for it, and thus materially eases the marketing task.

The maker of a food additive must have a release from the Administration, showing that its use will have no dangerous toxic effects on the people who consume the end products containing it. The manufacturer of a plant protective material or one designed to cure or prevent diseases of animals or fowl or to stimulate the growth of animals, poultry, or plants must obtain such a release, assuring that no toxic residue remains in the meat, milk, eggs, fruits, or vegetables when prepared for human consumption. This requirement adds all the handicaps mentioned above in connection with medicinal materials, but does not establish that the product will do what it is designed to do. It constitutes merely a manufacturer's hunting license to try to capture sales, and affords no particular help in doing so.

Aside from the benefits of the Administration's work in protecting the public health, most manufacturers of such materials welcome these restrictions because they tend to preclude irresponsible producers from plaguing them with a type of competition very difficult to combat.

The makers of many kinds of building materials and equipment must see to it that the safety and fire-resisting properties of their products meet the requirements of the Board of Fire Underwriters and the local building codes. Since the codes differ from city to city, meeting their standards may be very cumbersome, time-consuming, and expensive.

As a result of the semiworks stage, information is usually at hand concerning production methods for full-scale operation and estimates of production costs. Likewise, the product should have proved itself in market-evaluation tests, and information about probable uses should be available. Prices will have been set during the semiworks stage, and the expected price on full-scale production will be known. With this information, it is possible to reexamine the size of the market. With all of this information, profit return on the new product can be estimated. The report is presented to the new-products committee, and if the project is approved for full-scale manufacturing and marketing it may be sent to top management for final action. This is a point at which the company commits large funds.

Full-Scale Manufacturing and Marketing. New-product projects approved for movement into full-scale manufacturing and marketing are in the final stage of assimilation by the company organization. During the period required to get into full-scale production, various activities started earlier during the development process, such as providing packaging, shipping containers, advertising, technical literature, and the like, can be completed so that the new product will be ready for introduction to a market wider than could be served with the limited quantity available in the semiworks stage.

PLANNING THE INTRODUCTION OF A NEW PRODUCT

The final step in product development is making plans and programs for introducing the new product on the market, and merging it into the product mix. In the course of doing this, a number of questions must be answered. Some of the most important are the following.

1. What channels of distribution shall be used in marketing the new product? The situation is ideal, of course, when a firm can effectively sell its new product through the same channels used for its other products. This is not always possible, for the new product may serve different groups of buyers or require different marketing treatment from the items already in the line. Sometimes, plans for adding a new product must be abandoned because it cannot be marketed effectively through existing channels and cannot be sold in sufficient volume through its natural outlets to support the cost of cultivating them. Difficulties such as this should be faced long before a new product reaches the full-scale manufacturing stage, but often they are not.

2. What should be the relation of the new product to those already in the line? The new product may be a complete addition to the product mix and simply make the whole mix more attractive to prospective buyers. Or it may be a complete replacement of an old product, since it will perform all the functions of the old, and perform them more effectively. Again, the new product may perform some functions more effectively than the old one, but may serve other uses no better or even less efficiently. For example, a firm whose product was a preparation that when mixed with the feed of animals cured a certain disease developed a new preparation, which was a good preventive but no better cure. The management was faced with the problem of deciding the better policy: (*a*) to discontinue production and sale of the old product, for which it had built up a considerable demand and which was widely known to the trade; or (*b*) to produce the two side-by-side, thereby sacrificing some of the savings of large-scale production, and promote the one as a cure and the other as a preventive. Sometimes, a new machine replaces an old one used in con-

junction with another machine that must be replaced or scrapped when the new one is put into operation. For example, a dictating machine company brought out a new machine, which recorded on nonreusable, foldable, fileable belts instead of on wax cylinders that could be shaved and reused. Buyers of the new machine had no use for the shaving machines (also sold by the company) they had in operation. The dictating machine company had the alternative of (*a*) continuing to produce the old machines until all customers gradually shifted to the new, or (*b*) discontinuing manufacture of the old machine and putting all its eggs in the new basket.

3. At what price should the new product be sold, and what pricing policies should be adopted with respect to it? When the new article is entirely new and replaces no item previously in the line, this problem is highly complex. Complexity becomes even more confusing when it replaces an old product already in the line, for which there are established prices and pricing policies. If the new product is highly attractive and there is obviously a ready demand for it, should its price be fixed at a very high figure that will enable the firm to amortize all its development costs and the cost of special equipment needed in its production within the six-month to two-year period that usually elapses before serious competition develops? Or is it better policy to fix the price at about the level where it may be expected to settle under competitive conditions and thus perhaps discourage the development of competition? These and other matters affecting the pricing of new products will be discussed in a later chapter.

4. What should be the policy with respect to inventories of the new product? Enough will be needed to service an unknown and uncertain demand, but the amount stocked must be kept small enough so that the possible failure of the new product to capture demand will not result in an overly serious commitment of the firm's funds in inventory.

5. What appeals will be most effective in promoting the sale of the new product? It is a task of no small difficulty to find out why people buy or refuse to buy a product that is well known and has been long on the market. It is infinitely harder to discover what motivations will determine customer behavior toward a new unknown product. These difficulties are somewhat less with industrial goods than with consumer goods, since the former tend to be bought largely on the basis of a dollars-and-cents analysis, while sales of the latter occur to a great extent in response to consumer taste, whim, and emotion. Marketing research through the use of various product and market-testing devices can be of considerable aid in determining what buying motives are apt to be the most influential in effecting sales of a new product; but often a true appraisal of the power of its several sales appeals must await the application of the trial and error method in the market.

The Importance of Timing

Timing is usually the essence of good performance in introducing new products into the market. If the operations of the buying industries are subject to seasonal ebb and flow, a decision must be made on whether the new product shall be brought out during the slack season, when buyers can give more time to examining it and learning about it, or at the beginning of the busy season, when they may be expected to be more in the buying mood. There are strong arguments for both sides of this issue. In many cases, the matter may be settled by the incidence of the widely attended trade shows or expositions that operate in most industries. Such an event offers a highly effective platform from which to introduce a new product—so effective, in fact, that many firms as a matter of course utilize the show for this purpose. Of course, the developmental activities of competitors may supply the decisive factor in timing the introduction of the new product. If two competing firms are at work on the development of about the same kind of product—a situation that prevails more often than is commonly thought—the one that breaks the new product first enjoys a definite advantage.

Once the release date for a new product is fixed, plans must be made to synchronize a whole program of activities, each of which is vital to its successful and profitable launching. In some cases, new or additional production equipment must be procured, installed, and put into operation so that its output will be available in time to supply the expected demand when the new product is launched. Adequate inventory must be built up to service the demand that may be reasonably expected; if sales are to be made through distributors, a supply must be placed in the stocks of each according to his probable needs. If the new product supplants an old one, the stocks of the old product, both in the hands of distributors and of the industrial marketer, must be depleted to the minimum consistent with continuing service to customers. One machine maker uses an option plan whereby it announces new models a long time ahead of their introduction, and accords customers the option of buying old models during the interim to be exchanged for new models when they appear, less a $25-a-month use charge.

The salesmen of the manufacturer and of his distributors must be trained to handle the new product. The start of active selling work must be synchronized with the availability of the product in the stocks of the marketer or his distributors. The advertising must be timed to stimulate demand when the new product is released and to take advantage of the publicity value of its newness; but it must not effect this result too early, because orders that cannot be filled have a corroding influence on customer goodwill.

In the introduction of certain types of new industrial products, the timing of all these activities is complicated by the necessity or desirability of obtaining releases from governmental bodies, such as the Food and Drug Administration, or the approval of public or semipublic bodies, such as the American Medical Association or the National Board of Fire Underwriters.

PRODUCT DELETION

One more problem of product management remains to be discussed— deletion. Products die, just as they are born. Like people, many of them take a long time to die, and in the process they become decrepit so that their bills must be paid by others. A declining product usually yields little profit, or none at all; it uses capital, labor, and facilities for which it makes no adequate return; it demands an exorbitant amount of executive time and attention.

Unlike homicide, to kill aging products is no crime. Unless a firm in a dynamic industry has a procedure for doing so, and unless its management sees to it that the process of deletion is carried on consistently, its product mix is almost bound to be cluttered with items that do not pull their weight. Such a procedure includes several steps.

Selecting Candidates for Deletion

This involves examining the product mix to discover items that should be studied with the understanding that one of the possible outcomes of the study may be a decision to delete. Some factors that suggest a product as the subject of such a study are:

A declining volume of sales.
A falling rate of profit.
A declining share of the market.
The appearance of a substitute that represents an improvement.
An increasing cost of production.
A declining market.
The need for constant executive attention to prevent loss.

No one of these things is cause for deletion. The occurrence of any one or a combination of them does suggest the need for a careful examination of why it is happening and what can be done about it. Deletion is one of the things that may be done.

Gathering and Analyzing Information for Decision

Usually, the organization unit that has the job of selecting candidates for deletion should also be charged with the task of gathering facts about products that are suspect, analyzing them, and making recommendations for decision. Probably the first objective of such a study should be to discover why the product is going sour, and how far and in what directions the process of deterioration has gone. In the process of finding these facts, the group will probably uncover numerous suggestions on what to do about the matter and facts that indicate the feasibility of each alternative.

In the course of this study, the decision makers should seek the answers to several questions.

1. Is there any way in which we can salvage the product and restore its profitability? We may try earnestly, but not too optimistically, to cut costs. We may market it in a less costly or more effective way. We may change its design to increase its customer benefits or to reduce its costs. We may cut price, hoping to get enough increase in sales volume to make cost reductions possible.

2. If we delete the product, how much of the capital now used in making and marketing it can we salvage? The working capital—that invested in accounts receivable and inventories of materials, goods in process, and finished goods—will drain back into the cash account as final production runs of the product are made, sold, and paid for if the deletion process is done properly and before it becomes a crisis action.

The capital invested in equipment is another matter. The machines may be flexible so that they can be used to make some other product if one is available. Or we may be able to sell them for their unamortized value. Or we may face the choice of scrapping them and writing off the loss or continuing to make and sell the product as long as its price yields something more than the direct costs, or until the entire investment has been amortized.

3. If we delete the product, have we in sight for the capital and human resources released some use that promises to net the company more than the product now does? This matter of opportunity cost is one often overlooked.

4. What will deletion do to our labor relations and to our moral obligations to our employees? Theoretically, if we can make our peace with the union we should worry no further about the effect of a deletion on the lives of our employees. But if the demise of a product will take the jobs of a group of long-time pipe-bending shop workers who know nothing but pipe-bending and are too old to learn other skills, management may show a pronounced reluctance to dispense with its pipe-bending operations.

5. How will the deletion of this product affect our marketing operations? It may be that the resulting decline in sales will force a reduction in either the number or quality of our salesmen. A much more general danger, though, lies in the possibility that the product to be deleted is needed by customers who buy from us sizable volumes of profitable products and who will switch their entire patronage if they must go

elsewhere to get their supply of the product. This matter needs careful, cold-blooded analysis without the semihysterical assumptions a volume-conscious sales force is likely to harbor.

6. What will deletion do to operating costs? It is often assumed that dropping a product relieves a firm of all its so-called direct costs, mainly labor and materials. This is usually true of materials but not always of labor. The same people often work on several products. When one of these products is dropped, most of the people are still needed to handle the remaining ones. Dropping a product often causes a decline in direct costs that is less than proportional to the decrease in sales volume it brings about.

Very rarely will the deletion of a product enable a firm to make any reduction in its overhead costs. They remain about the same and must be respread over the surviving products.

7. What effect will a product's deletion have on total net profits? In answering this question, the decision maker must take into account its effect on costs, on volume of sales not only of the dropped product but of others as well, the effect of the shift of salvaged resources to the most promising alternative uses, the volume of gross profit, and other factors. If the volume involved is large, perhaps it will be worthwhile to compare an estimated budget after all foreseeable adjustments are made with the budget to be expected if the product is retained in the mix.

The Details of Deletion

Once a deletion decision is made, its details must be planned. It should be timed so as to cause the least disruption of the firm's operations and of those of distributors and customers. If the article is mechanical, a supply of spare parts must be provided for the soon-to-be orphan product. Customers should be informed far enough ahead to make new arrangements for their needs, but not far enough to prevent the cleaning out of company stocks and those of distributors. The move must be explained to customers in a way that will cause the least ill will.

Deletion is a drab, unexciting, depressing business, but it is necessary if the product mix is to be kept up-to-date and the firm's resources kept employed in the profitable projects that make for growth and survival.

SUMMARY

In this chapter, we have indicated the importance of the product-planning and management function in the industrial goods field, and have outlined some of its difficulties. We briefly discussed the general factors—technical research, competitors' product action, changes in market demand, shifts in customers' product mixes, shifts in customer location, seasonal or cyclical nature of demand, and government controls—that tend to emphasize the importance of product management as well as to complicate it. In addition, we referred to several factors that tend to force the industrial marketer to broaden his product mix, such as the buyer's desire to procure several product lines from a single source, the desire to reduce marketing costs by making full use of necessary facilities, the appeal of a wide line, and the desire to utilize excess capacity or waste materials.

We saw that good product management begins with a careful appraisal of a firm's strengths and weaknesses in its present product mix, production facilities and know-how, research abilities, technical service, marketing organization and capacity, financial strength, and the talents and attitudes of its management. We examined the organization for product planning and management. We outlined several steps in the process of product development, and discussed the problems most usually found in each of them. The steps we found convenient for our discussion were: finding new product ideas, screening them, research, semiworks operations, and initiating full-scale production and marketing activity. We concluded our treatment with a short description of some of the problems involved in a product deletion program.

CASES APPLICABLE TO PART III

PART IV

The Problems of Managing
Marketing Channels

ONE OF THE difficult problems faced by the industrial goods manufacturer is that of choosing marketing channels through which he will try to move his output to market. This is partly a matter of selecting the types of outlets through which he attempts to distribute. With the exception of manufacturers' branch houses and sales offices, these are known as middlemen because they intervene between the maker and the user of a product, performing a number of functions in marketing it.

A companion problem is that of negotiating and administering the relationships with and among the firms in the channel. For many industrial goods marketers, this is an executive activity fully as important as, and sometimes much more difficult than, managing the internal marketing organization.

Before we can intelligently discuss these problems, we must know something about the kinds of middlemen who sell industrial goods, how they operate, how many there are, how big they are, the kinds of services they render and the way they render them, and the rates of return they expect to receive for performing their part of the marketing task. For this reason, we will devote Chapter 9 to a description of these outlets, and follow it with a discussion of the problems of choosing and managing them in Chapter 10.

Chapter **9**

◇◇◇◇◇◇◇◇◇◇◇◇◇◇◇◇◇◇◇◇◇◇ **AVAILABLE OUTLETS**

FOR INDUSTRIAL GOODS

A MARKETING CHANNEL is made up of outlets through which a manufacturer's goods may flow to market.

Some of these outlets, such as manufacturer's branch houses and branch offices, are part of the internal organization structure of the manufacturing firms. Others, such as distributors or wholesalers, manufacturer's agents, sales agents, and other types of agents, are usually independently owned and operated enterprises, although some *tame cat* distributors are owned and controlled by the manufacturer.

Some of these outlets buy, own, and carry stocks of the goods they sell. Others act as agents and merely arrange contracts of purchase and sale. Let us first consider the most important group, the distributors.

INDUSTRIAL DISTRIBUTORS

Definition

The term "industrial distributor" is used with various meanings. The Bureau of the Census formerly employed it to mean an establishment that "handles a general line of industrial goods and sells largely to industrial users," not including houses that specialize in selling machinery or in serving specific industries. Some years ago, the Bureau abandoned the term and began to report its data on industrial distributors under eight major headings; some are broken down into classes, and some of these, in turn, into subclasses. In the 1963 census report, the breakdown looks about like the following:

Air conditioning, refrigeration equipment, and supplies.
Machinery, equipment, and supplies.
  Commercial, with four subclasses.
  Construction and mining.
  Industrial machinery, with seven subclasses.
  Industrial supplies, with six subclasses.
Professional equipment and supplies, with six classes.

Service establishment equipment and supplies, with six classes.
Transportation equipment and supplies, except automotive, with three
    classes.
Metals and minerals, except petroleum.
    Coal.
    Metals, with two subclasses.
Scrap and waste materials.
    Iron and steel scrap
    Waste materials, with four subclasses.
Lumber and construction materials.
    Lumber, with four subclasses.
    Construction materials, with four subclasses.

In addition, four general groups probably sell mainly to industrial
buyers, but also sell extensively for resale. They are:

Plumbing and heating equipment and supplies, with three classes.
Farm and garden machinery and equipment.
Paper and paper products, except wallpaper, with three classes.
Farm supplies, with four classes.

Several other groups, which sell mainly industrial goods, are classes or
subclasses of major groups whose sales are predominantly of consumer
goods. There are distributors of:

Trucks and tractors	Chemicals
Automotive equipment	Electrical supplies
Piece goods (jobbers)	Office and business furniture
Piece goods (converters)	Advertising specialties
Electronic parts and equipment	Forest products, except lumber
Textile bags, bagging, burlap	

You will notice that we have not included firms that handle farm
products, many of which are used as industrial materials. The reason, right
or wrong, lies in our feeling that the marketing of farm products is a
subject in its own right, and any attempt to treat the industrial part of it
here could, at best, be nothing more than a lick and a promise, which
could confuse the discussion of a subject that is by nature highly complex.

All the firms in the trades noted offer the industrial goods maker the
services of middlemen, taking title to and carrying stocks, assuming some
of the risks of marketing, and maintaining reasonably close contact with
users of his products.

Some of these houses are general in that they handle a wide variety of
industrial supplies and minor equipment, and sell to widely diversified
groups of customers. Others are specialty firms. Some specialize by handling a narrowly limited line of products, such as office stationery and
supplies, abrasives, mechanical rubber goods, or electrical wiring supplies,
sold to widely varying types of industries. Others specialize by serving
only a certain trade or industry, such as the shoe finders, the dental supply
houses, the hotel and restaurant supply firms, and the beauty and barber
supply houses.

TABLE 9–1
Statistics of Selected Groups of Industrial Distributors

	Number of Establishments				Sales per Establishment (000) Dollars				Employees per Establishment				Expenses as Per cent of Sales				Number of Days Stock on Hand			
	1939	1948	1958	1963	1939	1948	1958	1963	1939	1948	1958	1963	1939	1948	1958	1963	1939	1948	1958	1963
Industrial chemicals	746	1075	2805	3163	269	637	533	641	19	10	7	8	15.0	13.4	14.8	15.2	42	22	17	21
Electric wiring materials, equipment*	1162	2259	3106	7654	130	395	675	549	8	11	11	9	18.3	16.2	14.6	17.5	48	39	25	39
Construction materials	1633	2267	4467	5667	194	460	459	534	12	16	10	10	19.0	22.1	19.1	18.2	38	23	26	27
Commercial machinery	1643	1640	4255	5669	83	196	237	256	7	8	7	7	23.5	24.4	25.1	24.9	49	36	39	38
Industrial machinery (general)	116	839	2366	2361	606	1386	369	432	35	41	8	9	18.8	17.3	21.5	20.9	71	44	39	34
Oil-well supplies	896	1105	1444	1555	202	714	679	540	6	9	7	6	10.5	9.2	12.0	14.4	63	41	32	37
Industrial supplies (general and specialties)			6180	7267			415	502			9	10			20.3	20.2			40	39
Industrial supplies (general)				1112				821				15				19.3				46
Mechanical power transmission equipment			596	855			409	424			9	9			21.1	21.7			47	54
Professional equipment and supplies	1634	2253	3663	4567	106	239	366	463	11	12	11	11	28.8	25.7	24.3	23.8	68	55	42	45
Surgical, medical, hospital supplies		643	1387	1343		334	467	647		13	11	12		22.8	21.2	20.0	125	46	36	39
Service establishment supplies	3008	3520	4014	5658	89	211	259	274	6	7	7	7	21.1	19.1	24.7	26.3	51	46	35	40
Transportation equipment	244	809	1387	1650	267	416	444	518	11	10	9	10	17.9	18.6	21.7	21.2		38	37	44
Iron and steel products†		1866	3247	1803†		988	985	1,949		19	17	27		14.9	18.4	16.7		36	49	52
Nonferrous metals†		840	849	878†		2069	1677	2,166		21	14	23		7.3	8.1	13.6		20	23	35
Construction equipment	404	2006	2143	2358	239	861	936	1,108	13	20	13	17	20.1	16.5	18.8	18.2	59	52	62	68

* Includes electrical supplies and electronic parts and equipment houses in 1963.
† Drop shippers omitted in 1963.
SOURCE: Reports of the Wholesale Census, 1939, 1948, 1958, 1963.

Table 9–1 presents information about some of the more important groups of industrial distributors. A study of this table discloses the following significant facts about industrial distributors as a group.

1. They increased considerably in number from 1939 to 1963. An increase occurred in every one of the nine trades for which comparable figures in all four census years are shown in the table. This is probably due largely to the tremendous upward surge in industrial activity that took place during and after World War II.

2. Their total dollar sales also enjoyed a pronounced increase during the period. However, because of the very great increase in the number of firms in several trades the average sales per firm declined in some groups from 1948 to 1963.

3. Costs as a percentage of sales apparently tended to decline from 1939 to 1948, and to creep back up between 1948 and 1963. The reason probably was, in part at least, the decline in dollar volume of sales per establishment; many of the expenses of industrial distributors behave like overhead costs in that their total remains about the same in the face of wide shifts in sales volume.

4. The number of persons employed by industrial distributors tended to increase from 1939 to 1948, and then to decline or hold constant between 1948 and 1963. The average number of employees per establishment gives evidence of the relative smallness of the firms in this trade. Of the 16 trade groups, 11 in 1963 employed an average of less than a dozen persons per establishment.

5. During the 19-year period, there was a pronounced tendency among these firms to shrink their stocks in relation to sales. This may have been the outcome of the increased understanding of the true costs of carrying inventory that has developed during the period. There were some increases between 1958 and 1963.

Geographical Distribution

Industrial distributors are highly concentrated geographically. They may be found mainly in areas that have a heavy concentration of manufacturing establishments. Table 9–2 shows the percent of the total number of distributors in certain trades who are located in selected states of their greatest concentration, and the percentage of total trade sales volume made by the distributors in those states.

A noticeable feature of the table is the repeated appearance of a few heavily industrialized states, such as New York, Pennsylvania, California, Illinois, and Ohio. In recent years, Texas has increased in importance as a location for industrial distributors, as have Michigan and Florida.

A very large percentage of the industrial distributors with a heavy preponderance of total sales volume is located in large cities or in the industrial or trading satellites of such cities. This is shown by the following 1963 list of the percentages of the total number of establishments and total volume of distributor sales for several trade groups in cities of 500,000 or more population.

A similar table, showing the geographical distribution of the manufac-

Trade Group	Percent of Establish- ments	Percent of Total Distributor Sales
Electrical supplies, apparatus*.....................39		51
Electronic parts...............................38		48
Chemicals....................................44		58
Commercial and industrial equipment and supplies......39		44
Professional equipment and supplies...............51		58
Service equipment and supplies....................48		61
Transportation equipment........................49		52
Metals and minerals.............................45		62
Lumber and construction materials..................31		39
Air conditioning and refrigeration equipment and supplies.................................43		56

* These firms handle some consumer's goods.
SOURCE: U.S. Bureau of the Census, *1963 Census of Business, Wholesale Trade*, Washington, D.C.

TABLE 9–2

States of Greatest Concentration of Selected Groups of Distributors, 1963

	Transportation Equipment and Supplies	Service Machinery and Supplies	Metal Products	Industrial Supplies	Industrial Machinery and Supplies	Construction Materials	Construction Machinery	Commercial Equipment	Chemicals and Supplies
California	X	X	X	X	X	X	X	X	X
Florida				X					X
Illinois	X	X	X	X		X	X	X	X
Louisiana					X				
Massachusetts								X	
Michigan				X	X	X	X		
Missouri			X						
New Jersey	X								
New York	X	X	X	X	X	X	X	X	X
Ohio	X	X	X	X	X	X	X		
Oregon			X						
Pennsylvania		X	X			X	X	X	
Texas	X	X	X	X	X	X	X	X	X
Number of states checked	6	6	8	7	6	7	7	6	5
Percent of total number of establishments in the trade in states checked	52	44	37	41	48	51	56	45	53
States checked had distributors making following percent of trade sales	59	42	33	50	52	55	65	51	55

An *X* in the line of a state indicates that distributors in the column were heavily concentrated there. Compiled and computed from U.S. Bureau of the Census, *Census of Business, 1963 Wholesale Distribution*, Washington, D.C.

turing plants of the nation, indicates the existence of about the same degree of concentration in the same areas. Industrial distributors tend to cluster where industry is, for that is where the industrial goods market is.

Size of Industrial Distributors

The typical industrial distributor is a small firm. Table 9–3 shows the distribution of these firms by number and percentage of their sales among several size groups, classified according to annual dollar volume of sales. At the wholesale level, a concern that sells less than $200,000 annually is a small establishment. In 5 of the 26 trade groups included in the table, more than half of all the firms had yearly sales of less than $200,000. More than half of the firms in 16 of the groups had sales of less than $300,000 a year, and over half of those in 22 of the trades had annual sales of less than $500,000.

On the other hand, the large firms captured the lion's share of the business. In 19 of the 26 trade groups in the table, the firms that sold more than $1 million per year made more than one third of the total sales of the group, and in 16 groups they were responsible for one half or more of the total group volume. This means much to the industrial goods manufacturer. By selling aggressively to a relatively small number of the distributors in the average trade, he may put himself in a position to capture his share of the bulk of its total business. In this way, he may be able to reduce to a minimum his expenses of selling and physical distribution. Such a size pattern in relation to total sales volume tends to lead the manufacturers of many kinds of industrial goods to use selected distributors.

Another factor brought out in Table 9–4 emphasizes the advantages to the manufacturer of selling to selected larger distributors. This table lists, as percentages of sales, the average expenses of firms of different size classifications in the several trade groups. The most significant feature it shows is the pronounced tendency of expense percentages to decrease as the size of the establishment increases. This means that if the industrial goods manufacturer tries to cover the entire market by selling through every distributor in his trade the margin of gross profit he allows his distributors must be considerably greater than it need be if he confines his sales efforts to the larger firms in the trade. Such widening of the distributor's gross margin can be achieved in only two ways: the manufacturer may reduce his price to the distributor below what it would otherwise be, which means that his own margin of gross profit is less satisfactory; or his product must be sold to users at prices higher than those possible if the distributor's gross profit margin were narrower. This tends to limit the sale of the product.

This situation, more than any other, is probably responsible for a practice quite common in industrial goods marketing. Many manufactur-

TABLE 9–3

Distribution of Establishments and Sales by Sales Size (in $000) Groups, 1963 in Selected Trades

Part A—Establishments

Trades	Under $100	$100 to 200	$200 to 300	$300 to 500	$500 to 1,000	$1,000 to 2,000	$2,000 to 5,000	$5,000 to 10,000	$10,000 to 15,000	$15,000 to 20,000	$20,000 and over
					Number of Establishments in Sales Size Groups						
Industrial chemicals	167	856	345	371	432	257	148*	31	9	3	5
Electrical supplies and apparatus	27	26	69		120		91*				1
Electrical supplies only	631	526	402	573	732	472	231	32	7	1	1
Electronic parts and equipment	1081	920	563	478	358	173	83	20	2		
Office machinery	1550	659	230	180	94	28	8	3	1		
Restaurant and hotel supplies	272	203	153	139	155	81	20	3	1		
Construction equipment	324	300	197	288	401	400	298	59	11	1	1
General industrial equipment	608	460	325	331	324	169	45	11	1		
Power transmission equipment	118	143	133	147	185	88	6	1		1	
Aircraft and aeronautic equipment	246	174	107	119	107	56	48	6	1		
Marine machinery and equipment	164	114	89	77	95	44	9	2			1
Oil well and refinery supplies	277	268	177	276	294	113	68	5			
Printing machinery	105	78	105		63		10*				
Construction materials	380	306	178	221	257	127	48	6	1		
Dental supplies	130	116	86	112	126	30	4	1	1		
Surgical, medical, hospital supplies	320	191	107	148	206	139	63	92	30	10	14
Ferrous metals	7	151	53		114		317				
Nonferrous metals	6	17	131	258	366	398	77*				
Trucks and tractors, road type	261	310	250	296	428	259	84	12	2		1
Air conditioning equipment	551	432	268	320	298	136	35	1			
Materials handling equipment	98	98	60	67	69	34	8	5	1		
Metal working machinery	271	189	132	185	196	101	44	17			1
Industrial supplies, general	8	173	117	220	274	180	73	3			
Valves and fittings	9	68	44	87	100	80	35				
Welding supplies	30	388	246	243	178	37	5				
Scientific instruments and laboratory equipment	6	54	54		76		40*				

* Includes $2,000 and over groups.

SOURCE: U.S. Bureau of the Census, 1963 Census of Business, Wholesale Trade, Washington, D.C.

TABLE 9–3—Continued

Part B—Sales

Trades	Under $100	$100 to 200	$200 to 300	$300 to 500	$500 to 1,000	$1,000 to 2,000	$2,000 to 5,000	$5,000 to 10,000	$10,000 to 15,000	$15,000 to 20,000	$20,000 and over
					Percentage of Total Trade Sales Made by Firms in Each Size Group						
Industrial chemicals	1.9	3.7	4.1	7.0	14.8	17.1	21.8	9.7	5.2	7.3	7.4
Electrical supplies and apparatus	0.2	0.7	4.3	a	22.8	a	72.1	a	a	a	a
Electrical supplies only	1.2	2.9	3.8	8.4	19.5	24.6	25.4	8.2	3.0	—	3.0
Electronic parts and equipment	3.7	8.7	9.0	11.9	16.2	15.6	15.4	8.9	10.6	a	a
Office machinery	16.7	19.8	11.8	14.4	12.9	7.8	4.5	12.1	a	—	a
Restaurant and hotel supplies	3.0	6.4	7.8	11.4	23.1	22.7	12.1	13.5	a	a	a
Construction equipment	0.7	1.7	1.9	4.3	11.1	21.8	33.9	15.1	5.1	4.4	a
General industrial equipment	3.2	6.6	7.8	12.6	21.7	21.9	10.9	7.2	8.6	a	a
Power transmission equipment	2.0	6.4	9.5	16.5	37.9	21.1	6.6	a	—	—	—
Aircraft and aeronautic equipment	2.6	4.6	5.0	8.5	14.2	22.9	26.5	15.7	a	a	—
Marine machinery and equipment	3.6	6.8	8.8	11.6	26.9	22.9	19.4	a	—	—	—
Oil well and refinery supplies	1.8	4.5	5.2	12.9	24.4	18.5	23.3	9.4	a	—	a
Printing machinery	3.8	8.4	25.2	a	39.6	a	22.9	a	a	a	a
Construction materials	2.5	5.9	5.8	11.1	23.3	23.2	18.2	11.0	a	a	a
Dental supplies	2.4	6.8	8.4	17.7	35.3	16.1	13.3	a	a	a	—
Surgical, medical, hospital supplies	2.0	3.5	3.4	7.0	18.2	24.8	22.8	18.3	a	a	—
Ferrous metals	0.1	0.6	0.9	2.9	7.4	16.2	27.2	17.8	10.1	4.6	12.2
Nonferrous metals	Trace	0.5	2.9	a	20.9	a	75.6	a	a	a	a
Trucks and tractors, road type	1.2	3.6	4.4	9.1	23.9	28.3	29.5	a	a	a	a
Air conditioning equipment	3.6	7.8	8.0	15.1	25.5	22.3	17.7	a	—	—	—
Materials handling equipment	2.7	7.6	8.2	14.1	27.2	23.9	16.3	a	—	—	a
Metalworking machinery	2.2	4.3	5.9	11.5	21.9	22.2	21.6	a	a	—	—
Industrial supplies, general	0.5	2.6	3.0	8.9	20.6	25.5	23.1	15.8	a	—	a
Valves and fittings	1.3	2.7	2.9	9.0	19.2	30.5	28.4	4.8	—	—	—
Welding supplies	4.4	13.9	14.9	22.9	29.0	12.0	2.9	a	—	—	—
Surgical instruments and laboratory equipment	1.0	2.8	6.2	a	29.3	a	60.7	a	a	a	a

a—included in last previous entry.
Compiled and computed from U.S. Bureau of the Census, *1963 Census of Business, Wholesale Trade*, Washington, D.C.

TABLE 9-4

Distributor Size and Expenses, Selected Trades, 1963

(Size groups in $000 of sales; expenses as percent of sales)

	All	over 20,000	15,000 to 20,000	10,000 to 15,000	5,000 to 10,000	2000 to 5000	1000 to 2000	500 to 1000	300 to 500	200 to 300	100 to 200	under 100
Industrial chemicals	15.2	6.9	8.1	7.7	12.0	13.0	15.8	18.0	21.6	22.3	24.0	28.3
Electrical supplies and apparatus	12.6	b	b	b	b	12.3	12.6	a	17.5	a	14.5	30.3
Electrical supplies only	15.1	D	D	11.0	10.9	12.9	15.2	16.5	18.5	19.8	22.4	23.4
Electronic parts	21.6	D	D	D	13.3	19.3	20.1	22.0	24.3	24.4	26.1	27.7
Office machinery	31.7	—	—	D	D	30.9	26.4	33.0	33.3	34.1	34.6	23.4
Restaurant and hotel supply	21.5	D	D	D	D	19.8	22.6	22.3	23.6	24.4	23.7	27.1
Construction equipment	18.2	D	D	14.7	15.0	17.1	19.6	21.0	23.5	24.3	24.8	25.7
General industrial equipment	20.9	D	D	D	15.2	18.7	21.2	22.9	23.8	23.7	25.4	27.2
Power transmission equipment	21.7	—	—	—	D	D	21.5	20.5	21.8	22.1	25.4	28.8
Aircraft equipment	21.4	—	D	D	D	17.8	20.5	23.0	27.9	27.7	27.5	30.4
Marine equipment	21.1	—	—	—	D	D	21.7	20.7	24.2	23.3	23.5	25.5
Oil well, refinery supplies	14.4	—	D	D	D	10.6	12.6	13.8	18.5	24.2	24.4	27.5
Printing equipment	24.7	b	b	b	b	25.1	22.2	a	26.6	a	27.5	28.3
Construction materials	18.2	—	—	D	D	11.8	17.4	17.6	21.3	21.1	21.2	24.6
Dental supplies	26.9	—	—	D	D	D	28.0	26.3	27.4	27.7	25.5	27.5
Surgical, medical, hospital supplies	20.0	D	D	21.2	D	18.5	19.7	20.7	20.5	22.3	23.3	27.8
Ferrous metals	16.7	15.1	13.1	14.4	14.9	16.2	17.4	19.0	20.1	23.6	27.4	35.4
Nonferrous metals	13.6	b	b	b	b	12.4	16.7	a	19.9	a	19.1	26.1
Trucks, tractors, road type	17.5	—	—	D	D	15.0	16.7	18.8	21.6	21.0	21.0	24.5
Air conditioning equipment	22.9	D	—	—	D	D	22.2	24.6	24.0	26.3	26.9	30.1
Materials handling equipment	23.8	—	—	—	D	D	22.5	24.2	23.4	23.7	25.6	27.2
Metalworking machinery	17.6	D	—	—	D	14.4	16.7	19.1	21.1	20.6	22.0	24.8
Industrial supplies, general	19.3	—	D	D	D	18.3	18.4	20.3	21.3	22.1	22.9	28.5
Valves and fittings	16.9	—	—	—	13.7	13.6	15.9	19.5	21.8	23.5	24.1	26.4
Welding supplies	25.7	—	—	—	—	18.9	23.6	26.3	27.2	27.9	28.7	27.7
Scientific instruments and laboratory equipment	24.7	b	b	b	b	25.1	24.1	a	21.8	a	25.8	33.2

a—included in next larger group

b—included in $2000 to $5000 group

D—Census Bureau withheld information to avoid disclosure of individual figures.

U.S. Bureau of the Census, 1963 *Census of Business, Wholesale Trade*, Washington, D.C.

TABLE 9–5

Size Distribution of Distributors, 1963
by Number of Employees
Selected Trades

	1–3 Employees		4–7 Employees		8–19 Employees		20–49 Employees		50 or more Employees	
	Percent of:		Percent of:		Percent of:		Percent of:		Percent of:	
	Establishments	Total Sales	Establishments	Total Sales	Establishments	Total Sales	Establishments	Total Sales	Establishments	Total Sales
Industrial chemicals	48.4	13.0	23.8	15.1	19.1	71.9	7.2	a	1.4	a
Electrical apparatus, supplies	29.4	5.3	23.8	11.2	30.9	32.1	12.2	28.5	3.5	23.1
Electrical supplies only	32.3	6.8	24.7	12.9	30.1	36.4	10.9	29.7	1.9	14.0
Electronic parts	41.9	12.0	30.2	17.2	21.6	28.2	5.3	23.7	1.6	19.0
Office machinery	51.3	19.9	27.2	22.5	17.4	33.3	3.6	16.2	0.4	8.4
Restaurant, hotel supplies	37.0	8.5	26.9	15.1	25.5	33.7	8.6	23.5	1.8	19.5
Construction equipment	27.0	3.5	18.4	6.0	26.4	19.0	22.0	38.4	6.4	32.3
General industrial equipment	39.7	11.0	25.2	15.4	24.5	32.1	9.0	28.6	1.5	13.0
Power transmission equipment	28.8	8.4	31.0	21.7	32.6	47.1	6.7	18.2	0.7	4.6
Aircraf and aeronautic equipment	42.6	10.4	24.1	14.4	20.1	25.4	10.5	27.2	2.9	22.8
Marine equipment	40.8	D	26.6	18.0	24.6	36.4	7.7	27.2	0.5	D
Oil well and refinery supplies	46.0	18.5	34.3	35.6	15.8	29.9	3.6	13.3	0.3	2.9
Construction materials	35.6	10.0	25.8	17.5	27.0	36.8	9.8	24.5	1.9	11.1
Dental supplies	30.9	6.8	21.2	10.9	32.2	36.2	13.0	27.7	2.7	18.1
Surgical, medical, hospital supplies	38.3	6.0	21.2	9.4	24.5	25.5	12.7	32.3	3.3	26.6
Trucks, tractors, road type	26.3	6.6	22.4	10.7	32.6	32.0	16.5	36.1	2.3	14.6
Air conditioning equipment	40.5	12.3	27.9	20.5	23.0	35.6	7.3	23.1	1.0	8.6
Materials handling equipment	38.3	11.4	25.3	16.8	23.4	32.1	10.9	29.9	1.1	9.2
Metalworking equipment	42.0	10.6	26.6	19.0	23.7	36.8	6.8	25.1	0.9	8.5
Industrial supplies, general	18.2	3.5	26.0	10.0	34.5	28.8	16.5	31.0	4.9	26.8
Valves and fittings	31.8	6.1	23.9	12.7	29.8	37.0	12.4	32.7	2.1	11.7
Welding equipment, supplies	31.2	11.2	32.3	23.4	31.3	47.6	4.7	15.5	0.4	2.4
Surgical instruments, laboratory equipment	34.2	3.4	19.4	6.8	19.4	14.2	15.8	23.7	11.2	52.1

a—included in last previous entry.

D. Withheld by Census Bureau to protect confidential information.

Computed from U.S. Bureau of the Census, *1963 Census of Business, Wholesale Trade*, Washington, D.C.

ers sell to selected distributors at a distributor's discount. The firms selected are usually the larger, more aggressive houses. The manufacturer will also sell to other distributors, but at the same prices he charges their user-buyer customers. A few using firms are house accounts to whom he sells direct at special prices. Some manufacturers refuse to sell to nonselected distributors; then these small firms must buy from the larger selected distributors if they wish to handle the goods.

The figures presented in Tables 9–5 and 9–6 give some idea of the

TABLE 9–6

Relation of Small Size to Number of Salesmen

Volume in Thousands of Dollars	Number of Field Salesmen								
	1–2	3–4	5–6	7–8	9–10	11–12	13–15	16–20	20 and more
$500 or less............4	13	2							
$500–1,000............1	10	14	6		1				
$1,000–1,500..........		4	4	3		1	1	1	
$1,500–2,000..........		1			1				
$2,000–above..........		2		1		3	1	2	

This table indicates, for example, that 10 firms, selling between $500,000 and $1 million, operated either 3 or 4 salesmen apiece. These figures are from a study reported in *Industrial Distributor*, May, 1950. The number of salesmen employed by the typical distributor probably has increased somewhat, but not much.

facilities that industrial distributors of various sales size groups can offer the manufacturer whose product they handle. For example, a small general-line distributor with four or five employees, only one or two of whom are likely to be outside salesmen, can offer no very highly organized order-handling and filling service, nor can he put much sales effort behind the manufacturer's product.

Table 9–5 indicates that in many trades between one third and one half of the distributors offer the industrial marketer little or no aggressive selling service. A firm with only four employees almost certainly has no more than one salesman calling on the trade, and probably has none. Even a distributor with seven employees is not likely to have more than two salesmen among them.

Table 9–7 shows the approximate number of days stock the average distributor in each sales size group carried in 1963. It indicates that, in general, the smaller houses carry greater stocks in relation to their sales than do the larger ones. But in spite of this, the small house cannot carry a very representative or complete inventory of the products of the manufacturers he represents.

For example, the distributor with annual sales of $100,000 sells about $400 worth of goods a day. If his gross profit is 20 percent on sales, this merchandise cost him $320, and if he carries a 60-day stock his inventory is about $19,000—not more than enough to provide an adequate and representative stock for about one manufacturer with a wide line. You will note that most of them carry well under 60-days stock.

TABLE 9-7

Sales Size and Approximate Number of Days Stock Carried, 1963 Selected Trades

	$20,000 and over	$15,000 to 20,000	$10,000 to 15,000	$5,000 to 10,000	$2,000 to 5,000	$1,000 to 2,000	$500 to 1,000	$300 to 500	$200 to 300	$100 to 200	Under $100	Average
Industrial chemicals	36	26	8	20	19	21	22	22	23	26	26	21
Electrical apparatus, supplies	a	a	a	a	37	37	b	50	b	43	11	39
Electrical supplies only	D	D	25	22	29	31	35	41	44	46	50	32
Electronic parts	D	D	D	40	46	54	55	58	62	67	75	54
Office machinery	—	—	D	D	53	36	45	46	56	56	55	50
Restaurant and hotel supplies	D	D	D	D	39	37	36	43	45	55	50	37
Construction equipment	D	D	63	75	78	69	67	72	61	68	80	69
General industrial equipment	D	D	D	36	42	38	38	41	38	45	42	37
Power transmission equipment	—	—	—	D	D	58	51	66	49	62	50	49
Aircraft and aeronautic equipment	D	D	D	43	43	41	43	38	39	42	50	44
Marine equipment	—	—	—	D	D	57	43	46	45	59	77	47
Oil well and refinery supplies	—	D	D	D	30	38	37	46	53	53	70	37
Printing machinery	a	a	a	a	45	37	b	42	b	65	57	40
Construction materials	—	—	D	D	12	17	19	23	30	29	18	19
Dental supplies	—	—	D	D	D	53	56	63	67	60	77	69
Surgical, medical, hospital supplies	D	D	59	D	39	36	39	40	46	35	67	39
Ferrous metals	51	39	45	50	54	56	55	61	63	76	77	53
Nonferrous metals	—	—	—	—	29	15	b	37	b	30	20	32
Trucks, tractors, road type	D	D	a	a	35	33	37	36	40	42	45	36
Air conditioning equipment	—	—	—	D	D	36	39	38	47	44	37	38
Materials handling	D	—	—	D	D	37	33	38	22	24	43	34
Metalworking equipment, supplies	—	—	D	D	20	26	28	31	35	36	48	20
Industrial supplies, general	—	—	—	49	47	44	48	41	45	53	57	46
Valves and fittings	—	—	—	—	36	37	35	29	30	33	47	37
Welding supplies	—	—	—	—	15	34	37	37	53	44	39	38
Surgical instruments, laboratory supplies	a	a	a	a	61	51	b	55	b	43	50	59

Computed on the basis of a gross profit 1 percent higher than reported expenses.

a—included in $2000 to $5000 figure.

b—included in next largest group.

D—withheld to protect confidential information.

Computed from U.S. Bureau of the Census, 1963 Census of Business, Wholesale Trade, Washington, D.C.

In many trades, the industrial marketer can assure himself the benefit of practically all the aggressive selling effort distributors have to offer by maintaining contact with a surprisingly small number of them. With 3 salesmen, he can contact about 100 distributors every 2 weeks, which in most trades is an entirely satisfactory call frequency. In most trades, he will miss a surprisingly small percentage of the total volume if he makes no attempt to market through the small one-, two-, or three-employee distributors.

General Description of Distributors' Operations

General industrial distributors handle a large number of items of merchandise in a wide variety of lines. The mill supply house is reported to carry between 15,000 and 20,000 items in as many as 650 product lines, such as bolts, nuts, beltings, bearings, valves, fittings, cutting tools, hand tools, portable power tools, and some metal rods, bars, and tubing. A general electrical supply firm may handle some 60,000 items made by between 200 and 300 manufacturers. Some specialty houses are reported to carry from 30,000 to 50,000 items or more. Large steel warehouses handle 10,000 steel items, totaling from 25,000 to 30,000 tons in stock, although the average for all houses is probably nearer 1,000–2,500 tons. From the shapes such a warehouse carries in stock, it is prepared to shear and cut to an almost infinite variety of customer-specified sizes and shapes.

Often, the distributor does not sell competing lines of merchandise, especially in specialty articles and goods of high unit value. This is less likely to be true of highly standardized items. This tendency is doubtless emphasized by the trend away from the generalized house and toward the more highly specialized firm.

The typical industrial distributor has about 6 outside salesmen, each of whom handles about 140 accounts and makes annual sales of about $225,000. Almost two thirds of these men have had some college training, and the typical man has been with his company for slightly less than 10 years. He makes between seven and eight calls a day, seeing two people in most of the customer firms he visits. He works about nine hours a day, and spends slightly more than half of this time face to face with customers. He calls on a few customers twice a week or oftener; about a third of them he visits only once a month. He averages about one call on each customer every three weeks. His pay is about $8,500 a year, usually in the form of a salary combined with either a commission or a bonus.[1]

The metal warehouse is a specialized type of industrial distributor of sufficient importance to merit a brief separate treatment. About 80 percent of the total steel tonnage is sold direct by the mill to the user; the remainder goes to market through the steel warehouse. The warehouse

---

[1] This material is from a study of 1,500 salesmen of industrial distributors reported in *Industrial Distribution*, September, 1963.

receives no functional discount from the mill. It operates entirely on the differential between the mill price for standard base lots and the higher price the mill charges for smaller quantities. For example, at one time the base mill lot for cold-finished bars was 20,000 pounds, with an extra charge of $100 per 100 pounds for smaller lots. This means that except in very unusual circumstances the warehouse can sell only to buyers who purchase in less than standard mill lots.

The warehouse handles general steel products, such as structural shapes, plates, hot-rolled bars, cold-finished bars, tubing, and tool steel. It does very little business in specialties. It is prepared to cut and shear these items to the specifications of the buyer. Most of its customers are small buyers, although it is sometimes patronized by large users who buy fill-ins in an attempt to keep their stocks down. The warehouse is usually prepared to make deliveries on a 24-hour basis, which enables it to offer a service the mill cannot rival. As a general rule, the mills play no favorites among warehouses, although some mills sell special products to only two or three warehouses in a market area.[2] Nonferrous warehouses operate in much the same way in handling metals other than iron and steel.

Some additional idea of the nature of industrial distributors may be gained from a knowledge of how their assets are invested. A survey of 29 fairly large distributors, with average assets of $651,400 per firm, shows the following distribution of the funds invested in their businesses.[3]

Cash	7.5%
Receivables	21.5
Inventory	45.0
Fixed assets	23.0
Other	3.0

While this study was made about 15 years ago, the distribution of assets it found is probably reasonably representative of that still prevailing among houses of all sizes. The outstanding point is that almost half of the total funds of the average distributor is invested in inventory. Such a heavy investment is made necessary by the large number of items such houses must carry in order to serve the needs of their trade. Many of these are slow-moving articles that are required infrequently but, when needed, are vital to the operations of the manufacturer-customer. It is probable that the general emphasis on inventory control during recent years may have brought about some reduction in the importance of inventory. The rate of annual stock turnover in 1960 was 4.3 times; in 1962, 4.2 times; in 1963, 4.6 times.

---

[2] The material in this description is largely from C. A. Livesey, "Mill Supply Houses," *Harvard Business Review*, Summer Issue, 1945; and from *Industrial Marketing*, January, 1950. The nature of this business has not changed much during the past decade or two.

[3] *Industrial Distribution*, February, 1950.

Most of the larger firms publish and distribute catalogs to serve their customers. Some of these are big and rather costly volumes. For example, one large laboratory chemical house distributed 85,000 copies of its 1,000-page book, in which 15,000 items were listed and described. A distributor's catalog can be a very important part of his sales operation if it is well prepared and adequately distributed, and if his customers are properly guided in its use.

Many distributors maintain showrooms, which can be visited by customers and from which buyers can be served for small orders that require immediate delivery. Many manufacturers look on the distributor as a sort of retail store conveniently located where emergency requirements can be procured. A significant portion of many distributors' volume is handled in this manner. A showroom display maintained in connection with the facilities for handling such orders can often be a potent selling force.

The value of such displays to the distributor depends on several factors. If his warehouse is located near the factories he serves, he is likely to have many buying visitors who may examine his displays while waiting for their orders to be filled. Specialized houses derive more benefit from such displays than the more general house, since they are likely to have more novel items to show. However, some specialized distributors handle products that do not readily lend themselves to display. Much of the effectiveness of a showroom depends on the distributor himself. If it is to be effective, he must be willing to spend time and effort in making the displays attractive and instructive.

Industrial distributors are plagued by the problem of small orders. One steel warehouse reported that 31.7 percent of the orders it received averaged $7.50 per order, created 32 percent of its administration cost, and contributed only 6 percent to its total sales volume. A study of 100 distributors showed the following comparison of 7 firms especially troubled by the small-order problem with 93 concerns whose business was received in larger lots.[4]

	7 Small Order Distributors	93 Distributors
Average dollar value of order	10.09	26.88
Average value per billing line	3.87	23.28
Percentage of orders under $4	54.0	36.1
Percentage of value of orders under $5	12.4	4.0
Ratio sales to inventory	2.06	4.8

A study of the average size of the invoices issued by a representative group of distributors showed the following.[5]

[4] *Industrial Distribution*, June, 1949.

[5] *Industrial Distribution*, March, 1949.

| | Percentage of Firms Reporting |
Average Size Invoice Billed	Average
Under $10..............................	2.3
$10–$20................................	11.5
$20–$30................................	18.4
$30–$40................................	27.6
$40–$50................................	13.8
$50–$60................................	10.3
$60–$70................................	5.8
Over $70..............................	10.3

According to this study, 59.8 percent of all firms surveyed reported an average order size of less than $40, while only 26.4 percent had average orders of more than $50. In 1957, the size of the average order was reported to be $48.25; in 1958, $43.90; in 1960, $50.28; in 1961, $51.02; in 1962, $56.[6]

The significance of this tendency toward small orders will be appreciated if we bear in mind that the average cost of handling an order varies between $2 and $5 for different firms, and it probably averages somewhat more than $2.80 for all distributors.[7] While inflation has probably increased these dollar figures somewhat—they are more than 10 years old—the relationship between order size and handling cost remains about the same.

Some distributors have sought to meet this difficulty by trying to induce or force their customers to order in large quantities, either through persuasion, by means of discounts or price differentials, or through assessment of a surcharge on orders below a fixed minimum. This method probably will not be too successful, because the distributor is the chief source of supply for small manufacturers, whose orders are naturally small. Also, many large buyers look to him as a means of keeping their stocks at a minimum, through frequent small purchases, and as a source from which to buy emergency articles; both services, if rendered, force the distributor to sell in small quantities. By refusing to handle small orders or by making them expensive to the buyer, the distributor destroys several of the chief reasons for his existence.

The problem may be attacked in other ways. One firm cut the work of its pricing and billing departments by one third by issuing its price lists on a net basis rather than in the form of the time-honored list price with a string of discounts, which required a great deal of computation and numerous entries on the various documents involved in each transaction. For handling small orders, another worked out a special routine that

---

[6] *Industrial Distribution*, March, 1959; March, 1963.

[7] *Industrial Distribution*, January and December, 1950. In a pamphlet, *The Answer is $2.82*, the Research and Planning Committee of the National Supply and Machinery Distributors Association reported that in 1950 the average cost per order for 80 firms was $2.82.

short-cut some of the operations included in the regular routine that were not needed in handling the smaller order, thereby materially reducing the cost of filling such orders. Some houses follow the practice of simply giving the customer a sales slip in duplicate for each small purchase, accumulating the copies of slips and customer orders, and billing only at the end of a month or quarter, or when the amount outstanding reaches a fixed minimum. This amounts to handling the small order as a retail transaction, and the savings are considerable.

During recent years, many industrial buyers have become increasingly aware of the costs of preparing, placing, and receiving delivery of the small order. As a result, they seek ways either to reduce the number of small orders they place or to handle them less expensively. The systems they have worked out usually result in lower handling costs for the supplier as well as for the buyer. Some distributors have enjoyed reasonable success in trying to induce their customers to adopt the less costly ordering routines developed by other buyers.

Why Customers Buy from Distributors

The distributor's usefulness as an outlet for the manufacturer of industrial goods depends to a great extent on his usefulness to the consumers of the manufacturer's products. The manufacturer can market successfully through distributors only if the users of his products find it desirable to buy through distributors. In our endeavor to appraise the distributor as a marketing channel for industrial goods, we will find it worthwhile to examine the services he is equipped to render to the firms that use him as an outlet, the advantages users may enjoy as a result of purchasing from him, and the conditions likely to influence industrial buyers to patronize him.

The small manufacturer who must purchase in limited quantities is often forced to buy many of his supplies, materials, and items of equipment from the distributor. He cannot place orders big enough to justify the maker in selling to him direct. The larger user generally wishes to buy direct those materials he needs to purchase in lots large enough to justify quantity price allowances or to earn freight reductions. Some buyers make it a matter of policy to purchase direct from the manufacturer whenever possible. Many very large firms, however, find it good business to buy extensively from small local suppliers. It is good public relations to do so. In addition, this method of buying is often more economical. Aside from these considerations, the following factors tend to cause industrial buyers to patronize industrial distributors.

1. The distributor is usually able to deliver goods more speedily than the manufacturer. His warehouse is generally located nearer the factory of the average user than is the branch house of the manufacturer. Distributors operate many times the number of warehouses any manufacturer

can afford to maintain. They are widely scattered throughout the market. The delivery performance of the distributor is illustrated by the experience of an aircraft manufacturer, as shown by the following table.[8] Since

	Delivery Time		Days Saved Average
	Distributor	Manufacturer	
Valves	1 day	4–6 weeks	35 days
Chuck wrenches	1 "	4 days	3 "
Chucks	1 "	4 "	3 "
Files	1 "	14–21 days	16 "
Metal-slitting saws	1 "	5 days	4 "
Hose	1 "	30 "	29 "
Gears	1 "	5 "	4 "
Bearings	1 "	7 "	6 "

this study was made, improvements in air, truck, and rail transportation have somewhat reduced the distributor's advantage, but it is still overwhelming.

Speedy delivery enables the using firm to reduce its investment in inventory, tends to decrease the likelihood of inventory losses due to obsolescence and price declines, and cuts the cost of the space in which the inventory is stored. In addition, speed may sometimes make it possible for the buyer to time his receipts of materials so that they can be delivered to the machine site without being merged into stock, thereby reducing warehouse handling costs.

Speed and certainty of delivery may also increase flexibility in planning because it reduces the lead time—that is, the time that must elapse between the date an order is placed and the date on which the goods it includes are received. If this period is long, production plans must be made far ahead of the date on which their execution begins, and it is difficult, if not impossible, to change them. Estimates of the average annual cost of carrying inventory range from 10 to 25 percent of its value, and probably average nearer the higher figure. A buying firm may enjoy substantial economies through holding its inventory at a minimum.

2. The distributor may enable the buyer to reduce his cost of purchasing and paper work. The average industrial plant buys a large number of items produced by many manufacturers. If it purchases direct, its purchasing department must prepare a tremendous number of orders; its receiving department must take in, check, and merge into inventory an equal number of shipments; and its accounting and financial department must check and pay the same volume of invoices. If the firm buys from distributors, on the other hand, it can probably obtain its requirements from a few sources, often less than half a dozen.

[8] *Industrial Distribution*, November, 1950.

An example of this saving is supplied by a metalworking firm whose purchasing agent found that it was buying 144 supply and maintenance items from 66 manufacturers. A study showed that all the items could have been bought from four or five distributors whose competition was adequate to assure fair prices. The old method of buying involved upward of 30 times as much paper work as the new. In addition, the distributor would deliver many items in one shipment and bill for them on one invoice. The saving to be enjoyed is obvious.

3. In some cases, the distributor can deliver goods at lower prices than those the buyer must pay if he purchases direct. For example, several years ago a power and light company buying bolts for replacement parts on a machine found that for the 1 × 7-inch size it had to pay $1 a dozen from the manufacturer, but it could buy them for 52 cents from the distributor. For the 1 ×7½-inch size, the prices were: manufacturer, $1.026 a dozen; distributor 62 cents a dozen. The 1×8-inch size prices were: manufacturer, $1.10 a dozen; distributor, 62 cents a dozen. The distributor probably bought this item in quantity lots and enjoyed quantity prices.

Such a situation does not happen often. If the buyer compares prices on a delivered basis, however, he often finds a price differential favorable to the distributor because the distributor usually delivers with his own equipment without specific charge for so doing, while the manufacturer often ships f.o.b. factory, which means that the buyer must pay the freight.

4. The buyer can make adjustments much more easily and conveniently with the industrial distributor than with the manufacturer. When he has a complaint against the manufacturer-supplier, he must usually present it in writing and negotiate its settlement at long range. If he deals with a distributor, he can usually settle the matter within a short period of time by telephone or in a face-to-face conference with either the distributor himself or one of his salesmen, who generally call frequently instead of at long intervals, as the manufacturer's salesmen are apt to do. This is not a matter of vital import; but when other factors are equal or nearly so, it may tip the scales of buyer patronage toward the distributor.

5. The distributor may enable the industrial buyer to save on the freight that must be paid on incoming materials and supplies. The distributor is able to purchase many of the articles he handles in carload or truckload lots. Often, the industrial buyer cannot purchase from the manufacturer in such lots. On such articles the distributor is able to offer the purchasing officer the saving that results from a combination of a low carlot rate from the factory to the distributor's warehouse, plus a higher less-than-carload rate from the warehouse to the buyer's plant, as compared with the high less-than-carload rate the user would have to pay all the way if he bought direct. Of course, if the buyer is big enough to

purchase in carload or truckload lots, the distributor has nothing to offer in freight savings.

If the buyer does not have his own siding, the distributor can sometimes offer him a substantial saving in incoming transportation costs. If such a buyer purchases direct, he will receive many shipments, each of which must be picked up at the freight depot and carried by truck to the plant; if he buys from the distributor, he receives only one or a few shipments, and his cartage bill is correspondingly lower. Of course, if goods are shipped by truck, this saving is not possible.

6. The distributor sometimes offers the industrial buyer a quick general source of product information. He usually publishes a catalog that is a compendium of quality, price, and availability information about the products of many manufacturers. Through their frequent visits, the distributor's salesmen keep this information up-to-date. As a result of their wide contacts with the trade, these men can often supply their customers with general information about many lines, which the more highly specialized salesmen of the manufacturer-supplier do not have. Of course, when the buyer wishes highly detailed technical facts about specific materials, supplies, or equipment, he cannot always expect to get it from the distributor's salesman but must make contact with the manufacturer. The distributor's salesman should be a good source of broad, general information about many widely varied articles; the manufacturer's salesman must usually be relied on for more detailed data with respect to specific items.

7. To the small buyer, the industrial distributor should offer a convenient and reasonably liberal source of credit. Since the distributor is generally a local concern, he should be more familiar with the business, character, and financial needs of the small local buyer than the manufacturer-supplier can be. As a result, he ought to be able to extend credit in situations when the manufacturer, operating at long range, would not be justified in taking a chance. However, the census figures indicate that, in general, manufacturer's stock-carrying branches sell a slightly larger percentage of their total volume on credit than do the industrial distributors serving the same trades.

8. Because the industrial distributor is located near his customers and is thus in a position to have detailed knowledge of their operations, and because his salesmen visit the customer frequently, he is often able to give the buyer a type of service that cannot be duplicated by the manufacturer-supplier. For example, the metal warehouse offers to cut products to the specifications of the small buyer—a service the mill cannot afford to render, except to the large purchaser.

A machinery manufacturer who changed from using cast parts to parts cut from stock for a certain purpose found himself in difficulty. A call to a steel warehouse brought a technical specialist who not only solved the difficulty but, by supplying some parts and standardizing others, materially reduced the cost of the finished product. A small machine shop had an order that involved boring holes in 5,000 pieces of plate steel. The order was suddenly increased to 20,000 pieces at a lower price that, with the equipment in use, offered no profit. The manager put the problem up to a distributor, who sold and delivered to him the same day a multidrill head to install on his machine. The part enabled it to drill eight holes at a time instead of one. He was able to complete the order on time and at a profit. A manufacturer-supplier could undoubtedly have done the same thing, except that he was not on the spot and could not supply immediate delivery.

An analysis of this pattern of services offered by the distributor indicates the general circumstances in which he is likely to be able to command the patronage of the industrial buyer.

1. The small plant is compelled to purchase many items from the distributor. It must procure from him most of the articles it uses in lots too small for the manufacturer to supply economically. For example, the user of steel who buys in less than carload lots must procure his materials from the steel warehouse because the mill will sell only in carload quantities. The average small plant may buy a few items in quantities large enough to make direct purchase profitable, but their number probably will not be large.

2. The large industrial plant is likely to depend on the distributor as a source of supply for emergency items. The wise purchasing officer is well aware that the distributor cannot keep his business alive on emergency orders alone. Therefore, he is likely to divert enough of his routine purchases to the distributor to cause the distributor to regard him as a profitable account. Not all buyers take this intelligent point of view; it is likely that their emergency order handling suffers by reason of this lack.

3. The buyer for a large plant may look to the industrial distributor as a source from which to obtain articles he must procure in amounts so small that he cannot hope to enjoy quantity discounts in their purchase. By lumping a number of such items together in one order, he enjoys considerable saving in buying costs, receiving expenses, and paper work generally.

4. Even the large firm must buy from the distributor some articles it purchases in substantial quantities. This is true when the makers of such articles follow a policy of selective or exclusive distributor marketing and, to make it effective, protect their distributors by refusing to sell direct.

5. In procuring some articles, the large industrial buyer can save more through buying from distributors who can give quick delivery, thereby keeping his inventories at a minimum, than by purchasing in large lots at quantity discounts direct from the manufacturer.[9]

_____

[9] This analysis roughly follows that of C. A. Livesey in an article on mill supply houses in *Harvard Business Review*, Summer Issue, 1945. A study by the research

MANUFACTURER'S AND SALES AGENTS

Definition and Description

It has been estimated that about 80 percent of the companies making industrial goods at some time or another sell through manufacturer's or sales agents. About half regularly use agents in their marketing programs.

The manufacturer's agent and the sales agent operate in much the same manner. Each represents sellers only. Each operates on a commission basis. Each represents a limited number of principals with more or less continuity rather than playing the field as does the broker or the commission merchant. Neither takes title to the goods he handles, although many manufacturer's agents carry stocks on consignment.

The two agents differ in that the manufacturer's agent sells only a portion of the producer's output and limits his activities to a certain geographical area, while the sales agent usually sells to a given trade group wherever its members may be found and usually contracts to dispose of the entire output of his client-producer. By making an arrangement with a single sales agent, the producer can solve his entire problem of choosing marketing channels; if he markets through manufacturer's agents, he must make contracts with several of them in order to cover the entire market. Manufacturer's agents are much more important in the industrial goods business than in consumer goods marketing.

Tables 9–8 and 9–9 present the most recent statistics about the more important trade groups of these two types of industrial middlemen. In its reports after 1948, the Bureau of the Census does not differentiate between the two groups but lumps both with commission merchants and

department of McGraw-Hill Book Co., "The Industrial Buyer Tells You," supplemented by *Industrial Distribution*, May, 1958, showed that industrial buyers in eight cities bought the following percentages of their needs of the listed items from industrial distributors:

Coated abrasives.....83%	Hand tools..........97%	Pipe................84%
Bars, sheets, shapes...64	Motors.............52	Pulleys.............88
Antifriction bearings..79	Shears.............86	Pumps..............65
Plain bearings........78	Valves, fittings......92	Safety equipment.....84
Conveyor belts.......73	Wheelbarrows.......94	Saws, circular band...89
Transmission belts....77	Electric hoists.......77	Saws, hack..........99
V-belts.............77	Hose...............86	Portable electric tools.87
Bolts and nuts........75	Jacks..............91	Welding equipment...89
Brushes and brooms...82	Lamps.............79	Wire brush wheels...94
Machine screws.....82	Light machine tools...91	Portable pneumatic
Welding rods.......82	Accessory machine	tools.............83
Casters.............95	tools.............83	Hangers.............94
Chain..............87	Oils, greases.........44	Chain hoists.........84
Compressors.........60	Taps, dies, reams.....91	Cutting tools....70–100
Cordage............89	Vises...............96	Painting equipment...66
Twist drills.........96	Grinding wheels......78	Fasteners.......70–100
Fans, blowers........66	Packing.............76	Power tools.....70–100
Files...............99	Paint...............44	Shop supplies....70–100

brokers in one category, Agents and Brokers. An analysis of the figures for the classification suggests that what is said here about manufacturer's agents and sales agents is still substantially true. Notice that the nonstock-carrying manufacturer's agents are much more numerous than those who carry inventories, and that they sell a much larger percentage of the total volume of industrial goods marketed through this type of outlet. In most trades, the nonstock-carrying manufacturer's agent handles a slightly larger volume per establishment than does the one with stocks, although, as might be expected, the stock-carrying house is a much larger establishment in number of employees.

TABLE 9–8

Selected Trade Groups of Selling Agents, 1948

Trade Group	No. of Estab-lishments	Sales (in Thousands)	Sales per Estab-lishment	Employ-ees per Estab-lishment	Expenses as Per-centage of Sales
Industrial chemicals........	63	$103,463	1,642,000	4.3	4.6
Electrical wiring apparatus and supplies.............	67	28,853	431,000	2.2	6.3
Construction materials......	70	47,386	677,000	2.9	5.5
Commercial machines and equipment..............	98	12,353	126,000	2.9	12.6
Industrial machinery, equip-ment, supplies...........	282	80,567	286,000	2.3	8.8
Other machinery equipment, supplies.................	160	121,844	762,000	2.3	3.7
Iron, steel, and products.....	98	121,097	1,235,000	2.5	3.4
Nonferrous metals and metalwork..............	19	45,002	2,316,000	4.4	2.0

SOURCE: U.S. Bureau of the Census, *1948 Census of Business, Wholesale Establishments*, Washington, D.C.

In most trades, the sales agent disposes of a larger volume per firm than either type of manufacturer's agent. In average number of employees per establishment, it tends to be a somewhat smaller concern than the stock-carrying firm, although in this respect both types of agents are small enterprises in comparison with the average industrial distributor. This is to be expected in view of the more limited services they perform.

It is obvious that the manufacturer who sells through either of these types of agents can expect them to supply no very large force of salesmen to promote his goods. The sales force of the average sales agent can in the nature of things consist of no more than the owner or manager and perhaps one salesman. The same is true of the nonstock-carrying manufacturer's agent. The average manufacturer's agent who carries stock may possibly have two salesmen in addition to himself. All types, even the stock-carrying manufacturer's agent, sell mainly for delivery from the factory. The producer must usually perform all the functions involved in physical delivery, except the handling of emergency orders and other

TABLE 9–9

Selected Trade Groups of Manufacturer's Agents, 1948

	Stock-Carrying					Nonstock-Carrying				
Trade Group	No. Establishments	Sales (in Thousands)	Sales per Establishment	Employees per Establishment	Expenses as Percentage of Sales	No. Establishments	Sales (in Thousands)	Sales per Establishment	Employees per Establishment	Expenses as Percentage of Sales
Industrial chemicals..........	46	$ 63,767	1,386,000	5.4	3.7	95	$ 38,731	408,000	1.9	5.3
Electrical wiring apparatus supplies...113	113	49,824	441,000	4.0	8.0	710	368,514	519,000	2.2	6.2
Construction materials............	30	8,252	275,000	7.7	11.8	104	35,591	342,000	2.6	7.4
Commercial machines, equipment.....	88	17,455	200,000	4.5	12.4	123	41,489	337,000	1.7	5.7
Industrial machinery, equipment, supplies............	409	146,931	360,000	4.2	9.2	1180	417,156	354,000	1.9	8.2
Other machinery, equipment, supplies.	93	46,739	501,000	4.3	6.5	342	166,548	487,000	1.5	5.1
Metals and metalwork...........	47	30,528	650,000	4.4	4.9	414	280,309	677,000	1.5	4.2

SOURCE: U.S. Bureau of the Census, 1948 Census of Business, Wholesale Establishments, Washington, D.C. In later Census of Business reports, no separate figures are given for manufacturer's agents and sales agents. The dollar figures are now probably somewhat higher, but the relationships are probably about the same.

orders that require especially speedy delivery when he distributes through the stock-carrying manufacturer's agent.

When Manufacturer's or Sales Agents Are Useful

The maker of a single industrial goods item, or a narrow line of them, with limited sales volume in the average market area, faces a difficult problem in marketing his output. In most territories, he cannot hope to capture enough volume to support his own sales force and distribution machinery unless he is willing to job the products of other manufacturers; then he takes over all the managerial headaches that go with being an industrial distributor. On the other hand, since his line is limited he can hardly expect that the industrial distributor, if he decides to market through this outlet, will devote much sales effort to promoting his goods. His handicap is much more pronounced if his product requires special sales promotional effort.

The manufacturer may try to escape this dilemma by using the manufacturer's agent or the selling agent, who handles a narrow line of products—usually not over 30—and so may be expected to devote much more attention to each one and to know much more about each one than the distributor could possibly know. These agents may even prove useful to the full-line manufacturer who wants to market direct to users but finds demand so thin in certain portions of the country that such sales would be prohibitively expensive, or who discovers that a certain market for his products, although not yielding large sales volume, requires specialized technical knowledge and close customer contact. In either case, the large manufacturer is likely to employ manufacturer's or selling agents as part of his marketing system.

Both types of agents offer certain advantages as distributive outlets for a manufacturer's goods in the industrial market.

1. Their costs are low. Tables 9–8 and 9–9 indicate that for different trade groups costs range from 2.0 to 12.6 percent, and probably average in the neighborhood of 5 or 6 percent of sales. The *1963 Census of Business* reported the expenses of all manufacturer's agents as 6.0 percent of sales, and sales agents as 3.9 percent. Among the several trade groups of industrial distributors, expenses range from 13.6 to 26.3 percent of sales. Similar figures for manufacturer's stock-carrying branches are from 4.4. to 27.3 percent, and for nonstock-carrying branches from 2.1 to 23.0 percent of sales.

Of course, the figures for manufacturer's branches are not strictly comparable with those of either industrial distributors or agents, since to the cost percentages of distributors and agents must be added their net profit to compute their total contribution to the delivered cost of the manufacturer's products. In comparing the cost of marketing through agents with that of marketing through distributors, the expense of physical distribution must also be added to the agents' fees. In spite of all these adjustments, it is very likely that the cost of marketing through manufacturer's and sales agents is less than that of going through industrial distributors or branches, unless the manufacturers' products enjoy a heavy demand.

Both types of agents offer an advantage over the manufacturer's branch house; the cost of marketing through them remains the same in relation to sales, regardless of business conditions. They are paid a commission whose rate tends to vary but little in response to changes in business conditions. They offer the added advantage that the manufacturer has no selling costs unless sales are made, since all such costs are embraced in the commission payments. Neither of these advantages apply to marketing through industrial distributors.

2. Either type of agent usually will prove very valuable in introducing a new product, especially if the market is one in which the manufacturer has not sold before. The manufacturer's agent usually handles a line of products that complement one another. In selling them, he builds up contacts with buyers. When he adds a new product to his line, the new article benefits from the buyer contacts and goodwill established in vending those already in the line. This is true of the manufacturer who operates his own direct marketing outlets, but such a manufacturer is likely to make use of the agent when he seeks to enter a new market in which he lacks contacts.

The agent also offers established contacts with the market. When a manufacturer attempts to enter a market his rivals have already developed, the value to him of the agent's contacts is diminished somewhat because all the most desirable agents will be handling products of competing producers. On the other hand, a small, new manufacturer, lacking experience in the business of marketing, may find that through one sales agent he can obtain distribution of his entire output over the whole market, and that by making one arrangement he can solve his entire selling problem.

3. Either type of agent is likely to offer a better quality of sales service than does the industrial distributor. The distributor may have in his catalog as many as 30,000 items made by hundreds of manufacturers. It is obvious that his salesmen can devote little time or effort to selling any one of them, even if he handles most of them on an exclusive basis. He can be relied on to give little selling service other than that involved in listing an article in his catalog and price book, operating a force of salesmen who will take orders for it if the need is apparent, and, in some cases, supplying a limited amount of technical aid and service in connection with its purchase or use.

Conversely, the agent handles a limited number of items, usually not more than a dozen or two at the outside. As a result, he and his salesmen can devote to each of them an amount of promotional attention and effort that the distributor cannot rival. Even the manufacturer of an extensive line may discover that the agent can and will put behind a specialty article a quality and amount of sales pressure that he finds difficult to match through his own sales force. A salesman usually finds it impossible in one call to make a real pitch for more than four or five products at the most. Of course, the manufacturer who sells through sales agents must share their promotional effort with any other competing producers whose goods they handle; this is not true of the manufacturer's agent.

Since an agent handles only a few articles, he can afford to study them more exhaustively himself and to train his salesmen more intensively in selling them than the industrial distributor finds it profitable to do. In fact, the agent is probably able to do a more thorough job of sales training on the few products he handles than can the direct-selling manufacturer of an extensive line for many of the articles included in it.

Either the manufacturer's agent or the sales agent offers to the new manufacturer without market contacts, to the small manufacturer, to the producer of a narrow line, to the maker of a specialty item sold to a highly specialized trade, or to the producer of a heavy volume item or line in areas where volume is small a selling service that is generally superior to that of the industrial distributor, and sometimes more satisfactory than the manufacturer himself can afford. The agent can often do this at a cost that compares favorably with the distributor's cost, or with that of the manufacturer who sells through his own branches. If an article is bulky so that users generally buy in carload or truckload lots, or is of high value in relation to its bulk so that transportation and handling costs constitute no large element in its final delivered cost, the agent may be a valuable factor in the manufacturer's system of distribution.

Agents Have Drawbacks

Against these advantages must be balanced certain drawbacks in the use of manufacturer's and sales agents as channels through which to market industrial goods.

1. Industrial sales managers generally feel that manufacturer's and sales agents cannot be controlled so completely in their promotional activities as can the manufacturer's own sales force. The result is that the producer who relies on them as an important part of his marketing system thereby loses some degree of control over the process of selling his product to the user. It is especially hard to induce agents to do missionary work or developmental selling that does not immediately result in sales on which they can collect commissions. On the other hand, it is probably true that through these agents the manufacturer can maintain a greater measure of control over the process of marketing his products than he can if he sells through industrial distributors. Because of the small number of items he handles and the few manufacturers he represents, the agent can maintain a reasonably close knowledge of and relations with each of them, generally

much closer than the industrial distributor can achieve with his hundreds of suppliers and thousands of items.

2. Manufacturers who sell through agents also complain of their lack of flexibility in situations that involve competitive bidding. This is especially true of the manufacturer's agent who usually sells at a price fixed by his principal. The sales agent is much more likely to have a measure of discretion with respect to price and is able to vary his bids so as to get the business. It should also be pointed out that the industrial distributor suffers from the same weakness, and to an even more pronounced degree since his natural reluctance to vary bid prices is augmented by the knowledge that if he does, he may reduce his own margin.

3. When a product or product line enjoys a considerable sales volume, the cost of selling through agents, combined with the expense of handling physical distribution, may add up to a rather expensive marketing system. For this reason, many manufacturers make use of the industrial distributor, or set up their own branch house systems. Some manufacturers market through their own sales force and warehouses in areas of concentrated demand, and rely on manufacturer's agents to cultivate the regions in which potential sales are smaller.

4. The manufacturer of industrial goods who sells through sales agents must face the fact that with the commission he pays the agent he buys only a divided loyalty. The agent handles the products of competing manufacturers. It is often argued that by this method of operation he can procure a larger share of the potential business and then divide it among his clients in such proportions and in such a manner as to afford the greatest net profit to each of them. This is especially true of an agent that sells a semifabricated material, such as a fabric, made in several grades or varieties, whose costs are likely to vary among his manufacturer clients. But the fact that his clients must compete with one another for his services, even after the bargain of representation has been struck, remains a serious disadvantage of the use of the sales agent as a marketing channel.

5. If users wish to purchase a manufacturer's products in small lots and need quick deliveries, the cost of shipping direct from the factory may be prohibitive, and the delivery service demanded may be impossible. In some cases, it may prove practicable for the manufacturer of such a product to maintain stocks in strategically located commercial warehouses to which the agent sends his orders and from which deliveries may be made. It is usually more practical, however, for such an industrial marketer to sell direct or to make arrangements for his products to be handled by distributors.

6. When a manufacturer's product requires technical service in either selling, installation, or maintenance, he is apt to find that the agent is neither well equipped nor willing to render it. Then, he may seek to meet the situation by maintaining a force of technical specialists whose services are available to customers who need them. This system may involve

considerable difficulties in coordinating the efforts of the agents with those of the technical specialists so that the services of the specialist are applied when and where they are most needed and will be most beneficial to the manufacturer.

7. On the basis of pure theory and Ben Franklin's dictum, "if you want a thing well done, do it yourself," it might be expected that agent performance in supplying the sales service desired by both purchaser and marketer would not be so good as that of the manufacturer selling direct. This theoretical conclusion is supported by the evidence of the people in the best position to know—the purchasing agents. A study of 150 New York purchasing agents' experiences with manufacturer's agents and the manufacturer's own salesmen shows the following.

	Percent of Purchasing Agents		
	Manufac-turer's Agents	*Direct Salesmen*	*The Same*
Does better selling job............................ .28	53	19
Handles complaints better......................... .26	65	9
Better informed about product.................... .22	69	9
Times calls better................................ .24	40	36
Gets factory decision quicker..................... .25	67	8
Represents factory interests better............... .23	61	16
Represents customer interests better............. .40	48	12

New York Purchasing Review, March, 1959. A study made by N. J. Gallop and reported in *Journal of Marketing*, April, 1964, showed the same general conclusions.

BROKERS AND COMMISSION MERCHANTS

While brokers and commission merchants play no very significant part in industrial goods marketing, they can provide very useful distribution services to some manufacturers of such goods. Table 9–10 presents statistical facts about most of the types of brokers and commission merchants who handle industrial goods.

The commission merchant occupies a relatively insignificant position in the overall industrial marketing picture. The way this agent operates tends to disqualify him from functioning effectively in the industrial goods field. There is no reason why the average maker of industrial products should want to consistently consign them to an agent with whom he has no continuing contractual relationship and who may or may not be able to sell the products. It is highly probable that most of the commission merchants found by Bureau of the Census to be handling industrial goods function more like a manufacturer's agent than a true commission house. These observations do not apply to the marketing of basic agricultural raw materials, in which commission merchants play a highly significant role.

Conversely, in certain circumstances the broker can supply very worthwhile services to the manufacturer of industrial goods. If goods are standardized or can be conveniently described by grade or trade designations, the broker may offer a convenient method of selling them. Many materials, some supplies, and a few small tools and equipment items fall into this category.

Very few makers of industrial goods depend entirely on brokers or commission merchants to distribute their output. But very many make use of them, especially the broker, in certain conditions. For example, a manufacturer of a material finds himself with an excess supply on hand—more than he can sell to his usual customers within an economi-

TABLE 9–10

Brokers and Commission Merchants, 1948

	Industrial Chemicals	Electrical Goods	Construction Materials	Machinery, Equipment, and Supplies	Metals and Metalwork
Brokers					
Number of Establishments.....	41	31	55	195	82
Sales					
In Thousands..............$	43,602	$ 16,099	$ 26,024	$ 84,223	$ 49,776
Per Establishment.........$	1,063,000	$519,000	$473,000	$432,000	$ 607,000
Employees per Establishment..	2.5	2.1	2.0	1.7	1.9
Costs as percentage of Sales....	2.9	5.3	5.1	4.8	3.5
Commission Merchants					
Number of Establishments.....	13	17	8	98	19
Sales					
In Thousands..............$	8,425	$ 2,833	$ 1,996	$ 63,552	$ 23,507
Per Establishment.........$	648,000	$167,000	$249,000	$649,000	$1,237,000
Employees per Establishment..	2.5	1.5	0.8	2.6	1.6
Cost as Percentage of Sales....	4.1	6.4	7.7	4.5	2.1

SOURCE: U.S. Bureau of the Census, *1948 Census of Business, Wholesale Trade*, Washington, D.C. The *Census of Business*, 1954, 1958, and 1963, reported no separate figures for brokers and commission merchants in the industrial goods trades.

cal storage period. He may find a broker who, because of his wide, up-to-the-minute, and detailed knowledge of the trade and of the people in it, knows of someone willing to buy the excess. Such information and contact is amply worth the broker's commission.

In order to enjoy the savings of operating at optimum capacity, a manufacturer may produce more output than he can sell at his regular price through his regular outlets. He may sell the excess through a broker, often at reduced prices. This is often a short-sighted policy, for the material he sells in this way may find its way into the hands of his regular customers, to the disgust of his distributors or his own salesmen.

In the course of making a special order of a certain product, a chemical manufacturer found on his hands a stock of a by-product he knew to be useful in industry. But none of his regular customers bought it, and he did not know its precise usage. To have hunted a market through his own sales force would have been too costly to make the operation profitable, especially since it seemed unlikely that he would have frequent repeats of the special order in the future. Through a broker, he was able to dispose of the lot at a price that turned into an asset a product that otherwise would have been waste material. In order to have brokers available and willing to perform such services, this manufacturer and many others constantly sell a small portion of their output through one or more such agents.

In general, however, the broker and the commission merchant occupy only an incidental and not too significant position in the marketing structure of the average industrial goods manufacturer.

MANUFACTURER'S BRANCH HOUSES

Makers of industrial goods probably make less use of the manufacturer's branch house as a channel of marketing than do consumer goods producers. The firm that makes equipment to specification has little, if any, need for stock-carrying branches, except perhaps to maintain inventories of parts at points convenient to users; practically all its shipments must be made direct to the customer. The limited area within which an article that has a vertical demand can usually be sold because of the tendency of firms in any one buying industry to locate near one another restricts the need another fairly large group of industrial goods manufacturers has for branch houses. The large quantities in which the biggest volume of many industrial goods is bought tend to favor shipments direct from factory to user as against distribution through branch houses. These factors tend to limit the number of industrial goods firms that use branch houses, and to reduce the number operated by firms that do market through them. In spite of these limiting forces, however, the branch house occupies a significant position in the marketing system for industrial goods.

Types of Branch Houses

The two types of manufacturer's branch houses are stock-carrying and nonstock-carrying. As a general rule, goods are shipped to the stock-carrying branch in carload or truckload lots, thus permitting lower carlot or trucklot freight rates over the longer portion of their trips to market. They are then fanned out from the branch in smaller shipping lots to users or, in some cases, to distributors. This arrangement allows the manufacturer to enjoy a favorable combination of freight rates and to render a speedy and reasonably sure delivery service to his customers.

The nonstock-carrying branch house is primarily a sales headquarters.

It usually consists merely of an office from which operate the salesmen who travel the branch territory. Its chief function is usually to afford a convenient organizational unit through which to manage the sales activities of the company.

Statistics and Description of Branch Houses

Table 9–11 shows certain statistical facts about branch houses that handle selected types of industrial goods. From the material presented in it, a number of conclusions about the nature and functions of the two types of establishments can be drawn.

The stock-carrying branch is a good-sized concern, having a manager, and perhaps an assistant manager, a force of salesmen, a warehouse staff to handle the stock, and a clerical staff to carry on the order routine and, in many cases, to prepare and send out the invoices and maintain a fairly complete set of accounts. The salesmen in such an establishment are usually of two types. The inside salesmen remain in the office or show-room, and serve customers who visit the branch to seek information and advice, to place their orders in person, or to ask immediate service to satisfy emergency needs. The outside, or field, salesmen usually work out of the branch as a headquarters, calling on customers and seeking to make sales. The branch usually keeps its own inventory records; it may or may not perform its own accounting work and bill customers for the orders it fills. The varying extent to which these and other functions are performed explains, in part, the wide differences in the average number of persons employed by branch houses in the different trade groups.

The nonstock-carrying branch is usually a much smaller establishment in terms of employees, although not in sales volume. Its personnel may be composed primarily of salesmen and a small supervisory and clerical staff, usually confined to one or two persons. Its primary function is to sell; the orders it receives are transmitted to the factory or home office to be filled from there. It is thus able to handle a given volume of business with a much smaller staff than can the branch that maintains inventory. The difference in functions performed by the two types is also indicated by the difference in expenses as percentages of sales. In all the trade groups listed in Table 9–11, the expenses of the stock-carrying type are much greater than those of the branches that do not carry stocks—in some cases, several times as great.

Size of Branches

An examination of census data about the manufacturer's stock-carrying branch shows the following facts.

1. In most of the trade groups, a high percentage of the total volume of business is done by a small percentage of the establishments. In most of

TABLE 9-11

Statistics of Selected Groups of Manufacturer's Branches, 1963

Trade	With Stocks					Without Stocks			
	Number	Sales per Branch ($000)	Employees per Branch	Expenses as Per-cent of Sales	Number Days Stock	Number	Sales per Branch ($000)	Employees per Branch	Expenses as Per-cent of Sales
Industrial chemicals	563	6,438	36	11.1	125	793	8,066	18	3.6
Electrical supplies and apparatus	705	6,057	39	8.8	14	1,075	2,681	25	5.1
Electrical parts and equipment	121	3,238	21	10.6	16	334	2,390	7	4.7
Air conditioning, refrigeration equipment, supplies	48	2,431	23	12.3	32	170	1,884	8	6.3
Commercial machines and equipment	2388	1,371	35	27.3	21	305	1,316	26	23.0
Construction and mining machinery, equipment	96	2,999	18	9.2	38	53	4,590	12	4.6
Industrial machinery, equipment	1100	1,495	18	14.7	25	1086	1,449	8	8.4
Industrial supplies	677	1,834	16	12.1	23	617	3,051	7	3.9
Professional equipment and supplies	654	524	12	22.2	25	124	1,437	13	10.0
Service equipment and supplies	161	693	12	22.5	47	26	799	9	17.6
Transportation equipment and supplies	35	5,554	57	17.0	58	75	5,391	13	4.2
Metals	312	4,057	11	4.4	20	1364	10,359	13	2.1
Stationery and office supplies	191	975	21	25.5	24	388	905	12	15.0
Construction materials	476	1,421	22	16.1	24	583	3,778	13	5.8

Compiled or computed from U.S. Bureau of the Census, 1963 Census of Business, Wholesale Trade.

them, well over half of the sales volume is transacted by branches that sell more than $1 million annually; these usually constitute less than 30 percent of the total number of establishments in the group.

2. The advantages of the large branch in the matter of cost are very apparent. The manufacturer of industrial goods whose potential volume in an area is small will find it very expensive to distribute there through a branch house. For this reason, it is not uncommon for a firm to sell direct through branches in concentrated industrial areas and through distributors or manufacturer's agents in territories where demand is thinner.

Analysis shows an even greater concentration of manufacturer's branches in the big metropolitan centers than was found to exist among distributors. For example, over half of the manufacturer's branches that handle primary metal products, with about 80 percent of the sales, are in cities with a population of 500,000 or more; about 56 percent of the fabricated metal products branches, making slightly more than half the total sales, are in such cities; and over one third of the branches that market machinery, with slightly more than half the sales, are in such places. This tendency is emphasized by the fact that many producers of small-bulk items maintain branch warehouses in one or two cities such as Chicago, New York, San Francisco, or Los Angeles, out of which they make deliveries to large users and to distributors. Many distributors cannot order such items in carload or truckload quantities of a single article or of several products in the same freight classification. By using a few branch houses, producers are able to obtain a lower combined freight rate to many markets than they could get if they made all deliveries from the factory. For example, almost half of the sales of stock-carrying branches of fabricated metal products manufacturers are made to distributors. Slightly under one third of the sales of construction and mining machinery branches is made to such buyers.

What Trades Use Branches?

Manufacturer's branch houses and distributors are the two chief channels through which industrial goods flow to market. Their relative importance in different trades varies considerably. For example, of the total 1963 volume of industrial chemicals sold to industrial users by distributors, manufacturer's branches, and agents, 16 percent was handled by distributors, 80 percent by branches, and about 4 percent by agents. On the other hand, 80 percent of the construction machinery volume was handled by distributors, 16 percent by branches, and about 4 percent by agents. For construction materials, the figures were: distributors, 48 percent; branches, 45 percent; agents, 7 percent.

In general, supplies manufacturers seem to lean heavily on distributors to move their goods to market. Highly technical products, such as bulk chemicals and electrical apparatus, and bulky materials, such as metals, are marketed largely through manufacturer's sales branches. Logically, all machinery might be expected to be sold direct or through branches, but construction machinery and metalworking machinery are exceptions. The casebooks are replete with examples of relatively small firms making specialized types of equipment that market either through distributors or agents. In no small percentage of the cases, the reason is probably an engineering or production-minded management that prefers to settle the troublesome marketing problems by turning them over to specialists. Financial considerations may also be influential in this decision.

Objectives of Branch Distribution

Through branch house distribution, the manufacturer of industrial goods accomplishes several things. By means of the direct contact with customers that results from the efforts of the sales force, which usually constitutes a part of the branch staff, he is able to apply heavier and more highly skilled promotional pressure on users of his product than would be possible otherwise. This is true of both types of branches; in fact, it is usually the chief reason for the existence of the nonstock-carrying house. The distributors' salesmen, handling the products of many manufacturers, cannot be expected to devote much effort to selling any one of them or to be especially skilled in doing so. The branch house salesman has nothing to sell except the products of the firm that employs him, and he may be expected to know a lot about them.

By operating well trained technical specialists out of the branch, the technical goods maker can offer his customers expert information, help, and advice that his competitor, selling through distributors, will find difficult to match.

In his branch house, the equipment maker can maintain strategically located stocks of parts, as well as repair facilities and mechanics equipped to keep his machines in working order in his customers' plants. In some trades where it is customary to depend on the supplier for repair work, this is a factor of very great importance.

Through his branch houses located in industrial centers, the manufacturer of supplies, small tools, and materials is able to render a delivery service to his large customers that he might find difficult or impossible through distributors.

The direct contact with the trade that results from branch house operations serves a multitude of minor purposes. Through its salesmen, the branch can be a fruitful source of information about the market and developments that are taking place in it. One branch house in a system can be used as a guinea pig in which to try out new products, new methods of selling, new techniques of servicing customers, and other changes that may be very profitable if they prove sound but if applied generally throughout the company before testing in a small area might seriously disrupt the entire operations of the firm and prove extremely costly and wasteful.

Branch Distribution Can Be Costly

The chief drawback of the branch house system of distribution lies in its expense. Such an operation has a habit of developing costs of its own, often not anticipated before it is actually put into effect. It creates its own overhead costs, loads the company with an entirely new set of personnel obligations that may be difficult to diminish when costs must be cut, engenders a need for plant and equipment not otherwise required, and adds tremendously to the work of supervision and management, and to the staff required to carry it on. Establishing a branch house system is a major enterprise for a company of any size. For a company whose sales potential is limited, and whose market is thin, the cake may not be worth the candle.

SUMMARY

Let us summarize. Distributors are the most numerous and most important group of middlemen handling industrial goods. Some of them are general houses trading in a wide variety of products; others specialize in handling one or a narrow line of products or in serving one group of customers. As a group, their number has tended to increase, their average sales to decline, their costs to increase, their average number of employees to increase, and their stocks to decline in relation to sales.

They are highly concentrated geographically, and most of their volume is in the hands of relatively few large houses. We observed several of the operating features that affect their usefulness as outlets for the manufacturer's goods. Industrial users find it desirable to buy from the distributor because he usually can give quick delivery, his use saves paper work in buying, he can sometimes offer lower prices, adjustments are easier to negotiate, he may enable the buyer to save freight costs, and he is a good source of trade information. The patronage of the distributor thus comes mainly from (1) the firm too small to buy direct, (2) the large firm for emergency needs and items bought in small amounts or as a means of reducing inventory.

Manufacturer's and sales agents are useful outlets to producers of a single item or a narrow line of articles, to the manufacturer with limited finances, and to all kinds of manufacturers in areas where demand is thin or trade contacts are lacking. Advantages in using agents are that their costs are often relatively low and the producer incurs no costs unless sales are made, they offer contacts to the firm entering a new market, and their sales service is more specialized and intense than that of the distributor. But the manufacturer who markets through agents loses control over his marketing operations, lacks flexibility in bidding, incurs excessive costs when volume is large, loses speed of delivery, quality of technical service, and selling drive in comparison with his own sales force. Brokers and commission merchants are useful mainly in special situations.

Manufacturer's branch houses are of two types—those that carry stocks and those that do not. Through the branch house, the manufacturer gets better sales service, more adequate and representative stocks, and control of technical and maintenance service. But branch houses are often so costly as to be prohibitive.

Chapter 10

<><><><><><><><><><><><><><><><><><><><><><><><><><><> MANAGING

MARKETING CHANNELS

BOTH BUSINESSMEN and students of marketing often too narrowly define the problem of marketing channels. Many of them tend to regard the term "channel of distribution" as a complex of relationships between the firm, on the one hand, and marketing establishments exterior to the firm, by which its products are moved to market, on the other. This omits from the picture the part of the company's organizational structure devoted to this purpose.

A much broader and more realistic concept embraces both the internal marketing units of a firm and external agents or concerns handling its products as the marketing organization of the company. From this point of view, the complex of external relationships may be regarded as merely an extension of the firm's internal marketing organization. When we look at the problem in this way, we are much less apt to lose sight of the interdependence of the two structures, and more likely to be constantly aware that they are closely related parts of the marketing machine. The fact that the internal organization structure is knit together by a system of employment contracts while the external one is set up and maintained by a series of contracts of purchase and sale tends to obscure their common purpose and close relationship.

Also, the problem is too often regarded as merely a matter of choosing channels. This is only one part of the broader task of managing channel activities. Not only must the units that compose the channel be chosen, but their relationships with the firm and with one another must constantly be maintained and adjusted; the outside units and their employees must be informed and trained; incentives and compensations must be provided for them; and what amounts to supervisory contacts must be continually maintained.

NATURE OF CHANNEL RELATIONSHIP

In its essence, the relationship among elements within the channel of distribution is the same as that among the elements in any organization

254

structure. Any organization represents a composite of conflict and cooperation. It is made up of people and structural units joined together and
tolerating certain restrictions to achieve certain common, overall objectives. But each carries into this relationship a set of individual interests and
objectives, which often conflict with those of other members of the group
and, in some degree, with those of the organization. The organization is
strongest and functions best when those who comprise it see in it an
effective way of achieving most of their individual ends as well as the
common objectives of the group. This is a matter that management can
often do something about.

Since the marketing units outside a firm that belong to its channel of
distribution are often in hot competition with one another for the patronage of the same buyers, the conflict element in the organization structure
they comprise is especially pronounced. From this fact grow many of the
most difficult problems in channel management. These problems are aggravated because up to the moment of its final consummation each of the
series of contract or purchase-sale transactions that establish and maintain
the relationship between the firm and the several outside marketing units
in the channel occurs in an atmosphere of conflict. Both the selling
manufacturer and the buying channel unit know that to make profits they
must cooperate, but each is out to get for himself the best deal he can
within the area of cooperation.

If we bear in mind this natural conflict–cooperation atmosphere of the
channel relationship, we will find it much less difficult to understand the
problems of channel management.

Planning and Organizing Marketing Channels

The work of planning and organizing a system of marketing channels
involves at least three essential steps. The marketer must first conduct a
background analysis designed to isolate the various jobs or subjobs that
must be done in order to sell his products and move them smoothly to
market, and to discover and understand the implications of the factors
that influence the way these jobs must be done. He must then decide
which types of agents, or marketing units, can be expected to carry on
these tasks most effectively for him. Finally, he must select and establish
relationships with the individual units most suitable to his needs within
each type.

Comparatively few marketing managers ever face the job of setting up
a distribution channel system from scratch. A far more usual task is that of
making adjustments in existing channel systems to meet changing conditions or objectives. The three subtasks outlined above must be carried out
consciously or informally in either case if the whole job is to be well
done.

The job of modifying an existing channel is probably the more difficult of the two. Even in the initial planning and analysis stages of a rebuilding operation the marketing manager is likely to find his thinking obscured by a tendency to assume that the familiar—what is—is right. Once he visualizes the system he desires, he finds that in implementing it he is handicapped by the need to avoid disturbing his existing distribution system so violently that his firm suffers serious loss of volume, market position, and profits. Remedial action for a poor outlet may seem to threaten the position of a good one that may seek a new connection or lose some enthusiasm for the present one. Often, the marketer must move quite circumspectly, and erect his new structure a piece at a time over a considerable period.

Factors Affecting Channel Choice

Some factors that influence the choice and organization of channels arise from the nature of the market; others exist because of peculiarities of the product; still others grow out of the character and situation of the firm. Some factors are so peculiar to individual firms that their discussion is not profitable here. We will devote out attention to those that have reasonably wide applicability.

Is the Market Horizontal or Vertical? If a manufacturer's product can be sold only to the members of one or a few industries, and the number of firms in each industry is small, direct distribution probably is the most profitable method. Relatively few salesmen will be needed to make direct contact with all probable users. If branch warehouses are needed, the number necessary is likely to be small. Closer contact can be maintained with customers and prospective customers, and the opportunities to make sales are usually improved by this marketing method.

If, on the other hand, the market is horizontal and the product must be sold to buyers in many industries, the number of buyers probably is large, and the chances of economically reaching all or a large portion of them usually are enhanced by selling through distributors. The costs of setting up and operating a sales force large enough to directly reach all or a substantial portion of the users are liable to be excessive, and the expense of providing and maintaining branch warehouses to supply them may prove to be unbearable. For example, most industrial supplies producers make use of distributors in their marketing systems, as do the makers of small tools widely used by many industries.

Is the Possible Volume of Sales Large or Small in the Average Market Area? If the nature of a product is such that a substantial volume of sales is available in the average area served by a single salesman or branch warehouse, direct marketing may prove profitable. If, on the contrary, the probable volume of sales in a market area is small, the direct method may be too expensive.

Many people are not so familiar as they should be with the comparatively simple mathematics of direct marketing. Suppose a manufacturer makes industrial products that can be sold to 30,000 firms, which must be called on about once every two weeks. The average salesman of such industrial goods can make about 8 calls a day, or 40 a week. He can thus handle about 80 accounts. To maintain proper sales contact with 30,000 customers, the manufacturer would need about 375 salesmen. A conservative figure for the cost of such a salesman, including compensation and expenses, would be $15,000 a year, or a total of $5.625 million a year for the force.

In addition, such a sales force would need 1 field supervisor for about every 10 salesmen. Again this is a conservative estimate; about one for eight would be a more realistic ratio. The operating cost of each man would probably be about $20,000 a year, and if the company used 37 of them, the total cost of field supervision would be about $740,000 annually. The cost of the sales force involved in direct marketing would thus aggregate about $6.365 million, and this does not include the expenses of division managers and the supporting staff needed to administer such a force.

Add the cost of providing adequate warehouse space, which would vary widely in different parts of the country, the expense of office space for the administrative staff, and the costs generated by a staff of order-handling clerks, order pickers, packers, and shippers needed to service the large volume of relatively small orders, which are likely to characterize direct distribution, and we probably have another $3 or $4 million. If a firm with this sort of a distributive organization realizes a gross profit of 40 percent, it must have total sales of over $25 million just to meet its costs of distribution alone. If it is to get its distributive costs down to the general average of industrial concerns—somewhere between 5 and 15 percent—it must be a big business. Direct marketing, a simple answer to the problem of choosing channels, is often a very costly one unless there is a volume of sales sufficient to support the expense.

To What Extent Are the Possible Purchasers Concentrated Geographically? The tendency toward localization of industry makes it possible to market direct to the user many industrial products whose small sales volume would preclude the possibility of selling direct, even to retailers, if they were consumer goods. If 70 or 80 percent of the total possible sales volume of a product is concentrated in one or two limited market areas—not unusual with industrial goods—the makers of such a product are likely to find that there is enough volume available in those areas to support direct marketing. By marketing direct, a manufacturer may cut himself off from the remaining 20 or 30 percent of the total volume, although he may be able to capture part or all of his share of it through distributors located in the areas of thin demand.

What Are the Buying Habits of the User? If the user of an industrial good habitually purchases in small orders and for quick delivery, its marketer probably will find it least costly and most satisfactory to sell through distributors. By combining the user's needs for several kinds of items, the distributor may be able to turn previously small orders for any one manufacturer whose goods he handles into economically sized orders composed of products from several makers. By combining the sale of one manufacturer's goods, on which the gross profit is small, with those of other manufacturers, who make items that enjoy higher margins and are sold to the same users, although sometimes in small quantities, the distributor may assemble a line that has possibilities of satisfactory profit, even though it would not be profitable for any one of the manufacturers to try to sell his product direct through his own facilities. For example, dental supply houses sell dentists the supplies and materials they use, on which the margin of gross profit is modest, together with equipment, which carries a wider margin. This is true of many laboratory equipment and chemicals distributors, hotel and restaurant supply houses, and distributors of bottling extracts, equipment, and supplies.

If the user wishes to purchase supplies or materials on a volume or requirements contract, the goods to be delivered in increments throughout a year or half-year period, direct contact is more apt to be necessary, and direct factory shipments may be feasible. If, conversely, the user wants to buy on a hand-to-mouth basis, or attempts to control inventories by ordering when stock falls to a fixed point, the marketer must usually either maintain branch houses from which quick and reliable deliveries can be made—an expensive operation—or sell through distributors who, if properly selected, can be expected to carry stocks at points convenient to the users.

An ongoing change in buying habits may be expected to exercise a pronounced effect on the selection of marketing channels for certain types of industrial goods, notably supplies, standardized components, and materials bought in relatively small bulk. Formerly, it was almost a standard procedure of many purchasing officers in large firms to insist on buying direct in order to avoid paying the distributor's margin, and in the hope of getting quantity discounts. Two kinds of studies cast doubt on the soundness of this practice. Studies indicated that the cost of placing a buying order ranged from $20 to $40. Others showed that the cost of carrying inventory amounted to about 2 percent of its value per month. In other words, it costs about $24 a year to carry an average inventory of $100. The development of automatic record keeping suggested some things the purchasing officer could do about these expenses.

Many firms are streamlining purchasing practice by setting up continuing relations with selected suppliers, with whom orders are placed by telephone, unpriced simplified purchase order, or even a tub-file inventory punched card. Orders are totaled and paid every 10 days or at the end of the month instead of on an invoice created for each order. While each item may be bought in smaller quantities, many items are bought from one source and often on one order.

For this system to work, the purchasing officer must select one or two distributors and place all his orders with them. This vastly increases the importance of the distributor as an outlet for the makers of many supplies, materials, and component parts. It also may be expected to decrease the effectiveness of the limited franchise arrangement, whereby the manufacturer markets through only one or two distributors in a market area. For example, if a firm that uses abrasives concentrates all its purchases of supplies, materials, and minor equipment with one or two distributors, an abrasives manufacturer whose products are franchised to another distributor in the area has no chance to get the business.

This method of buying has been growing rapidly, and new refinements are constantly being added. How far it will go and how long it will last are unanswered questions. It seems likely that some streamlining of expensive order procedures and closer control of inventory are here to stay.

What Is the Gross Profit Margin? If a manufacturer's product or products carry a wide margin between production cost and the price the user will pay, he probably can afford a more expensive channel of distribution than he can when this margin is narrow. He may find it profitable to sell through his own sales force and make delivery himself, because by so doing he may increase cash inflow from added volume more than he augments cash outflow in the form of greater marketing costs. If the market situation is such that the spread between cost and selling price to user is narrow, the marketer is denied the necessary margin area within which to conduct such a maneuver. He must make his channel decisions primarily in the interest of low marketing cost rather than high sales volume.

The choice is usually not nearly so clear-cut as we have stated it here. The nature of the market for some narrow-spread items is such that while the use of the direct channel may increase the total dollar outflow for marketing activities the greater volume of sales it brings results in a smaller marketing cost per dollar of sales.

How Volatile Is the Price? The price of many industrial materials and some supplies is highly volatile. The maker of such an item who markets through distributors has a constant problem in adjusting their margins to compensate for shifts in price. If he does not make such adjustments, he finds that part of the time distributors are overcompensated in dollar receipts for the services they render, while part of the time they do not receive enough for handling his product to make satisfactory selling, stocking, and handling services worthwhile. As a result, the pressure is in the direction of marketing channels involving less complicated price–margin relationships, such as direct sale or the use of agents paid on a commission or per unit fee basis.

Must the Product Be Installed? Many industrial products must be installed in the users' plants or establishments. In some cases, such as heavy, complicated machinery, the nature of the product and the market is such that the work of installation must be done by the maker, or he must advise and aid the buyer in doing it. This tends to induce the use of direct channels of marketing. In other cases, such as communication equipment for use in apartment buildings, office buildings, institutions, and factories, specialized contractors have developed to do the work of installation. In such a situation, it is often desirable that the product be sold to the user by a local firm that can also make on-the-spot arrangements for installation and follow-through. This points toward the use of distributors. Sometimes, the local situation is such that the user who wants to buy direct and make his own installation cannot do so without danger of strike or boycott by unions or contractors' associations.

How Much Technical Service Does the Product Require In Use? Many materials, such as chemicals, and some types of highly technical equipment, such as accounting, recording, and statistical analysis machines, demand the services of carefully trained technical experts if the user is to enjoy the maximum benefit from them. The buyer of a chemical may want to mix it with a carrier not previously used or in proportions he has no experience with. He expects advice and help from the seller to obtain the desired result. If the user of electronic recording and computing equipment wants an analysis or a control result not contemplated when it was installed, he expects the equipment maker to tell him how to get it. Such service is usually more satisfactory when relations between maker and user are direct.

How Important Is Quality? The quality specifications for some materials must be very exact and the quality tolerances very narrow. This is especially so with materials that go into food or drug end products and with electronic or mechanical control components, although it is true of other items as well. Even the most meticulous inspection procedure will not prevent an off-quality lot from occasionally getting into the hands of customers whose use of it in their end products may have, at worst, lethal and, at best, unsatisfactory effects. When this happens and is discovered, a recall operaton must often be conducted to recover all the off-quality lot and replace it with satisfactory goods. When the article has moved to market through indirect channels so that the maker has no record of the users who finally bought it, this may be a highly expensive process and one of dubious success. Therefore, this characteristic points toward the use of direct channels of marketing.

It also sometimes happens that different users of a material or component want a variety of quality gradations so numerous that it is not practical to reduce them to a system of standard classes. In such cases, each batch or lot for each customer's order must be produced to specification. If such goods are marketed through indirect channels, it is hard to make sure that specification requirements are accurately communicated and that the proper lots are delivered to customers in the distribution process. In such a situation, the direct channel is much more effective and satisfactory to both maker and user.

In general, when an industrial product is made to specifications set by the user direct distribution is indicated. When it is made to standard specifications or in only a few variations or quality gradations, it may be marketed through indirect channels.

How Bulky Is the Item? If a product is so bulky that most of its users buy in carload or truckload lots, the tendency toward direct-to-user distribution is very strong. Unless speed of delivery is of prime importance to the buyer, or his rate of use of the commodity is subject to more than ordinary fluctuations, there is no reason for the manufacturer to maintain branch houses; he can sell direct through his own salesmen for factory shipment.

This is true if he makes an article so small in bulk that it is generally shipped by express or parcel post. Transportation expense usually constitutes a percentage of the total cost of such a product so small that the savings to be made by carload or truckload transportation would probably be much more than offset by the expenses of maintaining a branch house system. If his customers require speedy delivery, or the nature of their operations gives rise to emergency needs for a product, its maker may be justified in maintaining branch houses.

The same considerations apply to the marketing of such products through distributors. In handling them, the distributor lacks one of his big advantages—the saving in transportation cost he makes possible by buying in bulk lots and selling in less-than-carload or less-than-truckload lots—thus causing the goods to move at the lower bulk freight rate throughout the greater part of their journey to market. These difficulties do not apply to an agent in handling such articles, since he usually sells for factory shipment.

What Kind of Repair and Maintenance Service Does the User Need and How Much? If the product is so complex that it must be serviced by highly skilled specialists, the manufacturer must maintain some sort of service stations from which they can operate and in which stocks of parts may be carried. Such stations can just as well be used for branch houses. If the article is one the average mechanic can repair, customers will rely very little on the manufacturer for repair service. Then, the marketer may need to see to it that supplies of repair parts are conveniently available to users; this can be accomplished through distributors as well as, or better than, by branch houses.

Direct sale and delivery of parts may seem to be of some help to the machinery manufacturer in combating the pirate parts makers; on the other hand, by depriving distributors of the opportunity to handle the legitimate parts, he may stimulate them to take over marketing of the pirate products. Perhaps a sound policy consists in making sure that parts handling is a profitable business for the distributor and that he carries an adequate, but not burdensome, stock of them.

What Is the Firm's Size and Financial Position? Is the firm well financed and large, or is it small and without adequate financial backing? If a concern is in a strong financial position, it can support a program of direct distribution that requires the spending of money for sales effort, the long-time investment of funds in branch warehouse facilities, and the tying up of working capital in inventories and accounts receivable. On the other hand, if a firm lacks adequate capital, it must sell its output as quickly as possible after it is produced, get paid for it as soon as it can, and carry on the entire process of distribution at the least possible cost.

The use of distributors or agents helps to achieve these ends. Only a few salesmen are needed to sell to distributors; such outlets carry most of the stocks necessary to serve the trade; and they usually discount their bills. The agent offers the great advantage that while the firm that uses him must generally carry the stock needed to service his customers, it incurs no selling expense until after he has sold some of its goods, and the amount of its selling cost varies with the volume of sales made.

Sometimes, the small, poorly financed manufacturer of certain types of materials, components, and equipment may solve his distribution problem by selling his entire output to one big buyer. For example, a small firm in the Midwest concentrates on making several parts for one of the large motor manufacturers. It has only one customer; its production processes are entirely standardized; it has no sales expenses other than the time and effort of its executives in negotiating contract renewals; it moves its product directly from its machines to railroad cars or trucks; and it is paid twice a month. Its margin of gross profit enables it to earn a satisfactory net return. The only drawback lies in its complete dependence on its one customer. The motor company will probably protect this small supplier as long as his costs and prices are satisfactory; but if a reliable competitor is able to reduce the costs and undercut prices, the buyer may shift his patronage, provided his present supplier cannot meet the new offer.

What Are the Seller's Marketing Objectives? If a manufacturer is marketing his product locally and intends to expand to nationwide distribution, he will be wise to choose channels that will fit in with and facilitate that expansion. If he plans to diversify his product line, either through development of new products or by acquisition—particularly development—he should strive to build a channel system that is flexible in the sense that it can be expanded into new markets simply by adding new units rather than largely reorganizing to reach each new type of customer. If his objective is to make a profit by skimming the cream of the market through sale of a very high-profit product or provision of the maximum of service, he is likely to find direct channels most useful; if his policy is to seek a small profit per unit on a large number of units sold primarily on the price appeal, he may find it best to market through distributors. Other objectives either of a marketing or companywide nature may influence channel selection.

SELECTING CHANNELS

In the process of establishing his channel system, the industrial marketer must make three sets of selections. He must first choose the type of outlet or the combination of outlets that best fits his needs. Then, he must decide whether he will use only one or a limited number of these outlets in each market area, or will market through all outlets of the selected type available there. If he decides on the limited or selective policy, he must then choose the particular outlets in each market area that he will attempt to include in his system. In making all these choices, he will find it useful to apply the factors outlined in the previous section, plus others that may be peculiar to his situation.

Five general types of outlet or channel arrangements are available to him.

1. He may market direct to users through his own sales force, with or without his own branch warehouse system. An analysis of the list of factors discussed above suggests that this type of channel arrangement is desirable when:

   a) The product can be sold in volume large enough to support the cost of such a system.
   b) The market is concentrated so that the requirements of (a) are met in areas where the bulk of the volume is located, even though a minor part of the potential may be scattered outside these areas of concentration.
   c) There is great need for highly specialized technical service.
   d) The product must be delivered to the user either in carload lots or in small express shipment lots, provided its unit value is also high. Each of these situations means that the product can be sold for factory shipment, and expensive warehouse facilities are not needed.
   e) The manufacturer is well enough financed to be able to establish and maintain a direct sales force and branch warehouse system.
   f) The products are highly specialized or made to specifications of the buyer so that in any case there must be direct contact between maker and buyer.
   g) The market is vertical so that distribution is limited to a certain group or several well-identified groups of buyers.
   h) The price is volatile so that price changes must be made without the delay of transmission through intermediaries and without the shifts in price relationships between intermediaries that would otherwise have to be made.
   i) The margin between factory cost and price to the user is wide enough to support a direct distribution system.

j) The product is a piece of equipment that the maker must install or help to install, so that direct contact must be made in any case.

k) Adjustments must be made in quality to meet the needs of individual buyers, making direct contact necessary.

Not all these factors must favor a direct channel in any specific case in order to make its choice desirable. Their relative importance will vary with each situation. No small part of the skill of choosing channels consists in assigning proper weights to the various factors involved.

2. He may market to users through an agent or several agents. An agent may be a broker or commission merchant, or a manuatfcurer's or a sales agent.

A broker or a commission merchant will not be very useful to an industrial goods marketer unless the product is standardized and can be sold on grades or generally accepted specifications. The maker of a material with a very narrow margin between factory cost and user buying price may make use of brokers to keep the cost of distribution as low as possible and to meet price competition. How well this works depends on the amount of the broker's fee. In some lines of business, this may be as much as 5 percent of selling price, which is little, if any, below the usual cost–sales ratio for marketing industrial goods through other channels. Sometimes, manufacturers of materials use brokers to dispose of overstocks that occur when they misjudge the market or deliberately make more than they can sell through their ordinary channels in order to gain the cost advantage of optimum batch or production runs. Deliberate overproduction has the drawback that the overstocks sold through brokers may find their way into the inventories of users who ordinarily buy from outlets in the regular channels, to the acute unhappiness of the outlets.

Situations that seem to favor the use of sales or manufacturer's agents in marketing industrial goods occur when:

a) The manufacturer is poorly financed and must pay the cost of marketing an order for his goods out of cash received for them.

b) The manufacturer enters a market in which he has no contacts and about which he has little or no knowledge; among the chief stocks in trade of both these types of agents are market information and contacts.

c) The marketing of the product requires more than a little, but not too much, technical service. Because the agent handles a limited line of items, he and his salesman can know more about them than a distributor can, but his knowledge cannot be so extensive or so detailed as that of the manufacturer's own marketing staff.

d) The product is suitable for shipment from factory to user because of bulk or method of purchase.

e) The market is vertical or is composed of a number of vertical segments. By the use of different agents, each specializing in one or two of these segments, the manufacturer may put together an economical and effective channel system.

It should be pointed out that in order to use sales agents in his distribution channel a manufacturer must be willing to commit his entire marketing destinies to one agent in each buying trade, and that to employ manufacturer's agents he must rely entirely on one agent in each geographical area.

It should also be pointed out that while the manufacturer who uses agents gets from them a sales service probably somewhat better than the distributor can give to the multitude of items in his line the service still falls far short of what he could obtain from his own sales force. A study of purchasing officers and design engineers in the electronic equipment business showed that in the experience of these executives company salesmen were superior to agents in that they had more, and more reliable, technical knowledge, they gave better service, they had a better knowledge of the customer's needs, they were more effective in securing and arranging the cooperation of the supplier's technical people, and they occasionally were able to give better prices. Their superiority was indicated by the fact that many of these executives found it worthwhile to give company salesmen more interview time than they were willing to allow to agents.[1]

3. The maker of industrial goods may attempt to market them through industrial distributors who sell to users. As in other types of channel, certain situations favor the use of distributors. The most common are when:

a) The market is scattered so that sales volume in each area is too thin to support a direct marketing organization, or even to enable a sales or manufacturer's agent to operate profitably with his narrow line of products; a distributor, by handling many items, can develop a volume of business big enough to profitably market the entire group.

b) Quick sales and delivery service is needed, as in many maintenance, repair, and operation items; the number of distributors who can profitably handle a manufacturer's line usually far exceeds the number of branch warehouses the manufacturer can maintain, with the result that distributors' stocks are located nearer the user than are those of the manufacturer.

c) A product has an horizontal market, with the result that its volume is scattered and thin.

d) Customers want to buy the product in small, uneconomical orders; the distributor can often combine requests for small amounts with similar requirements for other articles in his line, and build orders of profitable size.

e) The margin between factory cost and user's buying price is too narrow to pay for a direct marketing organization, but through the economies of a wide line the distributor can profitably handle the product.

f) The quality required is fairly standard or the product is well identified

---

[1] N. J. Gallop, "Manufacturer's Representative or Company Salesman," *Journal of Marketing*, April, 1964.

by brand or make, and customers do not want special quality preparations that require direct manufacturer–user contact.

g) The product is of such bulk that significant savings in its delivered cost to the user can be achieved by taking advantage of the lower rates allowed for the carload or truckload shipments in which the distributor is able to buy.

h) A firm is financed well enough so that it can support the relatively modest outlay needed to operate the small sales force required to maintain contact with distributors, but is not rich enough to maintain the much larger force necessary to market direct to users. Even this outlay may be reduced by using agents to sell to the distributors.

4. Some industrial goods makers find it desirable to use multilevel channels of distribution. Every channel system is in part multilevel. Even the manufacturer who markets through brokers to users must have some unit in his organization that establishes and maintains contact with the brokers, as well as with sales agents or manufacturer's agents if he uses them as the sole extra-company unit in his channel. When he markets through distributors, he must use agents or maintain a specialized, although usually small, organization to keep contact with them and supervise their activities. In the building materials trade and in some phases of the equipment business, it is sometimes necessary to have an internal organization to keep contact with architects and builders, as well as distributors who sell to the contractors that do the work of making the final sale and installation. The need for these levels arises not only from one or more of the factors or situations we have mentioned, but also from established trade practices, customs, and sometimes coercion of one sort or another.

5. The industrial goods manufacturer sometimes finds it desirable to use what might be called a mixed channel of distribution. For example, when a market is heavily concentrated in certain districts but has some buyers thinly scattered over wider areas it may be profitable to distribute direct where the market is concentrated, and to rely on distributors or sales or manufacturer's agents to capture a share of the business where volume is thin.

The natural segmentation of the market may also make desirable the use of a mixed channel. For example, a manufacturer may make several products and sell to different markets, each with different types of service outlets, or he may market the same product to one group of buyers who are content to purchase a standard grade and to another who want special quality variations or demand very rigid tolerances with much technical service. Thus, he may find it desirable to reach the first through distributors and to market direct to the second.

An example is a firm that makes a liquified gas used as a refrigerant and an aerosol propellant. It markets through distributors to repairmen who recharge refrigeration systems, and through its own salesmen to manufacturers of refrigeration equipment, contract loaders of aerosol bombs, and firms that load and sell such bombs themselves. Some other firms in the industry use their own men to sell manufacturers where the market is concentrated, and employ manufacturer's or sales agents where it is thin.

Still another type of mixed channel occurs when a firm follows a policy of selling direct to large users while depending on distributors to handle the business of smaller users. For example, in 1965 the Abrasives Division of the Norton Company, which had marketed abrasive supplies through distributors, began to offer volume discounts to large users on an automatic reorder basis. In spite of the loud protests of the distributors, an executive of the company reported in *Sales Management*, July 1, 1966, that during the first half of 1966 new business showed a gratifying rate of increase.

Mixed channels probably are not used so extensively as they should be. Once having become familiar with the problems of marketing through a channel, manufacturers show considerable reluctance to add another, even when changes in market conditions or in their product lines indicate rather clearly the desirability of mixing channels. This is understandable, for the administration of such mixtures is often a complicated process. Then, too, if a manufacturer has his own direct marketing organization he probably wants to use it to the fullest extent possible, even though some parts of his marketing job may not be accomplished through it so effectively as through a combination of outlets. Also, the managers of an outlet that has enjoyed a long-standing relationship with a manufacturer are likely to develop the idea that they have a prior claim on his business, even when he brings out new products or enters new markets. This attitude may cause the manufacturer to fear that if he uses another type of outlet in a new situation he may endanger the effectiveness of his existing marketing system.

A study of 220 firms marketing industrial machinery, equipment, and supplies indicates that about 74 percent used the distributor as a major marketing channel. About 57 percent sold directly to the distributor, either from the factory or through branches, and about 17 percent reached him through a manufacturer's agent. The use of the distributor channel varied from about 87 percent for the small firms to about 44 percent for the large ones. It also varied according to product from 100 percent for valves and fittings to 44 percent for fasteners.

About 22 percent marketed direct to the user, either from the factory or through branch houses. This percentage increased from about 6 percent for small firms to about 56 percent for those with an annual volume of more than $100 million. It varied widely from zero for valves and fittings to about 56 percent for fasteners.

Less than 4 percent of the firms used manufacturer's agents as their major method of reaching the user. These were chiefly small firms that marketed abrasive products, cutting tools, materials handling equipment, steel products, and machine tools.

About 60 percent of the firms used the distributor as a secondary channel; about 46 percent serviced him directly from the factory or through branches, and 14 percent through manufacturer's agents. The rest used the manufacturer's agent to reach the user. There seemed to be no consistent variation according to size, although wide variations occurred on the basis of products.[2]

These percentages are somewhat deceptive because they are based on number of firms. The picture would probably be materially different if sales volume were used as the base.

The Use of Formulas

Some firms have experimented with the use of mathematical techniques in selecting channel types and even in choosing individual outlets within the types. There are at least four steps in this procedure.

1. Isolation of the controlling factors, the most common of which we have listed and briefly discussed. In doing this, the analyst should not be content with those treated in this book or in any other writings, but should be careful to include others that are peculiar to his firm, his product, or the market situation.

2. Assignment of weights to each factor. For example, the factor of product bulk might be assigned a possible weight of 10 points and technical service required, 15 points. This must often be done on the basis of managerial judgment, although sometimes mathematical analyses can be applied to past or estimated future operating statistics to determine the proper weights.

3. Assignment of specific weights to factors in specific situations. For example, one product might be awarded 8 out of a possible 10 points on the basis of bulk and the full 15 on the basis of technical service needed. This also is usually a matter of managerial judgment, although mathematic analysis can sometimes be useful.

4. Determination of a critical summary score. This may often be done on the basis of past experience, with the possible help of mathematic analysis.

Users of such formulas must be always alert to changes in company situation or objectives, product characteristics, or market conditions that invalidate factors in the formula, introduce new ones not in the formula, or cause shifts in the weights that should be assigned to factors. A formula offers no excuse for a manager to stop thinking.

All Outlets or Only a Few?

After the industrial marketer has determined the types of marketing units external to his firm through which he proposes to distribute, he must decide whether he will attempt to sell to all firms of each chosen type or will select only a few of them as his outlets. Each of these policies has its advantages and its weaknesses.

[2] W. T. Diamond, *Distribution Channels for Industrial Goods,* (Columbus: Bureau of Business Research, Ohio State University, 1963).

If he elects to market through all outlets of a type that will buy, he will find it much simpler to gain complete coverage of all parts of the market than if he adopts the selective policy. Merely by the laws of chance at least one oulet in each market area should be willing to handle his product. If he adopts the selective policy, he must fit the chosen outlets into a mosaic of the areas they operate in to be sure that all parts of the market are covered. He also has the problem of adjusting conflicting claims to districts where the trading areas of two or more selected outlets overlap.

The blanket policy usually does not afford the manufacturer the same degree of cooperation from his outlets that he can gain by use of the selective method. The selective policy tends to generate a much closer relationship, and to emphasize its cooperative aspects while diminishing its elements of conflict. Under the blanket policy, the relations between manufacturer and outlets are usually arm's-length contacts, with a purchase and sale transaction as their central element. The selected outlet is much more likely to feel that he has a stake in the manufacturer's success, and that it will be worthwhile to cooperate wholeheartedly in carrying out the producer's marketing programs. The selective relationship is much closer than the blanket one, and affords the manufacturer much more control over the field distribution of his products.

This more intensive spirit of cooperation plus the fact that the welfare of the selected agent or distributor is more closely tied to that of the manufacturer tends to afford the maker a higher quality of marketing service than he can expect from blanket outlets. This manifests itself in more aggressive selling effort by the outlet, greater willingness to carry adequate and representative stocks, more active cooperation in promotional programs, and greater willingness to equip himself and his sales people to render necessary service, technical and otherwise. The extent to which the manufacturer can expect to enjoy these advantages has definite limits. Within the outlet's operational pattern, his products are still in active conflict with those of other manufacturers for the limited time and effort the agent or distributor can afford to expend on his entire line.

The manufacturer who follows the selective policy can expect to enjoy some savings in marketing costs. He will have fewer accounts to call on than under the blanket policy. The saving will probably not be commensurate with the reduction in number of accounts, since the salesman's travel time will tend to remain about the same and the average call will tend to be longer. But the salesman can usually spend more of his calling time in constructive effort to move the product into the hands of the user and less of it in the struggle to get an order. Since the outlets are fewer, the average order is likely to be larger, with resulting reductions in order-handling costs.

The selective policy also is likely to provide the manufacturer with a distributor sales force that is better informed and better equipped to sell his product than one he can get by the blanket policy. If a distributor knows that the business he develops for a product in his territory belongs to him and can be served by no one else, he will feel it worthwhile to properly train his salesmen by sending them to the producer's factory and by cooperating in other training programs the manufacturer may develop. This is especially important to the maker of a highly technical product or one that requires service in installation or use.

The big drawback to the selective policy is that the manufacturer who uses it puts all his marketing eggs in one or two baskets in each area. The distributor who looks good on paper or under analysis may disclose clay feet in action, but by then the manufacturer is stuck with him. Usually, it is not possible to get the best distributor in every market; in some areas, it may not even be possible to get a good one unless the manufacturer is himself a prize catch for any distributor. The quality of the manufacturer's marketing performance in an area depends almost entirely on the excellence of his selected distributor there. If he sells on a blanket basis, he can expect to enjoy a fairly uniform quality of distributor performance everywhere, since in almost every market there are both poor and good distributors, all or most of whom will be handling his product.

This drawback is emphasized by the fact that a high percentage of manufacturer's and sales agents and many distributors are one-man firms or partnerships. This means that their continuity is highly uncertain. The manufacturer who follows a selective policy is likely to find that most of the time he must worry about replacing an outlet in at least one of his market areas, and in the meantime he is without good representation there.

If manufacturers' decisions are to be taken as a valid indication of sound policy, the advantages of the selective system seem to overbalance those of the blanket method in the marketing of industrial goods. The selective system seems to be used much more generally in the industrial goods field than in distributing consumers' goods. The streamlining of purchase procedure may reverse this tendency in some product areas. Of course, the manufacturer who markets through sales or manufacturer's agents must use the selective system because it is of the essence of their method of operation.

While the manufacturer can designate one distributor as his sole outlet in an area and make a valid contract to effectuate this policy, he cannot legally make a contract that requires the distributor to refrain from handling the goods of a competitor if, by so doing, he limits competition. The courts are so rigid in determining when such an agreement limits competition that, for all intents and purposes, all contracts limiting the distributor's choice of suppliers are to be avoided. While the case establishing this legal principle involved the marketing of a consumer good, gasoline, it applies to industrial products as well. The selected distributor policy, when carried to the extent of the so-called exclusive franchise, can be exclusive on only one side, that of the manufacturer. It thus leaves him in a weak position unless his product has unusual attractiveness and potentialities of profit to the distributor.

If the industrial goods manufacturer decides to market directly to users, his channel selection problem is narrowed to that of choosing salesmen, locations, and facilities for branch warehouses. We will discuss these choices elsewhere. If he decides to market through distributors on a blanket basis, he has the problem of selecting salesmen, but on a more limited scale. His choice among distributors very largely becomes a matter of who will buy from him. If, on the other hand, he decides to reach the market through agents or selected distributors, he must choose those he will try to include in his channel system.

In the main, the general factors that influence his choice are the same in the two cases. There is enough difference in the forms these factors take and in the emphasis he must place on them, though, to justify separating our treatment of the choice of agents and distributors.

Manufacturer's Choice of Agent

The general factors involved in selecting agents are as follows.

Sales Volume. The manufacturer is wise to choose an agent who has a sales volume big enough to be able to maintain a sufficiently large and well-manned establishment to afford adequate sales service for the products he handles.

Ownership. It is usually not wise to select one-man firms. They lack continuity. Many things may happen to terminate the relationship with such a firm, or to disturb its proper functioning—for example, crises in the agent's personal affairs or in his health, as well as business vicissitudes.

The Area Covered. This applies only to the manufacturer's agent. The sales agent usually undertakes to sell the entire output of his client to a specified trade. The producer who uses manufacturer's agents must select firms in various areas in order to adequately cover the market. The territories within which they operate should not overlap, since this is likely to cause friction.

Quality of Sales Personnel. Usually, most of an agent's selling work is done by one or two men. If they are not well qualified and able, the manufacturer is liable to suffer the penalties of poor sales representation.

Business Standing and Trade Contacts. When an industrial goods manufacturer makes a contract with a sales or manufacturer's agent, one of the important things he should expect is a set of already-made contacts with the trade. Therefore, before he finally formalizes the relationship he should check carefully to make sure that he gets what he bargains for. He should himself make enough contacts with the trade to judge the degree of respect and confidence the agent enjoys with the buyers to whom he must sell.

Other Products Handled.   The manufacturer should examine the articles already in the agent's line to make sure that his product will fit in. The agent's existing line should be composed of goods of the same general type and quality as those of the manufacturer; they should be sold to the same groups of buyers, and, if possible, they should have a standing and performance record in the trade that will add to, rather than subtract from, the prestige of the manufacturer's products.

In the work of selecting agents and making contracts with them, the manufacturer may find it worthwhile to take a critical look at himself and try to discover what he has to offer as a possible principal. He will be helped by a knowledge of the factors agents consider in choosing manufacturer-principals. One study found the following factors to be influential.

Factor	Percent of Agents Mentioning It
Compatability of product with current lines	65.0
Product quality	38.3
Good sales potential	36.7
Principal's trade reputation	35.0
Rate of commission	11.7
Principal's financial standing	11.7
Present volume of product sales	10.0
General company policy of principal*	8.3
Price of product	6.7
Availability of technical help	6.7
Principal's advertising	3.3
Quality of principal's management	3.3

* Mainly degree of commitment to use of agents.
J. M. Pierce, "A Comparison of Manufacturer's Representatives with Company Salesmen," 1962 unpublished M.B.A. thesis, New York University Graduate School of Business, reported in *Industrial Marketing*, January, 1964.

Manufacturers that want to use agents sometimes experience difficulty in obtaining lists of candidate firms. They are usually small concerns that do not require much capital, so there is a high rate of turnover in membership of the group. Probably the experience of 36 firms in the electronics business, reported in *Industrial Marketing*, January, 1964, is fairly typical.

Source	Number of Firms Using Source
National Association of Manufacturer's Agents	5
Electronic Representatives Association (Such associations are not found in all trades)	15
Advertisements in business publications	10
Directories (telephone and trade)	25
Recommendation of present agents	2
Recommendation of customers	4
Personal contacts	4
Newspaper advertisements	3

A few professional firms make a business of finding and assembling information about agents. They usually charge a general administration fee, a fee for each agent appointed as a result of their efforts, and a percentage of the agent's commissions for a limited period. Manufacturer's Agent Publishing Company, 554 Fifth Avenue, New York, N.Y., publishes a *Directory of Manufacturer's Representatives* (Agents), which lists 15,000 firms and indicates their areas of specialization.

This study also shows that after a candidate list is compiled information on which to base a final choice is collected through questionnaires to the agents, and through interviews and contact with general references, with the agent's present principals, and with customers. Probably the most fruitful of these sources is the interviews with the present principals and the customer firms. Financial sources, such as banks and credit-rating bureaus ordinarily so useful in this sort of work, are of little help here because of the limited capital needs of agent houses.

Manufacturer's Choice of Distributor

In choosing distributors for a selective channel system, the manufacturer will be wise to seek several kinds of information about each one he considers.[3]

Attitude of the Distributor. The manufacturer should assure himself that the distributor really wants to handle his line. Cases are not unknown in which distributors took on products of manufacturers primarily for the purpose of preventing competitors from handling them. Then, the manufacturer cannot expect from the distributor very satisfactory or energetic promotion work. If the manufacturer's products fit into and supplement or complement the rest of a would-be distributor's line, it is reasonably likely that the distributor really wants to handle them and will actively promote their sale.

Knowledge of the Product. The manufacturer should pick distributors who are adequately informed about his product, or whose managerial personnel has such knowledge. It will not always be possible to find distributors with a thorough technical knowledge of the product; but the ones chosen should be familiar with the industries the article is to be sold to, and, above all, they should show a willingness to learn about its technical features and to see to it that their employees, especially their salesmen, also learn about it.

Reputation and Standing. The manufacturer should inquire into the distributor's stability and his standing in the trade. The stability of such a firm may be judged from such matters as length of time in business, trend

---

[3] This discussion draws on material presented in *Sales Management,* September 15, 1951; *Industrial Distribution,* January, 1950, and July, 1958; and *Industrial Marketing,* November, 1949.

of the various items in its operating statement from year to year, capital structure, and general nature, average age, and quality of its management. Hints about a distributor's standing in the trade may be gleaned from his customers' attitudes toward him, and from what other manufacturers think about him. The kinds of merchandise the distributor handles and his methods of doing business should also be considered. For instance, the manufacturer of a quality line who sells on the basis of superior performance would be unwise to choose a distributor who consistently relies on price as his chief appeal and has a stock heavy with goods of doubtful quality.

Stock. If an industrial distributor is to do an adequate marketing job for a manufacturer, he must be willing to maintain a stock of the maker's goods sufficiently complete to enable him to supply all items demanded, and sufficiently large to prevent turning customers away because of stock shortages or ordering so often and in such small quantities that his business is unprofitable to the marketer. A fairly good idea of his willingness and ability to perform in this respect may be gleaned from an examination of his existing stocks. He will probably do a good job for the new line if his inventories of other producers' lines are complete and adequate.

Ability to Get Business. The industrial distributor's past selling performance with other manufacturers' goods affords some indication of the quality of selling job he is likely to do for a new line.

A manufacturer who is considering a distributor as an outlet for his goods should seek answers to such questions as: How aggressive is he in his sales work? How many of the important prospects in his territory does he sell? How many of them are missing from his customer list? How able are his salesmen? How well are they trained? What is his attitude toward the various forms of cooperative promotional effort we offer?

Territory Covered. The industrial goods manufacturer who intends to use selected distributors as a vital part of his marketing system must fit them together geographically into a sort of jigsaw puzzle pattern in order to achieve complete coverage of the market. In the process, he may be forced to be content in some areas with less desirable outlets in order to avoid overlapping areas and gain complete coverage.

Allied Products Carried. Other things being at all equal, the manufacturer will find it desirable to choose distributors who handle products that supplement or complement his own, and are equal or superior in quality and prestige. In such circumstances, the sale of one product facilitates the sale of another, and the combination provides an offering that is attractive to the customer and builds buyer loyalty to the distributor and the products he carries.

Finances. A desirable distributor should be financed well enough to assure that he can carry adequate and representative stocks of the manufacturer's line, to enable him to pay his bills and take his discounts, to assure the continuity of his services, and to make it possible for him to maintain and operate the kind of sales force and sales promotion program needed to achieve satisfactory volume for the manufacturer's goods. Lack of adequate finances is not always a fatal defect, however. There have been cases in which manufacturers have provided financial assistance for distributors whose qualifications were otherwise excellent but who lacked adequate funds to carry on the desired marketing activities. This is not a general practice, but it may be worthwhile when satisfactory representation is not otherwise available in a territory.

Facilities. The desirable distributor must possess facilities adequate to properly handle the manufacturer's line. These include: sufficient warehouse space, properly laid out, to enable him to carry adequate stocks of the line; convenient sidings or truck approaches to his warehouse; adequate receiving and shipping platforms; sufficient handling equipment to enable him to move goods into and out of his warehouse; a proper record-keeping system to keep him aware of what is happening in his business; and, in some cases, repair and maintenance equipment and staff to enable him to satisfactorily service the manufacturer's product. If the distributor does not have these facilities, he should possess the financial strength or backing and willingness to procure them.

Price Policy. It is desirable that the distributor follow a price policy consistent with that of the manufacturer. If the manufacturer sells on the basis of quality and prestige, he is not likely to get satisfactory marketing service from a distributor who consistently sells primarily on the basis of price appeal. If the producer wants to maintain uniform prices for his goods throughout the market, he should not tie himself up with a price-cutting distributor.

General. It may be taken for granted that a manufacturer in search of a distributor will very rarely, if ever, find one who satisfactorily meets all these requirements. Usually, he must seek the outlet that has the least weaknesses and is strongest with respect to the requirements he regards as most important.

A study conducted by William T. Diamond, under the sponsorship of the National Industrial Distributors' Association, the Southern Industrial Distributors' Association, and the Ohio State University's Faculty Committee on Research in Industrial Distribution, throws considerable light on the emphasis placed on the several factors in the manufacturer's choice of channels of distribution and of individual units within channels.[4] Professor Diamond asked 220 makers of industrial goods to indicate "the *most* important factor in choosing a channel of distribution." The results, on a percentage basis, were:

---

[4] William T. Diamond, *Distribution Channels for Industrial Goods* (Columbus: Bureau of Business Research, Ohio State University, 1963).

```
Market coverage.........................................25.4 percent
Ability to secure volume sales............................15.5
Willingness to carry local inventories....................15.0
Cost of distribution......................................  8.6
Technical familiarity with product line...................  7.7
Contact with trade........................................  6.4
Area of specialization in product line....................  5.9
Trade custom..............................................  4.1
Character of institution (outlet).........................  2.3
Other.....................................................  9.1
```

Several of these factors cut across or embrace several of the bases of choice we have discussed. For example, the excellence of the sales force is involved in ability to secure sales, contact with the trade, and probably market coverage.

Some of the steps a manufacturer may take in checking the suitability of a distributor as an outlet are as follows.

1. A check through Dun & Bradstreet and the manufacturer's bank discloses information that is chiefly financial unless a special report is requested; then it will cover a much wider area.

2. A check in the *Industrial Distribution Directory* discloses information on the nature of the distributor's business and his territorial coverage.

3. Inquiries to manufacturers of noncompetitive industrial goods should supply information about the nature and quality of the distributor's marketing service and should indicate how satisfactory he has been as an outlet for other makers of kindred products.

4. Interviews with customers or prospective customers of the distributor, usually with the purchasing agent or buyer of the kinds of goods the manufacturer has to sell, should afford a basis upon which to judge the distributor's standing with the trade he serves. In conducting such interviews, the manufacturer must be careful to avoid undermining the customer's confidence in the distributor.

5. One of the manufacturer's salesmen or an executive of the firm may spend some time in the field, calling on the trade with the distributor's salesmen. He can observe how they are received by customers, the degree to which they and the house they represent are respected, liked, and trusted by the trade they serve, and the extent to and manner in which they promote the sale of the products carried by the distributor.

6. An executive of the manufacturer's sales department may visit the firm being considered to inspect its equipment and facilities, to examine the adequacy and representativeness of its stocks, and to observe its methods of doing business, as well as to become acquainted with the managerial and office personnel who will be handling his products if he selects the distributor.

Other methods of checking the quality and ability of a prospective distributor may be employed, but those listed above are probably the ones most commonly used.

A manufacturer's success in recruiting and using a system of selected distributors depends to some extent on how he measures up as a source of supply in the eyes of the distributor. If he has the characteristics distributors look for in the producers whose goods they handle, his efforts are apt to be more fruitful than if he lacks these points. So it is probably worthwhile for the producer to try to look at himself through the distributor's eyes and understand his own strengths and limitations as a source. He may then be able to reenforce some of his strong points and eliminate or mitigate some of his weaknesses.

1. The distributor wants a source whose products are right. He wants a line that is well designed and engineered, and that fills a demonstrated customer need. He wants a source with a basic manufacturing position in the products it offers in the sense that its production facilities and know-how enable it to meet its competitors on a par in cost and quality. He favors a supplier who has shown an ability and willingness to keep abreast or ahead of competitors in new products and improvements in existing products. The manufacturer's appeal will also be strengthened if he packages his products in sturdy, well-marked containers of a size and shape that facilitate storage and fit in with customers' buying and using habits.

2. The distributor much prefers a supplier who has a clear, settled, consistent policy in dealing with distributors. He is favorably impressed if the manufacturer's policy is either written into the contract or is published in his advertising. But no amount of public or private profession can equal a record of faithful performance according to a stated policy. Figure 10–1 shows several statements of policy published in trade journals.

3. The distributor prefers a supplier who has earned a reputation for speed, consistency and reliability in making deliveries as promised. Delivery and paper work procedures that simplify the distributor's operations are an added plus factor. This involves a study of the typical distributor's buying, stock control, and payment procedures, and an attempt to construct the supplier's own order taking and handling and invoicing procedures so as to facilitate shortcuts in his paper work.

4. Of course, the distributor prefers a manufacturer whose prices are competitive and whose ideas of price as a promotional tool conform to his own. He wants a margin that allows him a reasonable net profit. Since not very many distributors have cost analysis systems that enable them to compute expenses by items or lines of merchandise, the desired margin tends to be figured on an overall or average basis. Distributors are not uniformly willing to accept margins adjusted to conform with differences in such things as rate of stock turnover, difficulty of selling, or technical service required. Once a distributor is brought to accept the idea of direct sale to house accounts or large buyers of components for original installation, he probably will be willing to tolerate a margin adjustment to compensate for his performance only of the functions of carrying stocks and making deliveries. The average distributor is apt to appreciate a net

FIGURE 10–1

Sample Statements of Policy

Acme Chain Company (*Industrial Distribution*, September, 1963):

1. Advertisements in 25 journals and 14 annual directories.
2. Referral of user inquiries to distributor (6,000 to date in 1963).
3. Engineering service.
4. Technical field service.
5. Sales training clinics.
6. Direct mail enclosures furnished.
7. Colored sound motion pictures available.
8. Seminars for executives.
9. Sales meetings.

Rex Chain Belt Company (*Industrial Distribution*, July, 1963)—items covered:

1. Territorial definition.
2. Handling inquiries and orders.
3. Review and return of stocks.
4. Field sales assistance.
5. Pricing and price protection.
6. Advertising and sales promotion services.
7. Inventory requirements.
8. Sales coverage requirements.
9. Sales training.
10. Sales meetings.
11. Customer services.
12. Warehousing aids.
13. Distributor Advisory Board (board of distributors to suggest marketing policies and programs).

Allen Manufacturing Company (*Industrial Distribution*, July, 1963)—makes socket screws:

1. Direct orders billed through distributors, who get regular discount on them.
2. Limited number of distributors in each market.
3. Suggested resale price schedule.
4. Assistance in promotion plans, sales clinics, missionary sales work.
5. Sales helps, such as circulars, catalogs, exhibit material, direct mail.
6. Engineering service on new applications and special problems.
7. No nonstocking distributor's discount allowed.
8. Product guarantee.

price quotation rather than a string of discounts that are difficult and costly to figure.

5. A good distributor will accept and appreciate a job assignment that is realistic and challenging. Such an assignment is usually expressed as a quota or sales potential for his territory. If it is too large, he is apt to resent it and his enthusiasm is dampened. If it is too low, he may doubt

whether the manufacturer knows what he is doing. An unrealistic assignment is worse than none at all.

6. The distributor favors a manufacturer who has a strong promotional program to back up his field efforts. Such a program may include general advertising and promotion of the product or line under the manufacturer's name. It should also almost always include cooperative advertising in which the distributor can participate and in which his name is featured along with that of the manufacturer. The program usually involves a variety of promotional materials the outlet can distribute under its own name.

7. The distributor usually appreciates a program of technical assistance. This may take many forms, depending on the nature of the product and its uses. In some cases, it requires maintenance of a group of technical service men to help solve difficult problems of product use. It almost always involves training for the distributor's salesmen, sometimes in the supplier's factory, sometimes in seminars or training sessions in the distributor's office, and sometimes in the field through men who travel with the distributor's salesmen and train them on the job. Technical assistance is a very definite plus factor when the supplier's training programs are obviously designed to be administered with the least expenditure of time and money by the distributor and his personnel.

CHANNEL SUPERVISION

Merely to properly select types of channels and channel units is not enough. The industrial goods manufacturer must supervise and support the units of his channel system if he expects to get a good marketing job. So far as his channel is composed of units within his firm, this process does not differ from the ordinary work of internal administration; we will discuss this aspect in various sections, especially those dealing with marketing organization and management, advertising, sales promotion, and physical distribution. The outside units present special problems, since results must be achieved entirely by persuasion and the manipulation of incentives without the help of sanctions that ordinarily arise from the employer–employee relationship.

The Contract

When the manfuacturer markets through distributors on a blanket basis or through brokers, the contractual arrangements usually consist of a series of purchase-sale or specific lot commitments. When he uses a sales or manufacturer's agent or selected distributors in a more continuous relationship, some sort of formal or semiformal statement of the agreement seems desirable. This may take the form of a written contract. Such a document may run for a definite period—a year, for example—and must be renewed if the arrangement is to continue. This creates the inconvenience of having to negotiate a new contract each year. It is probably better for the contract to run indefinitely, subject to cancellation by either party on proper notice.

The terms of such a continuing arrangement may be expressed in a statement of policy, such as those in Figure 10–1, issued by the manufacturer, which summarizes the services and prerogatives he intends to give his outlets and what he expects from them in return. This sort of document may also be useful to the manufacturer who markets on a blanket basis. Its disadvantage to the outlet is that since it is issued unilaterally the manufacturer can change it at will, and the only effective way the outlet can express disagreement is to cease buying from him. On the other hand, once the manufacturer has publicly committed himself to such a statement of marketing policy it is definitely not to his interest to change it, unless the conditions demanding modification are imperative.

Some statement of the terms of the continuing relationship between manufacturer and selected outlets is highly desirable, not so much because of its legal as of its practical advantages. A manufacturer would hardly be wise to hold an agent or distributor to an arrangement the outlet wants to terminate, because the essence of an effective marketing relationship is cooperation and mutual satisfaction; this is especially true in industrial goods marketing, where the user's devotion to brands tends to be weak or entirely lacking. But cooperation and mutual satisfaction are most likely to exist when each party to the relationship knows clearly what is expected of him and what he can expect in return if it works well. One way to help achieve this is by writing out the terms on which the relationship is based.

Protection

In administering the relationships with his channels, the industrial goods manufacturer must determine and make clear the degree of protection he proposes to give his outlets. Even if he markets on a blanket basis, he may limit his sales to one group of distributors—for example, mill supply houses or firms specializing in abrasives—and refuse orders from other distributors who might sell to the same users.

When he follows a selective policy, he may go the whole way and market through only one distributor in a market area—an exclusive outlet—or he may select two or three distributors as his only outlets in each area. By the second practice, of course, he gains the benefit of competition among the selected outlets, but loses the enthusiasm and cooperation that often results when the distributor knows that whatever business he generates for the product belongs to him.

A second phase of the protection problem arises in connection with government contracts and what are known as "house accounts." When the government buys on bids, the manufacturer who refuses to bid direct without the price addition resulting from the agent's commission or the distributor's margin is not likely to get the business. When the government buys on a negotiated contract, it will want to deal directly with the maker in an attempt to make sure that intermediaries' margins are not included in the price. It is probably more important that the outlet have a clear understanding of his place in the government business picture than that he share in its benefits.

In almost every industry there are certain firms, usually large, that prefer to buy industrial goods direct from the maker; some even refuse to purchase in any other way. Many manufacturers have a few customers whose patronage volume is so great that they cannot afford to take the chance of losing it. Such accounts are usually solicited by executives high up in the marketing organization, even by members of top management. Such customers are often called house accounts, and their denial to the firm's distributors or agents is usually a delicate matter in administering channel relationships.

But most distributors and agents are not without an understanding of the facts of business life, and unless the house account policy is carried to extremes they will usually accept it after due complaint and negotiation. The manufacturer may be able to work out an arrangement with his distributors whereby the outlets carry stocks for and make deliveries on blanket contracts with house accounts, and are compensated by receiving an agreed-on portion of their ordinary margin.

When the house account policy is carried to such an extreme that all the juicy, profitable customers are sold direct and the distributor is left with a prospect list composed mainly of cats and dogs, he is likely to view the whole arrangement with something less than unrestrainable enthusiasm. The distributor feels that he is allowed to handle only orders unprofitable for the manufacturer to solicit and deliver; the result would seem to be a situation in which the distributor cannot keep his business alive, let alone make a profit. This is not necessarily true. It is true that most of the customers left to the distributor under this policy will be little ones whose orders for any one manufacturer's goods are too small to be profitable. Yet, when the needs of such a buyer for the products of several manufacturers are lumped, as they are likely to be when placed with a distributor, the resulting total may be big enough to be profitable. It must be admitted, however, that this idea is hard to sell to a distributor who sees the manufacturer depriving him of a large volume of profitable business.

Some manufacturers follow the policy of crediting the distributor with all direct sales they make in his territory and allowing him his regular gross profit on the volume involved in them. In some cases, a selling charge may be assessed against such business, and the distributor credited with the net. Other producers of industrial goods take such orders but turn them over to the distributor for delivery.

Another matter that involves the manufacturer's willingness to protect his selected dealers is his handling of direct inquiries he receives as a result of advertising or general trade information. If he follows them up with his own marketing facilities and tries to turn them into sales, he is likely to arouse distrust and resentment among his agents or distributors. If, on the other hand, he sends the inquirer the desired information and refers the inquiry to the appropriate selected outlet, together with a copy of his reply, he engenders confidence that he has no intention of undercutting the agent or distributor.

When multiplant users buy centrally, the manufacturers of the goods they purchase must often protect the interests of one selected distributor or agent from infringement by another. This happens when the central buying office of a customer firm located in the territory of one selected distributor or agent makes a contract for equipment or material to be delivered to a branch plant in the territory of another. The second outlet may have done missionary or sales development work on the buying or operating executives of the branch plant, and then each selected agent or distributor feels that he has a claim on some or all of the commission or margin on the sale. Before such situations arise, the manufacturer must work out an equitable basis on which to split margins or commissions between his selected outlets—a basis understood and accepted by all the units in the channel system. It is not necessary that all outlets be enthusiastic about the basis on which splits will be made, but it is essential that all realize it is fair and reasonable, and recognize it as one of the terms of the selective arrangement.

Inventory Requirements

Most industrial products makers who market through distributors include in the arrangement some sort of requirement designed to assure that the distributor will carry a stock of the manufacturer's products sufficiently representative of his line and adequate in size to enable the distributor to fill all orders, except the very largest, without delay. This is an ideal earnestly sought but rarely achieved. Most manufacturers recognize that they must maintain stocks at convenient points from which they can supply distributors with goods to satisfy unusually large or emergency demands and requests for products needed infrequently.

If the manufacturer seeks to establish and enforce an inventory requirement that is too heavy, he is liable to lose the cooperation of his distributors. Probably the most sensible policy is that of starting each distributor off with a standard inventory based on the sales experience of the average outlet, and then working out an individual inventory requirement for him on the basis of his own experience during the first year or two after the relationship is established.

For example, a company that makes abrasives developed a formula by which each of its distributors could compute an economic order quantity for each of its products. The plan did not work well, because many distributors were in no position to compute their costs per order or carrying-cost percentages by products, which were essential factors in the formula. So the company arranged for each distributor to send in his raw accounting data, and used the company computer to prepare for each distributor an economic order quantity chart for each product.[5]

A distributor will be much attracted by the policy of the manufacturer who allows returns of obsolete merchandise and overstocks of slow-moving items. Such a policy goes far to enlist the distributor's cooperation in any inventory program the industrial marketer may set up. Many distributors favor the practice of reviewing their stocks once each year in cooperation with the manufacturer, who at that time takes back obsolete and slow-moving items and recommends new ones. Some manufacturers make a service charge, usually 1 percent, for returns of overstocks.

For example, a firm that makes industrial saw blades allows distributors to return for credit any slow-moving items. The distributor is authorized to extend the same privilege to his user customers. The net effect is to cut down the number of small, expensive emergency orders at both levels.[6]

Compensation

The compensation problem is just as important in administering the extracompany units of a manufacturer's channel system as it is in managing his own sales force. We will deal with the internal part of the problem in the chapter on managing personal selling.

The compensation of agents appears chiefly in the form of the commissions paid to them; that of distributors mainly as the margin between the price at which they buy the goods and that at which they can sell them.

The percentage an agent gets on sales is apt to be standardized to some extent within trades, although the usual figure may be varied according to the difficulty of selling the product, the volume of sales he expects to realize from it, and the expected duration of the agency relationship. Really, the amount of this percentage is not too important to the manufacturer so long as it is less than the marketing cost sales volume ratio for which he could get an equally good job by any other means.

Nor is the manufacturer wise to be disturbed by the total amount earned by the agent in selling his product. Too often, when an agent can make sales far above those the manufacturer expected when the agency relationship was established, the maker tries to reduce the rate of commission. This may cause considerable resentment and defeat the whole purpose of the agency relationship. The important question from the stand-

[5] *Sales Management*, January 4, 1963.
[6] *Sales Management*, April 5, 1963.

point of the manufacturer is not "How much is the agent making?" but "Am I getting a good job of selling done at a reasonable cost per unit or per dollar sold?"

Some firms allow their agents additional compensation for such services as submitting adequate reports of sales calls and carrying on long-range development programs, and other activities that are for the long-run benefit of the manufacturer but do not result in immediate sales.

Of course, the distributor is highly interested in the percentage of gross profit he will be able to make on a manufacturer's products. Theoretically, unless an industrial marketer practices price maintenance the distributor can charge whatever price he wants and thus, in some degree, control the amount of gross profit he receives. In many cases, even when the maker does not legally fix the resale price he may suggest it so strongly that it amounts to a command. This is especially effective when he sells on an exclusive or selective basis. Even when the distributor is free to price an article as he wishes, the prices at which similar products are sold by his competitors fix the limits within which he may choose. In addition, gross-profit percentages are often traditional in a trade; these sometimes command an acceptance equal, or superior, to that enjoyed by legally enforceable price contracts. The net effect is that the prime factor determining the distributor's margin is the price at which the manufacturer sells to him.

The manufacturer who wants to enlist the efforts of distributors on behalf of his product will do well to allow them a gross-profit margin at least equal to that accepted and prevalent in the trade; perhaps a percentage a little above this figure might prove attractive to the distributor whose support he seeks. But a gross-profit margin that is too liberal is likely to dampen the distributor's sales ardor, because it unduly rewards him for his effort and tends to fatten his selling muscles; it may also stimulate price-cutting. It is usually sound policy for the manufacturer to try to set a gross-profit figure the distributors will regard as attractive, but to allow no more than that figure.

It is sometimes possible for the manufacturer to make arrangements under which distributors perform only part of their normal functions and accept a narrower margin for the less complete service. For example, if the manufacturer does the bulk of the selling work through his own sales force, the distributor may carry stock and handle orders on a margin reduced by an amount approximately equal to the cost of his selling work. On the other hand, the manufacturer may increase the margin or add extras to it for the performance of extra services, such as carrying stocks earmarked for an important customer, rendering technical service beyond that usually expected, or carrying on unusual sales promotion activities, such as demonstrations or exhibits at industrial shows and exhibitions. None of these arrangements is very common.

Such variations in the prices at which a manufacturer's goods are sold to different distributors, as well as the payment of extras or allowances to some outlets but not to others, are fraught with legal dangers. They are apt to be regarded as illegal price discriminations under the Robinson-Patman Act. If the manufacturer follows an exclusive policy so that each agent or distributor sells within his own territory and does not overlap into that of any other, it is hard to see how such price differentials unfavorably affect competition, which they must do to be illegal. For the performance of a specific marketing service, an allowance that is not excessive relative to the cost of getting the same service done in some other way probably meets the law's tests of legality. All plans for such allowances and variations should be submitted to careful legal examination before they are put into effect.

In his study of 220 firms manufacturing industrial equipment and supplies, Professor Diamond found that the average margin allowed distributors declined from 31.9 percent among firms with less than $1 million annual sales volume to 21.5 percent among firms with sales of more than $100 million. The figure ranged from 23.3 percent for precision measuring tools to 35.0 percent for safety equipment and supplies. The range among different firms in the same industry was even wider. For example, one firm allowed 7.5 and another 36.0 percent on valves and fittings, and on power transmission equipment the range was from 15 to 40 percent. This wide range probably resulted mainly from different margins allowed on the several products within a single line—for example, high on new items and those hard to sell, and low on established, competitive articles in heavy demand.

This study indicates that trade custom is the major factor influencing the determination of gross margins allowed to distributors. Competition is also a very important factor. Cost of manufacture (cost-plus pricing), the distributors' costs, and the manufacturer's price on direct sales were found to be of lesser significance.

Price Policy

The industrial goods manufacturer who markets through agents or distributors can enlist their cooperation and enthusiasm by the price policy he establishes and by the way he administers his pricing practices. One policy feature most distributors are very much interested in is the way in which prices are quoted. Some makers of industrial products price their goods net—that is, the figure set down in the price list is the price at which the vendor proposes to sell. Others quote a list price subject to a chain of discounts, such as 40–20–10–10–5 percent. Each of these discounts is subtracted separately from the amount left after the deduction of the previous one.

Thus, in the case just given, if the list price were $1. per unit, we would first deduct 40 percent, or 40 cents, leaving 60 cents; we next subtract 20 percent of this, or 12 cents, leaving 48 cents. If we continue this process to the end, we find that the real quoted price is 37 cents. We also may wind up with the suspicion that if we had bargained more ruthlessly we might have forced another 5 or 10 percent discount from the seller. Industrial buyers generally, and especially distributors, prefer the net method of quoting prices. It avoids mistakes and inaccuracies, reduces paper work and laborious computations, and facilitates the computing of resale prices. In spite of these advantages, Diamond found that less than one fourth of the 220 firms he studied quoted net prices.

The manufacturer who sells through distributors will find it to his advantage to set up a quantity discount system that offers them some price inducement to buy in substantial lumps, at least in case or bulk lots, instead of in loose pieces. This is epecially desirable when the manufacturer sells on an open-territory basis and so has no contractual means of controlling the lot sizes in which his customers order. Unless he adopts some such pricing system, he is likely to be constantly plagued with the necessity of filling orders for 3, 4, 5, 6, or 8 units when the goods are packed 10 or 12 to the case. Filling such orders is highly expensive. A quantity discount system based on shipping case lots or bulk containers is usually not too difficult to legally defend under the restrictions of the Robinson-Patman Act. Diamond found that slightly more than half of the firms he studied offered quantity discounts.

The industrial products manufacturer who markets through distributors will do well to clearly state in his price book the freight allowances and equalization arrangements he is prepared to grant. This matter is equally important to the producer who sells direct, since both the distributor and direct buyer are likely to compute the purchase price of an article on a delivered basis, with freight charges included.

Distributors are divided on what should be the manufacturer's attitude on price-cutting. Of course, every distributor would be very happy if the manufacturers of the products he sells were to prevent other distributors from cutting the prices of those products. He is often not so enthusiastic about an attempt to fix the prices at which he must resell. The manufacturer's practice with respect to price-cutting is not so important when he sells to distributors on a selected basis, for then the distributor does not have to face the price competition of his rivals. It is usually very important to the success of the producer who sells on a blanket basis.

The distributor also wants to know what protection the manufacturer is prepared to offer him on the prices of his floor stocks in case of price reductions. Some manufacturers extend complete protection on all stocks the distributors hold when a price reduction occurs. Then, when the manufacturer reduces his price he simply credits each distributor's account with the amount of the reduction on all stocks held by the outlet. Often the distributor's statement on the amount of such stocks is accepted without checking.

Other manufacturers extend such protection only on stocks the distributor has purchased within the 30-day period immediately preceding the reduction date. Still others notify their distributors of an impending reduction at a set period, often 30 days, prior to the date it is to take effect. This allows the distributor an opportunity to diminish his purchases during the notification period and to approach the effective date with his stock at a minimum. From the standpoint of the manufacturer, this policy has the disadvantage that during the notification period the flow of orders may dry up, followed by a rush of emergency orders to replace stocks on or immediately after the effective date. Also, some distributors inevitably get caught with stocks on hand and are disgruntled. As the effective date approaches, moreover, users of the product are likely to be unable to buy it from distributors who have cut their stocks below the danger point in preparation for the price change.

The notification period policy also is weak in that it affords an advantage to nonstock-carrying and inadequately stocked distributors selling the goods of a manufacturer who operates on a blanket basis. During the notification period, such a distributor can be very busy taking orders for future delivery at a lower price, while his stock-carrying rivals are trying to work off their inventories at the old price. Users soon become aware that a price reduction is to be made, and they adopt a hand-to-mouth buying policy that tends to defeat the entire purpose of the practice. In addition, the policy penalizes the very distributors most valuable as outlets for the manufacturer's products.

Probably the prime drawback of the notification period practice is that competitors as well as customers hear about it, and the price-cutting firm loses all the advantages of surprise in its action.

Prestige of the Manufacturer and His Product

The manufacturer whose standing with the trade is high, and who has a reputation for the quality of his products and the constancy with which he honors his obligations, financial and otherwise, will be able to obtain the marketing services of good agents or distributors in almost any territory he wants to enter. He may find some desirable outlets tied up by contracts with competitors, but with patience and time he can attract a reasonable proportion of those he wants in his distributor organization. Outlets will also be willing to work with him in his cooperative marketing programs, because they will be confident of getting their fair share of the returns from the money and effort they spend on such programs.

The agent's or distributor's willingness to be an outlet for a manufacturer is influenced by the quality of the manufacturer's product and the consistency of its quality. He is especially anxious to know whether the manufacturer's product is of a type and quality standard that will fit into and be consistent with the rest of the line he handles. The agent or distributor usually seeks to build a line that will be consistent and will help to give his establishment an identity of its own. He may attempt to have his house known for the high quality of the goods it features; he may seek a reputation for handling good, reliable tools and materials at a medium price; or he may try to capture patronage by emphasizing the price appeal, with somewhat less attention paid to quality. When he is solicited to add a new product to his offering, he is apt to be influenced in his decision fully as much by his judgment on whether it fits into his line and sharpens the identity of his house as by his appraisal of its actual quality level.

The industrial goods manufacturer who markets through distributors can considerably increase his product's attractiveness to them by packaging it properly. The distributor will favor a package shaped and sized so that it is easy to handle and can be stored without loss of space, and one that protects its contents against the shocks and jars it is likely to undergo during handling in his warehouse. It should be clearly and simply labeled so that its contents are readily identifiable without the necessity of reading fine print in some not easily accessible spot on the package. A common complaint of distributors whose order pickers must handle goods speedily is that the symbols, figures, or words identifying many of the articles are in print so small as to be illegible without close examination, or are located on a part of the package that is covered up when the article is piled in a warehouse or on a shelf.

The number of units in a case is sometimes important to the distributor. If the manufacturer packs too many units to a case, he thereby magnifies the distributor's broken-package problem. If he packs too few, he is unable to allow enough price differential on full package orders to offer much inducement to the distributor to buy in such lots; in addition, he increases the distributor's handling costs. One possible method by which to choose the number of units per package is to try to ascertain the number the average customer of the distributor wants to buy in one order, and to use this as the standard size of the shipping case. This plan is not practical in all cases but often serves as a useful starting point.

From time immemorial, it has been customary to pack industrial goods, as well as consumer goods, in cases that hold a dozen or some multiple or fraction of a dozen units. During recent years, there has been some tendency to shift to the decimal system. Many distributors favor the change because it facilitates the computation of unit resale prices on broken-case lots. Others prefer the customary method. A manufacturer may be wise to consult the wishes of his distributors in this matter.

Types of Marketing Assistance

Most industrial goods manufacturers who market through agents or distributors find it necessary to mesh their own marketing activities into those of their outlets, and to provide various types of help for them. This may involve trivial operating adjustments or elaborate and very costly programs. We will confine our discussion to those most widely used.

Help in Handling Small Orders.   Many distributors feel that the manufacturer whose product is often bought by users in small, broken-package orders should bear some of the cost generated by this characteristic. Some manufacturers make a special allowance to distributors for handling such orders. Others pack their goods two, four, or six units to a shelf package; six, three, or two packages fit into the regular dozen-unit packing case, and each can conveniently be taken out by the distributor and sold as a unit, with considerable reduction in handling cost compared with the cost of breaking open the standard dozen packing case and handling the items one by one. Sometimes, the greater attractiveness of such packages to the distributor is more than worth the added costs involved.

Advertising.   The manufacturer can use his advertising to promote his distributors' cooperation. This process begins with the preparation of the advertising itself. If it is to mean anything to the distributor, its quality must be such that it will help to sell the manufacturer's goods. Its effectiveness as a tool for securing outlet cooperation will be augmented if it is constructed so that the distributor and his salesmen can use it in their selling work. This will not happen unless those who prepare the copy for the manufacturer study the distributors' sales problems and methods and the buying motives and practices of their customers to know what material will be useful in selling and in what form it will be most useful. This, in turn, will not happen unless the marketing manager insists on it. The manufacturer must then follow up by merchandising his advertising to the distributors—that is, by showing them how to use it in their sales work and by selling them on using it. But no amount of merchandising work will induce salesmen to use advertising that is not useful in the first place.

The manufacturer who markets through selected distributors can greatly increase the value of his advertising to them by including their names in the copy. The number of selected outlets used by the industrial goods maker is usually small enough so that he can include their names and the cities or areas in which they operate as a regular feature of his copy.

Cooperative advertising, in the sense of advertising that is paid for jointly by the manufacturer and the distributor, is not used extensively in the industrial goods field. Most of such advertising in the consumer goods business is placed in local media by the distributor or dealer and paid for, in part, by the manfuacturer. There are very few local media of any significance in industrial goods marketing.

But cooperative effort can be effectively applied in sales promotion work. It appears most often in the form of promotional pieces produced by the manufacturer and imprinted with the outlet's name and address, which are distributed by either manufacturer or distributor to a list of users or prospective users supplied by the distributor.

Here, again, effectiveness begins in the preparation of promotion material that will actually be of help to the distributor, and continues with the manufacturer's follow-through in selling the program to the distributor and in working with him in all phases of its execution. Technical brochures containing information about the characteristics of the product and advice and suggestions about its most effective use constitute one of the most widely used promotional pieces. Other types are direct mail pieces, product application sheets, catalog inserts, mobile displays, point-of-purchase displays for use in the distributor's showroom, envelope enclosures, and such novelty giveaways as blotters, calendars, rulers, and guages.

Missionary Men. Many industrial goods makers who market through distributors seek to supplement their efforts and enlist their cooperation by the use of missionary salesmen. These men are employed by the manufacturer, and their chief job is to call on the distributor's customers to promote the sale of their employer's products. Usually, when a missionary salesman gets an order he turns it over to the distributor for delivery, and the distributor enjoys his regular gross profit margin on it.

The number of missionary men a manufacturer utilizes is usually much smaller than the number of salesmen he would have to employ to market direct. They call on the customer much less frequently than the direct-selling salesman. In many cases, they call only on the largest and most important customers. In others, they may specialize on prospective users whom the distributor finds hard or impossible to sell.

The distributor tends to look on the missionary salesman with mixed emotions. He may be glad for the extra business represented by the orders the missionary man turns over, but he is by no means sure that all turnover sales represent added volume he would not have gotten without the missionary salesman. His own salesmen are usually quite sure that practically all such volume is merely business they would have gotten at the proper time in the course of their usual contacts with the trade. They may develop a feeling that the chief purpose of the missionary man is to show them up. This, in turn, may create a morale problem for the distributor.

The distributor may have a suspicion that the manufacturer's missionary sales force is really a disguised means of developing contact with the market so that at some appropriate future time the producer may shift to direct marketing. Such cases are not lacking. A thin-skinned distributor may feel that a force of missionary men is in itself evidence that the manufacturer suspects he is not doing a good job and is a sort of left-handed insult. But some industrial goods makers have for years marketed through distributors supplemented by missionary men, with confidence and cooperation on both sides. Such an attitude is usually the fruit of a long-continued relationship that supplies a sound basis for it.

The use of missionary men allows the manufacturer to depend on the distributor to supply such services as routine selling, stock carrying, order handling, delivery, and credit extension, while at the same time he may gain through his missionary force some of the benefits of specialized creative selling.

Training. The industrial goods manufacturer who markets through distributors usually finds it desirable to provide some sort of training program for his distributors' salesmen. Some such programs are very elaborate; others are quite elementary. Almost all are designed to give the salesmen a better knowledge of the manufacturer's product, how it is made, its technical properties, and how and for what it can be used satisfactorily. Some makers seek to train the salesmen in improved selling techniques, although this is usually left to the distributor.

Many manufacturers offer to train the distributor's salesmen at the factory. A firm that makes industrial tape required its salesmen to hold regular sales training meetings for its distributors' salesmen, mainly to impart product information. The company's salesmen were expected to train the distributors' salesmen in the field in groups of two or three at a time; they also had to help the distributors' men in selling accounts that required unusual technical knowledge or influence.

The expense of factory training is usually split between the manufacturer and the distributor. Most distributors will probably be content with something approaching an equal division of such expense. Often, the distributor pays the salesman's salary and traveling expenses while in training, and the manufacturer pays room and board, plus the costs of instruction. If the distributor is unwilling to forego the use of his salesmen's time in the field while they are undergoing such training, he is not likely to do a very good job in promoting the sale of the manufacturer's goods. A less expensive form of training consists of a series of seminars, in which the manufacturer's representatives train the distributor's salesmen and sometimes his executives.

The manufacturer who operates a force of missionary men may require them to travel with the distributors' salesmen and train them in methods of selling his goods. This requires a somewhat abler type of missionary man than is usually employed. The manufacturer is apt to find that he must not only train his missionary men to sell his products, but must also train them to train the distributor's salesmen.

Feedback

Channel relationships are like other human contacts in that areas of frustration and irritation tend to develop. They are also alike in that little sore spots tend to merge and grow into big ones if left untreated.

Therefore, the wise marketing manager tries to provide a feedback of information from the field so that he may know what is happening in his channels and in their contacts with the market. This is not always easy. Sometimes, agents and distributors are not sure in their own minds about the precise sources of dissatisfaction with the relationship. Often, if not too acute, dissatisfaction remains unexpressed. If the source of discontent is trivial or irrational or highly personal and selfish, as it often is, the agent or distributor is loath to bring it out into the open, but tends to rationalize by ascribing it to some logical cause that may be nonexistent.

Usually, a proper feedback system will disclose the existence of channel discontent, although often not its cause. Once the area of soreness is located, the manufacturer can set about finding its cause. There are several sources of feedback and diagnostic information.

1. The correspondence with outlets is a free source. This will inevitably contain complaints, and every complaint represents a possible point of irritation. Of course, some people are chronic complainers. They are easily spotted, and the marketer, having recognized them, must either live with them or drop them from his channel system. But when complaints are numerous and tend to cluster around one subject, something is wrong and it behooves the marketing manager to find out what it is. The general tone of outlets' correspondence may provide a tip-off of trouble. When warmth of expression gives way to politeness or business formality, the change will bear investigation. These tip-offs will not be picked up and utilized unless the correspondence is regarded as a source of information feedback and is systematically analyzed for that purpose.

2. If there is a trade press, it may provide a tip-off of impending trouble. This source will be useful only when some practice common to all or many manufacturers is resented, or when a change in the market renders some long-standing practice irksome. But it is worth watching.

3. The manufacturer's representatives whose job it is to maintain more or less regular contact with his outlets can be a very effective source of information feedback. If he markets through distributors, he will undoubtedly operate a force of salesmen to call on them. Contact with agents is often maintained by the marketing manager himself or some other executive in the marketing area. If contact with them is not regularly maintained, it should be.

Salesmen will not know what to look for or what to report unless they are trained for the job; they are not likely to recognize the importance of this kind of work unless its value is impressed on them and incentives provided to make it worth their while. Even the marketing manager is apt to find himself full of excuses for not leaving the comfort of his office chair to go out and hunt possible trouble among his outlets.

4. The trade grapevine carries bad news as well as good. Just how the marketer can get on it is hard to say. Probably helpful are personal acquaintance and association with his opposite numbers in competing firms and in those marketing complementary products, and a willingness to give information as well as take it. The manager will find that some of his salesmen and perhaps his advertising men are on grapevines at lower or

more specialized levels. The word that comes over the grapevine is not always gospel, but the truth content is often surprisingly high.

5. It is sometimes worthwhile to use field attitude surveys as a source of flowback. These are expensive and are probably used more often to find out exactly what the trouble is after an area of discontent has been disclosed by some other source.

None of these devices will be very effective unless the manufacturer has been able to establish a conviction that he is willing to listen, and to take fair and constructive action about what he hears. The best way to win such a reputation is to listen and to act fairly, with due consideration for the interest and the feelings of the other fellow.

Good marketing service from distributors or agents is not something the manufacturer can take for granted. He must earn it by intelligently selecting them, and by devoting to them the same sort of fair, conscientious, and consistent supervision he would have to give his own direct marketing force if he had one.

The manufacturer should watch several general trends in the industrial market, since they may dictate changes in his choice and administration of channels.[7] The most important trends are the following.

1. User-buyers are cutting their stocks to the minimum, and in the process are pushing the stock-carrying function back on their suppliers. This tends to make the use of distributors more economical and satisfactory, since the points at which they carry stocks are more numerous than the manufacturer can afford and nearer to the average user.

2. The use of blanket-order purchasing is increasing. This involves not only contracts covering the buyer's needs for a single product over a period of time, such as a year, but also commitments for groups of products not necessarily all belonging to the same line, such as supplies and maintenance items generally. This trend is a part of the general movement to reduce inventories. It has the effect of making the distributor a more attractive source for the user-buyer, since he carries a much wider line than does the manufacturer. The result is that the distributor becomes more valuable to the manufacturer as an outlet.

3. Buyers are tending to demand prices that vary according to the services suppliers render. This at once offers an opportunity to the distributor and creates for him difficult problems of management. As a result, it complicates the manufacturer's problem of choosing outlets and administering his relations with them.

4. New areas are being industrialized, with the result that the market is becoming more scattered geographically. This tends to make the distributor more attractive as an outlet.

---

[7] This discussion draws largely on the views of Walter Crowder, one of the keenest observers in the industrial goods field, as presented in *Marketing Keys to Profits in the '60s*, ed. W. Dolva (American Marketing Association, 1960).

5. The distributor is suffering from a net profit squeeze. During the late fifties and sixties, the average net profit has been less than one percent on sales—hardly enough to enable him to maintain his efficiency.

6. The increase in the complexity of production technology has tended to require specialization in marketing, to some extent along product lines, but to a greater extent according to industry customer groups. The specialization based on customer groups tends to diminish the value of the distributor as an outlet. This is for two reasons: first, the distributor cannot provide the highly skilled technical service whose need gave rise to the specialization; second, the small number of potential customers in the average industry enables the manufacturer to service them direct through his own sales force and technical specialists.

Attitudes and Interests

We started our discussion on the administration of marketing channels with the observation that the channel relationship is a complex of the mutual and divergent interests of the elements in it. The success of the industrial goods manufacturer in capturing the cooperation of individuals and firms that comprise his marketing channel depends in no small degree on the extent to which he is able to develop methods for making the achievement of his objectives promote their welfare.

In attacking this problem, the manufacturer's lip service is not enough. The attack must start with a careful study of his channel members' methods of operation, and of the factors that enhance or retard their success. For example, a promotional piece that simply stimulates sale of the manufacturer's products may or may not be used by the distributor, but a piece that does this and, in addition, stimulates the distributor's customers to patronize him is almost certain to be used. A program of training that merely informs the distributor's salesmen about the manufacturer's product is one thing; one that informs and, in addition, makes them better salesmen for the distributor is very definitely something else again.

Mutually profitable manufacturer–distributor relationships do not just happen. They will not occur unless the manufacturer and his marketing personnel are constantly aware of the natural areas of conflict and cooperation in that relationship, and are keenly conscious of the importance of narrowing the area within which the interests of the two parties are at war and of broadening the area within which they coincide. Such an awareness will tend to cause all levels of the manufacturer's organization to back up what his salesmen promise in their contacts with outlets. Good manufacturer–outlet relationships begin in the attitude that governs their administration.[8]

---

[8] Many of the ideas presented in this chapter are developed in greater detail in an unpublished thesis, "Managing Marketing Channels," prepared by Thomas Berg, available in the library of Columbia University.

SUMMARY

The manufacturer–outlet relationship is a composite of the conflicting and coinciding interests of the two parties. In setting up his channel system, the industrial goods manufacturer must discover the jobs he wants his channels to do, select the types of outlets best qualified to do them, and select and negotiate relationships with specific firms within those types.

Several factors affect the choice of channels, such as the horizontal or vertical nature of the market, sales volume, geographical distribution of the market, users' buying habits, gross profit margin, volatility of price, services required, importance of quality, the item's bulk, the producer's financial position, and his marketing objectives.

There are five general types of marketing channels for industrial goods: direct, through agents, through distributors, multilevel, and mixed channels. Each of these has its advantages and drawbacks. Within the selected type, the industrial marketer must decide whether to sell on a blanket basis or to selected outlets. We discussed the various factors the manufacturer must consider in choosing specific outlets when he markets on a selective basis.

The industrial goods marketer must administer his relations with his outlets and their relations with one another. Usually desirable is some sort of written contract, stating the manufacturer's position with respect to competition among them and with them in selling to house accounts. He finds it necessary to negotiate the inventory-carrying obligations of the outlet, and the form and amount of compensation allowed. His price policy is usually an integral part of the compensation. He needs to study the outlet's operations in order to adjust the details of his own operations to fit into them. Finally, he must set up and maintain a system of information feedback through which he can learn about the difficulties and irritations suffered by his outlets; then he can cure little troubles before they grow into big ones.

He must provide several forms of marketing assistance, such as help in handling small orders, advertising and promotion, sometimes missionary salesmen, and training.

CASES APPLICABLE TO PART IV

PART V

Management of Pricing

WHILE PRICE is not the most important factor influencing the demand for industrial goods and the patronage decisions of industrial buyers, it is significant enough to deserve careful study by the marketer.

The pricing process goes on against a background of competition and general trade and industry conditions. These tend to cause the general price movements and the stylized price behavior so often described in economic theory. So, in Chapter 11 we will discuss these background considerations.

The typical industrial marketer responds to these broad forces. In addition, he either accepts or adopts a set of specific pricing policies and procedures in response to the peculiar pressures that operate within his specific competitive situation. Many of these fall into patterns that are fairly uniform throughout industry. Chapter 12 is devoted to a description of some of the most important.

Chapter 11

PRICING INDUSTRIAL GOODS: BACKGROUND CONSIDERATIONS

ONE OF THE most important problems that confronts the industrial goods marketer is fixing the price at which his products shall be offered for sale. If he sets it too high, he may price himself out of the market; if too low, his income may not cover costs or, at best, will fall short of what it could be. Pricing is also important from the social point of view, since the proper functioning of the economic system as a whole depends to a considerable extent on the pricing policies of the businessmen in it.

The industrial goods manufacturer, like the consumer goods maker, is usually wise to seek the price that, in the long run, will yield him the greatest net return. This is easier said than done. Nor can he assume that once this best possible price has been found it will remain so for any length of time; shifting conditions of demand and cost tend to constantly change it. Before an industrial marketer can make intelligent pricing decisions, he must know the type of competition he faces, the nature of his costs, and the behavior pattern of the demand for his product.

NATURE OF COMPETITION

The competitive structure of the typical industrial market is characteristic of the structure of our industry as a whole. It usually includes: a big three or four group of firms, which handle the bulk of the business, a somewhat larger group of companies of medium size; and, sometimes, a considerable number of quonset hut or garage operators, who capture a very small percentage of the total business but exercise an influence out of all proportion to their share of the market.

The large firms in an industry are usually well financed. They capture the lion's share of the total sales volume. They are usually very active in research and are responsible for creating and introducing most of the technical improvements in the industry. They are set up to produce and market on a mass basis. These characteristics tend to liberally endow the big firms with overhead costs. Their product lines are usually broad, which means that many of their expenses are joint since the typical cost-generating activity plays a part in making and marketing a number of products. Their managers tend to think in terms of share of the market and "responsible competition." This means roughly that each competitor considers himself entitled to a certain percentage of the total sales volume, and that no responsible competitor takes pricing action to cause sudden shifts in market share. Their pricing philosophy seems to be live and let live, so long as the other fellow does not try to live too lustily. The sharpest kind of competition usually exists among them on the bases of product development, customer service, and, within generally accepted limits, price.

The medium-sized firms tend to model their competitive behavior on that of the big group. Their research activities are much less extensive. Their product lines probably are narrower. In some industries, many of them may be specialty houses in the sense that they handle customer requirements for types of products too specialized or needed in quantities too small for the large firms to supply profitably with their less flexible facilities. These concerns usually will not initiate price changes, partly because of fear of retaliation but primarily because they can make satisfactory profits by being responsible competitors.

The quonset hut operator manifests neither price responsibility nor respect for share of the market. His business is usually limited to one or a few products whose technology is simple and whose production does not require expensive equipment or refined operating know-how. His organization is the simplest, and he does not know the words, overhead or research. He rides on the technological coattails of other firms in the industry. His service is rudimentary. His sole appeal to the customer is price. Occasionally, he may grow to become a medium-sized or even a big firm.

Collectively, these operators usually capture a very small percentage of the total industry sales volume. But their disruptive effect on responsible competition usually far outruns their share of the market. The big house can do little to meet their price reductions without risk of generating a price war on the one hand or violating the antitrust laws on the other.

This description seems to indicate that price occupies a minor part in the total competitive picture of industrial goods. For the more highly technical and specialized products, this is true. It also tends to be true of capital equipment items, since a small difference in operating efficiency, aggregated during the life of the machine, can much more than offset a considerable variation in original price.

On the other hand, the typical industrial goods marketer can make little use of the brand advertising his consumer goods counterpart finds so effective as a protection against price competition. Industrial buyers are not particularly impressed by brands or volume of advertising.

Moreover, many industrial materials and items of equipment are standardized. Some of these sets of standards are established by the government, as are many materials used in making foods and drugs; others are set up by trade associations—for example, the NEMA (National Electrical Manufacturers' Association) standards for electric motors. Many of these standardization systems—for example, those applying to steel and other metal products—are highly complex, consisting of a basic specification for each product, with a series of ons and offs for the addition or lack of certain ingredients, variations in the amounts used, or the addition or omission of treatment processes. In each situation, all competitors offer for sale substantially the same product or a product whose quality equals or exceeds a common level.

By substantially removing quality from the competitive complex, standardization throws added emphasis on service and price as bases of competition. The result is that the marketer of standardized industrial products appears able to use price as a means of maximizing profits much more effectively than can the maker of unstandardized items.

Product Life Cycle

The competitive situation varies widely during the life cycle of an industrial product. When a firm introduces a new material, component, supply, or piece of equipment, it may expect to have a monopoly of the market for a period ranging from a few months to a couple of years. During this interval, possible competitors observe the behavior of the new product in use, learn as much as they can about making it, explore the possibility of modifications to increase its efficiency, prepare plans for making and marketing it, and acquire the necessary facilities.

Theoretically, if the innovating firm has a patent on the new product its period of monopoly may last for the life of the patent, 17 years. This rarely happens in practice. It is not easy to get a patent on a material or a supply, and when one is issued it usually covers the process of making the item rather than the item itself. Rarely is there only one way of making an article. So the holder of a process patent often finds that the best way to capitalize on it is to license rivals to manufacture and sell under it. This is less true of a patent that applies to a piece of equipment, for it is apt to be much more defensible. But even here the hazards of defending complete exclusiveness are so great that many firms find it desirable to license competitors to operate under their patents.

For a time after competition first develops, the market for the new product is usually still growing so that the rivalry consists more in the development and dividing up of new business than in the new competitors taking business away from the innovator. However, industrial buyers' desires for alternate sources of supply are likely to bring about the diversion of considerable volume from the innovator to his competition. At first, though, the competition emphasizes selling points other than price.

As the market becomes developed and use of the product becomes widespread, and as more competitors enter the market, price tends to become more important as a competitive factor. A new supplier can enter the market or an old one can increase his market share only by taking part of the market share of a supplier already there. The temptation to use price as an entering wedge is very strong, especially since by this time the product is likely to have been standardized so that quality no longer offers such an effective basis for competition.

There are exceptions to this general picture. The market for some industrial products, such as the metals, basic chemicals, and standardized machines, enjoys a general long-time growth in response to the basic growth of the ultimate consumer market, although it undergoes minor fluctuations along with cyclical ebbs and flows of business conditions. Competition in these products tends to become stabilized and responsible. In such cases, a condition of price leadership is likely to develop.

Price Leadership

Price leadership is probably much more common in the industrial goods market than in the consumer goods area. It is most likely to exist when one firm has a clear advantage in cost or productive capacity and enough financial reserves to stand the losses of a price war without being seriously crippled. The price leader's executives must also be willing to incur the risks of price war in order to establish and maintain leadership.

A price leadership situation has advantages for both the leader and the followers; it also imposes obligations and limitations on both parties. In such a situation, all parties know that destructive price conflicts are not likely to occur. Implicit in the very fact of leadership is a willingness to live and let live. Price wars severe enough to eliminate competitors are likely to be started only by firms that do not recognize the existence of a leadership situation. If such a war starts, the pricing actions of the leader are likely to be designed to discipline the rebel firm and to hold injury to others at a minimum.

The element probably most comforting to the followers in a price leadership situation lies in their knowing that so long as they operate within understood limits they are in no danger of price attack. They also avoid most of the really hard pricing decisions. After a situation of price leadership is established, it is probably maintained fully as much by the followers as by the leader. In fact, it is doubtful if under the present rigorous enforcement of the antitrust laws a price leader can take any very effective action to enforce his leadership. He must maintain it by making the right price decisions for the industry as well as for himself.

Price leadership imposes obligations on the leader as well as on the followers. He can maintain his leadership only by pursuing a definite and consistent pricing policy, by using his power with restraint, and by recognizing, tacitly at least, the rights of followers to their respective market positions. The history of such situations suggests that actually, over time, the price leader tends to lose relative market position, usually without impairment of his leadership unless the process of attrition goes too far.

It may seem that under conditions of price leadership there is no price competition. This is certainly true in the sense that it eliminates violent price action to capture individual orders. Such a condition may make individual buyers unhappy, especially when market conditions indicate that prices should be weakening. But this is in part compensated for because responsible price leadership affords the buyer a certain amount of protection against price squeezes when the market is temporarily tight.

Nor does price leadership eliminate the pressures that generate and direct price competition. The threat of independent pricing action is always there, ready to break out if the leader fails to make the right decisions. The leader is always aware that if the followers gang up on him they can probably beat him. For example, in the spring of 1963 the United States Steel Company, price leader in the steel industry, announced a price increase across the board under what seemed to many to be highly inappropriate conditions. President Kennedy brought such tremendous pressure to bear that the action was rescinded. But before the President acted, several other firms in the industry showed symptoms of sharp dissatisfaction and great reluctance to follow. Had the President not acted, it is entirely possible that some of the mills would have refused to increase their prices. If this had happened, there was probably little that Big Steel could have done about it. The net effect would certainly not have strengthened the leadership position of the United States Steel Company.

NATURE OF COSTS

Since value analysis affords the industrial buyer a technique for computing or estimating the costs of making many of the products he buys, cost is a factor more important in industrial goods pricing than in consumer goods pricing. The dominant factors in price determination are still on the demand side—what the buyer is willing to pay. But the buyer's knowledge, or shrewd guess, of what a product costs may have a considerable influence on what he is willing to pay. Cost is also an important element in pricing industrial goods, because it represents a floor below which a marketer will not go without strenuous resistance or drastic managerial action to maintain or restore a favorable balance between cost and price.

The Time Period

The importance of cost as a determinant of the price of an industrial good varies with the time period under consideration. If we think in terms of the length of time needed to sell goods already produced, we find that cost exercises little influence. At this point all costs are sunk in the sense that all the money needed to pay for making the goods has already been spent. This is just as true of expenses for materials and direct labor as it is of overhead. The important pricing objective is to get back the money spent, or as much of it as possible. In this situation, both direct and overhead costs have the same effect on pricing—practically none at all. What the buyer will pay becomes almost the sole determining factor, since to hold stocks is not only a risky but also a costly business; inventory carrying charges are usually estimated to run at about 1 to 2 percent a month of the value of goods held.

When we consider the pricing of goods during and beyond the coming production cycle, we find it desirable to distinguish between the expenses generated directly by the production and marketing of goods, those that arise from the existence of equipment and facilities, and those generated by the conduct of the business as a going concern—true overhead costs. If he leaves out of consideration such matters as market position and continuous employment for his people, the industrial marketer must be able to foresee a price that will at least cover direct costs and contribute something to the depreciation account of the equipment and facilities used before it is economical to put goods into production.

The choice is not always quite so sharply defined as this, since a going operation tends to develop a momentum of its own that induces an atmosphere of managerial inertia. But in the absence of considerations such as those mentioned above, good management will not long continue to produce and sell an article whose price does not cover direct expenses with something left over to apply to the sunk costs of facilities and equipment.

When the industrial goods marketer plans a long-range pricing policy that extends over the life of a product or of the equipment with which he makes a product, he must consider all three types of cost. At the time of such planning, no costs are sunk, except perhaps those of exploration and research. The same thing is true if the planning involves the procurement of equipment and facilities to expand production. None of the new money needed to service such a decision is yet committed. The pricing plan should be designed to recapture all such money, together with a satisfactory return on it.

In this discussion, we must distinguish several kinds of costs. It is time to review these concepts and to point out some of their implications in making price decisions.

Types of Costs

Controllable and Noncontrollable. The amount and sometimes the existence of controllable costs are subject to the manager's decision. Their identity varies according to the different levels of management. For example, the marketing manager has authority to add or not to add a salesman to the sales force. From his standpoint, the expense of operating the new salesman is a controllable cost. However, if he considers doing entirely without salesmen, and relying on advertising and direct mail or on manufacturer's agents to do the selling job, that decision is not likely to be his alone, although he is almost certain to have a hand in it. The expenses of operating a sales force are certainly controllable by top management but usually not by the marketing manager alone. Production costs, depreciation, and overhead expenses, aside from those of the marketing department, are uncontrollable as far as the marketing manager is concerned.

The point of this distinction for pricing is that the executive who has charge of it is obligated to seek the balance between the manipulation of price and controllable costs that will be most profitable to the company. Sometimes, it will be profitable to increase both price and controllable expenses. Again, price may be increased and controllable costs left unchanged or reduced. It may be impossible to change price, and the path to added profit lies through the reduction of controllable expenses. Occasionally, price may be reduced in the hope that added sales volume will more than pay the same or even added controllable costs. When the pricing executive deals with noncontrollable expenses, his field of maneuver is limited to manipulating price to cover them and leave a profit, or sometimes to merely cover as much of them as possible. Heavy noncontrollable costs narrowly limit his strategic choices.

Incremental and Sunk Costs. Incremental expenses are those added by a given project or program. Sunk costs consist of money that has already been spent and can be recaptured only by successful operations. For example, when a new product is ready to be introduced on the market all the funds that have been spent on research and development to bring it to that point are sunk costs; the money that may be spent to put it on the market is, at the moment of decision, incremental expense. If we buy equipment to make the new product, the funds we pay for it are, up to the moment of purchase, incremental to the project; after they are invested in the equipment, they become sunk costs.

In planning a new product or a new project, a manufacturer should see his way clear to realize a price that will cover both expected sunk and incremental costs, or he should abandon the new venture. If his estimates prove to be in error, or if something goes wrong after he is committed to the new venture, his primary pricing objective then becomes that of recovering the sunk costs. This may involve selling at a price below full cost as long as it covers incremental expenses with something left over to apply to the recovery of sunk costs.

Cash Costs and Book Costs. The conventional accounting procedure recognizes (1) certain expenditures that must be made currently in cash, such as purchases of materials and supplies, and wages and salaries—also called out-of-pocket costs—and (2) other sums that should be set aside from cash inflow and held in the business to maintain its capital structure or to provide for expenditures that may be expected in the future. For example, when a firm buys an expensive piece of equipment it does not charge all its cost as a current expense, but sets it up as a capital account that must be amortized by amounts of income held in the business during the life of the equipment. Since all the cash involved in the purchase goes out when the machine is bought, these charges to its depreciation are simply book transactions for which no checks need be written.

All this means that to remain solvent a firm must pay its out-of-pocket costs, but that over long periods of time it can ignore its book costs. They will eventually come home to roost, bringing disaster with them, but for the life of the equipment that generated them the pricing manager can leave them out of his calculations. It is probable that many quonset hut operators fix their prices without proper regard for their real book costs. The same thing is apt to be true of firms that are declining and near the dropout point. The presence of such firms in an industry tends to influence the pricing decisions of every other concern in it, however small their share of the market may be.

Opportunity Cost. This is what a manager gives up when he carries out one project instead of another. For example, if he is considering the market introduction of new product A he matches the returns he may expect against those he may expect to enjoy if he uses the same amount of money, facilities, and time in introducing product B, or in improving performance with the products already in the line. When he adopts one of these projects, he incurs as an opportunity cost the benefits he could probably have gained by carrying out the best remaining alternative.

This concept has an indirect, rather than a direct, effect on pricing. Of course, it is a factor in the constant series of choices management must make among manipulating price, cutting cost, changing quality, and varying service as alternative means of augmenting profits. It may cause a firm to continue to handle a product, even though profits are unsatisfactory, if no more fruitful use of the capital is available. This is likely to create very disturbing price competition for the other firms in the industry.

Overhead and Direct Costs. In analyzing cost data for purposes of pricing, the industrial marketer must distinguish between fixed or overhead costs and variable or direct costs. The total amount of fixed costs for the firm, at least in the short run, does not change in proportion to the volume of production or sale. Examples are rent, interest on owned or borrowed capital, real estate taxes, insurance, and many types of labor expense. It should be noted that labor costs incidental to assembly line or production line operation tend to behave like overhead within wide ranges of volume. On the other hand, are variable costs whose total increases or decreases more or less proportionately with the volume of production. Examples are most types of wages, raw material costs, and income taxes if the sales–profit ratio remains constant. These expenses are also called direct or operating costs. Sometimes, a third category of costs may be distinguished—semivariable costs, which vary only slightly with the volume of production or which vary as a result of executive decision. Certain kinds of salary payments and advertising appropriations may be placed in this category.

The study of overhead costs is highly important to pricing analysis. First, in making short-run pricing decisions about additional business management need not take overhead expenses into consideration so long as unused capacity is available, and the price received for an additional order covers something more than the costs directly attributable to that order. If the order contributes something more than direct costs toward overhead, net profit will be greater (or net loss will be less) than had the order not been accepted. Second, even in the long run many types of overhead expenses need not be met currently, since a losing business has the unhappy alternative of going out of business or simply using up its fixed assets until the time it is forced into bankruptcy.

Selling expenses, including advertising costs, payment to sales personnel, traveling expenses, and others, are usually treated as overhead costs. Really though, not all these are true overhead expenses, since changes in sales production volume may be caused by changes in the amount spent for advertising and sales work. Certain of these expenses are what we have referred to as semivariable costs. The advertising budget, for example, is generally flexible to the extent that it can be increased or decreased as sales exceed or fail to meet expectations. But in the very short run practically all these expenses may be treated as overhead, and there is no completely compelling reason, from the short-run point of view, why any particular order, any particular product, or, for that matter, any segment of a business should be made to bear its proportionate or fair share of the overhead, except when failure to do so results in pricing that is discriminatory under the Robinson-Patman Law.

In deciding whether or not to accept an order or to submit a competitive bid that will not pay all properly allocable overhead, the industrial seller must take into account his future relationships with the buyer and the reaction of his competitors. There is danger that a small company that accepts high-volume, low-margin business and expands to meet its production requirements will become dependent on such business and eventually will be merely an appendage of the large buyer. When competitors for a specific piece of business are likely to retaliate against a low offer with an equally low or lower one, the seller may not want to become involved in a destructive price war and may thus be restrained from offering a price that does not cover all costs.

In the very long run, it should be noted, all costs become direct in the sense that they must be met if a business is to survive. But businesses fail every day, and while they are in the process of failing they are, in fact, not meeting overhead costs. When patronage falls off to such an extent that these marginal businesses cannot meet all costs, the easiest short-run solution may be simply to cease paying certain deferrable expenses. Of course, the owners would probably like to sell out at this point and get their money back, but a business that loses money over any considerable period of time is not likely to bring much more on the auction block than its scrap value. The only way a substantial portion of sunk costs can be retrieved may be to continue to operate, paying only those overhead expenses that are absolutely necessary. Depreciation charges, for example, need not be met. Repair and maintenance costs can be reduced to those necessary for day-to-day operation, and need not include preventive maintenance. Reserves of various kinds can be entirely eliminated. Even payment to bondholders or preferred stockholders can be neglected until they threaten to exercise their rights by taking over and running the business themselves. The business may continue in this fashion either until the equipment assets become inoperative and are sold for their scrap value or until demand revives to such an extent that overhead costs can again be covered. It is often the expectation of revival that keeps a business alive and active through extended periods of unprofitable operation. Indeed, firms have been known to keep their doors open without even meeting direct expenses in order to hold their organizations together in anticipation of more prosperous times.

The considerations just given pose very interesting and serious problems in industries where a substantial portion of cost is represented by overhead, as with many manufacturers of industrial goods. What should be the price policy of company A whose competitor, company B, is selling at a price that does not cover fixed costs? The question becomes more acute when the product in question is Company A's main product but only a minor product or a by-product of the price-cutter. In some instances, company B is not even aware of its real costs, and therefore cannot be expected to make intelligent pricing decisions. Again, the motive may be a predatory attempt to drive company A out of the market. In any case, when the product cannot be easily differentiated, or when it is sold on the basis of standard specifications, company A is in a difficult position.

The problem of overhead costs becomes especially acute when a large producer of industrial goods, with an expensive research and development program and all the other outlays incidental to being a leader in the industry and a responsible, respected citizen of the business community, must meet the competition of the quonset hut or garage operator, who neither toils at research nor spins the future of the industry by development work, but whose offers to customers are often arrayed in highly attractive price concessions. No generally recognized defense is available to the big house against this kind of price competition. In most cases, its pricing executive must console himself with the knowledge that such an operator can take only a small segment of the market, and that as soon as he begins to get big he will learn the meaning of the nasty word, overhead.

Joint Costs

In many industrial goods businesses, the production of one product is inseparable from the making of one or more other products, with resulting joint costs. This usually occurs when two or more products are made from the same material or are processed by the same equipment. The second product, however, may require additional processing not needed to make the first; the expenses of such extra processing are separable costs. For example, cottonseed is produced as a by-product of the process of ginning cotton, and its costs cannot be distinguished from the cost of ginning the cotton. However, the cost of pressing the oil out of the seed is a separable expense.

Joint costs give rise to some very interesting pricing problems. Each joint product must obviously bring in a cash flow to cover its separable costs if it is to be marketed, but the price to ask beyond this minimum will depend on how much there is to be sold in relation to its demand, and this, in turn, on the volume of production of the main product. It often happens that over a period of time the by-product gains while the main product loses in importance, with the result that the by-product is able to bear an increasingly larger percentage of the common processing expense. Indeed, the by-product and the main product have, on occasion, exchanged roles—for example, kerosene and gasoline.

Sometimes, this change of roles creates serious problems. For example, a chemical house that makes an antibiotic developed an animal feed additive from the residue of the production process. The new business became more profitable than the antibiotic operation, and its volume grew so large that it required more of the essential ingredient than resulted from making the amount of the antibiotic the company could sell. But if this ingredient was made as a prime operation, its cost became prohibitive in relation to the price that could be obtained for the feed mixture.

In the coke industry, there are literally thousands of by-products. Here, the allocation of overhead and joint costs is quite arbitrary, and the pricing of the individual product must depend in very large measure on such factors as the seller's judgment about what the market will bear, his desire to expand the market for a new product, or simply his need to get rid of a certain amount of a given by-product. In certain instances, such as in oil refining, the amounts of the various by-products can be changed within rather narrow limits by alterations in technical processes. Hence, the pricing executive has some room in which to maneuver.

NATURE OF DEMAND

The term "market demand" refers to the amount of a product buyers may be expected to purchase at various prices at a given time. An industrial marketer can construct a schedule of demand showing the amount he might expect to sell at each possible price. This may be much less exact or reliable than the demand schedules in the average economics textbook would lead us to believe. Actually, the only facts about demand the seller can be sure of are those represented by his current price and quantity position. He may estimate the remainder of the schedule on the basis of anticipated buyer reaction, past experience, or the experience of companies that sell similar products. Since he must estimate physical volume at different prices in order to do any marketing planning at all, he is probably wise to make the process as systematic as possible. But he should be entirely aware of the uncertainties inherent in his schedule once he gets it constructed.

With most consumer goods, the higher the price, the smaller is the demand, and the lower the price, the greater is the amount taken. This tends to be true because of the composite thinking and attitudes of the market as expressed by the differing valuations different possible buyers put on a product in relation to money. That is, at a price of 75 cents only consumers who feel the product is worth that much money or more will buy. If the price is $1, all consumers who value the product at less than that much money will be out of the market.

The theory assumes a certain static characteristic in buyers' attitudes toward the relative values of money and the product; it assumes that the demand schedule stands still when price changes. This is not always true. The mere fact that a price change occurs may cause some buyers, sometimes considerable numbers of them, to change their attitudes toward the relative values of product and money.

As explained in a previous chapter, this is especially likely to be true in the short run with industrial goods, because of the professional nature of those who make buying decisions, their close familiarity with the market, and the factors that motivate them to purchase or refrain from purchasing. The value of a material to an industrial user is what it is worth at the time he uses it, and he generally uses it some time after he commits himself to its purchase. So he must constantly think in terms of price in the future—at the end of his purchasing turnaround time, plus his stock turnover period, plus the span of his production cycle—instead of at the current moment. A decline in price, therefore, may cause him to change his mind about the probable future price, and may lead him to adopt a waiting policy to see if it will go lower rather than entering the market or increasing his purchases. Thus, a drop in price may, for a time, have the effect of shrinking demand instead of increasing it.

The same sort of change in the reverse direction may happen over a longer range. For example, as a result of the drastic increases in the prices of steel products during the 1950's, many industrial buyers who had never given serious thought to the substitutions of plastics or aluminum for the heavier metal began to do so, with a consequent increase in the amounts of those products taken at certain prices, and corresponding decreases in the demand for steel products. Often, if the price of a material drops to certain levels industrial houses that never thought of using it before begin to hunt uses in their operations. For example, when the prices of vitamins dropped far enough, the bakers and flour millers began to use them in enriching flour and bread; when the cost of certain antibiotics fell far enough, the compounders of animal feeds began to find them useful and economical for stimulating animal growth. In both of these cases, the buyer's relative valuation of money and product was changed by events that occurred in the market.

An unusually penetrating economist remarked that to be truly reflective of actual conditions a demand curve must be drawn with rubber chalk on a rapidly vibrating rubber blackboard. This may be an overstatement, but not a flagrant one in the industrial goods field.

Behavior of Derived Demand

We pointed out earlier that the demand for industrial goods is derived rather than direct. This means that the total demand for an industrial product can increase only as a result of an increase in the purchase of the consumer end products it is used to make. Theoretically, of course, if the prices of the materials or equipment used in making a consumer product are reduced enough to allow its price to be cut its sales may be expected to go up, and the demand for the materials and equipment to be increased likewise. By reducing price, a firm may be able not only to increase its share of the market but also to enlarge the total market.

This looks a lot sounder in theory than it usually proves to be in practice. For the principle to work effectively, the demand for the consumer end product must be highly elastic in response to price changes. But even if such end product elasticity exists, it often happens that a considerable change in the prices of an industrial ingredient, component, or piece of equipment will not force or make possible any significant change in the end product price.

The cost of purchased materials usually runs between 40 and 50 percent of selling price of the finished product. Let us consider an end product sold to the consumer at $1 per unit. Let's assume that only one material is used in making it—a highly unrealistic assumption. Its price and cost structure might look as follows:

Retail selling price...............................$1.00
    Gross profit to retailer (30%).................... .30
Wholesaler's selling price.........................$ .70
    Gross profit to wholesaler (15%)................ .105
Manufacturer's selling price.......................$ .595
    Material (40%).............................. .238
    Other costs and profit.........................$ .357

If we reduce the cost of the material 10 percent and figure back from there, the cost–price structure becomes:

Material......................................$.2142
Other costs and profit........................... .3570
Manufacturer's possible selling price................$.5712
Wholesaler's possible selling price.................. .672
Retailer's possible selling price....................$.96

A reduction of 10 percent in the price of the material makes possible a decline of only 4 percent in the price of the end product to the consumer.

But suppose that our material is responsible for only one fourth of the cost of the materials used in making the end product. If we cut its price 10 percent, the picture will look somewhat like the following:

Old price of our material (¼ of $.238)............$.0595
Reduced price of our material...................... .05355
Other materials ($.238–.0595).................... .17850
Total materials.................................$.23205
Other costs and profit........................... .357
Manufacturer's possible selling price..............$.58905
Wholesaler's possible selling price................ .693
Retailer's possible selling price....................$.99

A reduction of 10 percent in the price of our material makes possible a decline of only 1 percent, or 1 cent in the price of an end product that sells for $1, not enough to make much of a dent in the consumer's consciousness or arouse in him any wild enthusiasm to rush out and buy more of it.

This illustration somewhat overstates the case. It leaves out of consideration that some industrial materials are to some extent interchangeable in use. Examples are steel and aluminum. The price of aluminum per ton is above that of steel, but it has certain advantages, such as appearance and lightness of weight. As the price of steel increases or that of aluminum falls, it becomes profitable for users to substitute the aluminum for steel for some purposes. By manipulating their prices in relation to those of steel, therefore, aluminum producers may expand their total market by taking over a part of the market for steel. Precisely this has been happening during recent years.

The fact remains, however, that for many industrial products a marketer's attempt to increase his sales volume by reducing price can succeed only when he takes business away from a competitor. This is so liable to provoke retaliation by the competitor that most industrial marketers are cautious about its use.

The derived nature of the demand for industrial goods affects the extent to which it is subject to influence by selling effort. When a manufacturer of a consumer good applies advertising and sales effort to its promotion, he may increase the demand for it in several ways. He may induce a rival's customers to buy from him instead. He may induce present customers to buy and use more of the product. Or he may persuade people who have never used the article to become customers of it.

By promotional effort, the manufacturer of an industrial product may hope to take customers away from a competitor. If his promotional work is directed at present users of his product, he can expect to do very little to increase their demand for it. That is conditioned by the demand for the end products it is used to make, and his promotion has no effect on that. A few industrial goods makers find it possible to advertise over the heads of customers to end product consumers. But this is usually rather expensive because, at best, the manufacturer can hope to get only about 40 to 50 cents of each dollar of new business his promotion may develop, regardless of whether this new business represents increased usage by old consumers or the demand of entirely new consumers of the end product. Occasionally, promotion directed at industrial firms may induce a few of them not now making the end product to go into the business; but such pickings are apt to be very slim.

In some cases, through a combination of research and promotion a maker of an industrial product can increase its total usage by developing new uses or new end products to be made of or by it. This is true of both materials and equipment. For example, a manufacturer of a plastics material may work with a customer in a joint program of research to develop a new end product made in part or entirely of a new form of the plastic. After a suitable interval, he is usually at liberty to promote and sell the material to other customers for the same purpose.

THE SELLER'S BEST PRICE

Economists have long striven to devise a theory to explain how a businessman can determine his best price.

A basic premise is that a pricing executive's general objective is to manage his firm's prices so as to gain the largest possible profit. This involves balancing the effect of price on sales volume, and through that on production cost, against the volume-generating effects of variations in service and sometimes in quality and the costs they give rise to. All this must be done within an environment set by the reactions of competitors to changes in any of these factors.

As a general rule, an increase in physical sales volume, and so in the amount produced, tends to make possible reductions in factory cost per unit. The greater the proportion of overhead expense in the cost structure, the more pronounced this effect is likely to be. So, if by reducing his price the manager can bring about a considerable increase in physical sales volume, it may be that the lower price, minus a reduced factory cost per unit, multiplied by the increased number of units sold will create a larger net cash inflow than will the former higher price. Whether this works or not depends to a considerable extent on competitors' reactions to the decrease.

Changes in factory cost due to shifts in volume produced can usually be estimated with reliable accuracy. Marketing management should be able to estimate with somewhat less accuracy the effect of a proposed price change on sales volume in the absence of competitive reaction. A pricing executive who knows his trade can probably make a considerably less accurate guess as to whether competition will react to a price shift and, if so, what the direction and extent of the reaction is likely to be. As a result of this process of estimating, the manager might wind up with a set of data somewhat like the following.

A. If we cut price 5 percent, the chances are:
   1. 50 out of 100 that competitors will not react; then our physical sales volume will increase 3 percent, and our factory cost per unit will decrease 1.5 percent.
   2. 5 out of 100 that competitors will cut price less than 5 percent; then our physical sales volume will increase 2 percent, and our factory cost per unit will decrease 1.3 percent.
   3. 40 out of 100 that competitors will meet our cut exactly; then our physical sales volume and factory cost will remain unchanged.
   4. 5 out of 100 that competitors will cut more than 5 percent; then our physical sales volume will decline 3 percent, and our factory unit cost will increase 2 percent.
B. If we cut price 10 percent, the chances are:
   1. 20 out of 100 that competitors will not react; then our physical sales volume will rise 25 percent, and our factory unit cost will decline 5 percent.
   2. 10 out of 100 that competitors will cut less than 10 percent; then our physical sales volume will rise 15 percent, and our factory unit cost will fall 4.5 percent.
   3. 40 out of 100 that competitors will meet our cut exactly; then our physical sales volume and factory unit cost will remain unchanged.
   4. 30 out of 100 that competitors will cut more than 10 percent; then our physical sales volume will decline 10 percent, and our factory unit cost will increase 5 percent.

The list of alternatives and the assumptions applying to each of them can be expanded indefinitely. We can carry this assumption analysis further by estimating the effects of several actions we might take for each competitor reaction. A formula can be developed for application by a computer to derive the probable effect of each alternative on company profits and to select the one promising the most profit.

It is true that this involves a tissue of assumptions; only one set—those applying to the effect of output volume on unit factory cost—has any pretense of reliable accuracy. (For some products, a statistical analysis of the time relation between a firm's price shifts and its sales volume may supply some basis upon which to forecast the effect of proposed price changes on sales. This is not true of as many industrial products as might be expected.) But without such a set of assumptions, recognized or implicit, no intelligent pricing decisions can be made. It is highly probable that they will be more carefully done and more accurate, and the probable results of the various alternatives will be more soundly weighed if both alternatives and estimated results are brought out into the open, set down in black and white, and examined with the best tools available.

The usefulness of this method of approach to industrial product pricing is limited by several factors.

1. The management of a firm may have prime objectives other than maximizing profits, such as share of the market, price leadership, company image, or growth. These goals may be of prime or dominant importance for considerable periods of time as long as profits are satisfactory, even though below the maximum possible. There may be and usually are intrafirm conditions that dictate what the price objective should be. For example, if a firm has heavy sunk costs in a product, such as research, special equipment, and market development expenditures, the best price may be a figure that results in the shortest payout period—the length of time required to recover the investment in the product out of the cash earnings it generates. This may result in a fantastic rate of net profit, or it may result in no book net profit at all. It is the figure that will most quickly return sunk costs and restore the capital structure of the company.

The best price may be one that enables the marketer to gain or hold a favorable market position, which means that under some conditions, and almost certainly during the early stages of a product's life, its price may bear little resemblance to the one that will return the greatest net profit. It may be argued that such a policy is really tantamount to pricing for the greatest net profit over the long run—the entire life of the product. This is probably substantially true, although implementing the policy requires the use of rather exact forecasts based on exceedingly tenuous estimates of future events that are very hard to predict.

2. The industrial goods firm is under considerable pressure to make and sell a full line of the kind of goods it deals in, because by so doing it can supply the customer's entire requirements and prevent competition from getting a foothold in his business. Each item in a line may react in a different way to price manipulation and may be subject to different competitive pressures and have its own cost structure. The problem of

pricing then ceases to be one of fixing prices for individual items and becomes one of creating a system of prices for all articles in the line, many of which react on one another. In such circumstances, the method outlined above tends to become almost impossibly complex.

3. In marketing many industrial products, price is a factor of relatively minor importance. This is true of all special kinds of equipment, materials, components, and supplies.

4. Even when price is a primary factor in determining patronage, the buyer's definition of price probably will be different from the figure on the seller's invoice. As we saw in the discussion of value analysis, the buyer tends to make his price comparison on the basis of the cost of the product in use, which reflects a variety of additional factors, such as cost of buying, cost of delivery, cost of carrying inventory, and value of special services. The customer's thinking and computations with respect to these matters are not apt to be known to the supplier.

5. In the case of most consumer goods, when a supplier reduces his price his action has a dual effect. It enables him to take volume away from competitors. And by making the product available at a lower price, he increases the total amount sold. As we have seen, with many industrial products this is not true, since their demand is derived from the demand for the end products they are used to make. Unless the price of a material or a component or a piece of equipment constitutes an element in the cost structure of its end product large enough so that a change in its price makes possible or requires a change in the end product price and, hence, the sales volume, no amount of manipulation of the industrial good price will have much, if any, effect on the total quantity of it sold.

This means that any attempt to maximize the profits of many industrial products by price shifts, particularly reductions, will be reacted to promptly and vigorously by competitors. A common comment of industrial goods price executives is, "If we cut price, they will cut, too, and then we will each be selling the same tonnage at less profit."

6. No firm that makes and markets widely used materials or components can operate without a weather eye on government attitude. Both the Federal Trade Commission and the Department of Justice are peculiarly sensitive to corporate pricing behavior, and they subscribe to the concept—often unacknowledged—of a "fair" price that by no means maximizes profits. A pricing policy designed to maximize profit will have features that irritate that sensitivity. During the late 1950's and early 1960's, Congress has shown a tendency to investigate pricing practices. A pricing scheme patently based on the objective of maximizing profit is not easy to defend before a congressional committee seeking publicity through the crucifixion of business management.

For these reasons, the precise use of graphs and complex formulas in pricing industrial goods are often rendered unrealistic by the intangible factors that exercise so potent an influence on the market for these goods.

Their very precision and exactness may mislead the pricing executive who tries to use them, unless he is endowed with a rare sense of the intangibles and an unusual power to weigh their importance.

Perhaps some guidelines may be set up to help the pricing executive set the profit objective to aim at in pricing his company's line of industrial goods. What is a reasonable profit or a proper profit for such a firm to seek? If the factors that make up or determine the limits of this concept can be isolated for a firm, perhaps a knowledge of them may be helpful in constructing the complex of prices to be applied to the firm's product line.

A marketer may approach the problem of putting the reasonable profit concept into figures by relating it to the average rate of profit on capital used that is achieved by firms in his industry, or to the median rate of the more successful firms in the industry. Or he may attack it by an analysis of what uses or objectives profits may achieve. For example, profits are needed to pay enough dividends to keep the stockholders satisfied or, at least, quiescent. They are needed to provide capital with which to seek out and exploit opportunities in the form of new products, new markets, or acquisitions. This may be done from retained earnings or by borrowing on favorable terms made possible by a satisfactory rate of earnings on capital already used. They may be needed to build up retained earnings against possible future reverses and to enable the payment of dividends in spite of them. It is possible to express all these needs in dollars, which set a profit objective toward which the pricing executive can work. Competition, the possibility of loss of customer good will and market position, and the threat of government action limit the extent to which he can attain or go above this objective. These factors may establish a range within which the dollar definition of reasonable profit and, thus, reasonable price falls.

But neither this sort of analysis nor any other yet devised lends itself to the preparation of a formula by which the industrial pricing executive can infallibly, or even usually, solve his day-to-day problems.

SUMMARY

To price intelligently, the industrial marketer must know the type of competition in his industry, the nature of his costs, and the way in which the demand for his product behaves.

The average industrial goods trade is composed of a small group of large firms, a more numerous group of medium-sized competitors, and often a group of very small concerns that sell mainly on the basis of price. The first two groups are likely to subscribe to the theory of responsible competition. The nature and intensity of competition changes with changes in the life cycle of a product. Price leadership is a common phenomenon in the industrial goods field.

The nature and pricing implications of costs tend to change with the time period—production cycle, equipment use cycle, or product life cycle—considered. Different kinds of costs—controllable or noncontrollable, incremental or sunk, cash or book, overhead or direct, incremental, and joint—exercise different influences on pricing.

The derived nature of the demand for industrial goods affects its behavior in response to price change. In spite of this, or perhaps because of it, the pricing executive may use a means-end-probability type of analysis to guide his decisions, although this has its drawbacks. The concept of the right price is highly nebulous but may afford some guidance.

Chapter 12

⟨⟨⟨⟨⟨⟨⟨⟨⟨⟨⟨⟨ PRICING INDUSTRIAL GOODS:

DECISIONS, POLICIES: PRACTICES

We have just examined some of the background concepts and forces involved in the pricing of industrial goods. Let us now look at some of the kinds of actual pricing decisions the industrial marketing executive must make in order to successfully distribute his products. Probably more has been written about prices and pricing than about any other function in the business system. But less is really known about how marketers actually determine their prices than about any other phase of economic or business activity. The paucity of information on the subject and the characteristic reluctance of the responsible executives to talk about it might lead one to suspect that pricing is habitually done with mirrors, or by consulting some highly specialized and occult commercial Delphian oracle.

SITUATIONS REQUIRING PRICING DECISIONS

It is possible, though, to analyze the process, to isolate at least some of the factors involved in it and some techniques for dealing with them, and to establish some guides that may be of help to the pricing executive in his work. It is probably worthwhile to distinguish at least three business situations that give rise to the need for making pricing decisions.

The first of these is the introduction of a new product. Before it can be offered on the market, someone must decide what price will be asked for it. This is a situation that requires positive decision. It cannot go by default or be expected to decide itself through managerial indecision.

A second situation that requires a pricing decision arises when a rival changes his price or a new competitor enters the market with a price different from the prevailing one. This confronts the marketer with the question: Shall I change my price in response to this new factor or shall I sit tight? In this situation, vacillation or indecision is really a decision to stick with our present price. Positive decision can be escaped. When this situation arises, the pricing executive is usually wise to seek the answer to such questions as: Why did my competitor change his price? What objective does he hope to accomplish by the change? If he can find reasonably satisfactory answers to these questions, they may point toward the counteraction he will be most wise to take.

A third situation that demands pricing decision arises when we consider initiating a change in our own price as a move in marketing strategy or tactics. This situation too is susceptible of resolution by indecision. Failure to decide whether or not a price change shall be made means that none will be made, and that the opportunity to profit from making it will probably lapse. Before the pricing executive initiates a pricing change as a strategic or tactical move, he will be wise to ask himself: "If I make this change, what counteraction is competition liable to take and which competitors are most likely to take it?" and "If one or more of them do react as I expect, what effect will that have on my likelihood of attaining the objective of my original move, or what additional action will I have to take to protect myself against their counteraction and to gain my objective?" The nature of these questions suggests the need for the pricing executive to study the pricing policies and practices of competitive firms and the behavior and emotional makeup of his opposite numbers in those firms.

TECHNIQUES OF DECISION

Each of these situations presents its own problems to the pricing executive, and each is fraught with its own uncertainties. The executive can use a number of techniques or methods of analysis in dealing with them. It might be worthwhile to examine these techniques, to explore the extent to which each can be applied to each of the situations just described, and to try to appraise their usefulness in pricing industrial goods.

Analogy—Historical Method

This is a very old technique, and is probably used consciously or unconsciously much more than most pricing executives realize. In its essence, it runs about as follows: "We faced a situation much like this once before and did so and so with pretty good results," or "company X handled this kind of problem in such and such a way and seems to have gotten away with it, so let's do the same thing." The memory of analogous situations undoubtedly forms a highly influential part of the mental and emotional atmosphere within which the pricing executive attacks his problems.

The chief drawback of the analogy approach is that business situations never duplicate themselves exactly, and seemingly trivial, even unnoticed, variations may cause a pricing action in the current case to work in a way entirely different than in the analogous one. Then, too, there is no assurance that the course of action followed in the analogous case was the best one, and by following it we cut ourselves off from the possibility of finding a better one.

There is little difference in the usefulness of pricing by analogy in the three decision situations just described. Nor are there significant differences between its use in the industrial goods and the consumer goods fields.

Following Competitors

A marketer must choose between the roles of a price follower and price leader. The medium-sized firm usually does not find this choice very hard, being more or less forced into a followership position because, although its cost structure may be as, or even more, favorable than that of its bigger rivals, it lacks the financial strength to wage a successful struggle for leadership. The medium-sized firm usually is able to exercise enough influence on the market to make it worthwhile for the price leader to apply disciplinary measures if it cuts price. On the other hand, while the very small competitor—the garage or quonset hut operator—can never aspire to price leadership, he can occupy a position of considerable price independence. He usually has little or no overhead cost. If he cuts price, most of the retaliatory counteractions open to the large firms in the trade are either of doubtful legality or are highly expensive in relation to the market segment objectives involved. About all the price leader can do about him is to suffer in dignified silence, knowing that the small operator can exercise no widespread influence on the market.

Being a follower materially simplifies the marketer's pricing problems. All that is necessary in pursuing this policy is to maintain an alert information system and to determine which competitor to follow and when and how far. On the other hand, by being a price follower a marketer relinquishes whatever prestige, timeliness, and other advantages are inherent in leadership, and resigns himself to an attitude of relative passivity compared with the aggressiveness that marks the leader.

The essential principles involved in following a competitor's price leadership are the same for the industrial goods marketer as they are for the firm that distributes consumer goods. But the circumstances surrounding the process differ significantly. In most consumer goods trades, brand advertising plays a vital role in achieving product differentiation. The degree of differentiation achieved depends heavily on the effectiveness of the advertising. Prices of branded goods are notoriously sticky, partly, at least, because the price is often a part of the advertising.

Branding plays a much less important role in industrial goods marketing, and product differentiation results much more from product differences that generate provable claims of benefits on which the buyer can put a dollar sign, or from superiority of services that he can also measure in dollars. This means that an industrial goods marketer may follow a competitor's price leadership without his prices being identical with those of the competitor. In order to follow effectively, he must calculate how much more or less than the competitor's price customers will be willing to pay for his product-service package because it has provable benefits the rival product-service package does not have, or it lacks provable benefits the competitor's package offers.

On the other hand, the industrial materials marketer finds it impossible or much harder to disguise price differences than does the firm that distributes consumer goods. Industrial materials or components are usually sold in units that are standard to all buyers and sellers, such as pounds, gallons, or pieces. Many consumer goods are sold by the package. Package contents are not necessarily all standard. Not all large tubes of toothpaste contain the same amount of paste or essential cleansing ingredient, nor will they all clean the same number of teeth. Ultimate consumers can usually find out how much is in a package if they want to; but how many of them do so? On the other hand, the industrial buyer is more than willing to check what he gets for the price he pays.

Trial and Error

This is one of the oldest methods of pricing and is really implicit in all the others. No matter how scientific a management is in setting a price for its product, it may make a mistake. So, in a sense, every pricing action is a trial. The important point in the use of this technique is to recognize a mistake as early as possible and to rectify it as soon as possible. It is almost always better initially to set a price too high rather than too low, because a price reduction usually generates less ill will than does an increase.

In the use of this method, there is little difference between the industrial goods and the consumer goods fields. In the consumer goods field, trial and error is often somewhat harder because price is often widely advertised, and to change it may mean to change the entire promotional campaign. In marketing industrial goods, a price change is usually announced in a price or discount list or through the salesman's call. Channels of distribution for consumer goods tend to be longer and to include more levels of marketing agencies than those used for industrial goods. This means that a change in the manufacturer's price requires adjustments all along the line.

Test Pricing. This may be viewed as a special variety of trial and error. It involves trying out several prices in carefully selected parts—usually geographical—of the market, under conditions as rigidly controlled as possible, and observing the results. Prices may be changed and the effect of the changes may be observed.

This method enjoys wide usefulness in consumer goods marketing. Its applicability to industrial goods is narrowly limited by several factors. First, as we learned in a previous chapter, the market for many industrial products is not a single homogenous unit but is segmented into a number of trade or industry groups, each using the product for a somewhat different purpose and, consequently, buying it on the basis of different benefits sought or enjoyed. What a test pricing campaign tells a marketer about one segment of his market will be of little use in other segments. Moreover, each of these segments may include relatively few firms, and there is usually a very active grapevine among them. So it is not possible to conduct a test pricing campaign without its becoming common knowledge to all buyers, with resulting generation of ill will because a lower price is being offered to some buyers and not to others.

In addition, as has been pointed out, each industry usually has a few large buyers and a number of smaller ones, and they tend to buy on somewhat different bases. What the marketer finds out by test pricing a sample of the smaller buyers will tell him little about the probable reactions of the larger ones. Because of these factors, test pricing is not nearly so widely used in industrial goods marketing as in consumer goods.

Marketing Research

On the other hand, research is probably a more useful and reliable guide in industrial goods than in consumer goods pricing. The consumer is notoriously unreliable in matching what he actually does about a product or a condition of sale in the market with what he said he would do about it before he came on the market. This unreliability reaches its peak in the pricing area.

In the industrial goods field, a careful and clever researcher can gather a lot of fairly reliable information to guide the making of price decisions. While pricing research in the consumer goods field usually attacks the problem by trying to find out how much the average consumer will be willing to pay for a product, the industrial goods price researcher tries to find out how much it is worth to the customer to have the product for use in his operations. This is the maximum amount the buyer will pay for it, and his willingness to pay is not apt to be influenced by changes in his mood or emotions.

In doing this kind of research, the industrial goods marketer can make use of the value analysis techniques described earlier. For example, a firm develops a new machine to perform a certain operation. In a given period of time, one of these new machines will turn out 25 percent more pieces of finished product than the machine it replaces. Each of the old machines required one man to run it; one man can tend three of the new machines. It is possible for a researcher in the firm that makes the machine to compute, with some approach to exactness, the dollar value to the customer of the savings generated by these two features of the new machine during its expected life. The only open-end question then becomes: How much of this total saving can the marketer take in a price premium on the new machine over the old and still sell it? Even this question may respond, in part, to analysis by the discounted cash flow method.

A chemical house develops a preparation that, without leaving toxic residue, will shorten by 15 days the period needed to cure meat. By studying the curing process and estimating the various elements in its cost, the marketing researcher for the chemical firm can compute a saving to the packer that will, at least, be in the ball park. If the price of steel were to increase by 20 percent, what kinds of steel users would find it profitable to turn to the use of aluminum, and how much tonnage would they shift? Market researchers in the steel industry can figure this out, and undoubtedly have done so. The aluminum producers are probably working the formula in reverse.

Marketing research by use of value analysis cannot usually tell the industrial marketer exactly what price to put on his goods, but it can establish fairly precise limits within which the right price falls.

Formulas

Undoubtedly, formulas are used more than they should be in pricing industrial goods, even though a higher percentage of the total consumer goods pricing decisions is probably made by formula than is the case in industrial goods pricing. A very high percentage of the pricing decisions of wholesalers and retail stores, small and large, is made by adding a set percentage of markup or a customary dollar amount to cost. The prevalence of persons with engineering training in the marketing managements of industrial goods houses tends to emphasize the formula approach to pricing in that field.

Pricing by formula is a comforting process in an area fraught with uncertainty and hazard. It is precise and logical, and fits in with the engineer's conviction of the universal verity of mathematical analysis. Its chief drawback is that the buyer-user knows nothing about the formula and cares less; in fact, as a result of his value analysis work the user may have a formula of his own that is quite at odds with that of the marketer. But the use of formulas may be of considerable help to the industrial goods pricing executive in establishing a floor below which the price of a product cannot profitably go, and in clarifying the influence on income that varying prices may exercise through their effect on volume and, hence, on cost of production.

Pricing formulas are generally based on cost. In using them, the pricing executive must be careful to distinguish the effect that differing pricing policies may have on direct or variable costs, overhead or fixed costs, and total costs. One very useful way in which to do this is by break-even analysis. The way this analysis works is best illustrated by a break-even chart, shown in Figure 12–1.

The distance between lines *AF* and *CE* represents total overhead costs,

which do not increase as the number of units ma⟨...⟩ ⟨...⟩e
distance between lines *CD* and *CE* represents ⟨...⟩ch
increase as the number of units made and so⟨...⟩ ⟨...⟩ce
between line *AF* and line *CD* represents tota⟨...⟩ and
direct. The distance between line *AF* and lin⟨...⟩ flow
from sales.

This chart indicates that the company do⟨...⟩ until
line *AB* intersects and passes above line *CL*⟨...⟩ point,
and that the farther line *AB* goes above *C*⟨...⟩e com-

FIGURE 12–1

Break-Even Ch⟨...⟩

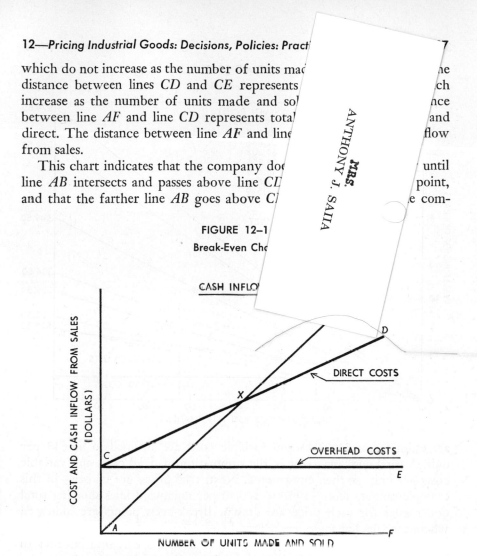

pany makes. For a new company or a new product, the best short-run
price is usually the one that will cause *AB* to pass above *CD* most quickly;
the best long-run price is one that will cause *AB* to go the highest distance
for the longest time above *CD*.

This basic type of break-even chart can be modified to show the
pricing executive what his profit position may be expected to be at
different price levels under assumed conditions of demand and cost. Such a
chart is shown in Figure 12–2.

A glance at the chart reveals the break-even points at various prices,
and also indicates the amount of profit or loss that would be forthcoming
at different prices and different volumes of output. In the figure, 80,000
units is assumed to be capacity production during the first year of operation. Therefore, the horizontal axis is scaled from 0 to 80,000 units.

Costs and sales are measured in dollars on the vertical axis. Fixed costs

FIGURE 12–2

Break-Even Points

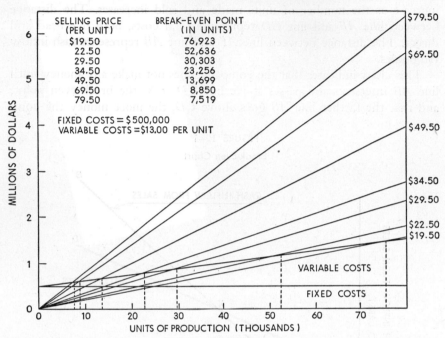

SELLING PRICE (PER UNIT)	BREAK–EVEN POINT (IN UNITS)
$19.50	76,923
22.50	52,636
29.50	30,303
34.50	23,256
49.50	13,699
69.50	8,850
79.50	7,519

FIXED COSTS = $500,000
VARIABLE COSTS = $13.00 PER UNIT

(Y-axis: MILLIONS OF DOLLARS; X-axis: UNITS OF PRODUCTION (THOUSANDS))

are estimated at $500,000, and variable costs are assumed to be $13 per unit. A total cost line—that is, the summation of fixed costs and variable costs per unit—is then constructed. Next, trial prices are chosen—in this example ranging from $19.50 to $79.50 per unit—and lines showing total dollar sales for each price are drawn. Break-even points are indicated where the sales line intersects the total cost-line.

We see that at a price of $19.50, 76,923 units must be sold in order to break even; at $22.50, 52,632 units must be sold in order to break even; at $29.50, sales of 30,303 units are needed to break even; and at $79.50, the break-even volume is 7,519 units. The calculation of break-even points is as follows:

$$\text{Fixed costs} = \$500,000$$
$$\text{Variable costs} = \$13.00 \text{ per unit}$$
$$X = \text{break-even point}$$
$$\text{(expressed in units)}$$

At $19.50 per unit:
$$(19.50)\,(X) = 500,000 + (13.00)\,(X)$$
$$6.5X = 500,000$$
$$X = 76,923 \text{ units}$$

At $22.50 per unit:
$$(22.50)\,(X) = 500,000 + (13.00)\,(X)$$
$$9.5X = 500,000$$
$$X = 52,632 \text{ units}$$

At $29.50 per unit:
$$(29.50)\ (X) = 500{,}000 + (13.00)\ (X)$$
$$16.5X = 500{,}000$$
$$X = 30{,}303 \text{ units}$$

At $34.50 per unit:
$$(34.50)\ (X) = 500{,}000 + (13.00)\ (X)$$
$$21.5X = 500{,}000$$
$$X = 23{,}256 \text{ units}$$

At $49.50 per unit:
$$(49.50)\ (X) = 500{,}000 + (13.00)\ (X)$$
$$36.5X = 500{,}000$$
$$X = 13{,}699 \text{ units}$$

At $69.50 per unit:
$$(69.50)\ (X) = 500{,}000 + (13.00)\ (X)$$
$$56.5X = 500{,}000$$
$$X = 8{,}850$$

At $79.50 per unit:
$$(79.50)\ (X) = 500{,}000 + (13.00)\ (X)$$
$$66.5X = 500{,}000$$
$$X = 7{,}519$$

Obviously, it is not feasible to calculate break-even points for every conceivable price. In choosing trial prices, the analyst must rely largely on experience and judgment. A few guiding principles, however, may be useful. An investigation of competitors' prices for similar products will give an idea of the practical price range. The concept of customary price is often a very useful one in pricing new products. A word of caution may be in order at this point. Instances can be cited in which whole industries were wrong in their pricing policies. Therefore, in choosing trial prices the analyst would be well advised not to be bound too closely by the price policies of others.

By this time, you will have observed that break-even analysis offers a technique by which the manager can manipulate price to carry out the policy of maximizing profits, which we discussed in the previous chapter. Its use in pricing is subject to several limitations.

First, break-even analysis may be misleading when applied to marginal business, that is, business on which, technically, the break-even point is not reached but which nonetheless contributes to increased profits at the end of the accounting period. As pointed out previously, as long as the price on additional business covers direct costs and makes some contribution to general overhead, it may be worthwhile to accept such business when capacity is available.

Second, break-even charts as they are customarily constructed are based upon the assumption that total variable costs increase proportionately as production is expanded. If a businessman accepts this assumption, he is assuming that full-capacity production yields the greatest net profit. In ordinary circumstances, this is not true. Actually, variable costs per unit may be expected to decline, reach a low point, and then increase as production expands. Not only do factory costs begin to increase as capacity output is neared, but also, more important, selling costs may become prohibitive as sales are pushed toward this volume.

Break-even analysis also assumes that the total amount of overhead costs will remain constant as volume produced increases. This is not necessarily true. As operations expand, staff personnel tends to grow and with it the overhead expenses it generates. Nor is the line between overhead and direct costs always clear and definite. It tends to be fuzzy in actual experience, although this fuzziness is not always recognized in the accounting records.

For example, it is generally accepted that costs generated by direct labor of men on a production line are of the direct type. But suppose that at a certain volume level a gang of 10 men is economical to perform a given operation, each completing 1 or more parts of it. Volume may have to undergo a substantial increase, sometimes double or treble, before it becomes economical to rearrange the work so as to divide it among 12 or 15 men, or to add a second gang of 10. Within this volume range, the cost of direct labor really behaves like overhead. This does not mean that break-even analysis is not a useful tool to the pricing executive, but merely that he should not rely on it as an absolutely accurate instrument, or that he should draw his direct cost line as a series of ascending steps instead of as a line with an even upward slope.

In using cost formulas, the pricing executive should always be aware that he is pricing for the future, not for the past, and that the costs important in his calculations are not those of the past but those forecasted for the future. Of course, it is true that since these forecasted costs never exactly materialize, he is thus making pricing decisions on inexact data. But very few of the business statistics in the books of account really attain the precise accuracy implied by the form in which they appear there. None of the overhead items do. The real difference in accuracy between forecasted costs and those reported in accounting statements is simply a matter of degree.

The formula approach to pricing industrial goods suffers from the difficulty that the customer does not know or care about the formula or, worse still, has one of his own. Since the seller's formula is usually based on cost, it has the added drawback that the important fact in pricing a product is not what it cost but what the customer will pay for it. Cost analysis and cost formulas help the pricing executive to set a floor, and he should make every effort not to go below it. Formulas and analysis provide some notion of the effect different pricing decisions will have on the margin between sales dollars coming in and cost dollars going out, and they give the executive reasonably exact knowledge about a matter—his own costs—that many industrial customers will be trying to estimate through the techniques of value analysis.

Hunch

The scholar or the scientist is apt to regard seat-of-the-pants judgments and decisions with some misgiving, even with contempt. The business executive, however, knows that hunch is not something to be disregarded. The feel that a certain price is right or wrong may be compounded of a number of things, such as memories of past experiences, subconscious understanding of competitor and customer emotions and attitudes, an unrealized appreciation of the condition of the market, a nebulous projection of a host of dimly remembered similar situations and decisions in the past, and probably other factors, most of which are pertinent although not clearly understood. In part, this feel may be a result of the working of the subconscious mind, which many people find so helpful in problem solving. In many cases, though, it is something more than this, since the result never rises to the level of the executive's thought processes but manifests itself in his feeling comfortable with one decision and ill at ease with another.

Because of the intangible nature of many of the factors that influence pricing decisions, the importance of hunches is probably greater in this area of business decision making than in most others. There is probably no great difference in its use in the consumer goods and the industrial goods fields.

The hunch is a pricing tool that must be used with discretion. The pricing executive is wise not to act on his hunches until all available evidence is in and thoroughly digested. It is also prudent to check the soundness of his hunching mechanism by keeping a record, as unbiased as possible, of his hunches and the outcomes of pricing decisions to which they apply in order to develop a batting average of his own performance.

PRICING DECISIONS AND SITUATIONS

Let us return to our initial classification of the marketing situations that give rise to the need for pricing decisions, and examine some of the factors usually involved in determining prices in each situation.

New Products

At the time a firm introduces a new product on the market, it is likely to have considerable sunk costs invested in it. All the expenses of such activities as research, planning, testing, pilot plant operations, buying and installing special equipment, readjusting factory operations, training salesmen, informing customers about the product, and building stocks of materials and finished units constitute cash that has flowed out of the business on account of the new product. This outflow causes an impairment of the firm's cash position.

Certainly, a very important objective in pricing the new product must be to get this money back into the business and restore the firm's cash position. How fast management should try to do this depends largely on such factors as the company's financial strength, the presence of other promising projects requiring cash, the probable length of life of the new product, and the speed with which competition may be expected to develop.

If fast recovery of the cash position is the prime objective, the pricing executive will seek to fix a figure that promises to bring in the largest possible number of immediate sales dollars. If this objective is secondary to another, such as capturing a strong market position before competition develops, he must modify his pricing decisions accordingly.

In either case, he is likely to have a choice between two policies—a skimming price and a penetration price. If a skimming policy is adopted, the initial price is very high; gross margin may be as much as 80 or 90 percent of sales. This price may be held for varying periods of time, perhaps indefinitely if the product enjoys valid and defensible patent protection, but usually not more than the time necessary for competitors to study the product's usefulness, to decide what to do about it, and to tool up for making it—a period ranging from a few weeks to as much as two years. Then, the price is apt to drop precipitately, and over a period of a few years to approach the usual or customary margin above cost that is common in the industry.

If the penetration pricing policy prevails, the initial price of the new product probably will be somewhere in the vicinity of what may be expected to be its level once competition enters the field, generally slightly above that level. If the initial price is properly picked, only minor adjustments need to be made if and when competition develops. Figure 12–3 shows graphically the behavior of these two types of prices.

An advantage of a skimming price policy is that it allows the innovating firm within a short time—before competition develops, if it is lucky—to recapture through cash inflow from sales all the cash outlays made for research, tooling and facilities, and market development, and perhaps to enjoy a profit besides. From that point on, the bulk of the cash inflow from the product, above direct expenses connected with it, can be applied to improvement of the firm's financial position, while competitors who enter the business must apply part of their cash inflow to the amortization of introductory outlays for such things as tooling, facilities, and market development work. This puts the innovator in a very strong cost position when competition develops.

On the other hand, by its high price the innovating firm may generate considerable ill will among customers that will increase its difficulties when competition develops. This may be offset or prevented to some extent by timely price reductions before competition starts.

The chief benefit of a penetration pricing policy lies in its tendency to discourage the development of competition. A lush gross or net profit ratio lures competitors just as effectively as nectar attracts bees; a lean one discourages them. The effectiveness of this strategy is diminished somewhat by the fact that where profit is satisfactory—what innovator wants a less than satisfactory profit from his innovation?—there competitors will gather.

Several factors tend to indicate which of these policies will be most useful in a specific case. If large expenditures have been made for research and heavy outlays must be incurred for equipment to make or introduce a new product, it seems prudent to use the skimming policy to get back as much of these sunk costs as soon as possible. If the innovator's capital is limited or he is short of cash, a skimming policy is apt to rectify the lack

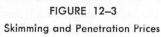

FIGURE 12–3

Skimming and Penetration Prices

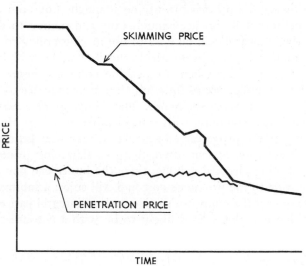

most quickly. If the life of the product promises to be a short one, sound policy seems to be to try to get as much out of it as fast as possible; if its life promises to be a long one, profit may be gathered more slowly. If a product enjoys valid patent protection, either a skimming policy of indefinite duration or a penetration policy may be adopted.

The latitude a patent gives in pricing should not be overemphasized. If the holder sets and maintains an exorbitant price, the complaints of gouged buyers may cause the Department of Justice to become interested in all his pricing operations. Nor are the competitive effects of such a policy to be ignored. It stimulates competitors to try to find a way to get around the patent. If the patent applies to a product, their efforts usually take the form of developing another machine or material based on a different principle to serve the same purpose. This may not be easy and may prove impossible. If a process patent is involved, as is usually the case with a material, would-be competitors seek a different process to make the same thing. And they are not unlikely to find it. The innovator can minimize the likelihood of both these developments either by setting a price that represents a compromise between the skimming and penetration levels, or by licensing other firms to manufacture under the patent, thus providing some measure of competition.

If a high degree of production skill and know-how is needed to make a product, so that it will be difficult and time-consuming for competitors to get into its production on an economical basis, a skimming policy may be useful, since they will be slow about deciding to enter and will probably suffer delays during the process of entry. If a new product looks so good that a ready-made market for it is apparent, a skimming price policy seems to be indicated; if, on the other hand, much time and money must be poured into market development work to build a market, little can be gained in slowing the process by pricing it much above the penetration level. Competitors will also need much time and money to develop demand, and the innovator will be wise to use pricing policy to shorten his own development process as much as possible so he will have an established market position when competition confronts him.

The skimming policy seems to be much more applicable to the pricing of industrial than of consumer goods. The innovator of a new industrial product can often compute with considerable accuracy the product's dollar benefits to the prospective buyer. This may bear little relationship to its cost. Therefore, he can often charge a skimming price with little danger of forgoing physical volume, since the buyer can pay a price out of all proportion to the product's cost and still enjoy a substantial benefit from its use. Nor is the innovator's price such an integral part of his brand and advertising complex as it is likely to be with a consumer good; this close tieup makes price changes difficult and sticky for consumer goods marketers.

When Competition Starts

The pricing problems that the innovator of a new product faces when competitors begin to make and market the product vary considerably according to the initial pricing policy he has followed. If he has used a skimming price, he faces a series of decisions, all involving questions about when to reduce price and how large a cut to make. Of course, the ideal timing of the first cut is the day before the chief executives of the most interested prospective competitor meet to decide whether to enter the business, and the ideal amount of the decrease is one big enough to discourage them from going ahead. Very rarely is the information service of a firm good enough to make this possible.

Probably, it is good policy to reduce a skimming price well before competition actually appears, even before its imminence becomes common knowledge in the trade. This is apt to prevent some of the customer ill will that may otherwise arise from the feeling that the innovator continued to charge exorbitant prices until competition forced him to cut. Such an early reduction can almost always be explained, with some approach to candor, on the ground of reductions in cost due to quantity operations and increasing production know-how, the benefit of which the firm is passing on to its customers.

Regardless of when the first cut in a skimming price is made, it should be substantial. A considerable reduction effected through a series of nibbles is not likely to attract much attention. The cut should be big enough to mean something to customers.

After competition has actually become active in the business, the innovator loses much of his control over price. From then on, at least some of his pricing moves will be precipitated or conditioned by the pricing action of competitors.

The innovator who follows a penetration policy faces a different set of problems when competition develops. If his pricing executives have been skillful, his price is already somewhere near the lowest figure his rivals can charge and make a satisfactory profit. There is not much room he can maneuver in. If his pricing policy has been successful, he has a very strong market position—probably more of the market than he can expect to hold over the long pull. The new competitor may rely on price reductions, even below cost, as a means of getting a foothold in the market. The innovator must decide whether to fight every encroachment and meet price cut with price cut, or accept as inevitable the loss of part of the market and hold to his original figure until the competitor gets a satisfactory market share and becomes responsible. This decision depends to a considerable extent on the innovator's estimate of how much of the market the competitor will be willing to accept as satisfactory, and of what part of his present volume he can hold on the basis of the buyers' inertia, the service relations he has built up, and the customers' reliance on his superior know-how and experience to provide dependable quality.

When a Product Is Mature

Once a product becomes mature, most of the decisions that must be made about pricing will probably arise from competitive pricing action. Speed of decision is usually of vital importance in such a situation. If a reaction to a competitor's price change is too long delayed, it loses much of its effectiveness. This is more true of a cut than of an increase. If we delay in following a sound price advance, we stand to lose only the added profit a prompt increase might give us. Our delay may actually cause some increase in volume to offset at least part of this loss. On the other hand, when our competitor cuts price and his decision to do so is correct, if we delay in following suit we stand to lose considerable sales volume, which may cost us a lot of time and money to regain.

It was suggested earlier that in deciding how to react to a rival's price change an understanding of why he made the change is very important. Of course, we can very rarely know all the factors that generate our competitor's action. But a knowledge of the condition of the market, of the competitor's operations, objectives, policies, and habit of thinking, and of his current position with respect to finances, inventory, and utilization of capacity may enable us to make some shrewd guesses about his motives.

For example, if his stocks are heavy or his cash dangerously low, his price cut is likely to be a temporary expedient that will be abandoned when the situation is corrected. If so, we may be able to ride it out without reaction. If he has been losing market share and has much unused capacity, he may very well be out to take some volume away from us and hold it. From the timing of a rival's move, the way in which it is made, and what is known about his general situation and pattern of behavior, a shrewd, well-informed pricing executive can often draw surprisingly detailed and accurate conclusions about the objectives of a rival's action. These may suggest not only what our reaction should be, but also what counteraction he is likely to take to any retaliatory move we may choose to make.

When a competitor changes price and our firm chooses to react, our pricing executive must decide on the extent of that reaction. For example, if the other fellow cuts price, should we simply meet his cut or go below it, or go down only partway? In general, it is probably better to sit tight than to move only partway to meet the competitor's cut. By a halfway measure, we merely call attention to his move without really countering it. An exception occurs when we have a quality or service advantage such that our quoted price can be somewhat above our competitor's and still be as attractive as his or more so on the basis of real cost to the customer, as shown by value analysis. If we react to a rival's price reduction by cutting below him, we invite a price war. Not the least of the factors that should guide us in this decision is whether we feel we can win a price war and, if so, whether we can afford the luxury of winning it.

If our analysis of a competitor's motives in making a price change, particularly a reduction, indicates that he has achieved a cost advantage, any price change we may make must be regarded as a sort of holding action while we seek to match his cost saving or add some premium to quality or service to offset his price advantage. Our specific pricing decision must depend on which of these alternatives we feel we are most able to carry out. If cost saving looks most promising, we probably should immediately meet his price and take our licking, while working to achieve the saving; if a quality or service improvement seems most feasible, we should probably make no price change.

Many factors may offer an opportunity to use price change as a strategic or tactical weapon. We may achieve a cost saving or foresee an opportunity to do so by increasing our sales volume. We may decide to try to increase our market share. We may need cash or have to dispose of an overstock. We may have improved quality or service and want to cash in on the advantage by increasing price. We may want to penetrate a new market. We may want to use a change in the price of one product to help increase the sale of another. Our pricing action in any of these and many other similar situations must depend very largely on our estimate of our competitor's ability and willingness to retaliate. In Chapter 11, we outlined one kind of analysis that may be used in trying to balance out these and other factors to arrive at a price that will maximize profit or help achieve other objectives.

Pricing Factors and Information

The excellence of pricing decisions depends not only on the quality of the analyses conducted by the executive who makes them, but also on his thoroughness and discretion in selecting the determining factors in each situation, and on the accuracy and completeness of pertinent information available for his use. The determining factors and pertinent information for each pricing situation differ from those applicable to any other. But certain factor and fact patterns are important in most industrial goods pricing decisions. Let us endeavor to segregate some of them in the form of questions whose answers the industrial goods pricing executive will be wise to seek.

New Products

1. What is the probable life of the product? If it promises to be long, pricing should usually be done to build a market position; if short, the idea is to clean up fast and get out.

2. How will per unit cost of production vary with volume? If cost drops rapidly with volume increases, the effect of price on physical volume of sales becomes a dominant factor.

3. Is the product of such a nature that it promises the development of many uses not visualized when it is first introduced? The fuel cell is an example. This characteristic suggests the desirability of an initial penetration price and of a high degree of pricing flexibility.

4. Do we have any sort of market protection for the product, such as a patent, the need for highly specialized research, expensive equipment, or great production skill or know-how? This greatly expands the area within which we can manipulate price.

5. How long will it take competition to get into production and how much will it cost to do so? If either the cost is high or the time is long, skimming pricing is suggested.

6. Who are our competitors likely to be and what are their patterns of pricing behavior?

7. What are the prices of products, if any, that serve the same general purpose as our new product?

8. What price for our new product will have the same effect as the price of the existing product on the cost structure of the customer's end product?

9. What is the dollar value of the benefit the customer will enjoy from using our new product?

10. How important will the price of the new product be in the cost structure of the customer's end product? If it is very important, there will be more resistance to a skimming price than if it is relatively unimportant.

11. Are prospective customers highly price-conscious or not?

Reaction to Competitive Price Changes

1. Why did the competitor change his price? If you can figure out what objective a competitor is trying to achieve by a price change, you are usually well along the way to deciding what to do about it.

2. Is the competitor's change an increase or a decrease in price? If it is an increase, we stand to lose only possible additional profits and may gain physical volume by sitting tight with our present price; if it is a cut, we stand to lose volume, market position, and profits.

3. Is this change a long-run or a short-run affair? If it is a short-run move—to clear out an overstock, for example—we can probably ride it out without drastic action.

4. How price-conscious is the trade concerning the product? If it is highly so, we cannot wait to see what happens but must react quickly.

5. If we allow ourselves to be at a price disadvantage on the product, will this affect the sale of our other products?

6. If we meet or go below the competitor's new price, what will he do about it?

7. How strong is the competitor financially, productionwise, and marketwise in comparison with our firm? If he heavily outweighs us, we may not be able to afford the risks of a price war with him, although he probably will not take drastic action if we merely meet his new price.

8. If we do not meet a competitor's new price, how much physical volume are we apt to lose, and what will this do to our costs?

9. How much of a thing is the competitor making of his price change publicitywise and sales promotionwise?

Initiating a Price Change

1. Why do we want to initiate a price change?

2. If we reduce price, how many more physical units must we sell to get the same or more dollar gross or net profit? Can we sell them?

3. If we increase price, can we sell enough physical units to gain the same or higher cash inflow or dollar profit?

4. Is price the primary factor influencing customer patronage for the product, or can we gain our objective more cheaply by manipulating some factor other than price?

5. If we change price, will competitors follow suit or retaliate by bettering our change?

6. If it is a price cut we intend, are we a price leader, so that competitors will feel they must follow but not exceed our cut? If we are not, how full is our financial war chest?

7. What effect will a price change on this product have on customer goodwill and our sales of other products?

DISCOUNTS

In many industrial goods trades, there are certain deductions from list price. In some lines, these deductions are standard, and thus the manufacturer has, in effect, no problem of price structure. He simply quotes the same discounts as his competitors, whether or not there are any logical reasons underlying them. When latitude in discount policy exists, however, there is much danger of confusion, inequity, loss of goodwill, and loss of sales. Therefore, in establishing discount policies it is important that definite objectives be set up and that each policy be analyzed in the light of its effect on these objectives. The principal types of allowances used in industrial goods marketing are trade discounts, quantity discounts—which may be based on either size of order or total amount purchased within a set period—and cash discounts.

Trade Discounts

When a manufacturer sells all or part of his goods to distributors, he customarily quotes a discount to the distributor designed to represent the outlet's operating expenses and profit. If a channel of distributution containing two or more middlemen or levels of customers is used, the price structure may consist of a chain of discounts subtracted successively from each new net price.

Several reasons underlie the use of trade discounts. First, the policy provides a means of suggesting or controlling the resale price. If a flat price were quoted rather than a list price less discount, the result might be a set of differentials in selling prices to final users, depending on the margin added on by each individual distributor. The discount off list, however, automatically defines what the manufacturer thinks the distributor's margin should be and strongly suggests that the outlet's selling price should be the list figure. This device is less useful in the sale of industrial than of consumer goods, since price maintenance is less widely practiced in the industrial field.

Second, the use of chain trade discounts makes it easier to implement a varying price policy among distributors. For example, a distributor in one district may have facilities for performing certain services that the manufacturer himself must perform in other areas. A simple means of compensating the distributor for these services is to allow him an additional discount. This skirts perilously near the edge of illegality under the antitrust laws.

Third, trade discounts are useful as a way to try to keep actual prices secret, not only among distributors but also from competitors and users. This advantage, however, may be more apparent than real, since an extra discount, like murder, will out however elaborate the measures to conceal it. Finally, expensive catalog revisions are diminished, since nominal list prices may be printed in the catalog and a separate discount sheet made up whenever a price change is desired.

The trade discount may also be used either to protect distributors against direct-buying users or to deny them the business of certain users. Large using firms often have a policy of purchasing direct whenever possible, hoping thereby to avoid paying the distributor's margin and profit. If the product is one the user cannot buy in amounts that are economical for its maker to handle, or if he feels that distributors are necessary to assure him a satisfactory volume, he may not want to sell direct. To refuse to sell to a user-buyer may prove embarrassing and engender ill will. The manufacturer of such a product may seek to accomplish his purpose with a discount system as follows.

> Price to distributors..........................25% off list
> Price to all other buyers......................list

Under this system, the user has nothing to gain pricewise by buying direct.

On the other hand, the maker of a product, such as an electric motor, that is sold as a component to manufacturers who install it as a part in their end products, and also to others for replacements and incidental use in their plants, may want to sell to OEM (original equipment manufacturer) buyers at a lower price than to other purchasers. This is because OEM customers buy in much larger volume and because their use of the product as a component creates a replacement market. He can accomplish this by a discount system like the following.

> Price to OEM buyers...................25 and 20% off list
> Price to distributors....................25% off list
> Price to other buyers...................list

The legality of the first of these discount systems has not been questioned. The legal status of the second is, at best, doubtful. The marketing manager who contemplates using it will be wise to first consult his company attorney.

It is important that the trade discount represent as accurately as possible the cost of the distributor's services plus a normal margin of profit. If the discount is too high, it may encourage price-cutting. On the other hand, if it is too low distributors will be reluctant to handle the product unless they can sell above the list price, which is not always feasible.

Many industrial buyers prefer the net price type of quotation over a list price less a discount or a chain of discounts. The purchasing officer who negotiates a contract involving a string of discounts is apt to be haunted by the suspicion that if he had bargained just a little harder he could have got an extra 5 percent. Moreover, the discount method of price quotation creates paper work costs. It has been computed that when the net price method is used 12 clerical operations must be performed by the manufacturer, distributor, and industrial buyer in moving a product from maker to user. If the quotation is in the form of a single discount from list, 24 such operations are needed, with further additions as more discounts are added. Since clerical activities generate what are perhaps the most insidious and crippling costs the business executive has to deal with, the marketer who quotes prices net will win favor with his industrial customers.

Quantity Discounts

Quantity discounts are price reductions varied according to amount purchased. They may be cumulative—based upon total purchases over some period of time, such as a month or a year—or noncumulative—based upon the amount of one order. In establishing his pricing policies, the industrial marketer must decide whether his interests are better served by selling at one price to all buyers on a given level of distribution or by quoting quantity discounts, and, if the second, whether cumulative or noncumulative or both should be offered.

Discounts Based upon Size of Individual Order. The objective of this type of discount is to encourage customers to purchase in large orders rather than on a hand-to-mouth basis. When customers buy in small lots, additional expenses are involved in packing, billing, transportation charges, and broken-package handling. If a buyer is willing to anticipate his needs more carefully and purchase in larger quantity, there is sound reason for passing on to him part or all of the resulting savings.

This kind of quantity discount may be expressed as a percentage off list or as a variation in price per unit, as follows:

Size of Order	Discount Off List	Size of Order	Price per Pound
Less than 10 units	0%	50 lb. carboy	$0.25
10 to 19 units	2	100 lb. drum	0.245
20 to 29 units	3	250 lb. drum	0.24
30 units or more	4	2 × 250 lb. drum or more	0.23

The per unit quotation creates somewhat less clerical work than the percentage off list variety.

Discounts Based upon Purchases over a Period of Time. The main purpose of basing discount structure upon purchases made over a period of time is to expand sales and reduce costs by increasing the amount of business placed by each customer. It also tends to hold the loyalty of the buyer during the discount period. This type of discount policy should be employed when lower distribution cost is a function of size of customer to a greater degree than size of order. An example is provided by the

	Size of Customer's Annual Purchases				
	Small	Medium	Medium large	Large	Distributor
Size of Discount (percent)......60–5		65–5	70	70–10	70–10

following system used by an abrasives manufacturer in pricing grinding wheels according to the size of the customer's annual purchases. From the customer's point of view, the cumulative type of discount has the advantage over the noncumulative type in that if the buyer who normally purchases in large quantities wants to order a small emergency shipment from time to time he is not penalized.

When small buyers habitually split their requirements among several sellers, the cumulative quantity discount policy may induce them to concentrate their purchases. By making small customers larger (at the expense of other sellers), the seller enjoys good possibilities for reducing costs. This may be beneficial not only to the customer and to the seller who receives the additional business, but also to competitors who are relieved from handling the unprofitable small orders they would otherwise receive from the buyer who is persuaded to concentrate his purchases.

Overall Considerations. It is argued that quantity discounts favor the large buyer and make it difficult for his small rival to stay in business. This brings about a situation detrimental to the seller in that he tends to become dependent on a few large buyers, who may then dictate his price policies and practices. This objection is more convincing in theory than realistic in practice, since the seller who sees it happening can easily remedy the situation by changing his discount practice.

The manufacturer's quantity discount policy may depend largely on competitors' practices. He may have no alternative but to follow trade custom. However, when his product is sufficiently differentiated or his service is unique he may find it possible and worthwhile to pursue an independent discount policy.

Many of the metals trades make use of a specialized form of noncumulative quantity discount system. A base price per ton is usually quoted on a carload lot. If a customer buys less than a carload, quantity extras are added to the base price; the smaller the quantity bought, the higher is the extra per ton. In some cases, deductions from the carload price are allowed for multicarload shipments. The quantity discount feature of this system is somewhat obscured by the fact that extras and deductions are also applied for variations of quality, size of pieces, service operations, and other factors, as well as quantity. This system defines the limits that steel and nonferrous warehouses and distributors operate in; the differential between the carlot price at which they buy and the net price, including extras, at which the mill sells to less than carlot buyers provides their margin of gross profit.

The quantity discount is most useful in marketing materials and supplies. In fact, it is not likely to be used as such in the major equipment and components areas. The size of a piece of equipment or the amount of it bought in a single contract is likely to influence the price, but any allowances granted for quantity appear, not as discounts, but as reductions in the quoted prices. Since components usually are bought on blanket or requirements contracts, about the same conditions apply. Quantity allowances may be made, but they are in the form of differences in contract prices and not as discounts.

Marketers of materials and supplies may use a quantity discount system to help solve the small order problem. Makers of many types of such industrial goods often find themselves doing what amounts to a wholesaling operation, which is especially costly because they are not set up to do that kind of business. By adopting a quantity discount system, they force the small buyer, as well as the large buyer who by purchasing in small quantities seeks to hold his inventories at a minimum, to compare the savings of inventory reduction against both the cost of preparing many small orders and the higher price resulting from the loss of discounts rather than against the former cost alone. This is a somewhat less drastic method than the alternative of refusing to handle orders for less than a set minimum, say $50.

The quantity discount may also be used as a means of classifying the marketer's customers into the large quantity buyers, whom he wishes to serve direct, and the small order buyers, whom he prefers to have serviced by distributors. The discount system may be so constructed as to make it economical for large users and distributors to buy direct and uneconomical for small users to do so. By employing the quantity discount for this purpose, the marketer is able to effect an actual classification of customers into direct and indirect without ostensibly doing so. This avoids much administrative work and many embarrassing problems of individual classification.

Cash Discounts

Cash discounts are deductions the buyer makes from the face of an invoice in return for payment of the bill before it is due. Their purpose is to encourage immediate payment, and thus enable the seller to avoid the

burden of extending credit. Certain costs are involved when credit is
extended, including use of capital, the expense of operating a credit and
collection department, and bad debt losses. There are also certain positive
gains when invoices are paid immediately, including faster turnover and
more efficient use of working capital, the fostering of goodwill due to
removal of possible sources of friction when customers are slow in paying,
and, in fact, increased sales, since customers in good standing are more
likely to buy than those in arrears.

Thus, certain advantages accrue to the seller when he is relieved of the
necessity of extending credit. So far as the value of these gains is passed on
to the buyer, it is a true cash discount; but when the discount exceeds this
amount, as is sometimes the case, the excess is not a cash discount but,
rather, a trade allowance or a price concession. Buyers, in effect, are
forced to discount their bills in order to compete successfully. Those who
do not take advantage of this so-called cash discount are the weak ones
among whom credit losses are most likely to occur.

The marketer must sometimes adjust his cash discount terms to the
accounting practices of his customers. Suppose, for example, a customer
follows a policy of paying on the 15th of each month all bills received on
or before the 10th, and on the 1st of the month all those received on or
before the 25th of the preceding month. The seller will probably be wise
to allow him to take his discounts, even though the stated terms are 2
percent, 10 days, net 30 days.

Legal Considerations

In establishing and administering his discount system—in fact, any
aspect of his pricing system that has the net effect of causing one customer or group of customers to pay a price different from that paid by
another—the industrial goods marketer must be careful to avoid violations
of the federal antitrust laws, particularly the Robinson-Patman amendment to the Clayton Act, which outlaws price discrimination. That the
framers of this law intended it to apply to industrial goods marketing is
doubtful. It was designed primarily to protect small retailers and wholesalers against the competition of mass retailing concerns. But since the
language of the act is couched in very general terms, it is clear that its
prohibitions affect the marketing of industrial, as well as consumer, goods.

Any treatment or set of terms granted to one buyer and not available to
another, and causing a difference in the final costs the two buyers pay for
the goods, probably falls under the definition of discrimination. Such
discrimination is not illegal if: (1) made on the basis of savings in costs of
production, sale, or delivery that result from differences in the manner or
quantities in which the buyers involved make their purchases; (2) the
goods are not of like grade or quality; (3) the discrimination does not
substantially lessen competition; (4) the goods are perishable; or (5) the

discrimination is made in good faith to meet an equally low price of a competitor.

This means that if an industrial product manufacturer wants to get the business of a prospective customer, he cannot offer him a special price unless he offers the same price to all other buyers of the same goods under like conditions. It means that a discount for quantity is not legal unless the seller can show, from adequate accounting records, that because of the quantity purchase he enjoys savings in the costs of making, selling, or delivering the goods that equal or exceed the amount of the discount, or unless he can prove that it is made in good faith to meet an equally low price of a competitor or that it does not substantially lessen competition.

At first blush, it might seem that a showing of savings offers the best out. But the Federal Trade Commission, which administers the Act, and the Department of Justice, which enforces it, have made a rather rigid interpretation of this defense. First, the seller who offers marketing savings as a defense must do so on the basis of a cost analysis system for marketing that meets the dictates of good accounting practice.

Then, too, the production savings defense is practically worthless. Suppose, for example, that a seller is approached by a large buyer whose purchases will double his sales volume, cutting in half his overhead costs per unit, and will even off the seasonal fluctuation in his operations, making possible further cost reductions. The Justice Department holds that this saving results from the seller's entire volume, and must be made proportionately available to all customers if it is allowed to any. Almost the only situation in which the production cost defense can be used occurs when one customer wants a product modification that causes manufacturing cost to be increased or decreased. The difference can be offered as a defense for a price differential. But the modification is probably a different product, anyhow.

The defense that has been found most useful is that of meeting the price of a competitor. Any firm in an industry plagued by garage or quonset hut operators can probably use this defense to justify price differentials in the areas where such operators are located. However, the marketing manager would be wise to allow such differentials only after consulting his company attorney.

The law is couched in very general and, in some spots, obscure terms. The language implications are well illustrated by a firm that made an industrial material sold to a trade that included one very large and numerous small and medium-sized buyers. The large user had been following the practice of purchasing about a month's supply at a time and treating each purchase as a separate transaction. He approached the supplier with the proposal that he commit himself to the purchase of a definite amount annually, to be shipped at the discretion of the supplier as long as a month's stock was maintained in the buyer's warehouse at all times, and asked for a price concession on the basis of this arrangement.

The marketing manager of the supplying house explored with its accounting department the possibilities of savings implicit in the proposal, and was assured that their amount was significant, although uncertain, because in computing it several accounting assumptions had to be made; a court might regard some as sound and some unsound. The legal department pointed out, however, that the total annual profit realized from the supplier's business with the large buyer amounted to about $100,000, while the cost of defending a suit through the courts would amount to some hundreds of thousands of dollars. Further, should the supplier lose such a suit, he would be subject to suits by all other buyers for three times the difference between what they had paid for their supplies of the product and the amount the favored buyer had paid during the period the arrangement was in force.

On the basis of this information, the management of the supplying firm decided not to run the risk of making the concession. The uncertainty of the law in this case probably had the long-run bad effect of causing the price of the end product made from this material to be more to its final buyers than it would have been had the arrangement been made.

The indefiniteness of the language in these laws and the refusal of enforcement authorities to make firm commitments on what that language means in specific cases, except as the outcome of hazardous and expensive litigation, discourage good business practice, handicap efficient and aggressive competitors, and over the long run in the aggregate tend to cost the consuming public heavily. This end result is rendered even more unhappy from the economic standpoint by the fact that the law was passed in the first place to protect a single, shrilly vocal group of businessmen, containing among its members an unusually large number of highly inefficient operators.

PRICE LINING

Many consumer goods makers follow the practice of price lining. This means that the manufacturer starts his planning with a price either presumed or proven to be one that users will be willing to pay—for example, $29.95 for a coat—and then builds an article that he can sell profitably at that price. This means that an adjustment of quality and costs (for instance, linings, buttons, trimmings, and workmanship for a coat) must be made so as to leave a satisfactory gross margin.

This practice is probably not so common in the industrial goods business, but the manufacturer of such goods, particularly materials and components, must occasionally conform to it. For example, a manufacturer of builders' hardware (locks, door handles, window catches, etc.), may be forced to compromise his quality standards by making a line of merchandise priced to attract the trade of development builders who want to trim their costs as much as possible. Since lower quality in a lock does not usually show up until after it has been in use for some time—long enough for the builder to get out of the picture—it is a good item on which to cut costs. The builders' hardware maker, therefore, must offer a second quality line made to sell at a price these customers are willing to pay or forgo his share of the development builders' volume.

Manufacturers of room air conditioning equipment do not need motors of standard quality and are loath to pay for them. Unless a motor maker is willing to cut quality and costs on a model built to meet their price standards, he can expect to get very little air conditioning business. While price lining as it appears in the consumer goods field is not the usual thing in the industrial goods business, the specialized forms we have just illustrated are probably more common than is generally recognized.

PRICE CHANGES

The prices of some raw materials or highly standardized products are continually changing as the forces of supply and demand act and react on each other. However, most industrial goods marketers have some degree of control over price, and therefore must make policy regarding price changes.

Except for changes brought about by cyclical variations, the manufacturer is best served when prices in an industry remain stable. This enables him to keep them in the background and to sell on a quality or service rather than on a price basis. As a generalization, then, prices should be maintained without change as long as possible. It follows that when a price change is decided on it should be a substantial one. The rationale of this policy is that on a declining market a series of small price cuts may cause industrial buyers to stay out of the market in anticipation of a further cut. On a rising market, a large increase is less disturbing than a series of small increases, since each price advance necessitates among distributors and customers a series of readjustments, which are a function of the change rather than of the magnitude of the change.

It is sometimes desirable for a manufacturer to guarantee or protect his customers against declines in the prices of his products held in their stocks. Such a guarantee may apply to all stocks, regardless of when they were bought, or it may be restricted to goods purchased within a specified time, such as 30 or 60 days, before a price change occurs. Stock protection is more likely to be extended for materials and a few kinds of supplies than for other types of industrial goods. It especially may be granted to distributors and on items whose demand or production is seasonal. The mechanism of stock protection usually consists in the seller's crediting the account of the buyer with the amount of any price reduction on goods sold to the buyer that are reported in his inventory at the time of the reduction. Most marketers do not willingly grant stock protection, but only under the pressure of competition. It is expensive and cumbersome to administer, although its practical effect on price is merely to antedate the reduction.

GEOGRAPHY AND PRICING

The industrial buyer tends to regard as a part of the price of a material, supply, or component the cost of transporting it to the place it is to be used. Many of these items are of such a nature that if they must be carried very far his cost becomes a significant factor in relation to the net price at maker's factory door. As a result, many industrial marketers must include as an integral part of their pricing systems some sort of arrangement for transportation cost. These arrangements may take two general forms— factory pricing and freight allowance pricing.

Factory Pricing

The industrial marketer who uses the factory pricing method almost always ships f.o.b. (free on board) factory or point of origin. This means that the buyer pays all the freight and is responsible for all the risks occurring during transport, except those assumed by the carrier.

This method has several advantages for the marketer. It assures him a uniform net price on all shipments, regardless of where they go. It relieves him of the necessity of negotiating adjustments of freight overcharges with the carrier. Since, in the absence of agreement to the contrary, title to the goods passes to the buyer when the marketer delivers them to the carrier, the seller avoids all risks of damage not assumed by the carrier, chiefly so-called acts of God. The passage of title at factory door also means that the seller assumes no responsibility for the length of time the carrier takes to deliver the goods to the buyer's plant. This advantage is more apparent than real, for the professional purchasing officer tends to value the supplier's delivery service on the basis of his actual turnaround time, regardless of whose fault it may be that delays, if any, occur.

Since many industrial goods are heavy and bulky, expense of transport is a much more important item in their final cost to the buyer than it is in most consumer goods. Therefore, many industrial marketers find that if they insist on f.o.b. factory pricing, they simply cannot compete in certain parts of the market unless they operate plants in or near all the areas in which it is concentrated. This may be very costly in terms of duplicate equipment and plants built to less than optimum capacity. It is often more economical to make some sort of adjustment in the direction of a delivered pricing policy.

Freight Allowance Pricing

The industrial marketer who finds it desirable to follow a policy of freight allowance pricing has several possible methods to choose from.

F.O.B. Destination or Delivered Prices. F.o.b. destination means that the seller pays freight charges and assumes the risks of transport not taken by the carrier. Title does not pass until the carrier delivers the goods to the buyer. When it is used, the marketer may receive a different net return from every customer. All customers, those far from the seller's plant and those nearby, pay about the same delivered price for the goods if we ignore other discounts. Minor differentials may occur among customers if shipment is by rail, since those without spur tracks serving their plants may have to pay a cartage charge. Even this may be avoided by the use of delivered prices that contemplate delivery by the seller to the buyer's plant either by some combination of common carriers or by trucks arranged for by the vendor.

The system enables the marketer to compete in all parts of the market on even price terms with competitors. This is the most extreme form of freight allowance pricing.

F.O.B. Shipping Point with Freight Allowance. Under this system, the buyer pays the carrier's charges, and either is allowed an agreed-on freight discount or deduction from his invoice or is authorized to pay the freight and deduct the amount of it from his bill before remitting. This arrangement relieves the shipper from risks of damage and delay in shipment, but it complicates the paper work of both parties and, if the seller suspects an overcharge, may lead to disputes between them as to just what the freight should have been.

Freight Equalization. In its mechanism, this is much like the plan just discussed. But it is quite different in the purpose it serves. Consider a firm with its plant in Newark, New Jersey, and a competitor in Chicago who sells f.o.b. factory. If its price is the same as the competitor's and it ships f.o.b. factory, it is at a freight disadvantage in serving all customers nearer to Chicago than to Newark. It may ship f.o.b. plant and equalize freight with Chicago; then a customer in Fort Wayne, Indiana, pays the freight bill from Newark to Fort Wayne, subtracts from it the freight on an identical shipment from Chicago to Fort Wayne, and deducts the remainder from his invoice before remitting. The Fort Wayne customer thus pays the same freight he would have paid had he bought from the competitor in Chicago.

The purpose of this is obvious; it enables the Newark firm to compete on even delivered price terms with the Chicago competitor. The firm may maintain a number of such systems of freight equalization, each one aimed at a specific competitor. The scheme has the advantage that it can be tailored with some exactness to the geographic distribution of competitors' shipping points and need not be applied over the entire market. Such a system can become almost incredibly complicated when competitors are numerous and scattered with proportionate multiplication of clerical costs and possibilities of error. It may also result in illegal price discrimination if a customer in a freight equalization area competes with one outside any such area in selling his end products.

Basing Point Pricing. This plan is really a form of freight equalization, perhaps identical with it if set up so that it is of unchallenged legality. It is used mainly in the metals industry. Under this system, one point, usually in the area of greatest concentration of the producing industry, is established as the basing point. All prices are then quoted f.o.b. this point, regardless of where the seller may be located. Thus, if Pittsburgh is the basing point for a steel item a steelmaker in the Chicago area will quote f.o.b. Pittsburgh, which means that the buyer is billed for freight from Pittsburgh to his plant, even though the merchandise is shipped from Chicago. So a buyer located farther from Pittsburgh than from Chicago pays more than the actual cost of transport, while one situated farther from Chicago than from Pittsburgh benefits.

An industry basing point is almost certainly illegal. A basing point established by an individual firm is probably legal so long as competitors have not chosen it for the same use; then, the presumption is that the common choice was the result of collusion among them. The whole idea is of such doubtful legality that its use is now very narrowly limited.

The courts and the economists have had much to say about the discriminatory effects of basing point pricing, freight equalization, and freight allowance systems. Certainly, the primary intent of the marketer who grants a freight allowance or equalizes freight is not to discriminate among customers but to put himself in a position to compete for their business on a delivered price basis.

But it is equally certain that regardless of the arrangements the marketer may make about freight he is bound to discriminate against somebody. If he ships f.o.b. factory, he discriminates against the customers farthest away from his plant. If he ships f.o.b. destination, he favors faraway customers at the expense of those nearby. If he sells f.o.b. factory with an allowance of all freight, he discriminates in the same way; if the allowance is a flat sum, he favors nearby customers who get the allowance without having to pay it all out in freight. If he equalizes freight with certain selected points, he discriminates against customers not within the equalization areas. If he quotes on a basing point system, he favors customers nearer to the basing point than to his plant at the expense of those nearer to his factory than to the basing point.

Since it seems impossible to administer this particular feature of the pricing function without discrimination, the industrial marketer will probably be wise to adjust his freight arrangements with the objective of improving his competitive position rather than of assuring fairness to all customers, to the extent possible without violating legal requirements. All such decisions are subjects for the careful scrutiny of the company attorneys.

ORGANIZATION FOR PRICING

In the small firm that makes and markets industrial goods, pricing decisions are usually made by the owner or the chief executive officer. This probably is true in a concern of any size whose business is concentrated on one or a few products.

In the larger house with a more varied line, the chief executive finds it difficult or impossible to maintain the close contact with and detailed knowledge of the market necessary to do the pricing job well. He is likely, therefore, to delegate much or all of the work to a pricing executive, who usually reports to him or to the man in charge of marketing. This does not always mean that complete power of decision is delegated. The chief executive may retain the power of review or approval over at least the most important pricing actions.

Regardless of who does the work or where it is done, the responsible official is likely to find it wise to try to develop policies to guide pricing decisions. The prices of materials that are basic or staple—commodities, as they are called—are likely to change rapidly. The executive who tries to price them without guiding policies is liable to find himself caught up in a series of crises that demand so much of his time and energy in making crash decisions that he has none left for really thinking his job through. The result is an inconsistent pricing pattern, shaped more by fright than by thought, that presents attractive opportunities to the competitor who approaches the problem with method and plan. In the big company where many of the pricing decisions must be delegated, it is generally desirable for top management to establish broad policies within which the pricing executive may work in making his day-to-day decisions.

Pricing policies may deal with such matters as:

1. What objectives do we wish to achieve by manipulating price?
2. On what products must we be price competitive, and on what ones can we afford to ignore price within limits, and what are the limits?
3. Do we want to be a price leader?
4. Whose competitive pricing actions are really dangerous, and whose can we safely ignore?
5. Under what conditions do we want to follow a skimming pricing policy, and when is penetration pricing better in introducing a new product?
6. If we use a skimming pricing system, when should we cut price and how much?
7. What price relationships do we want to maintain between different types of customers and between distributors and users?

This is a partial list of policy matters; others may grow out of the operating conditions and competitive relationships peculiar to each firm.

Throughout our discussion of pricing, we have emphasized its decision-making aspect. While it is true that decision leading to action is the target event in the pricing process, perhaps we need to restore the balance of this chapter's presentation somewhat by pointing out the paramount importance of market information in determining prices. In the industrial goods field, this ranges all the way from an analysis of the dollar benefits the customer derives from using the product to the latest rumor coming over the trade grapevine. Some of this information can be obtained by marketing research, some of it should be picked up by salesmen, some of it appears in the trade and business press, and a lot of it must be gleaned a fragment at a time by the pricing executive himself through his trade contacts. Finally, the pricing manager must conduct a sort of G-2 operation by which he seeks to fit together the odd bits of data received from all sources into a cohesive pattern pointing the way toward sound pricing action.

SUMMARY

Several situations require pricing decision: when a new product is introduced, when a competitor's price is changed, and when we want to use price as a weapon of marketing strategy. The factors that affect decision are different in each of these cases, but certain techniques are useful in all of them. The most common are: analogy; following competitors; trial and error, including test pricing, marketing research; formulas usually based on cost, and hunch or feel.

The marketer of a new product may choose a skimming price or a penetration price. Each has its areas of special usefulness. In responding to a competitor's pricing action or in using price change in our own marketing strategy, we must seek to analyze our competitors' attitudes, objectives, and probable reactions to any moves we may make.

The discount is a usual feature of industrial goods pricing. The most common types are trade discounts, quantity—both single order and volume bought over time—and allowances for cash payment. In administering his discount system, the industrial marketer must take account of legal as well as commercial considerations.

Price lining, while not common in the industrial goods area, is sometimes used. Changes in price may be facilitated by the practice of price guarantee. Problems of geographical price variations are especially acute in the industrial goods area. The chief devices used are factory pricing, delivered price arrangements, freight allowances, freight equalization, and basing point pricing. Several of these are of doubtful legality.

Pricing work may be done by the top executive of a business or by someone at a lower level who specializes in the job. In any case, the fullest possible information and the formulation of pricing policies are highly desirable.

CASES APPLICABLE TO PART V

PART VI

Getting the Goods Sold

THE SALE is the crucial point in the marketing process. The other marketing activities are directed toward bringing it about or consummating it by delivery and by provision of the services the customer needs to get satisfactory use from the product. It is to our interest, therefore, to examine the specific means by which the industrial marketing manager seeks to bring about sales.

In Chapter 13, we examine the organization structure that backs up the selling forces and directs them. Chapter 14 is devoted to a consideration of the problems and methods of managing the personal selling force. In Chapter 15, we treat industrial advertising, and Chapter 16 deals with the management of other methods of promoting sales.

Chapter 13

◇◇◇◇◇◇◇◇◇◇◇◇◇◇◇◇◇◇◇◇◇◇◇◇ ORGANIZATION FOR

INDUSTRIAL MARKETING

NATURE OF ORGANIZATION

THE MANAGERS of a firm engaged in making and marketing industrial goods may achieve top-notch performance in determining marketing policy and in planning marketing strategy, but their efforts are likely to be wasted unless they can develop an organizational structure to effectively implement the marketing policies and programs.

The marketing organization problems of a company that makes industrial goods do not differ much in kind from those of the average firm that makes consumer goods. Just about the same functions must be performed in marketing both types of goods. The chief differences consist in matters of emphasis and in the need to provide for a few functions not ordinarily required in the organization structure of a consumer goods marketer. Certain problems common to both are emphasized by the technical nature of many industrial products and by the methods customers use to buy them. But the basic nature of the problems and the methods, and organization structures available for solving them, are the same.

Bases of Organization

In thinking about organizing industrial marketing, we will probably be wise to bear in mind the fundamental nature of organization. An organization structure may be regarded as a way of gaining job specialization; that is, activities of the same kind, requiring the same or similar skills, are grouped together in a unit manned with people who have or can develop those skills. It may also be looked on as a system of avenues of communication for the transmission of information, instructions, and attitudes. Likewise, it may be viewed as a means of setting up desired relationships between the different parts of an enterprise. Perhaps it is most commonly thought of as a system of lines of authority and responsibility, determining who has power to do what, who gets credit or

357

blame for how it is done; who plays what part in making and carrying out what decisions, who is judged on the basis of how sound they are and how well they are executed.

As a corollary of this last concept, the organization structure is a means of delegating authority and creating responsibility. In thinking about this aspect, we will be wise to keep in mind a point that is often forgotten: authority can be delegated, but responsibility cannot. If I have power to do a thing, I can delegate that power or some part of it to you; but I still bear complete responsibility to my boss for how you do it. I have created a responsibility in you to me, but I have shed none of my responsibility to my boss. In industrial goods marketing, the importance of this concept is emphasized by the technical nature of the products and the multiplicity of buying influences within each customer firm; both make it necessary for several different units of the supplying firm to perform highly specialized parts of the marketing function according to a common plan. This at once forces more complete delegation of authority and increases the cost of lapses in responsibility.

Bases of Organization

A first step in organization is to classify into groups activities that are alike or closely related, or that require the same or similar skills. Marketing activities naturally cluster around several factors or bases. The broadest of these, and one always present, is the matter of function, which is really a composite of tools or methods and specific skills. Another factor found in practically every marketing enterprise is geography. Marketing activities also tend to cluster around products or types of products, and around customers or kinds of customers.

Functional Organization

The broadest classification of functions usually made is twofold—doing or operating on the one hand, and planning on the other. An industrial marketing organization set up on this basis might look somewhat like the one shown in Figure 13–1. Since in this structure plans will be made by people who specialize in planning, theoretically the resulting plans will be sounder and more carefully thought through than those resulting from other organization forms.

In practice, this conclusion is subject to limitations. The very fact that the planners are specialists means that they are removed from operations and are to some extent insulated from the impact of changes in the market and in competition. As a result, operating personnel may regard their plans as blue sky stuff that does not recognize the marketing facts of life. To some extent this is true.

Firms that use this marketing organization structure have sought to overcome this drawback by requiring a certain amount of personnel flow back and forth between the planning and operating groups. While the heads of both groups may recognize the desirability of this flow, each may drag his feet in administering it. The planning manager is just as loath to lose the services of a good planner for a time as the sales manager is to surrender the extra volume brought in by a good salesman. Then, too, a

FIGURE 13–1

Functional Organization (A)

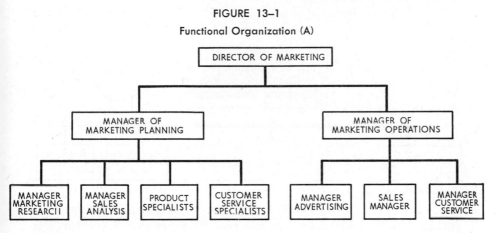

good planner is apt to be an indifferent salesman and vice versa. A compromise method is the requirement that people engaged in planning spend enough time traveling in the field with salesmen to learn what the fieldmen are up against in carrying out their plans.

Probably the chief real advantage of this type of functional organization structure is that it gets the planning done, since it provides a group of people whose sole job is planning. The business life of the operating executive tends to be largely made up of a series of crises. He must distinguish the things that must be done today from those that can be put off until tomorrow. Planning can be put off. It is not unlikely that enough such deferrals will occur so that the planning never gets done or is finally done under heavy pressure against a deadline, which means that it will be done with a lick and a promise.

It is very important that the planning of industrial marketing work be done well and in considerable detail. Because individual customers often take so large a part of total output, and because the buying influences are so numerous within each customer firm, it is often necessary to prepare a separate marketing plan for each customer. The different parts of the plan then must be carried out by different units in the supplier's marketing organization. For this reason, the operating–planning form of functional organization structure is probably found more often in the industrial goods field than in consumer goods marketing.

The form of functional structure illustrated in Figure 13–2 is the traditional type. If the operation is small or relatively simple, it will work satisfactorily. Its chief drawback lies in the danger that the top marketing executive's span of control will become overextended, and he will have so many functional executives reporting to him that he will be unable to afford proper direction to any of them. This is especially important in industrial goods marketing because of the necessity of coordinating the work of specialists whose skills are sometimes diverse and whose efforts all are necessary to effective operation.

The chief drawback to the use of any classification of functions as the

FIGURE 13–2

Functional Organization (B)

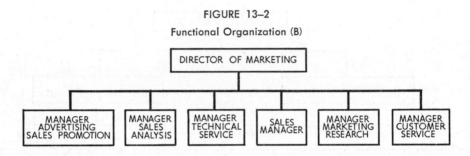

primary basis for the organization of industrial marketing departments lies in the nature of industrial goods and the customers who buy them. If a firm markets several highly technical industrial products or product groups of widely different technical characteristics, each marketing activity will have to be performed in a different way for each product or product group. This means that the nucleus about which activities cluster is the product or the product group. If a company markets its products to several industries that differ in the way they use the products or in the manner in which they want to buy them, the natural point its marketing activities cluster around is the customer or customer group, because it is of vital importance that each customer group be treated differently from every other.

Geographical Organization

Practically every marketing organization structure must to some extent reflect the influence of geography. The customers of most firms are scattered, and if they are to be served economically the smallest unit of the marketing organization, the salesman, must be set up on a territorial basis. A few industrial firms whose significant customers are geographically concentrated can ignore geography.

In general, geography is much less likely to be the central factor in the organization structure of an industrial goods marketer than it is in a consumer goods house. Geography makes a big difference in the things ultimate consumers buy and how they buy them. An industrial plant operates in much the same way wherever it is located, and it needs about the same equipment, materials, and supplies, and wants to buy them in about the same way. Differences in the activities involved in marketing industrial goods do not tend to cluster around geography but around products or customers. Geography must be recognized but is not emphasized in industrial marketing organization structure.

A fairly typical geographical organization structure is shown in Figure 13–3. Activities such as advertising, technical service, or marketing re-

FIGURE 13–3

Geographical Marketing Organization

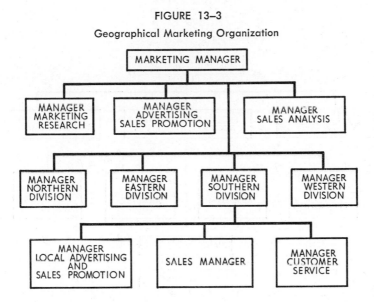

search can be carried on in the central office or shoved out into the area divisions, according to whether they are primarily national or local in character. The figure represents a compromise in which national advertising and generally used promotional material are handled centrally, and local material is prepared in the divisions. An activity like marketing research can usually be performed more economically in the central office.

Product Organization

Figure 13–4 shows a product type of organization. Because of the technical nature of many industrial goods and the resulting differences in methods of use and purchase, this form is much more common in the industrial goods field than in the consumer goods area.

Product organization has a big advantage in that it enables everybody involved in marketing a product or group of products, from marketing manager to field salesman, to concentrate on the one segment of technology involved in that product and become really expert in it. The result is better service to the customer, and a more intelligent and effective presentation of the product's benefits to him.

On the other hand, many products are used by several types of customers, who often belong to different industries. Each of these customer groups has its own technical problems in using the product, and each may want to buy it in a different way. Often, the differences in use technology between the customer groups are more pronounced and significant than the technological differences between products.

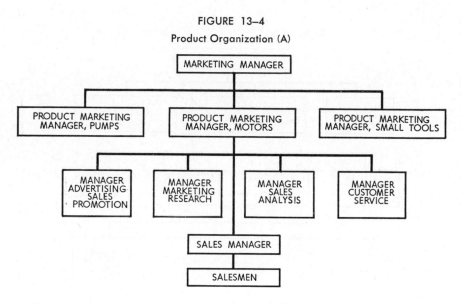

FIGURE 13–4

Product Organization (A)

Moreover, a firm that divides its sales force by products or product lines, each sold to several customer groups, may find that several of its salesmen must call on the same customer. This is expensive and may annoy the customer. Sometimes, this annoyance may be mild or nonexistent if the customer's buying work is specialized on a product basis so that each salesman calls on a different buyer.

When the product basis of organization is used, certain general functions may be kept at a staff level in the central area, as illustrated in Figure 13–5, instead of being pushed down into the product specialist level, as shown in Figure 13–4. This action depends on how much of each activity is common to and uniform in all product areas, and on the extent to which the activity has its own special techniques—for example, marketing research.

The differences between industrial products are sufficiently pronounced and important so that whatever the primary basis of a firm's marketing organization structure may be, provision for product specialization must be made at some level.

The product manager is an organizational device often used for this purpose. This title in an organization chart may imply a variety of patterns of authority and responsibility. In its broadest sense, it may involve complete authority to direct the manufacture and marketing of a product or group of products, subject to company policy and overall top management control. At the other extreme, the product manager may be limited to suggesting or recommending promotional programs, and may have no real authority. This situation is often found in the consumer goods field.

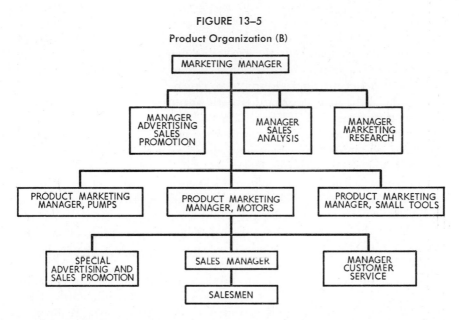

FIGURE 13–5

Product Organization (B)

In the industrial goods company whose manufacture, research, and marketing are set up on a functional, geographical, or customer group basis, a product manager group may be superimposed. In such a case, the product manager is essentially a staff officer, regardless of how his position description may be read. His real function is to be a source of information about his products, to study the markets for them, to recommend methods of making and marketing them, to plan or help to plan company operations involving his products, to check the efficiency of the firm's activities in making and marketing them, to suggest product modifications, and to make other studies and suggestions designed to improve the profit performance of the product.

Sometimes such a product manager is charged on paper with responsibility for the profit contribution of his products. This kind of assignment of responsibility is meaningless unless he is also given authority to issue orders to govern their research, manufacture, and marketing. The minute such power is given it conflicts with the authority of the heads of these functional areas, and the result is apt to be an organizational shambles. No able product manager will accept profit responsibility without authority over the activities that determine profits. No able functional executive will gracefully tolerate meddling in his area by a group of product managers. In many company organization structures there is a need for product managers at the staff level. In no organization is there a place for a product manager charged with a responsibility that forces him to grab for authority he does not have and, in the nature of things, cannot have.

Where the product manager belongs in the organizational structure is a matter of debate. In some firms, he reports direct to the chief executive officer or to a director of product managers who reports to the top executive. He may report to an administrative vice president in charge of staff functions. He may be in the marketing department; then he is usually expected to give product information service to other functional areas.

If the product manager reports to top management or to a nonoperational official, he may be regarded with suspicion and some hostility by the operating executives. They tend to look on him as a cross between a spy and a Meddlesome Mattie, and they are loath to give, let alone volunteer, the information he cannot function without, save in an ivory tower. If he is in an operating department, such as marketing, the marketing manager is liable to begrudge the time and energy (charged to the marketing budget) the product manager spends in providing information and other services to top management and other staff or functional executives. With the exception of top management, these outside officers are prone to complain that the product manager, owing first loyalty to the marketing manager, scants his services to them.

There is no right place for the product manager in the organization structure. The wise organization planner will consider the nature of the work the product manager is expected to do, the importance of each phase of his job, the psychological climate of the company, the urgency and difficulty of coordinating research, manufacture, and marketing, and the attitude of top management; then he will pick a spot he knows is not right in the sense of having no serious drawbacks, but one he hopes will, at least, prove to be the least wrong.

Customer Organization

If a company sells its product to several industries that differ markedly in the purposes for which they use the product and in the technical problems they encounter in its application, the most important basis of specialization in the firm's marketing work is the customer groups representing those industries. In a broader sense, an organization structure based on customer groups is an acknowledgement that the customer is the most important person who has anything to do with a business. The customer group type of organization is much more common in industrial goods marketing than in the consumer goods field. It is illustrated in Figure 13–6.

FIGURE 13–6

Customer Organization

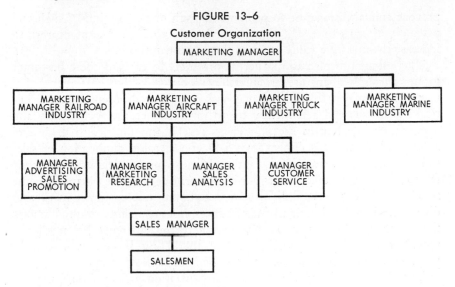

In this form of organization, as well as in the others, certain common functions, such as general advertising, and certain activities, such as marketing research and sales analysis, that because of highly specialized techniques or the use of specialized equipment can be performed more economically or efficiently by a central group are set up as staff operations in the marketing manager's office. The planning–operations functional division may also be introduced at the customer group level. In that case, the organization of the aircraft industry unit of the firm shown in Figure 13–6 would look somewhat like the following.

The use of the customer type of marketing organization structure is sometimes complicated by the tendency of customer firms to diversify. For example, a firm that makes fine chemicals has one line sold to pharmaceutical houses for use in preparing human medicinals, another sold to veterinary houses for use in making medicines for animals, a third to animal feed compounders for mixture with their feed products, either to prevent animal diseases or to promote growth or production of such end products as eggs or milk, and a fourth sold to food manufacturers to increase the nutritive value and tastiness of human foods.

The company's plan to market its products to each of these customer groups through a separate organization specialized from customer group marketing manager to field salesman was complicated because pharmaceutical houses showed a tendency to go into the veterinary business, and firms that made human foods, such as cereals and flour, also made and marketed animal feeds. This resulted in considerable duplication of sales calls and some customer dissatisfaction, because no one person could speak for the supplier or take orders for all his products. If the chemical house sought to overcome the difficulty by designating one customer marketing division to handle all such a firm's business, hot arguments resulted among the group marketing managers as to where the customer belonged and much of the advantage of specialized marketing service was lost. In practice, viable compromises were worked out in most cases.

The dominant form of marketing organization a firm should use depends on several factors. If it manufactures a number of supply items used by all kinds of industries and presenting no significant technical problems in use, the functional type is probably best. If the conditions of use or methods of purchase differ in different parts of the country, as they do for building materials, a geographical organization structure should probably dominate. If a firm's products are highly technical and their respective technologies differ widely, the product type of structure is probably best; certainly it is best if each product is sold to a different industry. If the use of the company's products differs widely among several customer industries, the customer type of organization is clearly indicated.

Centralized versus Decentralized Organization

Several decades ago, management experts were convinced that there was a one best way of doing each job, and that the secret of good management was to find that way and enforce its use throughout the organization. This led to a high degree of management centralization, which, in turn, emphasized the kind of marketing organization structure that centered control at the top or at general headquarters. During the years, management learned that there are several almost equally efficient ways of doing most jobs, and that the people in an organization—particularly the executives and those who deal with intangibles, such as salesmen—work more effectively when they are allowed to some extent to suit their methods of work to their own ideas and personalities. This has led to a program of decentralization in marketing organization, as well as in other departments of the business.

Decentralization in a marketing organization usually is in the form of delegation of wide powers to the geographical division heads, who are held responsible primarily for the results they obtain and only to a minor degree for the way in which they achieve them. In industrial goods marketing, there has been a considerable tendency to decentralize authority along the lines of customer or product groups. Under this system, the head of a customer division in a marketing department, for example, is charged with responsibility for marketing his firm's products to the members of that customer group. A similar arrangement may be set up for a product or a group of products. When this is done, each of these division managers has his own sales force, and perhaps his own advertising budget and technical service unit; he practically runs his own show and is responsible for the amount of his sales and the profit made from them. He may operate his own branch houses or utilize separate space in some or all of the branch houses maintained by the firm.

Geographical decentralization has not proved to be so applicable to industrial goods marketing as to the consumer goods field. Differences in the methods of buying and using most industrial goods are more pronounced between different groups of products or customers than between different areas. Usually, the members of the same industry require the same kind of service from the supplier, regardless of where they are located, although there are exceptions to this rule. It is important, therefore, that the same standard of service be rendered the country over. These factors point toward the use of the product or customer type of decentralized marketing organization, and away from decentralization on the basis of geography.

So strong is this pressure toward product or customer specialization that large industrial goods firms are often separated into semiautonomous operating divisions on one of these bases. This involves decentralization of management in all operations. Each division of such a firm is apt to have its own sales force and marketing organization. Even when considerations of cost dictate production in a central plant or complex of plants, marketing is often decentralized.

Decentralization of management, whatever form it may take, has an advantage in that it shoves the solution of problems and the making of decisions down nearer the area where the need for them arises and where all the conditioning factors and influences are known or readily discoverable in detail. This closeness promotes soundness and realism in decisions. It also creates a high degree of personal commitment in the people at the operating level. When a man makes a decision himself, he is much more enthusiastic about carrying it out than he is about executing a decision made by someone else. An imperfect plan carried out with vigor and drive often yields better results than a perfect one executed with lukewarm spirit. This is especially significant in industrial goods marketing, where the intangible factors and the coordination of diverse skills are so important to success.

A major problem of decentralized management is control. How can top management make sure that the head of a decentralized unit will make and carry out his decisions for the best interest of the firm rather than in the interest of his unit? The two do not always coincide. No surefire way to accomplish this has been found. Probably the most promising approach is that of sharply defining the firm's objectives and communicating them clearly to the men who make the unit decisions, and then judging their performance on the basis of the contribution they make to the achievement of these central goals.

For example, profit is almost always an objective. If the geographical, product, or customer group unit is made a cost-profit center and its head knows he will be judged on the basis of the contribution his unit makes to profit, he is likely to become very cost-profit conscious.

The management of a firm whose marketing department was set up on the traditional basis of a single sales force, with the necessary supervisory staff, that sold all products to all customers made repeated efforts to reduce marketing costs, with no results more significant than slight cuts in long-distance telephone tolls and the pruning of the more exorbitant excesses in expense accounts. The firm changed to a decentralized form of organization, with the managers of customer group units as cost-profit centers. Each unit was charged with the factory cost of the goods it marketed and was responsible for making a profit on them. The next budget-making time ushered in the most careful appraisal of costs and expected results of cost-generating activities that the company had ever seen. The unit managers were committed to making every dollar spent produce its profit quota. The danger here is that the unit heads will become Scrooges, unwilling to lay out dollars even when their expenditure would be profitable. But it is usually not too hard to teach them the art of spending money fruitfully.

An alert and ingenious top management can usually find some method of tying up the decentralized manager's interest with the contribution his unit makes to each of the nonmonetary objectives of the firm. This takes more imagination and inventiveness than is needed with the profit goal, but in most cases it can be done.

The experience of several electrical firms some years ago suggests that care must be taken not to put too much profit pressure on the managers of the decentralized marketing units. Several of their unit managers were convicted of agreeing to fix prices in violation of the antitrust laws and were sent to jail, to the great embarrassment of their top managements and with loss of goodwill and prestige to their companies. This danger of overemphasizing profit is especially acute in the industrial marketing area, where overoptimistic claims, high pressure selling, and cost-cutting skimpiness of service can be so devastating to the long-run welfare of the firm.

Compromises in Organizational Structure. Some managements are unwilling to delegate authority to the extent necessary to set up decentralized marketing units, but still want to have in their organization structure some recognition of the need for specialization according to product or customer groupings or geography. A mild form of such specialization is achieved by setting up a marketing organization structure that looks like the one shown in Figure 13–7.

Under this form of organization, the manager of sales to oil companies, manager of sales to drug companies, and manager of sales to chemical companies are staff officials. Their functions usually are to study the markets for their respective industries, to make suggestions to improve

FIGURE 13–7

Compromise Organization (A)

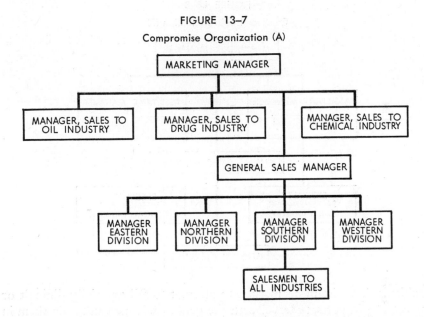

sales to those industries, to originate methods of improving sales service to them, and to give aid to the general salesmen who sell to all three industries. Sometimes, they may supervise the technical service to their respective customer industries. They have no authority to issue orders to any salesman; those must come from the general sales manager. They may suggest to him that orders should be issued to accomplish certain purposes, but their authority stops there. All too often, management attempts to tie up their lack of authority with a more or less complete responsibility for making satisfactory sales to their respective customer groups, as is frequently the case with product managers.

Usually, failure in attempts to fix responsibility without delegating authority is foreordained. If men willing to accept such responsibilities without commensurate authority can be found, they are usually not the kind who can accomplish much by the arts of persuasion. If strong men are induced to accept such positions, sooner or later they try to issue orders to the salesmen. This leads to a conflict of apparent authority over the salesmen, with consequent loss of efficiency and *esprit de corps* among them. Sometimes, because of the personalities involved, this system works fairly well, but the cases are not numerous.

A somewhat more positive compromise between complete decentralization and managerial reluctance to delegate complete authority on a customer basis is shown in Figure 13–8.

Under this system, each of the customer group managers has reporting to him a small force of specialists whose jobs are to handle special sales

FIGURE 13–8

Compromise Organization (B)

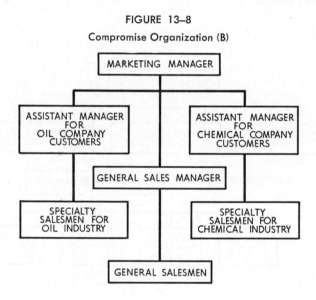

problems that arise in his market, to attempt to sell especially difficult or important prospects, to travel with the general salesmen and train them in selling to the kinds of customers in whose needs they specialize, and sometimes to visit customers in their respective groups to do developmental or missionary sales work. In this way, the customer group sales managers have at least some degree of control over the jobs they are responsible for. One of the obvious drawbacks of the system lies in the tendency for feuds to develop between the two types of salesmen.

There are innumerable modifications of each of these types of marketing organizational structure. In spite of the obvious advantages of a direct delegation of authority and responsibility on the basis of customers or products, several factors often force firms to adopt one of these compromise types of structure. For example, an attempt to have a separate sales force for each type of customer may result (*a*) in the need for a larger total number of salesmen and more miles of travel than a compromise system would require, especially in territories where customers are few and volume is thin; or (*b*) in having several salesmen from the same company call on the same diversified customer to his bewilderment and disgust. As mentioned earlier, this duplication may be mitigated by the fact that if the several products of a company differ enough to justify separate sales forces they probably are bought by different buyers in the prospect's purchasing organization. Sometimes, these difficulties can be resolved by setting up forces of specialists to handle customers or products in areas where business is plentiful, and allowing general salesmen to do the work for all products with all customers where volume is sparse.

Organization for Advertising

Advertising occupies a position much less important in the organizational structure of the average industrial goods marketer than it does in that of a consumer goods house. This is primarily because advertising is a less effective means of marketing in this field than it is in the consumer goods field. The annual statistical survey of industrial advertising by *Industrial Marketing* magazine indicates that the average expenditure for advertising industrial goods is somewhere near 2 percent of sales. The business of industrial marketing is not characterized by the multimillion-dollar advertising budgets common for consumer goods.

The marketing organization structure of many firms that make consumer goods places the advertising manager on a par with the sales manager. This is usually not the case in the structure of a house that markets industrial goods. Much of the publicity of such a concern often consists of catalogs, displays and exhibits, and direct mail material. It is not unusual to find this sort of work placed under the direction of a manager of sales promotion at a rank equal with the manager of advertising, whose functions are then largely confined to the buying and filling of trade journal and general business publication space and, occasionally, of radio or television time. Both of these officials—or the manager of advertising and sales promotion when there is one—are likely to report to the vice president for marketing.

Because different media are needed to carry different appeals to different buying influences in customer firms, and close coordination between all forms of nonpersonal promotion and the efforts of the salesmen is so vital, it is probably desirable that advertising and sales promotion be directed by one executive. Also, the resulting increase in the size of the budget to be administered justifies the employment of an abler manager.

Organization of Technical Service

The organization of the technical customer-assistance work, which is such an important factor in the marketing of many industrial products, presents something of a problem. In some companies, this work is performed outside the marketing department by a specialized group, often a section of the engineering department. When the work is organized in this way and the salesmen are technically trained, some lack of sympathy and cooperation is liable to develop between the two groups. This organization structure presumes that the salesman will call on the technician for help when customers pose problems beyond his depth. The salesman may be loath to admit the existence of such problems. The technical force, being thus deprived of occupation and seeking an excuse for its continued existence, is likely to begin making direct contacts with customers. Duplication of service, contradictory advice, and customer confusion follow as night follows day.

The technical advisory work may be assigned to a separate staff unit of the marketing department. This tends to avoid some, although not all, of the difficulties that flow from its location outside the marketing area. When a decentralized form of marketing organization divided along customer or product lines is used, it is probably better to assign this work to technical staff assistants who report to the manager of each decentralized department.

The location of this work in the engineering department assures that it will be done in a manner as thoroughly competent as is the personnel of the engineering staff; on the other hand, not much of it may be called for under this arrangement. Its location as a separate unit of the marketing department diminishes, but does not erase, this difficulty, especially if the organization is decentralized according to customer or product; the quality of the service may be lower, but not seriously so. When staff technicians attached to product or customer marketing managers are assigned the task, its purely technical quality may suffer somewhat; this loss may be more than offset by a greater realism and a more practical approach resulting from their greater familiarity with the use problems involved.

Relations to Research and Development

The marketing department of an industrial products firm must usually maintain close relations with the research and the commercial development departments. The research department, of course, conducts chemical, physical, and other technical research to discover new products or processes or to improve old ones. The commercial development department, called by many different titles in different companies, has varying functions, most of them centering around the problem of translating the need for new products or improvements in product or process into terms of research projects, and of carrying the test-tube or drawing-board results of research through pilot plant or other similar operations until the process has become a routine procedure, or the product an accepted member of the line.

Organization charts cannot reflect the relations the marketing department should establish and maintain with these or other departments. All too often, an active animosity is liable to develop between the members of the marketing department and the development group personnel. This is especially apt to arise because in the course of its work the development department must sometimes deal with marketing matters, such as the probable market for a new product or the effect of a process change on the salability of the product.

For example, in studying the sales possibilities of a new commodity the development department of one firm thought in terms of market potential, but reported its findings in terms of probable sales. When the marketing department fixed its budget estimates at a much lower figure, representing its estimates of company share of the total potential, general management was understandably bewildered, and a first-class feud was generated that, for several years, prevented the kind of cooperative effort between these two departments needed for the best interests of the company. The marketing department was partly at fault, because although it had an opportunity to examine a rough draft of the development department's report, before it was submitted to management, no one took the time and trouble to sit down with the appropriate members of the development group and, after explaining the difference between the two concepts, suggest a rephrasing of the report, which would have prevented the misunderstanding.

In some firms, the development unit contains both production and marketing staffs with which it conducts pilot plant and market introduction work. Such a unit is usually charged with the task of carrying each new product through the introductory production and marketing stages until it either fails and is deleted, or is ready to take its place as an established member of the line. At that time, it is turned over to the regular manufacturing and marketing departments.

This organization structure has both advantages and drawbacks. Such a specialized group develops expertness in making and marketing new products, which is often a quite different process from that of manufacturing and marketing established ones. It leaves the regular factory and marketing staffs free to devote their entire efforts to handling the established items in the line. On the other hand, it denies the marketing personnel, particularly the salesmen, the challenge and psychological lift that come from having something new to work with and talk about.

Its most serious drawback probably lies in the likelihood that the same mistake will be made twice. Mistakes are inevitable in new product work. If they are first made by a regular marketing staff, which is charged with handling both new and established products, they are not likely to be repeated. When they are made by a specialized development group, they may be repeated by the regular staff when it takes over unless it is very carefully briefed and unless the most cordial relations exist between the development group and the regular staff. Such relations often do not prevail, since a certain amount of jealousy is likely to arise between the two groups.

This difficulty may be minimized by transferring certain members of the development group to the regular marketing staff, along with the product. But this means that: the development group personnel must be constantly replaced with inexperienced people; those who are transferred have a difficult problem of adjustment to regular routines, procedures, and relationships; and the members of the marketing staff are denied the opportunities for promotion that often attach to the addition of a new product. Another compromise involves assigning one or two members of the regular marketing staff to development when it starts work on a new product. When the product is transferred to the regular staff as a full-fledged member of the line, they move with it and presumably carry with them much of the expertise developed during its introduction.

In other firms, pilot plant and introductory manufacturing operations are carried on by the production department, and market introduction work is done by the marketing department. The development group acts in a staff capacity, collecting information about the product, its characteristics, its possible uses, its probable market, the materials and equipment needed to make it, methods of production, estimated costs and profit—all of which it makes available to top management to assist in making decisions about the product, and to the operating departments for use in planning manufacture and marketing. The development men work with the marketing group in planning the introductory work, but marketing management is responsible for the quality of the plans and for the way they are carried out.

In the industrial goods business there are successful firms that use each of these organization structures or some modification of them. So there is no really solid ground on which to conclude that one is better than the other. My[1] preference is to keep all manufacturing operations in production management hands and all marketing activities under the marketing manager, with the development group as a staff unit. But that preference does not make it the only right way to organize the job.

REORGANIZATION

Not very many managers are called on to organize a marketing department from scratch. But practically every marketing manager at some time during his career faces the problem of reorganizing a going structure. In fact, in the tenure of the average marketing manager hardly a day passes during which he is not moved to wonder if some adjustment of the organization structure, major or minor, would enable his operation to run more smoothly.

Reorganization presents certain problems of its own. In contemplating it, the manager must recognize and make allowance for two conflicting psychological quirks that tend to distort his judgment. One of these is the

---

[1] R. S. A.

impulse to change for change's sake. This may be fortified by or rationalized on the basis of the tendency to blame the organization structure for performance failures caused by inevitable human error or by faulty administration. The other is the tendency to assume that what is, is right. This often has its rationalization in the maxim, let well enough alone. We hesitate to tinker with the machine as long as it works, even though the gears grind a little and it slips a cog now and then.

Once launched on a program of reorganization, the marketing manager is apt to find that his consideration for people tends to dominate his thinking. Ideally, he should build a structure designed solely around the activities to be carried on, and then hunt the people to fit into the positions he has created. But the reorganizer already has people on the job whom he knows as people and not merely as pegs to be fitted into holes. He inevitably finds himself building into his structure a job for Jim— a solid, conscientious, but uninspired worker, who has been with the company for 20 years, and supports 5 children in college and a sick wife. Probably, he will be wise first to design his organization as he thinks it should be; then if Jim doesn't fit anywhere in it, he can deliberately build in a job for him. At least, the basic structure will be right. And so will his action in making a place for Jim, because in a working group you can't heartlessly discard the Jims without destroying the morale and enthusiasm so important in marketing work.

When a manager is planning a reorganization of his unit, the grapevine inevitably learns about it, regardless of how circumspect he may be. The result is that everybody spends more time and energy in worrying about whether he will be around after the chairs are shuffled than in doing the job he now has. The work of the department may not be exactly at a standstill, but certainly it is performed in slow motion. Again, this loss of morale and enthusiasm is especially important in the marketing area.

After a reorganization is finished, there is an inevitable shakedown period while people are getting accustomed to their new jobs, establishing new relationships, and setting up new informal lines of communication to supplement those shown on the organization chart. If the changeover is not deftly carried out, the work of the department is bound to suffer severely. An important means of minimizing this loss is to spare no effort in making clear to each person in the new organization just what his powers and responsibilities are, and just how his new job fits into and is related to those of his fellow workers. This applies to all levels, from assistant manager to salesmen in the field. Such understanding is especially important in an organization that markets industrial goods because of the close teamwork needed to reach the various buying influences in customer firms with appeals that will be convincing to them.

Certain tools are especially useful in communicating an understanding of organization structure. The organization chart shows an overall picture of the formal lines of communication, authority, and responsibility. A position description lists the major activities involved in each job and describes each of them briefly. A procedure lists and describes briefly the detailed activities involved in a given process, such as preparing an advertisement, and indicates who is expected to do each and when. A very useful device is that shown in Figure 13–9.

FIGURE 13–9

Activity—Planning Advertising Program

Subactivity	Advertis-ing Manager	Customer Group Marketing Manager	General Marketing Manager	Advertis-ing Agency	Customer Group Sales Manager	Product Manager
Determining objectives						
Determining budget						
Determining target groups						
Determining appeals						
Selecting media						

In each square in the chart is written a brief but fairly complete statement of what the man whose title appears at the top of the column is expected to do about the activity listed at the left. For example, on the "Determining objectives" line the following might appear:

Advertising Manager—Consults with subordinates, agency, customer group marketing manager, and product manager, soliciting suggested objectives. Approves or rejects and recommends objectives to general marketing manager, after agreement, if possible, with customer group marketing manager.

Customer Group Marketing Manager—Consults with advertising manager and his own sales manager, and recommends objectives to advertising manager. Advises advertising manager on other recommended objectives. In case of disagreement, may appeal to general marketing manager.

General Marketing Manager—Initiates planning process. Reviews recommendations and decides.

Advertising Agency—Consults with advertising manager, recommends, and advises.

Customer Group Sales Manager—Consults with customer group marketing manager. Suggests objectives, and indicates how recommendations can fit into sales program.

Product Manager—Consults with advertising manager and customer group marketing manager, suggesting objectives for his products and advising.

If this chart is properly prepared, each man can, by reading down his column, observe exactly what he is expected to do in relation to the whole activity. By reading across, he can see exactly where and how his work fits into the work of others. This looks like a lot of work to accomplish a simple goal. But none of it is wasted if it prevents duplication of effort, bickering about who does what, and failure to perform seemingly minor but vital subtasks, and if it promotes the smooth running of a cooperative activity.

The ideal organization is an ideal structure staffed by people who believe in it and are enthusiastic about it. This is not always possible, especially in reorganization work. The people who carry on an operation are likely to have their own ideas about how it should be organized. Their notions do not always add up to the ideal structure.

An organization framework that seems something less than the best but is liked by the people in it will work better than an ideal one about which they are something less than enthusiastic. The wise organization planner will compromise the ideal set forth in books like this in order to wind up with a structure that has the support of the people who must operate it.

SUMMARY

In this chapter, we first summarized some of the basic factors of organization that are especially important in the industrial goods field. We then discussed several of the bases on which industrial marketing activities can be grouped into organization units, such as functions, geography, products, and customers, and listed the chief factors that indicate the use of each basis. We then took up the problem of centralization versus decentralization, seeking to show the characteristics of industrial marketing work that affect the use of each.

We also outlined several compromise structures between the extremes of centralization and decentralization. The chapter concluded with a discussion of several special problems in the organization of industrial marketing, such as the place of advertising and technical service in the structure, and the relations between marketing on the one hand and research and development on the other. Finally, some of the problems of reorganization were outlined.

Chapter 14

∞∞∞∞∞∞∞∞∞ MANAGING PERSONAL SELLING

THE ACTIVITIES carried on in managing the sales force of a firm marketing industrial goods are much the same as those involved in operating any other kind of sales organization. They include selecting salesmen, training them, assigning their tasks, supplying home office support for them when in the field, developing and administering a system of compensating them, administering their expenses, and supplying the day-to-day supervision and stimulation without which they cannot be expected to achieve their most efficient performance.

The basic characteristics of industrial goods and the circumstances in which they must be marketed affect the way the industrial marketer can perform some of these functions. These characteristics simplify the performance of some of the tasks listed above; others they emphasize or complicate. At the risk of some repetition, it might be useful to review several of the characteristics or marketing circumstances that are peculiar to or especially significant with respect to industrial goods, and that bear on this problem.

1. The need for technical information and skills in marketing many industrial goods creates special problems for the industrial sales manager. His salesman must have the technical background and training that will enable them to understand and talk intelligently about buyers' problems in using the product. However, often even the best educated and trained salesman encounters technical problems in the field that he is not equipped to solve. This makes it necessary for the home or the regional office to support the salesman with technical experts who do nothing else but study the characteristics and uses of the product and act as troubleshooters in problems of its installation and use. Some nice problems develop over the extent to which the salesman in the field should attempt to supply such technical service, how he may be trained to recognize matters he is not equipped to handle, and, even more difficult, how he may be induced to admit his own inadequacy and call for help.

2. The small number of prospective customers for the average industrial good means that, in general, the sales force of the industrial marketer is not so large as that of the consumer goods manufacturer. Each salesman

is more important, however. Greater care must be taken in his selection and training.

3. Since the purchase of many industrial goods must be approved by several persons in the buying firm, the average industrial salesman must spend a longer period of time in making each call; the number of calls he can make per day or per week is smaller—about 4 or 5 a day as against 20 or more for a consumer goods man calling on retailers—and he can handle fewer customers than his fellow who sells consumer goods.

4. Because the typical American industry tends to be characterized by the presence of a few large firms, generally less than a half dozen, which produce the bulk of the industry's total output, the marketer of an industrial good is likely to have a few large customers who take a disproportionate share of his total sales volume. These customers must receive special treatment, and the negotiations with them must sometimes be conducted at high executive levels within the two companies. But constant contact must be maintained with them.

5. The salesman of an industrial good usually has exceptional opportunities for creative selling or development work. By carefully studying the operations of prospective customers, he may be able to suggest ways in which his product can be used that may not occur to those in charge of such operations. Such study takes time, and much of it will produce no direct results. The industrial salesman must do much work that requires considerable originality and that does not result in immediate orders or contracts.

SELECTION OF SALESMEN

The industrial salesman is an important employee of the company that hires him. He must deal with well-trained, well-informed, highly responsible people in customer firms. The business he solicits for his company may aggregate hundreds of thousands or even millions of dollars annually. As a result, it is worthwhile to spend a great deal of effort and large sums of the firm's money to select and train him—in 12 companies, in 1964, the amount averaged $10,600 per man.[1] The long and expensive period of training he must undergo before he can begin to produce business for his firm makes it imperative that the greatest care be taken in choosing the right man so that this money and time will not be wasted.

JOB SPECIFICATIONS

The process of selecting an industrial salesman, like that of choosing any other employee, begins with the preparation of a job analysis or man specification. The details of any such specification usually grow out of the

---

[1] *Industrial Marketing*, March, 1964. In a study reported in *Sales Management*, November 20, 1964, the figure averaged $8,732 without the man's salary.

nature of the business of the employing company and the kind of selling job it has to do. But certain background traits and characteristics, included in such a description, are common to most industrial marketing firms and grow out of the attitudes of the average buyer, the way in which he purchases, and the kind of sales service he wants and expects from the salesman who calls on him.

Perhaps a good guide to follow in determining what basic characteristics an industrial salesman should have lies in the attitudes of the purchasing officers in manufacturing concerns. These gentry have been much more vocal and unanimous in indicating the traits they do not like in a salesman than in compiling a clear and comprehensive statement of what characteristics they think he should have. So we may be wise to sample their gripes about the shortcomings of the men that call on them, and from this negative approach to seek to discern the strengths industrial salesmen should have.

In November, 1963, *Purchasing*, the professional journal of industrial purchasing executives, listed in a somewhat less than serious vein some types of salesmen the buyer doesn't like.

Oscar the Order Taker whose sole idea is to get the buyer to sign on the dotted line.

Back Door Brumley who is expert in finding ways to sneak past the purchasing office and bother operating executives whose protection from just such intrusions is one of the reasons for the purchasing officer's existence.

Catalogue Calvin who refers all information seekers to his company's catalogue.

No Know Nelson who has none of the answers and gives the impression that he couldn't care less.

Mr. X, the mystery man, who refuses to tell the receptionist his name or the nature of his business but claims that he has some sort of secret deal the buyer can't afford to miss. Maybe he has.

Peeping Paul whose roving eye is ever seeking to read the material on the buyer's desk.

Sociable Sam who has a wonderful line of stories and seems to be glued to the caller's chair but never gets down to business.

In a more serious vein, *Sales Management*, June 1, 1962, reported the results of a survey of 3,000 industrial buyers to ascertain their specific complaints about the salesmen who call on them. The most common were:

Inability or unwillingness to provide product information and help—39.6 percent of those reporting.

Lack of knowledge of customer's products and the applications of their own products to them—34.3 of the respondent buyers.

Making of wrong contacts either too often or not often enough, which may be the fault of either the salesman or his management; a tendency to contact the wrong people, often going around the purchasing officer to do it, which may be the fault of the salesman, his management, or the purchasing officer who refuses to allow the salesman access to the people who really influence or make buying recommendations and decisions—30.1 percent of those replying.

Lack of the proper spirit of helpfulness that leads the salesman to try earnestly to understand the customer's problems and help him solve them—21.7 percent of the respondents.

Lack of technical background to enable the salesman to understand the customer's problems—13.9 percent of the purchasing officers replying.

To these might be added lack of elementary honesty. As one purchasing director phrased it: "We want salesmen to tell us what their companies can do and when they can do it. We want them to be honest in stating these facts. A salesman who honestly says he doesn't think his company can give us what we want builds his and his company's image and makes future sales when he is able to say that it can supply our needs."

The requirements for a good industrial salesman fall into several groups, some operational, others personal, and still others having to do with the core of his behavior as a representative of the marketing company. Some of them can be assured by proper selection, others by careful training, and others by the right kind of supervision.

The salesman should call regularly, on appointment if possible, and stay no longer than necessary to transact his business. He should also earnestly attempt to make himself available when his services are needed by the customer. Whenever possible, he should make his contacts through the purchasing agent instead of trying to short-circuit that official. The process of calling is sometimes complicated by the practice of many purchasing offices in limiting the hours within which salesmen can call. Often, the salesman must exercise considerable ingenuity to fit his visits into the patterns of his customers without loss of working time.

The average buyer likes the salesman to make a presentation of his products. His remarks should be intelligently suited to the operations and needs of the customer and should be based on the merits and usefulness of his products to the customer. A routine pitch is likely to fall on cold ears.

The salesman can warm the buyer's welcome by making himself a valuable source of market information. He should report price information, especially price changes, promptly and accurately. He should be prompt in submitting price quotations requested, and should include all facts the buyer needs to compute a delivered cost, such as quantity discounts, credit terms, and shipping terms. He should be alert to discover and transmit to his customers information about new or especially efficient uses of the products he sells. In doing this, he must be careful not to pass on to one customer information he has learned in a semiconfidential capacity about the operations of that customer's competitor. The favored customer will have a suspicion that facts the salesman learns about *his* business will be treated in the same manner.

The salesman should be careful to promptly handle special requests for information, consulting the technicians in his home office if necessary to insure completeness and accuracy. If he doesn't know the answer to a customer question, the good industrial salesman will be honest and say so. But in the same breath he will offer to find the right answer and supply it. And he will do that promptly. Refusal to give an answer of doubtful accuracy builds customer confidence, which is the industrial salesman's most priceless asset.

The industrial salesman should be alert to advise and help the customer in selecting the right materials or equipment to suit his purpose and in determining the proper amounts in which to buy them. It is sometimes wise for him to seek to dissuade a buyer from ordering an article that will not satisfactorily fit the user's purposes, even though such action loses a sale. It may occasionally be good business to urge a customer to reduce the size of an order when the amount proposed would possibly overstock him and tie up too much of his working capital. Both of these procedures will bring additional business later.

So far as his company organization permits, the salesman should follow up the orders placed by his customers and try to make sure that they are delivered according to the terms of the contract. He should be honest in making promises of delivery. The buyer usually prefers to know that he cannot get material until a certain date instead of being lulled with false promises of delivery at an earlier time. In case there is unexpected delay, the salesman should be careful to inform the buyer at his earliest opportunity. He should consider himself the buyer's agent in obtaining the earliest and most generous adjustment of complaints that may be justified under the policies established by his company.

These performance requirements for the industrial salesman suggest that the marketing manager may be wise to look for certain basic characteristics of mind and personality in the man he contemplates adding to his sales force.

The industrial salesman needs initiative and self-discipline, since he must be able to lay out a course of action for himself and follow it through. He must have the ability to study and to absorb knowledge. It goes without saying that he must have adequate knowledge of his own line. It is also important that he be well informed about his customers' operational problems and the application of his own products and services to their solution. The industrial salesman should be continually in search of information and ideas that will benefit his customers, regardless of whether such knowledge has direct commercial significance to him. He should be always alert to new ways of serving his customers.

Persistence is a necessary trait in industrial selling, for rarely is a sale closed the first time an item is presented. In selling an expensive piece of equipment, a long series of call-backs may be required. If the buying decision is important enough, the approval of several executives may be necessary before the order can be placed. This often takes a long time, and the salesman who continues his selling efforts persistently and tactfully, even after the sale seems lost, is sometimes rewarded by seeing the tide of purchasing decision turn in his favor.

This means that he must be a man of unusual patience and with the courage to keep on plugging with everything he has, even when the situation looks hopeless. Unlike the average consumer goods salesman, he must work for long periods without the emotional lift that comes from getting a buyer's signature on the dotted line.

One of the most important character traits that should be possessed by a man who sells industrial goods is adaptability. The salesman must be able to adapt his manner and his tactics to the individual prospect. In selling a single piece of equipment, for example, he may have to make his presentation to the man on the bench, the foreman, the shop superintendent, the purchasing agent, and perhaps one or more top executives, and he must be able to talk the language of each.

The industrial salesman must be basically friendly and considerate. Even more than the man who sells consumer goods, he must keep in mind the best interests of his customers, always seeking ways to be helpful. In doing so, he builds strong patronage motives that competitors find hard to break down.

He must be basically honest. This does not preclude enthusiasm in what he says about his product and his company. But when he states a fact about either, it should be solid and provable, and when he makes a promise about what either will do, it should be one that can be counted on. Misrepresentation by implication or omission destroys the buyer's confidence just as quickly and completely as positive untruth. Without that confidence, the industrial salesman is a weak vessel indeed.

Much more than his consumer goods counterpart, the industrial salesman must have the capacity and desire to learn. Not only must he study the technical and performance characteristics of his own and his competitors' products, but he must also learn all he can about the operations of his customers to find situations and ways in which his products, modifications of them, or new products that his employer can make can be used with profit. He must keep abreast of technical developments in both his employer's and his customers' industries.

In general, the industrial salesman must be a better planner than his brother selling consumer goods. He must plan, in great detail, not only his routes and schedules but also often his individual calls. His attempts to get a customer firm's business cannot be simply a series of isolated actions, but must have more of the nature of a carefully planned and well-coordinated campaign. Each contact must be carefully thought out and planned to achieve a specific minor objective that contributes to the final end result desired. Only the salesman himself can do this kind of planning; his manager cannot effectively do it for him.

The buyer prefers to deal with a salesman who is neat and courteous, who views his job, his product, and his company with enthusiasm, and who is the kind of person people like to know.

These requirements set the general pattern within which the job description of the industrial salesman is likely to be written. Other items stemming from the nature of the product or the marketing policies or practices of the employing firm may be added. From this description, a list of traits or characteristics a salesman needs to do the job can be compiled. It is often a good idea to divide the items on this list into two groups—a Must group and a Would Like group. This may be of great help early in the selection process in eliminating candidates who are unfit for the job.

Sources of Salesmen

The sources from which industrial salesmen may be recruited are much the same as those from which consumer goods salesmen are drawn, although there are notable shifts in emphasis.

Newspaper advertising is usually less effective than in the consumers' goods field. An abler type of salesman is sought, and he is less likely to be attracted by a newspaper advertisement. However, advertisements in the business opportunities section of better journals at times prove fruitful. Usually, the advertisement should be as specific as possible, setting forth the must requirements established in the job analysis, the nature of the work, the extent of the opportunity, and other facts the prospective salesman might like to know. Probably, it is generally desirable to include the company name in the copy, although some firms have been quite successful in the use of blind ads. One drawback of the unidentified ad is the embarrassing possibility that it may be answered by someone presently in the employ of the advertiser. Salesmen who are contemplating a change in jobs but are not yet ready to inform their present employers of their intentions may hesitate to reply to a blind ad in fear of the same possibility.

Many industrial firms have found trade journal advertising a fruitful source of candidates for sales positions. Its advantage is that only candidates who are qualified and interested in the business are likely to answer.

Technical schools and schools of business administration are often valuable sources of sales personnel material. The men recruited from the schools are almost certain to need extensive training in the practical aspects of selling work. Many of them also tend to look on a sales job as a stepping-stone to an executive position rather than an end in itself. Unless promotion into such positions is possible within a reasonable period, a policy of recruiting from the schools may result in a high rate of turnover of the sales force.

A study designed to correlate the success of industrial salesmen with their educational experience suggested that a college education was very important to success; for highly technical products, engineering graduates were more successful; for less technical products, a business administration training seemed to be most beneficial.[2]

The existing sales force itself may prove a source worth cultivating. If a salesman knows that his merit rating will be improved as a result of his suggesting suitable candidates for the force, he is likely to be on the lookout for them. The danger of such a policy lies in the tendency to suggest relatives and friends, and in the possibility that if the salesman suggests a man who does not make good he may feel that his own standing with the company has been damaged. This possibility is probably offset, at least to some extent, by the special interest a salesman takes in his protege, which may result in his passing on to the new man some of his own experience and selling techniques. This sort of personal coaching is especially important in the industrial field.

Departments of the business other than selling may be productive sources of sales personnel material. This is especially true of the technical divisions, the service units, and the shipping and order handling department. Candidates from within the business have advantages in that they come to the selling job with the feel of the merchandise and of the business, which outsiders must often spend a long time to acquire. In addition, the manager has already had an opportunity to observe them and form sounder judgments of their qualities and capacities then is possible by the ordinary selection procedure. Candidates from the technical and service departments are especially attractive because they come to sales work with much of the technical information and knowledge of product uses that outsiders gain only at the cost of expensive and time-consuming training. Insiders are likely to be already sold on the company and to understand and approve its personality, policies, and theories of operation.

Some firms regularly raid competitors for sales force candidates. In the long run, this is apt to be expensive, to result in a high rate of turnover of the sales personnel, and to cause a general lack of loyalty in the selling group. Men you can hire away from others, others can usually hire away from you. The hiring firm generally must offer a substantial increase in the salesman's earnings in order to get him. This is likely to result in a higher salary level than competitors are paying. This policy also may engender bitterness in the competition against the firm that practices it. On the other hand, it diminishes the need for expensive and time-consuming training programs. This advantage is subject to the reservation that the man hired away from a competitor may have to be untrained in some of the competitor's selling policies and techniques that do not fit the hirer's methods of operation.

The new salesman may bring along to his raiding employer some of his

---

[2] V. Harley Morgan, in *University of Washington Business Review*, October, 1960.

best and most loyal customers. In fact, this is sometimes the chief purpose of the user of this source. It is especially important in selling industrial goods bought on standard grades or specifications, where the salesman's personality is likely to be highly important. The firm that follows this practice must face the fact that customers whose primary loyalty is to a salesman can be taken away by him as well as brought by him.

Usually, customers are less important as a source of industrial than of consumer goods salesmen. If a customer has an employee with sales ability, he will want to use the man for that purpose himself and probably will resist and resent any attempt to hire him away. This is true even of distributors; in addition, the distributor's salesmen usually are able to earn about the same income as those representing the firms that sell to him. Since industrial marketers do not sell to retailers, who constitute a fruitful source of sales personnel material in the consumer goods trades, the customer reservoir of candidates is of little use in the industrial field.

Selection Devices

In selecting salesmen from among candidates, industrial marketers use all the accepted devices for elimination and choice. The nature of their sales problems and methods probably leads them to emphasize the application blank and the interview somewhat more than is the general practice.

Application Blanks. The application blank, with its record of technical training and experience, must necessarily be the backbone of any system of selecting industrial salesmen. By observing the schools the candidate has attended and the firms he has worked for, the industrial sales executive can gain a fairly reliable idea of the soundness of his technical preparation and of the extent to which and directions in which that preparation has been enriched by experience. Because the typical industrial sales force is so much smaller than that of the average firm selling consumer goods, the industrial sales executive finds little use for the technique of making a mathematical analysis of the application blank by means of applying weight factors to the several items of information recorded on it. He is limited to a more subjective appraisal of the information, since he lacks the volume of case histories in the experience of his firm, which is a necessary base for mathematical analysis.

Tests. The industrial sales executive can, if he wishes, make much more extensive use of technical tests than his brother in the consumer goods field. He usually does not take advantage of this opportunity. This is probably due more to wisdom than to inertia. The industrial sales manager does not need technical wizards in his force. He wants men with a technical background adequate to enable them: (*a*) to recognize the salient points of a production, engineering, or chemical problem; (*b*) to talk intelligently with the prospective buyer about it; (*c*) to realize when they should call for help from the highly trained and specialized technical staff with which he backs them up. A man who is too much of a scientist is not apt to be a good salesman; a salesman who is so much interested in the purely technical aspects of his field that he tries to keep abreast of all the developments in it probably does not have the time or energy left to do a good job of selling.

The technique of preparing, administering, and interpreting the results of sales aptitude tests has been developed to such a point that if an industrial marketer can afford to pay for the services of a psychological consultant he will find them of considerable help in selecting salesmen. This is especially important, since he has the difficult task of picking out from among the candidates with the necessary technical background those who are also endowed with the ability to sell and the personality and interest to use that ability. The aptitude or personal interest test, administered by skilled technicians, can be of value in this process. Its usefulness consists, not so much, perhaps, in indicating the exact candidate who should be chosen, as in calling attention to the technically qualified candidates who are not fitted temperamentally or by personality, interest, or aptitude for sales work. With these eliminated, the selecting executive is, at least, not liable to make very many serious mistakes in his choices.

References. While most industrial marketers ask references from candidates for sales positions, and the majority of them probably consult the references submitted, very little reliance usually is placed on this source in the process of selection. A candidate's technical qualifications are pretty well established by graduation from a recognized school. Whether his record was a B plus or a B minus is of little import. Hence, references from faculty members are of little help. Unless the candidate has had previous selling experience, and letters of appraisal can be obtained from his former employers, references can be of little aid in the work of selection.

When references are sought, the questions asked should be specific. It is usually desirable to request the person to whom the questions are addressed to complete a form that includes all the items of information desired. This is especially important when an attempt is made to obtain information about the character or the personality of the candidate. The general tendency of persons to whom such requests come is to report only complimentary information. If a general request for facts and opinions about a candidate is used, the average respondent tends to report only favorable facts and to forget to mention those that are unfavorable. A form composed of specific questions, with spaces for answers or a series of columns in which the respondent can rate the candidate on various specified characteristics and traits, tends to discourage this practice. A reference who will lie tacitly by omission will hesitate to do so by positive statement. The danger of this form is that it will fail to cover the precise area in which the candidate's shortcomings fall.

Some managers have been very successful in the use of telephone or personal interviews with references. The tone of voice, the facial expression, or a tactical hesitation may be more significant than what is said in this sort of conversation. When the reference gives evidence of an unexpressed reservation, polite probing will sometimes bring it to light.

On the whole, references are probably less useful devices for selecting industrial salesmen than for choosing consumer goods sellers. The type of information the reference is best adapted to supply can often be obtained much more satisfactorily and reliably by means of a credit investigation or an investigation by a bonding company. Because of the great financial stake represented by a salesman, and because the average industrial salesman stays with a given firm a relatively long time, the industrial marketer can usually afford the expense involved in making such an investigation.

The Interview. The most widely used tool of selection is the interview. Through it, the industrial sales manager is able to observe at first hand the personality of the candidate and to appraise the impression he makes. In using this device, the wise industrial sales manager will bear in mind certain limitations.

First, a man who is excellent at selling a product or a service for someone else may be much less effective when it comes to selling himself. Of course, it is taken for granted that a good salesman must sell himself to the prospect and that his ability to do so may be judged to some extent in an employment interview. But it is one thing to sell oneself as an adjunct to a product or a service, and an entirely different thing to sell oneself as the sole product offered. A man who is very adroit at the first may fail dismally in trying to do the second. The reverse is also sometimes true.

Second, the industrial sales manager must always keep in mind that it is his job to select a salesman for the prospects of his firm and not for himself. His thought should not be: How does this man impress me? but How is he likely to impress and get along with the customers of my house? Failure to approach the problem from this point of view is probably the mistake most commonly made in interviewing prospective salesmen.

Third, the industrial sales manager should see to it that interviewers employ some device designed to focus attention on and force judgment of specific traits and characteristics instead of allowing them to emerge from the interview with nothing more than a general impression, which is likely to become quickly confused or blurred. The most useful device for this purpose is a form on which the interviewer is required to enter his reactions with respect to specific traits or characteristics he may be expected to observe in the course of the interview. This has the added advantage of providing a written record of the interviewer's impressions and judgments to which he can refer when the time for a final selection comes. This is especially important in the choice of industrial salesmen. Because of the relatively small number of men in the sales force of the average industrial house, men are chosen at infrequent intervals and the process of selection may be a long-drawn-out one, with the resultant likelihood that things observed about candidates interviewed early in the process may be forgotten before the choice is finally made.

Fourth, the industrial sales manager should not place too much reliance on his own individual ability to judge the qualifications of candidates by the interview method. Not all of us are so good at sizing up other people as we think we are. No man in appraising other men can wholly escape the bias and unconscious prejudice engendered by his own background, previous experience, and emotional makeup. It is wise, therefore, to check his own impressions and judgments against those of other executives in his own organization. His use of the interview in selection should include the use of the jury method. This method may be implemented by providing that the candidate interview several executives in the course of employment negotiations. A method less widely used is that of asking the candidate to submit to a group interview. This technique probably has greater usefulness in the industrial goods field, especially heavy equipment, than in consumer goods, because selling such products often requires that the sales representative appear before a group of executives in the prospect firm. Such an interview may afford some notion of the candidate's ability to handle himself in the presence of a group.

TRAINING INDUSTRIAL SALESMEN

The relative fewness of customers and the large size of the average purchase of industrial goods lend unusual importance to the training of industrial salesmen. At the same time, the relative smallness of the average industrial sales force and the heavy stakes riding on each contact of the marketing firm with its customers render impractical many of the training devices commonly employed by concerns that vend consumer goods. The budding salesman cannot be allowed unchaperoned contact with a customer until his skill and knowledge of the selling job are reasonably complete.[3]

The task of training industrial salesmen is usually a long-drawn-out one, and it is costly. Rarely is a new salesman put on the road without

---

[3] That industrial marketers do something less than a perfect job of training is indicated by the results of several studies reported in *Purchasing*, the best of which appeared in August, 1953. The purchasing agents responding were of the opinion that only about 25 percent of the calls made on them represented sound aggressive selling; that less than 25 percent of the calls were truly constructive in the sense that the salesmen imparted useful information, gave assistance, or made worthwhile suggestions. About 87 percent of the purchasing agents felt that the answer was better training and supervision. This was supported by a study of 100 purchasing agents, reported in *Sales Management*, October 9, 1962. They rated 52 percent of the salesmen who called on them as deficient in selling skills, 70 percent as lacking awareness of customer needs, 50 percent as deficient in their efforts to service customers, 61 percent as failures in matching their products to end uses, and 72 percent as lacking overall creative selling ability.

some months of training, and some firms cannot hazard putting the new man in a territory until after several years spent in preparing for the job. To some industrial marketers, a new salesman going into the field represents a piece of property in which they have invested $15,000 or $20,000. To such a firm mistakes in selecting or training are exceedingly expensive.

Formal or Informal

Sales training is usually of two types—formal or classroom training and informal instruction or training on the job. The small size of the industrial sales force and the relatively low rate of turnover among industrial salesmen often make formal or classroom training impractical. The larger concerns with bigger forces, however, can make effective and economical use of classroom instruction in reviewing the new salesman's technical education, pointing it up, and making it more realistic and applicable to the company's selling job. Some firms base their classroom instruction mainly on the case method.

Other firms, for which the classroom method is impractical, make use of individual instruction. The prospective salesman learns while he works in a series of jobs in the sales department or in other divisions of the business, where he is likely to be exposed to information and attitudes that will be useful in his future task. For example, he may be put to handling and expediting orders, passing on credit applications, handling sales correspondence and answering inquiries, and working in the shipping department. He is apt to spend some time in a branch office, familiarizing himself with the procedure followed there. A firm that markets machinery or heavy equipment may give its prospective salesmen valuable experience by having them help in the work of installing and servicing the equipment. Although this is not the usual practice of such firms, it can be employed to give the new man the feel of the product and a very realistic understanding of the circumstances and manner in which it is used. For example, a firm that sells telephone systems and equipment to independent telephone companies starts its salesmen as installers. They then graduate to equipment engineers, and after a period spent in this work become salesmen.

One very real danger in informal training lies in the likelihood that it will be interrupted. The essence of informal training is that the student salesman works for a time in each of a series of departments or divisions of the business. If he is an able man, he is likely to make himself valuable to one or more of the executives for whom he works. The executive then tries to keep the trainee in his unit, with the result that the young man may be sidetracked. This may have tragic results on the personal career of the man, since it may interfere with his ultimate promotion to executive positions in the sales organization; selling experience is usually a requirement for such positions. The industrial sales manager who makes use of the informal training method—and most of them must do so—will be wise to set up definite limits on the length of time a trainee can stay in any one unit of the business during his training, and then be adamant in enforcing these limitations.

Subject Matter

Most of the subject matter for training an industrial salesman usually falls under four headings. The new man must learn about the company, its policies, and its methods of operation, particularly those that affect its capacity to service its customers. This not only equips him to do a better job of selling, but it also serves the purpose of indoctrinating and building up in him a sense of loyalty to and identity with the company. This part of the training can probably be carried on better in the home office or the branch office than in the field.

The new salesman needs to learn about the product—what it is made of, how it is made, its technical features, its place in the firm's product line, the uses for which it is designed, and its elements of strength and weakness in relation to competing products. This information also can probably be better imparted in the home or branch office than in the field, although a true understanding of the product's relation to its competitors probably can be had only as the result of field experience. Much of the technical information about the product the salesman needs can be made available in the form of a product or sales manual. The manual can be employed not only as a textbook in training, but also as a reference book to be used constantly in selling work.

The embryo industrial salesman must also be informed about the customers to whom he will sell. He must learn the types of concerns they are, the bases upon which they want to buy, the uses to which they put his company's products, their methods of operation, and the ways in which his company can most effectively fit its sales service into and supplement those methods. A beginning may be made in this instruction in the home or branch office, but the bulk of it must be carried on in the field. The way to learn to understand the customer is to meet him and deal with him.

The new man must be trained in selling techniques. Most of such instruction must be given in the field. A few marketers of industrial products who have large sales forces are able to make use of the services of specialized field trainers who spend all their time in training work. Many industrial houses do not have enough field training work to keep even one man busy, and so must rely on branch or regional managers, senior salesmen willing to train new men when the need arises, or even a home office executive if the house has only a few salesmen.

Selling techniques can be most effectively learned through the procedure of observation, trial, criticism, and perhaps reobservation and retrial. The new man accompanies his instructor and observes what he does. This process may continue for a few calls, or it may go on for months when the average purchase is very large and the selling task highly complicated. The new man is finally given the opportunity to try his own hand at the selling job, either under the observation of his instructor or alone, as personalities and circumstances seem to indicate. At some point in the learning process, he must perform in the presence of his instructor who later postmortems his performance and suggests improvements. This process of trial, criticism, and retrial may continue for a considerable period.

Training Experienced Men

The average industrial goods sales manager finds it desirable to do some training work with his experienced salesmen. This may be carried on in the field through visits of the branch manager, the supervisor, or the sales manager himself. This is probably the most effective method, but it also may be the most expensive and time-consuming. Conferences either in the home or branch office offer a useful means of imparting such training. It is usually wise to limit the number of salesmen in any one such conference group to six or eight so as to get the maximum participation by the men undergoing training. In such circumstances, no small part of the training will be supplied by the men themselves in their contacts with one another.

The technique of role-playing can often be used effectively. In this method, the instructor describes a sales situation and either himself assumes the role of the prospect or assigns it to one of the group. By a process of trial and error in which several members of the group may participate, the best method of handling the situation may be worked out. This method has the advantage of imparting to the proceedings a sense of realism that is otherwise liable to be lacking. A can company used the seminar method of training old salesmen. About 20 men were in a class. Cases were used, with a Harvard professor acting as discussion leader. No officials of the company were present, and it was felt that this tended to promote free discussion.

Conventions are sometimes used as means of training or informing experienced salesmen. Their effectiveness is doubtful. A convention can sometimes be used satisfactorily as a means of renewing the average salesman's sense of identity with the firm or his feeling that he belongs to the company family. If held at the factory, it may be a useful means of establishing or maintaining personal relationships between the salesmen and the home office supporting personnel with whom they have mail or telephone contact from time to time. It may also be used to present in a short period of time and at low expense a new product, a new sales program, a change of marketing policy, or any other similar general modification of the marketing method or task. Some mistakes commonly made in conducting sales conventions are well illustrated by the convention adventures of salesman Luigi Pacelli, shown in Figure 14–1.

Much of the really effective work of training experienced industrial

FIGURE 14–1

Death of a Salesman

Occasionally, as we try to do a good job, we build up so much steam that it pays to use a safety valve—to pause and laugh at ourselves.

Ethicon Suture Laboratories, New Brunswick, N.J., must have had that in mind at the company's national sales meeting last January. For Ethicon distributed at the meeting a 10-page, "unofficial, irresponsible, immaterial, undependable" issue of "Chicago Ethigram," a publication that burlesqued the sales meeting, the company, its executives, and products.

Across the top of two tabloid-size pages was a six-picture sequence for which Luigi Pacelli, San Francisco salesman, posed. The magazine was produced, the pictures were taken and the captions written by George A. Kellogg, the company's advertising and promotion manager, who, for all his barbed witticisms, must feel very secure in his job. As far as we know, he still has it. The pictures of Mr. Pacelli are below.

OPENING DAY—Signor Luigi Pacelli, star San Francisco salesman, applauds corny gags and fly-blown platitudes of stuffed shirts from home office. What a company! What a job!

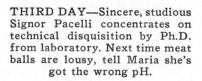

THIRD DAY—Sincere, studious Signor Pacelli concentrates on technical disquisition by Ph.D. from laboratory. Next time meat balls are lousy, tell Maria she's got the wrong pH.

FIGURE 14–1—Cont.

FIFTH DAY—Signor Luigi, fresh from 7 o'clock mass, responds with enthusiasm to abstruse gobbledegook from imported speaker. Wonder what's for lunch today?

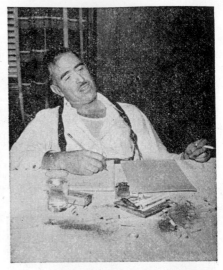

SEVENTH DAY–Pacelli makes careful notes of talk by market research expert on average operations per bed per hospital per 100,000 population, which prove he should be getting more business.

LAST DAY, A.M.—Luigi, crouching in back row, tries to figure out lawyer's talk on Retirement Plan. "Did he say tarts or torts?" Lawyers got more words than doctors.

LAST DAY, P.M.—It finally kills poor Luigi. Without sympathy, or even the last rites of the church, the exhausted salesman's remains await the mortician. *Sic transit gloria mundi.*

Courtesy of *Industrial Marketing* and Ethicon Suture Laboratories, makers of sutures.

salesmen must be done on an individual basis. It consists of diagnosing the man's strengths and weaknesses, trying to show him how to use his strengths more effectively, and inducing him to eliminate his weaknesses or learn to maneuver so that they no longer handicap his performance. Since some of these weaknesses may be in the area of personality, this is a very delicate matter. In the absence of professional psychiatric help, which is a pretty drastic measure, changes in personality traits must be made almost entirely as a result of the efforts of the individual involved. A manager can do little beyond trying to supply the incentive for making them and encouraging the salesman, during what is often a long and frustrating experience. If an undesirable trait is not too ingrained and is not a manifestation of a deep-seated emotional complex, certain procedures can be followed that may be helpful.

These steps may be stated rather simply. First, the salesman takes a personal inventory. A good way to start is to write out what he knows to be the strong points and the weak points of his sales personality. Since the individual is not likely to be aware of all his weaknesses and strengths, it is wise to enlist the aid of an interested second party—perhaps the sales manager or the company psychologist—who has had an opportunity to observe and appraise the various aspects of his sales personality.

When such an inventory has been honestly completed, the individual may be amazed at how little he actually understood himself. We are all too likely to take ourselves for granted, developing undesirable habits and attitudes without realizing it. The individual will often find that he has been at least partially aware of some of the defects that have hindered his sales effectiveness, but he has taken no conscious notice of them. An inventory of these traits, together with the good ones, is an important step toward self-improvement.

The second step is to determine which traits should be singled out for remedial attention. It is well to work on one or two at a time rather than to dilute one's efforts over the whole spectrum. It is also well to remember that it is much easier to develop and strengthen relatively strong points than to attempt radical personality changes. For example, it is probably impossible to change one's personality from introvert to extrovert, and it would be exceedingly dangerous to try except under the professional guidance of a skilled psychologist or psychiatrist. However, it is possible to compensate for a defect such as lack of aggressiveness by developing to a high degree such favorable factors as tact, power of observation, willingness to listen, and desire to be of service.

Having determined the trait to concentrate on, we develop a plan to bring about the desired results. If persistence is the trait we wish to develop, a frontal attack may be the best procedure. The simple expedient of persisting until a set number of refusals has been suffered before an order is given up as lost may do the trick. In most situations, a little thinking will reveal a suitable plan for improvement.

When more complicated or subtle weaknesses are involved, the problem is more difficult. For example, suppose that we have difficulty in remembering the names of people we meet—a rather serious deficiency in salesmen. Almost everyone is pleased by the sound of his own name, and its omission in a greeting is a lost opportunity for subtle flattery.

Psychologists tell us that the most important basic cause of poor name memory is faulty learning. A plan that has proved useful in developing name memory is, first, to make certain that the new name has been heard correctly by repeating it aloud. The salesman can then repeat it several times to himself or in the course of conversation. As soon as possible, the name can be written several times on a piece of scratch paper and in a notebook for future reference. As many associations as possible can be made between the sound or written appearance of the name and its owner or his surroundings. It is claimed that practice will enable any intelligent individual to become reasonably efficient in name memory.

The final, most important, and most difficult step is the follow-up. It is easy to make optimistic resolutions about improving oneself. We may even spend considerable time in making plans to do so. But it takes infinite internal fortitude to follow them through until the desired change becomes part of our makeup. The follow-up procedure involves periodic checking and self-analysis to make certain that the planned program is actually being carried out.

It should be pointed out that much of the task of self-improvement involves nothing more than the establishment of good habits of behavior or attitude patterns. Sincerity, helpfulness, enthusiasm, consideration, courtesy, honesty, and dependability are not attitudes that can be put on like a mask and then discarded as soon as we leave the presence of the customer. It is impossible for long to seem to be something we actually are not. It does not take long for such a mask to wear thin and reveal the true character.

It is undoubtedly true that strong behavior traits lend themselves more readily to development than do weak ones. But the fact that a desirable trait is rudimentary in an individual is no reason why it cannot be cultivated. The thesis is advanced that even such basic attributes as honesty, courage, and selfishness are capable of change, provided the effort is sufficiently long and concentrated.

It should be pointed out that this operation is not one that ought to be attempted by unguided amateurs. Though only the individual can do it for himself, no man should try it alone. In modifying a weakness, he may destroy a strength. Along the path of too much personal introspection lie many pitfalls of emotional disturbance. Only under expert guidance and counsel should a man seek to reconstruct his own personality.

EQUIPMENT FOR INDUSTRIAL SALESMEN

The task of providing the salesman satisfactory physical equipment to aid him in presenting the product to his prospects and in serving his customers is very important, as well as very difficult, for the industrial goods marketer. It is highly important, because the industrial buyer demands to know what a product will do, how it operates, and what its performance record is. It is often difficult, because the industrial product is a large, bulky item, and the salesman cannot transport samples to the buyer's plant or office. Probably, the types of selling equipment most commonly used in the distribution of industrial goods are sample cases, miniature models of products, portfolios of graphic presentations, and films or slides.

If the product is small in bulk, a well-arranged and convenient sample case in which the various types and sizes are displayed may be an effective sales tool. In preparing such sample cases, care must be taken not to encumber the salesman with an embarrassment of riches. A firm that makes container closures once developed a very compact, ingeniously constructed sample case in which all the several hundred items in its line were displayed. It was a flat failure, because the salesman found that the prospect's desire to examine all the items in the display and to discuss many of them so lengthened the average call as to reduce rather than augment his effectiveness. Comparatively few firms selling industrial products are apt to suffer from this difficulty, but, as a general rule, selectivity is likely to be a more desirable sample case feature than is completeness.

Many industrial goods marketers find it desirable to equip their salesmen with portfolios of pictures of their products in action on the job, charts, graphs, or tables showing performance records, and drawings or blueprints showing their construction. These should be of manageable size, and should be housed in a container that enables the salesman to present them on the prospect's desk without cluttering or confusion. They should also be placed in such sequence that the salesman can organize his presentation around them and use them as a positive tool of selling instead of as a crutch to fall back on when all else fails.

Many firms that sell large pieces of equipment or installations prepare miniature models to demonstrate how the product operates, where it can be installed, and what it is qualified to do. Most purchasing agents would welcome more extensive use of such models by salesmen calling on them, although some sales managers feel that their use tends to cause the salesman to lean too heavily on them and to neglect the wearisome task of keeping his detailed technical product knowledge up-to-date. Such models have been used by firms making a wide variety of industrial products.

Numerous devices akin to the miniature model have been developed. For example, a company that makes industrial lubricants prepared a tabletop demonstration unit of suitcase size to show its type of lubrication in use through a system of transparent walls and fluorescent lighting. It was a valuable aid in selling to machine owners and machine builders. A company that makes silencers and motor exhaust mufflers equipped its salesmen with a tape recording device to make recordings of various mufflers or silencing devices on the customer's equipment, which could be played back to the prospective buyer in the quiet of his own office. This was helpful in contrasting the results of the company's equipment with competing devices, as well as in selecting the particular type of silencer to do the best job in a specific situation.

Industrial marketers have made considerable use of motion-picture films and slides as selling devices. The drawback of film is that it is expensive to make. Many firms have found its production so costly as to be prohibitive unless the nature of the product or the selling job is such that the film can be shown to groups of prospects or to several interested persons in the average buying firm. Its great advantage is that the product can be shown in action, lending the presentation an air of realism gained in no other way except by a visit to the user's plant, which is often most difficult to arrange.

The use of film slides is much less expensive and affords many of the advantages of the motion-picture film, although in lesser degree. Another advantage is that a slide may be kept on the screen while the selling points it illustrates are discussed or while prospect questions are answered. It is a much more flexible selling tool than the motion-picture film, and the atmosphere of its presentation is apt to be much less formal and more convincing.

INCENTIVES AND COMPENSATION

The methods of compensating and providing incentives for industrial salesmen are influenced by the circumstances and manner in which industrial goods must be sold. The relatively high type of salesmen required, the fact that individual transactions are large and occur at infrequent and irregular intervals, the large amount of development and service work required, and the need for teamwork are especially potent factors in determining the method of compensation.

The straight salary is somewhat more widely used by industrial goods marketers than by firms marketing other types of products.[4] The irregularity with which orders are received creates the need to assure the salesman of some sort of regular income, which he could not count on if he were paid on the basis of a straight commission or if the bulk of his income were in the form of a commission. The large proportion of his

---

[4] A 1964 study of 400 industrial goods firms showed the following:

Straight salary..29 percent
Salary plus commission...............................31
Straight commission.....................................19
Commission with drawing account.........................9
Salary plus bonus...7
Salary plus commission plus bonus.....................5

Industrial Marketing, March, 1964.

time necessarily spent in developmental and service work that results in no immediate sales also creates the need for some method of compensation that provides payment for such work. The simplest form of payment to serve this purpose is the salary. The fact that many industrial sales must be made to firms that operate more than one plant but have interlocking buying arrangements among the several plants requires a high degree of cooperation among the salesmen of the firms that sell to them, and continual difficulty and dissatisfaction are created over the allocation of credit and commissions among the men responsible for making sales to them if the commission method is used.

A salary plus commission system offers one way of meeting this situation. If sales are big but few and far between, the salary assures the salesman a continuity of income, while the commission gives him some incentive to try to augment his total volume. If a man must do a lot of development work to secure the average contract or render time-consuming services to his customers, he is paid for it in the salary part of his compensation, while the commission gives him a cut in the volume that results when his spadework is successful. Obviously, the effectiveness with which this plan meets its objectives depends on how well it is drawn. The longer the time between sales and the more development and service work the company wants him to do, the larger the salary should loom in his total compensation. But the commission must be large enough to afford an incentive to increase volume.

Sometimes, a drawing account against commissions may serve the same purpose. This usually works about like the following. A man is authorized to draw $500 at the beginning of each month, and to receive 2 percent commission on sales. If his sales during a month are $40,000, his total income for the period is 2 percent of 40,000, or $800, and he is paid an extra $300 at the end of the month. If he sells only $20,000, he is entitled to only $400 and owes the company $100, which is charged against future commissions, although his drawing account continues without change. If a man has a run of bad luck that continues for, say, a year, in spite of his best efforts, his commission arrears may be adjusted or written off at the end so that he starts the new year with a clean slate. This should not happen too often, and usually no writeoff is allowed unless management is convinced that the situation is in no way the salesman's fault.

Another means of allowing for differences in the difficulty of selling different products and of providing incentives for working on those that require much development effort lies in varying product commissions according to this factor. This may be done by setting different rates for different products, or by more sophisticated methods. For example, the United Shoe Machinery, marketing certain shoe findings and equipment for making shoes, paid a salary graduated according to merit ratings, plus 2 percent commission on sales volume adjusted according to difficulty of sale. It worked somewhat as follows:

Product	Annual Sales	Factor of Selling Difficulty	Adjusted Annual Sales
A..	$ 38,000	100	$ 38,000
B..	200,000	20	40,000
C..	80,000	40	32,000
D..	15,000	200	30,000
Total............................	$333,000		$140,000

The salesman's commission is 2 percent of $140,000, or $2,800.

This is only one of the many ingenious schemes that can be used to accomplish this incentive objective.

The salary plus bonus method also affords a means of meeting several of the difficulties outlined above. The bonus is sometimes based on the amount of a man's sales either in absolute dollars or in relation to a quota or estimate of territory potential. In a few cases, the bonus is set as a percentage of net profits, either of the company as a whole or from operations within the man's territory. It may also be based on some sort of a rating system by which an attempt is made to measure the salesman's performance of the more intangible elements of his job.[5]

One sales manager in the chemical industry worked out an ingenious variation of the bonus principle in the form of rewards for performance above and beyond the call of duty. For example, a salesman who supplied a good customer with extraordinary service received a letter of commendation from the sales manager, with an enclosed check for $50. If the service was somewhat more unusual and of somewhat greater profit to the company, his letter was from the marketing manager and the check was for $250. A performance that was even more spectacular and saved a large, highly profitable customer or added a similar one to the customer

---

[5] The Republic Supply Corporation paid a basic salary plus a bonus based on ratings established by use of the following table.

Factor	Degree of Factor and Rating Assigned on Basis of Degree					
	Unsatisfactory	Acceptable	Fair	Good	Excellent	Outstanding
Teamwork..................	0	8	9.5	11	13	15
Selling activity..............	0	7	8.5	10	11.5	13
Balanced selling.............	0	6	7	8	9.5	11
Expense record.............	0	2	2.4	2.8	3.2	4
Public relations.............	0	1.2	1.4	1.6	1.8	2
Total..............	0	24.2	28.8	33.4	39.0	45

A salesman got no bonus if his total rating was less than 24.2. His excess rating over 24.2 was added to similar excesses of all other salesmen and computed as a percentage of the total of such excesses. He got that percentage of the total bonus fund established for the fiscal period. *Sales Management*, March 1, 1953.

list brought a letter from the executive vice president, with a $500 check. The ultimate recognition and reward of a letter from the president and a check for $1,000 went to the man who worked out a new application of a product to a customer's operations that promised substantial additions to the company's volume and profits. The kind of things for which each type of award would be given were spelled out in considerable detail and made known to the salesmen. This system had the advantage that it offered two kinds of incentives in one package, recognition and money.

Most sales managers experience great difficulty in administering bonus systems based on performance ratings, because they tend to become complicated and are not understood by the salesmen; consequently, they are regarded as unfair. This is somewhat less true of the firm engaged in selling industrial goods than of one in the consumer field. In the average industrial sales force, the man's characteristics and his familiarity with mathematics tend to make him more understanding and less suspicious of such systems. A cardinal principle in planning and administering a bonus system is that the bonus should be paid for the doing of specific things, and that the salesman should know what he must do to get it and should be entitled to it if he does that thing. It should not be in the nature of a Christmas present, whose payment or amount depends on the state of the manager's ulcers or liver at the moment of decision.

Industrial marketers find many types of nonmonetary incentives less useful than do other kinds of sales managers. Many such incentives, such as sales contests and similar plans, place great emphasis on immediate volume, with a resultant tendency of the salesman to oversell the customer. This is liable to be especially damaging to the industrial marketer. Moreover, the typical industrial salesman's relatively high intelligence quota and technical background tend to make him less responsive to the emotional hoopla often used to rouse and maintain enthusiasm for the typical sales contest.

On the other hand, these same factors tend to make the industrial salesman more than ordinarily subject to motivation on the basis of satisfaction derived from the knowledge and recognition of a good, workmanlike job well done. Many firms in this field have found nonmonetary rewards based on such recognition highly effective.

Salesmen's Expenses

The administration of salesmen's expense accounts is not entirely a matter of compensation or incentives. But it is a financial factor that may affect his take-home pay, and certainly affects his enthusiasm for his job and his company. If a firm's expense policy is too rigid or niggardly, its salesmen may have to pay part of their expenses out of their regular compensation. If, on the other hand, it is overly liberal or careless, the expense account may become a source of supplementary income to the men who choose to make it so. A firm's expense policy is almost always a factor the salesman takes into account in sizing up his job.

The task of administering salesmen's expenses is complicated by the need to adhere to the rulings of the Bureau of Internal Revenue, which will not permit what it regards as excessive expense allowances to be treated as costs in computing company profits. Such allowances may also constitute a problem to the salesman in submitting his own tax reports.

The expenses involved are usually the cost of travel, food, and lodging, expenses incidental to living away from home, and entertainment. Entertainment is an especially tricky item—so much so, in fact, that it is often treated as a separate problem.

There are at least three basic plans for the administration of salesmen's expenses. Each is subject to almost innumerable modifications. Probably the least widely used plan in industrial marketing is that of requiring the salesman to pay his own expenses out of his regular compensation, which supposedly contains an increment to cover them. This has the advantages that the firm is saved considerable record-keeping expense, a source of administrative friction is eliminated, and the man's expenses tend to be frugally managed.

On the other hand, since the management has no records from which to learn how much a salesman should spend or actually does spend, it is apt to be somewhat in the dark when it sets the increment added to the basic remuneration to cover expenses. This plan may also result in the man's managing his expenses too frugally for the company's benefit, since it is often hard for him to understand that to make money he must spend money. Then, too, the plan is usually tied up to a straight commission plan, and the same factors that make the commission less desirable in industrial goods marketing apply with even greater force to this method of handling expenses.

A second method of administering salesmen's expenses is that of allowing a lump sum per day or, in the case of travel costs, per mile. This avoids the hardship to the salesman of having to pay money from his own pocket in doing development work that does not result in immediate sales to cover its cost. Here too, it is not easy for management to decide just how much the lump sum should be. Moreover, having got the lump sum, the salesman may try to cut expense corners to save some of it, with the result that he may not do a selling job as good as management would like. Finally, the Bureau of Internal Revenue believes in specifics and prefers to allow as costs against profits only the expenses actually incurred.

A third method involves paying on the basis of a detailed expense account submitted by the salesman. This is the plan preferred by the Bureau of Internal Revenue. It was also probably the one most generally used even before the Bureau took an interest in the matter. It repays the salesman only funds he actually has laid out. It does not discourage him from spending more if by so doing he can sell more, but management can check his expenditures and try to keep them within reasonable bounds.

On the other hand, anyone who has traveled on an expense account knows that it is difficult to include all the extra outlays incident to living away from home, each trivial in itself but adding up to a considerable sum. Then, too, salesmen show a truly remarkable ingenuity in developing schemes for beating the expense account. If its administration is too rigid, priceless thought and imagination will be spent on doctoring the expense account, when they would materially increase sales if properly applied. Sales managers are usually convinced that salesmen's expense accounts contain some of the purest and most creative fiction to be found in the language. Probably the essence of good expense account administration is the manager's recognition that some salesmen will beat the game, and that he can only try to keep the overages within reasonable bounds. Due to the high quality and relatively high income level of industrial salesmen, their tendency to pad expense accounts is probably less pervading and urgent than among their consumer goods fellows; but, by the same token, they do a more finished job of it when provoked to try it.

The entertainment allowance is a special target for the attentions of the Internal Revenue Bureau. Probably, the soundest policy in administering it is to require careful reporting of such expenses and to allow only those that may reasonably be expected to contribute to making sales. Particularly to be avoided are spectacular ones and any with a predominating amusement aspect.

Assigning Salesmen's Tasks

Factory smokestack selling once was the expected and accepted thing in industrial goods marketing. Under this system, the salesman was assigned a territory. He was told very little about it, other than its geographical limits. He was supposed to work it on the theory that every factory building housed a potential customer. This system is still not too ineffective in the first stages of selling a new product whose uses have not been completely explored.

While the average industrial goods salesman still receives his assignment of duty in the form of a territory, most firms find it profitable to go far beyond the mere description of territorial limits. At this point, it should be noted that many industrial goods marketers find it desirable to define the tasks of at least some of their salesmen in terms of the assignment of specified customers. Such assigned accounts usually include the larger, more important users of the product, whose servicing is made the task of the older, more experienced salesmen, sometimes even of the executives of the selling house.

The cost of factory smokestack selling tends to force management to supply salesmen with information and aids in organizing and working their territories. A study made by the New York Sales Executives Club indicated that every 100 cold canvas calls resulted in 9.2 orders, which cost $187.39 each; the same number of calls made in response to leads received through advertising resulted in 16.0 orders, costing $107.75 each; and 100 calls made after the prospect had an opportunity to examine the catalog resulted in 38.4 orders, costing $44.89 apiece.[6] The performance part of these figures probably has not changed very much, although the costs have almost certainly gone up. The average cost per industrial salesman's call has increased from $17.29 in 1955 to $35.55 in 1965 according to a McGraw-Hill study reported in *Sales Management*, July 15, 1966.

The importance of training and equipping the salesman and affording him the utmost in selling support is emphasized by a study of a breakdown of the working time of 1,089 industrial salesmen, reported in *Industrial Marketing*, May, 1964. These men worked an average of 9 hours and 15 minutes a day. The typical salesman spent only 41 percent of this time, or 3 hours and 48 minutes, in face-to-face selling; 34 percent of his time was consumed in travelling or waiting; 20 percent went into paper work, making reports, and attending sales meetings; and 5 percent was spent in making service calls. These figures vary only slightly among industries. The highest percentage of face-to-face selling time, 46 percent, was found in the general electrical machinery trade; the lowest, 36 percent, was in the industrial chemicals business.

The salesmen in this study handled an average of 214 accounts—111 active customers and 103 prospective buyers. On each call, they visited an average of four persons. The average number of calls was 8.4 per day, although this figure is not too meaningful since the report fails to indicate whether a call represents a visit to a company or a person in a company; internal evidence suggests that in many cases a visit to a person was counted as a call.

It is the task of the industrial goods sales manager to institute and maintain continuing studies of the market and the prospects in it, to make the information thus obtained available to the salesman, and to see that he makes use of it. Much of this information must be gathered by the salesman himself. He cannot do it unless he is trained to do it; he will not do it unless he is properly supervised; and the facts gathered will not deliver their maximum usefulness for him unless they are properly digested, analyzed, and related to the details of his job.

The information that must be gathered and made available to the industrial salesman is quite varied. It includes such matters as:

1. Changes in the properties of the products made by his firm.
2. New purposes for which they have been found useful.
3. New conditions under which they can be employed.
4. Types of equipment owned by customers and kinds of materials that equipment can process.

---

[6] *Sales Management*, July 15, 1953.

5. Probable changes in the products or production processes of customers.
6. Changes in the products or selling methods of competitors.
7. Rumored or anticipated expansions or contractions in the operations of customers or competitors.
8. New technical information about the products of the employing firm or its competitors.
9. Names of and pertinent personal information about the persons in customer firms whose voices are decisive or influential in buying.
10. Total capacity of each customer to use the equipment, material, or supply made by the employing firm.

Numerous other items of detailed information also enable the salesman to make a planned instead of a blind approach to the selling task.

Part of this information can be collected by the salesman himself; part of it must be gathered by the headquarters or regional office staffs. To be useful, it must be digested, analyzed, arranged, and broadcasted so that what one salesman knows and what the sales executives learn can be used by all salesmen.

Supervision

The function of day-to-day supervision is especially important in the sale of industrial goods. But this supervision must be more a process of helping the salesman and less one of disciplining him than is the case in other fields of sales management. This is because of the high type of man employed, the technical nature of his job, and the importance of each transaction. The individual salesman will work best if he is given the feeling that he enjoys a high measure of autonomy in his work; the customer must be given the same impression if the salesman's prestige is to be fostered and preserved, and control must be exercised largely under the guise of cooperation, support, and help. The supervisory task of the industrial goods sales manager is more completely a study in the finer nuances of applied psychology than is so with the job of sales supervision in other fields.

The sales supervisor's job has many aspects. They vary with the industry, the company, the kind of product sold, the types of customers it is sold to, the nature of the salesmen, and the selling job. It is almost sure to include certain elements.

The supervisor is almost invariably a central factor in his firm's training program, especially in maturing the beginner into a seasoned salesman and in training the experienced men. A salesman, like every other type of worker, is prone to fall unawares into bad habits. It is the task of the supervisor to spot these lapses and seek to correct them. The process of correction usually requires considerable tact and finesse. The industrial salesman is apt to be an able, self-reliant citizen with strong opinions.

Often, he does not respond well to direct orders. On the other hand, his superior intelligence enables him to understand and accept suggestions offered through an oblique approach. Above all, the supervisor's training approach must be suited to the man.

The supervisor is usually expected to help his men plan their selling work, and occasionally to aid them in making specific sales when it seems that the participation of slightly higher brass may be effective. His participation in active selling work should probably be kept at a minimum. Often, he is expected to take the lead in planning the salesman's work, carrying through to the point of working with the man in developing campaigns and tactics for winning the business of individual customers. In doing this, he will probably be wise to maneuver so that the salesman winds up convinced that the plan adopted was of his own making. Able men are generally more enthusiastic about carrying out their own plans than they are about those made for them.

Marketing management usually looks to the sales supervisor to evaluate the men who work under him. He is generally involved in determining merit ratings. Many managements require the supervisor to periodically review the performance strengths and weaknesses of each man under him, and to discuss his report with the man before he submits it. This is one of the less pleasant parts of the supervisor's job.

It is the supervisor's task to explain the company to his men and them to his management. The man in the field cannot always see why management follows certain policies or makes certain decisions or behaves the way it does. Nor can the marketing manager always understand why the men in the field do the things they do. The able supervisor tries to see that company policies and decisions make sense to his men, and that management is aware of the difficulties and problems they face and of the way they feel. This mutual understanding is very important in industrial marketing because of the close coordination necessary among the different specialized, sometimes technical, groups whose actions can influence sales.

It is not always easy for the industrial salesman to maintain his morale. He often must go for long periods between sales. He must call on some prospective customers for weeks or months or years before a break comes that gives him a chance at the business. Much of the time he must negotiate with men further up in the business hierarchy than he is. Some of them have greater technical competence than his. And all of them regard him and his product and his services with critical eyes, and often speak of them with critical tongues. All these things tend to deflate the ego. And the ego is very important in maintaining the enthusiasm that is such an important tool of his trade.

He needs contact with someone who is on his side and has confidence in his capacities. Part of his supervisor's job is to be that person. Thus, his supervisor's work of training, discipline, and appraisal cannot be purely critical, but must be constructive and sympathetic in spirit and manner. It must be designed to build self-confidence and not destroy it.

Most salesmen want to do a good job. But now and then a man goes off the reservation and does things he should not. Often, this stems from an honest disagreement with company policy or procedures; sometimes, it is the outcome of carelessness and, occasionally, of plain cussedness. When this happens, his supervisor must become a disciplinarian. This feature of his job is probably less important in the industrial goods field than it is in the consumer goods area because of the superior endowments of the men under him. But, inevitably, he must do some of it. He cannot administer discipline according to any set pattern. It must be given in carefully compounded doses designed to fit his diagnosis of each individual case.

Finally, the supervisor must provide leadership for his men. Precisely what constitutes leadership and how it is exercised have never been adequately explained. Patton—conceited, arrogant, unpredictable, brash, dictatorial—was a great leader. Bradley—quiet, modest to the point of shyness, steady as a rock, almost completely without color—was a great leader. It is hard to see what common traits made them so.

We are practically forced to the expedient of defining leadership on the basis of its results rather than its innate elements. We can say that it is the thing about a boss that makes men proud of themselves, of their boss, and of the outfit to which they belong. It is that about a man which lifts the men under him out of their limitations and stirs them to perform better than they know how to. Whatever it is, the sales supervisor should have some measure of it, for it powerfully affects the enthusiasm and drive that men put into their work and that are so vital to good selling performance. Leadership is a scarce commodity, and no company has enough to go around. But its scarcity should not discourage marketing managers from seeking it in the supervisors they employ.

SUMMARY

The tasks involved in managing an industrial goods sales force are the same as those in the consumer goods area, but certain features of the industrial goods business change their nature and emphasis somewhat. The selection of salesmen begins with the preparation of job specifications from which a list of desired traits and abilities can be drawn. The main sources of industrial salesmen are trade journal advertising, technical and business schools, and nonselling divisions of the business; sources of lesser importance are newspaper advertising, suggestions of present salesmen, and competitors. In the process of selection, the application blank and the interview are probably most useful, although psychological tests and references can contribute valuable help if properly used.

Informal methods are much more widely used in training industrial salesmen than in training their consumer goods fellows. The subject matter is apt to be more technical and customer-oriented. Most training of experienced men is done on an individual rather than a group basis. The equipment supplied the industrial salesman consists mainly of samples, miniature models, portfolios of pictures, graphs, performance record tables, blueprints, films, and picture slides.

The compensation system must emphasize the salary or drawing account to provide continuity of income and to pay for development work. Various kinds of bonus arrangements and nonmonetary rewards are used to provide incentives. The administration of expenses involves the maintenance of a nice balance between excessive rigidity, which stimulates evasion, and overliberality, which wastes the firm's money and invites trouble with the Bureau of Internal Revenue.

The industrial salesman's assignment of tasks usually takes the form of a territory, although it may consist of a list of accounts. The work of the field supervisor centers around training his men, helping them to plan their work, providing support in handling difficult accounts, evaluating his men, explaining them to his management and management policies to them, maintaining their morale, and providing leadership.

Chapter 15

MANAGING

INDUSTRIAL ADVERTISING

INDUSTRIAL ADVERTISING is any paid form of nonpersonal presentation of industrial goods, services, ideas, or institutions by an identified sponsor. Its management is like that of consumer goods advertising in that the advertiser must measure his potential market, study buying habits and motives of possible users, determine his advertising objectives, set up his budget, select media, and prepare and place advertisements.

However, several distinguishing characteristics make industrial advertising different from its counterpart in the consumer goods field. The profit motive, rather than personal gratification, is the prime buying consideration. Rational appeals must be stressed instead of the emotional ones often so effective in consumer advertising. Industrial advertising is marked by the almost complete absence of the "hoop-la" and exaggeration that often characterize consumer goods copy. The language used must be very carefully checked, usually by technical experts, to eliminate all claims, overt or implied, that are not provable by analysis or examination of experience records. This serves to complicate and slow up the process of preparing copy and reduces the area within which the advertising agency can be useful in industrial advertising. Advertising typically performs a smaller part of the total selling task than it does for most consumer products. The fact that industrial advertising is directed at a relatively limited market has an important bearing on choice of media. In general, fewer types of media are useful to the industrial advertiser. These facts, coupled with generally lower gross margins for industrial goods, add up to a smaller percentage of the sales dollar that can profitably be spent for advertising.

Each year, *Industrial Marketing*, the trade journal of industrial advertising, publishes annual summary statistics of advertising budgets and expenditures of what seems to be a reasonably adequate sample of industrial goods marketers. Table 15–1 shows the figures for recent years. These include expenditures for both advertising as such and sales promotion.

TABLE 15–1

Advertising Expenditures as a Percent of Sales
For All Firms and for Firms in Selected Industries

	1961	*1962*	*1963*	*1964*	*1965**
Paper products...................	2.52%	1.4%	1.8%	0.6%	1.3%
Chemicals.......................	1.95	1.3	1.3	1.3	1.6
Primary metals..................	0.55	0.6	0.5	0.5	0.4
Fabricated metal products.........	2.05	1.8	2.2	1.8	1.7
Machinery (nonelectrical).........	1.98	1.9	2.2	1.9	1.7
Electrical machinery..............	1.80	2.0	2.4	1.7	1.7
Control and scientific instruments...	2.36	2.4	3.5	1.8	2.2
All.............................	1.86	2.0	2.1	—	1.6

* Budgeted expenditures as percent of expected sales.
Source: *Industrial Marketing*, January, 1962 and 1963; February, 1964 and 1965.

The figures in this table are averages from which the percentages of individual firms vary widely. For example, for 1963 the highs and lows in several industries were:

	High	*Low*
Chemical......................................	5.0%	0.5%
Paper and products.............................	11.0	0.3
Fabricated metal products.......................	4.0	0.4
Electrical machinery...........................	6.1	0.2
Rubber and plastics............................	1.9	0.4
Primary metals................................	1.5	0.2
Nonelectrical machinery........................	8.0	0.2
Instruments...................................	5.4	0.5

This variation was probably caused by such factors as new products being introduced, efforts to increase or keep market share, extent to which different firms rely on advertising as against personal selling in their marketing work, and, perhaps, the nature of management thinking in individual companies.

BASIC PROBLEMS

The basic task of industrial advertising is to show prospective customers that the product or service advertised will decrease cost, increase production, improve salability of the end product, or otherwise augment profit. The industrial product that does not promise a contribution to profit is extremely difficult or impossible to sell. If advertising can show that the product's use will increase profit, the task of the salesman is much easier. Advertising can also help the salesman by convincing buyers that the company is a desirable source of supply.

The industrial advertiser's task is often complicated because the thing he sells loses its identity in the end product. Producers of raw materials and process materials are particularly handicapped in this respect, as are, to a lesser degree, manufacturers of parts and fabricated or semifinished materials. This situation makes it difficult or impossible for the advertiser to build up a brand preference for his product, and is one of the reasons many basic industrial goods are sold on a highly competitive price basis, with resulting low margins.

The fact that several individuals in the prospective customer's organization normally have a hand in purchasing expensive equipment and items bought in large volume also complicates industrial advertising management. The maker of component parts or specialized materials often faces the same situation. For example, a manufacturer of precision castings found that since their substitution for machined parts could have a definite effect on the quality of the end product, the decision to use them was often made high up in the buying organization, sometimes even in the president's office. The advertiser must analyze buying policies and practices in the various industries or in the particular plants that make up his market in order to determine the key people who influence the purchasing decision. He must then choose media that will reach these individuals most effectively and at minimum cost.

In introducing a new product or an improvement on an old one, the marketer often finds it necessary to go beyond the primary customer and appeal to the customer's customer. This may be true, for example, when an improved part is developed for a machine manufactured by a prospective customer. Considerable resistance is often met because the machine is already presumed to work satisfactorily and because the immediate effect of installing the improved part will be to increase the cost of the machine. The advertising problem then becomes one of convincing the machine user of the merits of the new part and influencing him to specify it in his orders for the equipment.

OBJECTIVES

Advertising is a marketing tool. In order to use a tool effectively, the user must know what tasks it is suited for and decide which of these tasks he will use it for. The first step in planning advertising must be to decide what its objectives shall be—what part of the general marketing task management will expect it to do.

The objectives of a firm's advertising campaign grow out of the goals of its marketing activity. These, in turn, are determined by the overall company objectives. It is obvious, therefore, that the precise tasks assigned to advertising by any one company are apt to be different from those laid on it by another. Likewise, the advertising goals of each firm change from time to time, both in makeup and in the relative emphasis put on them.

Thus, any listing of advertising objectives we may make can not be expected to apply to all companies. But since advertising is a more effective tool for certain kinds of jobs than for others, certain goals are more or less common to all industrial advertisers. Let us examine some of these.

To Inform

A primary purpose of all advertising is to inform people about the advertiser and his products and services. This objective is more important in the industrial goods field than in the area of consumer goods, because industrial goods are usually bought much more on a factual, logical basis and less on emotional grounds than are consumer items.

If an industrial ad is read at all, it will be read rather carefully. The average consumer reads newspapers or magazines for pleasure; his advertisement reading is likely to be in the nature of an incidental excursion. The industrial buyer reads his trade journal as part of his job, to stay informed. He tends to regard the ads as a source of information and to look them over with some care.

This means that an industrial advertisement can and should contain many more facts than one for consumer goods. A man bent on pleasure has a short span of attention; one on serious business is willing to thoroughly examine each advertisement. This does not mean that the industrial copywriter can afford to stint the task of organizing the presentation of his facts around a central theme, but it does mean that he can use more facts to establish and clinch his theme than can the consumer goods advertiser. Also, he must know precisely what it is that he intends to communicate.

The facts should be precise, documented, and provable. Their presentation can be colorful and illuminated with personal interest and with all the skills of the copywriter's art. But the facts themselves should be solid.

To Bring in Orders

This is an end earnestly to be hoped for in almost all industrial advertising, but hardly to be expected. Very few buyers are willing to commit themselves to the use of an industrial product on the basis of the information that can be supplied in an advertisement. But some may be enticed to place trial orders for small test lots of materials, supplies, components, or auxiliary equipment. After such an order is received, considerable work remains for the supplier before he can count the ordering firm as a consistent customer. He must follow up and try to see to it that his product gets a fair trial in the use test, and that the people in the buying firm who apply it know how to get the best results through whatever procedure the customer firm follows in turning a test item into a routinely purchased article.

To Get Inquiries

Almost every industrial advertisement has as one of its objectives the stimulation of inquiries. Mainly, these may be expected to come from firms that are not currently users of the product advertised. Some may be from present buyers and may concern uses or using processes with which they are not familiar. A few may come from persons in using firms or firms recognized as prospects to whom the advertiser's salesmen have failed to gain access.

A procedure that is practically standard in dealing with such inquiries is, first, to reply by mail or by whatever other means of communication the inquiry is received, and then to turn them over to the salesmen or distributors from whose territories they originated for personal follow-up. That this procedure is not always followed through so aggressively as it should be is evidenced by a study made by the Industrial Publishing Corporation,[1] in which questionnaires were mailed to 8,164 persons who sent inquiries to advertisors in five trade journals. The replies indicated that 88 percent of them received a letter or pertinent literature from the advertiser, but only 18 percent were called on by salesmen, and only 15 percent bought the advertiser's product.

A firm making power industrial sweeping equipment,[2] which it marketed through distributors, mailed four follow-up letters to each of the senders of 1,421 inquiries brought in by advertising during a year at a cost of $45 each. Of the inquirers, 80 percent showed a positive interest and 25 percent eventually bought, but only 30 percent were called on by the distributor's salesmen to whom the inquiries were referred. A fork lift truck manufacturer found that his outlets called on only 39 percent of the inquirers referred to them. That the inquiries were hot was indicated by the fact that 28 percent of them bought.

This advertising objective is especially important in the introduction of new products. A company that brought out a new cord strapping advertised it in 9 publications and during the first year received 5,000 inquiries at a cost of about $10 each. Forty percent of them were turned into sales. A company breaking into a new market found that 23 percent of its new customers attributed their initial interest to advertising, 13 percent to salesmen, 34 percent to other users, 11 percent to trade journal articles, and the rest to other sources.

Industrial advertising can be an excellent means of getting leads for follow-up by salesmen and by other methods. We cannot overemphasize the importance of the follow-up and the unlikelihood of getting it without active pressure and control by marketing management.

---

[1] *Sales Management*, April 17, 1964.
[2] *Sales Management*, March 6, 1964.

To Get Name in Buyer's Resource File

Standard equipment in an industrial purchasing office is usually a resource file that contains the names of all firms selling the articles the office is expected to buy. This record also generally contains pertinent information about each supplier, such as his reputation for quality and service, his financial standing, his price performance, his reliability, and other facts that bear on his usefulness as a source. When bids are to be solicited, invitations to bid may be sent to all names in the file or to a list selected from it. When existing buying relationships are disturbed and new suppliers must be selected, candidate sources are apt to be chosen from the file.

When an industrial goods manufacturer moves into a new market or brings out a new product sold to a new group of buyers, one of his first tasks is to get his name in the resource files of as many of the firms in the new market as possible. An advertisement in the trade journal is usually a good way, since most buyers look to it as a means of keeping their resource files up-to-date. When a firm changes its productive processes or its product line so that its purchasing office must procure unfamiliar equipment or materials, the buyer must compile a list or file of possible suppliers. He is almost certain to consult the trade journal, especially its advertising pages.

To Reach Personnel Inaccessible to Salesmen

Advertising may be effective when the salesman is not able to contact all the individuals in the customer's organization who are influential in making buying decisions. These persons may range from the man on the bench to the research scientist or engineer, or to the outside director who controls the purse strings of the company. A steel company found that in one of its major customer firms 150 people influenced buying. Often, the salesman does not know who these key individuals are, and even when they can be identified they may be difficult or impossible to interview. By contacting them through advertising, the marketer may convince them of the virtues of his product or, at least, influence them to the extent that they offer no serious objection to recommendations made by others whom the salesman is able to contact.

To Provide Supporting Programs for Salesmen

An important objective of industrial advertising is to prepare the prospective customer for the salesman. Industrial advertising may inform the prospect of new products, indicate the extent of the marketer's line, show how the products may be used profitably, and explain the company's position in the industry and its policies toward customers. Preinforming the buyer in this manner saves the salesman's time and permits him to close sales more quickly. The salesman employed by a company that advertises consistently is likely to be received more cordially and his selling task is apt to be easier than that of one whose firm does not advertise regularly. Even the small industrial goods manufacturer, through effective use of a limited advertising budget, can open for his salesmen many doors that otherwise would remain closed. It is true that when a salesman has been calling on a customer over a period of time, advertising is relatively less useful, but when he contacts new prospects and, in particular, when his company is reaching out into a new industry, advertising can play an important supporting role in increasing his effectiveness.

To Reduce Selling Expense

All the factors we have listed tend to make the salesman's work more effective and, consequently, to reduce the cost of selling. The average salesman's call costs about $30. Obviously, anything that promises to cut that cost or to increase the sales volume resulting from the call is well worthwhile.

Effective selling requires that contact with the customer be made often enough to insure continued association in his mind between the seller and his need for the seller's product. In a competitive market, the seller who overlooks this fact very often finds that sheer weight of competitive contact loses the customers he thought were loyal to him. When there is little difference in quality and price among competitive products, even industrial purchasers are strongly influenced by aggressiveness in marketing. To make the necessary contacts through salesmen's visits is sometimes prohibitively expensive. However, because of advertising's relatively low cost per contact it is well suited to the task of maintaining the required association between salesmen's calls. When the purpose of the contact is to build goodwill or to keep the product dominant in the eyes of the customer, advertising is often more effective than are personal sales calls.

There is some statistical evidence to support this reasoning. The McGraw-Hill Company made several studies of the relationship between advertising expense as a percent of total marketing costs and marketing costs as a percent of sales. Table 15–2 shows the results of two studies. Since these studies were done by the publisher of a number of trade journals, their validity might be open to some question; but McGraw-Hill studies have a reputation for being carefully done and honestly reported.

To Help Get News Items

Even in trade journals, news items are more generally read than advertisements. When a manufacturer puts out a new product or enters a new market or discovers a new use for an old product or a new process for using it or adopts a new policy, it is worthwhile to try to get trade journal articles describing it. This is not always easy, since competition for news space is keen.

It would be unfair to suggest that publishers of trade journals allow advertising space considerations to dictate editorial policy. There is no blinking the fact, though, that news items of value to heavy and consistent

TABLE 15–2

Relation between Average Advertising and Marketing Costs

	1961			1963		
	Number of Industrial Goods Firms	Advertising Cost as Percent of Marketing Costs	Marketing Cost as Percent of Total Sales	Number of Industrial Goods Firms	Advertising Cost as Percent of Marketing Costs	Marketing Cost as Percent of Total Sales
Low advertisers.........	297	7.4	11.6	67	11.0	10.7
Medium advertisers......	300	17.6	9.9	63	22.0	8.7
Heavy advertisers........	296	38.1	8.7	65	43.4	8.2

Source: *Industrial Marketing*, June, 1964.

advertisers are bound to receive careful editorial attention. If such items lack real news value, they are not likely to be published. On the other hand, if two equally newsworthy items compete for limited space, one of benefit to an advertiser and the other to a nonadvertiser, the publisher would be more than human if he did not tip the editorial scales in favor of his advertising client. Advertising may not get news coverage but, like the rabbit's foot in the pitcher's mitt, "it doesn't hurt any."

To Establish Recognition and Reputation

The industrial goods manufacturer may find that straight product advertising does not bring the desired result, because his company or brand lacks the recognition and reputation enjoyed by leading firms in his industry. As an example, a manufacturer of stainless steel valves found that although its line of valves had been on the market for two years its brand was relatively unknown. Design engineers, plant managers, and purchasing agents were accustomed to specifying more familiar brands when buying new valves or ordering replacements. Distributors did not find the line particularly profitable and, therefore, did not make a special effort to sell it. In order to increase sales, the company embarked on an advertising campaign with the objectives of (1) building a reputation for its valves comparable to those of the most important competitors in the industry and (2) gaining recognition as a leader in the technical development of stainless alloys.

The main campaign element consisted of trade journal advertising, with heavy emphasis on institutional copy. A new external house organ described the applications of stainless steel valves and castings, and the company's association with important industrial users; industrial catalogs and directories were liberally used. Within two years, the company felt that its specific objectives had been gained because: (1) distributors who had previously been reluctant to handle the line were now trying to convince the company of their ability to sell its valves; (2) every prospect on the sales department's list of important potential customers had placed an order; (3) the number of inquiries had increased 25 fold. In the meantime, the company's stated goal in sales volume had been surpassed by more than 50 percent.

The catalog as an advertising medium can be very helpful in establishing a firm's standing, as well as in supporting its salesmen's efforts. For example, it has been found that if the prospect examines the firm's catalog prior to a call the salesman's efforts probably will be at least 4 times as effective in terms of orders per 100 calls and in terms of average cost per order, as compared with cold canvass calls.

To Motivate Distributors

When the industrial goods manufacturer sells through distributors or manufacturer's agents, one of his primary marketing tasks is to get them to devote sufficient time and effort to the line. The problem is, of course, complicated because other manufacturers whose lines the middleman carries are also competing for the outlet's time.

Advertising can be used in several ways to gain this objective. Copy directed at middlemen may point out the advantages of pushing the company's line, such as wide margins, large sales potential, rapid turnover, or the relatively small investment required. The company may identify distributors or agents in regional or national advertising and on direct mailing lists. Sales leads in the form of inquiries obtained through company advertising may be forwarded to the agent or distributor in whose territory the prospective customer is located. It is a common practice to undertake cooperative promotion either by supplying literature with the imprint of the middleman, which he can mail to his customers, or, less often, by remitting a portion of the cost, typically 50 percent, of space advertising up to a certain percentage of sales.

To Create a Company Image

The industrial goods manufacturer who is firmly established in one field may have difficulty breaking into a new industry, partly because his reputation in the primary market overshadows his entry into the new field. His advertising directed toward the second industry may fail to attract the attention or gain the interest of its intended readers because, in their minds, he is associated with a different industry.

This problem was faced by a watch company that sought to establish itself as a supplier of precision components for military weapons systems. A market survey showed that industry buyers thought of the company primarily as a manufacturer of consumer products. In order to create an industrial image, the company embarked on a two-pronged campaign, one series of advertisements directed at top management and the other at research, development, and production personnel. The same format appeared in general business publications used to contact top management and in specialized journals read by technically trained individuals. The company name was featured prominently enough to gain the advantage of the goodwill established in the consumer field. At the same time, use of a symbolic drawing or design, with photos and copy describing the company's technical capabilities, served to identify the firm as a manufacturer of precision instruments.

To Overcome Prejudice

Occasionally, advertising has the task of overcoming an unfavorable attitude prospective customers hold toward the company or its product. This may have resulted from the company's having produced a lemon. After the technical fault has been corrected, advertising may aid in rebuilding the prestige of the company or product through positive copy describing the difficulty, indicating how it was met, and stressing the product's strong selling points. When a company develops a synthetic product to compete with a natural one, such as leather, rubber, wool, or cotton, it must expect prejudice from users accustomed to the natural product. Marketers of the natural product are likely to foster this attitude through the implication that the synthetic product is an inferior substitute. Here, the problem is one of education. By instructing the prospective customer about the product's use and by supplying technical performance data, the advertiser attempts to destroy the idea that the new substance is an inferior substitute and to establish it as a superior product in its own right.

To Influence Users of Customer End Products

Now and then, an industrial goods manufacturer finds it desirable to advertise to possible users of the end products of his potential customers. This is usually for one of three purposes.

1. The advertising may be intended to induce the use of new products made of materials or by machinery manufactured by the advertiser. For example, the Excello Company advertised to persuade ultimate consumers to buy milk in paper containers put together, filled, and closed by milk compa-

nies with machinery made by Excello, which also furnished the especially prepared paper stock for the purpose. Even though the initial objective has long since been achieved, the company still continues consumer advertising to promote the superior virtues of its container.

2. The advertising may be designed to increase the sale of end products made of materials or by machinery manufactured by the advertiser. For example, a steel company advertised various types of home equipment made of steel.

3. When a material or component is branded and retains its identity in the finished end product, its maker may advertise to the end product users, hoping to induce them to specify end products containing the branded item.

Sales Management, November 19, 1965, reports several instances in which materials manufacturers advertised the branded end products of their customers. A firm selling nickel advertised that certain branded washers, dryers, and washer–dryers had tubs and drums made of its nickel stainless steel. Alcoa has advertised customer-branded aluminum siding, gutters, downspouts, storm windows, and porch lights. The American Viscose Division of FMC Corporation advertised customer brands of products made of its rayon fabrics.

General Considerations

Not all these objectives are sought in every industrial advertising campaign; not all are sought by any one firm. A firm's list of advertising objectives changes from time to time. If it does not, the company probably is not using advertising effectively as a marketing tool, for the marketing task changes as a result of shifts in the market and changes in the condition of the firm and its product mix.

Several objectives are usually sought in any one advertising campaign or plan. But rarely do they all have the same weight in marketing management thinking. If the advertising manager is to do a good job, he must be sure that he has a clear understanding of the goals his advertising is expected to gain and of their relative importance to management. Without this understanding, the tendency is to concentrate effort on the goal that is easiest to achieve.

The marketing manager will be wise to see to it that the advertising objectives are clearly stated and are as specific as they can be made. For example, "to help make sales" is a sort of umbrella objective whose achievement is almost impossible to measure. This general goal should be broken down into several subgoals that, if possible, are readily measurable. Examples might be: to provide leads for the salesmen in the form of inquiries, to influence engineers to specify our product, to inform purchasing officers about our company and our products. With ingenuity, ways can be found to measure the extent to which these more specific goals are achieved. Also, specific objectives supply a basis on which the people who prepare and place the advertising can make specific decisions about appeals, language, and media.

THE ADVERTISING BUDGET

How much shall we spend for advertising? Although the advertising manager is usually expected to recommend an answer to this question, final decision generally rests in the hands of the marketing manager or chief executive. The amount may be determined by several methods.

Some firms plan to spend on advertising a fixed percent of sales. The studies of industrial goods manufacturers' advertising budgets made annually by *Industrial Marketing*, and reported in its January and February issues, indicate that between 20 and 25 percent of industrial advertising budgets are determined in this manner, and that the percentage is decreasing. Most firms that use this method budget a determined percentage of expected sales for the year; a few fix the figure as a percent of last year's sales.

Budgeting a percent of expected sales for advertising makes more sense than does using last year's sales as a base. But neither method can be said to represent the ultimate in good management. Both are reminiscent of the mid-19-century theory of a Saturday night bath, without regard to the timing or urgency of need. Neither gives any assurance that either the percentage figure chosen or the base to which it is applied is the one that will result in the greatest profit to the firm or will make the most economical contribution to attainment of its nonprofit marketing objectives.

Much the same can be said of the practice of budgeting a determined percent of profits—last year's or expected. This practice is probably based on a vague notion that it is a good idea to spend as much as possible on advertising, but not enough to seriously reduce profits. Of course, the same theory might be urged with equal logic for research, purchase of new equipment, and various other activities that generate expense.

About a fourth of the firms reporting in the annual *Industrial Marketing* survey base the advertising budget on the tasks advertising is expected to do. According to this procedure, management first decides what tasks it wants advertising to do and then budgets the cost of doing them. Probably, the process is often a little more complex than this. In the course of planning advertising, several tasks are apt to be considered and cost estimates prepared for each. Management then decides which task or combination of tasks will be worth the cost and are within the limits of the firm's financial resources.

This method has much to recommend it. It forces a clear and precise determination of advertising objectives, for tasks are really objectives. It involves the process of matching the worth of what one wants to do against the probable cost of doing it, which is an essential feature of business planning. It focuses attention on what one wants to make happen in the future instead of on what has happened in the past, as the percentage method does. It forces a recognition that advertising should be a means of making sales or accomplishing other company objectives rather than a result or function of sales or profits, which by implication is its role under the percentage method.

On the other hand, the process of planning on the task basis is not so simple as it sounds. Many advertising objectives are naturally nebulous and hard to pin down. Some, such as creation of an attitude or dissipation of a bias, are of such a nature that it is hard to measure their achievement. The cost figures on which decisions must be made are estimates, and it is not always easy to forecast how much must be spent to achieve a nebulous result. But listing these drawbacks is simply another way of saying that planning deals with the future, and since the future is inevitably uncertain planning can never be an exact science. But we can try to make it so.

The *Industrial Marketing* studies show that between one third and one half of the reporting firms determine the advertising budget by a combination of the task and percentage methods. Probably, in most cases this means that the task method is used, with a top limit imposed by general management in the form of a maximum percentage of expected sales that can be spent. This method is probably better than the use of the straight percentage; how much better depends on the way top management sets the maximum percentage limit. If it is arbitrarily fixed and is not subject to change, there is little or no difference. If it varies according to changing circumstances and is carefully considered, the method has definite merit.

The theory that should govern the amount spent for advertising is fairly simple. The expected gross profit cash inflow sets an economic limit on all expenditures other than factory cost. Theoretically, money should be spent on all marketing activities as long as each dollar spent adds more than a dollar of total gross profit. Theoretically, this dollar of expenditure should be allocated to the marketing activity (personal selling, customer service, sales promotion, advertising), which promises to add the most to total gross profit.

Practically, this theory is very hard to apply, since it involves dealing with a number of variables, most of them unknown. Sometimes, it is possible to quantify the estimates of all these variable factors. When this can be done, mathematic techniques can be used to arrive at the combination of expenditure allocations to the various marketing activities that will contribute most to gross profit. It is true that this result is still uncertain, since it is based on numerous assumptions about factors that are themselves uncertain. But the manager must deal with these uncertain factors in any case, and anything that adds even a little precision to the process is pure net gain.

When advertising is considered for use in achieving an objective other than increasing current profits, the theory is equally simple. If management has decided that the objective is worth achieving, advertising should be allocated the budget appropriation estimated to be necessary to achieve it, provided this amount is smaller than the expenditure needed to accomplish it by any other means. If part of the job can be done by advertising and part by some other tool, advertising should be allocated the amount needed for the part of the job it can do most effectively and least expensively.

You well may wonder what is the good of all this fine-spun theory if the figures are rarely, if ever, available to enable the manager to apply it with precision. It is true that a mathematical model can very rarely be applied with exactness. But if a manager channels his thinking about the problem along the lines of a sound theory, he is much more likely to come out with a sound decision than if he decides on a catch-as-catch-can basis.

APPEALS

Having determined the objectives to be accomplished by a campaign, the industrial goods advertiser must next choose the appeals that will be most effective in attaining them. An effective appeal is something—an argument, a fact, an idea, or an expression of an attitude or emotion—that induces a prospective buyer to react favorably to the purpose of the advertiser. This something will not have the desired effect unless it promises to help the buyer to achieve his own objectives. As a result, the advertiser must learn what his prospective customers' buying motives are—what they hope to gain through the act of purchasing—before he can intelligently select advertising appeals.

Buying motives influence or trigger two kinds of decisions. Certain motives lead a prospect to purchase a certain type of article, regardless of the particular form of it he buys or the firm he buys it from. These might be called basic motives. Other motives lead him to buy one brand instead of another or from one supplier rather than another. These might be called patronage motives. We have discussed both types in previous chapters.

The buying motives of ultimate consumers are apt to be emotional at least as often as they are rational. This is not true of industrial buyers. They are more likely to be moved by appeals that involve thinking rather than feeling—thinking supported by facts that are soundly documented or claims that are or can be proved. It is the job of the industrial buyer to "look out for Number One" in the sense of purchasing articles that will add to the profits of his firm or serve to achieve its nonprofit objectives at the least cost.

This does not mean that emotion has no effect on his actions. But it is likely to mean that when there is such an effect it is against his will or without his awareness. Since consumer satisfaction—the objective of most consumer goods buying—flows fully as much from emotion as from reason, the consumer can often buy most wisely by giving rein to his emotions. The reverse is true of the industrial purchasing officer whose business it is to buy and not to be sold; by giving way to emotion he is apt to defeat the primary purpose of his buying.

In general, the basic motives that lead the industrial purchaser to buy a generic type of product are even less likely to be emotional than are the patronage motives. Materials, parts, supplies, and equipment are impersonal things and do not readily engender emotion. While their suppliers are usually firms, the firms are made up of and are represented by people who may engender love or hate, fear or confidence, or any of the other feelings man is heir to. This means that while emotional appeals may be of some use in advertising designed primarily to get buyers to purchase from one firm instead of from its competitors, they are likely to be wasted in copy whose primary purpose is to induce or increase the sale of a generic product.

A knowledge of prospective customers' buying motives may be derived from a study of their operating methods and the problems they meet in running their businesses, of their buying methods, of their objectives, and of their executives' attitudes and habits of thought. Certain industries are characterized by managerial conservatism. Others are of the growth variety, which means that their managers are more inclined to take chances and try new ways of doing things. Some are very price-conscious while others think mainly in terms of quality. The same differences prevail among individual firms of the same industry.

Appeals Used

At least two fairly extensive surveys of the appeals used in industrial advertising have been made, one by Vergil Reed, covering the years 1924–33,[3] and the other by the authors, covering 1936–40 and 1946–50, and published in previous editions of this book. A very sketchy check of the advertisements in a number of trade publications during 1962, 1963, and 1964 indicates that the appeals used have not changed much. Those used most frequently vary somewhat for different kinds of industrial goods.

Table 15–3 shows the first 10 appeals ranked according to frequency of use for 6 types of goods.

It should be understood that economy does not necessarily mean low selling price but more often means low cost in use, which may result from many factors other than price. Quality is a sort of catchall appeal, including such specifics as efficiency, dependability, power, strength, durability, accuracy. Service, complete line, experience, and popularity are strictly

---

[3] Vergil D. Reed, *Advertising and Selling Industrial Goods* (New York: Ronald Press, 1936).

TABLE 15–3

Most Commonly Used Appeals
(in order of frequency of use)

Major Equipment	Accessory Equipment	Supplies	Fabricated Materials	Parts	Process Materials
Economy	Economy	Service	Durability	Service	Quality
Efficiency	Complete line	Economy	Service	Complete line	General information
Dependability	Service	Quality	Economy	Economy	Economy
Service	Efficiency	Durability	Appearance	Durability	Service
Complete line	Dependability	Efficiency	Strength	Quality	Efficiency
Experience	Durability	Complete line	Low Maintenance cost	Dependability	Institutional
Low maintenance cost	Low maintenance cost	Experience	Institutional	Low maintenance cost	Uniformity
Quality	Accuracy	Low maintenance cost	Complete line	Efficiency	Increased output
Power	Experience	Protection from loss	Quality	Accuracy	Purity
Popularity	Space saving	Cleanliness	Light weight	Popularity	Dependability

patronage appeals. Most of the others are partly patronage and partly basic in character.

These lists are interesting as an indication of the appeals actually used. They can be of little help to the advertising manager in deciding the specific appeal or appeals to be used in any given campaign or advertisement. His choice must depend on: (1) the particular characteristics of the featured product that distinguish it from other products of the same kind, (2) the general plan of the personal sales force, (3) the types or functional groups of people in customer firms the advertising is designed to influence, and (4) the part of the overall marketing job assigned to advertising.

For example, in 1963 the Celanese Division of Celanese Corporation used a three-pronged advertising approach. Some pieces directed at general management used mainly relatively abstract conceptual appeals. A series designed to reach research and development people emphasized the help the division was prepared to give its customers in developing their own new products. A campaign in publications for members of customers' purchasing organizations was more nuts-and-bolts in character, featuring product and customer service information.

In 1962, the Minneapolis-Honeywell Company conducted a survey to find out what people in different technical and managerial groups in prospect-customer firms wanted in advertising copy. It was found that:

Vice presidents and those above wanted examples of the company's performance as a supplier and as an originator of new components and equipment.

Purchasing directors wanted copy that was attractively illustrated, could be quickly read, and featured the company's products and services.

Plant planning and test engineering people wanted clear descriptions of what the company had for sale, without much detail. They preferred to write for the details if they were interested.

Design engineers wanted specific details about capacities and circuitry.

It is very important that the industrial copywriter have a clear idea of the audience the advertising must reach. He also needs to know what part its members, by reason of their functional positions, are able to play in influencing or making the purchasing decision. He ought to know the kind of information about the product and the supplier each of them will find helpful in the work of decision. And he needs to be familiar with the language they talk; for example, the engineer wants to read about technical matters in technical language, while the president or executive vice president wants plain English. If he knows these things and bases his appeals and material on them, he can prepare copy that his audience will read and understand and have respect for, since it will help them to do their jobs.

INDUSTRIAL ADVERTISING COPY

Orientation of Copy

There are important basic differences between industrial readers and consumer readers that must be recognized in order to effectively orient industrial copy. Fundamentally, the difference is one of point of view. Normally, the ultimate consumer reads for pleasure and, in the course of doing so, may read advertisements that interest or attract him. Thus, artwork and catch phrases must be employed to gain his interest and attention. In contrast, the industrial user reads advertisements primarily to help him do his job. He is apt to assume a strictly objective attitude in reading them, since such reading is often done on company time, and resulting purchases involve the expenditure of company funds. Reliable surveys have indicated that industrial purchasers read advertisements intensively—on a par with editorials and articles—suggesting that the more expensive attention-gaining methods of consumer advertising are generally not warranted because the reader is interested in finding facts. It is not to the interest of his company for him to spend time reading industrial advertisements that do not provide worthwhile information.

This does not mean that advertising copy must be dull or devoid of color. Facts, even those of a technical nature, can be presented in an interesting way. Color that attracts the eye and layout that focuses attention on pertinent facts can add greatly to readability. Graphs, charts, pictures, cartoon strips, and human-interest stories serve to make copy easier and more enjoyable to read. While the user reads advertising copy as part of his job, he can have no reasonable objection to that task's being made easy or enjoyable.

Content

The industrial advertiser must determine the important points the prospective buyer needs to know about the product and the company in order to do his job well, and should stress this information in the copy, with supporting facts. Reed's able analysis disclosed the following list of types of information the industrial purchaser needs in order to make an intelligent decision about the purchase of the advertiser's product.

1. Nature and distinctive characteristics of the product.
2. Advantages over competing products.
3. Adaptability to the buyer's needs.
4. Experience of others in its use.
5. Gains to result from purchase.
6. Dependability of the supplier:
    a) as to claims made for product.
    b) as to delivery and fulfillment of contracts.
    c) as to servicing and repair or replacement.

Although in consumer advertising brevity is considered a virtue, this is not necessarily true of industrial copy. Long copy will not discourage the industrial reader, provided it is of interest and practical value. The industrial purchaser is seeking product and supplier news and will wade through long copy if the length represents informational riches rather than mere verbosity.

The effective industrial product advertisement typically contains a sequence of elements. A short headline presents an interesting or intriguing idea with enough significance to the reader so that he will want to pursue the idea further. An explanation or amplification of the headline then develops a limited number of specific appeals, which are carefully designed to show the potential user that the product or service can be useful to him and will fulfill an actual need. The copy then describes the distinctive features of the product, offering evidence of its desirability and proof of the claims made for it. Finally, the reader is urged to take some action, and, where feasible, specific courses of action are suggested.

Trademark versus Institutional Copy

One of the basic problems in industrial advertising strategy is whether to stress trademarks or company name. On the one hand, it is argued that the important thing is to sell the company, its name, facilities, and reputation rather than the importance of individual product trademarks, because once a purchasing officer has developed confidence in the company as a reliable maker and marketer of the products he buys, this becomes his most important consideration in making buying decisions. Furthermore, once the name of the company is well established, the effort and expense of developing brand names is not required. It may also be contended that as a company diversifies its line, and over a period of time trademarks a number of new products, the ensuing confusion and dilution of effort in company advertising makes the promotional task much more difficult and less effective.

In support of a policy of stressing product brands in industrial copy, several arguments are offered. Institutional copy featuring the company rather than specific products or services is apt to be based upon generalities and platitudes of little or no interest to the reader. Headlining individual products, which is implicit in brand advertising, gives the advertiser a broader range from which to draw worthwhile sales ideas. In a real sense, the brand policy may be more conservative. If, after heavy advertising and promotion, a branded product goes sour, the company's reputation is not directly jeopardized to the degree it would have been had the company name been stressed. Also, a branded product that becomes well known may be a means of enhancing the overall reputation of the company. Brands that indicate product use can be excellent headline attractions to focus the attention of potential users. They also may facilitate the firm's entry into areas where the company name is not well known.

The editorial type of copy has been found very effective. For example, a firm's advertisement may be introduced by a statement somewhat like "Here is what the X Company did with our product," followed by a description of the manner in which X Company fitted the product into its operations and the results it achieved by doing so. The advertisement tends to resemble the reading matter in the news columns of the journal. This may have the effect of promoting readership and of lending believability to the material presented.

Legal Requirements

All statements made in published advertisements are subject to the requirements of the Wheeler-Lea amendment to the Federal Trade Commission Act, and to the general prohibition of false claims in the Clayton Act. These laws, prohibiting misrepresentation in advertising and selling, were intended primarily to protect the ultimate consumer against false advertising by consumer goods vendors. But they also apply to the sale of industrial goods.

With most industrial marketers, these legal restrictions are likely to be of secondary importance in assuring truthful statements in advertising and promotional material. Because of the technical knowledge, skill, and testing facilities at the command of most industrial goods buyers, they are able to discover for themselves any product misrepresentations made by those who try to sell to them. Discovery of such a misrepresentation tends to have the effect of destroying the buyer's confidence in the maker-seller. Confidence, based on sound evidence of reliability, is a must in capturing the patronage of most industrial buyers. So, in complying with the laws against misrepresentation the industrial advertiser is simply satisfying the requirements of effective advertising.

MEDIA

An advertising medium is a vehicle through which the advertiser's message is carried to its audience. The consumer goods advertiser has a

TABLE 15–4

Breakdown of Industrial Advertising Budgets

| | *Percent of Total Budget* | | | |
Item	*1961*	*1962*	*1963*	*1966* **
Administrative salaries	8.4	7.5	8.4	8.3
Space in trade journals	37.5	35.0	41.5	40.8
Catalog	16.7	17.9	16.1	20.7
Distributor helps	3.9	2.9	4.3	
Direct mail	9.9	7.7	9.8	9.8
Exhibits	5.6	5.4	5.3	6.7
General management journals	3.4	4.2	1.7	
House organs	0.7	1.4	1.5	
Research	0.6	0.6	0.3	
Newspapers	1.0	1.2	0.7	
Advertising production*	6.1	5.9	X	
Radio, TV, outdoor	0.8	1.5	1.1	
Other nonmedia costs	5.4	8.8	9.3	

* Included in other media figures for 1963.
** Several media not reported for 1960.
Source: *Industrial Marketing*, January and February issues.

somewhat wider choice of media than does his industrial goods counterpart. For example, he can use newspapers, billboards, national consumer magazines, radio, and television—all of very narrowly limited usefulness to the industrial advertiser, if he can use them at all. In rare cases, an industrial goods manufacturer may find it worthwhile to place copy in a newspaper—for example, in the business or real estate section of the *New York Times* Sunday edition. A few equipment makers maintain physical or billboard displays in air terminals. Some TV commercials of a firm like General Electric have, at least, the secondary objective of informing and influencing industrial buyers.

But, in the main, the industrial advertiser must rely on trade journals, general management publications, catalogs, direct mail, and exhibits. Table 15–4 shows a breakdown of industrial advertising budgets by major items of expenditure, as reported in the *Industrial Marketing* annual survey. While items other than media costs are included, the table affords an idea of the relative importance of various media. The dominance of trade journal space and catalogs as industrial advertising media is obvious.

In the reports this table was drawn from, there is evidence that as advertising budgets increase in size, the percentages spent for administrative salaries, direct mail, and show and exposition displays decrease, while the percentage devoted to business publications increases.

Table 15–5 shows the distribution of advertising budgets among various categories of expense by firms making seven types of industrial goods.

You will note that some of these items, such as catalogs, distributor helps, exhibits, and house organs, are commonly classed as sales promotion

TABLE 15–5

Allocation of Advertising Budgets
Selected Industries, 1964

| | | Percent of Advertising Budget Spent* | | | | |
Industry	Adminis-tration	Business Publica-tions	Cata-logs	Direct Mail	Shows, Exhibi-tions	Other
Paper and paper products..	7.2	45.9	17.3	17.2	8.5	17.1
Chemical...............	15.9	46.8	15.7	13.3	7.0	14.4
Primary metals..........	11.0	50.2	14.4	10.9	8.4	13.1
Fabricated metal products............	13.3	39.8	24.6	12.5	4.6	19.0
Machinery, nonelectrical..	13.9	43.2	20.1	9.9	8.2	15.2
Electrical machinery......	19.5	39.0	25.7	8.7	9.3	9.7
Control and scientific in-struments............	17.8	33.9	19.7	11.1	8.2	18.1

* As these percentages are averages of the percentage figures of individual firms, they do not add up to 100.
Source: *Industrial Marketing*, February, 1964.

devices. They are included in many industrial advertising budgets, because in industrial goods marketing coordination between advertising and sales promotion is so important that the two are often handled by one organizational unit, usually the advertising department. Another factor that induces management to consolidate the two is the small amount of the total budget the typical industrial firm spends for advertising and promotion, usually one or two percent of sales. Unless a firm is very large, the total amount involved in either of the two is not enough to command the interest and justify the expense of a top-notch executive. When they are joined together, this difficulty is diminished.

The manager's choice of media depends to a very considerable extent on the audience he needs to reach. The choice is complicated by the number and variety of people who influence the buying decision in the typical customer firm. Top management reads one type of publication; operating management, another; design engineers, still another; purchasing officers have their own professional journals; and foremen, supervisors, and factory superintendents look to publications that deal with their peculiar problems. Some journals appeal only to people in one industry but try to offer wide functional coverage within the industry. The editorial and news content of others is directed to one functional group in all industries.

It is highly important that the media selector study the subscriber and reader distribution of the various media. Most publications are prepared to supply fairly detailed breakdowns of their subscriber lists. Such a list does not always tell the story, since a firm may subscribe for a journal and circulate it widely among its employees. Some publications research their readership and are able to supply a reasonably accurate picture of its distribution among functional groups. When this is not the case, it may be worthwhile for the advertiser to conduct his own research to get this information. A publication, Standard Rate and Data Service, supplies lists of trade journals, classified by trades and with some breakdown of the functional groups into which their readers fall.

THE USE OF ADVERTISING AGENCIES

Advertising agencies are specialist organizations equipped to provide a range of advertising services to their clients. They work on advertising strategy and campaigns, prepare copy and layouts, study markets, select media, and carry out the actual physical production of the advertisement up to the time it is sent to the medium. Agencies usually serve a number of noncompetitive clients.

Most media allow agencies 15 percent on the cost of the space or time purchased. In consumer goods marketing, this commission, plus fees for purchased services, usually represents the total agency income available to cover costs of operation and leave a profit. For many industrial goods marketers, this method of payment does not result in an amount large enough to cover agency costs, and the contract with the agency includes an additional lump-sum payment to compensate for the services wanted. This different relationship of cost to income arises primarily because the space rates charged by business publications are very much lower than those of consumer media with their much larger circulations. Closely coupled with this are the multiple markets involved in the sale of many industrial goods, and the higher cost of preparing a greater number of advertisements, each tailored to a particular group of prospects.

The advertising agency brings to an industrial client a wide breadth of experience in industrial marketing, which can rarely be matched by the experience of a single manufacturing company. It should also be able to provide the qualities of imagination and innovation to an unusual degree. Despite these advantages, agencies are not universally used by industrial marketers as they are by sellers of consumer goods. There are significant numbers of industrial goods manufacturers whose advertising departments perform all the functions the agency is equipped to handle.

The explanation lies largely in the technical and highly specialized nature of many industrial goods. Even when an agency staff includes men with engineering training, a substantial job of education must be done before they are fully conversant with the details of products and markets, and are able to prepare accurate and effective advertisements. Often, copy prepared by the agency must be submitted to the advertiser's technical experts for review. Sometimes, the resulting revisions are so extensive that it would have been more efficient and less costly for the company advertising staff, who are in closer contact with the technical people, to prepare the copy in the first place. Even more difficult for agency preparation are catalogs and direct mail copy; yet these are very important selling tools for the industrial marketer.

Some agencies specialize in serving industrial accounts. Others maintain special units to handle them. During recent years, there has been a tendency for agencies to expand the promotional services they offer and to charge on the basis of a fee for each job done. This tends to increase their usefulness to the industrial marketer.

There is no question that the advertising agency has an important place in industrial product marketing. It cannot perform some types of activities so well as company personnel, but it can do others better or more economically. The marketing executive's problem is to achieve the most effective integration of company and agency resources.

MEASURING ADVERTISING EFFECTIVENESS

Advertising is a marketing management tool. It is the marketing manager's job to combine the use of this and all the other marketing tools in a pattern that will be most effective and least costly. But he cannot intelligently plan the use of advertising or any other tool unless he can measure the results of its use.

Most attempts to measure advertising results do not go far enough. *Industrial Marketing* publishes, as a regular feature, a comparison of two or more advertisements on the basis of the extent to which they were noticed, read, and recalled. But this measure of effectiveness stops at about the halfway point. The essence of measuring effectiveness is to find out what influence, if any, the advertisement has on the thinking and actions of the people who make or influence buying decisions. No surefire, generally applicable technique has yet been developed for doing this.

It would seem that attempts to measure the effectiveness of advertising must be individual to the firm and must start, at the planning stage, with a clear understanding, in detail, of the purposes each advertisement or campaign is designed to achieve. Methods may then be developed to determine the extent to which it accomplishes each purpose. Earlier in this chapter we discussed a number of such purposes. Let us see if we can work out possible methods for checking the accomplishment of several of them.

If a unit of advertising is designed to bring in orders, we can check the flow of orders before and after it appears, compute the change in sales volume that occurs, and figure a cost of selling the added volume. This method has a few holes in it; the worst is that often we cannot tell whether the advertising or some other factor caused the change. But if we can find no other factor likely to have caused it, we are on fairly safe ground.

When advertising's primary purpose is to induce inquiries, the extent to which it does so can readily be measured. An inquiry usually contains internal evidence of the stimulus that triggered it. A cost per inquiry can be computed. If inquiries obtained by advertising are followed up and result in sales, a selling cost per dollar of sales can be computed for the resulting volume, and an advertising cost per dollar of business it initiated.

If an advertising campaign is intended to create an attitude or dispel a bias, it is possible, by conducting attitude surveys before and after publication, to check within reasonable limits of accuracy the extent to which it accomplishes its purpose. It is much harder to determine whether the purpose or the extent of achievement is worth the cost. But before the campaign was authorized, management must have decided that the goal was worth at least what was budgeted for it, and certainly the cost of complete or partial achievement can be computed to compare with what was planned.

If advertising is designed primarily to inform, the same technique may be used in before-and-after surveys of what sample members of the target audience know about the subject matter presented. The cost and value considerations are the same as those applying to an attitude campaign.

We have by no means covered all objectives, but we have dealt with enough to show that it is possible to develop methods of checking the results of much industrial advertising. If a marketing manager insists that his advertising objectives be as clear, definite, and specific as possible, and then applies his ingenuity to developing methods to measure the extent to which each is achieved, he can plan and control his advertising work much more exactly and intelligently. The cost of checking performance will sometimes be more than the measurement is worth. In such cases, there may be some question about the advertising's worth.

SUMMARY

Expenditures for industrial advertising as a percent of sales are much smaller than those for consumer goods advertising. The task of the industrial advertiser is complicated by the multiple buying influence characteristic of many industrial goods, the derived nature of their demand, and the fact that many materials lose their identity in the end product.

While industrial advertising objectives vary according to the firm and the situation, several are most common and most important. They are: to inform, to bring in orders, to induce inquiries, to get the advertiser's name on the buyer's list of sources, to communicate to influential persons in the buying firm whom the salesman cannot reach, to provide support for the salesman, to reduce selling costs, to help get items in the news columns of the publication, to establish recognition for the firm or its products, to motivate distributors, to create or change a company image, to create or change a buyer attitude, and to influence users of customer end products.

The advertising budget is sometimes set as a percentage of past or expected sales. A more intelligent method is to spend enough to accomplish the task assigned to advertising in the general marketing plan. This involves the use of marginal analysis.

The basic appeals tend to be rational, dollar benefits to the buyer or aid in achieving his nonmonetary objectives. Patronage appeals may be more emotional. Industrial copy should be largely factual, and the claims made should be specific and provable. Brand advertising is not nearly so effective as it is in the consumer goods field.

Trade journals are the media most generally used, followed by catalogs, direct mail, exhibits, general management publications, and distributor helps. Advertising agencies are much less useful in industrial than in consumer goods advertising. The basis of good advertising management is the measurement of results. While this cannot often be done with any approach to accuracy, thought and ingenuity can usually be used to devise measurements that will provide valuable guidance in planning and administering a firm's advertising program.

Chapter 16

<><><><><><><><><><><><><><><><><><><><><><><><><> SPECIAL MEDIA

AND SALES PROMOTION

IN THE LAST CHAPTER, we discussed the general problems of managing the work of industrial advertising. In the course of this discussion, we examined trade journals as an advertising medium. Although several other media—catalogs, trade show exhibits, correspondence, direct mail, advertising novelties—are also used in consumer goods marketing, they are of special importance in the industrial goods business. So it seems worthwhile to discuss them more fully here, and also to treat a number of methods generally used in sales promotion, such as distribution of samples, publicity and public relations, and customer entertainment.

INDUSTRIAL SHOWS AND EXHIBITS[1]

The modern industrial show, which traces its antecedents to the medieval fair, is an important tool in industrial goods marketing. It offers the manufacturer an opportunity to display and demonstrate his products to a large number of prospects within a short period of time, which otherwise would not be possible because of the widespread nature of his market.

Exhibitors' Objective

Since it is usually hard to trace sales that result from this type of promotion, the trade show's value to the exhibitor must often be measured in terms of more limited objectives such as the following.

Meeting Potential Customers. A trade show offers an excellent opportunity for the exhibitor to contact special groups of potential customers who are interested in his product. These include supervisory, technical, planning, and executive personnel, who are difficult to reach in their

---

[1] The material on industrial shows and exhibits was taken largely from Holmes Bailey, "The Value of Trade Shows as a Promotional Device in the Marketing of Industrial Goods," an unpublished thesis in the library of the Massachusetts Institute of Technology, written under the direction of one of the authors.

plants or offices but who are influential in making purchasing decisions. Many exhibitors feel that the primary value of the trade show lies in the opportunity to build goodwill among customers or among those who will eventually be in a position to purchase or influence the purchase of their products. In many instances, this is the only opportunity the exhibitor firm's office people have to meet and talk to customers with whom they correspond or speak by telephone. This element of personal contact tends to create a preferential position for the firm in the minds of customers and to smooth relations with them. It is also felt that participation in a trade show builds prestige among buying firms.

Making Direct Sales. While not usual, in a few industries direct selling is an important function of the trade show. The Leather Show is an example. Contracts are negotiated at these shows, and orders are taken for delivery of the exhibitors' products. By featuring specific items in the 1961 National Packaging Show, the Food Machinery and Chemical Company took on-the-spot orders for $500,000 worth of its products.

Building Prospect Lists. While sales are rarely consummated at a show, the exhibitor who keeps a record of visitors to his booth may expect to glean from it substantial additions of interested firms and persons for his prospect file. If these are followed up by correspondence and personal salesmanship, many are likely to place orders that had their initial impetus at the show.

Discovering New Applications for Existing Products. By exhibiting at trade shows, the industrial marketer can sometimes discover new applications for his products. Visitors often come to trade shows with a specific problem in mind, and they spend a considerable portion of their time there in looking for a product that will solve it. The possible application of a product to new needs may be unknown to the manufacturer until pointed out by potential users. From this source of information, for example, a sewing machine manufacturer got the idea that with a slight modification his machines had multiple uses in the light plastics industry.

Introducing New Products. When a new industrial product is developed, the trade show is often used as the medium of introduction. The trade show offers an excellent opportunity to present, within a day or two, complete facts on a new product that could be brought to the attention of the same audience through individual contact only over a period of many months. Most exhibitors regard this as a primary function of trade shows, and they make a special effort to have new developments ready for exhibition at such affairs.

Demonstrating Nonportable Equipment. Many industrial goods are too large or complicated to be set up and demonstrated in each prospect's plant by the salesman or manufacturer's representative. But the manufacturer can afford to display such equipment at a trade show, where he has reasonable assurance that his exhibit will be seen by many prospects.

Meeting Competitive Effort. That competitors are exhibiting at a trade show is a subtle, but nonetheless realistic, reason for taking part. While a leading company in its field may choose not to enter a particular show and will suffer no detrimental effects, a lesser known company may find that its lack of representation reflects on its competitive position. Even the leader may suffer if he stays out too long. That competitors have signed up is one of the best appeals of the booth space salesman. When there are readily observable quality differences in favor of a company's product, it may want to exhibit so that direct comparison may be made with competitors' products.

Hiring Personnel. In periods of high employment, one of the chief functions of the trade show is its role as a marketplace for exhibitors who want to add qualified personnel to their staffs and for men who are seeking employment. The show is sometimes referred to as the slave market.

Establishing New Representatives or Dealers. The trade show gives the exhibitor an opportunity to introduce new representatives or distributors to established clientele and to prospective customers. By having these representatives in the booth during the show, the industrial marketer can emphasize their relationship with his distribution activities, thus aiding their selling efforts. Perhaps an even more important objective is to recruit dealers or agents. These intermediaries often visit shows to look for new connections or new products to add to their lines. The wise manufacturer meets them more than halfway by being on the lookout for desirable outlet representatives and by seeking to interest them.

Scheduling Trade Shows

If an industrial marketer's objectives are such that the trade show promises to be a worthwhile part of his promotional program, his next step is to select the show or shows to be scheduled. This is sometimes a difficult problem, particularly for the manufacturer whose products are sold in several industries. Very often, he finds himself under pressure from groups of customers to buy space in a trade show; their real motive is to secure a contribution in support of the trade association sponsoring the affair. This is especially likely with local shows.

The prospective exhibitor should carefully evaluate the shows that cover the markets he is interested in to determine which ones most nearly meet his requirements. In evaluating trade shows, the manufacturer should obtain as much information as possible about such matters as frequency and location of each show, its audience, its acceptance in the trade, management reputation for good publicity and sound operating policies, rates charged for space, restrictions on exhibitors, and number and type of exhibitors who use the show regularly.

Some shows are sponsored by a trade association and are usually held in conjunction with a convention of the sponsoring association. An excellent example is the Radio Engineering Show, sponsored by the Institute of

Radio Engineers. Others like the National Materials Handling Exposition, promoted by an exposition management firm, established themselves without the trade association sponsorship. National shows are so called because they are sponsored by national trade associations or because the exhibitors sell on a nationwide basis. Other shows are local or regional in scope and are promoted primarily by local chapters of trade associations.

Some exhibitors feel that participation in trade shows should be timed to coincide with the development of new products, services, or ideas, and also with the ability of industries influenced by the show to absorb these new developments. Others feel that frequent and regular participation is desirable in order to build cumulative impact. Policy with respect to scheduling trade shows depends, of course, to a great extent on the overall promotional budget and on the exhibitor's judgment regarding the relative value of the show versus other kinds of promotion. A study of 397 industrial goods firms, reported in *Industrial Marketing*, June, 1962, indicated that the typical firm exhibited in 4 shows a year.

Planning and Operating the Exhibit

Exhibit planning is usually done by the exhibitor's advertising department. In large companies, a full-time exhibit manager may be employed for the purpose. The planning function includes the proper selection and dramatization of a theme, and the preparation of displays, headlines, illustrations, and copy that will attract and interest prospective customers. In addition, the background of the booth must be designed and built or purchased, and provision must be made for packing, shipping, and setting up the exhibit at the exposition site.

Operating the booth during the show usually is the responsibility of the sales department. For many technical products, it is essential to have engineering personnel on hand. Careful planning of the activity in the booth is necessary to gain the maximum benefit from personal contact, demonstration, and discussion with potential customers.

Many exhibitors follow the practice of giving away samples, souvenirs, or information folders during the show. Others feel that such giveaway material—especially when considerable cost is involved—can be distributed more effectively by mail on request to the prospect's home office. It is probably a good idea to give the visitor some sort of material to carry away that will answer most of his questions if he is interested enough to ask for it. The compilation of a prospect list from requests for information or other evidence of interest is one of the most important and tangible results of the trade show.

Follow-up

The importance of follow-up procedure in maximizing the value derived from trade show activity cannot be overemphasized. First, the exhibitor should promptly mail the information for which requests have been received. The people in the prospect list compiled at the show should be contacted by his salesmen as soon as possible.

Second, the exhibitor should critically review his performance at the show, including design and layout, registration technique, handling of traffic, efficiency of sales presentation, and accuracy and completeness of recorded information available for distribution. In this way, repetition of costly mistakes can be avoided at the next show.

Finally, an analysis and redefinition of objectives should be undertaken, and a judgment on the relative usefulness of the show as a promotional device should be formed. This involves an analysis of the firms represented by visitors, the functional positions of the visitors, the results of follow-up work in terms of sales or other marketing objectives, and the cost of results attained.

SAMPLING

Samples play an important part in the promotion and sale of many types of industrial goods. They may be used to introduce a new product; they may be used as a sales tool to gain a prospect's attention and interest; and in basic materials marketing they are often part of the sales contract. When samples are written into the contract, the seller guarantees that they are representative of the lot to be delivered, thus eliminating or reducing the necessity for inspection or testing by the buyer.

Sampling can be used very effectively in the introduction of a new product. Products that are compact, light, and not too expensive lend themselves most readily to this technique. For example, sample lots of newly developed chemicals are typically made available to prospective users as a step in the product development program. Information is sought on (1) possible uses and performance, (2) bugs that may not have been discovered in preliminary use tests, (3) the existence of a market, and (4) the extent of such a market.

In the sales presentation, the actual product may be used as a selling tool. Purchasing agents and other officials who influence the buying decision like to see and examine the article they are considering for possible purchase. It is well established that physical handling of a product is more conducive to its sale than is mere description. A good product, in effect, sells itself.

In some lines, samples are used as a means of gaining an entrée. For example, the pharmaceuticals detailer, a missionary salesman who calls on physicians, regularly carries samples of the products he wants to influence the doctor to prescribe. In return for their time, many physicians expect to receive such free goods to distribute to indigent patients who could not otherwise afford proper medication.

Products that are interesting in themselves or have a dramatic appeal suggest the best possibilities for use during the sales presentation. Many process and fabricating materials, parts, and operating supplies fall in this category. Samples of such supplies as cleaning compounds can be demonstrated in use during the salesman's call.

Samples of industrial goods are distributed in a variety of ways. They may simply be mailed to a list of prospective users with covering promotional literature. This procedure, while insuring adequate coverage of the market, suffers from the disadvantage that recipients may not examine, or perhaps even notice, an article that comes to them unsolicited through the mails. For this reason, some manufacturers follow the practice of advertising samples either through trade journals or by direct mail. Response is increased by inserting a coupon or return card for the interested party's use in requesting a sample. Many authorities believe that it is sound practice to make a nominal charge for samples as a means of imparting a value to the product, thereby insuring its careful examination, and to avoid waste. The waste problem may also be handled by distributing samples through salesmen, who are instructed to leave them only when the prospect appears genuinely interested. In many industries, the trade show offers an excellent opportunity to sample substantial numbers of interested potential customers within a short time.

Sampling as a promotional device may be criticized on the grounds that it is costly, that it has been overdone to such an extent that buyers no longer pay any attention to samples, that something received for nothing is regarded as not worth very much, and that the bulk of samples are taken by the sample hound, who is not a genuine prospect for the product. Further, many industrial products do not lend themselves to sampling because they are too costly, too heavy, or too bulky.

In answer to these criticisms, it can be pointed out that sampling may be a very inexpensive method of sales promotion, since the costs incurred in manufacturing samples should be viewed as incremental expenses. Through proper selection of mailing lists, or by distributing samples through salesmen, much waste can be avoided. The problem of heavy or bulky products can often be solved by constructing miniatures or models that operate like the actual product, but are portable and inexpensive.

PUBLICITY

Publicity is defined as "nonpersonal stimulation of demand for a product, service, or business unit, by planting commercially significant news about it in a published medium, or obtaining favorable presentation of it on radio, television, or stage, that is not paid for by the sponsor."[2] Publicity is generally considered to be a promotional activity that supplements advertising. Some industrial goods manufacturers, on the other

---

[2] "Report of the Definitions Committee," American Marketing Association, 1960.

hand, feel that publicity is a device more effective than advertising, and they look on trade journal advertising as a means of influencing or coercing editors to print free material that will benefit the advertiser. Others argue that editors are continually searching for information of value and interest to their readers, and if such worthwhile information is provided the editor will publish it, whether or not the sponsor has purchased space in his journal.

Some industrial goods manufacturers have been indifferent to publicity. When markets are concentrated and easily reached by salesmen, and when the product is a fabricating material or part or process material that cannot be readily identified in the end product, this policy may have merit. If the company is in a monopoly position, anonymity may aid in protecting that position. It is argued that in these circumstances publicity, at best, can have only limited value and, at worst, may be definitely harmful.

For most industrial marketers, however, publicity can be a powerful promotional tool. It may make a company known to potential customers and cause them to seek it out when they are in the market for products it makes. It may be used to increase a company's prestige and to establish it as a leader in its field. It is especially important in the introduction of a new product or for communicating information about new developments or improvements of existing products. It paves the way for salesmen, making the personal selling task easier, more effective, and less costly.

Techniques in Securing Publicity

Several types of publicity may be distinguished. Probably the most important from the point of view of the industrial goods manufacturer is technical information about the products he makes. It may also be worthwhile to publicize the general merits of the type of product the company manufactures—for example, plastics, steel, or synthetic rubber—or the type of equipment or service it provides—for example, shock and vibration control, materials handling, or air conditioning. News items of general interest about personnel in the firm or interesting information about the company itself, such as plans for expansion, community relations, or programs of customer service, may be worthwhile.

The industrial goods manufacturer typically assigns the publicity function to an individual whose duties consist of gathering and processing newsworthy information within the company or the industry, and making it available to the press. Employees may be encouraged to write technical articles for journals. Some companies have gone a step further and have made time available for highly competent men to write books in their fields. Valuable publicity has been gained by having employees speak before various organizations. Papers on current research or new-product development may be presented before scientific and engineering societies, or talks of a nontechnical nature may be made to civic and social groups. Many companies have found that showing visitors through their plants is an effective means of securing favorable publicity.

Many advertising agencies are organized to handle publicity for their clients, usually on a fee basis. Some companies find it worthwhile to hire a publicity expert who specializes in this type of work; others retain the services of a public relations firm, integrating publicity into their public relations program. The company house organ, when distributed to customers, may be a useful source of publicity.

Measuring the Effectiveness of Publicity

The tools for measuring the effectiveness of publicity are even less adequately developed than those for measuring the effectiveness of paid advertising. However, useful data can be compiled on the volume and type of publicity secured and whether it was favorable or unfavorable. Most trade journals assist in this effort by mailing published releases to the manufacturers concerned as part of their own promotional programs. Advertising agencies often keep track of such publicity as a service to their clients. Also, clipping service organizations may be employed to gather information, and radio and television monitoring services are available for this purpose.

PUBLIC RELATIONS

Public relations is defined as a planned program of policies and conduct that will build public confidence and increase public understanding. It differs from publicity in that it is much broader in scope; in fact, it has been said that public relations is 90 percent doing right and 10 percent talking about it. One may question whether public relations should properly be considered as a method of promoting sales, since many who have dedicated themselves to the field look on public relations as a way of corporate living. Some go so far as to place the building of public confidence and understanding above the profit motive as a basic business objective. No one would deny, however, that there is, at least, a close relationship between a sound public relations programs and a sound, long-range sales promotion program.

To be effective, public relations work must be directed at some specific, reasonably homogeneous group. The general public is not such a group; rather, it is a series of groups each having its own problems and interests, which must be met on a different plane. Each group may be bound together by a number of forces, including such factors as the racial, religious, occupational, political, professional, economic, patriotic, fraternal, and educational interests. A useful classification of so-called publics, prepared by the Committee on Industrial Practices of the National Association of Manufacturers, is as follows:

1. Customers.
2. Suppliers.
3. Competitors.
4. Employees.
5. Stockholders.
6. Creditors.
7. Local community.
8. The government.

The relative importance of each public differs with each industry and, in fact, with each company within an industry. The various classes of publics are not mutually exclusive. One individual, for example, might be a customer, a supplier, and a creditor, as well as a member of the local community. Despite these complications, it is an important first step in public relations to define as specifically as possible the various publics whose confidence and understanding are to be sought.

Planning the Public Relations Program

The planning operation involves two stages: (1) defining the problem, and (2) determining the action to be taken in order to solve the problem. Very often, company management becomes aware of a problem only after it has resulted in some major difficulty, such as a proposal for new legislation, detrimental to the company's interest, which is designed to correct a real or fancied fault. It is therefore important to conduct research that will illumine the inevitable blind spots, which every management suffers, and provide a clear, reliable picture of the ideas specific publics have about the company.

In conducting this research, two basic techniques are available—the historic method of impressionistic observation and the more objective method of opinion sampling. The historic method depends for its success on the experience and perception, or political or social sense of the individual making the observation. To the skilled observer, it provides a means of quickly sizing up a situation with a minimum of effort. Difficulty arises when two impressionistic observers arrive at different conclusions. Action may be blocked, since there is no sound means of reconciling their differences.

The opinion sampling technique, while less flexible and obviously more costly, will undoubtedly yield more accurate results if properly applied. In place of opinion about opinions, the survey provides actual facts about opinions. The intangible qualitative data public opinion is made up of are reduced to a form that can be charted, analyzed into classes or groups, and made more meaningful to management. The process involves defining the public, selecting a representative sample, designing a questionnaire that will yield unbiased results, obtaining the interviews, and then tabulating and analyzing the results.

Having gathered the facts and defined the problem, management is in a position to undertake the second stage of the planning program—determining what to do on the basis of the facts. This is a top-management decision of vital importance. In determining the course of action, executives must carefully weigh the objectives of the company, the facilities available, the size of the job to be done, the cost, and the value of having the job done. When the relative importance of these factors has been determined, a basic plan can be formulated to meet the situation. This plan is then issued as a major policy of the company and, as such, becomes the backbone of future public relations work. Day-to-day tactics must conform to the overall strategy and contribute to its successful achievement. Such a plan is a requirement for concerted and coordinated action throughout the company, which is necessary in order to insure the success of the public relations program. However, the plan must not be too rigid. Public opinion is continually changing as it reacts to what is seen, heard, read, and experienced; therefore, the basic strategy must be open to review and revision as events dictate.

Implementing the Program

The basic philosophy underlying public relations is sound performance in the public interest. No company can boast of a performance record that cannot be improved to some degree. Research may indicate that the company's products could be made cheaper or better. It may show that the company's waste disposal system pollutes the local water supply, that excessive smoke creates a health hazard, or that unsightly factory buildings depress local real estate values. A common source of public relations problems lies in the continual effort of operating officials in a large corporation to make the best possible showing on the current profit and loss statement, which sometimes results, despite top-management policy to the contrary, in taking unfair advantage of small suppliers and competitors. Before any attempt is made to meet a public relations problem through communication, every effort should be made to insure that actual performance with respect to that problem is sound. This involves management's acceptance of the thesis that, in general, the social interest and long-run company interest coincide.

Tools and Media

A sound public relations program, no matter how carefully formulated, will fall short of its objectives if not implemented with effective media. For example, the so-called open-door policy may provide a valuable tool for keeping in touch with employee opinion. In many instances, however, the open door has proved to be a barrier rather than an avenue for communication, and such machinery as the grievance committee or depth interviewing by an outside organization has been more effective in revealing workers' sentiments. In getting management's story across to employees, more positive media include the indoctrination handbook, bulletin board, payroll insert, newsletter, and house organ. Some companies have successfully used public address systems in building employee morale.

In reaching the community where the plant is located, the local press offers the advantage of adequate coverage at minimum cost. In addition, the various types of publicity mentioned in the preceding section are available for improving community relations. But, in the final analysis, nothing is so effective as personal contact with community leaders.

In dealing with customers and potential customers, smaller industrial goods manufacturers rely heavily on trade journals and direct mail, while the large corporation has made increasing use of national consumer media, including radio and television. Finally, in reaching the stockholder the trend has been toward dressing up the annual report to make it more interesting and informative, providing dividend check enclosures that explain company operation and policy, and encouraging direct communication with stockholders at the annual meeting.

Public relations is not a specific marketing tool that may be expected to result in immediate sales. Rather, it is a means of creating an atmosphere or a climate that is hospitable to the marketing efforts of a firm and tends to cause them to be more fruitful. So far as it does this, the activity is a worthwhile contribution to the industrial marketer's work.

CORRESPONDENCE

In organizing the customer correspondence function, the manager of an industrial goods firm must determine whether it shall be handled primarily by the company individual or division most directly concerned or by a central specialized section. In favor of decentralized correspondence is the fact that the writer is more likely to have accurate, up-to-date knowledge about the subject of the letter, whether it concerns products, pricing, competition, credits, adjustments, or any other aspect of the business.

A major disadvantage of this policy arises when the correspondence load becomes heavy and valuable executive time is taken away from other functions, or, conversely, executives may be so busy that they do not have time to adequately handle the function. Further, a specialized section is likely to produce more effective communications than those dictated by company officials, who are not primarily concerned with or skilled in letter writing. A correspondence section is better equipped to write letters that concern several departments of the business and to maintain uniform company policy in its correspondence. Because of its specialized staff and equipment, it is better able to deal with volume correspondence.

Some concerns seek to effect a compromise by setting up a sales correspondence section in the marketing department. Marketing personnel can give its communications with customers and prospects a sales emphasis and flavor and, at the same time, maintain a high standard of letter-writing performance and a high degree of conformance to company policy.

In several ways, effective customer correspondence can be an important auxiliary promotional device. In a few instances, the complete selling task may be accomplished by it. For example, when a machine designed for a limited market is being closed out, it can often be sold in this manner; when operating supplies can be offered at an attractive price, this method of sale is often satisfactory. When goods are bought on a bid basis—for example, by large institutions or government purchasing agencies—it may be mandatory that the seller keep his expenses at a bare minimum; then, correspondence may be the only practicable selling method.

The work of an industrial salesman can be greatly facilitated through correspondence. For example, a letter of introduction preceding his first visit will identify him with his house and will help to break down the natural barrier between strangers. Letters dictated for individual customers and timed to arrive between periodic visits of the salesman may be an effective method of keeping in touch with the customer. This is particularly important in selling heavy machinery and other lines in which purchase is infrequent. When the buyer is in the market only once in four or five years, the cost of continuous personal contact is apt to be excessive; yet the seller cannot safely assume that the buyer will get in touch with him when he wants to make such a purchase. A well-organized correspondence campaign can materially reduce the cost of sales solicitation in such a market.

Mailing pieces, such as advertising reprints, brochures, catalogs, and technical data sheets, receive much more attention when accompanied by an individualized covering letter. Salesmen might be expected to handle this task, since they are in the best position to know where, when, and to whom such mailing pieces should be directed. However, the difficulties are that most salesmen do not have time, cannot write well, or simply do not care for paper work.

A plan that has proved successful is to key the various mailing pieces, and then have the salesmen indicate to the central correspondence section by means of a form card the pieces that should be sent out and the customers to whom they should be sent. This system is flexible in that the salesman can indicate what should be said in the covering letter. When attempting to reach a lower echelon buying influence in the customer's plant, he may appeal to the man's ego by having the letter addressed direct to his home rather than to the plant.

Perhaps the most important area in which correspondence can influence sales is that of handling inquiries. These may be impersonal, in the form of coupons or cards supplied by the seller, or they may be personal letters asking for detailed information. In general, the response should correspond to the degree of formality of the inquiry. While form letters or printed material may be adequate for the more general kind of inquiry, a personalized letter is required for the personal inquiry. In any case, the reply should be prompt. If adequate information cannot be supplied on the day following receipt of the inquiry, a letter of acknowledgement should be forwarded, indicating when complete and specific information may be expected. No effort should be spared in making each letter an effective sales presentation. Results of this type of promotion can be improved by maintaining a tickler file system on sales inquiries and following them up at suitable intervals.

The possibilities of injecting salesmanship into other types of business correspondence should not be overlooked. In adjustment and collection letters, the emphasis should be on reselling a product so as to successfully conclude the sale and lay the groundwork for future sales. The credit manager has many opportunities to exercise positive salesmanship by inviting desirable prospects to open accounts, by encouraging the use of credit, and by writing letters of appreciation for the use made of accounts.

Letters following the receipt of an order furnish an excellent opportunity to promote sales, especially in new accounts, accounts that have been inactive, and large orders. All business correspondence, no matter how routine, should have as its major objective promotion of the idea that the company is a good one to do business with. The relatively small outlay required to improve company correspondence as compared with other promotional expenditures will pay large dividends to the industrial goods manufacturer in strengthening his competitive position.

Direct Mail

Direct mail is a specialized form of correspondence usually regarded as an advertising medium. It is especially useful in industrial goods marketing.

Analysis of the industrial advertising budgets of firms that replied to the annual survey made by *Industrial Marketing* indicates that about 84 percent use direct mail as part of their marketing program. The typical industrial advertiser allocates about 10 percent of his advertising budget to direct mail. There is some tendency for smaller firms to allocate relatively more to this medium than do the larger firms. Relatively larger amounts are spent for direct mail in the paper and chemical industries, as compared with such industries as machinery and instruments. It is not uncommon for industrial goods marketers to devote as much as 30 to 50 percent of their advertising budgets to this medium.

These facts suggest that the great majority of industrial advertisers make some use of direct mail, and that the smaller companies, with limited budgets and personnel, find it especially effective. Direct mail is particularly important where the market for a product is concentrated. Where the number of potential customers is limited, direct mail offers a much cheaper medium to maintain contact with them than does advertising in trade journals or other publications.

Another reason for the special usefulness of direct mail in marketing industrial goods is that it is not too difficult to compile lists of logical prospects. The most common sources of such lists are salesmen's prospect lists, the marketer's own customer records, trade directories, inquiries received from advertising, and trade magazines. Still another reason for its popularity in the industrial field is that results may be readily checked, most generally on the basis of number of inquiries received. It is usually not too difficult to trace these to the direct mail piece that generated them.

Objectives in industrial marketers' use of direct mail are quite varied.

1. It has been found effective in achieving quick distribution for a new product.
2. Some marketers use it to build prestige for the company name.
3. Some employ it primarily as a means of paving the way for a salesman's call.
4. Others follow up salesmen's calls with direct mail to emphasize and amplify points made in the oral presentation.
5. In certain instances, it may be used as a substitute for salesmen.
6. It is often employed as a sales aid to distributors, or is used to convince them of the desirability of handling a product.
7. It may be used as a means of testing the acceptance of new products.

CATALOGS[3]

In Chapter 15, we noted that catalogs are the second largest item in the advertising and sales promotion budget of the average industrial goods manufacturing house.

If a firm has a wide line of products, containing many items distinguished by size, shape, or other features that affect the precise uses to which they are adapted, it will probably be worthwhile to put out a catalog. For example, a medium-sized firm that makes electrical components listed in its 1,000 page catalog some 10,000 items. The book cost $10 a copy, and 50,000 copies were distributed to firms that might be expected

---

[3] Much of the material presented here leans heavily on pamphlets published by Sweets Catalogue Service, New York, N.Y.

to be in the market for electrical items—a lot of money for the company to spend on one medium. But if the distribution was properly carried out, a copy probably could be found in the catalog file of every significant firm buying this kind of industrial goods. The catalog file is one of the chief sources of reference in the average industrial purchasing office.

Even the firm that makes and markets a single item needs some sort of written material, describing the characteristics of the product, to place in the hands of prospective customers.

A general catalog is one of the type described above, which includes all the products of a firm. If a company sells its goods to several trades whose memberships do not overlap, distribution of such a general catalog to all of them is apt to result in considerable waste, since many of the items in it will not be usable by more than one of the customer trades. Such a house may find it worthwhile to issue a specialized catalog for each customer trade, listing only the articles its member firms may be expected to need to buy. A compromise method involves sectionalizing the general catalog according to customer groups so that each section or a combination of several sections can be distributed to the appropriate group as a specialized catalog, or the entire document can be sent out as a general catalog.

Preparing the Catalog

The first step in preparing a catalog is to find out which functional groups in customer firms will want to use it. Naturally following is an attempt to discover what kinds of information these groups seek in the catalog. Both of these sets of data tend to vary from industry to industry and, to a lesser extent, among customer companies. A knowledge of who uses the catalog should determine the method and scope of its distribution. An awareness of what these people expect to find in it should guide the determination of its content.

The purchasing officers of customer firms are almost certain to be prime catalog users. In fact, the purchasing office is often the recognized custodian of the company catalog file. The engineering staff, particularly the part of it engaged in designing work, is likely to have need for catalogs. For certain kinds of articles, the maintenance people and the factory management group are apt to be users. The research people may have occasional need to consult general catalogs and more or less constant need for laboratory equipment and supply catalogs.

Some kinds of information these functional groups commonly seek in the catalog are: who makes and sells what, the product's physical characteristics, its operating characteristics, how it can best be applied, its performance, its service needs, its dimensional specifications, methods of fabrication or assembly, illustrations or drawings, cost data, maker's facilities and services, and, if the product is marketed through distributors, names and addresses of local suppliers. Obviously, if a firm has a long product line an attempt to present all this information in detail will result in a document that is impossibly bulky and expensive. But it may be possible to summarize the most significant facts in each area and indicate the person to contact in order to get additional facts. The catalog builder must constantly be aware that a book that fails to give adequate information is a waste, and he must work out a satisfactory compromise between bulk and cost on the one hand and completeness of information on the other.

The information in the catalog should be presented simply and in language readily understood by users. The language requirement sometimes demands the use of technical terms, but, in the main, simplicity and compactness are earnestly to be sought. The material should be arranged so as to be readily available—so the user can find it where he thinks it should be without the need to master some esoteric classification system devised by the catalog maker.

Distributing the Catalog

The problems of catalog distributon are not always simple. If the book fails to get into the hands of those who need it, it is wasted. It is squandered if given to someone who has no use for it. To locate the persons in a customer firm who can make profitable use of the catalog is not always easy. Often, they are not readily accessible to the supplier's salesmen. Sometimes, he may not even be aware of their existence. Many firms make no effort to distribute to small buyers whose possible volume of purchases is not enough to justify the cost. This may be a dangerous policy, since little ones have a way of growing into big ones, and they may then resent having been ignored during their weak years. Since the catalog usually costs so much, it is generally worthwhile to spend considerable sums in research to determine the firms it will be sent to and the names and titles of the people in those firms whose use of it can be expected to be most profitable to the issuing firm.

In many trades, Sweets Catalogue Service offers valuable help in preparation and distribution. It maintains a staff highly skilled in preparing and printing catalogs. In addition, it is prepared to undertake distribution of the book to key personnel of important buying firms in six functional areas: light construction, architecture, industrial construction, plant engineering, product design, and machine tools. Distribution is made not simply to firms in these areas, but to specific individuals, by name and title, who are most likely to use the catalog. Many firms apparently find that this specialized service enables them to prepare, produce, and distribute their books either more cheaply or more efficiently, or both, than they could with their own facilities and manpower.

Purposes of Catalog

The objectives firms seek to achieve through the catalog vary from industry to industry and among individual companies. The following are the most common.

To Get Orders. Probably very few orders are placed entirely on the basis of the catalog, without the use of other sales devices such as correspondence or salesmen's visits. Undoubtedly, there are some, probably mainly for items in the maintenance, repair, and operations category. Orders received in this way have the advantage that the cost of getting them is comparatively low. Costly as the catalog is, its expense is apt to be less than that of one sales call.

To Develop Recognition by Buyers. To a very considerable extent, buyers rely on catalogs to find out who makes what. This means that the industrial goods maker finds the catalog useful in making reasonably sure that when a prospective customer wants the kind of product he manufactures he will be considered as a supplier. Very few firms find it profitable to rely entirely on it for this purpose. So far as they can rely on it, they will find that they can accomplish the purpose much less expensively with the catalog than by salesmen's calls, but more expensively than by advertising.

To Get Requests for Detailed Information. As was pointed out, it is usually difficult, if not impossible, to include in the catalog complete information about a product, especially if it is highly technical. But enough facts can be given to induce a prospective buyer to ask for more. This opens the door to wider contact through correspondence or salesmen's calls. By this means, the salesman often can establish contact with engineers, maintenance men, and operating executives whom he would find very difficult to reach without the catalog-inspired request as a door opener. Purchasing officers are not always willing to allow such contacts, but they find it hard to refuse a call requested by one of their own people.

To Get Invitations to Bid or to Solicit Business. When a buyer is asked to purchase an unfamiliar article, he is apt to consult his catalog file to find out from whom he can buy it. He may use the information thus compiled as the basis for preparing his bidders list—the list of firms he will ask to submit bids. If he does not buy on bids, he may ask the members of his suppliers list, thus compiled, to submit quotations and further product and service information. The catalog thus helps the manufacturer to be sure of obtaining his chance at all available business. He cannot safely rely on it as the sole means of achieving this purpose, but it is a fairly effective one.

To Get Specifications Adopted. When industrial goods are bought on specifications prepared by the buyer, it is important to the supplier that the specifications used are broad enough so that his product can meet them. If a firm's catalog describes its products by specifications and the buyer wants it as a possible supplier, he may have his own specifications drawn so as to include the supplier's if possible. Then, too, in drawing specifications for a product not previously bought, the purchaser's engineers may start with those of suppliers if available. If the supplier's are used as a model, there is a good chance that his product will be the only one, or one of only a few, that can meet the buyer's specifications when they are completed.

To Get Product Recommendations. Buying is usually influenced by a number of persons in the purchasing firm. Some of them have power only to recommend; others approve or disapprove the recommendations. At some point in the operation, the recommenders will work with catalogs or other promotional material. If the supplier's catalog contains adequate information, his chances of having his product recommended are increased.

To Help Get Approval. The product approval function is usually performed by someone fairly high up in the executive hierarchy. That someone is not always easily accessible to salesmen. The catalog can get to him if the supplier knows who he is and sends it to him personally. If he has it available, he probably will use it, with the result that he is not likely to refuse approval of a recommendation for the supplier's product without adequate knowledge of its characteristics.

The catalog is not the most important tool in the industrial marketer's kit. But its potential usefulness is usually enough to make it worth his while to devote considerable care and effort to its preparation and distribution, and to see to it that his selling personnel are trained in its efficient use.

ADVERTISING NOVELTIES

Advertising novelties are small, interesting, or personally useful items on which are imprinted the name and advertising message of the issuing company. In contrast to premiums, which are used extensively in consumer goods marketing, industrial advertising novelties are not usually tied in with deals, nor are they generally used specifically to induce a purchase or to promote brand preference. Rather, they are typically given away with no strings attached.

An effective advertising novelty should meet four requirements. First, it should be inexpensive. If it is obviously costly, it may be looked on with suspicion by the industrial purchaser who recognizes that its cost must be included in the price of the goods the donor is attempting to sell. Likewise, it is usually desirable to give out an advertising novelty to a number of people at different staff, executive, and operating levels in the customer firm. This would make a costly novelty quite expensive.

Second, the item should be unusual and eye-catching. A good example is a mechanical pencil used as an advertising novelty by an oil company.

The barrel of this pencil was made of transparent plastic filled with a heavy clear oil. Inside the barrel was a cylindrical sinker that moved slowly through the oil in an eye-catching manner as the vertical plane was changed. The company name was imprinted on the sinker.

Third, a good advertising novelty should have multiple impact—that is, the advertising message should be seen by a number of people over a period of time. For example, a calendar well placed in a customer's office or plant may be expected to provide constant exposure of the advertising message to a certain group of individuals over a period of a year.

Finally, the item should be useful. Such novelties as a pocket slide rule for an engineer or an atomic weight scale for a chemist are obviously much better than a gadget that has no conceivable use and is likely to be immediately discarded.

The results of using novelties are hard or impossible to measure. Probably, they serve fairly well the purpose of keeping buyers and those who influence buying constantly aware of the supplier's identity and of the general nature of the products he offers. They can do little more.

ENTERTAINMENT OF CUSTOMERS

There is an old adage that more important business deals are closed on the golf couse than over a desk. The industrial goods seller who overlooks the basic element of truth in this statement is being something less than realistic. The customer who resists a proposal from force of habit when approached in his office may be in a much more receptive mood while being entertained by the salesman or an executive of the marketing firm.

Whether or not to entertain, and the amount of entertaining that should be authorized, depends on the type of selling and the particular circumstances involved. In certain lines, especially when a standardized product is sold in bulk lots, entertainment may be undertaken to the extent that it becomes the primary promotional device. When the product is highly differentiated, or when only routine selling is involved, there may be little or no rationale or justification for extensive customer entertainment. During recent years, the entertainment wings of many firms have been drastically clipped by the Bureau of Internal Revenue, which now takes a very conservative view of the amount and kinds of entertainment expenditures that can be charged off as expense. It is not impossible that in this action the Bureau has done business a favor by putting competition back on a sound basis and discouraging all sorts of fantastic extravaganzas of entertainment formerly justified on the ground that Uncle Sam paid half the cost.

Entertainment may have a negative effect on the industrial purchaser: first, because he may feel it is contrary to good business judgment to accept such entertainment; second, because of considerations of propriety. With regard to propriety, the purchasing official may feel that it is his duty to his firm to purchase the best possible materials at the lowest possible price, and by accepting from suppliers something of value for his own satisfaction or pleasure he is not carrying out this obligation.

An instance in which entertainment backfired will serve to illustrate the first point. A group of buyers visiting New York were entertained lavishly at a banquet and taken to a heavyweight title fight by a firm interested in gaining their patronage. The next day, a competitor solicited the same group of buyers with the approach that as a matter of policy it never entertained customers. The competitor got the business by showing that because of this and other operating economies he was able to produce an identical product at a lower price. The amount of customer entertaining a firm should do requires careful consideration of common sense and propriety, as well as good business judgment.[4]

The same sort of reasoning applies to the practice of giving gifts to customers. Gift giving may occur ostensibly to express gratitude at the signing of a luscious contract or at its completion. It is more likely to occur at Christmas or on the buyer's birthday or some other similar occasion deemed appropriate. For the honest purchasing officer or other executive who influences buying—and most of them are honest—such gifts, if expensive, pose an embarrassing problem. To send them back seems to smack of ingratitude. To keep them may arouse in his boss suspicions about his honesty. Some companies have a firm, announced policy of neither giving nor tolerating the receipt of gifts. Others limit those given or received to a nominal value. A good point to remember about the matter is that business we can buy with an expensive gift can be bought by our competitor with a more valuable one.

SUMMARY

Industrial marketers typically use exhibits in shows or expositions to meet potential customers, to make occasional sales, to build prospect lists, to discover new uses for products, to introduce new products, to demonstrate nonportable equipment, to meet competitive effort, to hire new personnel, and to contact new distributors or agents. To be successful, participation in a show must be carefully timed and planned in great detail, and the contacts made must be followed up.

Samples are especially useful in introducing new products, although they may be employed generally as an aid to the salesman or as a means of

---

[4] Another classic example of this is the story of the salesman whose company's entertainment policy was modest, to put it mildly. He was unhappily constrained by a prospect, whose business he had never been able to crack, to be his companion at the very plush free bar maintained at a trade convention by the competitor who held the business. After an hour of liberal libations, the two left the competitor's entertainment headquarters. As they went down the hall, the prospect said, "Have you an order blank with you? I'll be———if I'm going to pay for any more of that kind of stuff in the price of the product."

describing the goods. Because they are expensive, great care must be used in planning their distribution.

Publicity most commonly takes the form of articles in trade journals. The most effective way to obtain publicity is to create newsworthy situations or events. The beginning of a firm's public relations program is to live right in its relations with the various subgroups that compose the firm's public. This involves careful study of how the company's behavior affects each of these groups, and what they think of the company.

Correspondence is a form of sales promotion activity largely initiated by the customer or prospective customer. If not well done, it is apt to have a negative effect. It should probably be handled by a specialized unit, although almost every unit of the business must participate by supplying information.

Direct mail is a relatively impersonal form of correspondence initiated by the marketer. It is especially useful when possible buyers are few. It can serve almost any purpose that does not involve personal contact with the customer or prospect.

Catalogs are a basic promotional tool for industrial goods. In preparing them, the marketer should attempt to find out what facts the probable users of a catalog hope to find in it, and then put those facts in the book. If properly distributed, the catalog may reach buying influences very difficult to contact by other means. Its main purposes are to get orders, to gain recognition by the buyers, to induce requests for information, to get invitations to bid or quote, to get specifications adopted, to induce product recommendations, and to facilitate their approval.

Advertising novelties are a secondary means of promotion, but may be useful as continuing reminders of the marketer and his products and service. Entertainment must be very carefully managed to avoid offending the customer's sense of propriety and to keep from violating the restrictions of the Bureau of Internal Revenue.

CASES APPLICABLE TO PART VI

PART VII

Managing Customer Service and Relations

SELLING THE CUSTOMER is not enough to assure marketing success. The sale must be followed by the provision of services designed to make sure the customer gets what he ordered when he wants it, and that the goods deliver the benefits promised.

Then, too, with respect to several phases of the customer-supplier relationship the marketer must establish and administer policies that are peculiar to the industrial goods market. Some have to do with services; some are fundamental to the nature of the relationship.

In Chapter 17, we examine the management problems involved in the physical distribution of industrial goods, or marketing logistics.

Chapter 18 is devoted to several crucial problems that often arise in the relations between the makers and users of industrial goods.

◇◇◇◇◇◇◇◇◇◇◇◇◇◇◇◇◇◇◇◇◇◇◇ MANAGING PHYSICAL

DISTRIBUTION—MARKETING LOGISTICS

IT IS GENERALLY agreed that about one half of the total cost of marketing is accounted for by the various activities involved in the physical movement of products from the production or assembly line of the seller to the receiving room of the buyer. These activities include production scheduling, storage, inventory control, materials handling, packaging, order processing, plant and warehouse site selection, transportation, and customer service. Their importance to industrial marketers varies from one company to another, but generally depends on the products sold and the characteristics of the distribution channel used.

A manufacturer of heavy equipment engineered for specific applications, for example, is not confronted with a finished goods inventory problem. On the other hand, such a firm may well face problems of scheduling production so as to meet promised delivery dates. Large equipment may also pose transportation problems if units exceed usual railroad or highway size limitations. Conversely, companies that assemble or manufacture for inventory usually face a wide range of storage, stock control, location, order processing, traffic management, and packaging problems. The seriousness of these problems generally depends on whether the companies are selling direct to original equipment manufacturers and users or to a limited number of stock-carrying middlemen for resale.

With the exception of customer service, the activities included in physical distribution are often referred to as marketing logistics. The analogy between them and the tasks required to supply weapons and material at proper times and places to support military operations is apparent. However, such additional activities as equipment leasing, provision of spare parts, engineering and technical assistance, and financial aid are not only closely related to the physical movement of end products, but also have an important bearing on the ultimate success of a logistics system. This is particularly true of industrial products; many are of a highly technical nature, presenting unique problems of installation, maintenance, and repair, as well as substantial outlays for purchase and operation.

Since these various logistical and customer service activities are often performed by different functional units within a business, each must be carefully integrated with the others in order to produce an efficient overall operation. In the interest of orderly discussion, however, the logistics aspect of physical distribution is treated in the present chapter while customer service is discussed in Chapter 18.

THE LOGISTICS SYSTEM

The concept of physical distribution as an operating subsystem within the larger system represented by total company activity has been current in management thinking since the 1950's. It is now widely recognized that the interdependence of the different distribution functions affords the opportunity for significant cost savings through proper coordination.[1] However, progress in this direction is often slow, due to the practice of splitting physical distribution among traditional functional areas of a company. Executives in charge of these functional areas are understandably concerned with the unique problems of their own departments and do not always take into account the effect of their operations on the business as a whole. This is not a criticism of department managers, because their perception of total system costs and the contribution of various system components to this total is often blurred by the traditional grouping and departmentation of functions.

Production managers, for example, tend to favor long production runs to smooth out operating cycles and to secure low unit manufacturing costs. The effect of such action on the company's inventory burden may not appear to them to be of much consequence. Indeed, if responsibility for inventory is assigned to another department, such as purchasing or materials management, manufacturing executives may have no ready access to data that enable them to compute inventory costs at various levels of production. Moreover, if manufacturing is their sole responsibility, they have little incentive to make such calculations.

By the same token, traffic managers may seek to reduce transportation costs by using relatively slow types of transportation and shipping in large quantities. Without carefully appraising the implication of these decisions, they may seriously weaken the company's competitive position. On the other hand, sales managers often insist on fast delivery service for all customers on all products, without appreciating the effect of such a policy on traffic costs or inventory requirements. Similarly, an

---

[1] Several significant textbooks are now available in this general area. Two of the most recent are: J. L. Heskett, Robert M. Ivie, and Nicholas A. Glaskowsky, *Business Logistics* (New York: Ronald Press, 1964); Frank H. Mossman and Newton Morton, *Logistics of Distribution Systems* (Boston: Allyn and Bacon, Inc., 1965).

economy-minded treasurer who wants to reduce the costs of inventory or prevent an escalation of clerical expense may limit both to the extent that he jeopardizes customer service or prevents the use of modern data processing equipment, which might conceivably speed up the operating tempo of the entire organization enough to save far more than its additional cost.

There is mounting evidence, nevertheless, that industrial marketers are becoming increasingly aware of the savings to be realized from careful integration of the various logistical elements of physical distribution into a single system. This is the result not only of a pressing need for increased operating efficiency, but also of a growing acceptance of the systems approach to marketing.

The Need for Efficiency

The importance of physical distribution as an element in the marketing mix stems basically from the carrying cost of inventory. In the typical firm, this cost may amount annually to as much as 20 to 30 percent or more of inventory book value. The major contributing factors are labor, interest, space charges, taxes, insurance, obsolescence, and shrinkage. Industrial buyers are therefore motivated to keep inventories as low as possible without causing production stoppages or interruptions in other operations as a result of material shortages. A key element in the success with which inventories can be reduced without unreasonable risk of shortages is the length and reliability of lead time, i.e., the period that elapses between placement of a purchase order and receipt of the goods ordered. The shorter and more dependable the lead time, the smaller is the inventory needed to reduce the risk of shortage to a given level. For this reason, industrial buyers typically place a high priority on fast delivery of materials carried in inventory, as well as the certainty of their receipt within a known and definite period of time. Control over inventories can be greatly simplified or vastly complicated by the efficiency with which suppliers perform the logistics function.

The need of industrial buyers for efficient logistical support by suppliers has grown with advances in technology. Increased mechanization and automation of production have motivated manufacturers to push the inventory burden on to suppliers by so scheduling the receipt of purchased materials that they can be moved directly into the production process without passing through a warehouse. As the seller becomes increasingly locked into the buyer's operations, he is increasingly compelled to meet a precise and consistent delivery schedule in order to retain the buyer's patronage. Such arrangements also place a premium on effective quality control by the supplier, because specification tolerances in automated plants tend to be much narrower than in other shops.

Similarly, industrial sellers are motivated by cost factors to keep their inventory investment as low as possible without jeopardizing their ability to meet all reasonable customer demands. Analysis often reveals that no more than 10 or 20 percent of the products offered for sale by a manufacturer account for as much as 80 percent of his total sales, while up to 50 percent of the products carried in inventory may represent less than 5 percent of company sales. Such differing rates of sale cause widely varying inventory costs among products and complicate the problem of inventory control. As a rule, they are the result of product diversification, which, in turn, is often due to intensified competition among sellers and a growing heterogeneity of demand. The last tendency has become more pronounced as industrial buyers themselves have been forced by competition and technology to offer new product lines as well as wider assortments of items within existing lines. A multiplicity of product offerings tends to divide any given level of sales volume into smaller segments and thus increases the inventory burden. For example, increasing the number of products offered from 1 to 3 could increase inventory requirements by 50 percent or more. Even if sales increased, inventory might increase at a faster rate.

Other forces are also at work, prompting industrial sellers to seek greater efficiency in moving their products from assembly line to customer. Perhaps the most important factors are the gradual shrinkage in profit margins over the past decade, important technological changes, and a growing readiness to accept logistics as a basic management function. Profits after taxes (as a percent of sales) of the 177 largest manufacturing corporations in the United States declined approximately 25 percent from 1950 to 1964, or from 9 cents per dollar of sales to 6.6 cents per dollar.[2] This results not only from increased competition in all its aspects, but also from steadily rising costs. The escalation in labor costs, particularly, has prompted recognition that the same type of analysis that reduced these costs in many manufacturing operations might well produce significant savings if applied to materials handling, order processing, packaging, and shipping operations.

Several technological developments have a demonstrated capacity to effect important savings when incorporated into a logistics system. Some of the more striking developments have been the piggyback handling of trucks, fishyback (coordinated truck–ship service), trainship, containerization, and air freight. Improvements in materials handling equipment permit faster and easier handling of palletized and unitized material, both within the warehouse and during order assembly. The availability and use of high-speed computers have made possible the development of wholly new concepts of communication, enabling management to keep abreast of very complicated traffic and inventory situations.

---

[2] Board of Governors of the Federal Reserve System, *Federal Reserve Bulletin*, selected issues, 1951–65. Percentages computed.

The inclination to regard physical distribution as a collection of separate activities has clearly given way to a growing recognition of it as a discrete function that deserves a place in the administrative structure along with marketing, finance, and production. This is evidenced by the attention given the subject in professional and trade literature, as well as the number of leading industrial corporations that have established physical distribution departments.[3] As information about successes in integrating and tying together the various activities in the physical movement of materials spreads, it is certain that top management of other enterprises will seek to incorporate similar improvements in their own operations.

The Components of the System

For discussion purposes, the various physical components of a logistic system can be separated into three broad categories—stationary facilities, the transportation network, and location. A stationary facility may be any geographical location in which there is storage or a transfer of goods from one mode of transportation to another. A transportation network includes all types of carriers—rail, water, pipeline, highway, and air—capable of being linked in the movement of merchandise from seller to customer. Location involves a choice of geographical points, which makes possible the most efficient utilization of both stationary facilities and the transportation network.

Stationary Facilities. The major type of stationary facility is the warehouse. It may serve as a storage depot, a transit facility for incoming or outgoing merchandise, or as a terminal facility for a transportation company. Industrial sellers utilize warehouses for a variety of logistical needs, such as storage of goods in process held temporarily outside the immediate production area, receipt and transshipment of finished goods coming off an assembly line, and in-transit storage and transshipment of finished goods when located at some point between the company's plant and its customers.

The chief use of storage warehouses generally occurs in relation to, and usually in advance of, various production processes. In the equipment part of the industrial market, it is unusual to store finished goods, ready to be delivered to customers, for any length of time. Situations may develop, though, in which a firm produces or purchases a large quantity of a

[3] See: H. Jay Bullen, "Physical Distribution Management," *Sales Management,* May 7, 1965, pp. 41–52; Kenneth W. Hessler, "Design and Phase-in a New Distribution System," *Transportation and Distribution Management,* January, 1965, pp. 35–43; Felix Kaufman, "Data Systems That Cross Company Boundaries," *Harvard Business Review,* January–February, 1966, pp. 141–55.
Some major industrial companies that have organized physical distribution departments are General Electric, American Cyanamid, A. E. Staley Company, Xerox Corporation, Monsanto Company, Du Pont, and International Minerals and Chemical Corporation.

material or component and must store some portion of it for later sale or use. If such situations occur frequently, or with predictable regularity, some form of stationary storage facility is needed. Makers of parts, auxiliary equipment, and MRO items made to stock instead of on order find it necessary to carry substantial stocks, often at widely scattered points, to service user demand.

Transit warehouses, sometimes referred to as distribution warehouses, serve as transshipment points for bulk breaking, accumulating stocks for larger unit shipment, or transfer from one type of carrier to another. Because of their different function, transit warehouses are designed differently and require more flexible, high-speed equipment for efficient operation than do storage warehouses. Merchandise often remains less than a day in such a facility. Consequently, unless such warehouses are highly mechanized their overhead cost tends to be much higher than a storage warehouse for a given level of average inventory.

The terminal and station facilities of transportation companies also serve (sometimes involuntarily) as storage depots for manufacturers as well as transit locations at which shipments can be combined or separated. Although terminal facilities are not under the shipper's control, they are as much a part of a firm's logistic system as the facilities it does control.

The Transportation Network. Available for use as transport components of a manufacturer's logistic system are railroads, trucks, ships, pipelines, and aircraft. Historically, railroads have accounted for the largest share of freight tonnage moved in the United States. The ability of these carriers to move large quantities of merchandise over long distances has assured them the major share of the nation's freight business.

Within the past 30 years, however, the motor truck has grown from a carrier that served limited requirements to the dominant element in the movement of local and regional intercity freight. Moreover, the structure of many individual motor carriers is now transcontinental in scope and includes a variety of services, ranging from city delivery to coast-to-coast operations.

Air freight has also shown significant increases in tonnage carried, particularly during the past decade. This reflects determined effort by air carriers to promote air freight as a regular element of a company's transportation network rather than as an emergency measure limited to rush orders. While air freight has been a satisfactory medium for suppliers of specialty and perishable items, manufacturers of heavy or bulk industrial products are deterred by the higher air rates. However, airline representatives argue that although air freight charges are relatively high its use can often reduce delivery time by enough to enable marketers to cut field inventories and even permit more highly centralized manufacturing operations. Either possibility may effect a significant reduction in the total cost of physical distribution.

Water carriers, like the railroads, have lost tonnage to other forms of transportation. They have been faced with restrictions on automation at the waterfront, wage rates in excess of those in other transportation industries, and selective rate cutting by competing carriers. In recent years, though, improved facilities have enabled river barge transportation to capture an increasing share of total traffic. As a group, water carriers still represent a sizable share of total tonnage moved. Pipelines carriers have sharply increased their share of total transportation revenue since 1950. Due to the demand for economical volume movement of fluids and solids in hydraulic suspension, pipeline carriers have extended their service to areas that as recently as 1950 were not considered feasible for pipeline transportation.

In addition to the carriers themselves, at least two auxiliary agencies constitute an important part of the transportation network. These are freight forwarders and freight pools. The freight forwarder provides a transportation service to the shipper by collecting l.c.l. (less than carload) lots of merchandise at a central point, shipping them in c.l. (carload) lots from there to a distribution station near their destination, and then distributing the goods in l.c.l. lots by truck to their respective destinations. The entire remuneration of the forwarder comes from the difference between the less-than-carload rate he charges the shipper and the carload rate at which he moves the merchandise through most of its journey.

A typical operation involving an l.c.l. shipment from Flint, Michigan, to Key West, Florida, might proceed as follows. The shipment is picked up at Flint by a trucking company under contract with the forwarder, and is carried to an assembly station at Detroit. The forwarder has a truckload of 20,000 pounds going south from Detroit, so he has a trucker carry it to Cincinnati, where he has enough goods consigned to Atlanta or Miami to make up a carload. Therefore, he ships the goods by rail in a c.l. lot from Cincinnati to one of the southern points. A trucker under contract with the forwarder then carries the shipment to its destination. The shipper has only one contract, with the forwarder, although four transport companies handle the shipment during its journey, and he pays the l.c.l. rate from Flint to Key West, which he would have had to do anyway.

From the standpoint of the shipper, the use of the freight forwarder has several advantages.

1. Speed. The forwarder usually ships in a c.l. lot on the same day on regularly scheduled trains.
2. Flexibility. The forwarder is in a position to use all types of transport to gain the most economical combination of speeds and rates. For example, if the nature of the goods permits, he may ship from an eastern port to Texas by trainship—a trip that requires only one day longer but offers a 50 percent saving in rates.
3. Simplicity. The shipper deals with one shipping company.

4. Savings. The shipper gets special carlot service for l.c.l. rates.

5. Tracing. The forwarder supplies the tracing service desired. Since he is a transport specialist, he can probably perform this task more efficiently than can the shipper.

6. Safety. The forwarder may repack shipments that need such service. He also assumes responsibility for collecting damage claims. His specialized knowledge enables him to do this efficiently.

Freight pools are also very useful devices for industrial manufacturers who habitually ship in l.c.l. lots. The freight pool is an association usually composed of a number of l.c.l. shippers. It is organized in the form of a cooperative, and operates just like a freight forwarder but saves for its members the difference between the c.l. rate at which it ships and the l.c.l. rates the members would have to pay if they shipped separately. That this saving can be substantial is evidenced by a comparison of c.l. and l.c.l. rates per 100 pounds on general drug products from the eastern seaboard to the Pacific Coast. If the l.c.l. rate by rail is given a value of 100, other rates compare as shown in the following table:

	Rail	Truck	Forwarder	Cooperative Association
l.c.l.	100	83	73	—
c.l.	44	58	58	55

Location.[4]   It is apparent that no seller can be equally near all customers or prospective customers, and that space and time impose significant limitations on the movement of goods from seller to buyer. In consequence, the location of the seller's production and distribution facilities in relation to those of customers is an important factor in his ability to deal with the limitations of time and space.

As a general rule, industrial companies tend to conform to one of four locational orientations: raw materials, labor, market, or power. Depending on the nature of the production process, the type of materials required, the characteristics of the end product, and the tendency of buying companies to cluster in a given area (tire manufacturers in Akron, Ohio; musical instrument makers in Elkhart, Indiana), proximity to raw materials may be an overriding consideration. For other manufacturers, proximity to an adequate labor supply or to customers may be the chief determinant of plant location.

While such factors as customer location, or the availability of power supplies, raw materials, or labor may have a primary influence on site selection, often more than one location would satisfy the primary need.

[4] Some of the more recent contributions of basic importance to location theory are: Melvin C. Greenhut, *Plant Location in Theory and Practice* (Chapel Hill: University of North Carolina Press, 1956); Walter Isard, *Location and Space Economy* (New York: John Wiley & Sons, 1956); August Lösch, *The Economies of Location* (New Haven, Conn.: Yale University Press, 1954).

This permits selection of the alternative that represents the most advantageous utilization of the transportation network and the warehouse facilities that have been or are to be acquired. Even if the primary constraints of market, power, labor, and raw material leave little choice among alternatives for plant location, distribution points can be selected to minimize transportation costs while maintaining the desired quality of customer service.

Finding the least cost combination by trading off (adding and subtracting) one category of cost from another, such as accepting higher transportation costs to realize a proportionately greater reduction in storage costs, is no simple task. Even in the case of small manufacturers, the multiplicity of possible tradeoffs can be staggering. Perhaps the most effective technique for dealing with this problem is linear programming—a mathematical formulation that assumes that the most important relationships are linear. For example, if transportation costs are linear in relation to volume, it will cost twice as much as one to transport two items of the same bulk and weight a given distance. While the assumption of linearity is not always tenable, recognition of this limitation to the technique should prevent gross errors in its application. Mathematical models often supplemented by the use of the computer can be used in choosing the most economical locations and sizes for distribution warehouses.

THE OPERATIONAL LOGISTICS SYSTEM

The operating logistics system requires not only warehouse facilities and transportation services, and the proper spatial relationship of both to the geography of the market, but also a coordinated group of purely functional activities concerned with the *how much, when,* and *where* of product movement. These are the functions of communication, scheduling, inventory control, materials handling, and traffic.

Communication

The communication element of logistics has both external and internal dimensions. Externally, communication is concerned with the flow of information between the company and its customers as well as independent firms and facilitating agencies that comprise the distribution channel. Internally, communication is concerned with the informational linkage among the various administrative units participating in the firm's logistics system.[5]

---

[5] For good general discussions of information systems, see: William R. Robins, "Theory and Design of the Management Information System," *Systems and Procedures Journal,* November–December, 1965, pp. 24–28; and John Dearden, "How to Organize Information Systems," *Harvard Business Review,* March–April, 1965, pp. 65–73.

External Communication.   Information feedback concerning sales, customer complaints, and operating problems in which the seller may be able to assist the customer are of great importance to a logistics system manager. The seller's exact information needs vary, of course, with the characteristics of the market and the dimensions of his marketing effort. Nevertheless, timely information feedback concerning sales to customers, customer credit, competitive prices, terms of sale, and services are essential for proper management of such functions as inventory control, production scheduling, order processing, and expeditious routing of both finished goods and goods in process within the plant and/or warehouse of the seller as well as through the transportation network.

The external communication system must also produce an information flow in the opposite direction. Since the customer's satisfaction and continued patronage is the end sought by the seller's entire organization, the customer must also be adequately informed of the seller's actions that affect his own operations. The seller's external communication should be designed to keep customers abreast of such information as expected arrival dates of shipments, any anticipated delays enroute, incomplete orders, and substitutions, as well as impending changes in price or design. Such status reporting becomes increasingly unnecessary, though, if the logistics system functions consistently as it is supposed to function. At the time of sale, the customer should be given such information as when the shipment will arrive and whether or not inventories permit immediate completion of the order. The cost of status reporting can reach serious proportions when it must be repeated for hundreds of accounts.

Internal Communication.   The proper functioning of a logistics system requires adequate informational links with the various elements of the system as well as with other functional areas of the firm. This does not mean that every informational detail must be incorporated into a system of formal reports and memoranda. In many instances, verbal communication between the persons involved is the most effective means of information exchange. What is necessary, however, is a recognition of the informational needs and some system of verification to assure that data necessary to the functioning of the system are properly transmitted and received. The most critical information categories are those concerned with product availability (amount and place of inventory), order collection (manner in which orders are placed), order processing, order routing, and credit clearance.

Scheduling

While responsibility for the logistics function seldom includes in-plant or in-process scheduling, complex logistics problems result if the two operations are not properly synchronized. While it is a marketing responsibility to determine how much the company may expect to sell over a given planning period, the production department usually determines *how* the products will be made, *when* they will be made, and in *what quantities*. A conflict of interest between the marketing and production managers may develop over these decisions because of the inconsistency between efficient production—i.e., production in economic lot sizes—and the maintenance of a finished goods inventory adequate to meet the requirements of customer service often desired by sales executives. Even if production were scheduled for the economic lot size, as determined by customer service and a defensible investment in inventory, the question of timing would still remain.

Fortunately, production scheduling techniques are sophisticated enough to reflect the influence on total costs of inventory carrying charges, transportation volume-shipping cost breakpoints, purchase discounts, and other costs not directly related to the manufacturing process. Consequently, it is possible to determine the true economic lot size if management decides it should be done. Unfortunately, determining the exact sequence in which the various economic lots should be produced requires the reconciliation of sales forecasts and desired operating standards for customer service, with the lead times required by the production department to manufacture products of the desired specifications. Conceptually, responsibility for this reconciliation belongs in the domain of logistics management. A logistics manager is the proper functionary to inform the production department about what quantities of which products must be produced on what schedule, and to provide the quantity and quality of raw materials at the time necessary to support the schedule. Neither the production manager nor the marketing manager is in a position to appraise the effect of his own actions on the operation of the other.

Proper scheduling of the production function is quite important, because once set, the schedule becomes a fixed element in the design of the logistics system. An utterly inflexible schedule can lead to unnecessary effort and exhorbitant overtime costs, while a schedule with too much flexibility can result in idle capacity and numerous forms of wheelspinning. A balance between these extremes can often be achieved by scheduling a relatively continuous level of output, while utilizing various transportation alternatives to either speed or slow the transfer of products from one phase of the system to another as needed to match marketing requirements with manufacturing capability.

Inventory Control

As previous discussion has indicated, finished goods inventory is the buffer between plant output and market demands. The crux of the inventory problem is to maintain assortments and quantities of finished goods in stock adequate for all reasonable customer demands, while maintaining a turnover rapid enough to keep the cost of inventory at a minimum. This requires a determination of the proper amount of each product to be carried, as well as a system of information feedback that will enable management to regulate the flow of finished products into inventory.

Determining Proper Inventory Levels. Since demand can never be predicted with accuracy, more inventory than the manufacturer expects to sell must be carried during any given period. This extra stock provides a cushion or safety factor that can absorb unexpected spurts in demand or interruptions in supply that otherwise would produce stock shortages and lost sales. This safety stock represents the real inventory burden, since it is seldom sold out. In this respect, it resembles a fixed more than a current asset. This is apparent in Figure 17–1 which shows the familiar sawtooth pattern of order cycles.

FIGURE 17–1

The Order Cycle

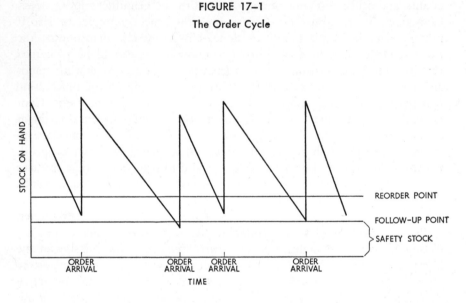

How much safety stock should be carried depends on the variability of sales, the costs of carrying inventory, and the seriousness of a stock-out. A stock-out of a widely used standard item ordinarily represents no serious consequence, because orders can easily be filled in from other sources. While inconvenient and perhaps embarrassing to the seller, the cost of completing an order from other sources of supply is usually nominal. But a specialized machine part with little or no interchangeability is another matter. Sales fluctuations in these items represent a serious problem of control. How much of a buffer management can afford to maintain against the contingency of a shortage depends in large part on the costs generated by various levels of safety stock.

Although some elements of inventory cost—rent, insurance, taxes, shrinkage—can be readily determined, other costs are more difficult to measure. Interest on invested funds, for example, presents a troublesome estimate, particularly if no substantial part of the investment represents borrowed capital. There is no consensus on what constitutes an appropriate rate of imputed interest in such cases. Some managers use the rate that would have to be paid on the funds if they were borrowed from an available source; others use opportunity cost, i.e., the rate of return that could be earned if the funds invested in stocks were applied to some other opportunity (short-term securities or new equipment); and at least a few managers completely ignore interest.

For items of limited life, such as certain types of chemicals, electronic components, and replacement parts, losses that result from obsolescence may be more important than all other costs combined. Unfortunately, obsolescence can be determined with accuracy only after the fact, even though inventory decisions must be made before and during the periods when obsolescence is likely to occur.

It is often very difficult to assign a quantitative value to the seriousness of a stock-out. If the effect is a stoppage on the customer's production line, with consequences that can be estimated, then the cost of a stock-out can be determined at least within a calculable margin of error. If inventory shortages result only in lost current sales and back orders, rather than in lost customers, their cost is the dollar contribution that would have been realized from those sales. Because it is so difficult to estimate the effect of inventory shortages on future sales, the practice of assigning stock-outs a much higher cost value than would be represented by the dollar amount of lost sales is widespread. However, available methods permit fairly accurate estimation of the proper size of the safety stock that should be included in the inventory of an item if realistic values can be assigned to inventory costs and shortages.[6]

The Information Feedback System. Information systems for inventory control may take a variety of forms, depending on the number and kinds of items carried, their speed of movement, and the seriousness of a stock-out. Most of the systems, however, can be classified as one of three general types—perpetual, stock count, or visual.

1. *Perpetual* Perpetual inventory systems provide a continuing picture of the inventory situation, i.e., stock on hand, stock on order, merchandise receipts, and sales. The unique feature of perpetual inventory systems is the collection and posting of sales data for each category of the material or part being controlled. To the stock on hand at the beginning of a period is added receipts of the product, and from their sum are subtracted sales and returns to vendors. The receipts are usually recorded at the end of each working day, while sales and returns are recorded as they occur. The result is a current stock-on-hand figure.

---

[6] See Robert Schlaifer, *Probability and Statistics for Business Decisions* (New York: McGraw-Hill Book Co., Inc., 1959), chaps. 4 and 15.

Most manufacturers and industrial distributors who use perpetual inventories keep records in terms of units rather than dollars. A unit may be either an individual physical item, such as a centrifugal pump or mechanic's vise, or a standard package, such as a box of washers or keg of nails. It is the lowest common denominator of the inventory practical for counting. Perpetual inventory records on a unit basis afford a complete and current picture of the inventory assortment, as well as the quantities of units in stock, without the need for visual inspection. The dollar value of the inventory can always be ascertained by multiplying the number of units in a given classification by their unit price, and then summing these values for as many classifications as desired.

2. *Stock count.* Stock count systems involve a physical count of products at specified intervals of time. They are, of course, unit systems, and stock on hand can be converted to dollar values by multiplying units by their price. The physical count reveals the stock on hand, items to be reordered, and items in excess supply. The unique feature of this system is that sales are derived from the stock on hand at two different times rather than being recorded separately, as in the perpetual inventory. To the stock on hand at the first count is added the net amount of items received, and from their total the stock on hand at the second count is deducted to determine the quantity sold.

Stock counts are usually made with the aid of a stock list on which is recorded the desired minimum stock of each item, the level at which reorders should be placed, and perhaps the level at which orders should be followed up. The stock on hand is then checked against this list. Since there is no item-by-item record of sales, it is difficult by this system to identify shortages or to determine whether stocks of particular items are being carried in proper relation to expected sales.

The stock count system works rather well, though, for staple items, particularly if the stock is arranged so it can be counted easily without crisscrossing and backtracking over the storage area. Since some items do not need so much attention as others, they can be counted less frequently, thus conserving the man-hours of time required to operate the system. Items that sell more rapidly can be counted more frequently than the others. It is often helpful to group together the items counted at the same frequency. One group may be counted every day, another every week, and a third every month. It is a relatively simple matter to so arrange stock lists in a file that the items to be counted each day automatically come to the attention of the stock clerks. Since stock lists are ordinarily much simpler than perpetual inventory records, there is somewhat less risk of error and the system is less expensive to operate.

However, stock count systems function only when the stock counts are made. Consequently, the system is a postmortem operation, revealing the situation of the immediate past but not offering a current day-by-day picture of the inventory—unless, of course, the stock count is made every day. But if daily counts are made, the cost of the system rises sharply and one of its major advantages disappears.

3. *Visual.*   Although the so-called visual system has many variations, all possess one characteristic in common—the absence of any formal record or list of stock. Typically, the amount of stock that represents the reorder level of an item is physically segregated in some way. When the order picker must go to this segregated stock to fill an order, he is reminded of the need to reorder the item. Sometimes, the segregation is more visual than physical, as when the reorder level is merely indicated by a stripe painted on the side of the bin in which the item is stored.

Depending on the physical characteristics of a product and the rate at which it is customarily sold, visual systems may also be applied by use of a bin ticket. A bin ticket contains such information as reorder quantity, code or lot number of the item, vendor indentification, and perhaps invoice cost. Presumably, every time an order is filled from the bin the picker will quickly observe the quantity in the bin and compare it with the reorder quantity on the ticket. If the stock in the bin is down to the reorder level, the picker places the ticket on a spindle or otherwise notifies the responsible executive.

Visual systems tend to work well for items in fairly constant demand and of a size and shape that make for easy observation when in storage. They are usually inexpensive to operate and give an automatic quality to reordering. However, the accuracy of such a system is entirely dependent on the memory and conscientiousness of the order picker. If pickers are deficient in either quality, the system fails.

Even the simplest of information systems entails cost, and any system is of value only when the results obtained from it outweigh the cost of installing and operating it. As a general rule, it is advisable to divide the inventory into classifications based on the urgency of control and to be selective in the application of information systems. For example, an inventory might be divided into thirds, as follows: first part—the 10 percent of the stock that accounts for 30 percent of the company's sales volume; second part—the 30 percent of the stock that accounts for 50 percent of the company's sales volume; third part—the 60 percent of the stock that accounts for 20 percent of the company's sales volume.

These proportions would, of course, vary from one manufacturer to another, but they are not unusual. Depending on the rate of sale and the value of items in these categories, a daily stock count might be used for the items in the first part. These are the fast movers, and the importance of maintaining proper assortments in a fast-moving item as well as the relatively small number of items involved make daily stock counts feasible. A perpetual inventory might be appropriate for items in the second class. These are slower moving than items in the first category, but important enough that a daily on-hand figure is needed. However, they are probably too numerous to justify a daily stock count. Since items in

the third part are clearly the slow movers, visual control would probably
be adequate for this stock and would be more economical than either of
the other alternatives.

Materials Handling

The chief activity conducted in warehouses is materials handling. Like
other functional elements of a logistics system, it must be carefully
planned and organized so as to mesh properly with the remaining parts of
the system. The efficiency with which materials are handled depends in
large part on the volume concerned, the degree of fluctuation in volume,
local wage rates, the relative cost of space, and the success with which the
activity can be organized to minimize idle time, overtime, breakage,
breakdowns, and errors. Modern facilities and the latest equipment do not
of themselves insure an efficient operation, although they are clearly
important contributing factors to efficiency.

A materials handling system includes not only equipment and various
storage aids, but also supporting components and warehouse layout.

Equipment. The trend to mechanization in the materials handling
operation continues, and it is to be expected that an increasing number of
companies will seek its benefits. The forklift truck came into wide use
with the advent of pallets and containers designed to accommodate forklift tines or blades. More recently, the clamp truck, which is capable of
picking up and moving loads not palletized or strapped, has received
substantial acceptance. Both types of trucks are available in a variety of
load capacities, speeds, and widths. Also available is a wide assortment of
towing tractors, trains, conveyors, hand-powered equipment, containers,
time devices, bins, drawers, and other storage aids.[7]

Supporting Components. The pallet or container, together with the
storage racks or other equipment required to stock them, are generally
referred to as supporting components. It is apparent that the pallet or
container size selected must be consistent with the equipment employed
and the design of the warehouse or other storage areas used. Many firms
have redesigned their product packages or containers to dimensions that
permit unitization—simultaneous handling of standard numbers of packages or containers—in the form of a cube or a hexagonal cross-section.
These two forms are thought to be the most effective for maximum space
utilization.[8] Such redesigning can lead to trouble, however, unless the
pallet package design also fits into the dimensions of transportation vehicles and the materials handling systems of customers.

Warehouse Layout. Layout of the warehouse involves space utilization
planning so as to achieve an orderly flow of materials from receiving, to

[7] See Robert M. Sutton, "Physical Distribution for Profit . . . Or Loss," *Transportation and Distribution Management*, August, 1965, pp. 19–24.

[8] "Product Flow," *Transportation and Distribution Management*, March, 1962, pp.
21–23.

storage, to order selection (which sometimes includes packaging or re-packaging), to shipping areas at minimal cost. Ineffective planning of space utilization can incorporate into materials handling systems a cost penalty that may be extremely difficult to overcome. As a general rule, space utilization is most efficient if goods can be moved in one direction through the warehouse, while some materials are still permitted to bypass one or more stages of the storage process. For example, it is usually advisable to expedite the handling of materials with a rapid turnover by so arranging layout that they can be moved directly from inbound transportation vehicles to the order selection and assembly area. By the same token, layouts should be planned to avoid crosshauling within areas and to make possible the concentration of the greatest quantity of stock at the point of greatest need. This serves to expedite order picking as well as movement to the next stage of the logistics function.

Layout of the storage area itself includes the pattern of storage locations as well as the surrounding network of aisleways. As a general rule, stock placement should be guided by the activity of the item, size per unit, compatibility with items stored in adjacent locations—e.g., nuts and bolts—and consistency with one directional traffic flow. The relative emphasis each of these factors should receive is, in turn, influenced by the system of order selection that has been chosen or is under consideration.

Order selection systems tend to belong to one of three general types: out and back, picker, or conveyor. The so-called out and back type of order selection makes use of forklift trucks and is generally appropriate where items are picked in large quantities. Order picker selection, on the other hand, is typically used for the selection of small items, i.e., manpower is used to pick and transport the items selected. Where the activity of the stock warrants a higher degree of automation, conveyors are often used in combination with pickers. In this instance, the pickers are stationed at various intervals along the conveyor, and transfer items ordered from storage racks in their assigned areas by hand to the conveyor.

Which of these selection methods is most appropriate depends on the weight and bulk of the item stored, the number of units typically included in an order, the frequency with which the item is ordered—i.e., activity—and the distance over which it must be transported to reach the next stage in the materials handling operation. Since each of these factors can usually be assigned a quantitative value, it is possible to develop an index number that can serve as a useful guide in arriving at the best combination of storage pattern and selection procedure.

Traffic Management[9]

The traffic function can be divided into two general areas of responsibility—traffic planning and traffic analysis. Traffic planning is concerned

[9] An updated and highly competent treatment of this subject is contained in Charles A. Taff, *Management of Traffic and Physical Distribution* (Homewood, Ill.:

with the use of transportation services, whereas traffic analysis deals with the evaluation of these services in terms of the efficiency of the logistics system. In many firms, the cost of transportation is the largest component in the total cost of logistics. However, the significance of transportation costs should not overshadow the importance of planning the service so that it is compatible with the overall logistics pattern of the firm.

Traffic Planning. Traffic planning involves the selection of carriers, documentation of shipments, payment of carrier charges, establishment of standards for carrier performance, and designation of action to be taken in the event of substandard performance. The documentation and information feedback, which provide data for specific comparison of traffic performance with standards, are of particular importance.

The basic documents of transportation are the bill of lading, the freight bill, and the freight claim. In general, they provide for proper identification of shipment, billing of freight charges, and adjustment of charges incorrectly billed as well as the settlement of claims resulting from loss or damage to products during shipment. These documents represent the legally enforceable obligation of carrier and shipper to each other, and they supply the information on carrier performance necessary to detect deviations from the shipper's performance standards.

The three most important indexes of carrier performance are billing, delivery time, and condition of delivered goods. Since carriers are not bound by rate quotations or routing promises made by their representatives, shippers must maintain their own traffic files and updated rate lists to assure that the rates they are charged are correct. To minimize the time and effort necessary to audit freight bills, many shippers confine their audits to bills above a certain dollar amount or engage the services of an independent traffic consultant.

In order to stay informed about the performance of hired carriers, traffic managers utilize an assortment of reports. The most common probably are the freight allocation report, the damage report, and the transit time report. Freight allocation reports indicate the amounts of freight offered by the shipper to various carriers, and can often be instrumental in exacting the desired level of performance from carriers. Damage reports are usually filed by customers at the request of the shipper, and not only assure that customers are compensated for goods damaged in transit, but also over time produce a record of the carrier's efficiency in handling merchandise.

Transit time reports are also typically submitted by the customer at the request of the shipper in order to reveal the consistency with which the carrier maintains a given delivery schedule. A basic traffic management objective is to standardize transit time from carriers. If the time required to deliver goods from seller to buyer can be predicted with accuracy, one

Richard D. Irwin, Inc., 1964). See, also: Heskett, Ivie, and Glaskowsky, *op. cit.*, pp. 416–43; and Mossman and Morton, *op. cit.*, Appendix B.

of the variables of inventory control is eliminated for the buyer, and an important sales appeal is created for the seller.

Traffic Investigation. Over time, the services of a hired carrier may deteriorate, and the shipper may be confronted with the necessity of a thorough reappraisal of the transportation function. In order to avoid the possibility that such decisions will be made without adequate investigation, a continuous program of traffic analysis is often advisable as an integral part of the logistics function. Such a program might include such projects as periodic estimates of the total cost of transportation, assessing the cost of privately owned transportation, and/or identifying the factors that influence rates as well as the course of rate negotiation.

The total cost of transportation is not reflected in published rates or accessorial charges; it must be estimated. Included in the total cost figure are such items as loading and unloading costs, packaging and dunnage, in-transit loss or damage not covered by carrier liability, obsolescence or deterioration of products due to transit time, and time devoted by management to the control of contract transportation services.

Loading and unloading costs alone could make a low-quoted rate the highest cost between two points. Different carriers require different types of loading facilities, and some offer more loading assistance than others. Moreover, the extra charges for this assistance tend to vary with the type of loading procedure employed by both buyer and shipper. In nearly all cases, no service of this kind is included in published rates.

Although carriers normally prescribe minimum specifications for packaging, the important consideration is the susceptibility of a product to damage. If products are highly susceptible to damage, it may be necessary to provide additional bracing or other protective devices, i.e., dunnage, for safe shipment. While some carriers provide crossbracing and compartmentized vehicles to reduce the possibility of damage, others do not. If not, dunnage must be furnished by the shipper and included in the cost of the transportation function. By the same token, shippers incur additional insurance costs if the carrier has quoted released value rates, i.e., rates under which the carrier's liability in a given shipment is limited to a certain amount.

A continuous program of traffic investigation might also include feasibility studies of owned versus hired transportation, as well as means for negotiating lower quoted rates. To many industrial firms, particularly the larger ones, owned transportation offers significant advantages. It gives the shipper more control over transit time, greater flexibility in adapting the service to the need and special equipment of customers, and a reduction in paper work associated with maintaining tariff files and allocation records, preparing bills of lading, and submitting claims.

Matched against these advantages, though, are costs that require careful appraisal. An owned transportation service requires a capital investment, and both the investment and the manpower needed to operate the service must be efficiently managed. Moreover, the management problems themselves run the gamut from insufficient equipment versus idle time to complex labor relations problems. The labor aspect can be a formidable drawback to a firm with no experience in managing a transportation facility.

Investigating the rate-making process with a view to securing either a downward adjustment of rates or a rate structure that includes more service is probably undertaken to some degree by all large shippers. While rate making is a very complex subject, well beyond the scope of the present discussion, it should suffice to say that rate adjustment is not a panacea for transportation problems, nor are negotiations aimed at securing rate reductions without their elements of risk and cost.

Analysis of the System

The Hypo Company, a creation of the General Electric Company's marketing service staff, provides a simplified example of an operating logistics system and offers a useful basis for discussing analysis of the total system's performance.[10] The company is assumed to have annual sales of $50 million through the manufacture of 500,000 units of a product selling for $100 each. Its plant is located in Indianapolis, and it sells to 10,000 customers scattered across the United States. A summary of the savings of nearly $3 million to be gained as a result of a change in the distribution process of the Hypo Company is shown in Figure 17–2. The explanation of

FIGURE 17–2

Summary of Hypo Company Distribution Cost Savings

1. Reducing the number of distribution points from 100 to 25 . . . .$1,460,000
2. Cutting warehouse replenishment time from 25 days to 10 days   811,000
3. Stocking slowest moving items in only 5 key warehouses   146,000
4. Stepping up the manufacturing cycle from 3 weeks to 1 week   506,000
   Total Savings $2,923,000

the detail for each of the four components is given in Table 17–1 and figures 17–3 through 17–5. It will be noted in Table 17–1 that as the number of warehouses decreases transportation costs go up, while inventory investment and annual costs of investment, plus handling and paper work costs go down. Also, the percentage of the market reached the first day after receiving the order decreases, but only to 90 percent for a level of 25 warehouses. The other 10 percent of the market can be reached with deliveries the second day after receiving the order. Total distribution cost is shown at the bottom of the columns, and a saving of $1.46 million is possible, using 25 instead of 100 warehouses.

---

[10] "The Case for 90 Per Cent Satisfaction," *Business Week*, January 14, 1961, pp. 2–85.

TABLE 17–1

To Reach the U.S. Market Hypo Company Found This Pattern

	Number of Warehouses				
	100	50	25	17	5
Percent of market reached:					
(1) First day after receiving order....................	99%	96%	90%	81%	33%
Percent of market reached:					
(2) Second day after receiving order	1	4	10	16	53
(3) Annual transportation costs....................	$ 1,847,000	$ 1,934,000	$2,082,000	$2,211,000	$2,632,000
(4) Amount of inventory investment................	14,418,000	11,423,000	9,079,000	8,004,000	5,475,000
(5) Annual cost (at 22% of investment)	3,172,000	2,513,000	1,997,000	1,761,000	1,205,000
(6) Handling and paper work costs.................	1,281,000	953,000	771,000	724,000	638,000
(7) Percent of market reached on second day (100% product availability)..........................	100%	100%	100%	97%	86%
(8) Total Distribution Cost (Lines 3, 5, and 6)......	$ 6,300,000	$ 5,400,000	$ 4,840,000	$4,693,000	$4,475,000

Result—Hypo found that it could save $1,460,000 by using only 25 warehouses ($6,300,000 minus $4,840,000).

As the second step, shown in Figure 17–3, the Hypo Company cut its warehouse ordering cycle from 2 weeks to every day, thus making possible a drop in replenishment time from 25 to 10 days. This made possible a substantial cut in inventory levels and a saving of $811,000 in cost of maintaining inventory.

Selective stocking of slow-moving items of types "C" and "D" at 5 warehouses, as indicated in Figure 17–4, yielded savings of $146,000. These represented 85 percent of the total items stocked and 33 percent of

FIGURE 17–3

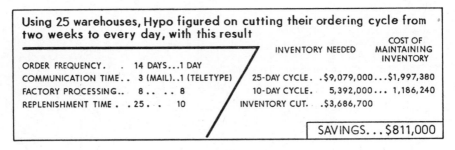

Using 25 warehouses, Hypo figured on cutting their ordering cycle from two weeks to every day, with this result

		INVENTORY NEEDED	COST OF MAINTAINING INVENTORY
ORDER FREQUENCY.	14 DAYS...1 DAY		
COMMUNICATION TIME..	3 (MAIL)..1 (TELETYPE)	25-DAY CYCLE. .$9,079,000...$1,997,380	
FACTORY PROCESSING..	8 8	10-DAY CYCLE. 5,392,000... 1,186,240	
REPLENISHMENT TIME . . 25 . . 10		INVENTORY CUT. .$3,686,700	

SAVINGS...$811,000

FIGURE 17–4

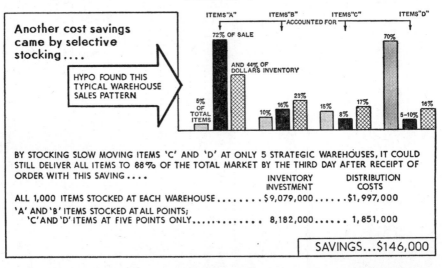

Another cost savings came by selective stocking....

HYPO FOUND THIS TYPICAL WAREHOUSE SALES PATTERN

ITEMS "A" ITEMS "B" ITEMS "C" ITEMS "D"
ACCOUNTED FOR

72% OF SALE
70%
AND 44% OF DOLLARS INVENTORY
5% OF TOTAL ITEMS 10% 16% 23% 15% 8% 17% 5–10% 16%

BY STOCKING SLOW MOVING ITEMS 'C' AND 'D' AT ONLY 5 STRATEGIC WAREHOUSES, IT COULD STILL DELIVER ALL ITEMS TO 88% OF THE TOTAL MARKET BY THE THIRD DAY AFTER RECEIPT OF ORDER WITH THIS SAVING ....

	INVENTORY INVESTMENT	DISTRIBUTION COSTS
ALL 1,000 ITEMS STOCKED AT EACH WAREHOUSE........$9,079,000.....$1,997,000		
'A' AND 'B' ITEMS STOCKED AT ALL POINTS; 'C' AND 'D' ITEMS AT FIVE POINTS ONLY.............8,182,000...... 1,851,000		

SAVINGS...$146,000

FIGURE 17–5

Hypo found factory inventories could be cut if each item were made each week, instead of every three weeks

	NEEDED FACTORY INVENTORY	COST OF CARRYING AND HANDLING INVENTORY
ALL ITEMS MADE EVERY THREE WEEKS. ....$3,970,000....... .$873,400		
ALL ITEMS MADE EVERY WEEK 1,670,000 367,400		

SAVINGS...$506,000

the inventory, but accounted for only about 15 percent of Hypo's sales. This saving was accomplished with a step-down of service on these classes of items to third-day delivery after receipt of order for 88 percent of the total market. Presumably, the remaining 12 percent of the market received longer delivery times for these items. Finally, as shown in Figure 17–5, Hypo was able to substantially cut factory inventories by producing each item each week instead of every 3 weeks, to reach a total saving of $506,000.

In the Hypo Company example, the penalty incurred by 2-day delivery for 10 percent of the market, and 3-day delivery of slow-moving "C" and "D" items for 88 percent of the market (12 percent received slower service) is not explicitly recognized in the form of a cost. The delivery of industrial products is part of the total marketing process, and a company's ability to hold or increase its market share can be seriously affected by delivery policies. Thus, one of the first steps in any study to improve logistics systems should be to determine the level of customer delivery service considered adequate by marketing management. Determination should not be made hastily, and there is always the danger that marketing executives may view it as a bargaining process within the company and hold out for levels of service that are not truly necessary. In arriving at such decisions, full information about company as well as competitor delivery performance should be available by types of customers in various sales areas, by sizes of customers, and by types of products. At the same time, all valid information available concerning customer complaints on delivery and general customer attitudes toward company and competitor delivery service should be assembled. Field surveys may be required. When this step has been completed, there should be a fairly firm companywide agreement on desirable levels of delivery service, as well as on estimates of the benefits in exceeding these levels and of the penalties for dropping below them.

Closely interwoven with this first step is a careful examination of whether inventory maintenance may serve some important company objectives other than adequate delivery service. In a seasonal demand business, management might elect to hold production at steady levels, thus giving steady employment to production workers at the cost of carrying very substantial inventories during parts of the year. Such a policy might produce a lower total cost than would a fluctuating work force, or the cost might be higher. If it is higher, management might still want to maintain steady employment for its workers and might be willing to accept the cost penalty. Whatever may be the case in a specific situation, knowledge of such overriding functions of inventory are important as the foundation for an analysis of possible changes in the distribution system.

An essential starting point in the study is a comprehensive analysis of sales and shipment records of customers for the past few years. This analysis would indicate such important characteristics as the concentration of sales among a few customers and the product mix purchased by customers of different sizes. At the same time, there should be an analysis of different industry markets found in the customer group and the purchasing habits of each market. Of particular importance from an inventory planning point of view is whether the same types of customers buy both fast-moving and slow-moving items in the line.

The next step should be an analysis of sales by products to determine statistically the amount of variation in the sales pattern in relation to the lead time for replenishment of stocks. The size of this variation clearly has an effect on the level of inventory that must be held to provide the desired level of customer service. The larger this variation, the larger the stocks must be throughout the entire distribution system.

Also of great importance is whether the variations from one time period to another are correlated. If they are highly correlated, the accumulated variations over the replenishment lead time are nearly in proportion to the length of the lead time. Thus, if the lead time were doubled inventory requirements would almost double, while cutting the time in half would almost halve the inventory requirements. If, on the other hand, time period variations are not correlated, increasing the lead time would mean a less than proportionate increase in inventories. Thus, if analysis of sales indicates high correlation between time periods emphasis should be on making the entire system react faster with lead times as small as possible. On the other hand, if correlation is low more use could be made of low-cost methods of transportation and information handling, with longer lead times and somewhat higher inventories.

Another type of sales variation that should be examined is one between areas, which will have an effect on warehouse location decisions. If chance variations in sales tend to offset each other between areas, there may be an opportunity for consolidation of warehouse stocks at fewer points, but if sales movements between areas tend to occur together, not enough may be saved to offset probable higher transportation costs. A final type of sales analysis is to look at the sales variations between items. With high variation in an item, stocking at a few central points may be desirable, despite higher transportation costs.

The next step is to obtain information on costs of maintaining inventory, physical handling, clerical processing, and transportation. Although many companies do not regularly accumulate costs covering physical distribution activities, it is usually possible to obtain reasonable approximations through statistical analysis of operating costs and the various activities that generate these costs. Data on a reasonably broad range of situations should be secured so that different alternative methods of organizing the distribution system can be studied. These alternatives can be studied on paper to see the probable results, and various factors can be modified in order to see how they affect the results. The analysis can be limited, as a first step, to existing company plants and warehouses with existing constraints on capacities, and then can be expanded if desired to include possible modifications of the present plant and warehouse complex. These investigations may suggest a variety of more detailed studies.

There are opportunities for effective application of quantitative analytical methods in many aspects of the physical distribution process. In fact, it is in this aspect of marketing that quantitative methods have so far had their greatest impact. The available literature is steadily increasing, and it can be said that the burden of proof is on the executive who is skeptical of the systems approach to the logistics function as well as the tangible benefits to be derived from the acceptance of quantitative techniques it implies.

SUMMARY

The management of physical distribution is a composite of production scheduling, storage, controlling inventory, handling, packaging, order processing, selection of plant and warehouse sites, and transportation. It is a matter of balancing the excellence of these services, with their resultant costs, against the value of customer satisfaction. Traditionally, these activities have been performed by different units in the marketing firm. There is an increasing tendency to put them all under a manager of a logistics system.

Logistics is essentially a function of facilities, their location, and a transportation network. During recent years, air transport and pipelines have been increasing their shares of the total movement of goods, although the railroads and water carriers are substantially improving their services.

Basic elements in logistics are information and communication. The customers' needs, the supplier's inventory situation, and the costs and performance of transport agencies must be known. Many firms are making significant savings by holding inventories at a proper level to balance costs against the losses resulting from out-of-stock situations. To do this effectively, management must create and operate a system that enables the manager to know at any time how much inventory there is, where it is, and how much will probably be needed where. The location of stocks and the provision of efficient handling equipment are vital.

Transportation management is essentially a matter of setting up and operating a system of information and communications to balance the total costs of transport—not merely freight rates—against the benefits of speed and certainty of delivery.

We have shown an hypothetical example of the way in which all of these factors can be combined into a system to effect substantial savings in comparison with the traditional fragmented method of managing them. Mathematical techniques can be of very great help in setting up and operating such a system.

Chapter 18

◇◇◇◇◇◇◇◇◇◇◇◇◇◇◇◇◇◇◇◇◇◇◇ *SPECIAL PROBLEMS OF*

CUSTOMER SERVICE AND RELATIONS

SEVERAL SPECIAL PROBLEMS arise in managing industrial goods marketing. Some of these, such as reciprocity, to sell or to lease, and the provision of technical service, are not encountered to any significant extent in consumer goods marketing. While some, such as the provision of parts and the financing service, are found in both the industrial and consumer goods fields, they assume such peculiar aspects in industrial goods that they demand special treatment.

These problems are so distinctive that they do not fit comfortably into any of (what we fondly hope are) the fairly logical divisions of this book. Also, they are so discrete among themselves that they may not seem to fit together in a harmonious chapter. They all have one characteristic in common, however: they are concerned either with the services the industrial goods marketer offers his customers or with his relationships with his customers. So, at the risk of confusing the reader with a disjointed and seemingly catchall chapter, we will treat them here and trust the student to discern and hold in mind the customer-relations thread that runs through them all.

RECIPROCITY

Meaning of Reciprocity

Manufacturers of many kinds of industrial goods must solve the problem of what to do about reciprocity. Reciprocity involves the use of a firm's purchases to augment its sales. Reduced to its simplest form, it means that one manufacturer says to another: "I'll buy from you if you will buy from me," or, "Last year I bought X dollars worth of your Product B from you; now you return the favor by purchasing Y dollars of my Product A from me." The proposal is usually phrased in somewhat more subtle language, but the meaning is the same. This is reciprocity in its direct form.

A watered-down form of reciprocity exists when, purely as a matter of trade relations, a firm in buying gives preference to customers when other patronage factors, such as price, quality, and service, are equal as between customer and noncustomer suppliers. Apparently, this is a very general practice throughout industry.

Reciprocity may involve a third party. Then, A says to B: "I'll buy your Product X from you if you will buy Product Y from C." A then informs C: "I can get you B's orders for Product Y if you will buy my Product Z from me." In a case on record, a firm making steel specialties gave favored treatment in its purchasing to companies that sold their plant maintenance products through mill supply houses. It wanted to build up mill supply houses as distributors of its own products. Indirect or three-way reciprocity is not so commonly practiced as is the direct form, but occasionally occurs.

Several years ago, *Purchasing*, the trade journal of the industrial purchasing profession, made a study that presented the most complete available picture of the reciprocity practice in American industry. The answers to some of the questions may have been colored somewhat, since they came from the chief purchasing officers rather than from the marketing executives or top managements of the participating firms. On the whole, though, the information is probably substantially correct. Table 18–1 shows a summary of the results of this survey.

From these figures, it is apparent that reciprocity is a managerial problem in half or more of the firms in the seven fairly typical industrial trades the survey covers. It is especially prevalent in the nonmetals supply trades and in chemicals, industrial petroleum products, and iron and steel. It is more widespread among large firms than among small ones, and its practice by big companies is more complex, tending more often to involve indirect or secondary arrangements.

Sales Advantages and Disadvantages

From the standpoint of the sales department in an industrial goods firm, reciprocity has definite and obvious advantages. At the very least, it offers an easy means of wooing the goodwill of customers or prospective customers whose goods the firm can use. When all other factors are equal, it seems a good idea to patronize a customer; it probably costs the buyer nothing and may serve to cement his relations with the favored supplier. When used aggressively, reciprocity offers the sales department an easy means of getting business without the apparent expenditure of much money or sales effort. Occasionally, the sales department of a firm may be driven to use reciprocity as a defense against its use by competitors, or as an offset to its use by potential customers.

From the standpoint of the sales executive, reciprocity suffers from the disadvantage that it is likely to weaken the morale and dull the fighting

TABLE 18–1

Prevalence and Management of Reciprocity
Survey of 300 Chief Purchasing Executives
(All figures in percentages)

Questions	Non-metals	Trades: Chemicals and Petroleum Products	Iron and Steel	Services	Fabricated Metal Products	Construction Materials	Electrical Equipment and Supplies	All Firms According to Volume (in $Millions): Under 10	10 to 50	Over 50
Is reciprocity a factor in the operation of your company?										
Yes	68	100	100	45	56	55	44	46	62	78
No	32	0	0	55	44	45	56	54	38	22
Should your supplier-customer divide his purchases between you and your competitors in proportion to your purchases from him?										
Yes	70	84	78	46	58	39	52	56	52	58
No	20	16	22	33	27	50	40	24	36	34
Don't sell to suppliers	10	0	0	21	15	11	8	20	12	8
Do you get involved in secondary reciprocity?										
Yes	40	64	38	17	22	24	16	20	28	41
No	60	36	62	83	78	76	84	80	72	59
Who handles reciprocity?										
Purchasing department	48	95	70	57	54	32	58	56	64	72
Marketing department	40	75	62	27	38	16	40	30	40	50
Top management	58	56	62	33	66	55	60	72	56	38
Trade relations department	12	11	15	0	3	6	2	2	2	8
No one	28	0	0	15	4	0	6	4	4	2
How does the purchasing officer help the sales department?										
Mentions company products to suppliers	53	71	63	21	54	45	58	60	54	62
Gives lists of sources and volume of purchases to sales department	40	71	39	15	28	16	28	12	26	54
Makes calls with salesmen	12	46	7	12	8	22	12	4	14	24
Gives other aids	15	31	15	12	10	16	2	2	18	20
No assistance	28	0	23	57	33	28	24	38	30	14

Source: *PURCHASING*, November 20, 1961.

edge of the sales force. To a salesman, an order obtained through reciprocity is something he gets for nothing; it is a handout from another department of the business. Salesmen who enjoy too many handouts tend to become beggars, leaning on the crutch of reciprocity, and may lose their capacity as business builders.

From the standpoint of the firm as a whole, reciprocity entails certain hidden costs. It is a way of buying business. If a customer knows that he will get part or all of his supplier's business on the basis of reciprocity, he loses much of the incentive to bid for it through prices that are lower, services that are better, or quality that is higher or more consistent than any his competitors offer. If customer-suppliers are favored over long periods, possible suppliers who cannot use the firm's products tend to lose interest in its business. This diminishes competition and, in the long run, tends to increase price, lower the excellence of service, and diminish the standard of quality. For some products, a minor cost of reciprocity is that it inhibits the buying officer from taking advantage of bargains that noncustomer suppliers may offer from time to time. The price a firm pays for reciprocity may be a long time coming and hard to measure, but it is fairly sure. It must be remarked, however, that in the eyes of many sales managers the blessings of reciprocity appear immediate, obvious, and highly enjoyable, while its costs seem remote, nebulous, and uncertain.

A Matter of Company Policy

For this reason, and because it affects the purchasing as well as the sales work of a firm, reciprocity should be, and often is, a matter of company policy—not merely of sales strategy. Since in its essence an order placed in a reciprocity program is a means of buying sales volume, its desirability from the company standpoint should be analyzed in the same manner as any other expenditure made for the purpose of increasing sales volume, such as the addition of a salesman or an increase in the advertising appropriation. If it costs more than the probable added business will return in net profit, it is a losing venture and should be shunned. If over the long run a single reciprocal transaction or the practice of reciprocity promises to bring about a net addition to profits, it is worthy of serious consideration; if not, the opportunity to engage in it should probably be ignored. For example, an aircraft manufacturing company was in the market for an order of small parts. A maker of satisfactory parts who wanted to buy a plane for use by his firm quoted $150,000. The officials of the airplane company found that they could buy the parts elsewhere for $125,000. The net profit on the plane was $15,000. They placed the parts order elsewhere.

Since reciprocity is a matter that involves the conflicting interests of at least two functional areas—purchasing and marketing—and is likely to directly affect the company net profit, top management should probably take an active interest in it. In some firms, this may mean that the chief executive handles all situations involving it. The purchasing study summarized in Table 18–1 indicates that this is the policy in many small- and medium-sized companies. A few concerns, mainly the larger ones, place the matter in the hands of a trade relations manager, who usually reports to top management.

Probably a much more common practice is for top management to set up a company policy with respect to reciprocity, and to delegate its administration to the purchasing and marketing executives. Certainly, the figures in the table indicate that in many firms more than one managerial area participates in making decisions about it. This is probably the way it should be.

One possible policy is that of enforcing on the sales department a measure of restraint in the use of reciprocity by charging as a sales expense all costs involved in its practice. This is easier said than done, since many of the costs of reciprocity to a firm's purchasing program are intangible and difficult to reduce to dollars and cents. Another apparently good policy is that no salesman shall attempt to get orders from customer-suppliers by threatening to take his firm's business away from them if they do not buy from him. If this sort of thing is allowed indiscriminately, it can get really vicious. It also appears to be sound policy to state that all individual cases of reciprocity must be decided and administered on the basis of net benefit to the firm as a whole rather than to the interest of any functional area.

Although several government agencies have investigated the practice of direct reciprocity, its legality has never been seriously challenged. Its ethical justification has often been questioned. But when reciprocity is administered on both sides for the benefit of the respective firms involved, it is not easy to draw against it an ethical indictment that will hold water. When it is administered entirely in the interest of the marketing area of either party, it may weaken both firms involved and so undermine the system of competitive enterprise. Any program of secondary reciprocity skates dangerously close to the edge of coercion and conspiracy, and at best is difficult, if not impossible, to defend on ethical grounds.

TO SELL OR TO LEASE

The maker of industrial or business equipment must decide whether he will sell or lease to users. By far the largest number of such manufacturers choose to sell their products rather than to lease them. A small number, including some large and influential concerns, follow the policy of leasing their machines. Others prefer to sell, and devote their best efforts to doing so, but will lease to customers who prefer that method of procurement. In addition, some firms in a few trades make a business of buying equipment from its builders and leasing it to users. Some leasing arrangements are primarily financial in character and purpose.

Equipment Leased

Some articles that have been or are leased instead of sold are:

Shoe-making machinery	Packaging machinery
Business machines	Glassware-making machinery
Doughnut-making machines	Riveting machines
Postage meters	Hospital X-ray equipment
Textile machinery	Machines to make paper milk cartons
Measuring devices	
Refrigeration equipment, includ-	
ing office water coolers	

In the construction industry, contractors often lease heavy machinery to one another. Such equipment is very expensive and may not be needed for continuous use by any one contractor. By buying such a machine and leasing it to another contractor when he does not need it in his own operations, the owner is able to gain income from equipment that would otherwise stand idle. This industry also includes dealers who make a business of buying construction equipment and leasing it to contractors. A contractor can lease from them almost any piece of equipment from a crawling, snuffling, mechanical behemoth that moves a ton or so of dirt in each bite, to an outdoor, portable toilet, appropriately christened Johnny-on-the-Spot, or Jobsite Johnny. The same practice is followed by firms that own trucks and lease them, either with or without drivers, to using concerns.

In an arrangement largely financial in purpose, a life insurance or a finance company buys freight cars or locomotives or tankships and leases them to a railroad or an oil company. Such a contract usually runs for 15 years, with a 10-year renewal arrangement. *Sales Management*, October 10, 1962, estimated that about 100 firms were engaged in this business.

The extent to which leasing has superseded sale throughout industry is unknown. A report in *Distribution Age*, November, 1962, stated that one fairly typical materials handling equipment maker leased about 25 percent of output, and it estimated that about 700,000 trucks are operated under leasing arrangements. The report also noted that a large chemical company was trying to lease all the transportation and materials moving equipment it used; a powder company and a meat packer leased about 95 percent of their freight cars; and an oil company, about 50 percent of its tank cars.

A survey by Wheels, Inc., reported in *Sales Management*, for January 17, 1964, found that about 31 percent of the cars used by industrial concerns were leased, and that the number of motor vehicles leased by business concerns increased 15 percent during 1963. A National Industrial Conference Board study of 220 firms, reported in *Business Management Record,* November, 1963, indicated that during the preceding 5-year period 34 percent of the participating companies had increased their leasing operations, while only 10 percent had reduced them. Leasing seems to be on the increase.

Terms of Lease

Under a leasing arrangement, the owner usually reserves the right to enter the premises where the user keeps or operates the machine in order to gain access to it whenever he wishes; he likewise reserves the right to remove the machine and reclaim custody over it if the user violates the terms of the lease. The owner generally agrees to keep the equipment in good repair, although in some cases the contract authorizes him to charge the cost of doing so against the account of the user. The rental payment may be in the form of a charge per day, per month, or per year, as is the case with most business machines, or it may be a fee per unit of use, as is the case with most shoe-making machinery, for example. A set charge per pair of shoes worked on is made, with a minimum fixed charge per month.

Trucks are customarily leased on four bases.

1. Long-term, full service arrangements, under which the owner provides everything involved in operating the vehicle except the driver. Rent is usually charged by the year or month.
2. Short-term, service rental, which is the same as the first, except that the rent is charged by the hour, day, or week.
3. Trip leasing, which includes the truck, the driver, and all operating costs for a specific trip. The charge is based on the tonnage loaded and the distance it is carried.
4. A financial arrangement under which the owner assumes the ownership and capital risk, and nothing more.

There are probably infinite variations of each basis, applying to trucks as well as other kinds of equipment.

Illegal Terms.   Certain types of lease arrangements have been declared illegal.

1. It is illegal to charge to a user who leases other equipment from competitors a higher machine rental than the amount charged for the same machine to a user who rents all his equipment from the supplier.
2. It is illegal to charge a rental based on the user's entire output of the article for which the machine can be used; the rental can be based only on the part of the output the machine is actually used to make.
3. It is illegal to specify that the leasing contract is invalid if the user rents other machines from any competing equipment manufacturer.
4. It is illegal to include in the leasing contract a requirement that the user

buy from the owner certain supplies or materials made or sold by the owner and generally used in connection with the operation of the equipment. Charging a higher rental to nonusers of the owner's supplies is also invalid.

5. It is of doubtful legality to lease equipment without also offering the user an opportunity to buy it. This proscription seems not to be so ironclad as the others. Any exclusively leasing marketing arrangement deserves the careful scrutiny of the company attorneys.

All but the last of these are line-forcing devices whereby the owner of a machine, who has a patent or other form of monopoly on it, seeks to force the sale or lease of other items in which his competitive position is less favorable. In spite of these legal restrictions, a machinery owner may sometimes exercise some degree of control over the user's purchase of other items. For example, it is probably not illegal for the owner to state that if a machine is used to work on, or with, materials not of his manufacture, he can no longer assume full responsibility for its satisfactory performance. This can have interesting implications with respect to his supplying the repair and maintenance function. If the owner does not want to run the risk of announcing a nonresponsibility policy, he can maintain silence and allow the quality of his repair and maintenance service to announce the policy for him.

The User's Appraisal of Leasing

Leasing has certain advantages and disadvantages from the standpoint of the equipment user. On close examination, some of the apparent advantages may lose much of their attraction.

Financial Factors. Leasing tends to reduce the amount of capital investment the user needs in order to operate his enterprise. For example, a firm can start in the business of making shoes if it has enough capital to buy materials and findings, to finance inventory, to carry credit outstandings, and to pay current expenses for a reasonable period. In the meantime, it is using the shoe machinery manufacturer's equipment, for which it would have had to provide thousands of dollars in capital funds if the equipment maker sold rather than leased his products.

To start his enterprise, the shoemaker needs little beyond working capital; the machinery company provides most of his fixed investment. Machine tool marketers offer lease contracts to their customers, many of whom are small operators. A large oil company leases tankers from an insurance company because it can make more profit from capital invested in refinery equipment rather than in tankers.

This does not always prove to be an unmixed blessing to the user. First, through the leasing arrangement he has exchanged the expense of servicing a capital investment for a monthly or per unit rental charge. However, the cost of servicing the capital investment could be less than the amount of the rental charge. For example, a certain piece of equipment worth $11,000 was leased for $275 a month, or $3,500 a year. The service costs on an $11,000 loan at 6 percent interest would be somewhat in excess of $660 a year. Unless depreciation charges and the costs of keeping the equipment in repair are very heavy, the rental contract will be a losing venture for the user. The ratio, cited above, between annual rentals and selling price is not unusual. For example, a firm that makes computers will sell them for prices ranging from $140,000 to $500,000, or will lease them for annual rentals ranging from $37,000 to $120,000. Another company sells its machines at $270,000 for the cheapest model and $1.5 million for the most expensive; it offers them for lease at $70,000 and $360,000 per year, respectively.

On the other hand, if a firm borrows money to buy a machine, it can charge off as expense in computing its income tax such items as repairs, interest paid on the loan, and depreciation. If it has paid for the machine entirely out of its own funds, it can charge off only repairs and depreciation, which are almost certain to be a lesser amount than the rental fee it can charge as an operating expense if it leases. By leasing in such circumstances, the firm is able to put itself into a better income tax position than it would occupy had it bought outright. In addition, leasing reduces the capital structure to which profits must be applied.

During recent years, an increasing tendency in the marketing of heavy, expensive equipment items has been to bring into the picture a third party in the form of a concern with money to lend or invest. For example, insurance companies and finance houses have been active in financing the distribution of railroad rolling stock and locomotives. One insurance company has set up an arrangement whereby it lends funds to a leasing concern that is the joint subsidiary of a freight car manufacturer and another concern that owns patents on several parts used in making the cars. The leasing company uses the funds advanced by the insurance company to buy the cars from the manufacturer. It then leases them to the railroads and services its debt to the insurance company out of the proceeds. Another insurance company that also buys cars from the manufacturer makes a down payment and agrees to amortize the balance in equal installments over a period of five years, provided rentals continue to be received from the railroad, which is also a party to the deal. A manufacturer has arranged to sell his lift trucks to a large commercial financing company and to turn over to it the leases negotiated for their use.

The reduction in capital requirements for entry into business that results from use of the leasing arrangement in equipment distribution tends to make entry easy for new firms with limited finances. As a result, a trade may be constantly plagued with excess productive capacity, and competition may be of the cutthroat variety. While leasing may make a business an easy and cheap one to get into, it may also cause it to be one not worthwhile being in.

Business Risk. The equipment user's business risk is reduced by the leasing arrangement. He does not venture his own funds in procuring his equipment. Moreover, if he makes a mistake and leases a machine that gives unsatisfactory performance, he can get rid of it without serious loss.

Servicing. The equipment user's servicing problems are likely to be diminished by the leasing arrangement. If a monthly rental is paid and poor service causes interruptions in production, he has a valid claim for exemption from rentals during the time lost when the machine was inoperable, or he may bring pressure to bear on the owner by threatening to return the machine. If the rental is on a per unit of product basis, the owner gets no return while the machine is inoperable and so is under considerable pressure to keep it in usable condition as much of the time as possible.

Trade Secrets. In some trades where secret processes are used, the leasing arrangement is disadvantageous in that the right of entry and examination of equipment may give the machine owner or his representatives access to knowledge of such processes.

Machine Maker's Appraisal of Leasing

The equipment producer must consider a number of factors in determining whether to lease or to sell.

Total Return. It is often possible for an equipment maker to get a larger total return from a machine by leasing it rather than selling it. Several years ago, the purchase price of machines made by a company that would either lease or sell amounted to between 54 and 60 months' rental. From this should be subtracted costs of maintenance, insurance, taxes, and interest. Even with these subtractions, it is probable that the manufacturer's investment in the machines was amortized by the end of six or seven years. Since the equipment had at least a 10-year life expectancy, the ultimate total of the rentals derived from it considerably exceeded the price received if it were sold.

A study of another company's rentals indicated that after an allowance of 6 percent interest on the estimated cost of the machines, and a liberal allowance for maintenance, insurance, and taxes, most items of the equipment were amortized from their rentals within a period of from 4 to 5 years. Some of these machines had been in service as long as 17 years, and most of them had a life expectancy of at least 10 to 12 years.

The United Shoe Machinery Company 1963 Annual Report showed that its net investment in leased machines was $51.996 million, from which it received rentals of $43.631 million during the year. The cost of leased machine operations was $14.696 million, and depreciation of the equipment, $1.662 million. Interest on investment at 6 percent would have been $3,119,760.

Even when an equipment maker offers his customers either a lease or a sales contract, he can usually charge a rental fee that will net him a larger ultimate return than the amount of a sale, because many prospective users lack the capital resources to buy and are willing to pay the higher cost to rent. This discrepancy between sales price and total rentals received is less than it seems, because the sales price is received at once, while most of the rental payment is deferred and its value must, therefore, be discounted.

The ratio between total returns received by lease and those obtained by sale is not always favorable. In many cases, equipment is leased at low rental charges in order to promote the sale of materials or supplies used in connection with operation of the equipment. For example, a riveting machine worth $10,000 was leased for an annual rental of $500. This would mean an amortization period of more than 20 years. The purpose of the deal was to promote the use of rivets. The rental on a doughnut-making machine leased by a firm that made doughnut mix involved an amortization period of about 19 years.

Stabilization of Income. The leasing arrangement tends to stabilize the income, both gross and net, of the equipment manufacturer who uses it. This is illustrated by the net income records of the International Business Machines Company and the United Shoe Machinery Company during the period of the 1929–33 depression, as shown below. While there was some

International Business Machines		*United Shoe Machinery* *	
Year	*Net Income (in Millions)*	*Year*	*Net Income (in Millions)*
1927	$4.4	1928	$ 8.5
1929	6.7	1930	9.7
1931	7.4	1932	7.5
1932	6.4	1933	6.0
1934	6.6	1935	8.8
1936	7.6	1937	11.3
1938	8.7	1939	9.5
1939	9.1	1940	9.9
1940	9.4	1941	8.2

* These figures are from R. B. McNeill, "The Lease as a Marketing Tool," *Harvard Business Review*, Vol. 22, No. 4 (Summer, 1944).

decline in the earnings of these firms during the depression, it was not catastrophic and they continued to make profits, which was not true of most equipment makers during the depths of the depression. The stabilizing effect of the leasing arrangement can be further observed by a comparison of the United Shoe Machinery Company's gross income figures, which were in the form of net sales of the items it sold, plus those received as royalties and rentals from machines it leased. During a seven-year period, they were as follows.

Year*	Net Sales (in millions)	Percentage of Fluctuation from Previous Year	Royalties and Rentals (in millions)	Percentage of Fluctuation from Previous Year
1945............42.8		+72%	20.7	+5%
1946............37.5		−12	20.8	+0.5
1947............45.7		+22	23.2	+12
1948............50.6		+11	24.4	+5
1949............49.1		−3	24.5	+0.4
1950............44.1		−10	24.5	0
1951............55.5		+26	27.2	+11

* Standard & Poor's Corporation Records, New York, 1952.

Variations in Returns. In some cases, the leasing arrangement allows the equipment manufacturer to obtain from the large user a greater total return per unit of his product than he can get from the small one. It enables him to discriminate in final price among his customers roughly on the basis of his product's usefulness to them. This is possible only when the rental charge is made on a per-unit-of-product-worked-on basis. The customer who uses the equipment most—generally the large firm—pays the most for it. This is likely to result in a larger total return on the machine than its sale would bring.

Financial Burdens. The leasing policy throws a heavy financial burden on the manufacturer who follows it. When he sells a machine, he gets back the working capital invested in it as soon as the bill is paid. When he leases it, his capital or credit remains tied up in the machine until the rental payments have amortized it—usually a period of 4 to 10 years. This greatly increases the capital requirements of the leasing firm.

In 1960, the Compo Shoe Machinery Company operating statement indicated that it received $1.488 million in income from leased machines in which $2.401 million of its capital was invested. Sales of cements, solvents, and other similar products amounted to $5.118 million. In inventories of these items, it had invested $907,000. In the same year, the United Shoe Machinery Company had an investment of $52.189 million in machines, from which it received a rental revenue of $27.865 million. It also sold $62.298 million worth of findings and machines; in these inventories, it had a capital investment of $22.602 million. The manufacturer who leases his product is likely to have a much slower rate of working capital turnover than does the one who sells.

Ownership Instinct. The machinery manufacturer who leases his product may be handicapped by the strong desires of some prospective customers to own their capital equipment. This attitude not only arises from the normal acquisitive instinct, but also often reflects a need for flexibility and freedom of decision, which the customer tends to feel will be hampered or infringed by outside ownership of leased equipment. The ownership instinct probably is buttressed by a general opinion that the practice of leasing is suspect from the standpoint of public policy. This opinion probably is thoroughly unjustified, because the leasing method enables operation of many small, poorly financed firms that could not otherwise hope to engage in business, but it undoubtedly tends to influence the action of some otherwise rational buyers. The equipment marketer can overcome these limitations by offering his customers the option to rent or to buy, as they wish.

Repair and Maintenance. The firm that disposes of its product by lease must set up and maintain a top-notch organization and staff for rendering repair and mainteance service to its users. This is apt to be expensive. One leasing firm maintains a stock of parts and a small staff of repairmen in the plant of one of its biggest equipment users—solely for servicing this one user. The owner of leased machinery is under much heavier pressure to maintain it in working condition than he would be had he sold it. If the machinery fails to operate, he gets no rentals or collects them under protest. Thus, the equipment marketer who leases may expect his costs of supplying repair and maintenance service to be higher than those involved in outright sale.

Since unsatisfactory equipment usually generates heavy demands for service, and since most machinery is expensive to install and remove, the equipment maker who leases must ensure that his salesmen do not oversell their customers. Installations that are canceled soon after they are made are very expensive, even though a charge may be made for removing them.

The usefulness of the leasing arrangement is largely limited to the distribution of standard designs of machines. It is rather dangerous to offer leasing in the sale of specialty items whose life is likely to be short and for which there are no alternative uses.

Expansion of the Market. On the other hand, the leasing method is likely to be of considerable help in the firm's selling work. When machines are sold outright, even on the installment basis, a substantial down payment must be obtained from the buyer. When they are leased, the user often does not need to pay a penny until the first rental bill comes due. As a result, the leasing firm creates many small customers who could not dream of going into business with their existing capital if they had to buy the necessary equipment. Also, the leasing plan dissipates the psychological hurdle that almost always inspires caution and reluctance in the commitment of a sizable chunk of the buyer's capital. In consequence, leasing may bring about a considerable expansion of the market.

Conditions Favoring the Leasing Method

Certain marketing conditions favor the use of the leasing method.

1. The leasing method is favored when the necessary equipment in an

industry is expensive in relation to the financial resources of the firms that must use it—for example, the shoemaking and construction industries. If the equipment makers in these industries sold their products instead of leasing them, their market for the heavier, more expensive machines, at least, would almost surely be confined to relatively few, large, well-financed customers whose equipment requirements would undoubtedly be much smaller than the total needs of the many small users whose existence is made possible by the leasing system.

2. When repair and maintenance service is an important factor in the life and use of the equipment, the leasing method has an advantage. This has been illustrated in the tire industry. Tire companies that lease their products for industrial use find that by taking proper care of the tires they can vastly extend the period of their usefulness and can supply them to the users at lower costs per mile traveled, while realizing a much greater ultimate return than they would on sales. The same factors operate when the equipment requires highly specialized and skilled service to assure its proper operation, as is the case with the more complicated business machines. Unless these machines are kept in repair by highly skilled technicians, and their users can call on the manufacturer's experts for advice and help in adapting them to the solution of unusual problems of record keeping and analysis, the services they give to users are likely to be unsatisfactory.

3. When equipment is used seasonally, or when any one user's need for it is sporadic and uncertain, as in the construction industry, the leasing method is favored. In such trades, distribution is accomplished best by local firms that engage in the business of buying equipment and leasing it to users nearby.

4. The leasing method has an advantage when the sale of a material depends on its use in connection with a certain type of equipment. Examples are rivets, which require special riveting machines in their use, metal containers, which need closing machines; material for paper milk containers, which must be made, as used, by expensive machines; and metal tape for wooden or fiberboard packages, which must be fastened by a stapling machine. Most of the machines mentioned are leased as a means of selling the supplies or materials used in connection with them.

THE PROVISION OF PARTS

The manufacturer of machinery or equipment must establish policies with respect to the distribution of parts. All machines have parts that wear out or break. When this happens, the machine is generally useless until the part is replaced. The availability of parts to the equipment users is, therefore, a vital factor in the manufacturer's effort to give satisfaction to the user. Some equipment manufacturers buy practically all their parts from firms that specialize in producing them; others make many of them in their own plants. Some parts, such as ball or roller bearings, are mainly standardized; others are made to specification to suit the needs of the machine maker who orders them. Both the manufacturer of standardized parts and the builder of the machines of which they are a component have an interest in seeing to it that replacement parts are supplied to machine users.

Standardized Parts

The manufacturer of standardized parts to be used for replacements must determine the channels through which he will seek to sell them to machine users. He may sell only to manufacturers of the machines, relying on the machine makers to distribute to users. Or he may also sell to the users, either direct or through distributors. If his chief market is for replacements, and his product is used in making many types of equipment so that for replacement use it has a horizontal market, he will find it desirable to sell through distributors. If he relies heavily on the distributors to cultivate and serve the replacement market, he must determine whether to sell direct to all manufacturers for original installation or to service some or all of them through his distributors. The distributor will undoubtedly bring pressure to get all the original installation business. Unless the distributor is able to handle original installation contracts at about the same price the manufacturer can supply the same buyers, the parts manufacturer must expect to lose a certain amount of the original installation business if he succumbs to this pressure.

The Machine Manufacturer as a Channel. As a distribution channel for standard replacement parts included in his machine, the machine manufacturer suffers from the disadvantages: (1) that his markup is usually higher, since it is likely to be tied to the markup he enjoys on the machines themselves; (2) his points of distribution, where he carries stocks from which to service users, are apt to be fewer than those of the distributors; and (3) his marketing organization is likely to be heavily preoccupied with the sale of machines, with the result that the sale of parts does not receive the attention it should. On the other hand, the machine manufacturer is under considerable pressure to furnish a good replacement parts service, since the reputation of his machines depends heavily on it. In addition, he may find that in the process of giving good replacement parts service he is able to maintain contact with the user between purchases of equipment. Usually, this works out with something less than complete satisfaction, because parts are generally a matter of routine procurement, handled entirely by the purchasing department, while the engineering department usually has a great deal to say about equipment buying. The replacement parts contact, however, is often close enough to enable the salesman who makes it to get advance notice of projected purchases of equipment, which enables the machine manufacturer to get in on the ground floor in the negotiations for them.

Unstandardized Parts

When the machine manufacturer makes his own parts, or has them made to his own specifications, he may sell them for replacement use either direct through his own organization or to distributors for resale to users. If he renders the repair and maintenance service himself and most of his customers depend on him for it, he may find it best to handle this business himself. If his customers are equipped to do their own repair work, he may find it desirable to service replacement parts demand through distributors. In this manner, he is likely to gain wider distribution through warehouses more conveniently located to his customers than are his own branch warehouses. Moreover, if he refuses to make his own parts available for sale by distributors, they are liable to turn to the pirate parts manufacturers as a source of supply. He may be able to head off this tendency or hold it to a minimum by making his own parts available to them.

The Pirate Parts Problem

If an equipment manufacturer's parts replacement demand is active and the business of supplying it is profitable, those parts are likely to be made and sold by producers who specialize in them. These are known as pirate parts manufacturers. Some of these firms make parts that are just as good as those of the machine maker; others use shoddy material and poor workmanship.

Purchasing agents patronize pirate parts manufacturers for two main reasons. First, such a producer is often a local firm on whom the buyer may rely to furnish other items, or to supply emergency needs. In order to keep him in business, the buyer gives him some of his parts business so that the local supplier can enjoy the advantages of mass production and sale. Second, the pirate can often supply parts at lower prices than can the machine manufacturer. Since he usually copies the machine manufacturer's parts, the pirate has little or no developmental and engineering costs; if he is a local operator, his shipping costs are generally low; and he is likely to have little sales cost and little or no service expense. In addition, as indicated above, the machine manufacturer often gears his gross profit margin on parts to his margin on the completed machines. The second is generally much higher than the first when handled alone.

The chief drawbacks to buying parts from the pirate manufacturer are the following.

1. The buyer may make himself liable to legal action by the machine

manufacturer if the part is covered by a patent giving the manufacturer the sole right to "make, use, and vend" the part. This is usually not too serious, as the machine maker is unlikely to jeopardize future sales of an expensive machine by alienating a customer through legal action over a relatively inexpensive part.

2. The source of supply is insecure. Most pirate producers are small and highly flexible, so that any one of them may at any time turn to the production of some other more profitable article. This also is not too serious, since the buyer can almost invariably call on the machine maker for the service. Some embarrassment may be involved, but usually little real loss.

3. The pirate producer often has little or no quality control. The parts are no more reliable than their maker.

4. The pirate maker gives little or no service, so that the user must carry larger inventories of parts than would be necessary if he bought from the machine manufacturer or one of his distributors. But this expense may be more than offset by price advantages.

5. The parts produced by the pirate are often not closely standardized and, hence, sometimes do not fit. This requires greater inventories, and the expense of returns and making claims. Also, they sometimes lack finishing. This requires a certain amount of machining by the user, which may offset any price saving enjoyed.

6. Buying parts from the pirate tends to weaken the machine manufacturer as a source of the much more important item—the machine itself—and may in the long run cost the buyer much more than the small saving he may enjoy in procuring the parts.

There are several steps by which the machine builder may attempt to diminish the inroads of pirate parts makers on his business.

1. He may offer users of his machines price concessions for an annual contract to supply parts. The contract will be effective only if the volume of parts bought by the average user is great enough to justify a concession that will be attractive to the buyer.

2. He may keep his prices down to a point where parts making offers no real inducement to the prospective pirate. This is probably the most effective method.

3. He may make stocks of parts readily available to users of his machines. If his own branch warehouses are not sufficiently numerous or conveniently located to the users, he may be able to achieve this end by marketing through distributors.

4. He may make his parts catalog complete and detailed. Since the parts business is an offshoot of the main machine business, it is often regarded as the stepchild and fails to receive the attention needed to assure its retention. The parts catalog is sometimes incomplete and inconveniently arranged for the buyer's use.

5. He may constantly improve the machine and keep down the prices

of the new models. This forces the pirate to constantly shift his production processes, and reduces the profit he can make from the business. But it also increases the development and engineering costs of the machine maker.

ENGINEERING AND TECHNICAL SERVICE

Manufacturers of several types of industrial goods must establish policy with respect to supplying engineering and technical service in connection with the sale and use of their products. This is especially true of equipment makers, although it is less so of standard machines than of those specially built to fit a particular need. In the distribution of standard types of machinery, this kind of service often consists chiefly in helping the customer choose a machine or combination of machines that will best perform the job he wants done; it may also involve making minor modifications of standard machines, or making and affixing attachments to them so that their operations more exactly fit the needs of the buyer. Rendering technical service also constitutes a problem to the sellers of some kinds of supplies, such as belting, abrasives, and lubricants, and many materials, such as metals, plastics, and chemicals.

Most firms that sell these types of industrial products are compelled to make available to their customers and prospective customers some sort of engineering or technical service. If such a concern fails to do so, its sales are likely to suffer because of customer resentment at the lack of a service expected, or because of gratitude to service-rendering competitors for their help in solving difficult problems. Such a firm may also find that its products are giving something less than satisfactory performance in use because they are not handled in precisely the proper manner.

Types of Technical Service

Engineering or technical service may assume any or all of the following forms.

1. It may include no more than provision of technical information about a product and its uses, generally on request of the customer or prospective buyer. Such information usually includes suggestions about the way in which the product may be applied to the specific operating needs of the buyer. Most firms that make industrial products probably do some of this kind of work.

2. Through his engineers or technicians, the seller may make a thorough study of a buyer's needs to determine exactly the kinds of machinery, supplies, or materials he should use, and precisely how they should be used. For example, a rubber belting manufacturer offers the services of a force of power transmission engineers who are prepared and equipped to

study the power transmission needs of the customer and recommend a complete program for satisfying them.

3. Engineers or technical men employed by the industrial goods marketer may work with a prospective buyer's technical staff in developing equipment to meet his needs or in developing a process by which he may most effectively use a material or supply. This work may involve designing a special machine or making changes in standard machinery. It may also involve the development or modification of a process employed, for example, by a chemical product user. The marketer who renders this sort of service must expect that some prospective buyers will accept it gratis and then, when plans are drawn, invite other suppliers to bid on the job.

4. The seller may maintain a force of technical experts to install his equipment in the buyer's plant after sale, or he may work with the buyer's technical staff in doing this job. The same kind of help may be supplied in getting a process or a service under way—for example, a chemical process or a mechanical record keeping system.

5. The seller may supply technicians to train the buyer's employees in the proper methods of using and caring for the equipment he sells. Probably the most widely known example of this sort of service is that supplied by manufacturers of mechanical record keeping and computing equipment, who are prepared both to train routine operators of such machinery and to teach executives in charge of the work how to use the equipment to get out of it the maximum service. Such technicians are constantly on call to give advice and help in working out difficult problems, even after the training period is over.

Organization for Technical Service

When an industrial goods manufacturer needs to render considerable technical or engineering service in the course of his marketing work, a special unit of the company is usually set up to take charge of it. There is no substantial agreement on where such a technical service unit should be placed in the organization. In some firms, it is an arm of the engineering department; in others, it is a part of the development department; in still others, it is lodged in the marketing area.

There are logical reasons for each of these locations. The marketing manager may feel that he should be in control so that the men in the unit will constantly be kept aware that its primary purpose is to make sales by creating satisfied customers. He feels that unless the men who do this work are under his control, they will not be sales-oriented. On the other hand, the men must be technicians. What they work out in the field, the plant technical men must implement. The engineering executives usually fear that if the men who do the field work are under marketing department control they will, in their anxiety to promote sales, promise technical features that cannot be delivered.

All technical service requires a detailed knowledge of the specifications and properties of the product. Some necessitates at least minor modifications in its characteristics. These matters are within the province of the engineering function, so engineering executives often feel that since their people and facilities are very likely to be called in to solve a technical service problem they should be in on it from the beginning and have charge of it. All this seems reasonable, although there is little doubt that such service administered by the engineers will emphasize its purely technical aspects and minimize its customer relations objective.

Location of technical service work in the development department probably represents a compromise of the issues between marketing and engineering. Its interests cross-section those of the other two; it is generally charged with the task of overseeing the commercial development of new products and new uses of existing products.

There seems to be no spot in the organization into which this unit ideally fits and should always be placed. Its location should probably be determined in each company on the basis of the nature and extent of technical service work to be done, and the executive personalities involved.

When technical service needed is not too complicated and does not require too much time, it is usually performed by the salesmen, who in such a case probably have some training as technicians. They may be supported by a technical service unit in the branch, or at the home office, to which they can refer problems and requests for information beyond their own ability to handle.

Difficulties of Rendering Technical Service

Administration. The administration of a technical service program is usually a difficult task. It is apt to be costly and, unless watched constantly, tends to grow to such proportions that it is prohibitively expensive. The men who render the service must be thoroughly trained technicians of considerable ability. If the service cannot be made thoroughly reliable and of outstanding quality, it is probably better not to try to render it.

Possible Abuse. The most painful managerial headache associated with rendering technical service, however, is its susceptibility to abuse. Firms that give such service are often called on to render it to companies or persons who have no intention of becoming customers. Many manufacturers can probably duplicate the experience of a chemicals maker whose technical service unit was called on by a small customer for help in working out the proper way to use imported competing materials of inferior quality. Small buyers demand services entirely out of proportion to any purchases they may possibly make. A buyer with a contract to place may ask for technical help from several suppliers in planning and preparing specifications for the article he proposes to buy, synthesize their proposals, and ask each of them to bid on the synthesis, perhaps in competition with other firms that do not offer such service.

For example, *Purchasing*, January 14, 1963, reports the case of a vendor who spent $6,000 in developing designs and specifications, used by the buyer who requested them, and then lost the order to another bidder. Another spent $7,000 on the same kind of a deal. A knowledgeable consultant estimated that between 60 and 90 percent of all engineering proposal costs in competitive bidding are lost to the firms that incur them. This practice is good for neither buyer nor seller. It is true that it seems to enable the individual buyer to get, free of charge, much expensive engineering service, but the cost is multiplied for the trade as a whole.

It is difficult, if not impossible, to avoid a certain amount of abuse in this service. Some firms have tried with varying success to charge for all or for certain parts of the engineering services they render. This is apt to work satisfactorily when business is good and demand is heavy; but few suppliers have the courage to stick to it when business is bad and orders are scarce. Perhaps to stick to it under such conditions would exemplify poor judgment more than courage. It might not be a bad idea for firms heavily committed to the supply of technical service to use the techniques of motivation research to try to find out just how influential it actually is in gaining patronage.

THE FINANCIAL SERVICE

The industrial goods maker, like his counterpart in the consumer goods field, must usually provide some financial service in the form of credit extensions or credit arrangements for his customers. The help the manufacturer is prepared to give the customer in financing the purchase of his product is very definitely a part of the product-service benefit package his marketing organization has to sell. So it is a matter of primary importance to the marketing manager. Of all executives in his company, he is in the best position to know how much of such help is needed and in what form it will be most useful and acceptable to the customer.

The stock-carrying service of the industrial goods manufacturer also creates a need for financial management decision and action. Stock-outs do not usually create or facilitate sales. The marketing manager is in the best position to know how much stock-outs cost the firm in lost sales volume and how much finished goods inventory is needed to prevent or to hold them to a planned percentage of orders received. He is not always equipped to balance the costs of stock-outs against the expense of carrying the inventory necessary to avoid or hold them to an economical minimum.

Both of these matters belong in the domain of either an executive in charge of physical distribution or the chief financial officer who manages the working capital of the firm. Some understanding of the costs and the mechanism for providing these customer services can enable the marketing manager to be much more helpful in making and administering working capital policy. He can hardly avoid having something to say about the formulation of such policy, nor would he be wise to avoid it if he could, for through his salesmen and his subordinate executives he must play a part in carrying it out.

Terms of Sale

When a sale is negotiated, the buyer and seller usually agree on certain conditions under which payment is to be made. These are commonly referred to as terms of sale or credit terms. They indicate the extent to which the seller is willing to use the credit service as a means of capturing the buyer's patronage. These terms tend to be uniform throughout a trade, with such minor modifications as individual firms may see fit to make. Table 18–2 shows the credit terms commonly used in a number of trades engaged in manufacturing and selling industrial goods.

Perhaps some explanation of the meaning of the terms most commonly used will aid us in seeking to understand their implications.

Net cash generally means that the buyer is expected to pay the full amount of the bill within 10 days after the date of the invoice.

Net 30 or net 60 means that the buyer obligates himself to pay the face of the bill within 30 or 60 days after the date of the invoice.

Two percent, 10 days, net 30 days, often written 2–10–30 or 2, 10, net 30, means that if the buyer pays within 10 days after the date of the invoice he is privileged to deduct 2 percent from the face of the bill, and that he is obligated to pay the full amount of the bill within 30 days after its date. One percent (or ½ percent), 10 days, net 30 has the same meaning, except that he is privileged to deduct only 1 percent or ½ percent as the case may be.

Net, 10 proximo means that the buyer is expected to pay the face of the bill on or before the 10th day of the month following that in which the invoice is dated. For example, if a firm buys materials on these terms and receives a bill dated January 15, it is obligated to pay the full amount mentioned therein on or before February 10.

Two percent, 10, E.O.M. means that if the buyer pays within 10 days of the date of the bill, he may deduct 2 percent from its face; otherwise he is obligated to pay the entire amount by the end of the month.

Two percent, 10, net 30, 60 extra means that if the buyer pays within 10 days of the date of the bill, he may deduct 2 percent from the face of it, but if he takes his full credit period, he has 90 days to pay the total amount of the bill. Such terms are generally used by firms that sell to customers who, in turn, either resell the merchandise or process it and sell the resulting product to buyers whose demand is seasonal. It is a way of helping the customer to meet heavy requirements for working capital caused by the seasonal nature of his business.

In general, the credit terms used by industrial goods firms are somewhat simpler than those offered by consumer goods makers. This is

TABLE 18–2

Terms of Sale of Industrial Firms

Type of Manufacturer	*Terms*
Chemicals	Net 30 days, most frequent 1%, 10, net 30, also Net 10 proximo
Concentrates, extracts, syrups	1%, 10, net 30
Cotton cloth	Net 10, on duck 2%, 10, net 30
Cotton goods converters	70 days, usually 2%, 10, 60 extra, sometimes
Foundries, gray iron	Net 30 ½ or 1%, 10, net 30, sometimes
Malleable iron	½%, 10, net 30
Brass and bronze	½ or 1%, 10, net 30, or Net 30
Machine shops	Net Cash or net 30 1 or 2%, 10, net 30
Industrial machinery	Net 30 after completion and delivery of smaller machines Agreed down payment, balance on delivery or on installments for large machines On special work for new customers one third down with order, payments monthly as work progresses, full payment on delivery
Metal stampings	Net 30, sometimes 1%, 10 New accounts, ⅓ to ½ on order, balance 10 days after delivery
Paper boxes:	
Setups	2%, 10, E.O.M.
Fiber boxes	1%, 10, E.O.M.
Structural steel:	
Fabricated	Net 10 proximo and net 30
Erection materials	Payment 10th of each month of 90% of value of all materials shipped, stored, or ready to ship, balance net 30 days after completion of contract
Airplane parts	1%, 10, net 30
Rayon, silk, acetate piece goods	Net 60 or 70

SOURCE: Abstracted from Roy A. Foulke, *Terms of Sale* (New York: Dun & Bradstreet, Inc., various years).

probably due, at least in part, to the fact that the channels of distribution commonly employed in the industrial goods business are more direct, and that such goods flow to market through a more limited variety of outlets. For example, the consumer good manufacturer may have to sell direct to some large retailers, such as department stores, chain systems, or mail-order houses, while at the same time distributing through wholesalers. Each of these types of buyer may demand a different set of credit terms. On the other hand, the industrial goods maker is not likely to find it necessary to sell through more than the direct channel and the industrial distributor.

On the whole, the terms used by industrial marketers seem to be somewhat less liberal that those offered by firms selling consumer goods. For example, cash discounts for payment within 10 days are somewhat less generally allowed, and net terms without discount seem to be rather more commonly required. Extra datings are less generally offered, although their place has been taken to a large extent by longer net terms, such as 60 days net. It is probably true that by and large the problem of administering credit terms is less complicated in the industrial goods business than in the consumer goods field. Of course, individual trades provide exceptions.

Financing with Warehouse Receipts

The warehouse receipt offers a means by which the industrial goods manufacturer can finance at least part of his inventory-carrying operations.

There are two types of warehouse receipts—negotiable and nonnegotiable. When goods are stored on a negotiable receipt, ownership of them can be transferred by an endorsement on the receipt by the person to whom it is drawn. In order to remove the goods or any part of them from storage, the holder of the receipt must present it and endorse an acknowledgment that he has received the goods removed. The merchandise covered by such a receipt belongs to the holder of the receipt properly endorsed.

When goods are stored on a nonnegotiable receipt, they belong to the person whose name appears on the receipt. He can transfer them to another only by assignment or by turning in the receipt and requesting the issue of a new one, drawn to the buyer. They can be withdrawn from the warehouse on presentation of a warehouse release order signed by the person to whom the receipt is drawn.

The industrial goods marketer can borrow on a warehouse receipt by signing a note to a financial institution, such as a bank, and depositing the receipt in proper form as collateral. If the receipt is a negotiable one, he must endorse it to the lending establishment. If it is nonnegotiable, he must have the receipt drawn to the lender and deposit it as collateral. Banks generally prefer the nonnegotiable document, since then the receipt need not be taken from the bank when partial withdrawals are made.

When merchandise is withdrawn from the warehouse for delivery to customers, the owner may either pay the portion of his loan representing the value of the amount withdrawn, or may execute a trust receipt for it. Such a receipt usually contemplates repayment of the value of the goods covered within a limited period of time; it is also apt to limit the uses that may be made of the goods while covered by the receipt.

The usefulness of warehouse receipts issued by a regular commercial warehouse to an industrial goods marketer is usually limited to the financing of reserve stocks of finished goods or stocks earmarked to service the needs of customers buying in substantial quantities. For example, a cabinet manufacturer is reported to use such receipts to finance supplies of cabinets held in the major radio and television manufacturing centers. From these, he can quickly supply the needs of customer firms. Can manufacturers customarily maintain large stocks at strategic points in canning areas during the packing season. Thus they are able to make quick deliveries to the packing plants, whose needs may vary considerably according to weather conditions. A manufacturer of copper wire and electrical parts stores products at points convenient to producers of electrical equipment and appliances. The same plan is employed by a maker of industrial cleaning compounds. All these firms make some use of warehouse receipts to finance these stocks, thereby making it possible to obtain the maximum use of their working capital while at the same time maintaining adequate stocks conveniently located to service their customers.

The manufacturer who wants to use warehouse receipts to finance the holding of materials in his own storeroom or of finished stocks in his own warehouse or distributive branch can obviously make little use of the traditional type of public warehouse receipt. To meet his needs, a practice known as field warehousing has been developed.

Field Warehousing

When this plan is used, the industrial marketer stores materials or finished goods in his own plant or distributive branch warehouse. He leases the warehouse or the part of it in which the merchandise is stored to a field warehousing firm, which takes legal possession of the premises. Usually, the warehousing concern hires one or more of the employees of the marketer as warehouse custodians: they are transferred by mutual consent from the payroll of the marketer to that of the warehouseman. The field warehousing firm issues warehouse receipts covering the merchandise held by its custodians. The marketer can then deposit these receipts with a financial institution as collateral for a loan on the merchandise. Advances ranging from 60 to 85 percent of the value of the goods may be obtained on such loans. The legal nature of these receipts and their acceptability as collateral differs little, if any, from the traditional type of warehouse receipt.

The field warehouse may also be located on the premises of a customer of the industrial marketer. For example, a can manufacturer customarily sells cans to a packer whose storage space is apt to be vacant, or nearly so, for several months immediately prior to the opening of the canning season. The packer stores the cans; the can manufacturer arranges for a field warehousing firm to lease the packer's storeroom and officially take custody of the cans until they are needed during the packing season. The warehousing firm issues receipts, which the can manufacturer is able to use as collateral for loans at his bank. The cans are where the packer can quickly get them when needed; the manufacturer frees working capital with which to make more cans.

The Use of Factors

For a long time, the factor has been an important element in financing marketing operations in the textile industry. His services have been used most extensively in the parts of the industry that make semifinished materials.

There is a strong tendency for the use of factors to spread to many other industries, some engaged in industrial goods production and marketing. No intrinsic feature of the factor's activities would prevent his use by the maker of almost any sort of industrial goods, except perhaps the manufacturer of very heavy and expensive specialized equipment, which must be financed on long-term commitments.

A manufacturer can effectively use a factor for two types of financing service connected with the marketing operation. The factor can be of material aid in financing the carrying of inventories. He can also be used to finance the extension of credit to customers through his accounts receivable service. The second service is his most typical and the one in which he is most skilled and proficient.

Accounts Receivable. When the manufacturer extends open-book credit to his customers on a 30- or 60-day basis, the funds he has tied up in the goods delivered are to all intents and purposes dead for the period of the credit extension. During this time, he cannot use them to earn additional profits. The factor offers two kinds of service to help the manufacturer avoid this loss.

The factor is prepared to buy his client's accounts receivable outright. Then, he usually collects the accounts from the customers and assumes all credit risks. Obviously, when this is done the manufacturer must maintain credit extension standards satisfactory to the factor or even allow the factor to check the credits when extended. In some cases, the arrangement provides that the client will make collections and remit them to the factor, although this is not the usual practice.

The manufacturer may also pledge his receivables to the factor as collateral for a loan. When this is done, the work of collecting the accounts is carried on entirely by the borrower, and the factor assumes no risk of their uncollectibility. The manufacturer's customers have no knowledge that their accounts have been pledged.

Which of these two arrangements the manufacturer chooses to adopt depends largely on four considerations. If he needs or wants some form of credit insurance on his accounts, their outright sale without recourse provides a means of getting it. Once the sale is made, he no longer stands to lose by reason of a customer's default. If the manufacturer wants to avoid the tedious and expensive record keeping work involved in maintaining accounts receivable and collecting them, outright sale offers the best method. Neither of these considerations are apt to be of prime importance to the industrial goods marketer, because his customers are usually relatively few in number, their credit standing is better than average, and their routines of payment are generally more or less standardized.

On the other hand, the manufacturer must consider the effect of his financial operations on the goodwill of his customers. Some may be disturbed by or resent the sale of their accounts. This is especially important to the industrial goods marketer. In appraising the reliability and financial strength of suppliers, the purchasing officer often examines their credit standings. The sale of accounts receivable accompanied by their collection by the factor may be interpreted as a dead giveaway of the lack of adequate working capital, and may lead to the witholding of orders when reliability and certainty of delivery are of the essence in the transaction. In some trades, also, there is a prejudice against the sale of accounts receivable. It is regarded as a confession of weakness on the part of the firm that sells them. This consideration also has special significance to the industrial goods vendor for the reasons just outlined.

The factor's charges for the accounts receivable service include two elements. He collects a commission ranging usually from 0.5 to 1.5 percent of the net amount of the receivables taken over. To this, he adds an interest charge of 0.5 percent a month on the funds turned over to the client. Cash discounts taken by the client's customers are offset against the first of these charges. The charges themselves may vary with business conditions.

Financing Inventory Holdings. The factor is also usually prepared to lend funds on materials held in warehouse pending sale. Such accommodations range from 50 to 80 percent of the market value of the goods, depending on the client's financial condition, the character of the goods, market conditions, and the reasons for the borrowing. When the factor makes such a loan, he takes a lien on the merchandise, which he registers with the appropriate official, thereby giving notice to other creditors of the client firm that the goods covered by the lien are not to be relied on to meet its general obligations. When such goods are sold, the factor is prepared to cancel the lien and substitute an accounts receivable transaction for it.

General Services. The factor sometimes extends loans on the client's general credit and, on rare occasions, lends funds to finance his clients' equipment purchases. In general, however, his services are designed to supply their working capital requirements rather than to augment their fixed capital funds.

Commercial Finance Houses

The commercial finance house is usually considered an institution that confines its operations to financing installment purchases of high unit value durable consumer goods—and many do. But numerous large houses of this type also carry on a considerable business in financing industrial goods marketing. They are especially well equipped to provide funds for the purchase and sale of equipment and somewhat less interested in or adapted to financing inventories or ordinary accounts receivable.[1] In 1964, one such house carried about $667 million of industrial financing.

Some of these firms are prepared to give the industrial marketer financial service for accounts receivable much the same as that provided by the factor. They tend more to make loans on such accounts as collateral rather than to purchase them. Their basic charge for this service is a rate of a fraction of 1 percent per day of the gross amount of receivables pledged. For the ordinary marketer of industrial goods, the commercial finance company probably offers a more readily accessible source of accounts receivable service than does the factor, because most factors specialize largely in the textile business. Therefore, their understanding of the problems peculiar to other industries is not so great.

Because of its wide experience in the medium- and long-term credit field, gained in its business of financing installment purchases of consumer goods, the commercial finance house is well qualified to render the same kind of service in the industrial goods field. Several firms of this type have developed very flexible arrangements for industrial installment financing. They are prepared to investigate a client borrower's operations and to work out a financial program that will enable him to pay off an equipment loan in a manner that will not handicap his operations or dangerously commit his future income or working capital.

These arrangements usually take the form of notes, which fall due at strategic intervals best suited to fit in with the borrower's expected receipts of income and other commitments of working capital, or a program of installment payments whereby he can pay for the equipment out of current income, which he is using the machine to produce. Sometimes, these arrangements become highly complicated. One case reported involved a four-way deal participated in by a printing machinery manufacturer, a printer who bought the equipment, a large customer of the printer for whose work the machine was needed, and the finance company.

Can manufacturers make and sell to packers machines for sealing filled cans. Two large can makers arranged with a commercial finance company to handle the installment selling programs by which they distributed these machines to the food packers. The same finance company operates an

---

[1] Much of the information used here was obtained from publications of the CIT corporation, and in conversations with its executives.

installment system by which an electronic and sonic device manufacturer sells to fishing vessel operators a sonic depth sounder for locating schools of fish. This firm also offers to dentists an installment arrangement to finance needed equipment purchases. This and other commercial finance companies have sought to adapt their services to fit into the distribution needs of industrial marketers.

Manufacturers of expensive industrial equipment, materials, or components, the inventories of which absorb a large part of the capital of the typical customer, often find it desirable to arrange with finance houses to make credit available to customers of good standing. Many buyers are likely to look on such ready-made financial arrangements as a distinctly worthwhile part of the service offered by the supplier. They may represent the difference between making and losing a sale.

Installment Sales

A considerable amount of industrial equipment is sold on an installment basis. There are no figures from which to make any reliable estimate of the extent to which this device is used. It is certain that in total dollar volume it falls far short of the volume of consumer goods installment sales. It is also probably true that the percentage of total sales of industrial equipment made on this basis is much smaller than that in durable consumer goods.

There is probably less real need for the installment sales contract in industrial goods marketing. Comparatively few machines are so high in unit price that their purchase constitutes a significant drain on the capital structure of the buying firm. The business house also has available sources of capital, such as sales of securities, bank loans, and loans from finance companies, which are denied to many consumers or available to them only on terms they do not want to accept.

On the other hand, an installment purchase contract for a piece of industrial equipment usually constitutes a sounder extension of credit than does such an arrangement applied to the sale of a consumers' goods item. First, the industrial buyer probably has planned his purchase somewhat more carefully and on a more businesslike basis than the consumer usually bothers to do. He is apt to match future income against future outgo a little more realistically. Second, more detailed and reliable credit information about the industrial buyer is usually available. Third, if the industrial purchaser's estimates of his future business are sound, he will generally be able to apply money earned by using the equipment to pay off the debt he incurred in buying it. To some degree, the equipment pays for itself. Installment credit seems a sound method of financing the sale of industrial equipment.

Some industrial marketers offer a sort of hybrid lease-installment arrangement. This works somewhat as follows.

The manufacturer of a machine selling at $48,000 leases the machine to a user under contract providing for a monthly payment of, say, $2,000. At the end of 12 months, the user has the option of buying the machine by applying, say, $12,000 out of the $24,000 he has paid during the year to a purchase price, which has been scaled down at a fixed depreciation rate. If the depreciation period were set at 8 years, for example, the scaled-down price would be about $42,000. The remaining $6,000 of the monthly payments received by the seller applies to financing charges, maintenance charges, and profit on the financial operation as such. Similar adjusted options are offered at various stages during the period of the lease. These figures are very rough approximations and probably are not entirely realistic; but they should convey an idea of the general nature of the transaction.

This arrangement has the advantage of enabling the user to have the benefit of the machine without initially committing any large block of capital to its purchase. At any of the stated option periods, he may acquire ownership of the machine if that benefits him financially. Seemingly, it may also enable him to charge off the lease payments as a current expense in his income tax computations. This may be a snare and a delusion, however, because the Bureau of Internal Revenue generally tends to take a dim view of such arrangements. Therefore, the marketer who is tempted to use this sort of contract should submit it to the careful scrutiny of his attorney and tax adviser, so that the arrangement he offers allows the user the maximum legitimate income tax benefits possible. He should also be very careful to see that his advertising and sales promotion materials and his salesmen give no false impressions of the tax benefits safely available to the user under the contract. The irritation generated in the user in the course of a losing encounter with the Bureau of Internal Revenue is very liable to rub off on the marketer who proposed the deal in the first place.

Financial Service Policy

The industrial goods marketer may adopt any one of three policies in his approach to the problems involved in the relations between marketing and finance.

1. He may completely ignore the sales possibilities of the credit service, aside from financing the necessary inventory, and devote his attention to stimulating sales by other methods, relying on the prospective buyer to provide his own purchase financing. This policy is apt to seriously limit sales, especially during periods when he must sell in a buyers' market. On the other hand, it means that he gets cash for all the sales he makes, and his rate of capital turnover is not reduced by the impounding of large sums in accounts receivable.

2. The industrial marketer may finance the stocking and sale of his

goods entirely out of his own capital through open-book account, install-ment sale, or some other credit arrangement. The execution of this policy requires large working capital; it results in a slow rate of turnover of working capital; it involves, in many cases, a high cost of record keeping and correspondence with customers; and it is apt to bring about losses of customer goodwill because of the sometimes drastic steps that must be taken in making collections. On the other hand, this policy enables the marketer to keep all his financial strings in his own hands, and to regulate his relations with customers unhampered by the ideas and interference of third parties whose primary interest lies in money management.

3. The industrial goods manufacturer may avoid the detailed activities involved in providing financial service to his customers but arrange with some sort of financial institution to supply such services. He usually cannot work through a bank to do this, but must turn to a factor, a commercial finance house, or some other type of concern specializing in industrial financing operations.

SUMMARY

In this chapter, we discussed several matters that, while apparently discrete, all center around the management of customer relations and service.

Reciprocity is widely practiced in industrial goods marketing. The practice of awarding patronage to customers when all other buying factors are equal is probably sound. Other forms of reciprocity are of doubtful desirability. Whether or not to practice reciprocity is as an issue for top-management decision. Probably the best ways to keep it within reasonable bounds are to charge its cost as a sales expense and to decide each case on the basis of its effect on net profit.

To sell or to lease is also an issue that demands top-management decision. The terms surrounding the leasing transactions vary widely. The buyer may favor leasing because: it reduces his capital investment and enables him to charge off as an expense claims on income not allowable on owned equipment; it reduces his risks; and it diminishes his problems of servicing the equipment he uses. The machine maker finds that: leasing may afford him a greater total return on output than he could get by selling; it tends to stabilize his income; it broadens his market; but it may augment his servicing problems; and it tends to increase his capital re-quirements. Leasing seems desirable when equipment is expensive, when repair and maintenance is unusually important, when equipment must be used seasonally or sporadically, and when a material must be used in connection with a certain type of machine.

The provision of parts is often looked on as a stepchild. The results are that poor parts service handicaps the original sale of new equipment or that the pirate parts makers get the business. Both of these difficulties can be minimized or eliminated by a sound system for marketing parts.

Engineering and technical service is necessary. Whether it should be rendered by the engineering department, the marketing department, the development unit, or some combination of them depends on the nature and importance of the service and the conditions under which it must be rendered. This service is subject to grave abuses.

The chief financial problems in marketing industrial goods cluster around the costs of carrying inventory and of carrying accounts receivable. Both may be financed out of invested capital at the cost of slow turnover of capital funds. Borrowing on warehouse receipts may be used to finance inventory. Factors may be used to finance both inventory and credit extensions, as may commercial finance houses. Industrial equipment is well suited to financing by installment sales.

CASES APPLICABLE TO PART VII

PART VIII

Control in Industrial Marketing Management

THE CONTROL FUNCTION is probably more important in managing industrial goods marketing than it is in the consumer goods field. A successful industrial marketing operation requires the carefully articulated and more or less precisely timed cooperation of a number of people in the marketing firm, most of whom are carrying on jobs that are highly specialized and often technical in nature. Such cooperation rarely occurs without careful planning and adroit control.

At the same time, the control operation is surrounded with unusual difficulties in the field of industrial goods marketing. The existence of the big three or big four in the average buying industry loads many of industrial marketing activities with very heavy stakes and makes each move of great importance. The multiple buying influence in the customer firm increases the number of points where controls need to be applied. And the long period involved in negotiating many industrial marketing transactions tends to obscure the causes of customer action and so to increase the difficulty of checking performance.

In Chapter 19, we will attempt to elaborate on some of these difficulties and indicate how the industrial goods marketer may attempt to handle them.

Chapter 19

CONTROL OF INDUSTRIAL

MARKETING OPERATIONS

NATURE OF THE CONTROL FUNCTION

THE ESSENCE of the control process lies in seeking to answer the question: How are we doing? The question is closely related to setting objectives and making plans. In fact, we can do little in the direction of measuring how well we are doing something until we know clearly what it is we want to do and how we propose to do it. So it is that controls should grow out of plans, which, in turn, derive from the objectives sought. Therefore, in discussing controls in industrial goods marketing we will revert to some of the material in the earlier chapter on planning.

The control process has three phases.

1. Setting standards of performance. Because the nature of marketing work is so intangible and the marketing of many industrial products requires so much preliminary development work, setting standards for it is very difficult.

2. Measuring performance against standards. The two phases of this operation are often done together. One consists of collecting information about what is happening; the other involves comparing this with the standards.

3. Correcting failures to perform to standard. This involves the analysis of such failures to find out why standards were not met, sometimes making plans to rectify the failures, and taking the necessary executive action to prevent their recurrence. When a standard is new and its validity uncertain, or when the conditions that governed its setting are found to have changed, corrective action may involve changing the standard.

STANDARDS OF PERFORMANCE

Too often, standards of performance for marketing, as for the other functions of business, are set entirely on an accounting basis or are borrowed from published or privately reported sets of marketing controls used by other firms, or are suggested by the people who write books on the subject. Such standards and the control instruments that implement

521

them are apt to be unrealistic when applied to the marketing activities of any one industrial goods house.

The marketing control standards of a company should grow mainly out of two things—the conditions under which the firm's marketing work must be done and its marketing objectives. For example, a firm new in a field needs to apply marketing performance standards that are different from those of a well-established one. In marketing a new product, a wise manager will apply standards that differ from those he uses in the distribution of one that is mature. Since an objective is what you want to get done, and control is an attempt to measure how well you are doing the things you set out to do, performance standards should bear a close relationship to objectives. This precept is so simple that it seems childish nonsense to state it, but it is also so commonplace that setters of performance standards tend to overlook it.

Since no two firms are likely to have the same marketing objectives nor to operate under identical market conditions, we will confine our discussion of marketing performance standards to those of wide application and general use.

Marketing Plans

The marketing plan is rapidly gaining importance as a standard of marketing performance. Since it should include a detailed statement of objectives and the steps the marketing organization proposes to take in order to achieve them, the plan seems to be a good device for measuring actual operations and results. The chief drawback to its use is that it offers no standard against which to measure the adequacy of the objectives or of the plan itself. This is not strictly true, because the objective is not likely to be achieved if the marketing plan is inadequate. But this means that the objective, and not the various parts of the plan, is being used as the real performance standard. And the system offers no means of checking the adequacy of the objectives. On the other hand, if the marketing plan and the objectives contained in it are carefully drawn, they represent the best judgment of the firm's marketing executives, at the time of preparation, as to what can be achieved with the resources available and how it can be achieved.

Short-run marketing plans are much more useful as control standards than are long-run plans. The maker of a long-run plan can only try to forecast what conditions will exist in his market 5 or 10 years ahead, to determine what future position he proposes to occupy, and to prepare a general program for capturing that position. A marketing plan covering a period of 5 or 10 years cannot realistically be prepared in detail as great as one for the coming year or half or quarter of a year. It can merely be sketched out with enough exactness to indicate the future profit possibilities, to suggest sales and cost objectives, and to guide financial and general management in forecasting the firm's future needs for resources, financial and otherwise, and in planning to provide them.

It is especially hard for the industrial marketer to make the long-range forecast that is basic to a long-range marketing plan. In order to forecast, he must deal with three major variables: the demand for the end products his goods are used to make, the technology of the industry that makes them, and the technology of his own industry in making his products. All these are highly uncertain.

As a result, long-term marketing plans are not generally used as standards of performance for control. The technique of long-range forecasting has not yet been perfected to the point where its results are exact enough to serve this purpose. Then, too, the longer the target period of a forecast, the more numerous and greater become the variable factors that may upset it and invalidate the plans based on it. Partly because of these factors, long-range plans usually are so general that they lack the necessary detail for use as standards of marketing peformance. So most firms that use marketing plans for performance standards employ the short-run variety—a year or less.

As we noted in an earlier chapter, if the short-run or project marketing plan is properly drawn it includes a statement of the objectives we propose to gain, together with a list of the things we intend to do and the resources we expect to use in the process of achieving them. These may be arranged into a schedule by the addition of the time element. This affords us four checkpoints for control work as the operation proceeds: (1) Have we done the things planned? (2) Have we used the resources committed? (3) Have we done these things on time? (4) Have the objectives been gained or how far along are we toward attaining them?

The marketing plan may be broken down by products or groups of products, by customer groups, by geographical divisions, or by functional activities. This affords the same control checkpoints for each subsidiary operation.

As a system of control standards of performance, the marketing plan has the same general advantages and disadvantages as objectives. It is better than objectives in that (*a*) the items in it are much more specific and (*b*) most of the items can be checked during the course of the operation, while objectives are usually achieved or lost only when the operation is complete or, in some cases, long after its completion. Checking performance of the marketing plan is thus much easier and more timely. But both suffer from the same weakness in that they offer no standard against which to measure the excellence of the objectives or the plan.

Marketing Budget

The marketing budget probably constitutes the most widely used standard of marketing performance for both industrial and consumer goods. If a budget is realistically prepared on the basis of marketing plans from which its dollar figures are drawn, it forms a logical and useful set of yardsticks by which to measure the effectiveness of marketing activities. When the budget is the result of a guessing process, without detailed marketing plans to assure its realism, it is probably worse than no standard at all. As a control standard, the budget presents about the same elements of weakness and strength as does the marketing plan.

Past Sales Records

Another very widely used standard of performance is the past sales record of the firm. Sales this day, this week, this month, or this year to date are measured against sales during the same period last year, or several previous years. The same technique may be applied to the several categories of marketing expense. To some extent, this is a process of measuring the garment of today against the pattern of yesterday. It is sometimes assumed that as long as improvement is demanded the method may be regarded as a good one. This is not necessarily true, since the method takes no account of the effect that changes in general business activity or in trade conditions may exercise on the sales of a firm. For example, a decline in sales that is less than the industry average may represent good performance, while an increase that leaves the firm with a shrunken market share or decreased profits can hardly be so regarded. Because of the unusual sensitivity of industrial goods demand to changes in business conditions, this method is probably less useful as a measure of performance in marketing industrial products than in selling consumer goods.

Activities

In some cases, standards may be set in terms of activity—for example, sales calls made, technical service rendered, catalogs distributed, or distributors' salesmen trained—rather than in terms of dollars. This sort of standard is especially useful in industrial goods marketing because so much of the work of promoting sales must be of a developmental type, which cannot be expected to bring immediate results. If an activity quota is used as a means of setting sales tasks, it may also be employed with reasonable effectiveness as a standard of performance.

Market Potential

A more fundamental standard by which to measure marketing performance, and one that is neither the product of a firm's managerial plans nor the outcome of its past activities, is the market potential. The market potential is the total amount of a product that may reasonably be expected to be sold by all competitors distributing it in a market. It is the volume of sales of a product that a firm would have if it got all there was to get. A market potential may apply to the entire country or to any portion of it, such as a district, a division, a salesman's territory, a product or product group, or a customer or class of customers.

The market potential for some products can be constructed from actual sales figures. This technique applies to such products as gasoline or liquor, which are subject to special taxes posted in public records on a local basis, or automobiles or trucks, which must be registered before they can be used. The seller of such a product can find out for any period of time almost exactly how much of it is sold by all vendors. This figure may be taken as the market potential for the period. Very few industrial goods are of this type.

Market potentials for most industrial products must be estimated on the basis of fragmentary facts. Such estimates are made by two chief methods. One employs statistical indexes or series that are found to be indicative of the product's sales possibilities. By a proper selection and weighting of such series or indexes, a reasonably reliable system of market potential figures can sometimes be built up. This method is of use chiefly in the consumer goods field, but it may also be applied to the development of potentials for some industrial goods, such as certain supplies or materials that have a horizontal market. The indexes or series most often used for this purpose are the Federal Reserve Board index of industrial production, electrical power consumed, number of man-hours worked in manufacturing establishments, number and value of building permits issued, and others applicable to specific industries.

The second method for arriving at an area or customer market potential figure is estimation of the product's total probable consumption by each possible user and addition of all these estimates to make up the area or market potential. This method is especially applicable for use in preparing market potentials for industrial goods bought by limited numbers of users. For example, if a product can be sold to only a few hundred or even to a thousand customers, a manufacturer who has developed the proper contacts with his trade should be able to make a shrewd guess about the product's total possible or probable consumption by each one. The accuracy of these guesses may be checked against the actual figures of customers known to buy all or a certain percentage of their requirements from his firm. By using this means, he is likely to obtain a final total figure much more accurate than one he could compute by employing any combination of available indexes or statistical series.

For example, a chemical house that makes a material used by pharmaceutical firms in producing certain drug products sold under their own brands estimated its potential as follows. The total number of units of the end products made and sold was computed from figures supplied by a marketing research firm that reports product sales of a representative sample of drugstores. From information on end product labels, the amount of the material used per unit of each end product brand was computed. By a simple process of multiplication and addition, the chemical maker then arrived at the total amount of the material used by each pharmaceutical house. This figure was then checked against an analysis of information fragments gathered by its salesmen through conversation and observation during their calls.

Once a market potential has been computed, the actual sales performance of a firm can be measured against it, and the percentage of the potential volume the firm is getting in any area can be computed. In this way, management may ascertain what part of the total market it is getting, and what part of the market it is capturing in each sales area. It thus has a measure of the effectiveness of its performance on an overall basis and in each sales territory.

A well-constructed market potential is by all odds the best standard of sales performance available. Each of the other types suffers from the difficulty that in one way or another it grows out of the plans or activities of the firm itself. If the plans are too timid or inept, or the activities are ineffective, the standard will not be high enough to afford a true or reliable measure of the quality of the sales job being done. The rub comes in computing an accurate potential figure.

A market potential is not a static thing but is constantly changing. As a result, it should undergo constant revision in order to keep it up-to-date. This is probably much more true of industrial goods as a class than of consumer goods. Changes in the basic factors that underlie demand for consumer goods, such as population and purchasing power, or even consumer attitude, usually occur slowly in an area; the opening or closing of a factory in an industrial goods salesman's territory may bring about a quick and drastic shift in his potential sales. The development of a new material that is a substitute for an old one, or of a new process that increases the yield from a material, may cause dramatic changes in potential. The industrial goods marketer who uses market potentials as a managerial tool should see to it that constant revision keeps them up-to-date, even though it may be highly expensive. If he cannot afford to keep them currently accurate, he cannot afford to use them.

Marketing Cost Analysis

A highly important means of checking sales performance, which has been developed during recent years, is the analysis of distribution costs through the application of cost accounting techniques.

Since the manufacturer's costs of distributing industrial goods are not so high as those of marketing consumer goods, this is not such an effective tool of marketing planning and control in industrial goods as it is in consumer goods, but it is still very useful. A study of 74 concerns making industrial goods, picked at random from Moody's Industrials, shows a range in costs of selling and general administration from 1.6 percent to 30.3 percent of total sales, with an arithmetic average of 11.8 percent and a median of 12.7 percent. The figures for 32 companies making consumer goods, picked in the same manner, showed a range from 6.1 percent to 51.7 percent of total sales, an arithmetic average of 22.8 percent, and a median of 20.2 percent. A number of the consumer goods firms reported marketing expenses separately from general administration costs, and in such cases the marketing cost figure was used in making the comparison. All industrial goods makers combined the two types of cost in one figure in their reports, so their percentages are somewhat inflated relatively.

This difference in distribution costs is to be expected, and arises from differences in the essential nature of the two types of goods and in the conditions under which they must be marketed. Industrial goods buyers are relatively few; consumer goods buyers are many. Industrial goods are bought by experts who can be influenced to a relatively small degree by persuasion; consumer goods are bought largely by nonexperts who are susceptible to the arts of persuasion through salesmanship and advertising. The purchasers of most kinds of industrial goods are concentrated within a small area; the buyers of consumer goods are scattered throughout the nation. The average industrial buyer purchases in relatively large lots; the average buyer of consumer goods, in small lots. All of these factors tend to cause the manufacturer's cost percentage of distributing industrial goods to be less than that of marketing consumer goods.

There is considerable variation in manufacturers' costs of distribution among the various types of industrial goods. Among firms included in the above analysis, the average cost of selling and general administration for concerns making machinery was 11.5 percent of sales; for firms making materials, the figure was 8.2 percent of sales; for producers of light equipment, the percentage was 19.0 percent; for manufacturers of supplies, it was 14.8 percent; for makers of fabricated components, it was 10.4 percent; and for producers of packages and packaging materials, it was 8.4 percent of sales.

At the wholesale level, this relationship between the costs of handling the two types of goods is reversed. In 1963, the average operating cost of 32 trade groups of wholesalers handling mainly consumer goods was 15.7 percent of sales; the median figure of the group was 15.1 percent. In the same year, the average operating cost of 33 trade groups of industrial distributors was 19.1 percent of sales; their median was 21.1 percent.[1]

This higher cost of industrial distributors may be due to the fact that several of their trade groups handle articles that move through inventory very slowly. In general, though, the stocks of industrial distributors are probably no greater in relation to sales than are those of wholesalers handling consumer goods. The difference in cost is more likely to be

[1] U.S. Bureau of the Census, *1963 Census of Business, Wholesale Trade.*

explained by the fact that many industrial distributors perform functions in the industrial field closely akin to those of the consumer goods retailer. They must sell many items in very small lots; they must usually render technical services that the consumer goods wholesaler does not supply; their salesmen must have at least some technical training and experience and, in consequence, must be paid more than the less expensively trained representatives of the consumer goods wholesaler.

However, the amount of the costs of marketing industrial goods, either actual or expressed as a percentage of sales, fails to completely measure the importance of their proper management as a factor in the process of marketing such goods. Distribution costs that are too high can either remove a manufacturer from price competition or, if he sells at competitive prices, force him to be content with an inadequate margin of net profit. But by far the most important benefit to be gained by the proper analysis and management of industrial marketing costs lies in the guidance it may give in making managerial decisions on planning products, programming production, selecting marketing channels, determining marketing policies, making marketing plans, formulating inventory policies and practices, and checking performance.

Cost Allocation. In analyzing distribution costs, for either consumer or industrial goods, the first step is usually that of determining what expenses to include. A fairly sound procedure is that of including in this category all expenses incurred after the goods leave the machines that make them. This is likely to be more important for industrial than for consumer goods, because industrial goods must often be packed to suit the buyer's specifications as to size, materials, and methods used in packing.

The various types of technical help, advice, and service rendered to the industrial goods buyer are expensive phases of the marketing process that are not usually found in consumer goods marketing. It is also especially important that the costs of handling, shipping, and transporting industrial goods be included in marketing costs, because these activities usually vitally affect the service element, which is one of the most important factors determining the patronage of the buyers of such products. This element is not so important in consumer goods.

It is highly important that the work of analyzing marketing costs be done by someone whose judgment the marketing executives have complete confidence in, and that it be carried on in close cooperation with those executives. The average marketing executive is vitally interested in sales volume. When a distribution cost analysis project is proposed, the chief outcome he visualizes from it may be the discovery that many of his customers and products are unprofitable and will be dropped from the catalog or account list, with resulting loss of volume. Therefore, from the time the project is begun he must be sold on the idea that its primary purpose is not to take business away from him but to enable him to manage the firm's marketing work more efficiently and to change unprofitable items and customers into profitable ones.

It is also quite necessary that the work of allocating costs be done in close cooperation with the marketing executives of the firm, because in the process of making such allocations many assumptions about where particular cost items logically belong must be made. The validity of such assumptions often depends on a knowledge and understanding of the minor details of the marketing process. The analyst who attempts to do this work without such knowledge is likely to produce a system of allocation that will be unrealistic at so many points that it will not command the support and confidence of either the top executives, who must approve it, or the marketing executives, who must use its results if it is to be effective. Also, a long-standing axiom is that often the best way to sell a project to a man is to get him to help carry it on.

The method used in allocating distribution costs depends to a very great extent on the type of cost results sought. Three basic types of cost results may be obtained from cost analysis—costs by product, by customer, and by transaction. From these can be derived costs by product or customer groups, by channels of distribution, by salesmen, and by territories, branches, districts, or regions.

One problem encountered in almost every distribution costing project is that of how far one should go in allocating costs. For example, is it desirable to allocate general overhead, research expenses, advertising, and general marketing overhead? The case for including advertising and general marketing overhead seems fairly clear. They are definitely a part of the marketing effort of the company. They vary to a considerable extent as the selling emphasis varies.

If the advertising features specific products in each piece of copy, its costs can be allocated directly to those products with almost complete validity. On the other hand, allocating the cost of general institutional advertising among products, either on the basis of sales volume or on the relative volume of other directly allocable costs, cannot be logically defended. Much industrial advertising features no specific product, especially when the advertiser makes a line of materials or supplies containing many items. An arbitrary basis of allocation is inescapable. An analyst can only try to make it as realistic as possible.

Marketing overhead is like general overhead in that: (1) there is no method of allocating it, except volume of sales, volume of other costs, or a study—bound to be highly inaccurate—of the ways marketing executives spend their time; (2) the deletion of a product from the line, or the dropping of a customer, will in no way change its total amount. If these costs, often so large that they constitute a significant portion of the total marketing expense, are allocated, they tend to distort the results so as to obscure the cost effect of activities whose amount and direction are subject to managerial control.

For this reason, it is sometimes good practice to exclude from the analysis all cost items for which there is no logically defensible method of allocation, or those that arise from activities not subject to the control of marketing management. This would exclude all general overhead, research,[2] and, in some cases, general marketing overhead and advertising. The final results of such an analysis would be expressed as the contribution of each customer, product, or transaction to general overhead and net profits—not as its contribution to net profits alone.

On the other hand, the inclusion of all cost factors in the analysis results in a job that has the appearance of greater completeness and finish. It must be admitted that this appearance is often spurious, sometimes misleading, and often handicaps management in the use of cost results as a basis for decisions, when it should facilitate or lend soundness to such use. But if cost results are to be used in checking the profit performance of products and in making product decisions, all costs must be included, or the firm may wind up with a mix entirely or largely composed of products that contribute to overhead without adding to net profits.

What we have said about the practicability of allocating overhead costs to products applies with even greater cogency to their allocation to customers or transactions. All overhead costs must be distributed on the basis of sales volume or volume of other directly allocable costs—even most of the advertising. In distribution costing work for consumer goods, advertising expenses can often be allocated directly to customers because such products are often promoted by means of local advertising, paid for jointly by the manufacturer and the retailer. This is rarely done in industrial goods advertising.

In his cost results, the marketing cost analyst must constantly compromise accuracy with the expense of getting it. When a few cents in cost one way or the other will make the difference between product A or customer X being profitable or unprofitable, there seems little point in spending dollars to obtain complete accuracy. The product or the customer merits managerial study in any case. If distribution cost analysis succeeds merely in focusing managerial attention on marketing events whose stories are written in red ink on the company books, it has achieved only half its mission. Borderline cases that tie up a firm's capital and human resources without adequate return are equally deserving of executive study and action.

It will serve no useful purpose here to enter into a detailed discussion of the methods used in allocating distribution costs to products or customers. It will be sufficient to indicate the general method employed and some of the problems encountered in the process.

Activity Classification. The first step in allocation is to classify the firm's marketing activities into several homogeneous groups. The classifications most generally used include: personal selling, advertising, stock-carrying, order handling—both paper work and physical order filling—

---

[2] When research is applied to modifying a product to suit the needs of a specific customer or group of customers, and is done at the request of the marketing executives, its cost may logically be allocated.

transportation, and supervisory work. Other classes may be used to fit the marketing conditions and methods of operation of the firm.

The second step involves segregation of the costs that apply to each of these activities. In doing this, it is necessary to divide such traditional accounting classes as rent and wages and salaries into several parts, and assign each marketing activity its proper share. In an industrial goods firm, the portion of the total marketing costs assigned to advertising and personal selling is likely to be considerably smaller than that in a consumer goods firm; the order-handling costs are apt to constitute a somewhat larger portion.

The third step involves the allocation of each activity cost to products, customers, or transactions on some basis that is sound and logical, or as nearly so as possible. It should be pointed out again that in order to produce cost results useful to management it is not necessary that every expense classification be allocated or that complete accuracy be attained.

The cost of personal selling, which includes all payments made to salesmen for salary, commissions, traveling expenses, maintenance expense, and entertainment, may be allocated to products, or groups of products, on the basis of a sort of time and motion study. A cost analyst accompanies a sample group of salesmen in the field and observes the amount of time each spends in selling each article or product group. This is often unsatisfactory because such a large part of the salesman's time is spent in general sales work not directly involving any one product. Then, too, a salesmen is very likely to depart from his normal behavior when he is under observation. The method is also very costly. About the same results will probably be obtained from a series of conversations with salesmen. The analyst then tries to appraise the relative emphasis the salesman puts on the several products or product groups, on the theory that selling time is a function of emphasis.

The techniques of time and motion study may also be employed in allocating the costs of personal selling to customers and transactions. This may be done either by traveling with the salesmen in the field or by requiring them to submit daily call reports in which they include a time schedule of their activities. Traveling expenses and the cost of salary time spent in travel may be allocated on the basis of mileage between call points. All this is tremendously time-consuming and costly. The final results often differ very little from those obtained by the simple process of allocating these expenses on the basis of an average cost per call for each salesman, computed by dividing his total costs by his total number of calls made during the period under consideration.

When advertising features specific products, its cost may be allocated directly to them. But much industrial advertising merely features the name and reputation of the firm. This cost may be allocated on the basis of the relative dollar sales volume of the several products, or according to the relative amounts of advertising cost that can be allocated directly to them. Either method is unsatisfactory, although the cost of advertising usually constitutes so small a proportion of an industrial goods manufacturer's general marketing cost structure that errors made in allocating it are not too serious.

The process of allocating advertising costs to customers and transactions is more difficult than that of distributing them among products. While the consumer goods manufacturer often engages in cooperative advertising with his dealers, which renders allocation easy, this is not often done by the industrial goods maker. Very rarely is an advertisement for an industrial product directed at, or for, the benefit of any specific customer. If the advertiser sells through distributors, the cost of trade journal advertising may be spread among distributor-customers according to the circulation of the journal among their user-customers. This may not be entirely sound, since, to a large extent, the advertisement is probably directed to prospective, as well as actual, customers. The bulk of the average industrial goods manufacturer's advertising expense must be distributed among customers on the basis of either sales volume or the amount of advertising cost, sometimes relatively small, that can be directly allocated on some logical basis. It is sometimes possible to allocate advertising expenses to customers by first allocating them to products, computed as a definite charge per unit or per dollar sold, and then to customers through the application of this factor to the number of units or dollars worth of each product bought by each purchaser.

The financing costs associated with the work of marketing are usually two—discounts for prompt payment, which may be treated as a cost or deducted from gross sales to get cash billings, and the cost of financing finished goods stocks held to service sales. Since discounts for cash are usually expressed in terms of a percentage of selling price, and since they must be credited to each customer's account, it is not difficult to allocate them directly to customers. If a firm has a large number of small customers, so that the work of checking cash discounts taken will be too expensive and time-consuming to be worthwhile, it may be possible to compute an average percentage taken by customers, and then use that figure across the board, except with the larger buyers, who may be expected to consistently take their discounts. For example, one firm that gave 2 percent, 10 days, net 30 days terms found that the average discount taken was 1 percent.

This cost may be allocated to products on the average percentage basis, unless it seems worthwhile to analyze invoices by item extensions, which is apt to be exceedingly expensive. The result would probably be somewhat more accurate for both customers and products if the consistent discount-taking customers were segregated and charged directly with their discounts taken, while the others were treated on an average percentage basis. In the course of this process, products and transactions could be treated in the same manner.

The cost of financing finished goods stocks is often treated as a part of the general expense of carrying them. This method is probably more logical and convenient than treatment as a separate operation; so we will defer it.

In an industrial goods firm, the expenses arising from the order-handling routine are likely to be a more significant portion of the total distribution cost structure than they are in a consumer goods business. The emphasis industrial buyers put on delivery service quality as a factor influencing patronage causes vendors to emphasize it as an activity and leads to greater expense. Such expenses naturally fall into two classes—those arising from the paper work involved and those growing out of the work of physically handling the merchandise in assembling the order and preparing it for shipment.

Two factors influence the amount of paper work involved in servicing either a customer or a product. One is the number of orders handled; the other is the number of line extensions handled. A line extension is one line on an order including, at least, the number of product units, the description or designation of an item, the unit price, and the total price for the amount of the item bought on the order. In the course of the usual order-handling routine, certain operations must be performed on an order regardless of whether it has 1 line extension or 100, or totals $1 or $10,000. The remaining paper work operations in such a routine usually vary according to the number of line extensions on the order.

The process of allocation, therefore, is carried on by ascertaining a cost per line extension and a cost per order, counting the number of orders and line extensions for each customer or each product, and multiplying. Such per unit costs may be obtained by means of time and motion studies that yield none too accurate results. A time and motion study may ignore the effects of alternate periods of intense activity and waiting time in order-handling, which result from the normal ebb and flow of orders through the house. It is possible to study the activities of each person in the order-handling group to determine what proportion of his working time is taken up with activities arising from the mere presence of the order, and how much time is devoted to activities arising from the number of line extensions. On the basis of this data and the costs originating from the work of these persons, it is possible to compute an average cost per order and an average cost per line extension, including waiting times. When machine bookkeeping is used, these items will be an average cost per customer card and per commodity or transaction card handled.

The analyst may allocate order-handling costs to customers by counting the number of orders received from a customer and the number of line extensions they contain, and by applying the cost factors just described, augmented by proportional allocations of cost of space, power, heat, light, machine time, etc. By a count of the number of line extensions involving each product, and the application thereto of the appropriate factor described above, the cost of that activity may be allocated to products. The costs peculiar to the order as a whole may then be allocated to products in proportion to the allocations of line extension costs. Some idea of the relative importance of these types of cost may be obtained from the experience of a firm whose order cost was computed to be $1.44, and whose expense per line extension was figured at 40 cents.

The costs of the physical handling of goods in filling orders may be allocated on the basis of the units in which they are handled. A material or supply is likely to be handled: (*a*) in car- or truckloads; (*b*) in bulk containers; (*c*) in the individual packages into which it is put for use, such as bottles or boxes; and (*d*) in the standard cases or cartons into which these individual packages are put for storage and transport. Small tools, for example, are likely to be handled a piece at a time or in cartons or cases containing tens or dozens or multiples of tens or dozens; a fine chemical may be handled in 50-pound or 100-pound bulk drums, in 5-pound, 1-pound, or ¼-pound bottles, or in cases containing a dozen or a multiple of a dozen such bottles; a heavy material is likely to be handled in carloads or truckloads.

If, in the process of filling orders, goods are handled in bulk, in cases, and in loose pieces, the cost analyst may seek to establish an average or normal cost for handling each unit. To compute this cost, he can make a time and motion study or a study of the operations of the average person engaged in order-filling work to determine how much of his working time he spends in handling each type of unit and how many units he handles. One firm, for example, found that its costs were: bulk containers, 56 cents each; case lots, 40 cents each; and loose pieces, 12 cents apiece. By counting the number of each type of units supplied a customer or handled in delivering a product over a period of time, and multiplying by the appropriate cost factors, a reasonably accurate allocation of these costs can be achieved. With machine accounting, this is not too expensive.

The cost of packaging may or may not be regarded as a part of distribution expense. In most cases, it is probably more convenient and less expensive to treat packaging costs as a part of production expense. When this done, the only packaging expense the distribution cost analyst must consider is that of putting loose pieces into shipping cartons, which can be allocated as a part of the physical order-handling expense. When the customer demands a special put-up, its cost should probably be regarded as a distribution expense, but it can be allocated to products in the same manner as other production expenses. If packaging costs are treated as a production expense, they are allocated to products and so to customers and transactions as part of the cost of goods sold. If, on the other hand, they are regarded as part of the costs of distribution, they must be allocated to products by the use of production costing techniques, and thence to the customers who buy the products.

Stock-carrying expense is a function of two factors—space and time. It includes the cost of funds invested in inventory and the expenses arising from maintenance of the space in which the inventory is housed, plus certain incidental outlays such as insurance. By dividing the number of usuable square feet in a warehouse not needed for aisles, etc., into the cost of maintaining the warehouse, the analyst may obtain a cost per square foot of usable space. He may then compute the average number of square feet set aside to house the stocks of a given product, and by multiplying these two will derive a total space occupation cost for the product over a period of time. Dividing this figure by the total number of units of the product passing through inventory during the period, the analyst obtains a space-occupation cost per unit of the product handled. When an article is of such a nature that it can be stacked from floor to ceiling, it may be more realistic to compute a cost per cubic foot.

The cost of the funds employed in carrying the inventory may usually be computed as the interest at a reasonable rate on the capital invested in the inventory during the time it is held. Probably the most convenient method of allocating this cost to products is to compute total interest charges for the period on funds invested in stocks of a product, divide this amount by the number of units of the product passing through the inventory during the period, and thus obtain a financing cost per unit.

While stock-carrying costs can be allocated more or less directly to products on a fairly logical basis, they can be allocated to customers only indirectly by adding the stock-carrying costs for each product to its cost of goods sold, or by charging against the customer the appropriate stock-carrying cost for each unit of each product he buys. An industrial goods vendor sometimes agrees to carry a specified stock of his product earmarked for a specific customer. In such a case, of course, inventory-carrying costs must be allocated to the customer by a special technique suited to the circumstances.

When industrial goods are shipped by common carrier, the cost analyst can allocate transportation costs on the basis of published freight tariffs or freight bills. A company's products are likely to be sufficiently homogeneous so that all or large groups of them take the same freight rate. If this is the case, the entire freight bill for the company or for the product group can be divided among the various products on the basis of the poundage shipped. If this is not the case, a more laborious and costly method must be followed in making the allocation. Transportation costs may be allocated to customers on the basis of an analysis of the company freight bills, or they may be computed less accurately and less expensively on the basis of the poundage shipped to the customer times a zone freight rate. The method to be used depends on the bulk of the products, the number and variety of them sold, and the importance of transportation expense in the total distribution cost structure. When the seller practices freight equalization, the allocation of transportation costs can become almost impossibly complex.

Some sales supervisory costs can be allocated directly to products or groups of products, or to groups of customers. Very few can be allocated directly to individual customers. The costs arise from the activities of executives and supervisors who are responsible for overseeing the work of selling specific products or product groups, or to groups of customers. These expenses can probably be best allocated to individual products and customers within a group on the basis of the volume of other directly allocable sales costs assigned to them. The same is true of expenses of the firm's general marketing executives; any attempt to divide their total costs among product or customer groups is rarely worth the expense involved.

Uses of Cost Information.   Cost information has such important uses in marketing planning, and its control uses apply on such a distinctive basis, that it seems desirable to discuss them here instead of in the general section on the uses of control information.

Marketing cost analysis is worse then wasted unless its results are used by executives in making managerial decisions. They will not be used for this purpose unless the executives who make the decisions are convinced of the value of the entire project and of the validity of its results. For this reason, the cost analyst must at all stages of the process constantly seek to sell the analysis and the facts it discloses to the responsible marketing executives of the firm. This has already been pointed out, but it is of such paramount importance that the admonition cannot be too often repeated.

While the analyst should, during the early stages of a distributive cost job, plan with some precision the nature and uses of the cost results he sets out to obtain, he should be alert at all times throughout the process to discover by-product results not contemplated in the original plan. Such results often appear and are sometimes fully as important as those he sets out to find.

Selecting Channels.   A cost analysis may be of value to a firm's executives in selecting the channels of distribution to be used. A company that made a chemical product used by many small processors was selling direct to user-customers. A cost of distribution analysis showed that the firm's business with most of these customers was in the red. It was apparent that if the firm dropped all its losing customers, the remaining volume would be so small that it could no longer produce under favorable cost conditions. It was found that these small customers were served by distributors who sold them other materials, supplies, and equipment. While the gross margin it was possible to allow distributors on the product in question was not enough to net them much, if any, profit, it was found that in the process of selling equipment and other materials on which they enjoyed a satisfactory gross margin they felt the need of making regular and fairly frequent calls on their customers. The product in question would both give an excuse for making such calls and pay the cost of making them. So it was possible to arrange for a satisfactory number of distributors, scattered strategically over the country, to handle the product, with a resulting volume that enabled the manufacturer to make and sell it profitably. Other similar cases could be cited.

Customer Selection. The results of a cost of distribution analysis may provide a basis upon which a firm's sales executives can select customers to be dropped from the customer list. This does not mean that all customers whose business is not profitable should be dropped. Nor does it mean that a customer's profitability should be the only factor, or even the primary one, to be considered in deciding whether to retain or drop him.

Unprofitability simply indicates that the customer's relation to the firm should receive careful attention. Obviously, the first thing to be considered in studying the problem of an unprofitable customer is what, if anything, can be done to make the firm's business with him profitable. It may be that the salesmen are calling on him oftener than is necessary. He may be getting more service than the firm is justified in giving. It may be that he is ordering in small quantities and oftener than he should. It may be possible to correct some or all of these cost-generating mistakes.

Other factors should be considered before deciding to drop an unprofitable customer. He may also be a supplier from whom the firm buys materials or equipment that it could not get on equally satisfactory terms elsewhere. It may be that he has connections in the trade whose patronage would be alienated by a refusal to sell directly to him any longer. It may be that while he is now a small buyer whose business is not large enough to be profitable, his potentialities for growth are such that he is likely to become a highly profitable account. Some years ago, a chemical house sold direct to a small buyer whose processing operations were carried on in a garage. Other houses refused to service him direct because his business was unprofitable. The faith the supplier manifested in his future was justified in later years when his purchases from the friendly house varied between $500,000 and $1 million annually, and he would buy from no other.

Some industrial goods manufacturers follow the policy of selling to certain customers direct and relying on distributors to serve others. Usually, the distinction is made on the basis of volume of purchases. The profitability of the account may offer a better guide in choosing customers to be granted direct status, which often carries at least a small price advantage as compared with the figure at which the distributor must sell. While cost analysis results should not be the only factor to be considered in selecting customers for direct selling status, it should be an important one.

Customer Emphasis. In the administration of customer relations, marketing cost analysis results may serve an important purpose by offering a basis upon which sales emphasis may be varied among customers. This type of analysis often discloses that much sales effort is being wasted on customers who are not profitable and give no promise of ever becoming so. For example, one cost study disclosed that a customer whose business would have been unprofitable without any personal selling expense charged against it was visited 26 times during a year by a salesman assigned to the account—the same number of calls he bestowed on his highly profitable customers. Nor was there any indication of the existence of future sales potential that might justify the selling attention through possible future profits. The firm that wants to stagger its salesmen's calls by varying the number of their visits to different customers will find a customer cost study a most helpful factor in arranging such a schedule.

Pricing. The use of cost analysis results in pricing has already been discussed. Of course, the most important part of the cost structure of almost all industrial products is composed of production or materials expenses, but marketing costs usually possess sufficient significance so that their improper allocation to products or product groups may cause a firm either to sell without profit or to price itself out of the market. Adequate marketing costing can be a very real help in price administration.

Product Deletion. An industrial goods concern with an extended line of products may find the results of distribution cost accounting a great help in administering its product deletion program. Such a firm must be constantly alert to add to its line new products that give promise of profitability, and to delete old ones that have outlived their usefulness. When applied to new products, of course, marketing cost analysis must be so largely guesswork that it is of limited value. But in dealing with old products, the situation is different. Presumably, any article in the line that is not realizing a profit is a candidate for deletion. This does not mean that every such item should be deleted, but it does mean that the justification for its continued existence as a part of the firm's product line should be carefully examined. Distribution cost analysis can be of very great importance as a guide to product deletion work.

Packaging. A by-product result of distribution cost analysis may consist of the information it discloses about the packaging work of the firm. It may show that packaging materials or supplies to the customer's specifications is too expensive to justify continuance. It may indicate that certain products in small demand are being packaged in job lots that are too small.

For example, a firm's long line of a certain type of materials included many bought in very small lots and infrequently. It packaged, in runs of 7 units at a time, an item of which 50 units were sold annually. A distribution cost study indicated that this item was one the company lost money on, even though other sizes of the same article were profitable. A further analysis to determine the reason disclosed that the cost of the item was out of line because of heavy packaging charges per unit. Examination showed that the bulk of the packaging charges of 95 cents a unit were the result of makeready and cleanup time in the packaging process. As a result of packaging a year's supply instead of 7 units at a time, the packaging cost was reduced to about 20 cents a unit. Even with the addition of 2 percent a month for stock-carrying costs, the saving was enough to change a loss item into one on which the company enjoyed a profit. The discovery of this minor loss product led to a search for other similar items, which, in turn, resulted in substantial savings throughout the line.

Direction of Sales Effort. A knowledge of the distribution costs of specific products enables a firm's marketing managers to direct sales effort so as to emphasize the products with greater profit possibilities and thereby to maximize earnings. In some cases, marketing cost analysis by products may indicate that the expenditure of greater sales effort on some of those not showing adequate profit results will increase volume and turn losing items into profitable ones. Much may be gained by a proper direction of sales emphasis; marketing cost analysis may be of great help in guiding the direction of such emphasis.

By combining the marketing cost results of customers, a picture of the profitability of a salesman's efforts may be obtained, making possible a more intelligent direction of his activities and affording a measure of their effectiveness. A further combination of the cost results for salesmen into cost results for a branch, district, division, or region may afford the same type of managerial benefits.

Order Size. Marketing cost analysis may disclose that orders below a given size are without profit. For example, a firm found that when one of its products was ordered in less than 250-pound lots the transaction was in the red. Since this article was usually bought alone and not in combination with others, it was apparent that any customer who habitually purchased in less than this quantity was a losing one. Such buyers were referred to distributors who, because they handled other products made by other manufacturers and sold to the same purchasers, were able to serve buyers of smaller lots without losing money on the business.

Those who make decisions on the basis of marketing cost analysis results must always bear in mind that within wide limits many such costs behave like overhead. Consider, for example, the expense of the paper work involved in handling orders. In a firm of any size, the order-handling routine is a sort of production-line operation in which each of a number of people perform a single function on each order. Once such an operation is set up and staffed, the volume of orders it can handle is subject to very wide variation.

For example, it may be economical to set up and staff a unit to handle 300 orders a day, but the same staff may be able to process twice that number of orders without expansion. If the volume of orders increases to more than 600 a day, the division of work must be reorganized and more people added. This means that if the order-handling routine of a firm is set up on a 300 order-per-day basis and is actually handling 450 orders there will be very little, if any, saving enjoyed by reducing orders to 400 per day. No real saving will result until the order volume is reduced below 300 a day so that cuts may economically be made in the order-routine staff.

To a considerable extent, the costs of personal selling behave in the same manner; several other important types of marketing costs follow the same pattern. Therefore, efforts to control distribution costs are sometimes regarded as bootless. On the other hand, the firm that labors to keep expense-generating factors trimmed within reasonable proportions will find itself able to respond to changes in its volume of business without excessive additions to cost when volume increases, and without drastic personnel changes when business declines. Moreover, its marketing costs will always be somewhere near what they should be, and are not likely to affect its competitive position adversely.

Marketing managers who rely on cost analysis results in making their decisions must also constantly bear in mind that it is sometimes good business for a firm to lose money on some of its operations. This loss may be justified on the ground of customer service and goodwill, the future possibilities of profit from those operations, and other like factors. For example, so long as its total business with them is profitable a concern may be willing to sell certain customers money-losing items that the customers need in order to conduct their enterprises. The supplier who is unwilling to supply products that are cats and dogs may find it difficult to win patronage on items that are profitable. It is no business crime to lose money on certain items. The crime consists in not knowing that items are being handled at a loss, and in not knowing why it is worthwhile to continue handling them without profit. Marketing cost analysis discloses such losses and often supplies a clue to whether they are worthwhile.

CHECKING PERFORMANCE

The process of checking performance against standards involves collecting, analyzing, and studying information about the firm's marketing activities and their results. This is done chiefly by two methods— observation and reports, mainly statistical.

Observation

For this purpose, observation is much less useful in marketing than in production, and it is less applicable to industrial goods marketing than to consumer goods. Unless his span of authority is very broad or his plants are widely scattered, a production executive can, by walking the shop, have a chance to see what practically every man under him is doing. Many marketing executives would spend months visiting and observing all the men under them. The executive in charge of marketing consumer goods can observe how a part of his operation is working every time he visits a retail store that can handle his product, views or listens to a TV or radio program, reads a newspaper or a magazine, or talks with his friends or neighbors. The industrial marketer can observe his advertising and talk with his customers at trade gatherings.

Aside from this, his observation of performance is largely limited to traveling with his salesmen, who are very likely to perform differently when he is with them than when they call on customers alone. But he can gather much information about the quality of their work from various telltale signs that indicate the respect in which they are held by their customers. If he or his salesmen command the confidence of his distributors, he can often secure permission to examine their stocks and thus judge the adequacy and representativeness of their inventories. In spite of its limitations, personal observation is useful to the industrial marketer in checking the performance of at least part of his marketing organization.

Statistical Analysis

The operating records, particularly of sales, expenditures, orders, shipments, and inquires, supply very useful control information if properly analyzed.

Sales figures may be broken down by products or product groups, customers or groups of customers, salesmen's territories or other geographical areas, or on any other basis that promises to be useful. These classifications can then be compared with performance during past periods, such as last year or several preceding years, last month or last week, or the same month or week last year. The consumer goods marketer may even find it useful to compare today's sales with those a year ago today. This is usually not worthwhile for the industrial goods marketer, because his sales occur in much larger lots and much more irregularly. Actual sales figures may also be compared with planned sales and with potential or desired market share.

When orders are taken mainly for future delivery, it may be worthwhile to analyze shipments and unfilled orders so that they can be measured against the same standards as those suggested above for sales. It may also be helpful to analyze orders by size and the manner of their receipt, through salesmen, by phone or mail.

It may be worthwhile to analyze inquiries on the bases of the types of firms they come from, the functional area or executive level that originates them, or the factor, such as an advertisement or trade journal article, that generates them.

Marketing expenditures should usually be analyzed so that they can be compared with past outlays or with budgeted expenditures. For example, to date we have spent 10 percent more on advertising than we had up to the same date last year, but 15 percent more of our advertising budget remains unspent today than remained at this time last year. In managing advertising, it may be worthwhile to make similar comparisons of commitments to spend.

Reports

All these analyses result in reports. The matter of reports should probably be viewed from two standpoints. How many and what kind of reports should operating personnel be required to submit? How many and what kind of reports should be supplied to management?

The factors governing the answer to the first question are fairly simple. Operating people hate to prepare reports. While they are preparing reports, they are not operating. So the reports required of them should be as few and as simple and as easy to prepare as possible, but still supply the information management needs to make decisions and guide action. It is amazing how much information can be reported by making check marks on a form if the proper amount of brain power is spent on constructing the form in the first place. It is also true that operating people usually talk better and more comfortably and willingly than they write. Sometimes, money spent on providing dictating equipment—to salesmen, for example—will be more than repaid in the completeness of their reports and in their more cheerful acceptance of the idea of making reports.

No item of information should be required that is not used. And operating morale is lifted if those required to report information are told how it is used, especially if its use makes their own work easier or more effective.

Control reports prepared for management are as various as the executives that use them, and they should be. A system of control reports should be built for the men who are to use it, for the conditions that govern the business they run, and for the methods they use in running it. It should supply the information they consider important, and that information should be arranged and analyzed in each report in the manner most convenient and immediately useful to the men who must make executive decisions based on it. Such control reports usually contain: daily, weekly, monthly, quarterly, yearly, or yearly-to-date sales figures; activities of salesmen; advertising expenditures or commitments; inventory position; price relationships; and other similar data.

Certain general principles may be laid down to govern the preparation of marketing control reports.

1. Any one report should not contain too much information. The executive to whom it goes may become so enmeshed in detail that he overlooks salient facts or relationships. It is a good idea to construct each report so that it deals with one subject or a small number of related subjects.

2. All significant relationships should be computed and included in the report in the form of percentages or ratios. The report that must be

studied with a slipstick is a time waster and often fails to call the executive's attention to the facts that really count.

3. The report should contain no facts or figures that are not used. The report constructer should always remember that when people compute figures and put them down on pieces of paper it costs money, and that in the course of a year or several years the compilation of unused information may become exceedingly wasteful. That information should be used but is not has no bearing on the subject; if the person supposed to use it does not do so, it is a waste of time to supply it to him.

4. The same principle suggests that reports not used should not be required. This is easier to say than to implement. Once a report gets into a system, it tends to become fossilized there and to persist long after its usefulness has ceased. It is probably good practice to conduct a periodic housecleaning and appraisal of marketing control reports to make sure they are needed.

5. The report should be so constructed that important facts or relationships stand out and call attention to themselves. This usually results from placing related items of information near each other on the report form. If a figure in one part of the form has to be compared with another in a remote part of it, the comparison may not always be made.

USE OF CONTROL INFORMATION

The uses of marketing control information are as varied as marketing situations and operations and the ways in which they can go wrong. They fall mainly into six general classifications, however.

1. It can be used to spot things that are going wrong so they can be remedied before the process has gone far enough to cause serious loss. For example, an advertising campaign may be designed to bring in inquiries. If the first few issues fail to generate a satisfactory volume of inquiries, the nature of the campaign can be changed or it can be abandoned. This is one of the two most constructive and fruitful purposes to which control data can be put.

2. It can be used to spot what has gone wrong and to guide marketing executives in picking up the pieces and trying to cut the losses resulting from failure. This happens when the debacle has gone so far that it is irreversible until it has run its course—for example, sales below the planned volume. In such a case, management may cut production and reduce inventories, cut price, increase advertising or sales pressure, modify the product, or take other remedial or salvage action.

3. It can be used to determine just how and why failure has occurred, and to suggest what steps may be taken to prevent its recurrence. For example, a firm analyzed several past failures in introducing new products to find out why they occurred. The same mistake was found to have been

a causative factor in a number of them. This also is a highly constructive use. Mistakes cannot always be avoided, but they need not be repeated.

4. It may be used to find out who is to blame for failure. In general, this is the least constructive of its uses. If it is consistently employed for this purpose, the people controlled become afraid to decide or to act. They develop the habit of wasting time and effort in thinking up excuses and in trying to conceal failure. A favorite concealment method is to operate in a way that permits one to blame failures on someone else if they occur. This leads to cumbersome operation and destroys the cooperation and mutual coordination of effort so vital to successful marketing work. Often, people become highly skilled at covering themselves, which tends to defeat the constructive purposes of the control system. A scared marketing force is likely to be an inefficient marketing force; for fear begets error. If a marketing control system is administered in the spirit of "Who is to blame?" it is apt to do more harm than good. If administered in the spirit of "What's going wrong, what can we do about it, and how can we prevent its happening again?" it may be a highly constructive part of a system of marketing industrial products as well as any other kind of goods.

5. If a control system is properly conceived and administered in the right spirit, it is apt to induce an attitude of self-examination in the operating executives. They are willing to admit their own failures and to critically examine them. Often, they even set up their own control devices so they can get the earliest possible checks on how their operations are going. They study their failures more assiduously than their successes, to the end that in the future they may avoid the mistakes that caused them. Controls can build men's self-reliance and initiative as well as destroy those qualities.

6. Control information can be of inestimable value in planning marketing operations. Basically, control work is an attempt to measure the effectiveness of marketing tools and activities in the situations to which they are applied. From it may come a better understanding of the jobs for which specific tools and activities are suited and an ability to forecast what their results will be if applied in the future. This is the essence of good planning for marketing or any other human endeavor.

SUMMARY

The function of control consists of three processes.

1. Setting standards of performance. The performance standards of a firm should grow out of the conditions under which it operates. Those most commonly used are marketing objectives, marketing plans, marketing budgets, past sales records, activity quotas, marketing potential, and marketing costs determined by cost analysis. Such cost analysis data can be especially useful in selecting and managing marketing channels, select-

ing customers, determining sales emphasis on products and customers, pricing, product deletion, packaging, directing sales effort, and solving problems of order size.

2. Checking actual performance against standards. This may be done by observation and reports. Reports should be selective in the information they show, they should emphasize pertinent relationships, and their content and form should depend on the use that is made of them.

3. Action. Control work may be used to head off failures or to stop them before they become serious, to enable marketing executives to salvage something out of otherwise hopeless situations, to determine the causes of failure, to induce a spirit of self-examination among executives, and to guide planning work.

Most of the success of control work depends on the spirit in which it is done—whether it is punitive or constructive.

CASES APPLICABLE TO PART VIII

CASES

ACME CHEMICAL COMPANY

◇◇◇

The Acme Chemical Company, located in New England, manufactured a great variety of products and distributed them through its 12 sales divisions, which were roughly broken down along product lines. The company initiated a study of its sales operations to determine distribution costs. A breakdown of the 12 sales divisions, showing the percentage of customers less than $100 during a typical year, was as shown in Exhibit I. This study focused attention on Division 16, the coverings division, and supplied information useful to the division sales manager, Mr. Bowden, about the relative profitability of customers, products, and orders. Since this study indicated the existence of relatively large numbers of low-profit-margin customers and product lines in the division, Mr. Bowden had to determine what action, if any, he should take.

As shown in Exhibit I, 62 percent of the division's customers accounted for only 2 percent of its gross sales, which totaled $608,000 for the year. A more detailed breakdown of gross sales by customer size was as shown in Exhibit II. This breakdown revealed that sales during the year to 12 customers (1.5 percent of the total number) were $306,000, which represented 50.3 percent of total volume for that year.

In order to get a better idea of the profitability of customers with low annual sales, Mr. Bowden requested the market research department to undertake an analysis of the minimum average order cost. Determination of the cost of an order was complicated by the different types of costs involved—variable, semivariable, and fixed. Furthermore, no clear-cut line of demarcation existed between these types. If fixed costs, such as rent, taxes, and depreciation, were to be considered, they had to be arbitrarily allocated. Furthermore, a serious question usually existed as to the propriety of the allocation, because even if the coverings division eliminated a substantial portion of its orders the fixed costs would continue at the same rate.

Therefore, the market research director, Eliot Snow, decided that a reasonable approach was to disregard fixed costs and to consider only the direct or out-of-pocket costs. These expenses increased or decreased in total as the number of orders increased or decreased. If the gross margin exceeded the cost of processing and filling an order, the excess revenue

EXHIBIT I

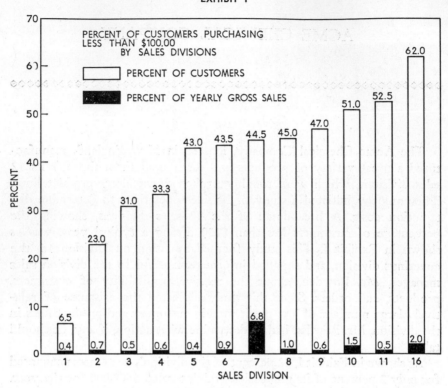

EXHIBIT II

Division 16, Coverings Division
Gross Sales by Customer Size

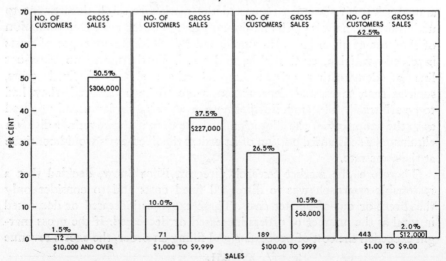

EXHIBIT III

Average Items per Invoice

Orders Typed by Order and Billing Department
for Month of May

Division	Total Invoices May	Total Items	Average Items per Invoice
16—coverings................	237	338	1.42
1.........................	222	258	1.16
2.........................	221	271	1.22
3.........................	8	12	1.50
4.........................	123	151	1.22
5.........................	245	319	1.30
6.........................	106	212	2.00
7.........................	19	54	2.84
0.........................	714	234	1.10
9.........................	82	133	1.62
10........................	187	314	1.67
11........................	13	17	1.30
12........................	57	71	1.24
13........................	74	110	1.48
14........................	6	7	1.16
15........................	135	237	1.75
Total, all orders........	1,949	2,738	1.40

contributed to the reduction of overhead; therefore, the order was worth handling.

The cost of processing an invoice depended largely on the number of items on the invoice. Mr. Snow made an approximation of an average number of items per invoice, as shown in Exhibit III. The average items

EXHIBIT IV

Cost of Processing an Order, Excluding Shipping Department Handling

Total company invoices typed January 1 through July 31:22,666

I. *Payroll:*

Allocable to order and billing..................	$ 9,940
Allocable to accounting......................	6,986
Allocable to IBM operations.................	357
All benefits at $0.068/$100 payroll................	12
Total................................	$17,295
Payroll per order—$17,295/22,666.............	$0.7630

II. *Cost of Paper:*

	Per Invoice	
Invoice set...............................	$0.0450	
IBM cards...............................	0.0055	
Bills of lading.............................	0.0155	
File folder................................	0.0188	
Three-cent stamp..........................	0.0300	
Invoice envelope..........................	0.0362	
Total................................		0.1510
III. *IBM Rental*............................		0.0385
Total Cost.........................		$0.9525

EXHIBIT V

Cost of Handling for Shipment

Container	Handling Cost
Single shipments	$0.221
55-gallon drums	0.292
30-gallon drums	0.237
15-gallon drums	0.174
5-gallon pail	0.077
1 gallon or smaller	0.104
No. 10 can case	0.043
Barrels—4 and 6 hoop sugar	0.050
Bags—burlap and paper	0.072
Cartons, fiberboard	0.208
5-gallon keg	0.122
Rolls insole	0.226
Empty drums	0.050
Empty pails	0.014
Miscellaneous shipments	0.472

per invoice for the coverings division was 1.42, as compared with an overall company average of 1.40.

The average cost of handling an order, based upon total invoices received by the company from January 1 to July 31, excluding the necessary handling in the shipping department, was 95 cents, as shown in Exhibit IV. The cost of handling for shipment varied widely, as indicated in Exhibit V, depending on both the size of the order and the type of container. However, in order to arrive at an average total cost figure, Mr. Snow computed the average handling cost for a single shipment as 22 cents, which added to the 95-cent processing cost gave $1.17 as the total cost of handling an average order.

Exhibits VI and VII revealed that 12 percent of all orders in this division were for less than $5, with an average gross margin of $2,

EXHIBIT VI

Coverings Division

Sizes of Orders by Product—April, May, and June
Total Orders: 472

Product	Number of Orders	$0–$5	$5.01–$10	$10.01–$20	$20.01–$50	$50.01–$100	$100–$500	Over $500
AB	144	19.5%	31.2%	13.9%	21.5%	12.5%	1.4%	...
AC	61	18.5	18.5	11.8	24.1	11.1	12.3	3.7%
AD	54	24.1	22.3	5.5	40.8	5.5	1.8	...
AE	24	...	12.5	33.3	29.2	25.0	...	...
AF	16	...	31.3	12.5	37.5	6.2	12.5	...
AG	5	...	...	40.00	...	...	60.0	...
AH	2	...	...	...	100.0	...	...	...
AI	40	...	...	...	15.0	7.5	57.5	20.0
AJ	126	1.6	7.9	5.6	7.1	20.6	53.2	4.0
All products	472	12.2	18.0	9.0	21.0	14.0	23.0	3.0

Coverings Division—April, May, June
Gross Margin by Size of Orders

Product	$0-$5 Total G.M.	No. of Orders	Aver. G.M.	$5.01-$10 Total G.M.	No. of Orders	Aver. G.M.	$10.01-$20 Total G.M.	No. of Orders	Aver. G.M.	$20.01-$50 Total G.M.	No. of Orders	Aver. G.M.
AB	$ 52.65	28	$1.88	$189.20	45	$4.20	$138.74	20	$6.93	$ 481.65	31	$15.50
AC	35.98	7	2.11	28.29	10	2.83	4.20	1	4.20	201.03	13	15.50
AD	24.80	3	1.91	37.55	12	3.12	18.12	3	6.04	278.44	22	12.70
AE	....	..	...	13.99	3	4.66	62.78	8	7.85	119.74	7	17.11
AF	....	..	...	9.84	5	1.96	8.13	2	4.06	69.56	6	11.59
AG	....	..	...	....	..	...	16.75	2	8.37	....	..	....
AH	....	..	...	....	..	...	....	..	...	17.88	2	8.94
AI	....	..	...	....	..	...	....	..	...	82.10	6	13.68
AJ	6.44	2	3.22	40.54	10	4.05	40.00	7	5.71	146.34	9	16.26
All Products	$119.87	50	2.00	$319.41	85	3.76	$288.72	43	6.72	$1,396.74	96	14.34

EXHIBIT VII—Continued

Coverings Division—April, May, June
Gross Margin by Size of Orders

Product	$50.01-$100 Total G.M.	No. of Orders	Aver. G.M.	$100.01-$500 Total G.M.	No. of Orders	Aver. G.M.	Over $500 Total G.M.	No. of Orders	Aver. G.M.
AB	$ 626.41	18	$34.60	$ 118.00	2	$ 59.00	$	..	$ .....
AC	176.23	6	29.37	851.45	12	71.00	705.04	2	352.52
AD	97.63	3	32.54	49.92	1	49.92	.....	..	.....
AE	136.36	6	31.06	....	..	....	.....	..	.....
AF	15.00	1	15.00	97.40	2	48.70	.....	..	.....
AG	....	..	....	168.70	3	56.23	.....	..	.....
AH	....	..	....	....	..	....	.....	..	.....
AI	68.80	3	22.93	3,263.47	23	142.00	2,430.59	8	303.82
AJ	1,019.51	26	38.80	7,392.56	67	110.50	2,025.46	5	405.09
All Products	$ 2,179.94	63	34.50	$11,941.50	110	108.50	$5,161.09	15	344.00

Totals:

AJ	$10,660.85
AI	5,844.96
All Other	4,901.00

(AJ and AI contributed $16,505 in gross margin. All remaining products contributed only $4,901 gross margin) and as many as 30 percent were orders for less than $10 worth of merchandise.

In comparison with other company divisions, this percentage of small orders was high. As shown in Exhibit VI, the preponderance of these small orders was in the product classes AB, AC, and AD. Large orders, on the other hand, were received for the classes of products AJ and AI; these two were by far the most profitable in the division. Exhibit VII shows that from April through June, AJ contributed $10,660 in gross margin, AI contributed $5,845, and all remaining products yielded only $4,901.

The AI product class was probably the most profitable in the division, since selling expense and research costs were properly allocable to AJ, and research costs were allocable to AB, AC, and AD. The AI product class had had no research expense during recent years, and it had practically no selling expense, since customers for that product ordered direct from the Acme Company and were seldom solicited by company salesmen. Thus, the class of products on which the coverings division directed the least effort—the AI group—yielded a greater profit than any other group of products in the division.

AGEX OIL COMPANY (A)

◇◇

The marketing executives of the Agex Oil Company were reviewing its sales organization with particular reference to the position of industrial salesmen.

The company's operating territories included most of the Atlantic seaboard area and several adjacent states. Its marketing organization consisted of three regions, as shown in Exhibit I. The three regions were made up of 11 sales divisions, which, in turn, were broken down into 55 districts. Typical division and district organizations at that time were as shown in Exhibit II. Not all districts had assistant district managers.

Industrial salesmen and dealer salesmen were paid on a straight salary basis. The industrial salesmen received training in industrial lubricants and specialty products, as well as general background on company organization, refining processes, and the marketing of company products to industry. Their jobs were considered highly specialized,

EXHIBIT I

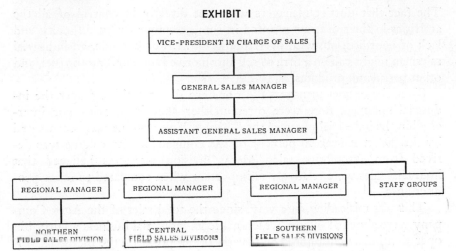

and their training was broader and more intensive than that of other sales groups.

While the general salesmen reported to and were under direct authority of the district manager, the industrial salesmen reported to the industrial products manager on the divisional level and, consequently, were not directly under the authority of the district managers in their respective territories.

This organization of the sales function resulted in many disadvantages.

EXHIBIT II

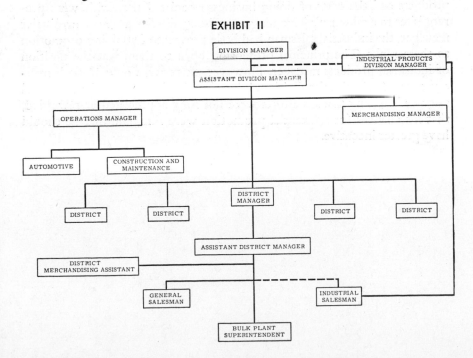

The fact that district managers were not directly in control of all the activities in their districts resulted in some communication difficulty and lack of coordination, with overlapping effort. For example, an industrial salesman might call on a firm to sell automotive lubricants, motor fuel, and other petroleum products.

Since the district managers did not have direct authority over the industrial salesmen, they were often neither acquainted with nor interested in the industrial phase of the business. This attitude was accentuated by the fact that over 90 percent of the company's sales volume was derived from automotive sales. Many division managers believed that industrial sales were relatively unimportant when compared to other product lines.

This was misleading, in a way, since the total sales of the Agex Company were about $1 billion, which made its industrial business a fairly big operation in its own right. The margin of net profit on the industrial volume was considerably higher than that on the automotive business. The industrial market was also geographically concentrated, although there were some industrial customers in every sales district. The bulk of the industrial volume was sold to large users who were few in number as compared with automotive products outlets. A relatively small percentage of the industrial business could be sold to the relatively large number of small manufacturing plants that were possible customers.

Perhaps the most important disadvantage of the sales organization structure was that since experience in sales and handling of automotive products and the costs of doing business associated therewith were prerequisites to a salesman's becoming an assistant district manager or district manager, the industrial salesman had little prospect of attaining promotion to these ranks. The principal promotion open to them was the position of industrial products manager. However, there were only 11 such managers, one for each sales division. This situation resulted in the industrial salesman's feeling that his efforts were not fully appreciated or rewarded, that his chances for substantial promotion were slim, and that he should have greater incentive.

AGEX OIL COMPANY (B)

◇◇

The executives of Agex Oil Company, a large integrated firm, were reviewing the training program for the company's industrial salesmen.

During its early history, the company had no training program for its industrial salesmen, so the men lacked adequate knowledge about specifications on many products in the line. About 30 years ago, a vice president of sales developed and instituted an industrial sales training course. During this three-week course, given at the company refinery, the trainees learned how industrial lubricants were manufactured and blended, and familiarized themselves with detailed product specifications. The trainees also received some sales product training in the refinery by means of a machinery audit, during which each trainee determined the type of lubricant required by a particular machine and attempted to sell the selected product to the plant superintendent. When these trainees returned to their districts, they were better informed about many products than their sales managers. To correct this situation, the company then made the product data and specifications used in the training course available to all sales personnel.

About 10 years later, company executives developed a series of lectures to be presented to industrial salesmen over a period of six months. One executive suggested that the lectures be printed in textbooks and used for class discussion groups to meet in New York City during a three-month period, with industrial sales staff men in the New York office as instructors. Several discussion groups were held, and the text material later formed the basis of a correspondence course for industrial salesmen, which the company adopted. The material covered practically all phases of the petroleum industry, including geology, production, refining, transportation, combustion, lubrication principles, product specifications and testing, prime movers, industrial lubricants, and other subjects.

The company suggested, but did not require, that its industrial salesmen take the correspondence course. The company furnished each division with a complete set of the various textbooks for each salesman enrolled in the course, as well as a list of questions on each book. The division supplied the salesman with only one book at a time, and he was supposed to submit written answers to the questions before being supplied with additional text material. The salesmen were required to submit a total of 85 papers, to be graded and returned. Initially, the New York office staff graded the papers; later, a model list of answers was developed and sent to each division office, and the paper grading was then handled on the divisional level. Although most salesmen turned in one to two papers per month, the company imposed no time limit for completion of the course.

The division manager of industrial sales, or a delegated assistant, usually graded the papers. For better instruction, the company naturally desired that the paper grader should write comments on the papers, explaining why a given answer was incorrect. Such attention required considerable time and effort on the part of graders, but most divisions handled this function reasonably well.

This correspondence course underwent several improvements: the papers were later assigned on a more definite schedule, plant visits were included, and the divisional industrial sales manager spoke to the salesmen after they completed a part of the course. The text material was revised to eliminate overlapping, and the subject matter on geology, production, refining, and transportation was eliminated. The revised course was called The Technical Sales Course.

For over a decade, the company used The Technical Sales Course in training its industrial salesmen. Gradually, the executives came to feel that this correspondence type of training needed to be supplemented with two additional courses—a basic industrial sales course and an advanced industrial sales course. Company executives believed that the basic industrial sales course should represent the minimum essential knowledge required for industrial sales work by providing up-to-date information on the technical aspects of the company's products, information on company research and development, and an analysis of its marketing operations. The proposed basic course covered general background on company organization, information on production, transportation, and refinery manufacturing processes concerning fuels, lubricants, and specialties. In addition, it provided some study of industrial marketing operations, sales techniques, laboratory work, and public speaking, as well as inspection trips to nearby plants. The executives believed that this type of training could best be given on a full-time study basis, which would require a two-month course. The basic course was not intended to provide detailed information on specific industries.

Company executives believed that the advanced industrial sales course should be a refresher course designed for industrial salesmen with extensive experience or for men who had taken the basic eight-week course at least two years previously. The course was to be of two weeks' duration on a full-time study basis, and was to provide up-to-date information on the latest petroleum developments in the industrial field. In addition to some information included in the basic course, the advanced course covered certain new areas, such as making a lubrication survey of a new power station, new developments in the machinery field, market analysis of industrial potential, study of laboratory analysis of used oils, sales demonstrations, study of additives, new synthetic lubricants, and study of more specialized products, including cutting oils, hydraulic oils, transmission oils, petroleum solvents, liquified gases, drawing compounds, quenching and tempering oils, and process oils.

Although company executives were in accord regarding the need for both a basic and an advanced industrial sales training course, there was some difference of opinion about the method through which these courses should be taught. Some executives favored division-level instruction by specially trained instructors from the New York offices to be sent to the company's 11 divisions. These instructors would themselves receive training in educational and teaching methods, as well as in the subject matter they taught. Executives favoring the instruction of salesmen on the division level believed that the basic two-month industrial sales training course should be taught on a full-time basis, but that the two-week advanced course might be taught on either a full-time or part-time basis.

Other company executives believed that both the basic and advanced courses should be taught at some central training center established by the company. Under this plan, both courses would be limited to a maximum of 20 salesmen, who would be selected from the various divisions. It was argued that by locating the central training center close to New York City, the instruction might be supplemented by management personnel from the headquarters office. Under this plan, the trainees participating in both courses would be housed conveniently to the training center and would remain there through the duration of the course.

Under both alternative methods of instruction, the division managers would select the salesmen to participate in the courses, and their selections would be subject to approval by sales management in New York City.

AGEX OIL COMPANY (C)

The Agex Oil Company operated large refineries in the New York area and in the Gulf, and conducted marketing operations contiguous to these manufacturing sources. The development of a considerable concentration of steel plants along the middle eastern seaboard made it desirable for the company to reevaluate its marketing operations as they pertained to the steel industry. The company's marketing organization is shown in Exhibits I and II.

The company manufactured almost every kind of petroleum product. The industrial product line included a wide variety of lubricants and other petroleum products, many specifically engineered and blended for specialized end uses. The importance of specialized engineering service to customers had increased greatly in recent years, since there was a growing tendency for industrial customers to evaluate competitive suppliers by the quality of such service rendered.

The company sold its industrial products through a sales force of more than 80 industrial salesmen, who worked out of district offices and were paid on a straight salary basis. An increasing percentage of these

EXHIBIT I

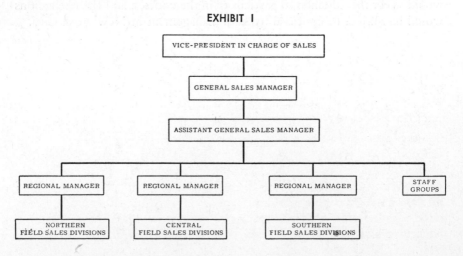

EXHIBIT II

Typical Division Organization

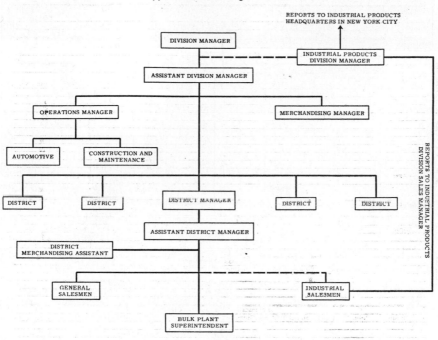

salesmen were graduate chemists and engineers, and were considered both salesmen and technical experts. A salesman sometimes encountered technical problems that demanded greater experience then he possessed; therefore, he occasionally had to call on the headquarters organization in New York City for assistance in solving them. The engineers assigned to the New York headquarters devoted their attention to customer engineering service and did not actively sell industrial products.

Company salesmen were required to submit a trade report (Exhibit III) for each customer. These trade reports provided data concerning customer purchases, supplies, units purchased, and, where obtainable, the price per unit.

Each industrial salesman also submitted a monthly progress report (Exhibit IV) to his division office. This report gave information on business the salesman had gained or lost during the preceding month.

Company executives believed that the shift in the steel mill industry made it desirable for the company to determine its position in this industry with regard to share of the market, end use of products, relative profits on different products, and volume. It was also necessary to determine what, if any, personnel changes were required in order to intelligently solicit business of a new type in certain marketing territories,

EXHIBIT III

Company Name							Indus. Code			P O R FO N G
Office	Street				Plant	Street				
	City			Ph.		City			Ph.	
Contacts			Title							

Lubricating Oils (Bbls.)						Grease, wax, pet. & Spec. (Bbls.)				
Competitive Name Comp.	Competitive E.Y.C.	Our E.Y.C.	Dely. Meth.	Brand Names	Competitive Name Comp.	Competitive E.Y.C.	Our E.Y.C.	Dely. Meth.	Brand Names	
Totals			Grand Total		Totals			Grand Total		
Contract Expires					Contract Expires					

Fuel Oils (Inc. Diesel)						
Grade	Dely. Meth.	Total E.Y.C.	Supplier	Cont. Exp.	Use, Spec. Requirements, Etc.	

Naphthas and Solvents						
Grade	Dely. Meth.	Total E.Y.C.	Supplier	Cont. Exp.	Use, Spec. Requirements, Etc.	

Automotive, Aviation and Marine					
Grade	Dely. Meth.	Total E.Y.C.	Supplier	Cont. Exp.	Use, Spec.

L.D.E. Record					
Equip.	Dispensing Pumps	Barrel Pumps	Lube Tanks	Grease Outfits	Underground Tanks
Number & Type					
Process Products					

Remarks:

Division	Salesman	Date of S-110

E.Y.C.—Estimated Yearly Consumption.
L.D.E.—Lubricant Dispensing Equipment.

and to determine whether the company should make certain steel mill lubricants at other refineries situated closer to the market.

While the trade reports and progress reports provided a general guide, they did not furnish all the information required for a complete evaluation of the market in the steel industry. Therefore, a special survey form (Exhibit V) was prepared. From trade directories and other sources of information, the marketing department in New York prepared a list that set forth the name of each customer, or potential customer,

EXHIBIT III—Continued

Sales 19			
Code No.			
Product			
Delivery Pt.			
January			
February			
March			
April			
May			
June			
6 Mo. Total			
July			
August			
September			
October			
November			
December			
12 Mo. Total			

Sales 19			
Code No.			
Product			
Delivery Pt.			
January			
February			
March			
April			
May			
June			
6 Mo. Total			
July			
August			
September			
October			
November			
December			
12 Mo. Total			

Sales 19			
Code No.			
Product			
Delivery Pt.			
January			
February			
March			
April			
May			
June			
6 Mo. Total			
July			
August			
September			
October			
November			
December			
12 Mo. Total			

and the name and location of the customer's plants for which full information was desired. The list was prepared in triplicate and sent to appropriate sales division offices. The industrial salesman concerned filled in a survey form for each company listed in his territory; the industrial sales manager in the division office reviewed the survey forms and sent a completed copy of each to the New York office. The survey covered all steel accounts, including mills, fabricators, and processors.

EXHIBIT IV

PROGRESS REPORT
(Show all quantities in Bbls.)

Salesman   Month   19

Business Gained

NAME OF ACCOUNT	ADDRESS	OUR PRODUCT	CURRENT RESULTS	E.Y.C.	NEW OR REPLACE-MENT*	COMPETITOR	REMARKS
NEW BUSINESS CONTACT					(*N for New: R for Replacement)		
ADDITIONAL BUSINESS--CONTRACT CUSTOMERS							
SPOT OR OPEN MARKET *	(*Indicate by X Whether Item Purchased Before)						

Business Lost

CONTRACT	ADDRESS	OUR PRODUCT	ACTUAL 12 MOS. SALES	COMPETITOR	REASON FOR LOSS
ITEMS--CONTRACT CUSTOMER					
SPOT OR OPEN MARKET					

Products under Test

CUSTOMER	ADDRESS	PRODUCT	QUANTITY DELIVERED	E.Y.C.	COMPETI-TOR	OUR OR COMPETI-TIVE ACCOUNT	RESULTS

This survey covered not only lubricants but also other petroleum products and specialties purchased by the steel industry, such as aromatic and aliphatic solvents, gasoline, kerosene, diesel fuel, distillate fuel, residual fuel, and liquified petroleum gas (LPG). The survey indicated the various classifications of products used in each steel mill; showed those steel mills and marketing territories in which the company had a satisfactory share of the business, as well as those in which the company was not well represented; provided a factual basis for evaluating and realigning the sales personnel in the various marketing territories;

EXHIBIT IV—*Continued*

| Contracts | | | | | |
CUSTOMER	ADDRESS	EXPIRATION DATE	RENEWED (Check ✓)	PENDING (Check ✓)	REMARKS

| Competitive Prices | | | | | | | |
CUSTOMER	COMPETITIVE PRODUCT BRAND	PRICE	E.Y.C.	DELY METHOD	OUR REPLACEMENT	PRICE	RECOMMENDATION

Competitive Practices

Business Conditions and Trends

Special Sales Activities

and indicated company products that were performing satisfactorily, products that should be improved to give optimum operating results, and new products that might be needed in the product line.

The elapsed time required to conduct the survey was four months— the time span between development of the survey form and tabulation and analysis of the completed forms in the New York office. The salesmen returned approximately 300 completed forms to the New York office, each form representing a separate steel company within the company's marketing territory.

This was the first such survey conducted by the company, and the management was well satisfied with the results obtained. One executive suggested that the company conduct similar surveys in other industries, such as textiles, chemicals, public utilities, and paper mills.

EXHIBIT V

Customer _____
Plant _____
Location _____

CLASSIFICATION OF STEEL MILL LUBRICANTS AND FUELS

Classification	Explanatory Remarks	Supplier*	Brand	Consumption Bbls. per Year	Price	Remarks
Absorbent Oil	Used only in by-product coke plants	1. 2.				
Transformer Oil	Transformers and circuit breakers	1. 2.				
Light Process Oil	Slushing or rust preventive oil Coal Spray Oil Quenching Oil Uncompounded roll oil Flushing Oil Light noninhibited hydraulic oil Low viscosity air filter oil	1. 2. 3. 4. 5.				
High Quality, Low Viscosity Lubricating Oil	Turbine oil Electric motor oil Hydraulic oil Low viscosity oil for circulating systems Air compressor oil	1. 2. 3. 4.				
Engine Oil	General purpose, medium viscosity lubricating oil Air filter oil Hydraulic oil	1. 2. 3. 4.				
High quality, high viscosity straight oil	Circulating systems serving backing roll bearings or gear and bearing systems where lubricant is continuously reused and EP properties are not required	1. 2. 3. 4.				
Black Oil	Rough journal bearings Low cost lubricating oil for once through application in old equipment	1. 2. 3. 4.				

(3)

Classification	Explanatory Remarks	Supplier*	Brand	Consumption Bbls. per Year	Price	Remarks
Open Gear Lubricants	Wire rope and open gear lubrication--to include solvent cutbacks and other specialties of type	1. 2. 3. 4.				
Multi-Purpose Grease	Generally used throughout a plant to simplify grease lubrication practices	1. 2.				
Miscellaneous Greases	Block greases Hot neck greases Cold sett greases Plug valve lubricants Pipe thread lubricants Wool yarn greases Replenishing grease Wire rope manufacturing lubricant Launching lubricants	1. 2. 3. 4. 5. 6. 7. 8.				
Specialties	Soluble and compounded cutting oils Drawing and forging compounds Tableway lubricants Compounded rust preventives and rust preventive bases Compounded roll oils and roll cleaners Palm oil substitutes Coating oils Petrolatum and wax	1. 2. 3. 4. 5. 6. 7. 8. 9. 10.				

EXHIBIT V—*Continued*

Classification	Explanatory Remarks	Supplier*	Brand	Consumption Bbls. per Year	Price	Remarks (2)
Cylinder Oil	To include both compounded and uncompounded cylinder oils Tempering oil Circulating oil for old gear and pinion sets not requiring EP lubricants	1. 2. 3. 4.				
Detergent Motor Oil	Diesel engines Automotive engines Blowing engines	1. 2. 3. 4.				
Mild EP Leaded Gear Oils	Gear and bearing systems requiring extreme pressure properties and suitability for long-time service	1. 2. 3. 4.				
Conventional EP Roller Bearing Grease	Rolling mill and highly loaded bearings	1. 2. 3.				
High Temperature EP Roller Bearing Grease	Rolling mill and highly loaded bearings	1. 2. 3.				
Lime Base General Purpose Grease	Miscellaneous bearings	1. 2. 3				
Electric Motor and High Temperature Grease	Soap type	1. 2 3.				
Electric Motor and High Temperature Grease	Nonsoap type	1. 2.				
Graphite Grease	Plate and blooming mill bearings Hydraulic plungers Miscellaneous journal bearings	1. 2. 3.				

Classification	Explanatory Remarks	Supplier*	Brand	Consumption Bbls. per Year	Price	Remarks (4)
Fuels and Solvents** LPG		1. 2. 3.				
Solvents (a) Aliphatic		1. 2. 3.				
(b) Aromatic		1. 2. 3.				
Gasoline		1. 2. 3.				
Kerosene		1. 2. 3.				
Diesel Fuel		1. 2. 3.				
Distillate Fuel		1. 2. 3.				
Residual Fuel		1. 2. 3.				

*To include Company sales.

**Remarks should indicate special restrictions as sulfur content, etc. LPG remarks should indicate whether used in conjunction with Natural Gas and any trend toward or away from the use of Natural Gas.

THE BARRY CORPORATION

◇◇

The Barry Corporation, a New England manufacturer of shock and vibration control equipment, developed a mounting especially engineered and adapted for use with machine tools and other heavy equipment. Because it lacked productive capacity necessary to manufacture the product on a large scale, the Barry Corporation made a 2-year agreement with 2 large subcontracting firms, under which they would make the mounting in production runs of 1,000 or more. With adequate manufacturing facilities assured, Edward A. Johnson, vice president in charge of sales, faced the necessity of deciding on the distribution channels through which the product should be sold.

The Barry Corporation was established in 1943. The firm initially engaged in the manufacture of improved shock and vibration isolators for military electronic equipment. The armed forces had determined that isolators designed for commercial applications in many cases aggravated, rather than improved, the shock and vibration conditions encountered on military equipment. The Barry Corporation was organized to supply isolators that would give maximum protection against the varying conditions surrounding the different military applications. Barry successively developed a line of shock mountings for use on Navy combat ships, shock mountings for use on Army land vehicles, and vibration isolators for use on military aircraft. In most of this work, Barry concentrated on developing isolators especially designed to protect electronic and electrical components from the unusual and difficult combination of mechanical conditions encountered on military equipment.

Following World War II, the Barry Corporation expanded its line of shock and vibration isolators to cover many commercial applications and also to offer improved mountings for military applications. Although the company manufactured a wide variety of mountings, these products could be grouped into four types.

1. Air damped. This type was made of a damper bellows (balloon) of freeze-resistant synthetic or silicone rubber. The damping action was caused by the displacement of air in and out of the bellows through a small orifice in its cap. The load was supported by a spring.

2. All metal. This type used wire mesh and coiled springs, with a nonlinear deflection curve for dampening effects. Employing no organic materials, these mountings were not subject to temperature influences that affected the performance of other mountings.

3. Rubber in shear. This mounting employed rubber between the baseplate and the object to be insulated. Shear forces were set up in the rubber to provide the dampening effects.

4. Rubber in compression. In this mounting, the utilization of rubber in compression in all directions provided a smooth deflection curve. Essentially equal stiffness in all directions characterized this mounting.

5. Rubber in compression and rubber in shear. This type is a combination of (3) and (4), above.

The Barry Corporation began research and development work on the machine tool mounting when a large manufacturing concern requested such a mounting for use on the 800 punch presses in its plant. This manufacturer had tried, with little satisfaction, most of the mountings available on the market, including felt, scored rubber, and rubber in shear types of vibration cushionings. This firm found that when it moved sensitive machine tools from one plant location to another the machines would not hold their tolerances. The firm's engineers believed the primary cause of these variations in tolerances was that the steel structure of the plant transmitted the vibrations received from the heavy street traffic outside the building to the machines mounted on the concrete plant floor, thus setting up resonance vibrations within the machine tools. Another major reason this manufacturer wanted a better mounting was the greater flexibility in machine use gained by avoiding the need for lagging them to the floor.

The Barry Corporation undertook the problem from an engineering rather than a marketing approach. After several months of close cooperation with this customer, during which Barry engineers worked in the manufacturer's plant, the company developed a new machine tool mounting that gave satisfactory performance where others had failed.

This new mounting was constructed on the sandwich rubber in compression principle of shock and vibration absorber. It consisted of two ¼-inch metal baseplates, with hard neoprene rubber between. The leg of the machine tool rested on the upper baseplate. The machines were typically set on the oily floors of machine shops, so the company used neoprene rather than natural rubber because of the oil and chemical resistant qualities of the synthetic compound.

Due to insufficient production facilities, the total sales of these mountings during the 2-year period were only 2,400 units, at an average price of $5.50 per mount. The company sold almost all of these mounts direct to the user at original equipment manufacturer prices.

After completion of the agreement with the two subcontracting firms, the Barry Corporation supplied them with technical assistance in the manufacture of the machine tool mountings, and incurred the expense of tooling them up in order to provide productive capacity adequate to meet the anticipated demand. Therefore, more attention to the methods of marketing the mountings was necessary.

The new mounting could be used on all types of heavy equipment requiring good insulation and maximum shock absorption. It was particularly suited for punch presses, lathes, drill presses, grinders, milling machines, and other industrial equipment. While the machine tool industry represented the major market, this mount also was applicable to any heavy equipment where noise and vibration were a critical factor, such as printing presses, motor generators, and power transformers.

The Barry Corporation had no direct sales force; it currently sold the bulk of its products through manufacturer's agents to any manufacturer who had a need for vibration isolators. The company sold 95 percent of its output to the electrical and electronics industry. The manufacturer's agents who handled the Barry line were located as follows:

Location of Manufacturer's Agents	Number of Salesmen Employed
New York City	2
Rochester	2
Philadelphia	3
Cleveland	3
Dayton	4
Washington	1
Detroit	3
Chicago	4
Minneapolis	3
St. Louis	2
Seattle	2
Los Angeles	5
Dallas	3
Toronto	2
Atlanta	2
Boston	2

The number of different product lines handled by these firms varied from 2 to 15, and the amount of goodwill and push the Barry line enjoyed also varied among them. Mr. Johnson stated that in New England, New York City, and Philadelphia, the Barry line was the most profitable line carried by the agents and, consequently, received considerable support from them.

The agents did not stock any of the product lines, nor did they assume any credit or billing functions. The Barry discount structure on the regular product line (not the new mounting) was as follows:

First $75,000 annual sales	10 percent
Second $75,000 annual sales	8 percent
Over $150,000 annual sales	6 percent

This discount structure was constant for all Barry products, with the exception of new products involving considerable application research by Barry engineers. In this instance, the discount was 5 percent.

When Barry developed the machine tool mounting, the product was turned over to the manufacturer's agents for distribution as another product in the Barry line. Distribution of the product through these concerns to machine tool users—a market the company subsequently realized was its major sales opportunity—was not satisfactory. Most sales of this mounting were made direct to customers, usually when a customer with a mounting problem contacted the company. When a Barry agent received a direct customer inquiry or an inquiry relayed from the Barry Corporation, he followed up the inquiry and attempted to sell the mounting. Lacking such direct inquiries, however, agents often did not push or actively sell the new mounting to the machine tool industry. The primary reason was that the mounting was essentially alien to the product lines handled by the agents, who normally contacted electrical and electronics industries rather than machine tool users.

Although the aggregate market for this product was very large, the order per customer was often less than $50, and the Barry outlets could not afford to call on the thousands of small alley machine shops comprising the major market. Also, there was little repeat business for the product, since once a customer had equipped a machine tool with this mounting he had solved the shock vibration problem relating to that machine for a 5- to 10 year period.

For the above-mentioned reasons, the Barry Corporation sold practically all of its 2,400 mounts during the first two years direct to users, without the assistance of manufacturer's agents, at the following quantity discount prices:

	Price per Mount	
Quantity Ordered	Type 670	Type 297
1–8	$5.42	$6.30
9–24	4.61	5.51
25–99	4.07	5.15
100–499	3.52	4.61

Each agent, however, received his normal commission on all Barry sales within his territory.

Until the Barry Corporation obtained adequate production facilities for the product, Mr. Johnson was not concerned about changing the distribution channels. However, when adequate production capacity was available he recognized that a change in distribution policy would be required to ensure the best possible product distribution. He thought that continued distribution of this product through manufacturer's agents was undesirable, since they did not provide adequate market coverage.

The new mounting developed by the Barry Corporation had the following advantages to machine tool users.

1. Lower mounting costs. Barry mounts were cheaper to install than those that had to be bolted to the floor. Also, the machines could be placed into service more rapidly.

2. Maximum utilization of capital investment. By making all machines portable, Barry mounts permitted the movement of idle equipment to other departments; they gained work space by allowing idle machines to be moved to storage; and they permitted rearrangement of machines for a particular operation, thus providing a more efficient work flow.

3. Maintenance of accuracy. Barry mounts absorbed the vibrations that destroyed precise adjustments, and they gave a greater percentage of isolation than many competitive mountings.

4. Reduction of employee fatigue. Barry mounts lessened noise carried through floors and walls, and protected employees from tiring machine vibrations.

5. Quality. Barry mounts were of the highest quality and yet were cheaper in price than many similarly styled mountings.

Mr. Johnson considered the following distribution channels for the mounting as possible alternatives:

1. Selling direct to machine tool manufacturers as original equipment.
2. Selling through machine tool distributors.
3. Selling through industrial supply houses.

The major products competing with the new Barry mount included a mounting of $5/16$-inch rubber sheeting, grooved on both sides so that the ribs produced by the grooving were in opposite planes. Another product consisted of a special felt material, varying from $1/2$ inch to 2 inches in thickness, which the user glued to the floor under the base or feet of the machine to be isolated. A third competitive product was a line of spring-type mountings that could be used on a wide variety of machines; the load range varied from 75 to 25,000 pounds per mount. Although competition currently controlled the bulk of the market, Mr. Johnson believed that the Barry mount, when properly installed, gave superior performance in many applications.

Manufacturers of machinery and machine tools exhibited a mixed response regarding use of the Barry mount as original equipment. Many of them were uninformed about it and did not realize its true merit. The company had encountered some resistance among these manufacturers, because a competitor had previously introduced a similar, but inferior, product that had not performed satisfactorily. Mr. Johnson considered the possibility of developing a direct sales force of from two to four sales engineers to cultivate this market. Mr. Johnson did not know how many firms made machines on which the mounting could be used as original equipment. He did not think that the total number was over 1,000, and he felt that not more than 200 controlled the bulk of the business. They would probably want to buy mountings in orders of dozens or hundreds at a time.

Another possible method of distribution was through machine tool distributors. However, these firms typically handled highly technical products whose cost often exceeded $50,000, and Mr. Johnson realized that persuading them to handle Barry mounts at $3 to $10 per mount might prove difficult.

Industrial supply houses offered perhaps the broadest market coverage for an industrial product. Many of the larger ones stocked more than 100,000 different items. Their salesmen usually had little engineering training and did little more than solicit orders.

One Barry executive recommended that, regardless of the channel of distribution decided on, direct mail advertising play an important part in supplementing the sales effort. Specifically, he felt that direct mail advertising might be useful in stimulating demand and securing inquiries, in educating potential users regarding the merits of properly applied mounts, in supplying technical application data, and in paving the way for direct selling efforts.

THE CHILDERS MACHINE COMPANY

◇◇

The Childers Machine Company, located in New England, manufactured a line of high-quality, precision industrial grinders. The company sold these grinders, priced from $7,500 to $150,000, through machine tool manufacturer's agents. The company had always sold through these channels, and although at various times the executives had considered selling direct to industrial users through their own sales force, they had always decided against it. In the fall of 1959, the Buffalo agent, whose territory comprised western New York State, decided to retire and to liquidate his distributorship. This brought about the necessity of securing new distribution channels for that area.

The company produced precision-machined products capable of grinding to extremely close tolerances, and it held a position of prestige among the ranking manufacturers in the machine tool industry. Although many product improvements were made since the company was founded in 1900, the basic line remained unchanged.

The Childers Company maintained its own design, engineering, and cost departments, where it designed its standard model grinders and made all subsequent improvements. These departments were also responsible for the product and development engineering work involved in special-purpose or custom-made machines the firm manufactured for its customers. These special-purpose machines were produced in lots of two or more. The sale of such machines required agents with not only technical selling ability but also managerial ability, and adequate financing as well.

In selling special-purpose grinders, the agent determined the general type of machine that should be used; then he submitted to the Childers Company engineers such technical data as amount of grinding required, number of surfaces to be ground, their planal relationship, size and shape of pieces, and desired production in pieces per hour. With this and other pertinent technical data, the engineering and cost estimating departments prepared bids, which the company submitted through the agent to the customer for approval.

Each of the 15 Childers agents handled from 15 to 18 lines of noncompeting machine tools. These firms covered the entire United States, each with a definitely assigned territory, and together employed 250 salesmen. They neither stocked the machines of the manufacturing firms they represented, nor did they maintain replacement parts for these machines. Mr. Gordon, the Childers Company sales manager, believed that his agents were the finest in the trade, and a bond of friendship and close cooperation existed between the Childers Company and its various agents and their salesmen.

The agents selling the Childers line neither handled used machinery nor offered trade-in allowances on old machines. The better manufacturers of machine tools demanded such a policy from their representatives because (1) they did not wish to be identified with outlets handling used machine tools, and (2) such a policy assured them that the agents would not push secondhand machines instead of new equipment.

The technical training of the agents' salesmen varied greatly; some were graduate engineers, and others had not finished high school. However, Mr. Gordon stressed the selling rather than the technical ability of his agents' salesmen, and pointed out that many salesmen, who were not high school graduates, were currently earning $30,000 a year in commissions.

The Childers Company maintained a staff of four demonstrators. Mr. Gordon assigned them to specific job installations, where they supervised the installation and adjustment of machines and demonstrated their operation. These men had no formal engineering training, but were skilled mechanics with a thorough knowledge of the Childers line.

Mr. Gordon visited his agents on regularly scheduled trips, attended sales meetings, talked with the individual salesmen, and generally kept them up-to-date on matters pertaining to the Childers line. One major purpose of these trips was to assure that his products received at least their proportionate share of the salesman's selling time and attention. Mr. Gordon accomplished this by determining the number of calls made per day, and by accompanying the salesmen on some of these calls. He observed and corrected their sales techniques and introduced new selling points for Childers equipment.

The Childers Company budgeted 2 percent of sales for trade paper advertising, reprints, and promotional literature. In addition, agents spent approximately 1 percent of sales for direct mail advertising, including the expense incurred in sending circulars and reprints supplied by the company. Mr. Gordon believed these figures were representative of the industry.

He further pointed out that an agent's major cost resulted from selling expenses and salesmen's salaries. A good machine tool salesman earned from $10,000 to $30,000 per year. According to Mr. Gordon, the average agent's commission was from 11 to 12 percent of the selling price to the customer, and the average agent's net profit on sales after taxes was approximately 2 percent.

Salesmen handling the Childers line had to be well versed in metallurgy, and thoroughly familiar with the various types of metals and alloys and their respective cutting characteristics. In addition, they had to know the cutting speeds, rates of production, and other technical aspects of their own as well as their competitors' machines. A machine tool salesman was expected to give unbiased technical advice regarding the machine best suited to meet the customer's requirement, even though the agent for whom he worked did not handle that particular machine.

It was customary in the machine tool trade for an agent to remit payment to the manufacturer within 30 days after shipment of the machine, although the agent often extended 90-day credit to the buyer. Sometimes, the agent financed the purchase by accepting a percentage down payment (often 25 percent) and receiving the balance in installments spread over, perhaps, 1 or 2 years. During the payment period, he retained a mortgage on the machine and charged an interest rate, which covered the cost of obtaining capital.

Mr. Gordon estimated that his agents financed approximately 10 percent of their sales, although the percentage varied among different territories. He also stated that an agent needed sufficient liquid capital to carry approximately 30 days' sales. Since some agents had annual sales of $50 million or more, the size of the capital or line of credit needed may be realized. They often assigned their accounts receivable to commercial banks as security for loans.

Such financing required strong agents who were able to maintain large lines of credit. Thus, manufacturers selling through these channels were primarily concerned with securing and maintaining a few important outlets who were financially strong and solvent and able to maintain themselves during recessions. Other important considerations were the agent's prestige and recognition in the industry and the quality of his sales effort.

In 1955, the president of the large agent firm covering New York State, New England, and northern New Jersey decided late in life to liquidate his business and retire. This agency employed 20 salesmen, and the capital stock was held largely by the president, who had made no provision for continuation of the firm.

At the time the president decided to retire, the executives in this agency included a treasurer, sales manager, and secretary, none of whom had the ability to assume the presidency. All the machine tool manufacturers whose product lines this firm handled sent representatives to a joint meeting, where the problem was discussed. The result of this meeting was a decision to bring in from the outside a man who had the requisite financial backing and managerial ability to undertake the presidency of a new organization.

In the meantime, the managers of the Buffalo and Syracuse territories expressed a desire to buy out their respective branches and set up independent agencies to handle all of New York State, with the exception of metropolitan New York City. These offers were accepted. Subsequently a suitable man was found to form, with executives of the former agency, the managerial nucleus of a new one, comprising the territory of New York City, New England, and northern New Jersey.

The above situation proved satisfactory until, in the fall of 1959, the president of the Buffalo agency decided to retire. Neither of the two salesmen in this firm had the necessary financial backing or executive ability to manage a selling organization. This situation focused attention not only on the Buffalo territory but also on the Syracuse outlet, which was a similar one-man firm employing two salesmen. Mr. Gordon feared a repetition of the Buffalo situation in the Syracuse territory some five years hence when that agency president reached retirement age.

Not only the Childers Machine Company but also the 17 other manufacturers served by this firm were without coverage in the Buffalo area. Mr. Gordon stated that there were no other desirable Buffalo area agents to take over these lines.

Mr. Gordon stated that he knew of one outlet in the Syracuse area that would be glad to take on the Childers line. However, he was reluctant to use this firm, since it handled used machine tools to a large extent. He further pointed out that any immediate plans concerning distribution in Syracuse should provide for and incorporate the existing Syracuse agent. Thus, while he wanted to ensure against a repetition of the Buffalo situation, Mr. Gordon did not want to abandon this Syracuse agent with whom the Childers Company had maintained friendly relations for many years.

COCCIDIOSTATS FOR THE BIRDS

◇◇◇

Coccidiosis is a germ disease that attacks the digestive tracts of chickens and turkeys. It is highly contagious, being transmitted through the birds' droppings, and if allowed to rage unchecked may decimate a flock before running its course.

Through experience, the large grower could estimate the cost of sanitary measures necessary to diminish the likelihood of an attack and to hold its ravages within bounds if one occurred. He could also predict with reasonable accuracy what the extent of his losses would be without preventive or curative medication. The sum of these costs, divided by two, determined about the price the average grower would be willing to pay for a preventive or cure.

About 8 or 10 years ago, a chemical manufacturer developed and put on the market Sulfaquinoxoline, a cure for the disease. At first, Sulfa Q was administered by the growers, who mixed it with the birds' feed or water. Later, feed compounders found it profitable, as an added bid for grower patronage, to mix it with the feeds they sold. Having better equipment than the growers could afford, they got a more uniform mix. At about the same time, several competitors developed and marketed rival products. SQ was clearly superior to these in several respects and captured the lion's share of the market.

The executives of most of the firms in the business felt that a cure was not the final answer to the problem of coccidiosis. During the period when birds had the disease, they lost weight and growth was stopped. It took them some time after recovery to recapture the ground lost during illness and recuperation. With over two billion birds annually vulnerable to the disease, the sales potential and profit possibilities of the business were great enough to justify extensive and expensive research for a preventive.

Again, the company making SQ was successful. About three years ago, it developed a highly effective preventive, which it marketed under the trade name Nicarb. This, like SQ, was administered in the feed, so it was sold primarily to poultry feed manufacturers, who mixed it with their prepared feeds and sold it to growers. The company continued to make and market SQ, since some poultry growers were careless about administering the preventives and others chose to chance having their flocks get the disease rather than pay the price of a preventive.

Nicarb, however, had certain drawbacks. There were mixing problems, although these could largely be solved by technical service. It could not be administered to laying hens because its residue caused the eggs to be slightly off-color, although it had no toxic effect on the people that ate the eggs. While this limited the market, the limitation was not severe, since laying hens constitute a very small percentage of the fowl grown. But the egg producers were very anxious to get some way to protect their flocks. Also the bugs began to display a disturbing ability to develop strains resistant to Nicarb and to other rival, but inferior, products that had been put on the market.

So research was instituted for an improved coccidiostat. The trade grapevine reported that competitors also were conducting heavy research programs, and the race was on to see who could first come up with a better product. Again, the leader in the industry won out, and by the end of last year had in the testing stage a new and apparently vastly improved product, Glycamide. It was to be administered in the same way as Nicarb, so the company planned to market it through the same channels.

Usually, a new product such as Glycamide is tested thoroughly under varying conditions before it is put on the market for general distribution, but the trade grapevine was again busy carrying the rumor that at least two competitors had in the testing stage new products that might be as good as, or superior to, Nicarb, and that they might be launched on the market at any time. The preliminary use tests of Glycamide showed results that were almost unbelievably good. No shred of evidence appeared to indicate that the new product had any serious weaknesses to offset its advantages, so the executives of the company offered the new product on the market early this year.

At first sales were very gratifying. But after Glycamide had been on the market for about three months, trouble began. The scientists engaged in research on coccidiosis had long observed that the germ producing the disease tended to develop strains resistant to any chemical medicinal cure or preventive applied over a long period of time. This usually did not occur within less than three years.

But strains resistant to Glycamide began to show up within about three months after it appeared on the market. Outbreaks of the disease occurred in flocks treated with the new product, and clinical tests disclosed that the germs taken from the stricken birds thrived on the prescribed doses of the new medicine. If it was administered in concentrations high enough to kill these strains, it was prohibitively costly. These outbreaks seemed to occur mainly in poultry-growing areas that suffered from damp, cool weather during the growing season.

The research division went into high gear in an exploration of the possibility of modifying Glycamide to make it effective against these resistant strains. The results were highly disappointing. The scientists held out practically no hope of product modification. The company's executives were puzzled about what to do.

In the meantime the production of Nicarb and SQ had been sharply cut back in anticipation of a shift to Glycamide. When sales of Glycamide fell off and those of Nicarb and SQ increased, there was a surplus of the Glycamide and the other two were in short supply. There seemed no hope of making a sales forecast for any of the three that could be used as even a rough guide to production.

But the news was not all bad. Competitors were having their troubles too. Their new products had also developed bugs, or perhaps one should say the bugs had not responded to them as expected. At the end of May, there were eight competitive coccidiostats on the market, including three new ones. All had defects that made them less useful, or at least no more useful, than Nicarb and Glycamide. There was a ninth competitive product on the horizon, but the ever active grapevine gave assurance that it could not be launched on the market before the end of the year. The same source indicated that this was an excellent coccidiostat. Nicarb was effective against all the strains resistant to Glycamide, and SQ would still stop any epidemics that developed.

Two facts made the picture worse: (1) this experience seemed to indicate that from then on the chemical medicinal coccidiostat business would be a wild research scramble to keep ahead of the blind ingenuity of the bugs in developing new strains and (2) it would be a toss-up as to which of the several competing manufacturers would be on top of the heap at any particular moment.

Management was certain that a plan or program had to be worked out for the coccidiostat business—the volume and profit potential of the business justified heroic measures.

COLLIS COMPANY

◇◇◇

The Collis Company, located in Cincinnati, Ohio, manufactured a variety of paper products, both consumer and industrial, among the nine divisions within the company. Alarmed that the company's gross profit margin had dropped 10 percent in the previous 2 years and believing that their sales expenses were excessive, the management introduced in November a new system of sales reporting and trade analysis. This system, which gave necessary and useful information of sales costs, as well as competition and market potential, was adopted by several divisions of the company but resisted by others. The industrial specialties division, particularly, objected strenuously to the new sales reporting system. Six months after its introduction A. M. Plumley, general manager of sales, was considering the best means of securing the complete co-operation of the various sales divisions, especially the industrial specialties division.

The Collis Company manufactured among its nine divisions corrugated and solid fiber shipping containers, corrugated and solid fiber packing materials, grocery bags and sacks, folding cartons, wrapping paper, asphalt laminated paper, folding paraffined cartons, and a line of industrial specialties, including insulating material and board and paper specialties.

During the previous 10 years, the company had greatly expanded its plant and equipment. At the beginning of the period, 72 percent of the company's output was used for food packaging, but after that year the company tried to achieve stability through product diversification. The result was that by the end of the period no one industry consumed more than 32 percent of the output.

The typical sales organization for a division included a divisional sales manager, in charge of all selling activities within the division, and under him at least one senior and one junior salesman.

The old sales reporting form had remained essentially unchanged since its introduction 18 years before. This sales report consisted of five duplicate copies in colors white, yellow, red, blue, and green, routed by color as office copy, salesman's copy, laboratory copy, file copy, and the copy to the vice president of sales. These reports were very unsatisfactory, because they gave only the barest information, such as the firm called on, date, salesman, person interviewed, and brief resumé of the interview. These resumés varied greatly, including such extraneous material as guest entertainment as well as desired information on customer needs, purchases, and so forth.

This sales reporting system was unsatisfactory in that the report gave little market data of value; difficulty was encountered in that the salesmen failed to use common units of measurement; and the form was not conducive to an orderly account of the interview. Also, since the company required every salesman to submit a sales report for each call made, the resulting number of reports was such that the sales managers did not have sufficient time to examine them in detail. The salesmen themselves soon realized that their reports were not being read, and many of them neglected to fill out the forms, or did so only in a perfunctory manner. Several top executives agreed that the company needed a new sales report form that would be more accurate, more flexible, more easily prepared by the salesmen, and would provide adequate market data.

Several of the executives concerned also felt that the company's weekly expense report needed revision, since it neglected certain data and was too detailed on other items, such as automobile expenses.

After thorough study of forms used by similar companies, Robert S. Dearfield, director of marketing research, developed a new trade report, shown in Exhibits I–A and I–B. Every Collis Company salesman was required to fill out this trade report once a year for each of his customers.

Mr. Dearfield also developed a new combined weekly call and expense report; on one side was printed the expense report, and on the reverse side (Exhibit II) the weekly call report. The weekly call report summarized a salesman's weekly calls, and each salesman was to send it to his sales manager at the end of the week. Combining the expense and weekly call reports into one form was considered advantageous, not only in that the company could more easily correlate a salesman's expenses to his trips and calls made, but also in that the use of this new form required the Collis Company salesmen to complete their weekly call reports before they could submit their expense reports for repayment. Salesmen were not reimbursed for expenses until they completed the reports.

The market research department transferred the data from the annual customer trade reports to sort cards for ready reference and to punch cards for machine analysis. Thus, for each customer, the Collis Company had available data on type of customer (manufacturer, processor, distributor), annual requirements, size, salesman handling the account,

EXHIBIT I–A

		Salesman
		Date of Interview
	COLLIS COMPANY	Date Written
	Trade Report	

Firm

Sales Admin.

Sales Div.   Interviewed

Laboratory

File

Patent Dept.   Sales, Service or Development
                              Information, Summary first,
Cincinnati   then details

Routing

1

2

3

4

Initial Report

Revised Data

Service Call

Typed by

- - - - - - - - - - -

Date - - - - - - - - - -

Confirmed
by Letter of

- - - - - - - - - - -

Is Market Information up to date? Check Reverse Side.

customer code number, major supplier, location, Standard Industrial
Classification Code, products purchased from the company, and the end
use of purchases.

The major problem in the use of these new report forms lay in selling the idea to the salesmen and gaining their willing cooperation.
While his department was preparing the new system for use throughout the company, Mr. Dearfield met with C. J. Cox, vice president in

EXHIBIT I–B

COLLIS COMPANY

Market Information

This Market Data required only on initial call or to show revisions or additions.

KEY PERSONNEL
(Names & Titles) _____

_____

_____

PRODUCTS MADE OR SOLD _____

_____

Manufacturer	
Processor	
Distributor	
Employees	_____
Annual Sales	_____
Floor Space	_____

COMPETITIVE INFORMATION: Report below purchases of all products in Collis Company's field.

Products Purchased (Name, Type and Grade)	Use	Supplier of Products	Yearly Purchases (Units)	Price & Unit

Sales, Service or Development Information--
(Continued from Front)

charge of sales, Mr. Plumley, general manager of sales, and the sales managers of the nine divisions to explain the plan, what it had accomplished in previous trial uses in selected company divisions, and its potential value on a companywide basis.

Mr. Dearfield then presented the completed trade analysis system at a quarterly meeting of the top 20 men in the marketing department, including Cox, Plumley, and all division sales managers. He explained the market and expense data, shown in Exhibit III, to be obtained from the proposed system through the use of discussions supplemented by bar charts, slides, and other visual demonstrations.

Meetings of a division sales manager and his salesmen were called at the discretion of the sales manager, usually about every two weeks.

EXHIBIT II

COLLIS COMPANY

Weekly Call Report

Date	Company and Individual	Check One			Purpose and Results of Call
		Customer	Prospect	Records*	

*Records: (Are records up to date?)
N New prospect. Trade report sent in.
C Correction. Trade report showing change sent in.
File data is complete. No change necessary.

Many of these division sales managers recognized the necessity of selling the system to their salesmen, and used skits, charts showing the flow of information from salesmen to market research department and back to salesmen, question and answer periods, and other selling devices. Mr. Dearfield attended many of these meetings and contributed to the further understanding of the new system.

One reason for the salesmen's resistance to the proposed changes was that very few of them had worked with other companies. Thus, they were not familiar with the similar sales reporting systems used by other companies and resisted changes in their own routine. The most prevalent

EXHIBIT III

Collis Company, Marketing and Expense Data
from Expense, Call, and Trade Reports

Type of Data	Type of Report			
	Expense	Call	Trade	Sales* Analysis
I. Selling Expense Data				
Analyses of selling and call expense:				
By territories......................	x	x	....	x
By salesmen......................	x	x	....	x
By customers or prospects............	x	x	....	x
By customer size...................	x	x	....	x
By class of trade and industry group....	x	x	x	x
Entertainment cost by types of customers..	....	....	....	....
II. Sales Control Data				
Analyses of sales coverage:				
By territories, by salesmen............	x	x	....	x
By customers or prospects............	x	x	....	x
By class of trade, by industry..........	x	x	x	x
By types of customers, by customer size.	x	x	x	x
Analysis of sales per call................	....	x	....	x
Qualitative analysis of calls..............	....	x	....	x
III. Market Data				
Analyses of product potentials:				
By class of trade....................	....	....	x	x
Analyses of competition:				
By company size....................	....	....	x	x
Analyses of Collis Company's share:				
By geographic area (territories)........	....	....	x	x
Trends in product consumption:				
By industries (markets)...............	....	....	x	x
By customers or prospects.............	....	x	x	x
By product and usage.................	....	....	x	x
By product types and grades...........	....	....	x	x
By consumption units.................	....	....	x	x
By prices of products consumed........	....	....	x	x
Key personnel and changes in personnel....	....	....	x	....
Plant capacities.......................	....	....	x	....

* Prepared by the Marketing Research Department from the expense, call, and trade reports.

reason for dislike of the new system was that the salesmen believed such reporting was not properly their job as salesmen, and they feared they would become paper form handlers. The salesmen also believed that dollar sales figures were most important, and they were not interested in the origin of the sales or the dimensions of the market potential. They felt that they had operated satisfactorily under the old system, and they regarded the weekly call report as a device for checking on their activities, indicating a lack of confidence and trust in them on the part of the sales executives.

Although most top executives generally favored the new system, several thought the existing system was satisfactory. Mr. Plumley wholeheartedly endorsed it and was its strongest supporter. Mr. Cox, his superior and director of marketing, supported the program primarily because he placed great confidence in Mr. Plumley's judgment and usually supported his decisions. The top-level decisions on the trade analysis system were under the jurisdiction of these two men.

Three of the nine divisions within the company cooperated fully. Three divisions were undecided about the new system, and although they complied to the extent of supplying the desired information, they were not enthusiastic but waited to see the turn of events. Two other divisions resisted weakly, one primarily because the manager had been with the company for over 30 years, and claimed he knew the desired information and could see no use for the new forms in his division. The remaining division, industrial specialties, represented the major source of resistance to the new plan. The personnel of this division consisted of the sales manager, H. D. Miner, and three salesmen, ranging in ages between 35 and 40. All had been with the company 15 to 20 years. These men were not college graduates, as were the majority of the company's salesmen, but they were excellent salesmen who had joined the company on graduation from high school.

Mr. Miner, who was 35 years old, was a college graduate who had been with the company for 10 years. He would not attempt to force the new sales reporting system on his salesmen against their wills, but stated that it was Mr. Dearfield's task to convince his (Miner's) salesmen of the merits of the new plan.

Mr. Plumley, general manager of sales, had been the industrial specialties sales manager prior to Mr. Miner. Mr. Plumley, in turn, had taken over the division when it was beset with problems of morale and low sales, primarily the result of mismanagement by his predecessor, Mr. Griffith. He had been a stubborn and strong-willed sales manager, and although he had had close personal and social contact with his men, his leadership often resulted in discontent among them.

Mr. Griffith had left the company three years ago, and Mr. Plumley had become the industrial specialties division sales manager. He attempted to establish better coordination and communication between his division and the company, and he greatly improved morale. When Mr. Plumley was promoted to general manager of sales two years later, Mr. Miner took over as sales manager, but Mr. Plumley continued in close contact with the division. Mr. Miner maintained closer personal and social contact with his salesmen than Mr. Plumley had.

The industrial specialties division salesmen were paid on straight salary, which was often a source of discontent, since salesmen in certain other divisions earned larger remuneration on the basis of an incentive payment plan.

When the company introduced the trade analysis system, the industrial specialties salesmen complained bitterly about the weekly call report. Mr. Miner invited Mr. Dearfield to discuss this report with his salesmen, but the discussion proved unsuccessful, largely because Mr. Miner had misrepresented the plan to his salesmen, and they voiced many loud, but ungrounded, objections. Whether Mr. Miner had done this intentionally, Mr. Dearfield did not know.

Mr. Dearfield then prepared a new presentation on the weekly call report, but when he appeared before these salesmen a second time to discuss it, the salesmen transferred their objections from the call report to the customer trade report. They objected that filling out the trade report would take too much time and that the information obtained would not be really valuable. Mr. Dearfield countered that it should not take more than five minutes to correctly fill out the report, and he explained how the company would use the data obtained. Nevertheless, the industrial specialties salesmen did not fill out the trade reports, and eight months after the introduction of the new trade analysis system the marketing research department had not received a single trade report from the salesmen of this division. While other divisions did not cooperate as fully as desired, industrial specialties was the only division that offered flat resistance to the trade report. Of necessity, the salesmen of this division turned in their weekly call and expense reports, since the company required these before it would repay the salesmen's traveling expenses.

Although Mr. Plumley strongly supported the new plan and spoke in favor of it at meetings with his sales managers, Mr. Dearfield hesitated to ask him to take coercive action aginst reluctant sales managers, since he believed that voluntary cooperation was most important. Therefore, aside from his endorsement of the trade analysis system at meetings with his sales managers, Mr. Plumley took no action to force compliance, although he felt that company efficiency and morale were reduced by what he considered unreasonable resistance.

THE CUNDY-BETTS CORPORATION

The Cundy-Betts Corporation, one of the large wholesalers of electrical and electronic supplies, apparatus, and appliances, has grown with the industrial expansion of the Midwest. Like most electrical distributors, this company stocks a considerable variety of goods. Its inventory of supplies and apparatus includes small items, such as wire, cables, switches, fittings, conduit, radio speakers, amplifiers, and residential and industrial lighting fixtures, as well as such major equipment as air conditioners, heating units, motors, transformers, and power tools. The company also carries a full line of small and major appliances, including TV sets. About 45 percent of gross sales comes from supplies and apparatus; the remainder is accounted for by appliances and TV.

Cundy-Betts has grown considerably since its 1922 beginning in a barn converted to a warehouse and only one full-time salesman. Today, it employs 65 salesmen, who sell to 20,000 accounts in a 5-state area. To serve these accounts, the company maintains 15 warehouses, with an average floor space of about 18,000 square feet. Stocked in these warehouses are some 30,000 items from nearly 3,000 suppliers. Sales volumn last year was around $7.5 million.

Competition in this 5-state area comes from some 200 other independent electrical wholesalers, as well as a number of direct-selling manufacturers. In recent years, the most aggressive competition has been from manufacturers, who maintain local warehouses and ship on consignment. This competition has not only resulted in the loss of some customers, but has also served to reduce throughout the area much of the selling appeal of Cundy-Betts' own complete local stocks. Moreover, the willingness of these manufacturers to sell on consignment and drop ship has encouraged a number of marginal operators to enter electrical wholesaling. Equipped with no more than a telephone and a list of prospects, these operators have been able to quote prices considerably below those of the established service wholesaler.

The company is faced with a difficult decision. It may retrench on inventories and services, and thus join the discounters in taking advantage of manufacturer's stocks and direct shipments to customers. While this step may enable the company to meet the lowest prices of competitors, it will eventually reduce the organization to the role of a broker. On the other hand, it is not difficult to appreciate the electrical manufacturers' position. To get the most out of their enormous productive capacity, volume selling is imperative. Yet, the weak-kneed selling efforts of many wholesalers and their failure to maintain adequate stocks are well known. This plus the natural craving of each manufacturer for a bigger share of the total market are the ingredients of an explosive situation.

It seems evident to company management that their growth, particularly since World War II, has been sustained by a wide and deep product coverage combined with quality service. Moreover, because of the new electrical products and the changes in old ones constantly being introduced, it seems all the more necessary to carry extensive stocks. It also has been the salesmen's experience that when customers want merchandise, they want it at once. As one salesman expressed it, "If our customers have to wait while we order merchandise from Chicago, they may as well order it themselves." At the same time, financial and inventory records have revealed a disturbing situation. Although gross sales have nearly doubled since World War II, gross and net profits and dollar earnings have declined steadily since 1950. The number of items classified as "slow" has doubled in two years, and turnover has declined for the fourth consecutive year.

In order to tighten up their operating efficiency without compromising what were regarded as the essentials of wholesaling, the following policy revisions were adopted in 1956.

1. Complete inventories but fewer sources of supply. Complete stocks were considered necessary to insure prompt delivery—an essential in wholesaling. While the same variety of items was maintained, the number of manufacturers represented was sharply reduced. The decision on which manufacturers to eliminate was made only after a careful analysis of vendors on the basis of sales, lead time, price, adjustments, and complaints.

2. Systematic and formalized training of salesmen. Although the company had always stressed knowledge as well as method in selling, there had been no organized attempt to instill these qualities in its sales force. A plan was therefore devised to bring every salesman to the home office every year for two weeks of formal training. When asked to supply representatives and educational aids for this training program, the manufacturers' response was immediate and enthusiastic.

3. Specialized selling. To make the fullest use of the individual salesman's competence and capacity, the company separated its supplies and apparatus business from appliances and TV. Each of these divisions was given its own sales force and its own warehouses.

4. Selective distribution. Management had known for some time that,

on the average, 30 percent of its customers accounted for 70 percent of its business, but this circumstance had never influenced policy. Now a determined effort was made to recruit big-order business as well as business less affected by price competition. The number of retailers company salesmen contacted was also cut in half so that they could concentrate on the high-volume outlets.

5. Full-service package. This included assistance to manufacturers in sales promotion and other selling campaigns, as well as specialized services to nonretail customers. For example, the company organized a complete lighting service, offered at cost to contractors and architects.

Putting these policy revisions into effect, however, created some perplexing adjustment problems. The gradual elimination of low-volume buyers and the solicitation of larger accounts involved disadvantages as well as advantages. Large buyers were more sensitive to quality, more demanding about service, and more conscious of price, generally speaking, than were small buyers. While the separation of appliances and TV sales from supplies and apparatus was logical from a product and customer standpoint, the significantly higher ratio of expenses to sales in the supplies and apparatus came as a distinct surprise to management. Indeed, the division had failed to show a net profit since its establishment in 1956. Although substantial increases in sales had been achieved, they had been largely offset by increases in selling expense.

This situation was largely attributed to the greater technical competence, longer period of training, higher salaries, more sales calls per sale, and greater emphasis on development work required of industrial salesmen as opposed to salesmen in the appliance and TV division. In order to meet the competition of direct-selling manufacturers for big-volume accounts, it was also necessary to establish an engineering department within the supplies and apparatus division. The old service division, which had been very successful in dealing with the repair and maintenance needs of small accounts, simply did not have the personnel capable of handling the production and design problems encountered in large establishments.

Although most Cundy-Betts suppliers provided technical assistance to end users of their products, this assistance was seldom available as quickly as customers demanded it. Moreover, most buyers expected satisfactory service from the distributor who had sold the product rather than from the product maker. While these facts helped to explain the poor profit performance of the supplies and apparatus division, they did not make it any easier for management to accept.

Mr. Dean, who had been appointed manager of the supplies and apparatus division, found it necessary to spend about half of his time with the new engineering department. He thought the change in the company's organizational structure from a functional to a more product-oriented basis was logical in view of the revision in company policies.

In his judgment, though, these changes had been pushed too rapidly. He thought that giving marketing a greater voice in management decisions and more influence over company budgets was more important than separating it into essentially consumer and industrial divisions. It was also his contention that the engineering department was woefully understaffed. He pointed out that it had only a quarter of the personnel and a fifth of the budget of the old service division—to carry out an assignment too big for the old division.

In the final analysis, he thought, it was the technical service man who brought in the repeat business. Consequently, the engineering department should, at least, be placed on an equal footing in terms of numbers, salaries, and prestige with the old service division and eventually with the sales force itself. However, management did not see the role of the engineering department in quite the same light as Mr. Dean, so he was unable to get a sufficient increase in the division's budget to add substantially to the strength of the department.

The general manager of Cundy-Betts was J. G. Van Allen. He had been with the firm for about 20 years, first as a salesman of appliances, then of television, and later as manager of the newly formed appliance and television sales division. When the top executive position became vacant in 1960 because of retirement, Mr. Van Allen was appointed to that office. Before becoming general manager, he had made no secret of his belief that the supplies and apparatus division constituted the company's foremost problem. On his appointment as chief administrative officer, he stated that his first objective would be to place this division on a paying basis.

Mr. Van Allen thought that one of the division's major weaknesses was inventory control. No one in the division knew, he declared, when deliveries were received, where they were stored, or how much of an item was on hand. Returned goods were accepted without inspection, damaged goods were not accounted for, and, worst of all, orders were not processed in any systematic way. The last condition, he insisted, frequently caused embarrassing situations with customers, and he cited several letters of complaint he had received from manufacturers regarding Cundy-Betts' allegedly unreliable delivery service.

The second major weakness of this division, Mr. Van Allen argued, was its failure to properly plan its product lines. While he conceded that stock turnover had improved and the ratio of inventory to net working capital had been lowered over the past four years, streamlining the inventory in a quantitative sense was not enough. Inventory must also be streamlined qualitatively, he stated, by adding new products with high demand potential and by weeding out old products that were no longer paying their way.

He reminded Mr. Dean that although every industry the division served was spending millions on product research and development,

Cundy-Betts had not added a half-dozen new products to its industrial lines in the past 10 years. For example, the National Building Material Distributors' Association had estimated that in the Midwest alone over 50,000 homeowners would install automatically operated garage doors in the next 3 years, and another 30,000 homes would be either built with or converted to electric heat. Yet, Mr. Van Allen pointed out, the supplies and apparatus division did not carry a single piece of equipment that could be used in either type of installation. By contrast, over 50 percent of the sales volume in the appliances and television division came from products the company did not stock 10 years ago. He cited upright freezers, transistor radios, tape recorders, color television, electric can openers, and battery operated clocks as a few examples of such products.

Mr. Dean hotly contested this diagnosis of the supplies and apparatus division. His comments are quoted below.

"This division has made every possible effort to tighten inventory control. There is a limit to what we can do, however, because the real responsibility for this function rests with the purchasing division. All inventory records are maintained by the purchasing staff, and we simply tell them what products we want and when we want them; what happens after this is out of our hands. However, we have adopted a new simplified order form for salesmen, which replaces the old multicopy, snap-out form with a single punch card. This card has all the pertinent information about a product prepunched in it, and requires only the salesman's signature to authorize shipment. Use of the punched card not only reduces the time required to process an order, because the processing procedure can be mechanized, but also permits the recording of more complete information about the product and customer. Faster order handling with more product information should make possible more efficient control over inventory. If purchasing is not doing a satisfactory job of maintaining proper inventory levels and assortments, it is they who should answer for this and not us.

"Complaints about the unreliability of delivery service on industrial products are news to me. My salesmen send their orders directly to the purchasing department, where the merchandise sold is deducted from the stock-on-hand and the new stock-on-hand figure posted. Four copies of the order card are then reproduced; three are sent to the warehousing division and one to us. Warehousing immediately sends one of these cards—it is labeled "invoice" and has all pertinent information printed on it—to the purchaser to acknowledge receipt of his order. When the order is shipped, the second card is sent to the accounting division, and the third is retained for warehouse records. The accounting department then bills the customer for the amount of the order less discounts at the end of the month. If delivery service is unreliable, it is because of a time lag between mailing of the order acknowledgment card and shipment of the order.

"Frankly, this is the first time I have heard of complaints about our delivery service. Why a company would write to the general manager of a supplier about such a complaint rather than bring it to the attention of the salesman who took the order is more than I can understand. Besides, when we sell more than 8,000 accounts annually I can't be very upset about a half-dozen complaints. I think that is a pretty good record of service. When Mr. Van Allen brought these letters to my attention, I personally checked all our call reports for the past year. None of the salesmen had reported any complaints about delivery. They would have no reason to withhold such information, because poor delivery service would be no reflection on them. Making delivery is the responsibility of the warehousing division.

"The allegation that our product lines are poorly planned because we have failed to add enough new products and to eliminate enough old products reveals Mr. Van Allen's abysmal ignorance of this division and the market it serves. Manufacturers *are* spending a lot of money on product development, but our customers are not gadget-happy. They will not replace an old piece of equipment or apparatus with a new one simply because the new one is better looking or possesses greater snob appeal. The new product must be demonstrably superior in a profit sense before it has a Chinaman's chance of displacing an established product. Based on Department of Commerce statistics, a new product introduced today has only 1 chance in 50 of being accepted by the market. In other words, approximately 98 percent of the new products introduced fail to win acceptance in the marketplace. This means that somebody gets stuck with a lot of unsalable merchandise. And this division's record of increasing stock turnover and decreasing ratios of inventory to net working capital indicates that we have been successful in avoiding this pitfall.

"It is true that the division has eliminated suppliers rather than lines, but we are not carrying a single product for which we do not have buyers. We are also cautiously adding some new lines—notably, television focusing magnets, coin boxes for pay television, telephone-answering devices, and color television scanning equipment. Admittedly, these lines do not represent a very substantial portion of our total sales, but they are growth lines for which there is an established demand.

"We do not stock parts for automatically operated garage doors or control equipment and devices for electrically heated homes because these items are typically installed by builders. We have never sold to building contractors because we have never regarded the construction industry as a very healthy market. Not only is it subject to severe seasonal and cyclical swings, but also most builders are small- to medium-sized operators, whose prime consideration is almost always price and who never seem able to pay on time.

"We could undoubtedly get more volume if we chose to enter the construction market. But we would be obliged to add new lines, which I presume would please Mr. Van Allen, and increase the amount of working capital committed to inventory, which I presume would not please him. Since our present sales force is spread about as thin as we dare to spread it, entering a new market would most assuredly require an expansion of the field sales force and additional promotion; the net result, at least in the short run, would be to increase expenses by a greater proportion than sales. Moreover, the price situation in the construction market is about as bad as I have seen in my lifetime. To penetrate it we would have to be prepared to reduce prices to the level of drop shippers and other non-stock-carrying middlemen. This would mean taking losses as high as 20 percent on some lines. No company can afford to sell inventory at 80 cents on the dollar to get more business.

"Industrial selling requires a competent engineering service department as well as a competent field sales force. Neither can be created overnight. While this company has always sold in the industrial market, it has never attempted to systematically recruit, train, and promote industrial sales personnel. As a result, whenever one of our men develops into a really competent salesman one of our suppliers hires him away from us. In fact, a really ambitious man will not stay with us because he soon realizes that there is no place to go in this organization. It is the consumer product salesmen who have always received the promotions to managerial positions. And there are few career salesmen in this business, the work is too hard, the hours are too long, and the weekends on the road too frequent. As this division develops, however, with its own field offices and warehouses, there will soon be some attractive management positions to hold our good men. We will not have the men to fill these positions, though, unless the program of systematic personnel recruitment and training I have begun is continued. If a profit-making sales and service staff is to be developed in this division, the company must be willing to make a substantial investment in it. This, Mr. Van Allen seems unwilling to do."

The executive in charge of all purchasing at Cundy-Betts was Louis Schlarmann. The purchasing department staff included 25 buyers who specialized by product line and about 20 clerk-secretaries who handled correspondence and maintained inventory records. Mr. Schlarmann was aided by four assistant division managers. One manager supervised industrial goods purchases, another supervised consumer goods purchases, a third was responsible for inventory control, and the fourth was office manager.

Mr. Schlarmann did not believe the inventory situation was either so confused as Mr. Van Allen thought or so completely the purchasing department's responsibility as Mr. Dean seemed to think. He admitted that some confusion probably did exist when industrial product sales were separated from consumer sales and separate warehouses were established for each division. But he was not aware that any misunderstanding still existed regarding merchandise receipts, stock-on-hand, and stock location. His remarks were essentially as follows.

"Initially, only the fastest moving lines were stocked in the field warehouses. The slow movers of both divisions were carried in our main warehouse at the home office. The reason was that we were obliged to use rented warehouse space until we could construct our own facilities. During this period, there were delays in making delivery whenever a salesman sent in an order listing some items warehoused locally and others warehoused at the home office. In these cases, the customer received his order in two installments. Since customers usually want their entire order as soon as possible, our classification of slow-moving and fast-moving goods didn't give them much satisfaction. A customer is understandably confused when part of his order is delivered in four days and the remainder doesn't arrive for another week. It seems to me, though, that the salesmen could have done more to explain this situation to our customers. Complaints about delivery eventually filter back to us and we endeavor to give the customer a reasonable explanation, together with an apology. I don't recall how many such complaints we handled last year, but it wasn't enough to be alarming.

"There was also apparently some misunderstanding on the part of our personnel about which items were classified as slow moving and which as fast moving. As a result, items were occasionally reported as out-of-stock at local warehouses when they were actually in the main warehouse. Since we now have adequate storage space, we have abandoned the slow-moving–fast-moving classifications and carry complete stocks at our field warehouses. This source of confusion has therefore been largely eliminated. There are probably still some delays when an order received at a division warehouse contains items stocked by the other division. For example, one of Mr. Dean's salesmen might submit an order for a freezer or an electric can opener to be used in a company's kitchen. Neither of these items are stocked in the apparatus and equipment division, although salesmen in this division may take orders for them. Such orders must be sent to the nearest consumer products field warehouse or to the main warehouse.

"However, we now have in operation a rather effective system of cross-listing all items carried by the company. It enables the stock pickers at any field warehouse to determine quickly where any item not in their own facility is located. If a telephone call to this warehouse reveals that the item is in stock, the order is sent there and filled immediately. As you may know, we have a division office at each warehouse, and every item stocked has a separate punch card, prepared when the item is received. The card is stored in a tub file until the item is sold. That is, we maintain a perpetual inventory of items by keeping a physical inventory of cards. An order clerk can determine in a matter of minutes whether an item is in stock and where it is located if not carried in that particular warehouse.

"The only factor currently causing delays in delivery is an out-of-stock situation. Since our buying is done on the basis of forecasts formulated by the sales divisions, we can do nothing if these forecasts are in error. The forecasts submitted by Mr. Dean's division have frequently been too conservative on a number of products. Consequently, in a number of instances we have been obliged to place emergency orders with suppliers in order to fill orders submitted by his division. This is not only an expensive way to order—it usually means a long-distance telephone call or a telegram—but it also delays delivery to the customer.

"We in purchasing have nothing to do with the planning of product lines, either quantitatively or qualitatively, as Mr. Van Allen phrases it. The sales divisions tell us what products they want us to stock, and we endeavor to secure these on the most advantegous terms. When we recently discontinued a number of our former suppliers, the names of the firms to be dropped were submitted to us by the sales divisions. Our function is exclusively that of serving other divisions of the company. We make no decisions with regard to what is purchased or from whom; we fill orders, we do not initiate them. The only product decisions solely ours concern the proper quantity to order, the most economical ratio of stock to sales, and the various terms of purchase, that is, price, delivery, scheduling, discounts, insurance, and so on.

The company controller was Dale Torrence, who was also secretary of the board of directors. He explained that the organizational changes undertaken in 1956, while not affecting his department directly, made it impossible to allocate costs. He had estimated the company's break-even volume at about $7 million. While break-even estimates for the two divisions were still provisional, he felt that the break-even point for the supplies and apparatus division would not be much less than $3 million. Although sales for the division had not yet reached this figure, results for the present year were expected to slightly exceed the break-even volume. Mr. Torrence also stated that company sales had exceeded break-even volume every year since 1956 because of appliance and television sales to retail dealers. The accounting division charged all direct expenses against the division that incurred them, and allocated overhead on the basis of nonselling personnel or square feet of floor space, as appropriate.

Mr. Torrence thought the difficulties plaguing Mr. Dean stemmed from his zeal to increase sales on the assumption that volume beyond the break-even point was pure profit. The controller observed that additional sales volume invariably requires more inventory and more money invested in accounts receivable. Cundy-Betts simply did not have the working capital for such an expansion and, borrowing was proving to be expensive. As Mr. Torrence expressed it, borrowing working capital "eats up profits faster than they can be made." The situation became critical in the last part of 1958 when the company lost $200,000 in 4 months, but fortunately this experience has not been repeated. He added that he would like to see sales level off at about $7.5 million until earnings provided enough capital to support further expansion.

Mr. Torrence was also interested in Mr. Van Allen's views concerning product line programming, i.e., the addition of new products and the elimination of old ones. During the past year, the accounting staff had endeavored to make some distribution cost analyses to ascertain the contributions various products were making to company overhead. The sales tabulation they assembled is shown in Exhibit I.

EXHIBIT I

Sales Trends by Product Group
Supplies and Apparatus Division

Product Group	Percentage of Total Company Sales Volume		
	1954	*1956*	*1960*
Power tools	35.7	28.0	21.7
Heating units	13.3	12.6	10.1
Color scanners	*	1.5	3.0
Lighting fixtures	11.3	10.4	5.3
Switches	7.6	8.0	6.1
Wire recorders	4.0	5.0	4.1
General-purpose tape recorders	5.3	4.5	5.6
Type A speakers	5.7	8.0	10.0
Type B speakers	13.1	15.0	18.2
Conduit	4.0	7.0	10.9
Focusing magnets	*	*	1.5
Coin boxes	*	*	.5
Automotive parts	*	*	2.0
Telephone parts	*	*	1.0
Total Product Sales	100.0	100.0	100.0

* Not stocked that year.

Due to the expense of making a comprehensive study of all products, Mr. Torrence's cost analysis was of a fragmentary nature. Nevertheless, it disclosed that several of the company's products were priced at figures that put them in the red on a gross profit basis or resulted in no contribution to net profit and general overhead after estimated selling costs were deducted from gross profit. Mr. Dean, however, had defended the company's pricing policy on the basis that some of these loss products constituted an element of considerable importance in the cost structure of the typical buyer, and that these buyers also purchased other products on which the firm made a profit. He was unable to say whether or not this was true of all products on which his division was sustaining losses.

Mr. Torrence's conclusion was that it would be ridiculous to add new products without first eliminating some of the unprofitable ones now carried in the supplies and apparatus division. He warned that the company's financial position would not permit the continued sale of products at a loss. He was not prepared to say, though, which of the losing products should be discontinued.

THE HANCOCK COMPANY (A)

◇◇

The Hancock Chemical Company is a manufacturer of fine chemicals and drug materials. Its annual sales volume is between $60 and $80 million. The company makes about 1,000 products, some 200 of which are responsible for 70 to 80 percent of its sales volume. The company conducts an extensive program of chemical, pharmacological, and medical research, and is firmly committed to the proposition that such research is vital to leadership in the fine chemical business. About 60 percent of its present sales volume is in products developed through research during the past 15 years. Its present sales volume is about 5 times that of 15 years ago.

The importance of different products or groups of products in the sales volume pattern of the company varies widely from year to year as is shown by the following table.

Product Group	Percentage of Total Company Sales Volume		
	1940	1950	1960
A	11.3	10	5
B	9.6	8	5
C	7.7	2	*
D	7.3	5	1
E	7.0	12	0.5
F	6.9	3	2
G	3.9	4	3
H	3.9	2	0.3
I	3.8	4	1
J	*	15	27
K	*	7	6
L	*	*	15
M	*	*	12
N	*	*	9

* Not in the line.

The products of the company can be grouped in the following classes:

a) Antibiotics (penicillin, etc.)   e) Agricultural
b) Medicinal chemicals   f) Food
c) Vitamins   g) Industrial
d) Hormones   h) General

While the research and production problems of each group differ from those of the other groups, they do not differ too much from one another in the methods or problems of selling.

The products of the company are sold to the following types of buyers:

a) Pharmaceutical manufacturers, who use them in compounding preparations sold chiefly under their brands over the retail counter. Some of these preparations are sold only on doctor's prescription. There are about 900 such manufacturers—about a dozen very large, most small. They are heavily concentrated around New York, Chicago, and St. Louis, although there are a few in all parts of the country.

b) Veterinary houses, which use Hancock products to compound medicines sold chiefly under their own brands for use in treating animals. There are about 200 such houses.

c) Cosmetic manufacturers, about 1,000, who use certain Hancock products in preparations sold under their own brands.

d) Industrial buyers, who purchase Hancock products for a variety of uses; the most important is the vitamin enrichment of foods and animal and poultry feeds. About 15,000 industrial firms can use Hancock products; only about 6,000 can use them in sufficient quantity to justify direct sales service. These firms must be canvassed by salesmen qualified to offer technical advice and service.

e) Laboratories of industrial firms and educational institutions, about 1,000 of significance. Most of them buy from laboratory supply distributors, of which about 30 are of any real importance.

f) Chemical supply and laboratory supply and equipment wholesalers, about 200 worth carrying on the company's customer list.

g) Governmental units, buying mainly for health and hospital work. They purchase chiefly on bids.

h) Competing manufacturers, who buy from Hancock items that Hancock can make more cheaply than they can. Hancock also purchases certain items from them. There are about 30 of these, a half-dozen really important. It is very important to maintain cordial relations with some of these firms.

Gross profits are usually about 40 percent on sales, although the gross profit figure on individual items fluctuates widely from as much as 90 percent on sales to as low as zero. Selling and other distribution expenses are generally about 6 percent of sales. Net profit before taxes usually averages about 15 percent of sales, and after taxes about 7 percent of sales. Both selling expenses and net profit percentages vary widely among the different products as percentages of sales.

The introduction of a new product into the line is usually an expensive process. It often happens that during the test-tube and pilot plant stages, costs of as much as several millions accrue against a possible new product. Sometimes, these costs must be written off to profit and loss when it proves impossible to develop a prospective new product to the marketable point. If a new product gives evidence that it will be demanded in considerable quantities, it may be necessary to build or buy new equipment, sometimes costing several millions. The firm usually has a large sum of money invested in a product in the form of sunk costs before a nickel's worth of it is ready to be sold on the market.

The officials of the firm feel that three aspects of the company's pricing policies and practices should be reexamined.

1. In the chemical business, as in several others, there are two schools of thought about pricing policy and practice on a new product. When a firm brings out a new product, it usually has a virtual monopoly for a period varying from a few months to one and one-half or two years. During the early part of this period, competitors may be expected to watch the product's reception on the market and to attempt to appraise its market possibilities. After they become convinced that its production and sale will be a profitable venture, they must spend considerable time in procuring or developing equipment with which to make it, and in developing production and selling know-how by a process of trial and error.

During this period of monopoly, some firms follow the policy of pricing the product at the highest figure they can get for their supply, which is usually limited in relation to the demand. Sometimes the gross profit on such an item will run as high as 80 or 90 percent on sales during this period.

Other companies prefer the policy of trying to compute the level at which the price of the product will settle when it has become an established member of the line and after competition has developed. Such a firm then fixes its initial price at or near this level.

The Hancock Company has followed the first of these policies, but some of the executives are dissatisfied with it. They feel that it tends to invite competition, to cause embarrassment because of the deep price cuts that must be made when competition appears and begins to be established, and to create customer ill will because buyers feel that during the early stages of product marketing they were gouged by unreasonably high prices. It is usually not easy to explain the theory underlying such a policy, because many customers find it hard to believe that developmental costs are as high as they really are. Nor is it usually desirable to disclose such costs to customers in detail.

2. The company is one of the oldest in the field and commands great prestige throughout the industry. From the beginning, it has been meticulous in maintaining the most exhaustive system of checks and tests to assure the quality of its products. Hancock quality is a byword in the trade. It has also placed great emphasis on service, both in the form of delivery and in technical aid and advice on the use of its products.

As a result, there has been a feeling among some company executives that it is beneath Hancock's dignity to engage in too active price competition. The outcome of this has been a certain slowness in meeting competitors' price cuts. When a competitor cuts the price of an item, Hancock has a tendency to assume a somewhat haughty and righteous air, designed to indicate that such cheap practices are beneath its dignity and standing in the industry. Often, this attitude is maintained until the competitor makes serious inroads into the Hancock volume; then price is reduced to the level set by the competitor. The salesmen then have to struggle mightily to recapture customers enticed away by the lower price.

The routine necessary to initiate a price reduction may also have contributed to this slowness of response to competitive price cuts. Price changes are originated in the marketing department by the manager of price policy, who reports to the vice president in charge of marketing. A recommendation of the price policy manager must be approved by the vice president for marketing, who transmits it to the executive vice president and the president, without whose approval it cannot become effective. One of these men is a graduate of sales and the other of controllership; both are very much interested in pricing and carefully study proposed price changes. Their studies sometimes require considerable time.

Several of the younger executives feel that both the system and the policy should be changed in some way so as to bring about a quicker, more responsive, and more competitively effective pattern of pricing policy and practice.

3. Various cost of distribution studies have disclosed that many of the company's products are priced at figures that put them in the red on a gross profit basis, or result in no contribution to net profit and general overhead after distribution costs are deducted from gross profits. A few of these products are items that the company sells in considerable volume and are footballs of competition. They constitute an element of considerable significance in the cost structure of the typical customer who buys them. Most of them, however, are sold in small volume. The average customer who buys such an item purchases only a few dollars, or at most a few hundreds of dollars, worth of it a year. It constitutes no significant element in his cost structure. A few are articles whose prices are closely watched as barometers of price movements and indicators of competitive price position in the trade.

Some of these loss items are bought by customers who purchase from the Hancock Company significant volumes of profitable products. Others are bought largely by customers who purchase nothing else from the company.

Several executives of the company feel that this entire area of the company's pricing policy and practice should be studied, and that certain general principles and procedures should be established to administer prices of individual items belonging to this unprofitable group.

THE HANCOCK COMPANY (B)

◇◇

The Hancock Company is a chemical manufacturer. Its products are sold for use by pharmaceutical and drug manufacturing concerns, veterinary products manufacturers, food and beverage manufacturing houses, educational, commercial, and industrial laboratories, industrial establishments, and ultimate consumers, to whom they are dispensed by hospitals or physicians or on physician's prescription through retail drugstores.

The company's sales have grown very rapidly from $8.1 million in 1929 to $55.4 million in 1946, $108.5 million in 1952, and $200 million in 1960.

No small part of this great expansion of sales is the fruit of the extensive research program, which the company began in the early thirties and has continued to the present time. This research work is organized under a separate department; its chief reports directly to the company president and is a member of the operations committee, which includes the chief operating officials of the firm. This department contains units specializing in organic and biochemical research, microbiological research, and physical and inorganic chemical research. It also includes a development unit, which specializes in problems of chemical technology and production and has control of the pilot plant operations involved in carrying a new product from the test tube to the factory processing stage.

During one period of the company's development, there was considerable dispute between the research group and the engineering group over which should have charge of carrying a new product through the pilot plant stage of its development and readying it for full-scale plant processing operations. The research men felt that since they had lived with the idea from its inception and knew all its past history they were best qualified to carry its development right through to the floor of the factory and supervise the ironing out of all the difficulties that might occur in integrating it as a full-fledged member of the line. The engineering group felt, on the other hand, that since the umbilical cord binding a new product to research had to be cut at some time, and that since the test tube was the scale of operations at which the research men functioned best, while plant operation was the particular province of the engineers, the new product should be transferred to the control of the engineering department when it entered the pilot plant stage. The engineers finally won out, and the development section of the research department was transferred to the engineering department. While the research department members were not exactly happy about the outcome, they gradually became reconciled to it, more readily perhaps because the engineering department was under the leadership of a new chief who gave better technical service in the work of introducing new products than the research group had formerly been able to do.

But this happy resolution of the company's attempt to organize the technical aspects of new product work failed to solve all the problems connected with it. When a new article is ready for production and commercial use, it still must undergo the procedure of being tested and released for distribution by the Food and Drug Administration, and must be worked into the sales line as a full-fledged member of the company family of products. If this work were left until the test-tube and pilot plant stages were completed, the ultimate results from a profit standpoint might prove to be far from satisfactory. The commercial aspects of a new product need to be explored concurrently with its technical features. Current stories in the industry tell of a firm that spent $500,000 developing a new product, only to find that its total possible sales were about $50,000 a year. The sales department was too heavily burdened with the day-to-day crises that attend the work of capturing and holding customers to do much with the task of exploring the market possibilities of a new product, let alone that of appraising its probable effect on the cost and profit structure of the firm.

Top management felt that a separate unit of the company was needed to do this work. As a result, a product development department was established shortly before the beginning of World War II. It did not really get started before its operation was rendered unnecessary because of the company's preoccupation with war work, when all new product activities were dictated by the demands of the armed services. After the end of the war, the department was revived under a new head, Mr. Stanton, who set out to explore the areas within which his unit might operate to the profit of the company.

Mr. Stanton soon felt himself handicapped by what seemed to him a lack of product policy on the part of the company. For example, there seemed to be no clear-cut determination on the extent to which the company should sell such products as insecticides, which were somewhat outside the drug field. There also seemed to be some confusion of policy about the question of whether the company should develop a line of products to be sold over the retail drug counter under the Hancock label. Mr. Stanton finally worked out the following statement of the responsibilities and authority of his department for inclusion in the organization manual of the company.

Manager Product Development Department

Reports to: The President

In carrying out his responsibilities he:

1. Correlates and directs all matters related to the establishment of new products by the company.
2. Surveys and analyzes the sales and market possibilities for present and new products in existing and new fields.
3. Determines sales potentials for products in development or suggested for development.
4. On the basis of market surveys and analysis, recommends development or production of new products.
5. Estimates actual sales of new products to guide the planning of necessary production and sales facilities.
6. Coordinates the company's efforts in developing new products, including the recommending of manufacturing capacity, sales programs, and distribution plans.
7. When necessary, carries out initial sales of new products prior to turning them over to the marketing division.
8. Studies and reports on the probable effects of the introduction of new products on the financial, cost, and profit structure of the company.

Mr. Stanton attempted to build up the organization of the product development department and to expand its activities. In the process, he engendered antagonism among several of the operating divisions to such a point that neither he nor his assistants were able to obtain the cooperation so vitally necessary to the proper performance of the department's functions. For example, he urged that the product development department employ a small force of specialty salesmen with whom to conduct pilot marketing programs when introducing new products to the market, and he thought most new products should not be turned over to the marketing division until in the course of such pilot programs the bugs had been worked out of their distribution and production systems. This did not exactly serve to endear his department to members of the marketing division. After about ten years, Mr. Stanton made a connection elsewhere and left the company. His place was taken by Mr. Boyle, a very able young man with excellent technical and business training, pleasing personality, and great vigor and drive. He previously had been an executive of a smaller company.

About this time, at the suggestion of the administrative vice president Mr. Ross, careful study was given to the problem of establishing a marketing research department. This step was finally decided on at about the time Mr. Boyle assumed direction of the product development department, now elevated in the organization hierarchy to the status of a division. The new department was made a part of the enlarged division. Since Mr. Boyle was not immediately able to dissipate the lack of sympathy between his division and the marketing group, and since the tasks of sales analysis and making sales estimates still remained in the sales planning department, a unit of the marketing division, the work of the marketing research department was confined mainly to market explorations for new products and to economic studies for top management.

The large number of products made by the company and their diversified nature caused other complications. Each product, or at least each group of them, possessed problems of its own with respect to its improvement, the control of its quality, its production, and its marketing. For example, the problems involved in handling narcotics were especially unique in the rigid control required because of governmental regulations and the socially dangerous nature of the products themselves. The management decided that these problems required special attention, so a product manager was appointed to devote all his attention to the narcotics line. Other persons were assigned to this type of work, and in due course there were 10 product managers, each dealing with the problems of a separate group of products.

An executive of the company described the duties and authority of a product manager as follows.

The general responsibility of a product manager is that of a business manager for a specific product or group of products. He is responsible for coordinating all activities that have an effect on the profit contributions of the product or products assigned to him. Acting in a staff capacity, he works closely with operating and staff executives to maintain and improve the position of the product or products and the profits.

While he has no line authority, he has the responsibility of keeping top management informed on important operating problems and also on such other information as industry trends, the company's competitive position, sales forecasts, and any other significant matters. He makes recommendations on policies and practices that will improve the profit position, and assists operating executives in carrying out programs in accordance with instructions from the operations committee.

At first, each product manager reported directly to the chairman of the operations committee. Later, control of their activities was concentrated under a director of product managers, Mr. Angus, who reported to the chairman of the operations committee.

The responsibilities of a product manager were described in the organization manual of the company as follows.

The product manager is responsible for assisting general management and operating executives in improving the profit contribution of the products assigned to him. Acting in a staff capacity, he is responsible for continuous analysis, evaluation, and coordination of all company activities affecting these products, including sales, production, scientific, purchasing, engineering, financial and related matters. Serving as a focal point in the company for information about his products, he makes recommendations, after close collaboration with interested operating departments, on policies and programs designed to strengthen their competitive position and increase their profits. He is responsible for assisting in the management of contracts affecting the products, and for maintaining outside contacts and relationships as assigned.

The results were not always happy. The operating executives sometimes complained that the product managers got in their hair. For example, a product manager often felt the need of visiting members of customer trades in order to get a more realistic idea of the market conditions for his products than could be obtained from a desk in Baltimore, headquarters of the company. This was resented and opposed by the marketing division executives, who felt that relations with a customer were a delicate matter and should not be disturbed by other representatives of the company whose questions might raise embarrassing doubts in the customers' minds. Likewise, the sales executives were sometimes embarrassed by the estimates of sales possibilities issued by product managers. In estimating the sales of a product, the product manager usually dealt in terms of sales potentials—the volume Hancock would get if it got all the sales of the product there were to get. When the sales executives submitted their estimates of what they actually expected to sell during a coming budgetary period, general management sometimes did not remember to distinguish between the differing bases upon which the estimates were made, to the chagrin of the marketing group.

Some overlapping also developed between the work of the product managers and that of the product development division. For example, the head of the product development division felt that his unit should have primary responsibility for all new products, even when there was a product manager assigned to the general group of products to which the new product belonged. The director of product managers felt, on the other hand, that when a product manager was assigned a group of products he should be held primarily responsible for all new products developed in his group, and that the product development division should get into the picture only on request of the product manager. On the other hand, the director of product development was of the opinion that, of necessity, his group should interest itself in existing as well as new products. He expressed his attitude as follows.

"Product development is not merely a matter of taking new products proffered by research, coordinating the various matters relating to initial sale, and then dropping them. It must be concerned on a continuing basis with the various product lines, their profitability and competitive strength, the long-time as well as the short-run picture, changes in the economic position of industries served by Hancock products, and the relation of existing and potential facilities to demand.

"In order to properly evaluate the position of a potential new product, it is essential that those studying the problem be thoroughly informed about the past and present history of similar products, and the development in the line of products of which the new product will be a part.

"Furthermore, once all the necessary work has been done to understand whether a new product should be added to the line and what its competitive position should be, it seems to me wasteful at that point for the individual who has conducted the preliminary study to drop the item and no longer be concerned with it. This individual should follow and keep in touch with the inventory position and markets and prices and costs of the article, not for the purpose of exerting line authority over the operating departments, but to be able to warn of significant trouble ahead or to interpret accumulating inventories, changing costs, and other factors of the competitive situation and the need for the development of new or improved products or the abandonment of existing products or product lines.

"The establishment of product managers in addition to the product development division cannot help but result in duplication and extra overhead for the company. To be competent in his field, a product manager must give consideration to the competitive position of his assigned products and to the development of new products to strengthen the line within his field of responsibility. He must, therefore, overlap the responsibilities of product development. On the other hand, in order to consider new products intelligently and to evaluate their profitability and proper distribution, product development must keep informed of the status of existing product lines, thereby duplicating the work of the product managers."

These conflicting attitudes led to the development of the following personnel picture (secretarial help excluded).

Product or Activity Group	Product Development		Product Managers	
	Men	Money	Men	Money
General administration............1		$15,000	1	$12,000
Miscellaneous products............1		10,000		
Industrial products................1		8,500		
Narcotics and vitamins............1		8,500	3	18,000
Veterinary products...............1		8,500	1	8,500
Pharmaceutical products...........2		17,000	1	8,500
Specialties......................1		4,000		
Antibiotics.....................			3	19,500
Laboratory chemicals.............			1	8,500
Inorganic chemicals...............1		8,500		
Total....................9		$80,000	10	$75,000

This resulted in an overlapping of about $37,000 in the salaries of men in the two groups who were performing identical functions with respect to the same products.

Top management felt that the time had come to attempt to eliminate as much as possible of the overlapping and misunderstanding that resulted from this situation.

The director of product managers and the director of the product development division suggested that they be allowed to work together to divide up the area between them and set limits to their respective fields of authority and responsibility. In fact, they had made tentative steps in that direction, although they had not been able to agree on substantial areas.

Mr. Ross suggested that both product managers and the product development division be abolished, and a director of merchandising be set up. The responsibilities of this new official would include:

1. Studying the product line as to sales, profits, and competition.
2. Evaluating the outlook for the company's products in all commercial aspects.
3. Deleting or modifying existing products.
4. Studying containers and labels in order to reconcile the interests of sales, production, and scientific divisions.
5. Evaluating the markets and all commercial aspects of new products, and making decisions with respect to all new products involving a financial outlay of less than a fixed amount; recommending with respect to other proposed new products.
6. Studying inventories of finished goods and recommending policies in order to reconcile the interests of sales, production, and finance.
7. Studying price policies and practices.
8. Acting as a focal point for all company information about products.
9. Making decisions about finished inventory levels within limits of established policy.

In making this proposal, Mr. Ross sought to solve another problem that had long been a matter of vexation—the control of inventory. From time to time, the operations committee established overall policy on the amount and composition of inventory, both of materials and finished goods. This policy was carried out by the manufacturing planning department, which also made the necessary decision in the absence of a policy decision to cover a specific situation not of major importance. On occasion, a series of such minor decisions on inventory had worked into a policy pattern of major import. Mr. Ross felt that the inventory management was a matter in which at least three major operating parts of the company—production, sales, and finance—had an interest, and that, therefore, it should not be under the control of the production division.

EXHIBIT I

The Hancock Company

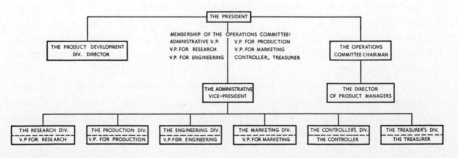

THE HEFLIN CHEMICAL SUPPLY COMPANY (A)

◇◇

The Heflin Chemical Supply Company is a large distributor of agricultural chemicals, fertilizers, and animal medicines. It is located in Ohio and sells through a force of some forty salesmen. One of the company's most successful products is a medicinal powder, trade-named Promaine. When added to animal feed, Promaine not only protects the animal against certain diseases but stimulates growth as well. The company holds a manufacturer's franchise on the product which makes it the exclusive supplier in a territory including western Ohio, most of Indiana, and eastern Illinois.

The chief purchasers of Promaine are feed manufacturers: large hog, broiler, and beef cattle raisers who prepare their own feed mixtures; country elevators which do custom mixing of feeds for farmers; and farm supply stores. Since Promaine is a potent drug, only a few ounces need to be added to a one hundred pound batch of feed to obtain the desired results in growth stimulation and disease prevention. While usage in excess of recommended quantities has no harmful effect on animals or the consumer end products obtained from them, neither does it provide any additional benefit. Consequently, failure to follow directions in mixing represents a waste to the user.

The principal competing product is a preparation made by the Roudebush Chemical Corporation of Buffalo, New York. It is marketed under the trade name Viotin, and is sold throughout the midwest chiefly by manufacturers' agents. Viotin is a crystalline compound of considerably greater bulk than Promaine powder. Its price is somewhat less per pound than Promaine, but it must be used in larger proportions to achieve the same results. Other preparations with medicinal characteristics similar to those of Promaine and Viotin are also on the market. Some are in dry crystalline form to be used as feed additives, others are in liquid or tablet form to be added to the animals' drinking water. Promaine, however, is the only powdered form in which such preparations are available.

Laboratory tests by the manufacturer have indicated that in comparison to Promaine, the use of other feed additives increases the cost of a one hundred pound batch of feed from 10 to 15 per cent when the same degree of potency is achieved. Tests conducted by agricultural experiment stations corroborate this and have established the fact that there is no difference in mixing qualities between the powdered and crystalline forms of such preparations. Either form becomes uniformly distributed through a batch of feed when ordinary types of mixing machinery are used. Tests by experiment stations also confirmed the superior effectiveness of Promaine in reducing the incidence of certain animal diseases. The same tests further proved the growth stimulating properties of Promaine to be equal to that of other similar feed additives including Viotin.

Recently, the Hoosier Feed and Milling Company, a well established manufacturer of livestock feeds and an important customer of the Heflin Company, circulated the announcement shown below in its monthly promotional letter. This letter is sent to a substantial list of farmers, feeders, elevator operators, and farm supply stores in the Midwest.

"During the coming year we plan to discontinue the use of all growth and disease preventatives in our line of Banquet Feeds except the drug Viotin. Our reasons for this decision are the proven facts that:

a) only crystalline preparations, such as Viotin, can be uniformly mixed in the batching process because a certain amount of bulk is needed in relation to potency.

b) the action of Viotin is less severe than other preparations; Viotin has no harmful after effect on animals, and

c) the lower price per unit of active ingredient in Viotin will permit us to supply our customers with Banquet Feeds at lower prices than we would otherwise be obliged to charge.

It is our considered judgment that Viotin is the only feed additive whose potency and safety have been scientifically proven and laboratory tested. We are confident that this change, made in the interest of the many farmers and feeders who use our product, will meet with their approval. We believe that our demonstrated policy of supplying only the finest feeds will further the confidence that Midwest farmers and livestock men have always placed in products of the Hoosier Feed and Milling Company."

This announcement came as a complete surprise to Heflin management. Although sales records had indicated that Hoosier Feed and Milling placed no orders for Promaine for a period of about ten weeks prior to their announcement, this had not been regarded as significant. The company had never placed order more frequently than once every two or three months. These orders were ordinarily large enough so that the Heflin company typically drop-shipped them to give Hoosier Feed and Milling the best possible discount. Call reports submitted by the salesman serving this account indicated no dissatisfaction with Promaine and no complaints from its users.

Heflin management immediately retained a law firm to study the situation and advise them as to what legal steps, if any, they should take. Legal counsel later reported that sufficient evidence existed for Heflin to bring suit against Hoosier Feed and Milling with every expectation of recovering heavy damages. There was no indication whatever that the Roudebush Company or any agent representing it had anything to do with the action of Hoosier Feed and Milling except to sell it Viotin.

Soon after the appearance of the announcement, Hoosier Feed and Milling's chief competitor, the Garver Feed Company, approached Heflin management with a proposal. The Garver president thought that this situation presented his company with a golden opportunity to discredit Hoosier Feed and Milling by exposing its brazen misrepresentation. The plan was to accomplish this expose with an extensive direct mail campaign as well as space advertising in local newspapers throughout the market area served by the two feed companies. Without specifically naming Hoosier Feed and Milling, the advertisements would recite Hoosier's claim and then refute it by presenting the true facts of the matter supported by quotations from technical bulletins of the agricultural experiment stations. The Garver Company and Heflin would split the costs of the campaign.

The Garver company had used Promaine in its feeds since the product was first introduced and, like Hoosier Feed and Milling, had been one of Heflin's best accounts. It was a somewhat smaller firm than Hoosier Feed and Milling but well managed by a young and aggressive staff. The marketing area served by both companies included most of Indiana, east central Illinois and western Ohio.

At a meeting of the Heflin executive group several other suggestions for dealing with the situation were also forthcoming. One proposal was to try to get the Roudebush Company to bring pressure on Hoosier to clean up its advertising. From all that could be ascertained, Roudebush had nothing to do with the Hoosier announcement. Consequently, it was argued that until further information indicated the contrary to be true, it would be reasonable to proceed on the assumption that Roudebush was a reputable company whose management would not condone outright misrepresentation. If all the facts of the matter were laid before the Roudebush Company, it would be in a position to exert pressure on Hoosier Feed and Milling to either retract their statement or at least to refrain from making any further such statements.

Moreover, those who advocated this alternative emphasized that Hoosier Feed and Milling was still a potential customer. If Heflin sued them or entered into a "plot" with one of their competitors to discredit them, their patronage would be lost for all time. It was suggested that the objective in dealing with this problem should be to keep Hoosier Feed and Milling as a customer, not to punish them. There was general agreement that Hoosier Feed and Milling should be brought back "into the fold," if that were possible. There was some skepticism, however, that Roudebush would have any incentive to correct their customer's misinformation—if indeed that was really the cause of the trouble. And even if Roudebush should urge them to make a retraction, it was doubtful whether a manufacturer could exert much influence over a customer anyway. Once a product has passed from the hands of the manufacturer to those of the customer, the manufacturer no longer has much control over what the customer does with it or says about it.

Another suggestion was that Heflin should approach Hoosier Feed and Milling at the highest administrative level and candidly discuss the whole affair. This would at least shed some light on what prompted the announcement and afford Heflin an opportunity to "call any bluff" Hoosier might be running. There could be nothing lost in letting Hoosier management know in a tactful way that Heflin executives were aware of the insecurity of Hoosier's legal position. Moreover, restitution could be made at such a meeting without any loss of face for either party.

If such a meeting were approached in a constructive and positive manner, it was argued, Heflin could do a real selling job at the policy making level of the Hoosier organization—an opportunity seldom afforded a salesman. On the other hand, if such a meeting should reveal Hoosier management to be truculent and unwilling to consider the affair objectively, then it would at least be clear that more forceful measures would have to be used. The position of those who advocated this approach was that every effort should be made to settle the disagreement as amicably and peacefully as possible. Only when such efforts proved to be fruitless should action be taken that would produce an altercation with Heflin's former customer.

A final suggestion was that Heflin undertake an extensive promotional campaign, entirely on its own, that would place before the market the verified facts about Promaine's performance for all to see. It was argued that no one who had been in the feed business as long as the men who were managing Hoosier Feed and Milling could be that misinformed about two such widely used products. Therefore, Heflin might as well accept the fact that Hoosier executives were being influenced by ulterior motives. And, it was argued, the most effective way to combat such deliberate deception as that being attempted by Hoosier, was with the truth. A campaign to spread the truth could embrace space advertising, pamphlets, direct mail, and all other appropriate promotional media. Salesmen could be briefed on the situation and be supplied with experiment station reports and other documentary evidence for distribution to customers on regular sales calls.

The particular virtue of this alternative, its advocates stressed, was that it could be implemented quickly and without setting any dangerous precedents—as in the case of the Garver proposal. It was important that any erroneous impressions created in the minds of customers by the Hoosier announcements be emphatically corrected. It was also important that this be done without creating the impression that the company was playing favorites or trying to take advantage of an awkward situation.

An aggressive, factual, and comprehensive promotional campaign would meet both needs—or so the proponents of this alternative believed.

The president listened patiently to these suggestions and to the various arguments advanced for and against each. He then adjourned the meeting and retired to his office to mull over the different alternatives and try to reach a decision.

THE HEFLIN CHEMICAL SUPPLY COMPANY (B)

The Heflin Chemical Supply Company is a large distributor of agricultural chemicals, fertilizer, and animal medicines located in Ohio. Its operations are divided into four functional divisions: warehousing, finance, sales, and maintenance. The warehousing division is responsible for all receipts, shipments, storage, and internal movement of merchandise, for physical inventory, and for custody of all equipment used in handling merchandise. The maintenance division is responsible for the physical operation, repair, and service of office and warehouse facilities. All accounting records including dollar and unit inventory records, costing, budgetary control, the authorization of monetary receipts and disbursements, the management of credit and insurance, office services, and the custody of petty cash are the responsibility of the finance division. The sales division is responsible for all activities connected with the buying and selling of merchandise with the exception of pricing, which is shared with the finance division.

The sales division is headed by R. G. Dunn, who started with the company 34 years ago as a bulk fertilizer salesman. He is a firm believer in the "personal touch" in matters of supervision, and in permitting salesmen as much individual initiative as possible in the administration of their territories. Consequently, each salesman is assigned a specific territory in which he can operate pretty much as he pleases. In his territory, a salesman is virtually an independent businessman with Heflin supplying the capital. All that Dunn insists upon is that each territory contribute its fair share of company profit.

This does not mean that a Heflin salesman can operate with complete freedom from budgetary control. But he does develop his own budget of anticipated expense and revenue for his territory, which he submits each year to the company's administrative board. The board, which is composed of the four division heads and the president, compares each salesman's budget with a budget which has been developed independently for his territory by the finance staff. This latter budget is based on statistical projections of past cost and revenue experience together with what influence anticipated business conditions, competitors' tactics, or Heflin's own plans would be thought to have on costs and revenues in the territory.

If the two budgets involve substantial differences, a conference is arranged between the salesman and a member of the finance staff to reconcile the points of difference. If this meeting fails to produce agreement, the matter is then referred back to the administrative board for a decision. Since the sales plan contained in the territorial budget becomes, upon approval, the salesman's quota, most disagreements arise over projected increases in the sales plan. Salesmen have tended to be distrustful of the statistical procedures employed by the finance staff and are apt to challenge any sales projection which exceeds last year's sales by more than 10 percent. Over the last 3 or 4 years, however, the administrative board has been obliged to make the final decision in only 3 cases out of 10.

Each salesman's territory includes about 11 counties. The largest territory includes 13 counties and the smallest 8. Salesmen whose territories are in northern Ohio, Indiana, and Illinois reside there, and typically maintain sales offices in their homes. Although there is no formal procedure with regard to visiting the home office, Mr. Dunn customarily holds a general sales meeting each year in January. He also calls salesmen to the home office for individual consultation any time a situation arises which either the salesman or management regards as requiring a change in plans for the territory.

Marketing and financial plans are formulated for each calendar year. Requests are usually sent to salesmen for their preliminary estimates of costs and revenue in September and firm plans are to be ready for top management approval in December. The master plan for the coming year is then usually introduced to the organization at the general sales meeting in January. Also at this time any additional training which would be called for by the plan is conducted. However, the general sales meeting is not entirely a business affair. It is looked upon as a social occasion as well and a good deal of entertainment and levity are included in the program. Wives are welcome to accompany their husbands to these affairs, and a number of them do, sometimes against the wishes of their husbands—so it is rumored. Other than the studied attention given to a review of the operating details of the plan, the general sales meeting is a gala occasion.

In addition to this annual meeting and periodic visits of salesmen to the home office. Mr. Dunn also visits each territory at least once each year. During these visits, which typically last two or three days, he makes calls with salesmen and endeavors to get a first-hand picture of conditions in the field. He believes that such visits not only give him the best indication of how well salesmen handle customers, but also serve to impress both salesmen and customers with the sincerity of management's interest in them.

Although Mr. Dunn personally directs the sales force and contributes a number of the promotional ideas employed, he has a merchandising manager who develops and plans all activity of a promotional nature. He is also aided by a field service manager. The latter handles those customers whose service needs are beyond the knowledge of the salesman. The merchandise manager supervises a staff of six, five of whom give their full attention to advertising and other promotional work. The sixth man devotes most of his time to the assembly, analysis, and presentation of information contained in sales reports. His primary responsibility is the operation of the sales reporting system. The field service manager has one assistant.

Most of Heflin's salesmen have been with the company for a number of years. Their average length of service would probably be at least ten or twelve years. Only one, the youngest of the group, holds a college degree. The others are graduates of the school of experience and hard knocks, an accomplishment which is not to be disparaged. Their morale is considered by Mr. Dunn to be very high. He has seldom found it necessary to discipline anyone in his division and turnover is practically zero. Salesmen are paid a straight salary plus a bonus. The bonus is based on a weighted average of three factors: number of years of service with the company, percent by which territorial sales exceed quota (a negative weight is used if territorial sales fall below quota), and company net profits after taxes.

Dunn has become increasingly concerned in the past few months with evidence that the feedback of information from field salesmen was faulty. In 1957 the company had inaugurated what was thought to be a well designed sales reporting system. It consisted of a weekly call report, a weekly expense report, and a monthly summary report. The call report summarized the salesman's activity for that particular week giving the names and addresses of firms or farmers called on, whether the salesman had ever called on the party previously, the type of activity in which the firm or farmer was engaged, and the purpose of the call. If the purpose was to make a sale, the salesman was asked to report the results of the sales efforts. If the call was of a service nature, or a combination of sales and service, the salesman was asked to report the nature of the service problem.

The expense report included the customary items of meals, lodging, automobile expense, and entertainment. It covered the same period and was due at the same time as the weekly call report. In fact, salesmen were not reimbursed for their expenses until the weekly call report had been received. Upon receipt of the reports the office staff transferred the data they contained to punch cards and compiled a master summary with details classified by territory. Thus, Heflin had a master punch card for each customer containing data on type of customer (feeder, elevator, farm supply store, etc.), location, annual requirements, size, salesman handling the account, customer code number, products purchased, and other suppliers serving the customer, as well as a territorial breakdown of expenses.

While information supplied by the call reports seemed to be fairly complete, suspicion was aroused that salesmen were careless in filling out the reports. A detailed comparison of orders taken with information contained in call reports following difficulties with one of the company's best accounts confirmed these suspicions. The problem now arose as to what should be done about this situation. As an initial step management proceeded to hold a series of conferences with each salesman at which the discrepancies between the record of orders submitted and information contained in call reports were tactfully called to his attention. Almost all salesmen were guilty of some carelessness in completing call reports. While results of these conferences were mixed, three conclusions seemed to stand out: 1) design of the call report form could be improved with a view to lessening the amount of time required to complete it, 2) salesmen generally did not realize the importance of information requested in the call report to management, and 3) the sales force was spread so thin over the Heflin market area that time which otherwise might be available for filling out reports was usually spent in traveling.

Redesigning call report forms and educating salesmen with regard to the importance of completing them accurately were largely matters of internal adjustment. Dunn thought that these problems could probably be worked out satisfactorily by his own staff working in cooperation with salesmen. What to do about an overextended sales force, however, was another question. Two alternatives were available: 1) to increase the size of the sales force, or 2) redesign the sales territories with a view to identifying areas of greatest potential and limiting the use of salesmen to them. Areas of low potential could either be served by mail order or ignored altogether.

The first alternative did not have much appeal to any member of the administrative board. To recruit and train additional salesmen without any real assurance that a larger sales force would increase sales volume faster than it would increase costs bordered on recklessness. Whether the increased accuracy of sales reporting and the more effective administration to which this should contribute would be worth the cost of an enlarged sales force was very difficult to answer. Also difficult to answer was the question of how many additional salesmen should be hired if this alternative were chosen.

In view of the urgency of the problem and the weight attached to the disadvantages of expanding the sales force, it was decided to experiment with the second alternative J. R. Osborn, the man in charge of the sales reporting system, was given the task of assembling all pertinent data needed for the measurement of market potential. An additional secretary was assigned to his office and he was told to procede with the job in any way he wished, but to get it done as quickly as possible.

The original territorial boundaries had been drawn with a view to equalizing travel distances as well as to make it convenient for salesmen to cover their territories from their homes. Osborn therefore decided to first try to measure the potential within each territory. He proposed to determine the areas of greatest and least potential within each one so that the territorial boundaries could be adjusted with least disruption of the present pattern. Since the basic geographic unit was the county, Osborn planned to rank each county in each territory on the basis of its potential. When each county had been ranked, territorial boundaries could then be easily redrawn so that each salesman would have a territory of roughly the same potential which in most instances he should be able to serve without changing his present location.

Osborn decided to begin his analysis with the central Illinois territory, which was the one farthest west. This territory was assigned to R. M. Barnett and included Iroquois, Ford, Livingston, McLean, DeWitt, Piatt, Macon, Moultrie, Douglas, Edgar, Champaign, and Vermillion counties. It covers an area of approximately 8800 square miles and was thought to include counties of widely differing market potential. The data pertaining to these counties assembled by Osborn are shown in Exhibits 1 and 2.

In addition to unpublished data provided by the State Departments of Agriculture in Ohio, Indiana, and Illinois, Osborn utilized material from the following standard references.

U.S. Census of Agriculture, 1958 Vol 1, *Counties,*

U.S. Department of Commerce, 1959, *City and County Data Book,* 1962.

U.S. Census of Manufactures, 1958, *Location of Manufacturing Plants,*

U.S. Census of Business, 1958, Vol. II *Retail Trade Illinois Agriculture Statistics,* 1959, Bulletin 59-1

EXHIBIT 1

Statistical Analysis of Farms and Farm Products

	Cham- paign	DeWitt	Douglas	Edgar	Ford	Iroquois	Liv- ingston	Macon	McLean	Moultrie	Piatt	Ver- milion
Employment in Agriculture	3405	1155	1338	1915	1457	3318	3119	1750	4119	963	1247	2621
Number of farms	2620	1094	1136	1611	1207	2976	2825	1540	3189	996	1966	2435
Size of county (sq. mi.)	1000	399	420	628	458	1122	1043	1173	576	345	437	898
Percent of total land area in farms	93.8	95.2	92.1	92.1	95.8	94.0	95.5	89.4	96.2	92.9	98.6	87.3
Average size of farms (acres)	229	222	219	230	248	227	226	214	227	206	262	206
Value, land & buildings ($1000)	128	107	114	88	104	90	96	112	106	101	127	78
Value of crops ($1000)	24.6	9.7	10.9	13.0	10.2	24.4	24.4	15.3	27.2	8.8	13.4	19.1
Commercial fertilizer used (T)	32.6	8.7	15.8	17.2	10.2	33.7	27.3	19.2	36.0	10.2	18.1	29.1
Value of livestock & livestock products sold ($1000)	8047	3787	2445	5893	4836	9383	10,229	3733	19,197	1882	4375	8699
Value of poultry & poultry products sold ($1000)	868	141	397	276	519	1479	2122	199	860	164	418	377
Number of livestock farms	227	156	66	331	183	278	354	130	662	55	98	354
Number of poultry farms	30	10	—	5	10	50	56	5	20	10	6	10
Cattle and calves (1000 head)	41	20	14	29	29	55	64	21	90	13	21	40
Hogs and pigs (1000 head)	50	42	31	70	42	85	86	36	185	15	28	72
Chickens (1000 head)	181	31	89	80	178	372	564	57	248	44	54	103

EXHIBIT 2

Statistical Analysis of Agricultural Supply and Service Establishments

	Champaign	DeWitt	Douglas	Edgar	Ford	Iroquois	Livingston	Macon	McLean	Moultrie	Piatt	Vermilion
Number of grain elevators	0	0	2	1	1	3	3	3	2	1	—	1
Number of farm, garden supply and feed stores	26	—	—	1	—	—	31	17	29	—	—	27
Total sales of farm, garden, supply & feed stores ($1000)	1583	—	—	10	—	—	3574	1282	4198	—	—	4856
Number of feed manufacturing plants	7	4	3	1	4	6	—	7	10	4	3	14
1–19 employees	1	—	—	—	2	2	2	2	2	—	1	3
100–250 employees	—	—	—	—	—	—	—	—	1	—	—	—
1 products	3	1	1	—	—	2	—	2	2	—	—	4
2–3 products	3	3	1	1	—	1	—	1	2	2	1	3
4–6 products	—	—	1	1	1	1	—	1	2	2	1	3
7 or more products	—	—	—	—	2	—	—	1	1	—	—	1

JACKSON CHEMICAL COMPANY

◇◇

In July last year, E. F. Bryce, Jackson Chemical Company vice president and Potomac Division general manager, acting on a directive from central headquarters to concentrate on development of fewer specific lines, decided to more closely integrate the research and development functions of the division. In March, a division directive had united the previously separate departments of research and development into a single research and development department, headed by Mr. Newman. In this organization, the original development department was maintained as a separate group within the new research and development department, but in July another company directive abolished the development group as a separate entity, and each of the three development men was placed on a team of research chemists. Each of the three research teams was concerned chiefly with research work along separate product lines, and the development man linked with each team concentrated his activity primarily along those product lines. While the proposed closer integration resulted in better liaison between research and development, it was recognized that the development function would probably be limited in its scope of operations. It was questionable whether the new organization structure represented optimum organization of the research and development functions.

The Jackson Chemical Company had assets of $250 million and annual sales of $300 million. The company, composed of 30 plants in the United States and abroad, was highly decentralized so that its divisions were autonomous and, with the exception of decisions regarding major expenditures for new plant and equipment, were practically self-controlling units. Thus, each of these company divisions, roughly divided along product lines, had its own sales, production, research, and development departments.

The Potomac Division engaged in a continuing search for new products and processes. Although the handling of new product development varied among different company divisions, the joint efforts of separate research and development departments usually carried on this function.

While coordination of the development of a single new product was not a difficult problem, this function became very complicated when a large number of products had to be followed simultaneously. During the development stage, many different groups within the division were concerned with the product. The marketing department, for example, entered the picture through its technical sales group, which adapted the new product to the customer's use. This technical sales service required a staff of men who had good chemical backgrounds, a flair for practical research, and a realistic sales approach, so that they could go into the plants of potential customers and determine what was required to make the new product most valuable from the customer's standpoint.

The Potomac Division's organization chart, operative from the time of its formation, was as shown in Exhibit I. Under this plan, a director of re-

EXHIBIT I

Organization Chart—Potomac Division
(During past 20 years)

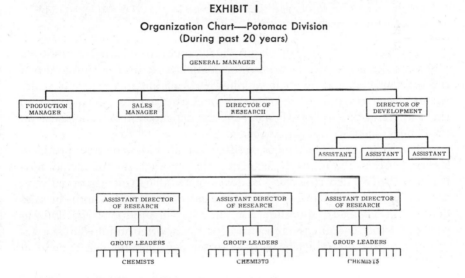

search headed the research department, and a director of development similarly had charge of the development department. Both directors reported to the general manager and were on the same organizational level as the directors of the production and sales departments.

The development department augmented division growth by its idea-finding and fact-finding functions. It took possible ideas for growth coming from within or without the division and refined them into realistic proposals, which it presented to management for a decision on whether or not to proceed. The development department acted as a service unit for other division departments, and it also called on these other departments for assistance in its assigned functions. It planned a development program, subject to management's approval, and remained alert to possible changes in the market situation.

In the course of its activities, the development department considered and solved many business problems confronting the division; studied the markets for products being produced, the industries consuming the division's products, the potentials for expanding production, and the market potentials for new products; and evaluated new facilities that might be acquired.

Some of the most important functions of the development department were as follows:

1. To survey and test markets for chemicals.
2. To assist in determining the exact form of new products desired by industry and to characterize the product by establishing specifications.
3. To prepare technical information sheets, brochures, and advertisements describing a product, and to encourage prospects to use the product.
4. To work with prospects to modify the new product to meet their requirements or to change their processes so that the product could be satisfactorily used.

The development department provided the eyes and ears of research, observing the needs of industry and guiding the research program down the most profitable avenues. It supplied information to the research department and transmitted information from the research department to the field. Thus, research department success depended in large measure on the commercial development program.

The development department communicated its ideas on new products and processes to the research department by the exchange of memoranda between the two departments. The development department worked with the new product and handled most of the customer contacts until the sales department assumed responsibility at the finished product stage. During the development period, the research department often supplied a man acquainted with the product to work with the development department on field tests and similar projects.

The major advantage resulting from the separation of the research and development functions was the complete freedom the development department enjoyed in the innovation and selection of new products and pocesses. Thus, the development department, concerned with ideas and planning far into the future, was independent and unfettered in its operations under this separation.

The major disadvantages of the separation resulted from channelization and layering. The necessity of going through channels was often time-consuming, and sometimes impeded the flow of information and the ability to reach immediate decisions. Further disadvantages were that the development department sometimes submitted to the research department ideas that research did not act on, and there was sometimes a lack of follow-through in projects initiated by one or the other.

In March last year, the Potomac Division combined the functions of the research and development departments under the authority of Mr.

Newman, newly appointed director of research and development. This new organization is shown in Exhibit II. Under the new arrangement, the three development men and the research chemists reported to the same superior, and Mr. Newman believed this resulted in closer liaison and coordination between the research and development functions. However, the division achieved this closer coordination only through a narrowing of the development department's scope. Thus, the development group was required to work more intensively on existing projects before it could consider newer or more remote ideas.

The analytical laboratory, employing five chemists, analyzed the products developed by chemists in the dye stuff, animal feed, and inorganic chemical fields for purity and quantitative analysis. The application laboratories in paper and textiles carried on research and pilot operations under simulated plant operations. Use of these laboratories, which contained the complete machinery involved in paper and textile manufacture, enabled the research department to develop special products for those industries and to evaluate their use and merit on a pilot plant scale. The development men associated with these application laboratories were concerned *only* with the field of application work carried on in them. Thus, it lacked the divisionwide scope of the development group, which reported to the director of research and development.

The development group consisted of three men: Mr. Kent, the group leader; and his two assistants, Mr. Wilson and Mr. Clark. As leader of the group, Mr. Kent occupied an unusual position in the organization hierarchy, shown in Exhibit II. He did not have the title of assistant director; yet his position as group leader was above that of the group leaders in the research group, since he reported directly to Mr. Newman and attended conferences with the assistant directors of research and development.

In July last year, Mr. Newman proposed that the functions of research and development be still more closely integrated. Under the proposed reorganization, Mr. Newman placed the two development group assistants, Mr. Wilson and Mr. Clark, on two research teams. Thus, each research team consisted of four to six chemists and the newly assigned development man, with a group leader (chemist) in charge of each team. Under the proposed arrangement, Mr. Wilson and Mr. Clark were to work closely with the research chemists on their respective teams, and each reported to and was responsible to the leader of the group with which he was connected. Under Mr. Newman's proposed arrangement, the development group would cease to function as a separate entity.

Mr. Newman proposed that Mr. Kent be both the group leader and the development man on the third research team. Thus, Mr. Kent again would occupy an unusual position in the organization hierarchy in that he would be group leader of the third research team—and, consequently, act in a research capacity—and would also be the development man connected with this third research team.

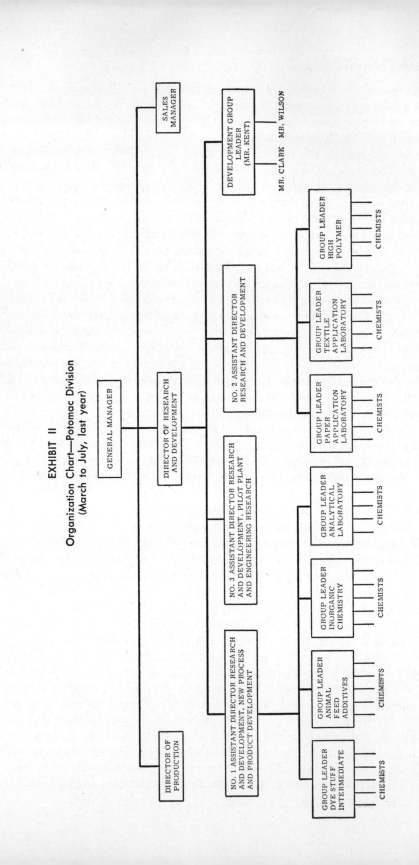

EXHIBIT II

Organization Chart—Potomac Division
(March to July, last year)

EXHIBIT III

Proposed Organization Chart—Potomac Division
(July, last year)

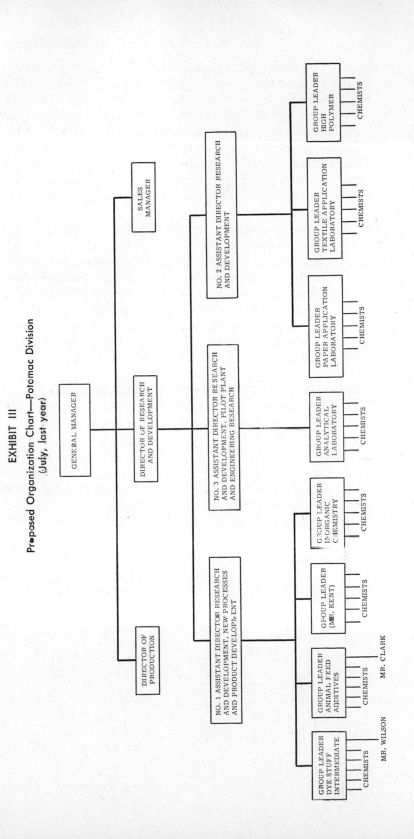

As in the current organization (Exhibit II), each of the three research teams under the proposed organization specialized chiefly in specified products and industry fields; consequently, the development man connected with each team was concerned primarily with these products and industry fields. Thus, the proposed reorganization would tend to limit the scope of the development men's activity to the extent that it forced them to perform a more thorough job on existing and current projects before they could plan and think ahead to new projects and products. The new plan also tended to channel thinking into the particular product and industry fields with which each was connected.

Under Mr. Newman's proposed reorganization, the organization chart would appear as shown in Exhibit III.

Under the proposed arrangement, each of the research teams handling new process and product development associated with dye stuff intermediates and animal feed additives had a development man on the team. Two anomalies were apparent: the research team headed by Mr. Kent did not have specified product fields along which to concentrate its efforts, as did the teams to which Mr. Wilson and Mr. Clark were attached; the research team dedicated to inorganic chemicals did not have a development man connected with it.

The application laboratories and other functions handled under the supervision of the No. 2 assistant director of research and development remained the same under the proposed reorganization.

The activities delegated to the No. 3 assistant director of research and development remained the same under the reorganization, except that Mr. Newman placed the analytical laboratory, previously under the supervision of the No. 1 assistant director of research and development, under the supervision of the No. 3 assistant director of research and development.

KENDALL MILLS[1]

◇◇◇

The executives of the Kendall Mills Division of the Kendall Company faced the problem of educating shirt manufacturers in the correct use of Clex, Kendall Mills' new fusible collar interlining. Clex fusible interlining was a specially treated textile material, which when placed between two pieces of broadcloth or similar fabric and subjected to heat and pressure joined itself with the two outer layers of fabric to the extent that the three pieces of material for all practical purposes, became one.

Since the introduction of Clex in the previous year, Kendall Mills had received many customer complaints about the product. On the basis of a study by their technical men, the company's executives believed that these complaints were due primarily to shirt manufacturers' incorrect use of the product rather than to quality deficiencies. However, they realized that they must take the initiative to correct the situation before customer dissatisfaction prevented successful marketing of the new product.

There were two general types of fusible interlinings—dry fuse and wet fuse. Clex best exemplified the dry fuse type of material, which the company developed because patent protection on the wet fuse process limited competition. After development work on the dry fuse material was completed, the resulting product was named Clex, and was sold direct to shirt and neckband manufacturers. Licenses were granted to those who wanted to capitalize on the trade name Clex in their promotion and advertising. The application of dry heat and pressure brought about the fusing of the dry fuse type of material so that its thermoplastic mass softened and injected itself into the interstices, or windows, of adjacent fabrics and became inseparable from them after cooling.

A product manufactured by a competitor best exemplified the wet fusible interlining. Instead of a coated product as was Clex, a combination of synthetic and natural yarns formed the wet fusible interlining. Prior to the fusing, the wet process involved treating the fabric with a solvent, which was usually a combination of acetone and alcohol. This application, when

---

[1] Readers familiar with the technology of the textile industry will recognize this as an old case. However, the problems it raises are so timeless and so typical in new-product development work that it is too useful and interesting to omit.

combined with heat and pressure in the press, caused the synthetic yarns to become thermoplastic and to fuse with the outer fabrics.

Approximately 50 percent of all dress shirt collars manufactured had fusible interlinings to give stiff-collar appearance and, at the same time, soft-collar comfort. Until the introduction of Clex, the wet fuse process had dominated the shirt collar interlining market. The wet interlining sold for 70 to 80 cents per yard, as compared with 60 to 65 cents for the dry interlining. The difference resulted largely from royalties on the wet process.

Kendall Mills employed rigid inspection tests at various stages in the production of Clex in order to maintain high standards of quality. Quality consciousness had to be foremost in the manufacture of this product, since even minor defects in the material, ordinarily disregarded in most textile operations, showed up unfavorably in a finished dress shirt collar. Common defects, such as grey cloth imperfections, oil spots, stains, and minute coating mass gobs, had to be spotted and marked. Even fingerprints had to be classified as defects.

Because of the glossy surface of the material, it was impractical to call attention to defects by placing a mark or sticker at the exact spot where the defect occurred. As a result, the company inspectors used a hand punch to make a hole opposite or near a defect in the material. For each punch hole made, the company included an additional eighth of a yard in each roll of material. When the material was wrapped for shipment, the inspector labeled the invoiced yardage, for example, 100 yards, as well as the gross yardage, which included the allowance for defects. In order to call attention to the purpose of the punch holes in the material, the inspectors placed a special cautionary label printed in red letters on the outside wrapper of each roll.

Color was a very important feature of Clex interlining, and Kendall Mills exercised great care to insure the proper color depth. It was necessary to incorporate enough blue in the material to result in a fabric that, when fused with white broadcloth, would blend exactly with the outer fabric.

The company produced Clex in two styles: a medium-weight fabric designed to meet the general overall demand of users of fusible interlinings, and a heavier material designed for use in making a thicker, but not a stiffer, collar.

A shirt manufacturer could not make a proper comparison of the wet and dry fuse interlinings by merely comparing the two fabrics; he could make a correct judgment only by comparing the results after he had fully fused the material and had subjected the fused collars to repeated launderings. When properly fused, Clex formed a permanent bond, and repeated launderings and wearings would not cause the plies to separate. A correctly bonded Clex collar might be washed and worn to such an extent that the outer fabrics were completely worn out before the Clex was affected.

The Clex dry fuse process required the users to practice much closer adherence to strictly defined production standards than did the wet fuse process. In the wet fuse process, the solvent's action greatly aided the bonding, and a satisfactory bond could be obtained despite wide variations in fusing time and in the temperature and pressure used in the bonding presses. But to achieve satisfactory results, the dry fuse process required a combination of correct press temperature, pressure, fusing time, and press padding.

The dry fusing operation required heat to soften the plastic Clex mass, thus enabling it to flow into the interstices of the shirting material. Steam was the source of heat generally employed to raise Clex interlined collars to fusing temperature, and it had to be used in both top and bottom press bucks to thoroughly heat the collar assembly. The solid Clex mass gradually softened as its temperature increased, in a manner typical of thermoplastic materials. Then, in a relatively narrow range of temperature, it softened rapidly and began to flow like a liquid. At higher temperatures, it became still thinner and flowed even more readily.

It was necessary to heat Clex fusible interlining above the point at which it began to flow, and experience established the correct working temperature. There was an upper limit above which Clex should not be heated; if the mass was too hot and fluid, it tended to flow through to the outer surface of the shirting material and caused a condition known as bleeding. Excessive fusing temperature also tended to scorch the fabric.

There was also a critical lower limit in the fusing temperature, and a fusing temperature too low caused various imperfections to appear in the collar fabric after a few washings; for example, bubbles, creases, and other visible defects soon appeared because of delamination. The company recommended a steam pressure for fusing of 90 pounds per square inch. This corresponded to a temperature of 330 degrees F. in the press bucks.

The padding used in the press bucks affected the pressure actually applied on the collar during the fusing operation. If a press pad was initially too hard or became hard through aging, it could not conform to the different thicknesses at collar faces, tips, and edges, and the results were often poorly fused collar faces and edges that showed bleeding. A rubber pad that was too soft dissipated the available pressure over the entire surface of the buck instead of concentrating it on the area occupied by the collars. This factor was sometimes responsible for insufficiently fused collars. The company developed a ⅜-inch rubber padding, which it made available to its customers at cost for use with the Clex process. This padding, which Kendall Mills engineered to the proper thickness and resilience for optimum results, would not stain or impart odor to the goods.

In spite of the light weight and relative thinness of a Clex collar assembly, it had a definite resistance to heat and fluid flow. Consequently, heat and pressure had to be applied for sufficient time to heat the entire assembly to fusing temperature and to force the Clex mass into the layers of fabric on either side. To complete this process, the company determined, by experience, that the fusing time of 20 seconds was essential. The method of fusing first on one side and then on the other was inefficient, since it involved an extra handling operation and required more than 20 seconds total fusing time because of the need to reheat the collars. Collars fused faceup for 20 seconds gave the ultimate in finish, bond, and customer satisfaction. All these features were discovered by Kendall technicians in an experimental pilot plant collar factory set up for the purpose.

Despite the necessity of adhering to narrow tolerances in temperature, pressure, fusing time, etc., during the bonding of Clex, this product had several definite advantages over the wet fuse method.

1. Elimination of solvent. The acetone and alcohol solvent usually used in the wet fuse method was very inflammable and explosive, with consequent fire hazards and high fire insurance rates. The acetone was also toxic to human skin, and since prolonged exposure could be harmful to factory personnel precautionary measures were necessary.

2. Elimination of solvent cost. This cost amounted to approximately 5 cents per yard of wet fuse interlining.

3. Extra process necessary in the wet fuse method. In the wet fuse method, the press operator had to wet out the collars in a so-called wetting-out machine before putting them in the press. The dry fuse method eliminated both this intermediate wetting-out step and the cost to the manufacturer of the wetting-out machine, approximately $275.

4. Production per press operator was greater when the dry fuse method was used. Use of the dry method enabled the average press operator to run between three and five presses simultaneously. Use of the wetting-out machines in the wet process reduced the production rate of these operators to such an extent that they could run only two presses and one wetting-out machine simultaneously. The fact that the wetting-out machine consumed more time than did the presses accounted for this slower rate. Furthermore, the necessary use of both presses and wetting-out machines in the wet fuse method prevented a layout of raw materials and production flow of finished goods as efficient as was possible with the dry fuse method.

Kendall Mills received many customer complaints about Clex soon after its introduction to the trade. Shirt manufacturers pointed out that they were getting too large a percentage of rejects during factory shipment inspection, mainly because of bubbles and creases in the collar and lack of bond. They also stated that the retail outlets handling their shirts received many customer complaints, primarily that bubbles and creases appeared in the collars after several washings. This resulted in attempted cancellations of orders, return of goods, backing up of inventory in the Kendall Mills

plant, and channeling of the company salesmen's time more into investigating customer complaints than into active selling.

The company's executives knew that Clex, when properly fused, gave
results in finish, appearance, and wearing qualities that were equal to, or
better than, the wet fuse process. It was recognized that a small percentage of the complaints were due to defects in the Clex product, and the
company therefore tightened inspection standards. The executives were
sure, however, that improper or faulty fusing techniques in the shirt
manufacturer's factory caused the great majority of complaints.

In an effort to educate their customers in the proper use of Clex,
Kendall Mills compiled a *Clex Manual,* which gave pertinent information
on fusing temperature, pressure, fusing time, padding of presses, and other
useful technical data. The company supplied this manual to shirt manufacturers, and urged that the factory foremen discuss the points covered in
the manual with their press operators. Use of this manual brought some
improvement in the fusing techniques in the factories, but these improvements were usually of short duration.

The weak link in the shirt manufacturer's factory was the press operator, who was usually an unskilled female worker with below-average
intelligence and little mechanical or technical skill. When the foreman
pointed out the correct fusing techniques to be followed and the need for
observing these techniques, the press operators usually made an effort to
improve their practices but soon lapsed back into their previous faulty
habits.

Another difficulty the company faced was mechanical maintenance of
the presses in the customers' factories. Most of the shirt manufacturers
developed their mechanics by sending workers with mechanical aptitude
to the trade schools operated by several of the large sewing machine
companies. At these trade schools, the recruits became very proficient in
the maintenance and repair of the scores of sewing machines operated by
the shirt manufacturers. However, they knew little about the maintenance
of presses, which involved knowledge of their adjustment, correct temperature, pressure, padding, repair, and maintenance of boilers, steam
lines, and traps.

The service policies of the press manufacturers varied widely among
the different firms. Several of the companies sold presses through their
own sales forces, and supplied customers with technical and engineering
service. However, one of the largest press manufacturers sold its line
through dealers and had no organization to service its presses. This company shipped presses to customers with instructions regarding assembly,
but with little data as to proper use and maintenance.

There was considerable difference of opinion among Kendall executives on how they might best handle the situation. One group believed
that the company should seek to establish an arrangement with the press
manufacturers whereby Kendall Mills would instruct the salesmen of the

five or six largest press manufacturers, who used a direct sales force, in the proper fusing of Clex. Under this arrangement, Kendall Mills personnel would instruct the press manufacturers' salesmen in these matters, and these salesmen might spend a short time at the company plant in order to learn firsthand about Clex and the dry fuse process. These executives believed that such a plan would enable the press manufacturers' salesmen to educate the shirt manufacturers in the proper use of Clex.

Another possible plan involved the use of a Clex engineer or specialist—a company engineer who would visit the shirt manufacturers' factories to explain the proper use of Clex. This proposed Clex engineer would spend his full time on such work, talking with foremen and press operators, explaining the necessity of adhering to established standards of temperature, pressure, fusing time, and other technical data; inspecting presses, steam lines, and traps; and making recommendations for mechanical changes.

A third possible plan was to improve Clex to the point where it was foolproof and would bond under all fusing conditions. This plan involved considerable expenditure for additional research work, and might be expected to increase the selling price of the improved Clex approximately 25 to 30 percent above the present price.

Other executives suggested that the company contact several of the large press manufacturers and have them design and manufacture presses specially built for use with Clex. The press manufacturers would equip these presses with automatic timing devices, temperature and pressure regulators, correct press buck padding, and other custom-made mechanical features, which would ensure optimum results with Clex after being installed by the shirt manufacturers. A press for this work cost about $500.

The company executives agreed that they had to take some action in order to ensure customer satisfaction before the ill will created by shirt manufacturers' improper use of Clex became widespread throughout the industry, eventually preventing successful marketing of the product and seriously damaging the Kendall Company's reputation.

THE LELAND LOCK COMPANY

◇◇◇

The Leland Lock Company manufactures a wide line of residential and industrial door locks, handles, and assorted hardware. The company is an old, established New England firm with a reputation for quality and dependability. The Leland cylindrical lock is generally regarded by building contractors as the finest obtainable. The company distributes its products through two principal channels—its own branches in New York City, Jersey City, Chicago, Los Angeles, and San Francisco, and approximately 45 hardware wholesalers scattered throughout other parts of the United States. A sizable export business is also transacted with Central and South American countries, the Philippines, Australia, and New Zealand. Net income, net sales, and other statistics for the company are shown in Exhibit I.

EXHIBIT I
Leland Lock Company, Inc.
Financial Report

Year	(Millions) Net Sales	(Millions) Net Income	Earnings per Share	Total Assets
1964	44.8	.99	$1.12	33.6
1963	40.8	.74	.83	31.3
1962	39.6	1.1	1.18	31.6
1961	32.9	.30	.34	27.3
1960	39.0	1.1	1.25	29.1
1959	36.5	1.3	1.47	28.0
1958	30.9	.39	.44	25.1
1957	35.2	1.9	2.17	26.1
1956	39.3	2.7	3.01	26.3
1955	34.2	2.3	2.54	23.3
1954	28.9	1.8	2.07	23.1

It has been estimated that current demand for locks is about 10 million units annually. This figure is probably a conservative one, since it is based solely on estimates of new construction and contains no estimate of the replacement demand. The figure was calculated by multiplying the total amount of floor space represented by all classes of residential and nonresidential building by a conversion factor reflecting the number of outside doors per square feet of floor area. Of the total lock market represented by new construction, 11 percent is in nonresidential and 89 percent in residential building. Roughly, 75 percent of the residential market is in one- and two-family dwellings. Annual estimates, projected to 1970, indicate that during the remainder of the present decade new residential starts will average more than one million per year.

Although Leland's hold on the heavy-duty industrial market seems secure, aggressive competition for lock sales has developed in the residential market. The Scriber Hardware Company and Delta Locks, Inc., have both introduced new lines of cylindrical locks. The Delta locks, especially, have made inroads on Leland's sales. The Delta recessed lock, competing with Leland's Y-type, sells for $6.45 as against Leland's $7.45. However, the Delta lock is a die-cast product, whereas Leland's is all-steel. The Delta 5-pin tumbler lock sells for $9.75, while Leland prices its 5-pin at $11.45. But, again, compared to the Delta product Leland locks are better constructed, longer lasting, more difficult to tamper with, and capable of a greater variety of master key combinations.

It is generally agreed that either the architect or the contractor has more influence on the choice of hardware used in the typical residential building than does anyone else. Nevertheless, it is also recognized that hardware manufacturers could do more than they are presently doing to make ultimate users aware of their products. In the final analysis, the homeowner must be satisfied with the hardware used in his home, even though the lock failure usually does not occur until after a residence has been occupied for awhile.

Although it would be possible for Leland to conduct an intensive advertising campaign to inform consumers of the Leland lock's superior features, top management has been cool to such a plan. It was thought that any effective effort to pull the product through the channels of distribution would be very costly, because the typical home buyer does not have much technical knowledge about locks and probably would make little effort to study information about them. Moreover, even if home buyers could be made sufficiently aware of differences in lock quality to request the Leland product, company management believed that an architect or contractor could still switch them to another lock at the last minute. The Leland sales manager contended that any contractor who said, "Well, the Delta lock will give you just as much service as the Leland lock and you can save $60 on hardware," could always outweigh the influence of Leland's advertising. The sales manager believed that on any hardware item whose quality is difficult for the home buyer to appraise, the architect or contractor would always have the last word, regardless of how much money the company spent on advertising.

Despite their respect for the sales manager's opinion, the majority of

Leland executives believed that the superior quality of their product would enable Leland to retain the major share of the higher priced residential market, i.e., houses selling for $35,000 and over. They felt that people buying homes in this price range are more particular about quality, especially in furnishings and details. Furthermore, surveys conducted by Leland generally indicated that persons who buy the more expensive homes are more discriminating, and builders are more willing to accept selling help from manufacturers of established quality lines of hardware, plumbing, heating, and kitchen equipment.

On the other hand, it has become evident to Leland executives that the day of the individually designed home is passing. The trend toward development housing is unmistakable, and with it the demand for materials going into houses can be expected to become increasingly price-oriented. Accordingly, materials that meet minimum standards are as desirable as materials of the highest quality. The truth of this was pointed out by the purchasing agent of a large development company. He said, "All homes, even the $30,000 ones, are speculative construction. We build about 500 homes a year; in addition, we are one of the few residential tract builders who employ regular architects to plan our developments. We use Delta locks on the basis of price, ease of installation, and appearance, and because in all our experience the locks have been holding up. It would cost us about $70 more per house to put in Leland hardware instead of Delta. We have not received any complaints from occupants about the locks on our houses."

The purchasing agent of another residential builder stated, "We can afford to put a maximum of only $60 in the locks we use in our tract homes. We are building homes in the $12,000–$15,000 price range, and as you can realize, price is a big factor. We cannot afford Leland products in our price range. We build about 600 homes a year, and we use Delta and Scriber locks."

Other tract builders emphasized the same factors. Although they were aware that the Leland lock was a quality product, and although a number of purchasers had requested that Leland locks be installed on exterior doors, they were of the opinion that to the average person inspecting a home one lock is as good as another.

Several of Leland's district sales managers have expressed their concern that unless the company manufactures a cheaper lock much of the effort in working with tract builders will be wasted. The district managers argue that since tract builders operate on very narrow margins they are not going to include more expensive hardware unless they can get a greater price differential on completed houses than appears likely at present.

If Leland is going to tap the tract home market, district managers believe it will be necessary to produce a low-priced lock to compete with Delta. They argue that the tract market is continuing to grow, and there is no technical reason why Leland cannot produce an acceptable, i.e., standard quality, low-priced lock. They are less certain whether Leland should use a different name on a low-priced lock. Unless a different name were used, though, there would always be the danger that many builders and architects might actually believe, or unwittingly lead home buyers to believe, that the best Leland locks were being used when, in fact, the cheaper lock had been installed. On the other hand, using a different name involves the problem of market acceptance, which is always uncertain and invariably involves a time lag, particularly with products whose quality the average home buyer finds so difficult to appraise.

A contrary view is held by most top-management executives at Leland, who believe that Leland should limit production to quality locks for the more expensive residential and industrial markets. Their argument is that these are the markets in which Leland holds an undisputed advantage and can best capitalize on it. Besides, as the treasurer expressed it, "The aim of the company is profits rather than expansion, and the two do not necessarily go together."

There has been no consensus on how a lower priced lock should be promoted and distributed if the company should decide to produce it. It has been argued that while home buyers want hardware that is durable they also want hardware that will add to the beauty of their homes. The question was whether durability, safety, and operational qualities of a low-priced lock should be stressed, or whether attention should be drawn instead to its contribution to the decor of the house. Could promotion successfully stress both? The sales manager thinks not, and is pessimistic about the whole idea of diluting the company's image with a cheap lock.

THE MARGEANN CHEMICAL COMPANY

Some years ago, an executive of the Margeann Chemical Company on a visit to Japan was told of a compound, gibberellin, which when sprinkled on certain plants stimulated growth and caused considerable increases in foliage, fruit, and seeds. He brought a sample back to America. Small-scale experiments indicated that the reports he had received from his Japanese friends were justified.

The Margeann Chemical Company made and marketed bulk chemicals to the pharmaceutical manufacturing industry, the veterinary trade, the food business, the animal food industry, makers of plant protective and growth-promoting compounds, and to general industrial houses. All Margeann products were used by the buying firms as materials in their end products. Total sales were about $100 million. The management was aggressive and definitely growth minded. The firm had financial resources to enable it to launch any new venture of reasonable proportions. During recent years, corporate earnings had averaged about 14 percent (before taxes) on investment.

The marketing research department and the product development group were instructed to study the gibberellins as a possible addition to the product line.

The product development report stated that the Margeann Company had existing production facilities to make the product. While initial costs of producing small amounts would be high, the costs of making it in quantity should be somewhere between $30 and $50 a pound. The product could be applied to plants in five ways:

1. As a spray on the foliage.
2. As a paste in an inert carrier.
3. As a dust composed of the compound and a carrier.
4. As a dip solution.
5. As a solution in which seeds could be soaked.

Each of these methods required that the material be compounded with other ingredients, since the amount needed for any one application was almost infinitesimally small.

Provable claims showed that gibberellin caused certain kinds of flowers and ornamental plants to grow much larger with more foliage and more luxuriant flowers. To exploit this market, the product had to be packed in very small units suitable for the retail trade, and the company would have to advertise it to ultimate consumer-users and develop channels of distribution to reach them. The company was neither experienced nor skilled in this kind of business.

Field tests in west Texas indicated that the application of 8 grams per acre to cotton plants on well-irrigated land increased the yield about 20 percent. The average yield per untreated acre was about 3.5 bales. These results indicated nothing about the effect of the material when used on cotton planted on land that was not well irrigated, or what it could do in cotton areas other than west Texas. About half of the two million west Texas acres planted to cotton were well irrigated. Cotton acreage in the country totaled about 10 million. In addition, the treatment of cotton seed with a special form of the material at the rate of ½ gram per 100 pounds of seed considerably shortened the germination period and greatly increased the percentage of the seed that germinated. About 20 pounds of seed were planted per acre.

Field tests in the grape-growing area of California also showed that

TABLE I

Experience with Grapes

Kind of Grapes	Costs	Per Acre without Treatment Returns Gross	Per Acre without Treatment Returns Net	Per Acre with Treatment Cost of Applying	Per Acre with Treatment Gross Returns	Material Used per Acre (Grams)	Total Number of Acres Planted to Grapes
Table (in Coachella Valley) . .	$800	$1,200	$400	$145	$1,800	16	7,000
Table (in San Joaquin Valley) .	645	875	230	75	1,250	8	18,000
Raisin	375	550	175	50	605	8	119,000
Wine	375	500	125	50	600	8	52,000
Canning	375	600	225	50	660	8	4,000

application of the material to vines increased the size of the fruit so that it commanded a higher price on the market and increased the output per acre. During one season, treated grapes sold for $8.80 per 24-pound lug as against $5.78 per lug for the untreated fruit. From the grower's standpoint, the economics of its use in the California area worked out about as shown in Table 1.

In addition, use of the material relieved the table grape grower of the necessity of girdling, at about $15 an acre, and thinning, at about $200 an acre in Coachella Valley and about $45 an acre in San Joaquin Valley. Some growers were afraid of the effect that continued application of gibberellin might have on the vines, which took from 10 to 15 years to grow to bearing maturity. For example, no one knew whether the increased productivity it generated would exhaust the plants before their normal time or whether it might prove poisonous to them if applied over a number of years. About 500,000 acres were planted to grapes in the United States. While the results shown in the table above might be representative of the possible effects of gibberellin wherever applied to grapes, no valid claims of effectiveness could be made outside the California area.

It might be expected that the application of gibberellin to some other crops would yield results worth exploration. To find out which crops would respond to it enough to justify commercial development was a costly process, requiring several years of experimentation and controlled field tests. So the management of the Margeann Company decided to pursue a vigorous campaign to capture the markets represented by the California grape growers and the west Texas cotton planters. It was hoped that the cash inflow from these operations might provide some of the funds needed to explore the effectiveness of the product on other crops and to develop provable claims for its use.

A study of the market indicated that a sales force to distribute the product directly to users or even to local dealers would be entirely too expensive. Such a force would have only one product to sell and there was no reasonable assurance that the company could develop within the near future a plant product line with enough volume to make possible direct distribution. Furthermore, management was aware that its skills did not lie in the direction of marketing to some millions of farmers through the various types of dealers who served them.

It was decided, therefore, to market the product as a bulk item to formulator distributors who either resold it without change of form or mixed it with carriers needed to assure convenience and control of application. It was estimated that about 25 to 30 such formulator distributors would be needed to provide adequate coverage throughout the country. The formulator-distributor could be expected to resell the product at a price about 50 percent above the figure at which Margeann sold it to him. The local dealer would probably add about 33 percent to the price he paid the formulator-distributor to arrive at his selling price. Thus, if Margeann's price for a given amount of the product were $1, the formulator-distributor would probably charge about $1.50, and the local dealer, $2 for the same amount.

It was known that at least three other companies were interested in developing the business of making and selling gibberellins to the agricultural trade. According to all reports, Margeann was about a year or a year and a half ahead of the rest of them in its developmental work. Two of the rival firms were hard-hitting and aggressive, but none of them were habitual price cutters. It was certain that the process of developing the market for the product in any crop area would be slow—from three to six years—and costly. Margeann management did not feel that for some years, at least, price would become a very decisive patronage appeal.

The executive vice president asked the director of marketing to recommend a specific price or structure of prices at which Margeann should offer the product. He also requested the formulation of a pricing policy to be followed as the market was developed and competition became active. Margeann's general policy had been to try to be price competitive without being either a price cutter or a price leader.

THE MEADOWS COMPANY

◇◇

The Meadows Company made and marketed a complete line of abrasive products and was a leader in the abrasives industry. Its annual sales of abrasives were about $150 million.

On the basis of marketing characteristics, the company's products could be divided into two types—standard and special. The standard items included grinding wheels and other abrasive devices used to do jobs that were widely prevalent throughout all using industries. These articles were made in sizes and to basic specifications common throughout the abrasives industry. They required a limited amount of technical customer service that was relatively simple and often supplied by users.

The special items were used on much more intricate and specialized jobs, and some of them were fitted only for those jobs. Some were made to order to suit the very highly specialized needs of particular customers. They required a lot of expert technical service. The total dollar volume of the standard items was well above that of the specialties, but the gross margin on specialties was higher. Most of the large customers needed specialties, although there was also an active demand for them among small shops that made highly fabricated products. The typical large abrasives user tended to buy his standard items from the source that gave him satisfactory technical service on his specialty needs.

The Meadows Company marketed its abrasive products through about 50 selected distributors, each assigned an exclusive territory. Many of them operated branch warehouses. The distributors were mainly general industrial supply houses that handled a variety of other products and, sometimes, the abrasives of Meadows' competitors. Some were houses that specialized in abrasives, and a number of these concentrated mainly on Meadows products. All the houses together employed about 1,000 salesmen, many with special training in selling Meadows' products. They were able to handle most of the simpler service problems. Meadows maintained a small force of highly expert technicians to handle the more complex problems.

This system of marketing channels was adopted by the Meadows

Company in response to the market conditions. The number of abrasives users is very large—probably 100,000 or more—and plants are widely scattered. In order to reach them and render adequate service, the Meadows executives felt it necessary to depend on distributors whose warehouses were well scattered. Through the exclusive territory arrangement, they hoped to gain aggressive selling effort and at least some technical service work by the distributors.

A few hundred manufacturing firms, however, control a large percentage of the total volume of abrasives bought. Most of these large concerns operate more than one plant. When such a firm also buys centrally, its total purchases of abrasive products are apt to be a very significant addition to or subtraction from the sales volume of any supplier. Some of these concerns bought in larger order quantities and greater annual volume than did the average distributor.

The Meadows Company executives had followed a policy of protecting its distributors by refusing to sell direct to users. At the same time, they had recognized the necessity of bidding for Meadows' share of the large buyers' business by offering a discount system that was compounded of a flat 20 percent discount to all distributors and a quantity discount that enabled the distributor who sought a big user's business to meet competitive prices. He might have to shade his margin of gross profit a bit to do it, but by means of comparison the Meadows sales force had been able to show distributors that such reductions were worthwhile because in handling the business of large accounts their selling expenses, delivery costs, and record keeping and collection costs were less per dollar of sales. For a time, this plan worked very well.

During recent years, manufacturers have become increasingly aware of the savings to be made by reducing inventories and procurement costs. Their efforts in this direction have been aided by the techniques of computerized control of stocks and by the development of automatic reordering arrangements. Computers make it possible to keep an almost up-to-the-minute count of every item in stock; automatic reordering diminishes the expense of the buyer's preparing orders and of the seller's handling them, and reduces the costs of invoicing and paying.

Large buyers have been especially active in making these arrangements, and many of them have used their buying power to squeeze from the supplier the lion's share of the savings he enjoys from these streamlined operations. The Meadows Company first took the position that contracts of this nature were the business of its distributors.

Two things happened to call this attitude in question. First, the marketing executives noticed a considerable increase in drop shipments—orders placed with Meadows by the distributors for shipment from the factory direct to the user. On such orders, the distributor got his regular discount, but Meadows had to assume the costs of carrying inventory and arranging delivery. Second, the Barrows Company, a large user, approached Mr.

Hurley, the Meadows Company marketing manager, with a proposal that the two agree to an automatic direct ordering arrangement and split the distributor's margin between them.

The marketing manager met with Mr. Stone, chief purchasing officer of the Barrows Company, to discuss the matter. During the conversation, he explained the Meadows policy and the reasons for it. Mr. Stone intimated that he proposed to discuss the matter with at least one of Meadows' competitors. He also indicated that the Barrows Company president was personally interested in making as many such arrangements with suppliers as possible, and that he would probably talk with the Meadows Company president at a forthcoming industry convention, which both men customarily attended. Mr. Hurley then suggested that Mr. Stone reduce the proposal to writing so that he could study it more carefully. An added purpose of this request was to provide a solid basis on which to discuss the proposal with his president and possibly with the executive committee of Meadows.

In a few days, he received from Mr. Stone a letter containing the following passage.

Subject to development in detail, we propose that:

1. We contract to buy from you and you agree to supply our entire annual requirements of abrasive products.

2. On the 1st and 16th of each month you will ship us a standard stock order as designated in a schedule of stock orders, one for each month, which we will supply you at the beginning of the year. By teletype you will advise us of each shipment.

3. Through our computerized system of inventory control we will inform you by teletype when the stock of each item falls to the order point between stock order shipments, and within 24 hours you will ship us from your nearest warehousing point a standard fill-in order of the item as shown in a standard fill-in order list, which we will supply you and keep up-to-date. We plan to link up our computer to a teletype transmitter so that our end of the process will be entirely automatic. We suggest that you tie yours into a receiver that will activate your computer to produce an order and perhaps initiate your order-filling process.

4. You will teletype us a notification of the composition and amount of each shipment as made. On the 25th of each month you will bill us for all unbilled shipments made up to that date, and on the first of the succeeding month we will pay you after checking your billing against our accumulated teletypes.

5. We estimate that our monthly stock orders will be as large or larger than the average order you receive from distributors. Your costs of shipping them will be the same as those of your present drop shipments to us—perhaps a little less because our monthly stock orders will probably be somewhat larger than the drop shipments have been. We have not called on our distributor for any service on standard items, and you have handled all our specialty service needs. So your service costs will not change. If you now bill your distributor for each order, you will make some saving in billing costs. In

short, we estimate that your costs of handling our business in the proposed manner will not be any more than they now are, and they probably will be less. We will make a considerable saving by getting rid of the order preparation work.

We will both save the distributor's margin, which we understand averages about 20 percent on the price we pay. We feel that since we initiated this arrangement we should get somewhat more than half—say, 75 percent—of this in reduced prices. For example, on items on which you allow your distributor a 20 percent discount from your list, you will allow us a 15 percent discount.

This is the gist of our proposal. We expect that some changes in detail and procedure may be necessary in order to cause the minimum dislocation of our mutual order handling systems.

Permit me to urge you to give this matter early and serious consideration. Sharp rises in the cost of labor and many materials make it necessary for us to push strenuously to achieve every possible increase in the efficiency of our operations. Mr. Hicks (president of Barrows) is very much interested in this program and is very anxious to get something worked out with you or with some other supplier.

Mr. Hurley showed this letter to the president of Meadows, who suggested that he explore the proposal's implications within the company and gather facts that might be useful in its discussion by the executive committee.

The president was leaving two days later on an extended trip that would wind up at the trade convention, so he wanted to talk the matter over with the executive committee before he left. This did not give Mr. Hurley time to do much more than collect the most readily available information on the problem.

Mr. Hurley first consulted the company attorney, who expressed the opinion that the amount of the discount allowed Barrows could not legally be more than the savings Meadows enjoyed by reason of the quantity and the way in which Barrows bought. He also pointed out that if Meadows made such an arrangement with Barrows it would have to make a similar arrangement available to all other customers who could and were willing to buy in the same way. Probably different discounts to different customers would be legal if in each case the amount of the discount did not exceed the amount of the saving. Mr. Hurley's next call was on the controller to obtain estimates of the proposal's effect on costs. After they had discussed the mechanics of carrying out the proposal so that the various cost factors seemed reasonably clear, the controller promised to supply an estimate of its impact on costs. The next morning, Mr. Hurley received a preliminary analysis, indicating that the cost savings and additions could be expected to just about cancel out each other.

The customer service manager who controlled the inventory of finished goods felt that the semimonthly stock order feature of the proposal would enable him to manage inventory a little more closely and perhaps would have the effect of reducing it slightly, but that the handling of fill-ins would probably cause an increase that would be at least, offsetting, since the distributor had previously handled most small orders out of his own stock. The additional volume of orders could be handled by the present staff without increase.

When the proposal was put before the vice president for production, he pointed out that, while the Barrows Company deal alone would have little effect on production operations or costs, the adoption of a similar automatic ordering technique by several of Meadows' largest customers should make it possible to plan manufacturing operations more closely and to effect some savings through longer production runs, with consequent reductions in makeready and setup expenses per unit. He estimated that his saving should amount to about 0.5 percent of total costs.

Mr. Hurley now had all the information he could collect before preliminary discussion of the matter by the executive committee, composed of himself, the president, the vice president for production, the treasurer, and the controller. He felt that such a discussion was highly desirable before the president attended the trade convention.

At this meeting, to which the company attorney was invited, the committee was able to discern several alternatives.

Meadows could turn down the Barrows proposal. This would carry with it a strong probability that the Barrows account would be lost. The president felt that in the course of his expected conversation with Mr. Hicks he could arrive at a reasonably sound judgment of the chances of this outcome.

Meadows could accept the proposal as made. This would involve a violation of its long-established policy in dealing with distributors. The distributor who handled the Barrows business would undoubtedly cry to high heaven. The fact that a turndown of the Barrows proposal would probably lose the Barrows business for both him and Meadows would not temper his reaction much. Meadows' acceptance of this proposal might be expected to disturb its relations with all its other distributors, especially those handling large accounts. They were not unaware that if Meadows allowed such a deal to Barrows the law required that it make the same deal available to all others who could and were willing to buy in the same manner. Meadows might expect its action to lose some distributors— probably the best ones—and lower the quality of the marketing services rendered by the others.

Meadows might accept the Barrows deal provided: monthly stock orders would be drop shipped and fill-in orders would be handled by the distributor, to whom Meadows would telephone them when they were received; a combined bill would be submitted to Barrows once a month by the distributor and payment received by him; the distributor would accept a reduced discount on the volume of both kinds of orders, amounting to about 5 percent, which ought to more than cover his stock-carrying costs and reduced order handling expenses. On all the distributor's other Meadows business, he would continue to receive his regular 20 percent discount.

This would mean that Meadows would benefit by (*a*) keeping the Barrows business and (*b*) keeping any internal savings in production, marketing, and inventory carriage resulting from the deal. It was also felt that there might be some give in Barrows claim for 15 percent of the distributor's regular 20 percent. The arrangement might also serve to mitigate the distributor's unhappiness to some extent, for he would have no selling expenses and his order handling costs and billing costs would be reduced to a minimum—in short, he would salvage something out of the relationship and would probably emerge with enough income to cover the real expenses of handling his part of the Barrows business, plus some profit, although not so much as he was used to. The alternative for him would be the probability of completely losing the Barrows business.

It was agreed that if the Barrows proposal or some modification of it was accepted, Meadows would have to offer the same deal to all its customers. Only a few, perhaps 15 or 20, used enough abrasives so that a semimonthly stock order would equal in volume the average order placed by distributors. It was agreed that this was the proper criterion of eligibility to participate in the deal. To extend the deal to customers whose volume did not meet this requirement would be uneconomic and would render the legality of the whole arrangement very uncertain indeed.

Opinion in the executive committee was sharply divided over what action Meadows should take on the Barrows proposal. All members agreed that accepting it would involve abandoning the exclusive distributorship policy, which had worked very well. Several members were much disturbed by the ethical aspects of the situation; they felt that Meadows had an obligation to its distributors, who had tied their abrasives business to Meadows products. On the other hand, if Barrows action represented a general trend due to changed conditions—and it apparently did—the distributors were likely to lose the business of big buyers in any case.

All committee members were disturbed about the effect an acceptance would have on Meadows' share of the business of small users, who must continue to be served by distributors. There were so many of them and their individual volume was so small that it would be prohibitively costly to market to them direct.

There seemed to be no clear consensus on what Meadows should do about the Barrows proposal.

NOTE.—Persons familiar with the details of the abrasives industry may notice some minor discrepancies in this case, because it was necessary to transpose the case from another industry in order to obtain clearance. That the problem is not unrealistic in the abrasives trade is evidenced by trade journal reports that the Norton Company recently offered its customers an automatic reorder deal apparently quite closely akin to the one described in the case.

THE ORDWAY COMPANY

◇◇◇

Management at Ordway is currently debating the advisability of adding a line of electronic parts and supplies to their present lines of industrial supplies, equipment, and automotive parts. The company is a large industrial supply house with a long history of service to manufacturing firms in Chicago, Whiting, and Gary. At present, about two thirds of Ordway's sales volume comes from the Chicago metropolitan area. The principal industries its customers represent are crude petroleum mining, electrical contractors, processors of food and kindred products, manufacturers of broad-woven fabrics and knitted products, furniture and fixture manufacturers, producers of paper and allied products, chemical and pharmaceutical plants, petroleum refineries, primary metal and fabricated metal makers, all types of machinery manufacturers, and manufacturers of transportation equipment.

The company was established in 1902 as a wholesale distributor of steel, heavy hardware, machinery, and blacksmith supplies. The founder, James J. Ord, emigrated from England where he had held an administrative post in a large steel mill. The Ord Steel Company, as the business was named, retained its original lines of merchandise until 1927, at which time blacksmith supplies were discontinued and automotive parts were added. The increasing importance of the automobile soon led Mr. Ord to seek a partner who could help him develop the automotive segment of the business. The man who finally became his partner was Willard Way, a former executive of the now defunct Overland Motor Car Company. The Ord Steel Company subsequently became the Ordway Steel Company. The word "steel" was dropped from the company name in 1948 when it was decided to discontinue warehousing steel and concentrate sales effort on hardware, machinery, and automotive parts. At the present time the Ordway Company carries about 22,000 different items in these three major lines and serves approximately 6,000 customers in five states.

Since 1952 the company has experienced a steady decline in its sales of machinery and heavy hardware. Sales of automotive parts and supplies, on the other hand, have risen sharply. The result has been a substantial amount of excess storage space, since auto parts require so much less space per volume of sales than the other lines. The decline in machinery and hardware sales is attributable to several influences, but chief among them has been the loss of several major suppliers. The growth and prominence of Chicago as a major industrial center provided these manufacturers with sufficient volume to justify the establishment of their own branch houses in the area. Moreover, the continued growth of heavy industry in Chicago has led Ordway management to expect further shifts in the distribution pattern of machinery and heavy hardware toward direct distribution for all but the smallest producers. However, there are still a number of machinery and hardware buyers in Chicago who for one reason or another prefer to deal with local suppliers. Some value the greater attention they receive from local suppliers, others have credit or service needs which local suppliers can serve better than a distant manufacturer, while a few purchase in quantities too small to interest direct selling manufacturers. While Ordway receives a sufficient amount of business from customers of this type to warrant retaining for the present its machinery and hardware lines, the sales outlook is not encouraging.

Management is therefore considering the addition of another product line, or lines, to compensate for the declining importance of machinery and heavy hardware in its sales picture. Initially, at least, electronic components and instruments appear to be an inviting possibility. These products have the same relationship to industrial users of electronic equipment as tools, abrasives, chains, pulleys, and other industrial supplies have to users of mechanical equipment. Also, a wholesaler of electronic parts and components has essentially the same problems of finance, stock control, warehousing, and selling as a wholesaler of industrial hardware or automotive parts. The only major difference between wholesaling electronic devices and wholesaling other industrial lines is the type of technical selling involved.

Electronics is a branch of electrical engineering pertaining to the conduction of electricity through a gas, vacuum, or solid. Electron tubes, semi-conductors, and photo-sensitive devices emit, control, and direct the flow of electrons. The market for such products includes manufacturing establishments, the military, broadcasting and television companies, technical research agencies, firms offering radio and television repair services, and individuals who operate ham radio stations. Producers of electronic products constitute the nation's fifth largest industry. Moreover, it is a rapidly expanding industry. Industrial-commercial electronics sales rose from $750 million in 1955 to $1.38 billion in 1958. The trade publication *Electronics* (McGraw-Hill) predicts sales of $4.75 billion by 1970.

Television receivers, computers, marine and air navigation systems are examples of electronic products purchased by consumer, commercial, and military buyers. Testing and measuring equipment, control devices, and components—such as tubes, semi-conductors, and other replacement parts—are the principal products purchased by industrial buyers. Electronic components are also used in large quantities by the military and by firms that service and sell television and radio receivers.

Impressed by the growth and dimensions of the electronics market, the president of Ordway appointed an executive task committee to study the industry and determine whether there was a niche in it for Ordway. The committee reported its findings early in 1962. The highlights of their report are given in the following summary.

Executive Committee Report

To businessmen accustomed to the fairly orderly pattern of established industries, the electronics industry presents a bewildering picture. The industry produces standard parts for replacement sales as well as for original equipment; standardized tools and instruments; and custom-made apparatus. These items are produced, though, in an unbelievable variety and many of them are highly technical in nature. Moreover, both special and custom-made products are constantly being converted into standard items, and makers who once limited their operations to standardized products are now expanding into a job-shop business. To add to the confusion, manufacturers who once made only nonelectronic products have either added electronic features to these products or introduced completely new lines of electronics.

Patterns of distribution are extremely fluid. The industry is crowded with small producers, most of whom appear to have no settled policies. They literally sell to everybody—agents, electrical wholesalers, general line distributors, franchised dealers, retailers, repair shops, specialized electronics houses, and specialized wholesalers in power transmission, machinery, instruments, and air-hydraulics. A few of the larger makers also sell direct to users. The marketing channel can be best described as wide open.

Supply firms with electronics as key lines or with separate electronics departments are relatively scarce. However, the few which do fall into this category appear to be very successful. A number of specialized supply firms have added electronics as a logical means of extending their present lines. For the most part, these are wholesalers specializing in mechanical instruments, although some specialize in power transmission equipment, and a few in precision tools. Paradoxically, electrical wholesalers have shown a reluctance to become very involved in the electronics market.

On the other hand, a number of supply firms are emerging which are difficult to classify except that they specialize in electronics. Some operate as agents, with no stocks except what may be held on consignment; some started as radio or television repair shops, built up inventories of parts and gradually added salesmen to push parts as well as service. A relatively few are bona fide merchant wholesalers. As a group these supply firms are small and poorly equipped. But there is at least one in every major city with impressive facilities and a well-trained staff. Like all specialists in newly developing industries, they tend to distribute over wide areas. It was discovered that salesmen from many of these firms cover an entire state.

Interviews with a fairly representative sample of electronics makers seems to indicate that they would welcome the kind of representation an established local distributor could give them. They are disturbed by the lack of management know-how, uncertain financial strength, and spotty representation which now characterize the present distribution picture. Except where military sales predominate, there is evidence that direct selling has become an increasingly burdensome expense. A few random comments of electronic executives are given below.

"Our business is growing so fast that the production department has a difficult time keeping up with sales. We are presently distributing through electronic specialists, not by choice necessarily, but because they are the only people who appear eager to handle our product. However, we have had to recruit a small army of these firms, because so few have enough working capital to stock our complete line. A supplier must be prepared to invest from $4000 to $8000 per line to carry an adequate stock of our products."

"Established wholesalers seem determined to shut their eyes to opportunity. I doubt that any significant number of them will wake up and re-equip themselves in time to be a factor in the electronics market. We are setting up a network of specialists to handle our lines. While results have been generally good, most of these people are new to management, and frankly, are poor risks. They are mostly ex-salesmen and ex-engineers who are not only without administrative experience but find it difficult to think in terms of marketing rather than selling or service."

"We would prefer to sell through product specialty houses, but users of our products are not familiar with these new firms and prefer to buy direct. We have tried without success to interest established industrial supply houses in our products. They lack men with the necessary training to sell our products and they are understandably afraid of obsolescence in a changing field."

"The manufacturer must do a great deal of market pioneering in a field like electronics. For this reason we always start a product with our own sales force. However, as soon as the market for a product is established, we like to turn it over to a distributor."

"We are organizing a highly selective distributor network to get the jump on our competitors, most of whom sell direct. Our products have so many applications that we would miss the boat without strong local coverage."

After reviewing the various segments of the non-military electronics market, it appears that components, particularly instruments and controls, are the products best suited to our type of operation. They are basic shelf supplies for every plant which has an automated process or which employs electronics in its shop or office. The great majority of manufacturing plants in our own area would certainly fall into this category. For the most part, electronic components are small, packaged items which take a minimum of warehouse space.

Three major product types can be identified within the general category of electronic components: testing and measuring instruments, control devices, and nuclear electronics. Instruments and controls include the counters, sorters, timers, gauge and related mechanisms used as the actuating "brains" of automated machines. They are extensively used as basic tools in quality control and are increasingly used for operations control in fluid process industries, such as chemicals and petroleum refining. Applications range from the counting of pills being packed in bottles at a pharmaceutical plant to measuring the speed and consistency of chemicals flowing through a pipeline. These products are also playing an important role in progress toward miniaturization and closer tolerance in manufacturing.

Nuclear electronics includes, among other things, geiger counters and radio-isotope thickness gauges. These, as well as many instruments and control devices, are highly specialized pieces of equipment—often custom made—and tend to be sold direct or through specialized agents. However, there has been a definite trend toward standardization as applications have become more numerous.

Sales of electronic components reached the billion dollar mark in 1960 and are still rising. What part of this figure represents sales to industries which we presently call on would be impossible to estimate. A substantial portion of it, however, is undoubtedly to original equipment manufacturers (o.e.m. accounts) who tend to buy direct. But it is also true that an undetermined number of o.e.m's are too small to justify direct manufacturer calls. Add to these the non o.e.m. buyers and there would appear to be substantial opportunity for an established distributor such as Ordway.

On the minus side, however, electronics is an unknown area to Ordway management. If we decided to enter this market, it would be necessary to institute an extensive training program that would include everybody in the company from the president to the stock clerks. The most urgent need would be to train, hire, or otherwise develop a sales staff with the necessary knowledge of product application. Due to the technical nature of these products, we would undoubtedly find it necessary to seek assistance outside the company.

The president of Ordway read the above report with genuine interest and hope. However, he was still undecided as to what action should be taken. A lengthy conference with representatives of the Association of Electronic Parts and Equipment Manufacturers confirmed the findings of the executive committee. However, the discussions shed little additional light on what types of firms represented the largest users of electronic components, except that purchases were closely related to capital expenditures.

REYNOLDS PRODUCTS COMPANY[1]

In February, 1946, E. F. Reynolds, president of the Reynolds Products Company, received a report from H. B. Miner, marketing research director, outlining a study made by Mr. Miner on the suitability of Buffalo, New York, as the location for a branch warehouse. The company had been considering the establishment of a warehouse in this city for some time, and Mr. Reynolds relied heavily on Mr. Miner's report in arriving at a decision on the matter.

The company sold both Reynolds-manufactured piping products and allied products purchased from other manufacturers. The items made by the company included pipe fittings, valves, and certain industrial piping specialties.

In addition to distributing the products manufactured in its various plants, the company sold piping products purchased from other makers—pipe, pumps, and plumbing and heating equipment. The company sold these manufactured and purchased products to a wide variety of customers, including contractors, industrial plants, refineries, textile plants, railroads, iron and steel mills, utilities, mines, and institutions.

About 200 company salesmen worked out of 26 warehouse locations. The company warehouses closest to Buffalo were in Philadelphia, Pennsylvania; Cleveland, Ohio; and Hartford, Connecticut.

The company salesmen sold both Reynolds-manufactured and purchased products within the metropolitan area surrounding each ware-

---

[1] This case is rather old, but it presents an extensive analysis of the warehouse location problem, together with some very intriguing lapses and omissions in such analysis. The principles and techniques involved are timeless.

house, while outside of these areas the company marketed its manufactured products through distributors. These distributors bought only Reynolds-manufactured products from the company, although they purchased other products from the original manufacturers.

Thus, the company warehouses served a dual purpose. They were outlets for company-manufactured products, sold in metropolitan areas by Reynolds salesmen and in outlying areas by distributors who bought from the company. They also were outlets for purchased products sold by company salesmen to customers within the metropolitan limits of the city where the warehouse was located. The typical sales office obtained 50 percent of its total sales in the metropolitan area where it was located, while the other half of its volume came from purchases of Reynolds-manufactured products by distributors in the outlying areas.

The number of salesmen attached to a Reynolds warehouse varied from 3 to 10; the average was 7. Approximately 15 percent of the Reynolds salesmen were graduate engineers. These men specialized in serving large accounts in the metropolitan area, rendered piping engineering service to these firms. The balance of the Reynolds salesmen devoted full time to contacting distributor accounts in their territories.

Each warehouse acted as a jobber in that it sold purchased pipe and plumbing and heating products as well as Reynolds-manufactured products in the branch city. The company found that whenever it opened a new warehouse approximately 20 percent of its sales were in the purchased product category. The reason was that customers usually bought pipe and pipe fittings and valves from the same source. Thus, company sales always increased in a territory after establishment of a warehouse, since prior to its establishment the company enjoyed only jobber sales of Reynolds products, while after its establishment company salesmen also sold purchased products in the branch city.

The 1946 sales of the Cleveland, Hartford, and Philadelphia warehouses which were closest to the proposed Buffalo warehouse, amounted to approximately $1.5 million each. These warehouses each had a sales force of from 8 to 10 salesmen. The report Mr. Miner submitted to Mr. Reynolds on the Buffalo warehouse question follows.

BUFFALO, N.Y., AS A LOCATION FOR A BRANCH WAREHOUSE

Buffalo, located at the eastern end of Lake Erie, is the terminus of much lake shipping coming east from the iron mines of northern Michigan and the automotive plants of Detroit. It is also one of the most important rail junctions in the country, being on the main lines of 12 railroads. It is 183 miles northeast of Cleveland and 300 miles from New York.

The city of Buffalo covers an area approximately 8 miles by 4 miles, with a metropolitan area that extends some 15 miles north, east, and south to cover a good part of Erie and Niagara counties.

In population Buffalo is the 14th largest city in the United States, with approximately 600,000 people. Its metropolitan area contains close to 1 million people, including the municipalities of Niagara Falls, 78,029; Lackawanna, 24,058; North Tonawanda, 20, 254; Kenmore, 19,612; Lancaster, 17,236; Tonawanda, 13,008; Hamburg, 5,467; and East Aurora, 5,253. The population has not increased greatly during the past 2 decades, and growth during the war was only about 3 percent. Lockport, a city of 24,379, is just beyond the metropolitan area.

Although Buffalo ranks 14th in population size, in buying power per capita it ranks only 118th.

EXHIBIT I

Buffalo Branch Warehouse
Estimated Operations

	First Year
Sales volume (not including Erie):	
In Buffalo metropolitan area	$ 540,000
To distributors outside Buffalo	460,000
	$1,000,000
Gross profit (after discounts)	15%
	150,000
Expenses	103,000
Operating profit or loss	47,000

ESTIMATED EXPENSES

Sales and office:	
Salaries	$ 50,000
Travel	10,000
Telephone and telegraph	4,000
Postage and miscellaneous	2,000
	$ 66,000
Shop:	
Salaries	25,000
Trucks	2,000
Light, heat, and power	1,500
Supplies, services, and miscellaneous	2,500
	$ 31,000
Fixed overhead:	
Rent	5,000
Insurance and taxes	1,000
	$ 6,000
Total	103,000

This area is highly industrialized, ranking 9th in the country, with 1,470 establishments in Erie and Niagara counties, of which 1,000 are in the city of Buffalo. Manufacturing is fairly well diversified (see Exhibit II). The principal industries are: aircraft—Bell, Curtiss Wright; flour and grain milling—Washburn Crosby, Pillsbury, Standard Milling; iron and steel—Bethlehem, Republic, Wickwire-Spencer; chemicals—Du Pont, National Aniline; motor vehicles—Chevrolet, Ford Assembly.

Of the 1,470 manufacturing establishments in Erie and Niagara counties, only about 170 are worthwhile from a Reynolds Company sales viewpoint, as follows:

Dun & Bradstreet *Financial Rating* *(Net Worth)*	*Number of* *Worthwhile* *Plants*
Over $1,000,000...............................	91
$500,000–$1,000,000.........................	26
$200,000–$500,000...........................	25
$75,000–$200,000............................	28
Total................................	170

Industry in the Buffalo area is highly mechanized, being greater than any other industrial area except Youngstown and Pittsburgh in horsepower installed per wage earner, and second only to Chicago in total horsepower installed. It is true that most electricity for this area is developed in hydroplants. However, the Buffalo Niagara Electric Company has one sizable steam power station, and, of course, many industrials have steam power plants for heating and process requirements.

Construction activity, particularly nonresidential building, has been substantial and unusually steady since the depression. That it rose only moderately in the wartime building boom of 1941 and 1942 might be considered a factor favorable to postwar construction activity. Because it is a long-established industrial center, many plants are obsolete and will have to be replaced or practically rebuilt to meet competition from newer plants in other parts of the country.

The distributor competition in Buffalo does not appear unusually strong for a city of its size and potential business, although there are 12 legitimate distributors plus 6 or 7 plumbing contractors who sell supplies. Only six houses

EXHIBIT II

Number of Industrial Establishments
Buffalo, Rochester, Jamestown, and Erie Industrial Areas

Product	*Buffalo*	*Rochester*	*Jamestown*	*Erie, Pa.*
Food and kindred products........	438	218	71	83
Tobacco manufactures...........	6	..	..	1
Textile mill products.............	21	6	5	..
Apparel.......................	54	46	1	4
Lumber products................	28	10	16	9
Furniture.....................	57	44	42	22
Paper.........................	44	31	1	7
Printing, publishing.............	175	113	22	26
Chemicals.....................	123	34	3	9
Petroleum and coal products......	12	4	..	5
Rubber products...............	6	1	..	1
Leather.......................	13	21	1	3
Stone, clay, and glass............	73	21	7	12
Iron and steel..................	121	41	21	42
Nonferrous metals..............	60	27	5	12
Electrical machinery............	15	13	1	11
Machinery.....................	108	77	12	37
Automobiles and equipment.......	22	4	2	1
Other transportation equipment....	12	5	1	3
Miscellaneous..................	82	87	7	21
Total..................	1,470	803	218	309

would offer really serious competition: Dave & Brown Company, Ureka Company, City Heating Company, and Mackie Company in Buffalo; Foster Company in both Buffalo and Niagara Falls; and Apex Supply Company in Tonawanda.

The only distributor with whom Reynolds does a substantial business is Dave & Brown Company, the leading house. They also buy from a competitor of Reynolds Company. Note the following:

Reynolds Sales to Dave & Brown Company

| 1939 | ....$2,261 | 1941 | ....$11,396 | 1943 | ....$27,146 |
| 1940 | .... 7,755 | 1942 | .... 33,812 | 1944 | .... 21,941 |

Foster Company, whose business is mostly with the plumbing trade, does not buy from Reynolds. Ureka Company is an industrial supply house handling competitive fittings. City Heating Company carries all makes of short-line fittings at extreme prices. Mackie Company, which is not well liked because of apparent indifference, buys only a few hundred dollars worth from Reynolds each year. Apex Supply Company has been a spotty customer, buying $443 in 1943 and $4,650 in 1944.

Total Reynolds sales in the Buffalo metropolitan area have run between $35,000 to $40,000 in the past 3 years. Compared to this, if Reynolds had a warehouse the 1946 Reynolds potential sales would be about $540,000 (see Exhibit I). The potential for the city alone, $420,000, slightly exceeds that of Seattle and Atlanta, where Reynolds now has branches, and only 5 locations that deserve immediate consideration as branch locations have greater sales potentials:

Cities	1946 Potential	Cities	1946 Potential
Boston................	$900,000	Buffalo................	$420,000
Baltimore..............	780,000	Indianapolis............	360,000
Pittsburgh..............	600,000	New Orleans............	360,000
Cincinnati.............	480,000	Kansas City............	360,000
Milwaukee.............	480,000	Dallas................	360,000

These potential sales values presume sales effort and competition similar to the average at established Reynolds branches. Of course, actual sales could not be expected to equal potentials until after some months of operation.

The makeup of the Buffalo market suggests a greater opportunity for a branch handling a considerable line of purchased material, including pipe, valves, and plumbing and heating supplies, than for one specializing primarily in engineer piping products.

. . . .

Within the territory extending 100 miles or so east and south from Buffalo, in which distributor accounts could be economically sold and serviced out of Buffalo, the only industrial cities of any importance are Rochester, New York, Jamestown, New York, and Erie, Pennsylvania. Consideration might be given to handling Syracuse, Auburn, and Elmira, New York, out of Buffalo—they are now serviced out of Hartford, Connecticut. On the other hand, it is questionable if any advantage would be obtained in transferring Erie, Pennsylvania, from Cleveland to Buffalo—it is only a few miles nearer Buffalo and would be no more easily sold or serviced from Buffalo.

However, with a branch at Buffalo and with greater solicitation of distributor business, sales could be considerably increased in Rochester, Jamestown, and the 17 smaller towns in the 15 westernmost counties of New York State and also in the several towns in Warren and McKean counties, Pennsylvania, such as Warren, Bradford, and Kane in the oil field district. During the past three years, total sales in this territory (not including Buffalo metropolitan area and Erie) have run only about $65,000 a year—this could certainly be doubled in short order.

. . . .

Rochester, 70 miles east of Buffalo—located on Lake Ontario and served by 4 railroads—is important enough itself to be considered for a small warehouse. The population of its metropolitan area is about 426,000—a decline of 3 percent from 1940. In New York State, it ranks next to metropolitan New York and Buffalo in industrial importance. In the United States, it ranks 14th in industrial importance.

Rochester is primarily important in the manufacture of precision instruments; it is the home of such well-known concerns as Eastman Kodak, Bausch & Lomb Optical, Folmer Graflex, and Defender Photo Supply. Industry is fairly well diversified, with a great deal of activity in iron and steel products, chemicals, optical glass, and apparel (Exhibit II). In Rochester, a few large plants are accountable for the greater part of industrial buying power; only 86 of 803 establishments in Monroe county have more than 100 wage earners, and only 82 are considered worth real sales attention. Of the 82 worthwhile plants, 37 have Dun & Bradstreet financial ratings over $1 million.

Financial Rating (Net Worth)	Number of Worthwhile Plants
Over $1 million	37
$500,000–$1 million	16
$200,000–$500,000	9
$75,000–$200,000	20
Total	82

Electric power in Rochester is mostly hydro, but the Rochester Gas & Electric Company operates a fair-sized steam plant. This company has not indicated any plans for expansion in the next two years.

Construction in Rochester has been considerably less over a period of years than in Buffalo.

There are eight or nine distributors in Rochester, including a branch of Foster Company and Mackie Company, both of Buffalo. Reynolds customers are Plumley & Company, who bought $12,000 in 1944, and Palmer & Cox, who bought $4,000. (Complete list in Exhibit III.)

Other than the 2 aforementioned distributors, only 4 accounts bought more than $1,000 in the past 3 years, and none of these over $2,000. Total Reynolds sales in Rochester have run between $20,000 and $30,000 a year.

. . . .

Jamestown, on the Erie Railroad 70 miles south of Buffalo and 56 miles west of Erie, Pennsylvania, is a city of 43,000 population. Its 218 industrial establishments are primarily engaged in the manufacture of wood and metal

EXHIBIT III

Principal Distributors in the Buffalo, Rochester, Jamestown, and Erie Industrial Areas

	Reynolds Sales (Rounded to Nearest $100)				
Distributors	*1940*	*1941*	*1942*	*1943*	*1944*
BUFFALO AREA					
Buffalo:					
City Heating Company........	.....	.....	.....	.....	.....
Foster Company..............$	200	$ 1,000	$ 500	.....	.....
Malden Pipe Supply Company..	.....	.....	600	$ 1,900	$ 600
Kelly Supply Company........	700	1,400	2,100	800	800
Mackie......................	40	300	700	400	1,600
Baldwin Supply..............	5,100	2,400	700	100	.....
Johnson & Cox..............	.....	.....	.....	.....	.....
Supreme Supply..............	100	500	300	.....	300
Ureka.......................	.....	.....	300	2,000	1,000
Stoller Plumbing..............	1,000	100	.....	.....	400
Dave & Brown..............	7,800	11,400	33,800	27,100	21,900
Niagara Falls:					
Foster Company..............	200	1,000	500	500	300
Tonawanda:					
Apex Supply Company.........	700	2,200	100	400	4,600
ROCHESTER AREA					
Rochester:					
Foster Company..............	.....	.....	.....	.....	.....
Mackie......................	.....	300	400	300	400
Duing........................	.....	.....	.....	.....	.....
Plumley & Company.........	18,100	20,000	24,500	15,600	12,200
Palmer & Cox................	3,200	5,500	4,300	1,000	4,400
George Supply................	.....	.....	.....	.....	.....
Hill Plumbing Supply..........	2	30	.....	300	10
Howard Fixture Company......	10	200	.....	20	300
JAMESTOWN AREA					
Jamestown:					
Foster Company..............	.....	.....	.....	.....	.....
Dane Hardware..............	8,300	13,100	5,600	5,200	5,100
ERIE AREA					
Erie, Pa.:					
Uniform Plumbing............	5,800	3,900	23,800	17,400	6,500
Foster Company..............	.....	.....	.....	.....	.....
Worthington Steel Supply	.....	.....	.....	.....	.....
Stevenson Manufacturing.......	300	.....	.....	.....	.....

furniture and other lumber, iron, and steel products. Very few are large concerns or worth Reynolds' direct solicitation.

There are only two important distributors in Jamestown—a branch of Foster Company of Buffalo and Dane Hardware. Dane buys $5,000 a year from Reynolds. Undoubtedly, sales to this account could be substantially increased if the business was more strenuously solicited.

....

There is little point in discussing Erie, Pennsylvania, because, as indicated

EXHIBIT IV

Reynolds Customers in the Proposed Buffalo Territory to Whom Sales
Were Over $1,000 in Any Year, 1942, 1943, 1944

Customer	Type of Customer	1942	1943	1944
NEW YORK STATE				
Erie County				
Buffalo:				
Malden Pipe Supply Co.	Distributor	$ 600	$ 1,900	$ 600
Kelly Supply Co.	"	2,100	800	800
Mackie	"	700	400	1,600
Buffalo Dye Works	Industrial	.....	900	2,300
Ureka Co.	Distributor	300	2,000	1,000
Dave & Brown Co.	"	33,800	27,100	21,900
Tonawanda:				
Apex Supply Company	Distributor	100	400	4,600
Niagara County				
Niagara Falls:				
Industrial Chemicals Corp.	Industrial	.....	1,300	200
Lockport:				
Fox Products Co.	Distributor	17,400	3,900	7,300
Genesee County				
Batavia:				
Hillman Supply Co.	Distributor	.....	200	1,000
Monroe County				
Rochester:				
Photo Products Co.	Industrial	600	1,200	1,600
Plumley & Co.	Distributor	24,500	15,600	12,200
Palmer & Cox Co.	Distributor	4,300	1,000	4,400
Benson Instrument Co.	Industrial	.....	.....	1,300
Doe & Hart Co.	Contractor	1,000	400	1,300
Seneca County				
Seneca Falls:				
Cox Pump & Valve	Industrial	.....	100	1,500
Steuben County				
Painted Post:				
Jones Company	Industrial	11,700	5,800	4,300
Allegany County				
Bolivar:				
Jeffrey Co.	Distributor	700	1,600	1,300
Chautauqua County				
Jamestown:				
Dane Hardware Co.	Distributor	5,600	5,200	5,100
PENNSYLVANIA STATE				
McKean County				
Bradford:				
Heslow Mfg. Co.	Industrial	500	2,700	1,200
Kane:				
Jones Piping Co.	Unclassified	600	1,100	300

previously, there appears to be no advantage in selling and servicing it out of
Buffalo instead of Cleveland.

There are only three important distributors beside Stevenson Manufacturing, whose home office is Erie—Uniform Plumbing who represents us, a branch
of Foster Company, and Worthington Steel Supply. We sell Acme Electric
and Johnson Motor Company direct, and it may be advisable to sell more in-

dustrials direct if we cannot increase our business with Uniform Plumbing. Note the following:

	Reynolds Sales				
	1940	1941	1942	1943	1944
Uniform Plumbing	$5,800	$ 3,900	$23,800	$17,400	$ 6,500
Acme Electric	4,500	15,000	7,600	4,600	1,600
Johnson Motor Co	4,500	8,600	5,400	4,700	19,000

Erie has 69 worthwhile plants, of which 21 have a financial rating of over $1 million. The chief products are electrical machinery and apparatus, machinery, meters, iron and steel forgings, hardware, and specialties—not altogether a hot prospect list for Reynolds.

The foregoing discussion indicates that a branch warehouse at Buffalo could be successful to the extent that the estimated volume and profit figures shown in Exhibit I are considered satisfactory. Estimates presume the inclusion of plumbing and heating material, as well as pipe, valves, and fittings. Outside the Buffalo metropolitan area, sales would be through distributors only.

EXHIBIT IV–A

Customers in Additional Territory Considered for Buffalo to Whom Sales Were Over $1,000 in Any Year, 1942, 1943, 1944

Customer	Type of Customer	1942	1943	1944
NEW YORK (NOW HARTFORD TERRITORY)				
Chemung County				
Elmira:				
Kennedy Bluing Co	Industrial	$ 1,200	$ 1,100	$ 400
Kennedy Valve Mfg	"	26,000	11,500	8,800
Gould & Lester Co	Distributor	1,500	.....	.....
Onondaga County				
Syracuse:				
Davis Supply	Distributor	19,400	17,600	22,600
Acme Electric	Industrial	20,300	12,400	8,200
John Miner	Distributor	100	800	1,800
Oswego County				
Oswego:				
Benson Company	Distributor	1,300	2,700	5,300
PENNSYLVANIA (NOW CLEVELAND TERRITORY)				
Erie County				
Corry:				
Kier Steel Works	Industrial	8,400	36,700	21,300
Erie:				
Uniform Plumbing	Distributor	23,800	17,400	6,500
Acme Electric Co	Industrial	7,600	4,600	1,600
Brocker Engine Co	"	5,400	4,700	18,900
Johnson Motor Co	Contractor	1,100	1,200	.....

EXHIBIT V

Reynolds Sales in Buffalo Metropolitan Area and Surrounding Territory

Year	Buffalo Metropolitan Area			Outside Buffalo Metro. Area, Not Inc. Erie County, Pa.	Total	Erie County, Pa.*
	Distributors	Direct	Total			
1939	$21,000	$6,000	$27,000	$47,000	$ 74,000	$10,000
1940	17,000	5,000	22,000	60,000	82,000	20,000
1941	22,000	9,000	31,000	72,000	103,000	47,000
1942	38,000	1,000	39,000	70,000	109,000	46,000
1943	34,000	3,000	37,000	45,000	82,000	65,000
1944	32,000	3,000	35,000	55,000	90,000	49,000

* Handled out of Cleveland.

EXHIBIT VI

Buffalo, Metropolitan Area

				% of U.S.
Market value of trucking area				0.8%

With no branch warehouse:
Potential sales (based on company experience in cities without branch warehouses) 0.5

Actual Sales		Distributors	Direct	Total	
	1939	$21,000	$6,000	$27,000	0.22
	1940	17,000	5,000	22,000	0.17
	1941	22,000	9,000	31,000	0.13
	1942	38,000	1,000	39,000	0.13
	1943	34,000	3,000	37,000	0.14
	1944	32,000	3,000	35,000	0.15

With branch warehouse:
Estimated potential sales first year 540,000   1.8

Market Value Factors (City)	% of U.S.
Population	0.6%
Effective buying income	0.8
Building permits	0.9
Value plumbing and heating work	0.6
Number industrial plants	0.6
Value manufactured products	0.8

Pertinent data:

Distance from Cleveland—183 miles northeast.

Railroad service—Main line of N.Y. Central and 11 other railroads.

Size of trucking area—15-mile radius; north, east, and south. Parts of Erie and Niagara Counties, including cities of Niagara Falls, North Tonawanda, Lancaster, Hamburg, East Aurora.

Population—Buffalo: 603,000; rank, 14: wartime growth, 4.7%. Other cities over 25,000 in area: Niagara Falls, 78,000. Counties of Erie and Niagara: 961,000.

Effective buying income per capita—Buffalo: rank, 118.

Industry—Buffalo: 1,034 plants; value manufactured products, rank, 9. Counties of Erie and Niagara: 1,470 plants; worthwhile plants 170; plants rated $1 million, 91.

THE SILAS OATES COMPANY
A General Round-up Case

◇◇

The executives of the Silas Oates Company are engaged in appraising the present position and planning the future course of the company.

The Silas Oates Company was organized in 1940 to exploit the skills and know-how in making metal castings, which Mr. Oates had developed while a graduate student and instructor in Pennsylvania State College. It started operations in an old auto repair shop on the outskirts of the town of State College (now University Park), Pennsylvania. The firm was barely organized when the defense program got under way, and until 1946 almost all its facilities were devoted to war work.

According to Mr. Oates, the business of the company consists in "making castings that can't be made." Most castings are lacking in surface smoothness, dimension precision, and uniformity of quality. In addition, some metals are tricky to handle in the casting process, so that it is very difficult to make certain shapes from them. The process requires not only a high degree of skill in techniques, but also ability in metallurgical research to develop alloys that, when properly handled, will give the desired effects.

The Oates Company specializes in making castings from aluminum. By use of patented processes and special alloys developed by Mr. Oates and his sister, a metallurgical engineer, the company is able to make aluminum castings that fall within very narrow dimensional and quality tolerances and will take a very high polish. Several years ago, the research group under the leadership of Miss Oates developed a process for making castings of ductile iron, which possess the same characteristics.

The firm operates two plants. One is in a thoroughly modern building with specially built machinery, several miles outside University Park, and specializes in aluminum alloy castings. The other is in Houserville, about six miles away, and is equipped to produce castings of ductile iron. The firm employs about 300 persons—250 in the University Park plant and about 50 in Houserville. The capacity of each plant is about twice its present output.

Many of the Silas Oates Company assets are intangible. Among them are a high degree of skill and experience in research in the field of metallurgy as applied to castings, a large fund of know-how throughout the executive and working force in the making of intricate and difficult castings, a spirit of insistence on precision and accuracy that pervades all ranks of the personnel, and a willingness to try new things.

Another intangible asset of the firm is its relations with its employees. It provides vacations with pay and a retirement fund based on contributions by both company and employees. It operates an employee stock ownership plan in which about half of the employees participate, with an ownership interest in 1956 of 50.3 percent of the total common stock. In addition, the Oats Company maintains a profit sharing plan whereby between one fourth and one third of the profits before interest charges are paid to the employees. The books of the company, aside from confidential figures on classified governmental orders, are open to the employees.

As a result, the employees take an active personal interest in the affairs of the firm and highly prize their close personal relations with the management. Some years ago, a strenuous effort was made to unionize the plant, but the employees defeated it, preferring their existing relationship. The management is very sensitive to the advantages of this situation, and devotes the most thoughtful attention and effort to maintaining it.

Tables I and II show certain financial statistics of the Silas Oates Company in recent years.

The company's chief product is tire molds. More than two thirds of the total volume is in this item. The Oates Company supplies about 80 to 90 percent of the tire mold purchases of companies that make new tires. This is a matter of some concern to executives of the firm. The rubber companies change their tire designs about every two or three years. During the period of six months to a year when a tire company is

TABLE I
OPERATING STATISTICS
Silas Oates Company

	1964	1963	1962	1961	1960
Net sales.......	$4,405,590	$4,207,684	$3,640,399	$5,030,136	$4,433,438
Other income...	38,628	34,487	6,365		
All costs.......	4,018,292	3,858,504	3,679,097		
Employees' profit*.......	140,522	126,615	16,581		
Income tax.....	128,228	131,671	−19,772		
Net profit......	157,176	125,371	−29,142	171,670	124,893
Dividends......	42,877	43,100	64,872	66,616	67,044
Retained earnings.........	114,299	82,271	−94,014	105,054	57,849
Cumulative retained earnings†........	993,821	879,522	797,251	891,265	786,211

* Includes contribution to retirement fund.
† At end of year.

TABLE II

ASSETS

Silas Oates Company

	1964	1963	1962	1961
Cash.......................	$ 239,911	$ 523,570	$ 127,416	$ 471,081
Accounts receivable...........	632,232	401,040	517,540	559,466
Inventory—materials.........	237,545	179,431	246,801	279,798
Inventory—in process........	316,791	198,384	175,308	139,650
Total Current Assets...	$1,426,479	$1,302,425	$1,067,065	$1,449,995
Land and improvements.......	161,843	157,706	147,786	147,786
Buildings...................	1,114,610	813,290	783,724	787,868
Machinery and equipment.....	1,887,753	1,712,161	1,674,014	1,584,492
Total...............	$3,164,206	$2,683,157	$2,605,524	$2,520,146
Less reserves for depreciation..	1,996,292	1,886,272	1,757,022	1,623,058
Fixed assets—net.............	1,167,914	796,885	848,502	897,088
Prepaid expenses, etc.........	24,261	26,380	32,761	34,061
Total...............	$2,618,654	$2,125,690	$1,948,328	$2,381,144

developing new designs, its purchases of old-design molds shrink drastically. Then, when it begins to retool for the new design its demand for molds expands tremendously.

This effect is multiplied by the fact that because of competitive pressures the redesigning and retooling activities of the different companies tend to coincide with each other timewise instead of being staggered so as to offset one another. This behavior of demand causes a wide fluctuation of sales from year to year, with consequent fluctuations in the number of workers needed and in profits. This, in turn, tends to nullify the effectiveness of the firm's personnel policy, to dissipate the know-how of the working force, and to weaken its spirit of insistence on quality and precision, which are so vital to the company's welfare.

In their off-the-road tire business (tractors, farm equipment, construction equipment, etc.), the rubber companies do not follow the same pattern of behavior as in their on-the-road business. Design changes are less frequent, and their timing tends to be staggered among the several companies. But the molds used to make off-the-road tires do not require quite the same accuracy and precision as do those used to make passenger car and truck tires. However, the Silas Oates Company makes them, although usually at a somewhat narrower margin of gross profit than it enjoys on its other tire mold business. The number of such tires produced is small in comparison with the on-the-road volume. The Oates Company has made no serious effort to get this type of business.

Tire molds are also needed in the retread business. The Silas Oates Company has not made a serious effort to get into this business for several reasons. First, many of the firms supplying the retread service do not require molds of the precision and finish the company is accustomed to supplying. To seek heavy volume in this business, therefore, the Oates Company would be obliged to offer price concessions that would reduce the average gross margin. In the process of producing retread molds of poorer quality, the company might also dilute the habit of precision and accuracy on which its business is founded.

Second, many of the firms doing retread work are small establishments that need only one or two molds. They are also widely scattered. The company would thus face a difficult task in getting its retread molds distributed. Third, this difficulty is emphasized by the fact that the Lido Company has been very successful in making retread molds and distributing them. The Lido Company sells some of its molds, leases some of them to firms doing retread work, and uses some of them in an extensive retread business it conducts itself. Its total volume from all sources is almost double that of the Oates Company. Two tire companies have bought retread molds from the Oates Company, which they lease or sell to their new tire dealers who want to offer a retread service.

About one fourth to one third of the Silas Oates Company's sales volume is in specialty castings not connected with the tire industry. Quite a bit of business is done with the airplane manufacturing industry. Some of this comes from defense and space exploration contracts, some of it from civilian business. Oates castings can be used wherever rotors must operate inside pipes or other fittings within narrow tolerances—for example, in various types of pumping apparatus. The company's executives are convinced that Oates castings could be substituted for many parts or assemblies that numerous equipment manufacturing firms now produce by other processes. This more diversified market has not been extensively explored by the Oates Company, partly because of marketing difficulties and partly because of research and production considerations.

The Silas Oates Company's tire mold contracts are handled by the tire mold sales manager, Mr. Soames, and two sales engineers. Mr. Soames is a very capable man who has been with the firm since he returned from the Navy.

The miscellaneous or specialty mold sales are handled by a force of five salesmen under the direction of Mr. Rogers, who is in his early or middle thirties. Since Mr. Rogers' background before coming to the company about three years ago was in the advertising business, he also functions as advertising manager.

Both these men are under Mr. Upton, a man between 45 and 50 years of age, who has been with the company from its beginning. Mr. Upton explains that the Oates Company has not more than scratched the surface of the miscellaneous, nontire-mold castings business. The present sales force is about as big as the volume of the company can support. Total marketing expenses run somewhat under 5 percent of sales.

Mr. Upton points out that most of the work of selling the miscellaneous or specialty castings is in the nature of bird-dogging; that is, the salesman visits a prospect in the hope of being able to learn enough about his operations to uncover some part or assembly in which Oates castings can be used profitably by the customer. This method is very expensive and time-consuming, and with the sales force available not so much of it can be done as seems desirable. Mr. Upton wishes some way could be developed by which the sales force could call its shots, that is, call only on firms that actually have a use for the company's products.

Some attempt has been made to do this by advertising. Space has been taken in several engineering publications. Thought has been given to trying direct mail to a prospect list culled from Thomas Register. The executives wonder whether advertisements in *Business Week* or *Fortune* might be worthwhile, since these journals are read extensively by production executives concerned with the kinds of components problems the Oates Company is equipped to solve.

Miss Oates, head of research, and Mr. Wheat, manager of the University Park factory, point out that the kind of selling described above is apt to be very expensive from a factory point of view. Many of the inquiries received from advertising or uncovered by bird-dogging involve situations in which only one or two castings are needed. Many of them also require extensive research and factory experimentation to develop precisely the casting needed. In such a situation, a run of less than 40 or 50 castings results in a net loss to the company.

Miss Oates and Mr. Wheat also point out that many of the miscellaneous or specialty inquiries involve considerable research and production planning effort to produce experimental models, which must be tested by the customer and may or may not result in volume orders. About two or three in every five such experimental models result in orders of sufficient volume to make them pay. Usually, six months to a year or two must elapse after the model is supplied to the customer before an order is received.

All the company executives are agreed that Oates castings could be used in many industrial situations, and that their discovery and exploitation would greatly add to the firm's sales and stabilize its volume from year to year. They are not all in agreement about the best way to locate these situations. They perhaps do not entirely accept the notion that in moving into this area the firm must put out a lot of seed corn over a long period of time before it can expect much of a harvest. Mr. Oates is an exception to this general attitude.

The Oates Company salesmen are technical men. Most have had experience in the factory. Their assignments are not in terms of specific territories, but rather in terms of customers or prospective customers. In most cases, a salesman is assigned the prospects he asks for, provided no other salesman also wants them. In such cases, the sales manager adjudicates the matter. The sales manager also makes specific assignments of leads received by mail or as a result of advertising.

When a salesman finds a customer who seems able to use a specialty casting of the kind the Oates Company can make, he collects all the necessary information about it. He then brings this material to the factory and spends whatever time is necessary with the research and production people to make sure that they understand the problem involved. When they come up with a casting or a plan for making one to fit the requirements, he prepares a proposal for the customer and transmits it either in person or by mail. Such a proposal may involve the supply of a test sample or a contract to supply the casting in quantity. The average salesman spends from one third to one half of his time in the factory.

Mr. Oates is convinced that a key marketing problem of the company is lack of contacts with possible customers. In the bird dogging process, the salesman must first locate a firm that looks promising and then try to get sufficiently acquainted with some responsible person in it so that he can learn about its production operations and discover processes in which Oates castings can be used. This is a rather tall order and takes a lot of time.

Mr. Oates wonders whether a manufacturer's agent might not be able to supply the contact and entrée to the confidence of potential customer firms to make possible a study of their operations for places where Oates castings might be used. He has discussed the possibility with a manufacturer's agent of his acquaintance, who informed him that some agents specialize in serving the trades most likely to have uses for Oates castings. He pointed out that such an agent could not be expected to render the kind of technical service Oates products needed, but that he could get an Oates technical expert into the plants of many possible prospects for a look at production operations. An agent would probably want a commission of about 7 or 8 percent on sales he initiated.

The company has done very little in the Pacific Coast market, although Oates castings could be economically shipped there. Mr. Oates is toying with the notion of trying to make contracts with one or two agents who, between them, could cover that territory. To get the market opened up, he feels that the company can afford the agents' commissions and the cost of sending technical specialists to see hot prospects. If the scheme works well there, it might be extended into territories already developed. While this plan would increase marketing costs as a percent of sales, Mr. Oates feels that if it worked it would provide more complete selling coverage than the company can afford through its own salesmen. He also hopes that once a market is developed for the company's products and less sales effort is needed, the commission rate may be reduced.

The Oates Company executives are convinced that in many industrial situations manufacturing firms would profit from using the company's research skills and knowledge, as well as its production know-how in developing specifications for castings, which would then be bought on an open-bid basis. This is particularly true of government subcontract arrangements. In fact, the company has been asked a number of times to do this kind of work on a development contract basis, under which it would be paid a fee for the development work and then might bid or refrain from bidding on the contract to supply the castings developed.

The executives have discouraged this type of arrangement on the theory that it might drain off research talent and interest from projects more likely to result in casting sales for the firm. Also, in one or two unfortunate instances the Oates Company spent a lot of time and money in developing specifications, only to lose the contract to another casting house that, lacking the necessary know-how, proved unable to meet the specifications, and by its failure soured the customers on the use of castings in general.

Promising opportunities are opening up in the direction of making special castings of such metals as steel, titanium, and zirconium and their alloys. To enter this field would involve broadening the area of research interest and knowledge, and developing new techniques and skills in production. The demand for castings of titanium and zirconium is still in the development stage.

Silas Oates, founder and president of the company, is about 50 years of age. He is a very pleasant person to work with, usually issuing requests rather than orders to his subordinates, and freely tolerating—even welcoming—their expression of opinions contrary to his. Under his genial manner, however, is a firmness and drive that enables him to play, concurrently, the somewhat contradictory roles of spark plug and balance wheel of the company.

Mr. Oates is gratified by the profitable history of his company and is

TABLE III

LIABILITIES

Silas Oates Company

	1964	1963	1962	1961
Accounts payable	$ 218,983	$ 85,434	$ 135,828	$ 137,406
Mortgage payable	....	....	22,572	25,914
Accrued items*	289,325	241,261	212,360	234,642
Federal income tax	88,289	113,993	....	170,784
Retirement fund	76,676	54,056	....	97,789
Total Current Liabilities	$ 673,273	$ 494,744	$ 370,760	$ 666,535
Long-term debt:				
20-year 5% notes	198,000	186,700	194,900	199,900
Notes to bank	175,000	....	....	....
Total Long-term Debt	$ 373,000	$ 186,700	$ 194,900	$ 222,472†
Capital stock	547,800	532,550	540,800	546,750
Premium on stock sales	27,028	1,513	13,956	23,463
Contingency reserves	3,732	30,661	30,661	30,660
Reinvested earnings	993,820	879,522	797,251	891,265
Total Net Worth	$1,572,380	$1,444,246	$1,382,668	$1,492,138
Total Liabilities	$2,618,653	$2,125,690	$1,948,328	$2,381,145

* Includes payroll tax reductions.
† Includes $22,572 due on old mortgage.

pleased with its current profit performance. He wonders, however, if perhaps there may be in it elements of weakness for the future. Next week, he plans to hold a meeting of his management group to canvass the present situation and probable future of the firm to the end of developing policies and establishing objectives for the business.

THE TAYLOR MARINE SUPPLY COMPANY

In January, 1964, George Taylor, president and principal stockholder of the Taylor Marine Supply Company, a privately owned corporation, met with Jeffrey Paul, sales manager, to review the company's operations and to make plans for future activities. They were primarily concerned with an available opportunity to further diversify the company's line of products.

The Taylor Marine Supply Company had been organized by its president in 1953, shortly after his separation from the Naval Supply Corps. At that time, he had obtained the exclusive East Coast replacement parts distributorship for a manufacturer of oil burners. These burners, which atomized oil with steam to control the burner flame, were used mainly on ships and in oil refineries. In the following years, Mr. Taylor had added to his line air hoists used on docks and piers, and also replacement parts for steam turbines and ship pumps. In addition, the company bought and sold a wide range of used ship equipment. Exhibit I shows a summary of the company's sales and earnings over the 11 year period from 1953 through 1963. Exhibit II shows the company's financial condition as of the end of 1963, while Exhibit III presents selected balance sheet accounts for earlier years.

Mr. Taylor had been seeking to expand the company's operations into an area that would be different from, but yet compatible with, the firm's present field of activities. He had been offered a distributor's franchise by the Armitage Pump Company to handle pumping equipment replacement parts and service in the Philadelphia, Pennsylvania, area. Actually, it was Mr. Paul who had conceived and then promoted the idea of obtaining the Armitage franchise. Prior to joining the Taylor Marine Supply Company in 1960, Mr. Paul, a mechanical engineer, had been employed for several years by a large oil company as a purchasing manager handling replace-

EXHIBIT I

Summary of Sales and Earnings 1953–63
Taylor Marine Supply Company

Year	Net Sales	Gross Profit	Selling, General, and Administrative Expenses	Other Deductions	Net Profit*	Executive Compensation	Net Profit†	Federal Taxes on Income	Earnings Available after Taxes
1953	$ 411,150	$ 159,200	$ 110,432	$ 460	$ 48,308	$22,300	$ 26,008	$ 6,284	$ 19,724
1954	598,500	224,612	156,620	781	67,211	30,100	37,111	12,168	24,943
1955	870,571	351,306	229,308	1,702	120,296	48,200	72,096	27,396	44,700
1956	1,317,402	520,600	334,200	890	185,510	60,620	124,890	47,458	77,432
1957	1,649,206	653,204	445,522	1,122	206,560	75,705	129,855	49,789	80,066
1958	2,446,701	1,023,191	576,190	210	446,791	78,291	368,500	181,513	186,987
1959	2,506,307	1,084,000	459,002	488	624,510	83,910	540,600	268,855	271,745
1960	2,563,400	1,129,283	442,331	3,802	683,150	83,910	599,240	298,615	300,625
1961	3,670,862	1,569,604	614,000	7,691	947,913	83,910	864,003	443,782	420,221
1962	4,856,207	1,988,444	984,670	9,603	994,171	83,910	910,261	467,835	442,426
1963	5,266,357	2,147,644	1,070,102	10,702	1,056,840	83,910	982,930	505,624	477,306

* Before executive compensation.
† Before federal taxes on income.

EXHIBIT II

Taylor Marine Supply Company
Balance Sheet, December 31, 1963

ASSETS

Current Assets:

Cash	$155,289	
Accounts receivable	478,860	
Inventory	779,080	$1,41...

Fixed Assets:

Building and land	$ 52,000	
Machine shop equipment	30,500	
Office equipment and fixtures	5,381	
Delivery equipment	12,070	99,951

Prepaid Expense:

Unexpired insurance	450
Total Assets	$1,513,630

LIABILITIES AND NET WORTH

Current Liabilities:

Accounts payable	$272,572	
Accrued salaries and commissions	12,803	
Provision for federal taxes on income	126,870	
Notes payable	300,000	$ 712,245

Net Worth:

Capital stock	$550,000	
Earned surplus	251,385	801,385
Total Liabilities		$1,513,630

ment parts for pumping equipment used in refinery operations. In his capacity as purchasing manager, Mr. Paul had numerous dealings with the Armitage Pump Company, and through these contacts became aware that this company was faced with a serious distribution and service problem.

The Armitage Pump Company had experienced rapid growth over a short span of years. It had expanded from a relatively small company that manufactured only pumping equipment to a large corporation engaged in the design, manufacture, and sale of various types of mechanical equipment used in industrial manufacturing, mining, quarrying, oil production and refining, chemical manufacturing, and in rail, automotive, and marine

EXHIBIT III

Taylor Marine Supply Company
Selected Balance Sheet Accounts

Year	Accounts Receivable	Inventory	Total
1954	$ 33,016	$ 61,988	$ 95,004
1955	49,327	93,972	143,299
1956	70,278	127,816	198,094
1957	109,183	199,901	309,084
1958	139,017	249,804	388,821
1959	203,859	352,875	556,734
1960	209,873	354,864	564,737
1961	214,617	358,089	572,706
1962	309,905	526,319	836,224
1963	478,860	779,080	1,257,940

transportation. Another major activity of the Armitage Pump Company was the designing of steam cycle and pump equipment for nuclear power plants. Also, the company was currently participating in projects for the development of nuclear power for aircraft, naval and merchant ships, and land-based electric generating stations. Company sales had amounted to $155 million during the previous fiscal year.

During this period of rapid growth, the Armitage Pump Company management, preoccupied with the problems of expansion and diversification, had not given adequate consideration to establishing facilities for replacement parts and service, but had concentrated on building up sales in the original equipment market. The company had authorized four small companies in the Philadelphia area to distribute Armitage pumping equipment parts, but these companies also handled replacement parts for several competing pumping equipment manufacturers. Therefore, they did not stock a complete line of Armitage parts, nor did they have service facilities for rebuilding pumps. Parts that were not maintained in inventory had to be ordered from the Armitage regional warehouse in White Plains, New York, and all pumps to be rebuilt had to be shipped to the company's service division in Norfolk, Virginia. Under the existing system, it took from one to six weeks to get a defective pump back into operation. This was a serious problem for companies using Armitage pumps, particularly in industries that utilized a continuous flow process in their operations. As a result, when an Armitage pump was depreciated or became obsolete, many companies were replacing the equipment with pumps made by competing manufacturers who provided better replacement parts service.

Since Mr. Paul suspected that Armitage management was confronted with the strong possibility of seriously declining new-equipment sales because of poor maintenance service, he believed that the company would be anxious to franchise a distributor who would specialize in the Armitage line and provide customers with a complete and efficient renewal parts service on a 24-hour basis. Acting on Mr. Paul's suggestion, Mr. Taylor contacted the Armitage Pump Company and expressed his company's interest in the possibility of becoming a franchised distributor in the Philadelphia area. Within three weeks, Armitage had offered Mr. Taylor a distributorship with territorial rights extending from Trenton, New Jersey, to Wilmington, Delaware.

Mr. Taylor believed that a minimum of 15,000 square feet of warehouse space, with adjoining offices, would be needed to maintain a complete inventory of parts, and to provide facilities for a machine shop to service and rebuild pumps. The company rented its present warehouse facilities and could rent additional space as it was needed. Mr. Paul estimated that the cost of the inventory would be between $150,000 and $200,000, depending on the requirements of the Armitage pumping equipment users in the Philadelphia area. Mr. Paul also estimated that the rate of stock turn on the new business would be about the same as on the old. Initially, service work would be handled at a machine shop owned by the Taylor Marine Supply Company in New York City, a distance of approximately 100 miles from the center of the Philadelphia marketing territory—about 2 hours by the New Jersey Turnpike.

Warehouse equipment would include storage bins, hand trucks, and chain hoists; the office would need the usual type of equipment and fixtures, such as typewriters, file cabinets, desks, and chairs. The cost of these items would amount to $20,000. A pickup truck would be needed for pickup and delivery service. Personnel would include an experienced warehouse man and at least two sales engineers. These salesmen would be equipped with company owned and maintained station wagons. It was believed that a secretary would not be needed, but a telephone answering service would be used to receive incoming calls.

Under the terms of the proposed franchise agreement, the other distributors already handling Armitage replacement parts in the Philadelphia area would continue to do so. However, any present user of Armitage equipment was a potential customer. Mr. Taylor believed that the key to a successful operation would be the service his company could provide. He felt that many customers would be attracted by the availability of replacement parts and service on a 7-day, 24-hour basis.

Basically, three types of pumping equipment would be handled—rotary, centrifugal, and reciprocating. The rotary pump was used for moving heavy, thick material like plastics and tar. Both the centrifugal and the reciprocating pumps, used to move lighter liquids, were extensively employed in the oil refining and chemical industries. However, the trend seemed to be away from the reciprocating to the centrifugal, mainly because the centrifugal pumps were more compact and required less space.

Generally, pumps were overhauled every six to nine months, depending on the severity of the operating conditions. At that time, such parts as the shaft, bearings, wear rings, and impellers were replaced. Primarily, the three kinds of metals used in replacement parts were cast iron, bronze and copper, and steel. The cost of these parts varied with the size and the type of metal involved. For example, a 3-foot stainless steel shaft would cost about $300, whereas, a standard steel shaft of the same size would cost much less. Stainless steel parts were required in pumps used to move fluids that attack and corrode metal, such as acids. Also, industries under the jurisdicton of pure food and drug regulations, such as bakeries, breweries, and pharmaceutical manufacturers, were required to use stainless steel parts in pumping equipment.

In Armitage's pricing structure, all parts were to be sold at a prescribed list price. However, industrial discounts were to be given, depending on the number of pumps a customer had in operation. This discount would range from 47 percent for an oil refining company, an extensive user of pumping equipment, to 20 percent or less for a small manufacturer with only a few pumps.

If Mr. Taylor accepted the distributorship, he would be selling the parts at an average gross profit of 40 percent. Also, if his company were successful in its Philadelphia area operations, Armitage would seriously consider giving the Taylor Marine Supply Company additional distributorships in other parts of the country. Mr. Paul was in favor of the proposed venture, but the decision was up to Mr. Taylor.

THOMSON ELECTRIC WELDER COMPANY

The Thomson Electric Welder Company manufactured resistance welding machines varying in price from $2,000 to $100,000, and had total annual sales of $500,000. Elihu Thomson, who amassed a total of 700 patents during his lifetime, founded the company after he had perfected the Thomson process of electric resistance welding. Mr. Thomson pioneered the engineering work in this field, and the company he founded has maintained its leadership in the development and perfection of this type of welding. The company was using space advertising in the metalworking trade papers, but the executives questioned whether this type of advertising was the most effective or profitable. They pointed out that the company's major problem in selling its products lay in educating potential users on the merits of the resistance welding process, and in showing them how Thomson resistance welders could be used for their particular operations. Thus, the company management reviewed its previous advertising program and considered whether the advertising policy should be changed.

For many years, steel was the only resistance welded product, and the Thomson Company manufactured equipment primarily for welding the coarser formed, stamped, or forged steel structures, which tolerated such undesirable welding aftermaths as severe electrode marking, warping, blacking, and scaling. But resistance welding was developed into a precision process, and its application was expanded to a wide variety of the modern alloy metals, such as stainless steel, brass, and bronze, as well as nonferrous metals of sharp fusion point, such as aluminum. Resistance welding was used for both subassemblies and final assemblies in almost every metal fabricating industry, especially the aircraft, automotive, and home appliance industries, where it speeded production and cut costs by reducing the need for rivets, bolts, couplings, and other fastening devices.

Essentially, resistance welding is a method of joining metal parts by passing a large volume of current at relatively low voltage through the pieces of material to be welded in order to heat the abutting surfaces to fusion temperature, while applying pressure to form the joint or weld. The basic principle can be applied in many ways: *spot welders* pinch the work between tapered electrodes to produce localized and individually formed welds; *seam welders* use circular electrodes to produce a continuous seam or series of overlapping spot welds; *projection welders* hold the work together under pressure, while the welds are localized by means of projections or embossments previously formed in the work; *flash-butt welders* produce a weld over the entire area of abutting surfaces, and may be used to join metal parts in end-to-end T or miter shapes. All of these types of resistance welders are available in standard models capable of a wide range of work, as well as in the form of special-purpose machines designed to mass-produce a single product. The special equipment is frequently equipped with jigs, fixtures, automatic feeds, or similar work-handling devices. Welders range in size from bench models capable of making precision welds on extremely small work, such as electronic tube parts, to huge machines that produce tons of road reinforcement matting made of heavy wire or rods.

In spite of the extreme diversity in size and capability of resistance welding equipment, most prospective users were not capable of thinking of the process in terms of practical application to their products. The problems resistance welding could solve were not always recognized as problems. In many cases, changes in product design were required to take full advantage of resistance welding methods—a situation that made it even more difficult for prospective users to recognize the opportunities and advantages of using resistance welding methods.

Since a high order of expensive engineering skill was required to sell resistance welding equipment, it was obvious that the Thomson Company could not rely on a large sales force to find likely prospects in a market thinly spread across the entire metalworking industry. District offices staffed by sales engineers were located in the principal metalworking centers. Sales agents or welding equipment distributors were used in the secondary market areas.

In addition to the limited availability and high cost of specialized sales talent, there was the further problem of engineering cost. Frequently, considerable study and experimental work was required to quote on or even pass an opinion on a proposed application. Advertising or sales methods that produced a high percentage of dud prospects would overburden the engineering staff and saddle the company with excessive sales costs.

It became clear that the Thomson Company's advertising had to accomplish a threefold objective:

1. To educate prospective users in the application and advantages of resistance welding and keep them abreast of new developments.
2. To encourage a higher percentage of enlightened inquiries.
3. To establish the Thomson Company as headquarters for the best in resistance welding equipment.

Arguments were advanced for various forms of advertising, such as trade journal space, selective direct mail, and a monthly technical bulletin. Those in favor of space pointed out the opportunities of low cost and mass coverage. Those opposed thought that the simplified, generalized appeal of journal advertising would not accomplish the purpose.

Advocates of selective direct mail pointed out the opportunities to canvass groups of manufacturers of similar products, and to talk in terms of specific operations and equipment. Opponents objected to the high cost of including adequate illustrative and descriptive material, and the expense or time required to cover the field.

Those in favor of a monthly bulletin saw opportunities to cover a representative range of equipment in each issue, to discuss equipment and applications in adequate detail, and to provide a worthwhile contribution of resistance welding news, ideas, and information that would enhance the prestige of the Thomson Company. Opponents objected on the basis of cost, the difficulty of compiling and keeping alive an adequate list, and the burden of producing a lively and interesting publication on a monthly schedule.

VELTING MACHINE COMPANY

The Velting Machine Company produced a line of machine tools, consisting of both standard and special machines. The special machines were individually designed tools or standard items extensively modified to meet specifications of individual customers, and represented about 50 percent of the company's sales volume. Unit prices varied from $500 to as much as $100,000. Most of the standard machines sell for $20,000 or less. Annual sales were about $50 million.

The company employed a force of 15 salaried salesmen who sold directly to metalworking plants in concentrated manufacturing areas. Machine tool dealers were utilized in markets where the expense of maintaining full-time salesmen would have been excessive. Most of the salesmen were graduates of engineering colleges, although a few without formal engineering training had been employed in the Velting factory and had demonstrated an aptitude for sales work. The sales manager recommended to the executive committee that the company make its machines available on a lease basis to those customers who preferred to buy that way.

The usual terms of sale for Velting machines were payment of the full amount within 30 days. For many years, the company had sold a limited number of machines on an installment contract, under which purchasers were required to make a 25 percent down payment. The installments were spread over periods ranging from several months to a few years. The company was in a strong financial position, and since these installment sales were but a small portion of total volume the treasurer had elected to finance from company funds instead of using an outside lending institution.

In recommending equipment leasing when desired by customers, the sales manager pointed out that during recent years there had been a rapid increase in the availability of lease arrangements among metalworking equipment manufacturers. He stated that he had been closely following this development, and now thought it wise to offer this type of contract. He felt that this would represent extra business that could not otherwise be secured, and pointed out that since the company was operating below production capacity any additional business would be welcome. Another factor leading to his recommendation was the apparent growth in volume of lease business being done by machine manufacturers. No overall figures were available, but information on the experiences of a few companies indicated that lease business, while small, had grown steadily and promised to continue to increase.

The other executive committee members, president, treasurer, and production manager, listened with interest to the sales manager's suggestion, but were skeptical. The president pointed out that excessive risk of loss would be incurred if lease contracts were offered on special-purpose equipment, because it would have little resale value at the end of the lease period or earlier if the lease were broken by default on the part of the lessee. Therefore, leasing would have to be confined to the standard line of machinery, which represented only one half of the company's total sales. He believed, further, that customers who leased machinery would tend to use it more intensively and to be less careful in maintenance than they might with their own equipment. He recognized that, in part, this risk could be compensated for by higher depreciation charges the Bureau of Internal Revenue might permit because of the leasing arrangement, but he questioned whether such allowances would be a satisfactory offset to this risk. He also was concerned about the possibility that the company might be held responsible for injuries to customers' employees caused by the equipment, or damage to customers' premises caused by installation and removal of the equipment. As a final objection, he stated that there was a deep-seated desire on the part of most customers for total owner-ship of capital equipment and an aversion to leasing.

The sales manager admitted that the idea of leasing machines was quite new to many buyers in metalworking industries and that some viewed it with suspicion, but he felt that this attitude could not stand up under logical analysis and he believed that it would change. So far as the other risks cited by the president were concerned, the sales manager stated that these could be adequately covered in the contract. Furthermore, he rec-ommended that there should be a required deposit of 10 percent of the purchase price, which would be held by the company until termination of the lease as a protection against any expense caused by nonperformance on the part of the lessee.

The treasurer asked that the sales manager review the specific benefits to a customer through equipment leasing as opposed to outright purchase or installment purchase. In answering this question, the sales manager quoted and summarized material in an article by Frank K. Griesinger of the Lincoln Electric Company, "Pros and Cons of Leasing Equipment," in *Harvard Business Review*, the March–April, 1955.

1. The lease provides cash-flow advantages for those companies that can use additional working capital for profitable alternative investment. This cash-flow may be superior to that of other financing methods.

The user is able to pay for machines out of the income produced by their use. Rental payments are deductible as an expense item, whereas payments on an installment purchase plan are not. Many leases are written for shorter terms than those normally used for depreciation of purchased equipment. Because rental expenses are deductible, less income is reported, and less cash is needed since taxes are lower.

2. The total dollar financing cost of the lease is high but profits on the freed capital may far outweigh the additional expense.

For example, consider a piece of equipment with a useful life of 10 years. The cash price is $100,000, but it can be rented at an annual rate of $24,000 for a 5-year period, and $4,000 a year for a 5-year renewal period thereafter. A firm that leased this equipment on these terms would retain, during the first year of use, free capital in the sum of $79,026, which would have been sunk in the machine if it had been purchased for cash. If the firm could apply this capital to some use on which it could realize 25 percent, it would enjoy added earnings of $19,757 for that year as a result of its leasing policy. Even though such added earnings would decline in succeeding years, the using firm would enjoy, during the entire 10-year

EXHIBIT I

LEASE CONTRACT

THIS LEASE between THE WARNER & SWASEY COMPANY, an Ohio corporation, hereinafter called "Lessor," and..................................

....

hereinafter called "Lessee,"

WITNESSETH:

WHEREAS, Lessee has need for the use of the machine tools hereinafter described, the duration of which need is not now known to the Lessee, and for this reason the Lessee desires to lease such equipment with the rights and privileges herein granted rather than purchase the same,

NOW, THEREFORE, in consideration of the mutual rights and agreements herein set forth, the Lessor hereby leases to the Lessee and the Lessee hires from the Lessor the machine tools, auxiliary attachments, equipment and tools described as follows:

(said machine tools, attachments, equipment and tools being hereinafter called the "leased property").

TO HAVE AND TO HOLD the same unto the Lessee for the term of seven years, commencing on the...day of ...., 19............, and ending on the...day of.., 19............, unless sooner terminated as hereinafter provided, and upon the following terms, covenants and conditions:

1. Rental: The Lessee covenants to pay to the Lessor annual rentals in accordance with the following table:

First Year $ Second Year $ Third Year $ Fourth Year $

Fifth Year $ Sixth Year $ Seventh Year $

payable quarterly in advance on the date of commencement of the term hereof and each quarter thereof.

2. Advance for Security: In addition to the rent, Lessee shall pay to the Lessor on or before the date of execution hereof the sum of $..................................., which shall be security for, and may be applied by the Lessor at its option at any time upon, any obligations under this lease of the Lessee to the Lessor on which Lessee shall be in default of performance, whether the same be obligations to pay money or perform acts, or other obligations, either in tort or contract, which may arise out of the transaction evidenced by this lease. Upon the termination of this lease and the return of the leased property to the Lessor as herein provided, or its purchase by the Lessee or any other person, the Lessee shall be entitled to the return of the balance, if any, of such security deposit which has not been so applied to the obligations owing from the Lessee to the Lessor.

3. Transportation and Handling Charges: The Lessee shall pay all transportation charges, handling charges, demurrage and similar expenses in connection with the delivery of the leased property to the Lessee and the return of the leased property to the Lessor and the cost of preparing the leased property for the return shipment.

4. Taxes: The Lessee shall pay all taxes and assessments (and interest and penalties, if any, thereon) which may be levied, directly or indirectly, against the leased property or any interest therein or with respect to the use thereof, whether said taxes be levied against the Lessor or the Lessee. Such taxes to be paid by the Lessee shall include, without limitation, property, sales and use taxes and any tax measured by the gross rent payable hereunder, but shall not include net income or franchise taxes payable by the Lessor. If such taxes are levied against the Lessor, it shall notify the Lessee of such fact. The Lessor shall have the right, but not the obligation, to pay any such taxes, whether levied against the Lessor or the Lessee. In such event the Lessee shall reimburse the Lessor therefor within ten days after receipt of invoice, and for the failure to make such reimbursement when due, Lessor shall have all remedies provided herein with respect to the non-payment of rent.

5. Use of Equipment; Return: Lessee agrees to exercise due and proper care in the use and servicing of the leased property, and at all times and at its expense to keep and maintain the same in good working condition, order and repair. Lessee agrees to make no alteration to the leased property without the written consent of the Lessor. Upon the termination of the lease for any reason except the purchase thereof by the Lessee, the Lessee shall forthwith return the leased property to the Lessor at 5701 Carnegie Avenue, Cleveland 3, Ohio (or at such other place not more distant from Lessee's place of business as Lessor shall designate) in good working condition, order and repair.

6. Insurance: Neither party shall have any obligation to the other party to keep the leased property insured against loss by any casualty, and in the event of casualty loss of the leased property, any insurance proceeds shall be the sole property of the party procuring the insurance.

7. Casualty: In the event that the leased property is damaged or destroyed while in the possession of Lessee, the Lessor shall have the right, but not the obligation, of substituting under this lease other property of the same design and equivalent, or better, age and condition, or of repairing and restoring the leased property to its condition prior to the damage, in either of which cases this lease shall remain in full force and effect with respect to such substituted or repaired property and without abatement of rent. If the Lessor fails to make such substitution or repairs within thirty days after receipt of notice from the Lessee of the loss or damage, and if the Lessee shall not intentionally or negligently have caused the loss or damage and shall have fully performed all of its obligations hereunder, the Lessee shall be entitled to terminate this lease without further liability. If the leased property is lost or damaged by the intentional action or inaction or negligence of the Lessee, this lease shall not terminate and the Lessee shall be obligated to repair or replace the leased property and shall remain liable to pay the rent and perform its other obligations hereunder.

8. Place of Use; Prohibition against Removal of Plates, Subletting, etc.: Lessee agrees that the leased property shall be installed and used on Lessee's premises at..

....and that it shall not be removed therefrom without the prior written consent of the Lessor. The Lessee agrees not to remove, deface or conceal any plate or sign which the Lessor has placed on the leased property showing the ownership thereof. Lessee agrees not to part with the possession of, sublet or otherwise dispose of or in any manner encumber the leased property or its leasehold estate, nor to permit any lien to exist upon it, other than a lien for property taxes not in default. This lease cannot be assigned by the Lessee, even by operation of law, without the prior written consent of the Lessor.

9. Right of Inspection: The Lessor, its agents, dealers and representatives shall have the right at any time during usual business hours to inspect the leased property and for that purpose to have access to the place where the leased property then is and Lessee shall on request furnish such supplemental information as may be reasonably necessary to determine whether or not Lessee is performing the several conditions of this lease on its part to be observed or performed.

10. Leased Property constitutes Personal Property: The leased property shall at all times during the term of this lease be and remain personal property notwithstanding its attachment or affixation to any real estate. Lessee shall be responsible for any damage done to any real estate, building or structure by the removal of said leased property.

11. Default: (a) On occurrence of any event of default the Lessor may terminate this lease by written notice to the Lessee, whereupon the Lessee shall be obligated forthwith to return the leased property to the Lessor and shall also be liable to the Lessor for all unpaid rentals, including the full current annual rent, and for all damages which Lessor may sustain by reason of

EXHIBIT I—Continued

Lessee's breach, including without limitation, all attorneys' fees and other expenses incurred by the Lessor in attempting to enforce the provisions of this agreement or to recover damages for the breach thereof and in addition shall have such other and further remedies and rights as may be available at law by reason of Lessee's default. In the event of such termination by the Lessor and breach by the Lessee of its obligation forthwith to return the leased property, Lessor shall have the right to enter upon any premises of the Lessee in which the leased property is located and repossess the same without prejudice to any other rights and remedies herein stated.

(b) The following shall constitute "events of default:" (i) the failure of the Lessee to pay any installment of rent or the breach of any other covenant or condition contained in this agreement; (ii) the subjection of the leased property to any lien, levy or attachment; (iii) any assignment by the Lessee for the benefit of creditors or the admission by the Lessee in writing of its inability to pay its debts generally as they become due; (iv) the appointment of a receiver, trustee or similar official for the Lessee or for any of its property; (v) the filing by or against the Lessee of a petition in bankruptcy or a petition for the reorganization or liquidation of the Lessee under any federal or state law; (vi) any action by the Lessee in furtherance of any of the aforesaid purposes.

12. Termination: The Lessee, having fully performed all its obligations hereunder, may terminate this lease as of the end of the................year of the term or at the end of any subsequent year of the term by giving the Lessor not less than thirty days prior written notice of termination.

13. Renewal: After the expiration of the full term of this lease, the Lessee, having fully performed all of its obligations hereunder, shall have the option of renewing this lease from year to year for not more than nine successive years upon thirty days written notice to the Lessor prior to the end of the term and the end of each such year, in which event the rental rate shall remain the same as for the seventh year of the lease, and shall be paid semi-annually instead of quarterly.

14. Holding Over: In the event of any termination of this lease including, without limitation, the failure of the Lessee to give a notice of renewal as provided in paragraph 13 hereof, the Lessee, if in breach of its obligation forthwith to return the leased property to the Lessor, shall not be deemed to be a tenant holding over but shall be deemed to have converted the leased property.

15. Option to Purchase: The Lessee shall have the option to purchase the leased property as of any anniversary of the commencement of the lease at the following price, payable in cash:

First Year $ Second Year $ Third Year $ Fourth Year $

Fifth Year $ Sixth Year $ Seventh Year $

If the lease shall be renewed as provided in paragraph 13 hereof, the option price as of the end of each renewal year shall be computed by subtracting from the option price at the end of the original term of the lease an amount equal to $................ multiplied by the number of years which have elapsed since the end of the original term of the lease. The option to purchase shall be exercised by the Lessee giving the Lessor ten days written notice of such exercise prior to the end of any year of the term or any renewal year and the payment of the purchase price on or before the end of such year. Upon payment of such price in full, Lessee shall be entitled to the return of the security deposit provided in paragraph 2 hereof.

16. Notices: Any notice required or permitted to be given by the Lessee to the Lessor shall be deemed to have been properly given if deposited in the United States mail, postage prepaid, addressed to the Lessor at 5701 Carnegie Avenue, Cleveland 3, Ohio, or such other address as the Lessor shall specify in writing. Any notice required or permitted to be given by the Lessor to the Leessee shall be deemed to have been properly given if deposited in the United States mail, postage prepaid, addressed to the Lessee at................................ ...., or such other address as the Lessee shall specify in writing.

17. Miscellaneous: This lease contains the entire understanding of the parties with respect to the subject matter hereof, and no agreement or representation, verbal or written, not contained herein shall be binding on either party. This lease may be amended and supplemented only by written instrument signed by both parties or their authorized representatives. The paragraph headings herein contained are for reference only and do not constitute a part of the lease.

IN WITNESS WHEREOF, the parties hereto have caused this lease to be executed this................day of ...., 19........

Executed in the presence of: THE WARNER & SWASEY COMPANY

By................................

Title................................

STATE OF OHIO } SS.
COUNTY OF CUYAHOGA

Personally came before me this................day of................, 19........, the above named ....of The Warner & Swasey Company, Name   Title known to me and known to be such officer, who acknowledged that he executed the foregoing lease, and that the same is the free act and deed of The Warner & Swasey Company and of himself as such officer.

My Commission expires:................

Notary Public

Executed in the presence of:

NAME OF LESSEE

By................................

Title................................

life of the machine, added earnings after taxes in the amount of $52,463, according to Mr. Griesinger. The article contained elaborate tables, showing exactly how this desirable result was worked out.

3. Some companies classified as good credit risks are leasing as a supplement to bank credit or to overcome presumed disadvantages inherent in bank borrowing.

EXHIBIT II

DEFERRED PAYMENT PLANS

Example—Selling Price: $10,000   Minimum Down Payment: (25%) $2,500   Balance: $7,500

	1 YEAR TERM	2 YEAR TERM	3 YEAR TERM	4 YEAR TERM	5 YEAR TERM
Unpaid cash balance	$7,500.00	$7,500.00	$7,500.00	$7,500.00	$7,500.00
Finance charge	243.75	618.75	956.25	1,275.00	1,593.75
Time balance	7,743.75	8,118.75	8,456.25	8,775.00	9,093.75
Payable Monthly in					
1st year	645.00	338.00	355.00	298.00	254.00
2nd year		338.00	237.00	220.00	200.00
3rd year			112.00	140.00	155.00
4th year				73.00	100.00
5th year					48.00

Terms longer than two years are made available under C. I. T.'s "pay as you depreciate" plan and are subject to their approval. One and two year terms are handled and financed directly by Warner & Swasey.

RENTAL PLANS

Can Be Written With or Without Option to Purchase

Plan No. 1—Lessee can cancel at the end of the second year and at the end of any subsequent year.

YEAR	MONTHLY RENTAL RATE	OPTION PRICE	YEAR	MONTHLY RENTAL RATE	OPTION PRICE
1	3%	74%	5	½%	28%
2	3%	43%	6	½%	27%
3	1½%	30%	7	½%	26%
4	½%	29%	8	½%	25%

Plan No. 2—Lessee can cancel at the end of the third year and at the end of any subsequent year.

YEAR	MONTHLY RENTAL RATE	OPTION PRICE	YEAR	MONTHLY RENTAL RATE	OPTION PRICE
1	2%	86%	5	1%	34%
2	2%	67%	6	1%	27%
3	2%	48%	7	½%	26%
4	1%	41%	8	½%	25%

Plan No. 3—Lessee can cancel at the end of the fourth year and at the end of any subsequent year.

YEAR	MONTHLY RENTAL RATE	OPTION PRICE	YEAR	MONTHLY RENTAL RATE	OPTION PRICE
1	1½%	92%	5	1½%	40%
2	1½%	79%	6	1½%	27%
3	1½%	66%	7	½%	26%
4	1½%	53%	8	½%	25%

All Plans
- After seven years, Lessee may renew from year to year up to nine additional years. For such renewal periods the rate is ½% per month, and the option price is reduced 1% each year.
- If option is provided, Lessee may purchase at the end of the first year and at the end of any subsequent year.
- At the start of the contract, a 10% security deposit will be made. This deposit is held until the purchase option has been exercised or until Lessee cancels the contract and returns the equipment.
- Rentals are paid quarterly in advance for seven years—then semi-annually.
- Only standard machines, equipment and tooling will be rented. All special items must be purchased.

A company with a high credit rating may prefer to gain capital through leasing as opposed to bank loans, in some circumstances, such as unwillingness of banks to finance fixed assets or differences in time periods required.

4. Certain miscellaneous advantages include protection against rapid technological obsolescense of equipment, a hedge against inflation, conditions of severe usage, etc.

The sales manager showed the committee a lease contract offered by a well-known machine tool producer. This contract is shown as Exhibit I, and three different rental plans as Exhibit II. The treasurer pointed out that all of the arrangements contained purchase clauses that permitted lessees to buy the equipment for stated amounts at specified time periods during the life of the lease. He wondered if these leases might not be construed by the Bureau of Internal Revenue as the equivalent of an installment sale contract, and lease payments disallowed as expense charges. He had been told that leases with purchase option clauses had, in some cases, been held not to be true leases.

The treasurer went on to question whether it would be wise for the company to utilize its funds for financing lease contracts. The sales manager replied that this would not be necessary, since specialized companies or leasing brokers could be used. In this procedure, the Velting Company would quote a customer in the normal manner and would ask the specialized leasing company to propose a lease arrangement. If the customer accepted the proposal, the leasing company would purchase the equipment outright from the Velting Company and would collect the rent from the user. In this situation, the Velting Company could consider the lease an outright sale, since the title would pass to the leasing company. If desired, an arrangement could be made with a leasing company to offer used equipment to the Velting Machine Company for purchase or for reconditioning. A second possible method of financing leases would be to borrow from banks.

Index

Index

Product offering—*Cont.*
  organization case study, 604 ff.
  policy of company, 182, 183
  product mix; *see* Product mix
  production facilities, processes, materials and labor, 184, 185
  research and development, 185
  single line of products, 172
  technical service, 185
Product organization, 361–64
Product planning
  competitive behavior, 173
  new products; *see* New product development
  organizing for, 188–91
  scope of tasks involved, 188, 189
  types of organizations, 189–91
Product policy, 182, 183
Product quality, 35, 36
Product research, 138, 139
Product specifications, review of, 90, 91
Product types; *see* Market levels
Production movement; *see* Logistics system
Production scheduling techniques, 468, 469
Professional groups, industrial customers, 51
Project plans, 118, 119
Promotional devices; *see* Sales promotion media
Public relations
  defined, 441
  implementing program of, 443
  media for, 443, 444
  planning program of, 442, 443
  types of publics affected by, 441, 442
Publicity
  defined, 439
  effectiveness of, measurement of, 441
  promotional tool, 440
  techniques in securing, 440, 441
Purchase order form, 81
Purchasing department, internal organization of, 58, 60
  company organization, 62, 63
  educational institution, 61
Purchasing officer, nature of, 86

Q
Quantity discounts, 341–43
Quantity production, 172, 173
Quotation request, 76

R
Raw materials, 27, 28
  marketing of, 28
Reciprocity in buyer-seller relationship, 11
  company policy regarding, 487, 488

Reciprocity in buyer-seller relationship
—*Cont.*
  meaning of, 484, 485
  prevalence of, 485, 486
  sales advantages and disadvantages of, 485, 487
Reorganization of marketing, 374–77
Reports
  requirements of, 542, 543
  salesmen's, case studies, 562 ff., 615 ff.
Research in industrial marketing; *see* Marketing research

S
Sales agents, 6
  advantages of, 241–43
  area covered, 271
  business standing, 271
  defined, 238
  disadvantages of, 243–45
  groups of, 238–41
  listing sources, 272, 273
  manner of operation, 238–41
  ownership of, 271
  principal's offerings to, 272
  products handled, 272
  quality of sales personnel, 271
  sales volume, 271
  selection of, 264, 265
    factors in, 271–73
  trade contacts, 271
  usefulness of, 241–43
Sales analysis, 164–66
Sales force; *see* Salesmen
Sales forecasting, 166–68
Sales and market research, 138, 139
Sales promotion media
  advertising novelties, 451, 452
  case studies, 663 ff., 675–77
  catalogs; *see* Catalogs
  correspondence, 444–46
    direct mail, 446, 447
  entertainment of customers, 452, 453
  industrial shows and exhibits; *see* Industrial shows and exhibits
  public relations, 441–44
  publicity, 439–41
  sampling, 438, 439
Sales supervisor, 405–7
Sales training; *see* Salesmen
Salesmen
  activities involving, 378
  advertising in support of programs of, 414, 415
  application blanks, 386
  assignment of tasks to, 403–5
  bonus systems, 400, 401
  classroom training of, 390
  commission variations, 399, 400
  compensation, 398–407

This book has been set in 10 and 9 point Janson, leaded 2 points. Chapter numbers are in 14 and 30 point Deepdene; chapter titles are in 18 point Deepdene. Part numbers and titles are in 24 point Deepdene. The size of the type page is 27 by 47 picas.